T. R. MALTHUS
AN ESSAY ON
THE PRINCIPLE OF POPULATION
VOLUME I

T. R. MALTHUS
AN ESSAY ON THE PRINCIPLE OF POPULATION;

or

A View of its past and present Effects on
Human Happiness;

With an Inquiry into our Prospects respecting
the future Removal or Mitigation of the
Evils which it occasions

The version published in 1803,
with the variora of 1806, 1807, 1817 and 1826

EDITED BY

PATRICIA JAMES

VOLUME I

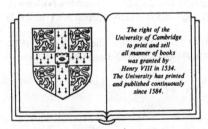

The right of the
University of Cambridge
to print and sell
all manner of books
was granted by
Henry VIII in 1534.
The University has printed
and published continuously
since 1584.

CAMBRIDGE UNIVERSITY PRESS

CAMBRIDGE

NEW YORK   PORT CHESTER

MELBOURNE   SYDNEY

FOR THE ROYAL ECONOMIC SOCIETY

CAMBRIDGE UNIVERSITY PRESS
Cambridge, New York, Melbourne, Madrid, Cape Town, Singapore, São Paulo

Cambridge University Press
The Edinburgh Building, Cambridge CB2 8RU, UK

Published in the United States of America by Cambridge University Press, New York

www.cambridge.org
Information on this title: www.cambridge.org/9780521323604

First published 1989
This digitally printed version 2008

A catalogue record for this publication is available from the British Library

Library of Congress Cataloguing in Publication data
Malthus, T. R. (Thomas Robert), 1766–1834.
An essay on the principle of population, or a
view of its past and present effects on human happiness.
"The version published in 1803, with the variora of
1806, 1807, 1817 and 1826, edited by Patricia James."
Includes index.
1. Population. I. James, Patricia, 1933–
II. Title.
HB861.E7   1987   304.6   87–9372

ISBN 978-0-521-32360-4 hardback (volume I)
ISBN 978-0-521-07134-5 paperback (volume I)

ISBN 978-0-521-32363-5 hardback (volume II)
ISBN 978-0-521-07132-1 paperback (volume II)

CONTENTS

VOLUME I

Book I
Of the Checks to Population in the less civilized Parts of the World, and in Past Times

Book II
Of the Checks to Population in the different States of Modern Europe

Book III
Of the different Systems of Expedients which have been proposed or have prevailed in Society, as they affect the Evils arising from the Principle of Population

Contents

VOLUME II

RE-WRITTEN CHAPTERS

Book IV
Of our future Prospects respecting the Removal or Mitigation of the Evils arising from the Principle of Population

EDITOR'S INTRODUCTION

Thomas Robert Malthus was born on 13 February 1766, with a hare-lip and a cleft palate, at a small country house in Surrey called The Rookery. He was the sixth child and second son of Daniel Malthus and his wife Henrietta Catherine, formerly Graham; another daughter was born some five years later. The family connections were with medicine and the law, but Daniel Malthus had inherited enough money to live comfortably in various parts of the Home Counties as a cultivated gentleman, with sufficient means to travel abroad, and to make the acquaintance of Rousseau, whom he idolised. The education of his son Robert (he was never called Thomas) was entrusted to a well-known pedagogue, the Rev. Richard Graves, at Claverton Rectory, near Bath; then, when he was 16, he was sent to a Unitarian tutor, Gilbert Wakefield, first at the Warrington Dissenting Academy, and then at the Wakefields' home near Nottingham.

Gilbert Wakefield had been a Fellow of Jesus College, Cambridge, and there Malthus took up residence as a student in November 1784. In 1788 he graduated as Ninth Wrangler, which meant that he was the University's ninth best mathematician of his year, and in 1793 his college gave him a Fellowship. While Malthus was an undergraduate at Cambridge, his family settled permanently in Surrey, in the neighbourhood of Albury and Shere; they had been 'wandering about' for the previous 18 years. Here, in his first settled home, Robert lived quietly with his parents and two unmarried sisters for a whole decade after leaving college.

Malthus's only known occupation at this time was that of a country curate: on 8 June 1789 he was licensed by the Bishop of Winchester to serve 'Oakwood, *alias* Ockwood, in the County of Surrey'.[1] Okewood (as it usually spelt) was a little chapel of ease in a remote woodland area, too isolated to be licensed for marriages; the remarkable thing about its late eighteenth-century register was the small list of burials and the prodigious number of baptisms, all children of 'the poor'. It is impossible to tell from the records for how long the young Robert Malthus actively served this curacy, but he

---

[1] The actual date has only recently come to light, and the editor is grateful to Dr John Pullen for drawing her attention to it.

obtained the title in 1824, and held it until his death: this occurred at his father-in-law's house in Bath on 29 December 1834.

As is well known, at some time in 1797 Daniel Malthus had an argument with his younger son about the perfectibility of mankind: Robert maintained that the utopian schemes of William Godwin could never be realised, on account of the excessive population which would result from them. On the advice of his father, Robert dashed off *An Essay on the Principle of Population as it affects the future Improvement of Society, with Remarks on the Speculations of Mr. Godwin, M. Condorcet, and other Writers*. This octavo volume was published anonymously, by Joseph Johnson, in 1798, and aroused much attention.

Anonymous books and pamphlets were common at the time, but Robert Malthus appears to have made no attempt to conceal his authorship. He immediately set about compiling a very heterogeneous reading list to reinforce his sombre thesis that population tended perpetually to press upon subsistence, held in check only by vice and misery. In 1799 he travelled with friends by way of Hamburg to Scandinavia and St Petersburg, and in 1802 a large family party took advantage of the Peace of Amiens to visit France and Switzerland.

Both these foreign tours are mentioned in the great quarto of 1803, on which are based all subsequent editions of the *Essay on Population*, including this one. Malthus himself called his monumental work 'the second edition' of the anonymous first *Essay* of 1798, and on the title-page was printed 'A New Edition, Very Much Enlarged'. Much of the first *Essay* was incorporated verbatim in the quarto, and these passages are indicated in the present variorum edition; the pagination used here is that of the original first *Essay*, reprinted by Macmillans in 1966.

On the title-page of the quarto the author was given as 'T. R. Malthus, A.M.' – the Latin form of M.A. – 'Fellow of Jesus College, Cambridge'. By the time Joseph Johnson brought out 'the third edition' in two octavo volumes in 1806, Malthus had to be described as 'Late Fellow of Jesus College, Cambridge'. He had forfeited his Fellowship, as the rules then were, by ceasing to be a bachelor; his marriage, to his first cousin once removed, Harriet Eckersall, took place in April 1804. This wedding was made possible by the death in 1803 of the Rector of Walesby in Lincolnshire, which enabled the patron of the living, Henry Dalton of Knaith, to present it to his love-sick cousin Robert. As was customary at this period, Malthus drew the income from the rectory of Walesby for the rest of his life, while a poor curate did all the work for a small salary.

Following the advice of friends, Malthus set about revising the two main statistical chapters of Book II almost immediately after the publication of the quarto, and these re-written versions were printed in 1806. Also in 1806 Malthus added an *Appendix* to the *Essay*, which was entitled *A Reply to the Chief*

Objections which have been urged against the Essay on the Principle of Population: he wrote

I should feel greatly obliged to those who have not had leisure to read the whole work, if they would cast their eyes over the few following pages, that they may not, from the partial and incorrect statements which they have heard, mistake the import of some of my opinions, and attribute to me others which I never held.

This Appendix was also printed separately on quarto sheets – it occupies 35 such pages – and sold as a sort of pamphlet, so that people who already possessed the 1803 edition could have it bound in with the earlier volume if they wished.

As may be seen from Malthus's *Advertisements*, the 1806 edition of the *Essay* was a very botched affair. The 1807 edition, also in two octavo volumes, was a great improvement, being evenly divided, with Books I and II in the first volume, Books III and IV with the *Appendix* and index in the second. The title-page in 1807 describes Malthus as 'Late Fellow of Jesus College, Cambridge, and Professor of History and Political Economy in the East India College, Hertfordshire'. At this time the Company's college for training its civil servants was inconveniently housed in temporary quarters in Hertford Castle; the Malthuses with their little children, a son and two daughters, lived in a Company house somewhere in the town.

In 1809 the four-year-old East India College moved to what would now be designated its own campus at Haileybury. It is important to remember that the College at no time had more than one hundred students, so that Malthus should not be regarded as a professor in the modern sense of the word. But he lectured; he contributed to the current discussion on the Poor Laws; he wrote articles for the *Edinburgh Review* on the problems of Ireland, and what is now called inflation; he defended the East India College when it was attacked in Parliament; and he published three significant pamphlets on the Corn Laws and *The Nature and Progress of Rent*; these last subjects were a seething political issue and the occasion of smashed windows and general rioting in 1815.

What Malthus called 'the fifth edition' of *Population*, 'with important Additions', was published by John Murray in three octavo volumes in 1817. This is the first version of the *Essay* to have a modern look, as Murray did not use the long S. Yet one is still conscious of the economical habits of the eighteenth century, for a separate volume was published at the same time, entitled *Additions to the Fourth and Former Editions of an Essay on Population &c. &c.* Thus readers who already possessed one of the three previous versions of the greatly enlarged *Essay* had only to buy a single new volume to bring themselves up to date.

The most conspicuous changes are what one might expect, at a time when the relationship between the price of food and the wages of labour –

especially manufacturing labour – was the subject of serious discussion as well as mob violence. Malthus re-wrote four chapters in Book III:

Of increasing Wealth, as it affects the Condition of the Poor.
Of the Definitions of Wealth. Agricultural and Commercial Systems.
Different Effects of the Agricultural and Commercial Systems.
Of Bounties on the Exportation of Corn.

It is perhaps typical of Malthus that six new chapters replaced the four old ones (these are chapters A–F of Book III in Volume II of this edition) and that he himself was well aware of how his critics would react.

In a letter to Ricardo dated 28 December 1815 Malthus wrote:

If I complete the subject, and say what I meant to say with respect to Restrictions on the importation of foreign corn, and the effects of high prices on foreign commerce, I fear I shall be led into too great length, and yet if I shorten it I shall probably be thought obscure. It would have been better perhaps in many respects to leave out the whole of the practical question relating to Bounties and Restrictions.[2]

On 9 March 1816 Ricardo wrote to his friend Hutches Trower:

Mr Malthus has been staying a few days with me . . . . He is yet doubtful whether he shall add an additional volume to his Essay on Population, or whether he shall publish a separate and independent work, containing his present views on the interesting subjects of Agriculture and Manufactures, and the encouragement which is afforded them by natural and artificial causes.[3]

As late as 9 September 1816 Malthus had still not made up his mind, and was writing to Ricardo: 'I have nearly determined to leave out the questions about bounties and restrictions, or only allude to them very shortly, as far as they are concerned with population.'[4] But he finally decided otherwise.

In 1817 Malthus also inserted additional chapters on the checks to population in France and in England, on the Poor Laws, on the Effects of the Knowledge of the Principal Cause of Poverty on Civil Liberty, and on the Different Plans of Improving the Condition of the Poor. He excised the chapter on a pamphlet which Godwin had written in 1802, and replaced it with one about Robert Owen, an idealist who was not only more financially successful than Godwin, but also some 15 years younger. This substitution probably gave rise to Godwin's own book on population, bitterly attacking Malthus, which was published in 1820.

---

[2] *The Works and Correspondence of David Ricardo*, edited by Piero Sraffa with the collaboration of M. H. Dobb, Cambridge University Press for the Royal Economic Society, 11 vols, 1951–1972, vol. VI, p. 346.
[3] *Ibid.*, Vol. VII, pp. 26–27.
[4] *Ibid.*, Vol. VII, p. 68.

Malthus himself castigated two contemporary writers, John Weyland and James Grahame, in a supplement to the original *Appendix* of 1806. In this occurs the crucial sentence overlooked by the nineteenth-century pioneers of birth control who called themselves Malthusians: 'If it were possible for each married couple to limit by a wish the number of their children, there is certainly reason to fear that the indolence of the human race would be very greatly increased; and that neither the population of individual countries, nor of the whole earth, would ever reach its natural and proper extent.'

With the 1817 edition of *Population* finally published, Malthus devoted his whole attention to his *Principles of Political Economy*, which came out in 1820. He wrote the article on Population in the 1824 *Supplement to the Encyclopaedia Britannica*, most of which was reprinted by Murray in 1830 as *A Summary View of the Principle of Population*.

In 1826 there appeared the last edition of the *Essay on Population* to be published during Malthus's life-time, neatly arranged by Murray in two octavo volumes. There were a few statistical additions, and the author could be styled on the title-page as the Rev. T. R. Malthus, A.M., F.R.S., he having been elected to the Royal Society in 1819. On this 1826 edition were based the Victorian one-volume octavo versions of 1872 and 1890; these both included Malthus's very important *Appendices* of 1806 and 1817. When the Everyman Edition was first printed in 1914 (in two volumes) these *Appendices* were omitted, so that about 22 000 words of Malthus's views on population have been virtually suppressed, at least as far as most twentieth-century readers are concerned.

Suppression of an author's opinion, contrary to his published intentions, is one kind of sin; it might be argued that those responsible for the present edition are guilty of a worse one, in bringing before the public passages which Malthus himself had cancelled. Our editorial defence must rest on Malthus's continuing fame and influence, especially outside his own country, which makes everything he wrote, and all his changes of mind, of permanent significance. The patchwork nature of the *Essay* is in itself a lesson in that sort of humility which is essential for any scientific pursuit of the truth.

More specifically, it was the *Essay* of 1803 which made the greatest impact on contemporary thought, and the effect of some of the more famous passages, cancelled as early as 1806, extends even now – almost like shock waves – over discussions on demography and economics. To give but two instances: first, Malthus is still condemned for the paragraph about there being no room at nature's mighty feast for those whose labour society does not want; to this day students search in vain, in modern editions, for this quotation, unaware that it was expunged three years after it was written.

Again, Malthus is labelled a doctrinaire physiocrat because he wrote in 1803: 'Manufactures, strictly speaking, are no new production, no new creation, but merely a modification of an old one, and when sold must be paid for out of a revenue already in existence, and consequently the gain of the seller is the loss of the buyer. A revenue is transferred but not created.' All this Malthus struck out in 1806, but it is still half-remembered against him in the nineteen-eighties.

To argue the need for a variorum edition of the *Essay on the Principle of Population* is easier than trying to make one. After much thought, it was decided that all the eight re-written chapters (two of 1806 and six of 1817), with their subsequent emendations, should be printed together in the second volume; thus readers who wish to make comparisons may do so by using the two volumes side by side. Where detailed comparison is irrelevant, the completely new 'additional' chapters are printed immediately after the earlier ones, as was done in 1817. In the case of the substituted chapter iii of Book III, the same applies, and it is inserted after the original chapter which it replaced. This arrangement means that the numbering of the chapters in this edition, of Books II and III, will be different from that of any other, which may cause some inconvenience; it appeared to be the least of a wide choice of evils.

It was not considered necessary to record changes in paragraphing, the use of capital letters, and small verbal alterations made merely for the sake of euphony or correct grammar: they indicate the care with which Malthus revised his work, but would be distracting to readers who are rightly more concerned with his subject-matter. As Malthus himself wrote in his *Errata*, printed at the beginning of the quarto: 'Obvious typographical errors and omissions are not noticed': we hope that they have all been unobtrusively rectified. Nor did it seem important to comment on when 'valleys' replaced *vallies*, 'chase' was substituted for *chace*, or even when Dr Smith became Adam Smith, which was not until 1817. On the other hand we have deliberately retained the archaic spelling of peoples and places, because nobody can control their unconscious word-associations: a modern oil-sheikh has little in common with Malthus's chaik, and Tahiti today is nothing like the Otaheite which Malthus read about.

In short, our main dilemma was to make the *Essay on Population* pleasantly readable, while at the same time bearing in mind the fact that Malthus wrote with his goose-quill pen a long time ago, and that much has changed since, including our attitude towards such minor matters as consistency in notes and references. Finally we agreed that the peculiarities of Malthus's footnotes should be left as they are (they may be followed up quite easily) but that it was essential to modernise his eighteenth-century punctuation, and this the editor has done.

Equally essential was the provision of a new index; Malthus's, however, are not without interest, and a short note on them has been printed immediately before the index to the present edition.

Editor's Introduction

One of Malthus's characteristics is that his long footnotes were sometimes more important than his text, and it seemed right to stick to his own arrangement – or the lack of it. All footnotes in this edition are numbered consecutively by chapter, not page by page, as in the author's day. Following the usual practice, Malthus's footnotes are given in their original form, while explanatory notes by the editor are enclosed in square brackets. Where there is an alternative in the text, the note relating to this begins with a square bracket, to indicate an editorial interruption of Malthus's prose; but since the content of these variora are the author's own words, there is no square bracket at the conclusion of the note. Straightforward permanent additions to the text are inserted in the appropriate places without note numbers. Where passages have been excised or re-written, note numbers and a large black dot have been used at the beginning as well as the end of the passage concerned (thus $^{15}\bullet \ldots \bullet^{15}$) so that the reader may be forewarned of a lengthy alteration. The same method has been adopted to draw the reader's attention to passages taken from the *Essay* of 1798, only in these cases an asterisk has been used to mark the beginning and end of the paragraphs or sentences closely following those of the first *Essay*. Notes to notes and notes to inserted matter are indicated by superscript letters.

To avoid overcrowded pages and excessive editorial intrusion Malthus's authorities, and information about them, are listed alphabetically at the end of the Volume II. It is hoped that this Alphabetical List will be of interest in itself, for the light it throws on an Englishman's literary heritage and social environment at the beginning of the nineteenth century. Malthus assumed that his readers had a working knowledge of French, as well as a background of Greek and Latin, Shakespeare and Milton, Pope and *The Tatler* and, of course, the Authorised Bible of 1611; he also took it for granted that they kept up with all the serious publications and political events of their own day. That day is long past, but some knowledge of it should help a modern student to appreciate the lasting contribution which Malthus has made to the scientific investigation of the nature and causes of poverty.

Apart from the conventional tasks performed by the editor, the present two volumes are the result of the team-work and technical expertise of the Cambridge University Press, especially Francis Brooke, Sheila Shepherd, and John Trevitt. We have all tried to meet our different challenges with as much ingenuity and professional dedication as we could muster; we are aware that we cannot hope to please all Malthus's readers of the twentieth and twenty-first centuries, all over the world, utterly diverse in religion and race, tradition and experience; in the language of his period, we can only crave the indulgence of the public.

PATRICIA JAMES

PATRICIA JAMES, 1917–1987

Patricia James died in March, 1987, after delivering the typescript of these volumes, but before the proofs were available for her expert attention. In undertaking the final stages of preparing this variorum edition for publication, I would like to thank John Pullen for taking the time from his companion edition of Malthus's *Principles of Political Economy* to compile the index: and R. D. Collison Black for lending another pair of eyes to an exacting task. All those who were fortunate to know Patricia James would like to think that this edition will serve as a fitting monument to a remarkable scholar, the culmination of her long labour of love on behalf of Robert Malthus.

DONALD WINCH

PREFACE

The Essay on the Principle of Population, which I published in 1798, was suggested, as is expressed in the preface, by a paper in Mr. Godwin's Inquirer. It was written on the spur of the occasion, and from the few materials which were within my reach in a country situation.[1] The only authors from whose writings I had deduced the principle, which formed the main argument of the essay, were Hume, Wallace, Dr. Adam Smith, and Dr. Price; and my object was to apply it to try the truth of those speculations on the perfectibility of man and society, which at that time excited a considerable portion of the public attention.

In the course of the discussion, I was naturally led into some examination of the effects of this principle on the existing state of society. It appeared to account for much of that poverty and misery observable among the lower classes of people in every nation, and for those reiterated failures in the efforts of the higher classes to relieve them. The more I considered the subject in this point of view, the more importance it seemed to acquire; and this consideration, joined to the degree of public attention which the essay excited, determined me to turn my leisure reading towards an historical examination of the effects of the principle of population on the past and present state of society; that, by illustrating the subject more generally, and drawing those inferences from it, in application to the actual state of things which experience seemed to warrant, I might give it a more practical and permanent interest.

In the course of this inquiry I found that much more had been done than I had been aware of, when I first published the essay. The poverty and misery arising from a too rapid increase of population had been distinctly seen, and the most violent remedies proposed, so long ago as the times of Plato and Aristotle. And of late years the subject had been treated in such a manner by some of the French Economists, occasionally by Montesquieu, and, among our own writers, by Dr. Franklin, Sir James Steuart, Mr. Arthur Young, and

---

[1] [This PREFACE of 1803 was reprinted in all subsequent editions, but from 1806 onwards the word *spur* was replaced by 'impulse', and Malthus wrote of
... the few materials which were then within my reach ...

I

Mr. Townsend, as to create a natural surprise that it had not excited more of the public attention.

Much, however, remained yet to be done. Independently of the comparison between the increase of population and food, which had not perhaps been stated with sufficient force and precision, some of the most curious and interesting parts of the subject had been either wholly omitted or treated very slightly. Though it had been stated distinctly, that population must always be kept down to the level of the means of subsistence; yet few inquiries had been made into the various modes by which this level is effected; and the principle had never been sufficiently pursued to its consequences, and those practical inferences drawn from it, which a strict examination of its effects on society appears to suggest.

These are therefore the points which I have treated most in detail in the following essay. In its present shape it may be considered as a new work, and I should probably have published it as such, omitting the few parts of the former which I have retained, but that I wished it to form a whole of itself, and not to need a continual reference to the other. On this account, I trust that no apology is necessary to the purchasers of the first edition. [2]●I should hope that there are some parts of it, not reprinted in this, which may still have their use; as they were rejected, not because I thought them all of less value than what has been inserted, but because they did not suit the different plan of treating the subject which I had adopted.●[2]

To those who either understood the subject before, or saw it distinctly on the perusal of the first edition, I am fearful that I shall appear to have treated some parts of it too much in detail, and to have been guilty of unnecessary repetitions. These faults have arisen partly from want of skill, and partly from intention. In drawing similar inferences from the state of society in a number of different countries, I found it very difficult to avoid some repetitions; and in those parts of the inquiry which led to conclusions different from our usual habits of thinking, it appeared to me that, with the slightest hope of producing conviction, it was necessary to present them to the reader's mind at different times and on different occasions. I was willing to sacrifice all pretensions to merit of composition to the chance of making an impression on a larger class of readers.

The main principle advanced is so incontrovertible that, if I had confined myself merely to general views, I could have entrenched myself in an impregnable fortress; and the work, in this form, would probably have had a much more masterly air. But such general views, though they may advance the cause of abstract truth, rarely tend to promote any practical good; and I thought that I should not do justice to the subject, and bring it fairly under

---

[2] [This sentence was omitted in 1806 (Vol. 1, p. xi) and all subsequent editions.]

discussion, if I refused to consider any of the consequences which appeared necessarily to flow from it, whatever these consequences might be. By pursuing this plan, however, I am aware that I have opened a door to many objections and, probably, to much severity of criticism: but I console myself with the reflection that even the errors into which I may have fallen, by affording a handle to argument, and an additional excitement to examination, may be subservient to the important end, of bringing a subject so nearly connected with the happiness of society into more general notice.

Throughout the whole of the present work, I have so far differed in principle from the former, as to suppose another check to population possible, which does not strictly come under the head either of vice or misery;[3] and, in the latter part, I have endeavoured to soften some of the harshest conclusions of the first essay. In doing this, I hope that I have not violated the principles of just reasoning, nor expressed any opinion respecting the probable improvement of society in which I am not borne out by the experience of the past. To those who shall still think that any check to population whatever would be worse than the evils which it would relieve, the conclusions of the former essay will remain in full force; and if we adopt this opinion, we shall be compelled to acknowledge that the poverty and misery which prevail among the lower classes of society are absolutely irremediable.

I have taken as much pains as I could to avoid any errors in the facts and calculations which have been produced in the course of the work. Should any of them nevertheless turn out to be false, the reader will see that they will not materially affect the general tenour of the reasoning.

From the crowd of materials which presented themselves in illustration of the first branch of the subject, I dare not flatter myself that I have selected the best, or arranged them in the most perspicuous method. To those who take an interest in moral and political questions, I hope that the novelty and importance of the subject will compensate the imperfections of its execution.

London, June 8th, 1803

---

[3] [In 1817 (Vol. 1, p. ix) this was altered:
... as to suppose the action of another check to population which does not come under the head either of vice or misery ...

ADVERTISEMENT TO THE THIRD
EDITION[1]

The principal alterations in the present edition are the following:

The chapters which were the fourth and sixth of the second book are nearly rewritten, on account of an error into which the author had fallen in an attempt to estimate the fruitfulness of marriages and the number of the born living to be married, from the data in registers; and as the chapters, in their present state, are not suggested by those which immediately preceded them in the same manner as they were before, they are transferred to the latter part of the book, and now form the ninth and tenth chapters.[2]

In the chapter of the same book, which treats of the Checks to Population in England, a remark has been added to show the incorrectness of considering the proportion of births as nearly uniform throughout the last century, and consequently of founding an estimate of the population at different periods on such grounds.[3]

In the fifth chapter of the third book an observation has been inserted on the policy as well as duty of assisting the poor through temporary seasons of distress;[4] and in the seventh, eighth, ninth, and tenth chapters of the same book, some passages have been omitted and others added, particularly in the tenth, which treats of bounties on the exportation of corn, on account of the present importance of the subject, and the discussion which it has lately received.[5]

In the sixth chapter of the fourth book, one passage has been omitted,[6] and a passage has been added on the effect of good government in diminishing poverty.[7]

In the seventh chapter of the same book a passage has been omitted;[8] and

---

[1] [This ADVERTISEMENT TO THE THIRD EDITION was placed immediately after the title-page in 1806, before the reprinted 1803 PREFACE. In 1807 it followed the PREFACE; it was still headed ADVERTISEMENT TO THE THIRD EDITION.]

[2] [Chapters iv(b) and vi(b) of Book II in this edition, Vol. II, pp. 1–22.]

[3] [Vol. I, p. 263 of this edition.]

[4] [See Vol. I, p. 357 of this edition.]

[5] [These changes are noted where they occur, in chapters viii, ix, x and xi of Book III in this edition.]

[6] [This was the paragraph about 'nature's mighty feast', Vol. II, pp. 127–8 of this edition.]

[7] [Vol. II, pp. 130–31 of this edition.]

[8] [This deleted passage shows Malthus's understanding of the attitude of the poor towards 'them', Vol. II, pp. 139–40 of this edition.]

in the eighth chapter a passage of some length, relating to a comparison of the married and unmarried,[9] has been omitted, and an observation added on the propriety of not underrating the desirableness of marriage, while we are inculcating the duties of moral restraint.

These are the most prominent alterations. The rest consist merely of a few verbal corrections, and here and there a short passage or explanatory note, to prevent misconceptions. These minor corrections occur principally in the two first chapters.

The reader will see that the alterations here mentioned do not affect the principles of the work, and therefore do not essentially lessen the value of the quarto edition.

In an appendix, an answer is given to the principal objections which have been urged against the Essay; and for the accommodation of the purchasers of the former edition it is printed in quarto, and may be had separately. Those who have not leisure or inclination to read the entire work, will find in the appendix such a notice of its most prominent arguments, as will give them a good general idea of the aim and bent of the whole.

[10]●For the sake of making the volumes more equal, the printer has placed the Index to both at the end of the first. It was not at first foreseen that the Appendix and Index would be so long; or a preferable division of the volumes would have been adopted.●[10]

---

[9] [These deleted pages contain an appeal for more courtesy to unmarried women, Vol. II, pp. 148–50 of this edition.]

[10] [This paragraph was omitted in 1807 (Vol. I, p. xiii), when the first two Books of the *Essay* were printed in Vol. I, the remaining contents in Vol. II. In 1806 the text of Vol. I ended at p. 505, at the conclusion of the chapter on Scotland and Ireland; this was followed by the index to both volumes; Vol. II began with the remaining three chapters of Book II, and finished on p. 559 with the end of the Appendix.]

PREFACE TO THE FIFTH EDITION[1]

This Essay was first published at a period of extensive warfare, combined, from peculiar circumstances, with a most prosperous foreign commerce.

It came before the public, therefore, at a time when there would be an extraordinary demand for men, and very little disposition to suppose the possibility of any evil arising from the redundancy of population. Its success, under these disadvantages, was greater than could have been reasonably expected; and it may be presumed that it will not lose its interest after a period of a different description has succeeded, which has in the most marked manner illustrated its principles, and confirmed its conclusions.

On account therefore of the nature of the subject, which it must be allowed is one of permanent interest, as well as of the attention likely to be directed to it in future, I am bound to correct those errors of my work, of which subsequent experience and information may have convinced me, and to make such additions and alterations as appear calculated to improve it and promote its utility.

It would have been easy to have added many further historical illustrations of the first part of the subject; but as I was unable to supply the want I once alluded to, of accounts of sufficient accuracy to ascertain what part of the natural power of increase each particular check destroys, it appeared to me that the conclusion, which I had before drawn from very ample evidence of the only kind that could be obtained, would hardly receive much additional force by the accumulation of more, precisely of the same description.

In the two first books, therefore, the only additions are a new chapter on France, and one on England, chiefly in reference to facts which have occurred since the publication of the last edition.[2]

In the third book I have given an additional chapter on the Poor-Laws;[3] and as it appeared to me that the chapters on the Agricultural and Commercial Systems, and the Effects of increasing Wealth on the Poor, were not either so well arranged, or so immediately applicable to the main subject,

---

[1] [In 1817 this PREFACE was printed immediately after that of 1803, the ADVERTISEMENTS of 1806 and 1807 being omitted.]

[2] [Chapters ix and xi of Book II in this edition.]

[3] [Chapter vii of Book III in this edition.]

as they ought to be; and as I further wished to make some alterations in the chapter on Bounties upon Exportation, and add something on the subject of Restrictions upon Importation, I have recast and rewritten the chapters which stand the 8th, 9th, 10th, 11th, 12th, 13th, in the present edition;[4] and given a new title, and added two or three passages to the 14th, and last chapter of the same book.[5]

In the fourth book, I have added a new chapter to the one entitled *Effects of the Knowledge of the principal Cause of Poverty on Civil Liberty*; and another to the chapter on *the different Plans of employing the Poor*; and I have made a considerable addition to the Appendix, in reply to some writers on the Principles of Population whose works have appeared since the last edition.

These are the principal additions and alterations made in the present edition. They consist in a considerable degree of the application of the general principles of the Essay to the present state of things.

For the accommodation of the purchasers of the former editions, these additions and alterations will be published in a separate volume.[6]

East-India College, June 7th, 1817

---

[4] [Chapters A–F of Book III in this edition.]   [5] [Chapter xiii of Book III in this edition.]
[6] [This paragraph was still included in this PREFACE when it was reprinted in 1826.]

ADVERTISEMENT TO THE SIXTH EDITION
Jan. 2d, 1826[1]

The additions to the present edition chiefly consist of some further documents and inferences relating to the state of the population in those countries, in which fresh enumerations, and registers of births, deaths and marriages, have appeared since the publication of my last edition in 1817. They refer principally to England, France, Sweden, Russia, Prussia, and America,[2] and will be found in the chapters which treat of the population of these countries. In the chapter on the Fruitfulness of Marriages an additional table has been given, (vol. i. p. 498.)[3] which, from the per centage increase of population in the interval between those decennial enumerations which are now taking place in some countries, shews the period of their doubling, or the rate at which they are increasing. At the end of the Appendix my reasons for not replying to the late publication of Mr. Godwin are shortly stated. In other parts of the work some inconsiderable alterations and corrections have been made, which it is unnecessary to specify; and a few notes have been added, the principal of which is one on the variations in the price of corn in Holland under a free trade, and the error of supposing that the scarcity of one country is generally counterbalanced by the plenty of some other – Vol. ii. p. 207.[4]

---

[1] [This ADVERTISEMENT was printed after the PREFACES of 1803 and 1817.]

[2] [There is no chapter on America as distinct from the 'American Indians', but readers of this edition may refer to the index for information about the United States.]

[3] [Vol. II, p. 17 in this edition.]   [4] [Vol. II, pp. 74–6 in this edition.]

ESSAY, &c

BOOK I

OF THE CHECKS TO POPULATION IN THE LESS CIVILIZED PARTS OF THE WORLD, AND IN PAST TIMES

CHAPTER I

Statement of the Subject. Ratios of the Increase of Population and Food

In an inquiry concerning the future improvement of society,[1] the mode of conducting the subject which naturally presents itself, is

1. An investigation of the causes that have hitherto impeded the progress of mankind towards happiness; and

2. An examination into the probability of the total or partial removal of these causes in future.

To enter fully into this question, and to enumerate all the causes that have hitherto influenced human improvement, would be much beyond the power of an individual. The principal object of the present essay is to examine the effects of one great cause intimately united with the very nature of man; which, though it has been constantly and powerfully operating since the commencement of society, has been little noticed by the writers who have treated this subject. The facts which establish the existence of this cause have, indeed, been repeatedly stated and acknowledged; but its natural and necessary effects have been almost totally overlooked; though probably among these effects may be reckoned a very considerable portion of that vice and misery, and of that unequal distribution of the bounties of nature, which it has been the unceasing object of the enlightened philanthropist in all ages to correct.

---

[1] [In 1806 Malthus altered this to:
   In an inquiry concerning the improvement of society . . .

9

The cause to which I allude is the constant tendency in all animated life to increase beyond the nourishment prepared for it.

It is observed by Dr. Franklin that there is no bound to the prolific nature of plants or animals but what is made by their crowding and interfering with each other's means of subsistence. Were the face of the earth, he says, vacant of other plants, it might be gradually sowed and overspread with one kind only; as, for instance, with fennel: and were it empty of other inhabitants, it might in a few ages be replenished from one nation only; as, for instance, with Englishmen.[2]

[3]*This is incontrovertibly true. Through the animal and vegetable kingdoms Nature has scattered the seeds of life abroad with the most profuse and liberal hand; but has been comparatively sparing in the room and the nourishment necessary to rear them. The germs of existence contained in this spot of earth, with ample food, and ample room to expand in, would fill millions of worlds in the course of a few thousand years. Necessity, that imperious all-pervading law of nature, restrains them within the prescribed bounds. The race of plants and the race of animals shrink under this great restrictive law; and the race of man cannot by any efforts of reason escape from it.*[3]

[4]*In plants and animals the view of the subject is simple. They are all impelled by a powerful instinct to the increase of their species; and this instinct is interrupted by no reasoning or doubts about providing for their offspring. Wherever, therefore, there is liberty, the power of increase is exerted; and the superabundant effects are repressed afterwards by want of room and nourishment, which is common to plants and animals; and among animals, by their becoming the prey of each other.*[4]

The effects of this check on man are more complicated. Impelled to the increase of his species by an equally powerful instinct, reason interrupts his career, and asks him whether he may not bring beings into the world for whom he cannot provide the means of support. If he attend to this natural suggestion, the restriction too frequently produces vice. If he hear it not, the

---

[2] Franklin's Miscell. p. 9.
[3] [This paragraph is taken almost verbatim from p. 15 of the 1798 *Essay*, but in 1806 (Vol. 1, p. 3) Malthus altered the third sentence:
    The germs of existence contained in this earth, if they could freely develop themselves, would fill millions of worlds ...
[4] [This is from p. 27 of the 1798 *Essay*. However, in 1806 (Vol. 1, pp. 3-4) Malthus made three alterations; the paragraph then read:
    In plants and irrational animals ... this instinct is interrupted by no doubts about providing for their offspring.
[The concluding words were:
    ... by want of room and nourishment.

human race will be constantly endeavouring to increase beyond the means of subsistence. But as by that law of our nature which makes food necessary to the life of man, population can never actually increase beyond the lowest nourishment capable of supporting it; a strong check on population, from the difficulty of acquiring food, must be constantly in operation. This difficulty must fall somewhere, and must necessarily be severely felt in some or other of the various forms of misery, or the fear of misery, by a large portion of mankind.

That population has this constant tendency to increase beyond the means of subsistence, and that it is kept to its necessary level by these causes, will sufficiently appear from a review of the different states of society in which man has existed. But before we proceed to this review the subject will, perhaps, be seen in a clearer light if we endeavour to ascertain what would be the natural increase of population if left to exert itself with perfect freedom; and what might be expected to be the rate of increase in the productions of the earth under the most favourable circumstances of human industry. [5]●A comparison of these two rates of increase will enable us to judge of the force of that tendency in population to increase beyond the means of subsistence, which has been stated to exist.●[5]

[6]*It will be allowed, that no country has hitherto been known where the manners were so pure and simple, and the means of subsistence so abundant, that no check whatever has existed to early marriages from the difficulty of providing for a family, and that no waste of the human species has been occasioned by vicious customs, by towns, by unhealthy occupations, or too severe labour. Consequently in no state that we have yet known has the power of population been left to exert itself with perfect freedom.

Whether the law of marriage be instituted or not, the dictate of nature and virtue seems to be an early attachment to one woman; and where there were no impediments of any kind in the way of an union to which such an attachment would lead, and no causes of depopulation afterwards, the increase of the human species would be evidently much greater than any increase which has been hitherto known.

In the northern states of America, where the means of subsistence have been more ample, the manners of the people more pure, and the checks to early marriages fewer, than in any of the modern states of Europe, the population was found to double itself for some successive periods every

---

[5] [This sentence was omitted in 1806 (Vol. I, p. 5).]

twenty-five years.*[6] Yet even during these periods, in some of the towns, the deaths exceeded the births;[7] and they consequently required a continued supply from the country to support their population.

In the back settlements, where the sole employment was agriculture, and vicious customs and unwholesome occupations were unknown, the population was found to double itself in fifteen years.[8] Even this extraordinary rate of increase is probably short of the utmost power of population. Very severe labour is requisite to clear a fresh country; such situations are not in general considered as particularly healthy; and the inhabitants were probably occasionally subject to the incursions of the Indians, which might destroy some lives, or at any rate diminish the fruits of their industry.

According to a table of Euler, calculated on a mortality of 1 in 36, if the births be to the deaths in the proportion of 3 to 1, the period of doubling will be only $12\frac{4}{5}$ years.[9] And these proportions are not only possible suppositions, but have actually occurred for short periods in more countries than one.

Sir William Petty supposes a doubling possible in so short a time as ten years.[10]

But to be perfectly sure that we are far within the truth, we will take the slowest of these rates of increase; a rate, in which all concurring testimonies agree, and which has been repeatedly ascertained to be from procreation only.

[11]*It may safely be pronounced therefore, that population when unchecked goes on doubling itself every twenty-five years, or increases in a geometrical ratio.*[11]

---

[6] [This sentence, and the two preceding paragraphs, are based on pp. 18–20 of the 1798 *Essay*.]
[A footnote was added in 1806 (Vol. 1, p. 6):

It appears from some recent calculations and estimates that, from the first settlement of America to the year 1800, the periods of doubling have been but very little above twenty years. See a note on the increase of American population in Book II, chap. xi. [chap. xiii of this edition, Vol. 1, p.295.]
[At the same time Malthus considerably altered the actual text of the whole paragraph:

In the northern states of America ... the population has been found to double itself, for above a century and a half successively, in less than twenty-five years. Yet ... in some of the towns the deaths exceeded the births, a circumstance which clearly proves that, in those parts of the country which supplied this deficiency, the increase must have been much more rapid than the general average.

[7] Price's Observ. on Revers. Pay. vol. i. p. 274.

[8] Ibid. p. 282. [In 1806 (Vol. 1, p. 7) this sentence was changed:

In the back settlements, where the sole employment is agriculture, and vicious customs and unwholesome occupations are little known, the population has been found to double itself...

[The present tense was continued throughout the paragraph:
... probably are occasionally subject to the incursions of the Indians, which may destroy some lives ...

[9] See this table at the end of chap. iv, book ii. [Chapter iv (a) of Book II in this edition, Vol. 1, p. 191.]

[10] Polit. Arith. p. 14.   [11] [This is on p. 21 of the 1798 *Essay*.]

The rate according to which the productions of the earth may be supposed to increase, it will not be so easy to determine. Of this, however, we may be perfectly certain, that the ratio of their increase must be of a totally different nature from the ratio of the increase of population. A thousand millions are just as easily doubled every twenty-five years by the power of population as a thousand. But the food to support the increase from the greater number will by no means be obtained with the same facility. Man is necessarily confined in room. When acre has been added to acre till all the fertile land is occupied, the yearly increase of food must depend upon the amelioration of the land already in possession. This is a stream[12] which, from the nature of all soils, instead of increasing, must be gradually diminishing. But population, could it be supplied with food, would go on with unexhausted vigour; and the increase of one period would furnish the power of a greater increase the next, and this without any limit.

From the accounts we have of China and Japan, it may be fairly doubted whether the best-directed efforts of human industry could double the produce of these countries even once in any number of years. There are many parts of the globe, indeed, hitherto uncultivated, and almost unoccupied; but the right of exterminating, or driving into a corner where they must starve, even the inhabitants of these thinly-peopled regions, will be questioned in a moral view. The process of improving their minds and directing their industry would necessarily be slow; and during this time, as population would regularly keep pace with the increasing produce, it would rarely happen that a great degree of knowledge and industry would have to operate at once upon rich unappropriated soil. Even where this might take place, as it does sometimes in new colonies, a geometrical ratio increases with such extraordinary rapidity that the advantage could not last long. [13]●If America continue increasing, which she certainly will do, though not with the same rapidity as formerly, the Indians will be driven further and further back into the country, till the whole race is ultimately exterminated.●[13]

These observations are, in a degree, applicable to all the parts of the earth, where the soil is imperfectly cultivated. To exterminate the inhabitants of the greatest part of Asia and Africa is a thought that could not be admitted for a moment. To civilize and direct the industry of the various tribes of Tartars and Negroes would certainly be a work of considerable time, and of variable and uncertain success.

---

[12] [In 1817 (Vol. I, p. 9) the word *stream* was replaced by 'fund'.

[13] [This sentence was altered in 1817 (Vol. I, p. 11):

If the United States of America continue increasing, which they certainly will do, though not with the same rapidity as formerly, the Indians will be driven further and further back into the country, till the whole race is ultimately exterminated, and the territory is incapable of further extension.

Europe is by no means so fully peopled as it might be. In Europe there is the fairest chance that human industry may receive its best direction. The science of agriculture has been much studied in England and Scotland; and there is still a great portion of uncultivated land in these countries. Let us consider at what rate the produce of this island might be supposed to increase under circumstances the most favourable to improvement.

14*If it be allowed, that by the best possible policy, and great encouragements to agriculture, the average produce of the island could be doubled in the first twenty-five years, it will be allowing probably a greater increase than could with reason be expected.

In the next twenty-five years, it is impossible to suppose that the produce could be quadrupled. It would be contrary to all our knowledge of the properties of land.*14 The improvement of the barren parts would be a work of time and labour; and it must be evident to those who have the slightest acquaintance with agricultural subjects that, in proportion as cultivation extended, the additions that could yearly be made to the former average produce must be gradually and regularly diminishing. That we may be the better able to compare the increase of population and food, let us make a supposition which, without pretending to accuracy, is clearly more favourable to the power of production in the earth than any experience that we have had of its qualities will warrant.

15*Let us suppose that the yearly additions which might be made to the former average produce, instead of decreasing, which they certainly would do, were to remain the same; and that the produce of this island might be increased every twenty-five years by a quantity equal to what it at present produces: the most enthusiastic speculator cannot suppose a greater increase than this. In a few centuries it would make every acre of land in the island like a garden.

If this supposition be applied to the whole earth, and if it be allowed that the subsistence for man which the earth affords might be increased every twenty-five years by a quantity equal to what it at present produces, this will be supposing a rate of increase much greater than we can imagine that any possible exertions of mankind could make it.

It may be fairly pronounced therefore, that, considering the present average state of the earth, the means of subsistence, under circumstances the most favourable to human industry, could not possibly be made to increase faster than in an arithmetical ratio.

The necessary effects of these two different rates of increase, when brought together, will be very striking. Let us call the population of this island eleven millions; and suppose the present produce equal to the easy support of such a

---

14 [These two sentences and the preceding paragraph are from pp. 21–2 of the 1798 *Essay*.]

number. In the first twenty-five years the population would be twenty-two millions, and the food being also doubled, the means of subsistence would be equal to this increase. In the next twenty-five years, the population would be forty-four millions, and the means of subsistence only equal to the support of thirty-three millions. In the next period the population would be eighty-eight millions, and the means of subsistence just equal to the support of half of that number. And at the conclusion of the first century, the population would be a hundred and seventy-six millions, and the means of subsistence only equal to the support of fifty-five millions; leaving a population of a hundred and twenty-one millions totally unprovided for.

Taking the whole earth instead of this island, emigration would of course be excluded; and supposing the present population equal to a thousand millions, the human species would increase as the numbers 1, 2, 4, 8, 16, 32, 64, 128, 256, and subsistence as 1, 2, 3, 4, 5, 6, 7, 8, 9. In two centuries the population would be to the means of subsistence as 256 to 9; in three centuries as 4096 to 13, and in two thousand years the difference would be almost incalculable.

In this supposition no limits whatever are placed to the produce of the earth. It may increase for ever, and be greater than any assignable quantity; yet still the power of population being in every period so much superior, the increase of the human species can only be kept down to the level of the means of subsistence by the constant operation of the strong law of necessity acting as a check upon the greater power.*[15]

---

[15] [The concluding paragraphs of this chapter are based on pp. 22–6 of the 1798 *Essay*.]

CHAPTER II

Of the general Checks to Population, and the Mode of their Operation

[From 1806 (Vol. 1, p. 15) this chapter began thus:

The ultimate check to population appears then to be a want of food, arising necessarily from the different ratios according to which population and food increase. But this ultimate check is never the immediate check, except in cases of actual famine.

The immediate check may be stated to consist in all those customs, and all those diseases, which seem to be generated by a scarcity of the means of subsistence; and all those causes, independent of this scarcity, whether of a moral or physical nature, which tend prematurely to weaken and destroy the human frame.

These checks to population, which are constantly operating with more or less force in every society, and keep down the number to the level of the means of subsistence, may be classed under two general heads – the preventive and the positive checks.

The preventive check, as far as it is voluntary, is peculiar to man, and arises from that distinctive superiority in his reasoning faculties which enables him to calculate distant consequences. The checks to the indefinite increase of plants and irrational animals are all either positive, or, if preventive, involuntary. But man cannot look around him and see the distress ...

The checks to population, which are constantly operating with more or less force in every society, and keep down the number to the level of the means of subsistence, may be classed under two general heads; the preventive, and the positive checks.

The preventive check is peculiar to man, and arises from that distinctive superiority in his reasoning faculties, which enables him to calculate distant consequences. Plants and animals have apparently no doubts about the future support of their offspring. The checks to their indefinite increase, therefore, are all positive. But man cannot look around him, and see the distress which frequently presses upon those who have large families; he cannot contemplate his present possessions or earnings, which he now nearly consumes himself, and calculate the amount of each share, when with very little addition they must be divided, perhaps, among seven or eight, without feeling a doubt, whether if he follow the bent of his inclinations, he may be able to support the offspring which he will probably bring into the world.[1]*In a state of equality, if such can exist, this would be the simple question. In the present state of society other considerations occur. Will he not lower his rank in life, and be obliged to give up in great measure his former society?[a] Does any mode of employment present itself by which he may reasonably hope to maintain a family? Will he not at any rate subject himself to greater difficulties, and more severe labour than in his single state? Will he not be unable to transmit to his children the same advantages of education and improvement that he had himself possessed? Does he even feel secure that, should he have a large family, his utmost exertions can save them from rags, and squalid poverty, and their consequent degradation in the community? And may he not be reduced to the grating necessity of forfeiting his independence, and of being obliged to the sparing hand of charity for support?

These considerations are calculated to prevent, and certainly do prevent, a great number of persons in all civilized nations from pursuing the dictate of nature in an early attachment to one woman.*[1]

[2]●If this restraint do not produce vice, as in many instances is the case, and very generally so among the middle and higher classes of women, it is undoubtedly the least evil that can arise from the principle of population. Considered as a restraint on an inclination otherwise innocent, and always natural, it must be allowed to produce a certain degree of temporary unhappiness; but evidently slight, compared with the evils which result from any of the other checks to population.

When this restraint produces vice, as it does most frequently among men, and among a numerous class of females, the evils which follow are but too conspicuous.●[2]

A promiscuous intercourse to such a degree as to prevent the birth of children, seems to lower in the most marked manner the dignity of human nature. It cannot be without its effect on men, and nothing can be more

---

[1] [These sentences are based on pp. 28–9 of the 1798 *Essay*.]
[a] [Here, however, Malthus simply wrote:
Will he not lower his rank in life?
In 1806 (Vol. I, p. 16) he altered this again:
Will he not lower his rank in life, and be obliged in great measure to give up his former habits?
[2] [From 1806 (Vol. I, pp. 17–18) this passage read thus:
If this restraint do not produce vice, it is undoubtedly the least evil that can arise from the principle of population. Considered as a restraint on a strong natural inclination, it must be allowed to produce a certain degree of temporary unhappiness; but evidently slight, compared with the evils which result from any of the other checks to population; and merely of the same nature as many other sacrifices of temporary to permanent gratification, which it is the business of a moral agent continually to make.
When this restraint produces vice, the evils which follow are but too conspicuous.

obvious than its tendency to degrade the female character, and to destroy all its most amiable and distinguishing characteristics. Add to which, that among those unfortunate females with which all great towns abound, more real distress and aggravated misery are perhaps to be found than in any other department of human life.

When a general corruption of morals, with regard to the sex, pervades all the classes of society, its effects must necessarily be to poison the springs of domestic happiness, to weaken conjugal and parental affection, and to lessen the united exertions and ardour of parents in the care and education of their children; effects which cannot take place without a decided diminution of the general happiness and virtue of the society; particularly as the necessity of art in the accomplishment and conduct of intrigues, and in the concealment of their consequences, necessarily leads to many other vices.

The positive checks to population are extremely various, and include every cause, whether arising from vice or misery, which in any degree contributes to shorten the natural duration of human life. Under this head therefore may be enumerated, all unwholesome occupations, severe labour and exposure to the seasons, extreme poverty, bad nursing of children, great towns, excesses of all kinds, the whole train of common diseases and epidemics, wars, pestilence,[3] plague, and famine.

On examining these obstacles to the increase of population which I have classed under the heads of preventive and positive checks, it will appear that they are all resolvable into moral restraint, vice, and misery.

Of the preventive checks, the restraint from marriage which is not followed by irregular gratifications may properly be termed moral restraint.[4]

Promiscuous intercourse, unnatural passions, violations of the marriage bed, and improper arts to conceal the consequences of irregular connexions,[5] clearly come under the head of vice.

---

[3] [The word *pestilence* was omitted in 1806 (Vol. 1, p. 19).]

[4] [In 1806 (Vol. 1, pp. 19–20) this footnote was added:

It will be observed that I here use the term *moral* in its most confined sense. By moral restraint I would be understood to mean a restraint from marriage from prudential motives, with a conduct strictly moral during the period of this restraint; and I have never intentionally deviated from this sense. When I have wished to consider the restraint from marriage unconnected with its consequences, I have either called it prudential restraint, or a part of the preventive check, of which indeed it forms the principal branch.

In my review of the different stages of society, I have been accused of not allowing sufficient weight in the prevention of population to moral restraint; but when the confined sense of the term, which I have here explained, is adverted to, I am fearful that I shall not be found to have erred much in this respect. I should be very glad to believe myself mistaken.

[5] [From 1806 (Vol. 1, p. 20) this read:

... irregular connections are preventive checks that clearly come under the head of vice.

Of the positive checks, those which appear to arise unavoidably from the laws of nature may be called exclusively misery; and those which we obviously bring upon ourselves, such as wars, excesses, and many others which it would be in our power to avoid, are of a mixed nature. They are brought upon us by vice, and their consequences are misery.[6]

[This paragraph was inserted here in 1806 (Vol. i, pp. 21–2):

The sum of all these preventive and positive checks, taken together, forms the immediate check to population; and it is evident that, in every country where the whole of the procreative power cannot be called into action, the preventive and the positive checks must vary inversely as each other; that is, in countries either naturally unhealthy, or subject to a great mortality, from whatever cause it may arise, the preventive check will prevail very little. In those countries, on the contrary, which are naturally healthy, and where the preventive check is found to prevail with considerable force, the positive check will prevail very little, or the mortality be very small.

---

[6] As the general consequence of vice is misery, and as this consequence is the precise reason why an action is termed vicious, it may appear that the term misery alone would be here sufficient, and that it is superfluous to use both. But the rejection of the term vice would introduce a considerable confusion into our language and ideas. We want it particularly to distinguish that class of actions, the general tendency of which is to produce misery, but which, in their immediate or individual effects, may produce perhaps exactly the contrary. The gratification of all our passions in its immediate effect is happiness, not misery; and in individual instances even the remote consequences (at least in this life) come under the same denomination. I have little doubt that there have been some irregular connexions with women which have added to the happiness of both parties, and have injured no one. These individual actions therefore cannot come under the head of misery. But they are still evidently vicious, because an action is so denominated, the general tendency of which is to produce misery, whatever may be its individual effect; and no person can doubt the general tendency of an illicit intercourse between the sexes to injure the happiness of society.

[Malthus did not amend this controversial footnote until 1817 (Vol. i, pp. 23–4); the third sentence then read:

We want it particularly to distinguish those actions, the general tendency of which is to produce misery, and which are therefore prohibited by the commands of the Creator, and the precepts of the moralist, although in their immediate or individual effects they may produce exactly the contrary.

[Instead of saying *I have little doubt that there have been some irregular connections* ... Malthus wrote in 1817:

There may have been some irregular connections ...

[Of individual actions which 'cannot come under the head of misery' he continued:

But they are still evidently vicious, because an action is so denominated which violates an express precept, founded upon its general tendency to produce misery, whatever may be its individual effect ...

[The 'express precept' is the Seventh of the Ten Commandments given by God to Moses: Thou shalt not commit adultery. (Exodus xx, v.14, Bible of 1611).]

In every country some of these checks are, with more or less force, in constant operation; yet notwithstanding their general prevalence, there are few states in which there is not a constant effort in the population to increase beyond the means of subsistence. This constant effort as constantly tends to subject the lower classes of society to distress, and to prevent any great permanent amelioration of their condition.

[7]*These effects, in the present state of society, seem to be produced in the following manner. We will suppose the means of subsistence in any country just equal to the easy support of its inhabitants. The constant effort towards population, which is found to act even in the most vicious societies, increases the number of people before the means of subsistence are increased. The food, therefore, which before supported eleven millions, must now be divided among eleven millions and a half. The poor consequently must live much worse, and many of them be reduced to severe distress. The number of labourers also being above the proportion of work in the market, the price of labour must tend to fall, while the price of provisions would at the same time tend to rise. The labourer therefore must do more work to earn the same as he did before. During this season of distress, the discouragements to marriage and the difficulty of rearing a family are so great, that population is nearly at a stand.[8] In the meantime, the cheapness of labour, the plenty of labourers, and the necessity of an increased industry among them, encourage cultivators to employ more labour upon their land, to turn up fresh soil, and to manure and improve more completely what is already in tillage, till ultimately the means of subsistence may become in the same proportion to the population as at the period from which we set out. The situation of the labourer being then again tolerably comfortable, the restraints to population are in some degree loosened; and, after a short period, the same retrograde and progressive movements, with respect to happiness, are repeated.

This sort of oscillation will not probably be obvious to common view; and it may be difficult even for the most attentive observer to calculate its periods. Yet that, in the generality of old states, some such vibration does exist,[9] though in a much less marked, and in a much more irregular manner, than I have described it, no reflecting man who considers the subject deeply can well doubt.

---

[7] [These passages, beginning with 'These effects . . .' are based on pp. 29–32 of the 1798 *Essay*. In 1798, however, Malthus added that:
    A satisfactory history of this kind . . . would require the constant and minute attention of an observing mind during a long life.
[8] In 1826 (Vol. I, p. 18) this was altered to:
    . . . that the progress of population is retarded . . .
[9] Changed in 1817 (Vol. I, p. 27) to:
    . . . some alternation of this kind does exist, . . .

One principal reason why this oscillation has been less remarked, and less decidedly confirmed by experience than might naturally be expected, is that the histories of mankind which we possess are, in general, histories only of the higher classes. We have not many accounts that can be depended upon of the manners and customs of that part of mankind where these retrograde and progressive movements chiefly take place. A satisfactory history of this kind, of one people and of one period, would require the constant and minute attention of many observing minds in local and general remarks on the state of the lower classes of society, and the causes that influenced it; and to draw accurate inferences upon this subject, a succession of such historians for some centuries would be necessary.*[7] This branch of statistical knowledge has of late years been attended to in some countries,[10] and we may promise ourselves a clearer insight into the internal structure of human society from the progress of these inquiries. But the science may be said yet to be in its infancy, and many of the objects, on which it would be desirable to have information, have been either omitted or not stated with sufficient accuracy. Among these perhaps may be reckoned the proportion of the number of adults to the number of marriages; the extent to which vicious customs have prevailed in consequence of the restraints upon matrimony; the comparative mortality among the children of the most distressed part of the community, and of those who live rather more at their ease; the variations in the real price of labour; the observable differences in the state of the lower classes of society, with respect to ease and happiness, at different times during a certain period; and very accurate registers of births, deaths, and marriages, which are of the utmost importance in this subject.

A faithful history, including such particulars, would tend greatly to elucidate the manner in which the constant check upon population acts; and would probably prove the existence of the retrograde and progressive movements that have been mentioned; though the times of their vibration

---

[10] The judicious questions which Sir John Sinclair circulated in Scotland, and the very valuable accounts which he has collected in that part of the island, do him the highest honour; and these accounts will ever remain an extraordinary monument of the learning, good sense, and general information of the clergy of Scotland. It is to be regretted that the adjoining parishes are not put together in the work, which would have assisted the memory both in attaining and recollecting the state of particular districts. The repetitions and contradictory opinions which occur are not in my opinion so objectionable, as, to the result of such testimony, more faith may be given than we could possibly give to the testimony of any individual. Even were this result drawn for us by some master hand, though much valuable time would undoubtedly be saved, the information would not be so satisfactory. If, with a few subordinate improvements, this work had contained accurate and complete registers for the last 150 years, it would have been inestimable, and would have exhibited a

must necessarily be rendered irregular from the operation of many interrupting causes; such as, the introduction or failure of certain manufactures, a greater or less prevalent spirit of agricultural enterprize; years of plenty or years of scarcity; wars, sickly seasons, poor laws, emigration, and other causes of a similar nature.

A circumstance which has, perhaps, more than any other, contributed to conceal this oscillation from common view, is the difference between the nominal and real price of labour. It very rarely happens that the nominal price of labour universally falls; but we well know that it frequently remains the same while the nominal price of provisions has been gradually rising.

[The two following sentences, together with footnote 11, were inserted in 1817 (Vol. I, p. 31):

This, indeed, will generally be the case if the increase of manufactures and commerce be sufficient to employ the new labourers that are thrown into the market, and to prevent the increased supply from lowering the money-price.[11] But an increased number of labourers receiving the same money-wages will necessarily, by their competition, increase the money-price of corn.

This is, in fact, a real fall in the price of labour; and, during this period, the condition of the lower classes of the community must be gradually growing worse. But the farmers and capitalists are growing rich from the real cheapness of labour. Their increasing capitals enable them to employ a greater number of men; and, as the population had probably suffered some check from the greater difficulty of supporting a family, the demand for labour, after a certain period, would be great in proportion to the supply, and its price would of course rise, if left to find its natural level; and thus the wages of labour, and consequently the condition of the lower classes of society, might have progressive and retrograde movements, though the price of labour might never nominally fall.

In savage life, where there is no regular price of labour, it is little to be doubted that similar oscillations take place. When population has increased

---

better picture of the internal state of a country than has yet been presented to the world. But this last most essential improvement no diligence could have effected.

[11] If the new labourers thrown yearly into the market should find no employment but in agriculture, their competition might so lower the money-price of labour as to prevent the increase of population from occasioning an effective demand for more corn; or, in other words, if the landlords and farmers could get nothing but an additional quantity of agricultural labour in exchange for any additional produce which they could raise, they might not be tempted to raise it.

nearly to the utmost limits of the food, all the preventive and the positive checks will naturally operate with increased force. Vicious habits with respect to the sex will be more general, the exposing of children more frequent, and both the probability and fatality of wars and epidemics, will be considerably greater; and these causes will probably continue their operation till the population is sunk below the level of the food; and then the return to comparative plenty will again produce an increase, and, after a certain period, its further progress will again be checked by the same causes.[12]

But without attempting to establish these progressive and retrograde movements in different countries, which would evidently require more minute histories than we possess,[13] the following propositions are intended to be proved:

1. Population is necessarily limited by the means of subsistence.

2. Population invariably increases, where the means of subsistence increase, unless prevented by some very powerful and obvious checks.[14]

3. These checks, and the checks which repress the superior power of population, and keep its effects on a level with the means of subsistence, are all resolvable into moral restraint, vice, and misery.

---

[12] Sir James Steuart very justly compares the generative faculty to a spring loaded with a variable weight, (Polit. Econ. vol. i. b. i. c. 4. p. 20.) which would of course produce exactly that kind of oscillation which has been mentioned. In the first book of his Political Economy, he has explained many parts of the subject of population very ably.

[13] [From 1806 (Vol. i, p. 28) this read:
... require more minute histories than we possess, and which the progress of civilisation naturally tends to counteract, ...

[14] [In 1806 (Vol. i, p. 29) Malthus added a footnote here:
I have expressed myself in this cautious manner, because I believe there are a very few instances, such as the negroes in the West Indies, and one or two others, where population does not keep up to the level of subsistence. But these are extreme cases; and generally speaking it might be said (and the propositions in this form would be more neatly and distinctly expressed) that,

2. Population always increases where the means of subsistence increase.

3. The checks which repress the superior power of population, and keep its effects on a level with the means of subsistence, are all resolvable into moral restraint, vice, and misery.

[In 1807 (Vol. i, p. 29) Malthus deleted the passage in brackets.]
[In 1817 (Vol. i, p. 34) he altered the first paragraph of this note:
I have expressed myself in this cautious manner, because I believe there are some instances where population does not keep up to the level of subsistence. But these are extreme cases ...
[Also in 1817, he added another paragraph to the footnote:
It should be observed that, by an increase in the means of subsistence is here meant such an increase as will enable the mass of society to command more food. An increase might certainly take place, which in the actual state of a particular society would not be distributed to the lower classes, and consequently would give no stimulus to population.

The first of these propositions scarcely needs illustration. The second and third will be sufficiently established by a review of the past and present state of society.[15]

This review will be the subject of the following chapters.

---

[15] [This sentence was altered in 1806 (Vol. 1, p. 29):
    The second and third will be sufficiently established by a review of the immediate checks to population in the past and present state of society.

CHAPTER III

Of the Checks to Population in the lowest Stage of Human Society

The wretched inhabitants of Tierra del Fuego have been placed by the general consent of voyagers at the bottom of the scale of human beings.[1] Of their domestic habits and manners, however, we have few accounts. Their barren country, and the miserable state in which they live, have prevented any intercourse with them that might give such information; but we cannot be at a loss to conceive the checks to population among a race of savages, whose very appearance indicates them to be half starved, and who, shivering with cold, and covered with filth and vermin, live in one of the most inhospitable climates in the world, without having sagacity enough to provide themselves with such conveniences as might mitigate its severities, and render life in some measure more comfortable.[2]

Next to these, and almost as low in genius and resources, have been placed the natives of Van Diemen's land;[3] but some late accounts have represented the islands of Andaman, in the East, as inhabited by a race of savages, still lower in wretchedness even than these. Everything that voyagers have related of savage life is said to fall short of the barbarism of this people. Their whole time is spent in search of food; and as their woods yield them few or no supplies of animals, and but little vegetable diet, their principal occupation is that of climbing the rocks, or roving along the margin of the sea, in search of a precarious meal of fish, which, during the tempestuous season, they often seek for in vain. Their stature seldom exceeds five feet; their bellies are protuberant, with high shoulders, large heads, and limbs disproportionately slender. Their countenances exhibit the extreme of wretchedness, a horrid mixture of famine and ferocity; and their extenuated and diseased figures plainly indicate the want of wholesome nourishment. Some of these unhappy beings have been found on the shores in the last stage of famine.[4]

In the next scale of human beings perhaps we may place the inhabitants of New Holland, of a part of whom we have some accounts that may be

---

[1] Cook's First Voy. vol. ii. p. 59.   [2] Second Voy. vol. ii. p. 187.
[3] Vancouver's Voy. vol. ii. b. iii. c. i. p. 13.
[4] Syme's Embassy to Ava, ch. i. p. 129. and Asiatic Researches, vol. iv. p. 401.
   [This should be pp. 389–90. See ASIATIC RESEARCHES in the Alphabetical List.]

depended upon, from a person who resided a considerable time at Port Jackson, and had frequent opportunities of being a witness to their habits and manners. The narrator of Captain Cook's first voyage having mentioned the very small number of inhabitants that was seen on the eastern coast of New Holland, and the apparent inability of the country, from its desolate state, to support many more, observes: 'By what means the inhabitants of this country are reduced to such a number as it can subsist, is not perhaps very easy to guess; whether, like the inhabitants of New Zealand, they are destroyed by the hands of each other in contests for food, whether they are swept off by accidental famine, or whether there is any cause that prevents the increase of the species, must be left for future adventurers to determine.'[5]

The account which Mr. Collins has given of these savages will, I hope, afford in some degree a satisfactory answer. They are described as, in general, neither tall nor well made. Their arms, legs, and thighs, are thin, which is ascribed to the poorness of their mode of living. Those who inhabit the sea-coast depend almost entirely on fish for their sustenance, relieved occasionally by a repast on some large grubs which are found in the body of the dwarf gum-tree. The very scanty stock of animals in the woods, and the very great labour necessary to take them, keep the inland natives in as poor a condition as their brethren on the coast. They are compelled to climb the tallest trees after honey, and the smaller animals, such as the flying squirrel and the opossum. When the stems are of great height, and without branches, which is generally the case in thick forests, this is a process of great labour, and is effected by cutting a notch with their stone hatchets for each foot successively, while their left arm embraces the tree. Trees were observed notched in this manner to the height of eighty feet before the first branch, where the hungry savage could hope to meet with any reward for so much toil.[6]

The woods, exclusive of the animals occasionally found in them, afford but little sustenance. A few berries, the yam, the fern root, and the flowers of the different banksias, make up the whole of the vegetable catalogue.[7]

A native with his child, surprised on the banks of the Hawksbury river by some of our colonists, launched his canoe in a hurry, and left behind him a specimen of his food, and of the delicacy of his stomach. From a piece of water-soken wood, full of holes, he had been extracting and eating a large worm. The smell both of the worm and its habitation was in the highest degree offensive. These worms, in the language of the country, are called

---

[5] Cook's First Voy. vol. iii p. 240. [It is possibly significant that in 1806 (Vol. i, p. 38) Malthus omitted the word *perhaps* when designating the Aborigines of Australia as third lowest in 'the scale of human beings'.]

[6] Collins's Account of New South Wales, Appendix, p. 549. 4to.   [7] Id. Appen. p. 557.

cah-bro; and a tribe of natives dwelling inland, from the circumstance of eating these loathsome worms, is named Cah-brogal. The wood natives also make a paste formed of the fern root, and the large and small ants bruised together and, in the season, add the eggs of this insect.[8]

In a country, the inhabitants of which are driven to such resources for subsistence, where the supply of animal and vegetable food is so extremely scanty, and the labour necessary to procure it is so severe, it is evident that the population must be very thinly scattered in proportion to the territory. Its utmost bounds must be very narrow. But when we advert to the strange and barbarous customs of these people, the cruel treatment of their women, and the difficulty of rearing children; instead of being surprised that it does not more frequently press to pass these bounds, we shall be rather inclined to consider even these scanty resources as more than sufficient to support all the population that could grow up under such circumstances.

The prelude to love in this country is violence, and of the most brutal nature. The savage selects his intended wife from the women of a different tribe, generally one at enmity with his own. He steals upon her in the absence of her protectors, and having first stupified her with blows of a club, or wooden sword, on the head, back, and shoulders, every one of which is followed by a stream of blood, he drags her through the woods by one arm, regardless of the stones and broken pieces of trees that may lie in his route, and anxious only to convey his prize in safety to his own party, where a most brutal scene ensues. The woman thus ravished becomes his wife, and is incorporated into the tribe to which he belongs, and but seldom quits him for another. The outrage is not resented by the relations of the female, who only retaliate by a similar outrage when it is in their power.[9]

The union of the sexes takes place at an early age, and instances were known to our colonists of very young girls having been much and shamefully abused by the males.[10]

The conduct of the husband to his wife, or wives, seems to be nearly in character with this strange and barbarous mode of courtship. The females bear on their heads the traces of the superiority of the males, which is exercised almost as soon as they find strength in their arms to inflict a blow. Some of these unfortunate beings have been observed with more scars on their shorn heads, cut in every direction, than could well be counted. Mr. Collins feelingly says: 'The condition of these women is so wretched that I

---

[8] Id. Appen. p. 558. [In 1817 (Vol. I, p. 41) 'water-soaked' was substituted for Collins's own *water-soken*.]

[9] Appen. p. 559.
[In 1807 (Vol. I, p. 35) Malthus omitted 'where a most brutal scene ensues'. He had already in 1806 (Vol. I, p. 35) changed *ravished* to 'treated'.]

[10] Appen. p. 563.

have often, on seeing a female child borne on its mother's shoulders, anticipated the miseries to which it was born, and thought it would be a mercy to destroy it!'[11] In another place, speaking of Bennilong's wife being delivered of a child, he says: 'I here find in my papers a note that for some offence Bennilong had severely beaten this woman in the morning, a short time before she was delivered.'[12]

Women treated in this brutal manner must necessarily be subject to frequent miscarriages, and it is probable that the abuse of very young girls, mentioned above as common, and the too early union of the sexes in general, would tend to prevent the females from being prolific. Instances of a plurality of wives were found more frequent than of a single wife; but what is extraordinary, Mr. Collins did not recollect ever to have noticed children by more than one. He had heard from some of the natives that the first wife claimed an exclusive right to the conjugal embrace, while the second was merely the slave and drudge of both.[13]

An absolutely exclusive right in the first wife to the conjugal embrace seems to be hardly probable; but it is possible that the second wife may not be allowed to rear her offspring. At any rate, if the observation be generally true, it proves that many of the women are without children, which can only be accounted for from the very severe hardships which they undergo, or from some particular customs which may not have come to the knowledge of Mr. Collins.

If the mother of a sucking child die, the helpless infant is buried alive in the same grave with its mother. The father himself places his living child on the body of his dead wife, and having thrown a large stone upon it, the grave is instantly filled by the other natives. This dreadful act was performed by Co-le-be, a native well known to our colonists, and who, on being talked to on the subject, justified the proceeding by declaring that no woman could be found who would undertake to nurse the child, and that therefore it must have died a much worse death than that which he had given it. Mr. Collins had reason to believe that this custom was generally prevalent, and observes, that it may in some measure account for the thinness of the population.[14]

Such a custom, though in itself perhaps it might not much affect the population of a country, places in a strong point of view the difficulty of rearing children in savage life. Women, obliged by their habits of living to a constant change of place, and compelled to an unremitting drudgery for their husbands, appear to be absolutely incapable of bringing up two or three children nearly of the same age. If another child be born before the one above it can shift for itself, and follow its mother on foot, one of the two must almost

---

[11] Collins's N. S. Wales, Appen. p. 583.   [12] Appen. note p. 562.   [13] Appen. p. 560.
[14] Collins's N.S. Wales, Appendix, p. 607.

necessarily perish for want of care. The task of rearing even one infant, in such a wandering and laborious life, must be so troublesome and painful, that we are not to be surprised that no woman can be found to undertake it, who is not prompted by the powerful feelings of a mother.

To these causes, which forcibly repress the rising generation, must be added those which contribute subsequently to destroy it; such as the frequent wars of these savages with different tribes, and their perpetual contests with each other; their strange spirit of retaliation and revenge which prompts the midnight murder, and the frequent shedding of innocent blood; the smoke and filth of their miserable habitations, and their poor mode of living, productive of loathsome cutaneous disorders, and above all, a dreadful epidemic like the small-pox, which sweeps off great numbers.[15]

In the year 1789 they were visited by this epidemic which raged among them with all the appearance and virulence of the small-pox. The desolation that it occasioned was almost incredible. Not a living person was to be found in the bays and harbours that were before the most frequented. Not a vestige of a human foot was to be traced on the sands. They had left the dead to bury the dead. The excavations in the rocks were filled with putrid bodies, and in many places the paths were covered with skeletons.[16]

Mr. Collins was informed, that the tribe of Co-le-be, the native mentioned before, had been reduced by the effects of this dreadful disorder to three persons; who found themselves obliged to unite with some other tribe to prevent their utter extinction.[17]

Under such powerful causes of depopulation, we should naturally be inclined to suppose that the animal and vegetable produce of the country would be increasing upon the thinly scattered inhabitants, and, added to the supply of fish from their shores, would be more than sufficient for their consumption; yet it appears, upon the whole, that the population is in general so nearly on a level with the average supply of food, that every little deficiency from unfavourable weather, or other causes, occasions distress. Particular times, when the inhabitants seemed to be in great want, are mentioned as not uncommon, and at these periods some of the natives were found reduced to skeletons and almost starved to death.[18]

---

[15] See generally, the Appendix to Collins's Account of the English Colony in New South Wales.

[16] Appendix, p. 597.   [17] Id. Appendix, p. 598.

[18] Id. c. iii. p. 34. and Appendix, p. 551.

CHAPTER IV

Of the Checks to Population among the American Indians

We may next turn our view to the vast continent of America, the greatest part of which was found to be inhabited by small independent tribes of savages, subsisting nearly in a similar manner to the natives of New Holland on the productions of unassisted nature. The soil was covered by an almost universal forest, and presented few of those fruits and esculent vegetables which grow in such profusion in the islands of the South Sea. The produce of a most rude and imperfect agriculture, known to some of the tribes of hunters, was so trifling as to be considered only as a feeble aid to the subsistence acquired by the chase. The inhabitants of this new world, therefore, might be considered as living principally by hunting and fishing;[1] and the narrow limits to this mode of subsistence are obvious. The supplies derived from fishing could extend only to those who were within a certain distance of the lakes, the rivers, or the sea-shore; and the ignorance and indolence of the improvident savage would frequently prevent him from extending the benefits of these supplies much beyond the time when they were actually obtained. The great extent of territory required for the support of the hunter has been repeatedly stated and acknowledged.[2] The number of wild animals within his reach, combined with the facility with which they might be either killed or ensnared, must necessarily limit the number of his society. Tribes of hunters, like beasts of prey, whom they resemble in their mode of subsistence, will consequently be thinly scattered over the surface of the earth. Like beasts of prey, they must either drive away or fly from every rival, and be engaged in perpetual contests with each other.[3]

Under such circumstances, that America should be very thinly peopled in proportion to its extent of territory is merely an exemplification of the obvious truth, that population cannot increase without the food to support it. But the interesting part of the inquiry, that part to which I would wish particularly to draw the attention of the reader, is the mode by which the population is kept down to the level of this scanty supply. It cannot escape

---

[1] Robertson's History of America, vol. ii. b. iv. p. 127. et seq. octavo edit. 1780.
[2] Franklin's Miscell. p. 2.
[3] Robertson, b. iv. p. 129.

observation, that an insufficient supply of food to any people does not shew itself merely in the shape of famine, but in other more permanent forms of distress, and in generating certain customs which operate sometimes with greater force in the suppression of a rising population than in its subsequent destruction.

It was generally remarked that the American women were far from being prolific, their marriages seldom producing above two or three children.[4] This unfruitfulness has been attributed by some to a want of ardour in the men towards their women; a feature of character which has been considered as peculiar to the American savage. It is not however peculiar to this race, but probably exists in a great degree among all barbarous nations, whose food is poor and insufficient, and who live in a constant apprehension of being pressed by famine or by an enemy. Bruce frequently takes notice of it, particularly in reference to the Galla and Shangalla, savage nations on the borders of Abyssinia;[5] and Le Vaillant mentions the phlegmatic temperament of the Hottentots as the chief reason of their thin population.[6] It seems to be generated by the hardships and dangers of savage life, which take off the attention from the sexual passion. And that these are the principal causes of it among the Americans, rather than any absolute constitutional defect, appears probable from its diminishing nearly in proportion to the degree in which these causes are mitigated or removed. In those countries of America where, from peculiar situation or further advantages in improvement, the hardships of savage life are less severely felt, the passion between the sexes becomes more ardent. Among some of the tribes seated on the banks of rivers well stored with fish, or others that inhabit a territory greatly abounding in game or much improved in agriculture, the women are more valued and admired; and as hardly any restraint is imposed on the gratification of desire, the dissolution of their manners is sometimes excessive.[7]

If we do not then consider this apathy of the Americans as a natural defect in the bodily frame, but merely as a general coldness, and an infrequency of the calls of the sexual appetite, we shall not be inclined to give much weight to it as affecting the number of children to a marriage; but shall be disposed

---

[4] Robertson, b. iv. p. 106. Burke's America, vol. i. p. 187. Charlevoix, Hist. de la Nouvelle France, tom. iii. p. 304. Lafitau, Mœurs des Sauvages, tom. i. p. 590. In the course of this chapter I often give the same references as Robertson; but never, without having examined and verified them myself. Where I have not had an opportunity of doing this, I refer to Robertson alone.

[In 1806 (Vol. 1, p. 53) *their marriages seldom producing above two or three children* was excised.]

[5] Travels to discover the Source of the Nile, vol. ii. pp. 223. 559.

[6] Voyage dans l'Interieur de l'Afrique, tom. i. pp. 12, 13.

[7] Robertson, b. iv. p. 71. Lettres Edif. & Curieuses, tom. vi. p. 48, 322, 330. tom. vii. p. 20. 12mo. edit. 1780. Charlevoix, tom. iii. pp. 303, 423. Hennepin, Mœurs des Sauvages, p. 37.

to look for the cause of this unfruitfulness in the condition and customs of the women in a savage state. And here we shall find reasons amply sufficient to account for the fact in question.

It is finely observed by Dr. Robertson that: 'Whether man has been improved by the progress of arts and civilization, is a question, which in the wantonness of disputation has been agitated among philosophers. That women are indebted to the refinement of polished manners for a happy change in their state, is a point, which can admit of no doubt.'[8] In every part of the world, one of the most general characteristics of the savage is to despise and degrade the female sex.[9] Among most of the tribes in America their condition is so peculiarly grievous, that servitude is a name too mild to describe their wretched state. A wife is no better than a beast of burthen. While the man passes his days in idleness or amusement, the woman is condemned to incessant toil. Tasks are imposed upon her without mercy, and services are received without complacence or gratitude.[10] There are some districts in America where this state of degradation has been so severely felt, that mothers have destroyed their female infants, to deliver them at once from a life in which they were doomed to such a miserable slavery.[11]

This state of depression and constant labour added to the unavoidable hardships of savage life must be very unfavourable to the office of child-bearing,[12] and the libertinage which generally prevails among the women before marriage, with the habit of procuring abortions, in which they rarely fail, must necessarily render them more unfit for bearing children after-wards.[13] One of the missionaries speaking of the common practice among the Natchez of changing their wives, adds, 'unless they have children by them', a proof that many of these marriages were unfruitful, which may be accounted for from the libertine lives of the women before wedlock, which he had previously noticed.[14]

The causes that Charlevoix assigns, of the sterility of the American women, are the suckling of their children for several years, during which time they do not cohabit with their husbands; the excessive labour to which they are always condemned in whatever situation they may be; and the custom

---

[8] Robertson, b. iv. p. 103.

[9] Robertson, b. iv. p. 103. Lettres Edif. passim. Charlevoix Hist. Nouv. Fr. tom iii. p 287. Voy. de Pérouse, c. ix. p. 402. 4to. London.
   [See LA PÉROUSE in the Alphabetical List.]

[10] Robertson, b. iv. p. 105. Lettres Edif. tom. vi. p. 329. Major Roger's North America, p. 211. Creuxii Hist. Canad. p. 57.

[11] Robertson, b. iv. p. 106. Raynal, Hist. des Indes, tom. iv. c. vii. p. 120. 8vo. 10 vol. 1795.

[12] Robertson, b. iv. p. 106. Creuxii Hist. Canad. p. 57. Lafitau, tom. i. p. 590.

[13] Robertson, b. iv. p. 72. Ellis's Voyage, p. 198. Burke's America, vol. i. p. 187. [In 1807 (Vol. 1, p. 48) Malthus excised the words 'in which they rarely fail'.

[14] Lettres Edif. tom. vii. pp. 20. 22.

established in many places of permitting the young women to prostitute themselves before marriage. Added to this, he says, the extreme misery to which these people are sometimes reduced takes from them all desire of having children.[15] Among some of the ruder tribes it is a maxim not to burden themselves with rearing more than two of their offspring.[16] When twins are born, one of them is commonly abandoned, as the mother cannot rear them both; and when a mother dies during the period of suckling her child, no chance of preserving its life remains, and, as in New Holland, it is buried in the same grave with the breast that nourished it.[17]

As the parents are frequently exposed to want themselves, the difficulty of supporting their children becomes at times so great, that they are reduced to the necessity of abandoning or destroying them.[18] Deformed children are very generally exposed; and among some of the tribes in South America, the children of mothers who do not bear their labours well, experience a similar fate, from a fear that the offspring may inherit the weakness of its parent.[19]

To causes of this nature we must ascribe the remarkable exemption of the Americans from deformities of make. Even when a mother endeavours to rear all her children without distinction, so great a proportion of the whole number perishes under the rigorous treatment that must be their lot in the savage state, that probably none of those who labour under any original weakness or infirmity can attain the age of manhood. If they be not cut off as soon as they are born, they cannot long protract their lives under the severe discipline that awaits them.[20] In the Spanish provinces, where the Indians do not live so laborious a life, and are prevented from destroying their children, great numbers of them are deformed, dwarfish, mutilated, blind, and deaf.[21]

Polygamy seems to have been generally allowed among the Americans, but the privilege was seldom used, except by the Caciques and chiefs, and now and then by others in some of the fertile provinces of the South, where subsistence was more easily procured. The difficulty of supporting a family confined the mass of the people to one wife;[22] and this difficulty was so generally known and acknowledged, that fathers, before they consented to give their daughters in marriage, required unequivocal proofs in the suitor of his skill in hunting, and his consequent ability to support a wife and children.[23] The women, it is said, do not marry early;[24] and this seems to be

---

[15] Charlevoix, N. Fr. tom. iii. p. 304.
[16] Robertson, b. iv. p. 107. Lettres Edif. tom. ix. p. 140.
[17] Robertson, b. iv. p. 107. Lettres Edif. tom viii. p. 86.   [18] Robertson, b. iv. p. 108.
[19] Lafitau, Mœurs des Sauv. tom. i. p. 592.
[20] Charlevoix, tom. iii. p. 303. Raynal, Hist. des Indes, tom. viii. l. xv. p. 22.
[21] Robertson, b. iv. p. 73. Voyage d'Ulloa, tom. i. p. 232.
[22] Robertson, b. iv. p. 102. Lettres Edif. tom. viii. p. 87.
[23] Lettres Edif. tom. ix. p. 364. Robertson b. iv. p. 115.   [24] Robertson, b. iv. p. 107.

confirmed by the libertinage among them before marriage, so frequently taken notice of by the missionaries and other writers.[25]

The customs above enumerated, which appear to have been generated principally by the experience of the difficulties attending the rearing of a family, combined with the great proportion of children that must necessarily perish under the hardships of savage life, in spite of the best efforts of their parents to save them,[26] must, without doubt, most powerfully repress the rising generation.

When the young savage, by a fortunate train of circumstances,[27] has passed safely through the perils of his childhood, other dangers scarcely less formidable await him on his approach to manhood. The diseases to which man is subject in the savage state, though fewer in number, are more violent and fatal than those which prevail in civilized society. As savages are wonderfully improvident, and their means of subsistence always precarious, they often pass from the extreme of want to exuberant plenty, according to the vicissitudes of fortune in the chase or to the variety in the productions of the seasons.[28] Their inconsiderate gluttony in the one case, and their severe abstinence in the other, are equally prejudicial to the human constitution; and their vigour is accordingly at some seasons impaired by want, and at others by a superfluity of gross aliment, and the disorders arising from indigestions.[29] These, which may be considered as the unavoidable consequence of their mode of living, cut off considerable numbers in the prime of life. They are likewise extremely subject to consumptions, to pleuritic, asthmatic, and paralytic disorders, brought on by the immoderate hardships and fatigues which they endure in hunting and war, and by the inclemency of the seasons to which they are continually exposed.[30]

The missionaries speak of the Indians in South America as subject to perpetual diseases for which they know no remedy.[31] Ignorant of the use of the most simple herbs, or of any change in their gross diet, they die of these diseases in great numbers. The Jesuit Fauque says that, in all the different excursions which he had made, he scarcely found a single individual of an advanced age.[32] Robertson determines the period of human life to be shorter among savages than in well-regulated and industrious communities.[33]

---

[25] Lettres Edif. passim. Voyage d'Ulloa, tom. i. p. 343. Burke's America, vol. i. p. 187. Charlevoix, tom. iii. pp. 303, 304.

[26] Creuxius says, that scarcely one in thirty reach manhood. (Hist. Canad. p. 57); but this must be a great exaggeration.

[27] [In 1817 (Vol. 1, p. 61) Malthus excised the words *by a fortunate train of circumstances*.

[28] Robertson, b. iv. p. 85.

[29] Charlevoix, tom. iii. p. 302, 303.

[30] Robertson, b. iv. p. 86. Charlevoix, tom. iii. p. 364. Lafitau, tom. ii. pp. 360, 361.

[31] Lettres Edif. tom. viii. p. 83.   [32] Lettres Edif. tom. vii. p. 317 et seq.

[33] b. iv. p. 86.

Raynal, notwithstanding his frequent declarations in favour of savage life, says of the Indians of Canada that few are so long lived as our people, whose manner of living is more uniform and tranquil.[34] And Cook and Pérouse confirm these opinions in the remarks which they make on some of the inhabitants of the northwest coast of America.[35]

In the vast plains of South America a burning sun, operating on the extensive swamps and the inundations that succeed the rainy season, sometimes produces dreadful epidemics. The missionaries speak of contagious distempers as frequent among the Indians, and occasioning at times a great mortality in their villages.[36] The small-pox every where makes great ravages as, from want of care, and from confined habitations, very few that are attacked recover from it.[37] The Indians of Paraguay are said to be extremely subject to contagious distempers, notwithstanding the care and attentions of the Jesuits. The small-pox and malignant fevers, which, from the ravages they make, are called plagues, frequently desolate these flourishing missions and, according to Ulloa, were the cause that they had not increased in proportion to the time of their establishment, and the profound peace which they had enjoyed.[38]

These epidemics are not confined to the south. They are mentioned as if they were not uncommon among the more northern nations;[39] and, in a late voyage to the northwest coast of America, captain Vancouver gives an account of a very extraordinary desolation apparently produced by some distemper of this kind. From New Dungeness he traversed a hundred and fifty miles of the coast without seeing the same number of inhabitants. Deserted villages were frequent, each of which was large enough to contain all the scattered savages that had been observed in that extent of country. In the different excursions which he made, particularly about Port Discovery, the skulls, limbs, ribs, and backbones, or some other vestiges of the human body, were scattered promiscuously in great numbers; and, as no warlike scars were observed on the bodies of the remaining Indians, and no particular signs of fear and suspicion, the most probable conjecture seems to be, that this depopulation must have been occasioned by pestilential disease.[40] The small-pox appears to be common and fatal among the Indians on this coast. Its indelible marks were observed on many, and several had lost the sight of one eye from it.[41]

In general, it may be remarked of savages that, from their extreme

---

[34] Raynal, b. xv. p. 23.   [35] Cook, third Voy. vol. iii. ch. ii. p. 520. Voy. de Pérouse, ch. ix.
[36] Lettres Edif. tom. viii. p. 79, 339. tom ix. p. 125.   [37] Voyage d'Ulloa, tom. i. p. 349.
[38] Id. tom. i. p. 549.   [39] Lettres Edif tom. vi. p. 335.
[40] Vancouver's Voy. vol. i. b. ii. c. v. p. 256.
[41] Id. c. iv. p. 242.

ignorance, the dirt of their persons, and the closeness and filth of their cabins,[42] they lose the advantage which usually attends a thinly peopled country, that of being more exempt from pestilential diseases than those which are fully inhabited. In some parts of America the houses are built for the reception of many different families, and fourscore or a hundred people are crowded together under the same roof. When the families live separately, the huts are extremely small, close, and wretched, without windows, and with the doors so low that it is necessary to creep on the hands and knees to enter them.[43] On the north-west coast of America, the houses are in general of the large kind; and Meares describes one of most extraordinary dimensions, belonging to a chief near Nootka Sound, in which eight hundred persons ate, sat, and slept.[44] All voyagers agree with respect to the filth of the habitations, and the personal nastiness of the people on this coast.[45] Captain Cook describes them as swarming with vermin, which they pick off and eat,[46] and the nastiness and stench of their houses, he says, is equal to their confusion.[47] Perouse declares that their cabins have a nastiness and stench, to which the den of no known animal in the world can be compared.[48]

Under such circumstances, it may be easily imagined what a dreadful havoc an epidemic must make, when once it appears among them: and it does not seem improbable that the degree of filth described should generate distempers of this nature, as the air of their houses cannot be much purer than the atmosphere of the most crowded cities.

Those who escape the dangers of infancy and of disease are constantly exposed to the chances of war; and notwithstanding the extreme caution of the Americans in conducting their military operations, yet as they seldom enjoy any interval of peace, the waste of their numbers in war is considerable.[49] The rudest of the American nations are well acquainted with the rights of each community to its own domains.[50] And as it is of the utmost consequence to prevent others from destroying the game in their hunting grounds, they guard this national property with a jealous attention. Innumerable subjects of dispute necessarily arise. The neighbouring nations live

---

[42] Charlevoix speaks in the strongest terms of the extreme filth and stench of the American cabins: 'On ne peut entrer dans leur cabanes qu'on ne soit impesté'; and the dirt of their meals, he says, 'vous feroit horreur'. Vol. iii. p. 338.

[43] Robertson, b. iv. p. 182. Voyage d'Ulloa, tom. i. p. 340.

[44] Meares's Voyage, ch. xii. p. 138.

[45] Id. ch. xxiii. p. 252. Vancouver's Voy. vol. iii. b. vi. c. i. p. 313.

[46] Cook's 3d Voyage, vol. ii. p. 305.

[47] c. iii. p. 316.

[In 1817 (Vol. 1, p. 68) this was changed to:
... pick off and eat, and speaks of their habitations in terms of the greatest disgust.

[48] Voy. de Perouse, ch. ix. p. 403.   [49] Charlevoix, Hist. N. Fr. tom. iii. 202, 203, 429.

[50] Robertson, b. iv. p. 147.

in a perpetual state of hostility with each other.[51] The very act of increasing in one tribe must be an act of aggression on its neighbours, as a larger range of territory will be necessary to support its increased numbers. The contest will in this case naturally continue, either till the equilibrium is restored by mutual losses, or till the weaker party is exterminated or driven from its country. When the irruption of an enemy desolates their cultivated lands, or drives them from their hunting grounds, as they have seldom any portable stores, they are generally reduced to extreme want. All the people of the district invaded are frequently forced to take refuge in woods or mountains, which can afford them no subsistence, and where many of them perish.[52] In such a flight each consults alone his individual safety. Children desert their parents, and parents consider their children as strangers. The ties of nature are no longer binding. A father will sell his son for a knife or a hatchet.[53] Famine and distresses of every kind complete the destruction of those whom the sword had spared; and in this manner whole tribes are frequently extinguished.[54]

Such a state of things has powerfully contributed to generate that ferocious spirit of warfare observable among savages in general, and most particularly among the Americans. Their object in battle is not conquest, but destruction.[55] The life of the victor depends on the death of his enemy; and, in the rancour and fell spirit of revenge with which he pursues him, he seems constantly to bear in mind the distresses that would be consequent on defeat. Among the Iroquois, the phrase by which they express their resolution of making war against an enemy is: 'Let us go and eat that nation.' If they solicit the aid of a neighbouring tribe, they invite it to eat broth made of the flesh of their enemies.[56] Among the Abnakis, when a body of their warriors enters an enemy's territory, it is generally divided into different parties of thirty or forty; and the chief says to each, 'To you is given such a hamlet to eat, to you such a village', &c.[57] These expressions remain in the language of some of the tribes in which the custom of eating their prisoners taken in war no longer exists. Cannibalism, however, undoubtedly prevailed in many parts of the new world;[58] and, contrary to the opinion of Dr. Robertson, I cannot but think that it must have had its origin in extreme want, though the custom might afterwards be continued from other motives. It seems to be a worse compliment to human nature, and to the savage state, to attribute this horrid

---

[51] Ibid. Lettres Edif. tom. viii. pp. 40, 86, & passim. Cook's 3d Voy. vol. ii. p. 324. Meares's Voy. ch. xxiv. p. 267.
[52] Robertson, b. iv. p. 172. Charlevoix, N. Fr. tom. iii. p. 203.
[53] Lettres Edif. tom. viii. p. 346.
[54] Robertson, b. iv. p. 172. Account of N. America, by Major Rogers, p. 250.
[55] Robertson, b. iv. p. 150.
[56] Id. p. 164.   [57] Lettres Edif. tom. vi. p. 205.   [58] Robertson, b. iv. p. 164.

repast to malignant passions, without the goad of necessity, rather than to the great law of self-preservation which has, at times, overcome every other feeling even among the most humane and civilized people. When once it had prevailed, though only occasionally, from this cause, the fear that a savage might feel of becoming a repast to his enemies might easily raise the passion of rancour and revenge to so high a pitch, as to urge him to treat his prisoners in this way, though not prompted at the time by hunger.

The missionaries speak of several nations which appeared to use human flesh whenever they could obtain it, as they would the flesh of any of the rarer animals.[59] These accounts may perhaps be exaggerated, though they seem to be confirmed, in a great degree, by the late voyages to the north-west coast of America, and by Captain Cook's description of the state of society in the southern island of New Zealand.[60] The peoples of Nootka Sound appear to be cannibals,[61] and the chief of the district Maquinna is said to be so addicted to this horrid banquet that, in cold blood, he kills a slave every moon to gratify his unnatural appetite.[62]

The predominant principle of self-preservation, connected most intimately in the breast of the savage with the safety and power of the community to which he belongs, prevents the admission of any of those ideas of honour and gallantry in war which prevail among more civilized nations. To fly from an adversary that is on his guard, and to avoid a contest where he cannot contend without risk to his own person, and consequently to his community, is the point of honour with the American. The odds of ten to one are necessary to warrant an attack on a person who is armed and prepared to resist; and even then, each is afraid of being the first to advance.[63] The great object of the most renowned warrior is, by every art of cunning and deceit, by every mode of stratagem and surprize that his invention can suggest, to weaken and destroy the tribes of his enemies with the least possible loss to his own. To meet an enemy on equal terms is regarded as extreme folly. To fall in battle, instead of being reckoned an honourable death,[64] is a misfortune, which subjects the memory of a warrior to the imputation of rashness and imprudence. But to lie in wait day after day, till he can rush upon his prey, when most secure, and least able to resist him; to steal in the dead of night upon his enemies, set fire to their huts, and massacre the inhabitants, as they

---

[59] Lettres Edif. tom. viii. p. 105, 271. tom. vi. p. 266.

[60] Cautious as Captain Cook always is, he says of the New Zealanders, 'it was but too evident that they have a great liking for this kind of food'. Second Voy. vol. i. p. 246. And in the last voyage, speaking of their perpetual hostilities, he says, 'and perhaps the desire of a good meal may be no small incitement'. Vol. i, p. 137.

[61] Cook's Third Voy. vol. ii. p. 271.   [62] Meares's Voy. ch. xxiii. p. 255.

[63] Lettres Edif. tom. vi. p. 360.

[64] Charlevoix, N. Fr. tom. iii. p. 376.

fly naked and defenceless from the flames,[65] are deeds of glory, which will be of deathless memory in the breasts of his grateful countrymen.

This mode of warfare is evidently produced by a consciousness of the difficulties attending the rearing of new citizens under the hardships and dangers of savage life. And these powerful causes of destruction may, in some instances, be so great as to keep down the population even considerably below the means of subsistence; but the fear that the Americans betray of any diminution of their society, and their apparent wish to increase it, are no proofs that this is generally the case. The country could not probably support the addition that is coveted in each society; but an accession of strength to one tribe opens to it new sources of subsistence in the comparative weakness of its adversaries; and, on the contrary, a diminution of its numbers, so far from giving greater plenty to the remaining members, subjects them to extirpation or famine from the irruptions of their stronger neighbours.

The Chiriguanes, originally only a small part of the tribe of Guaranis, left their native country in Paraguay, and settled in the mountains towards Peru. They found sufficient subsistence in their new country, increased rapidly, attacked their neighbours and, by superior valour or superior fortune, gradually exterminated them, and took possession of their lands, occupying a great extent of country; and having increased, in the course of some years, from three or four thousand to thirty thousand,[66] while the tribes of their weaker neighbours were daily thinned by famine and the sword.

Such instances prove the rapid increase, even of the Americans, under favourable circumstances, and sufficiently account for the fear which prevails in every tribe of diminishing its numbers, and the frequent wish to increase them,[67] without supposing a superabundance of food in the territory actually possessed.

[68]●That the increase of the Americans is regulated more by the means of subsistence, than by any of the other causes that have been mentioned as affecting their population; or rather, perhaps I should say, that these causes themselves are principally regulated by the plenty or scarcity of subsistence,●[68] is sufficiently evinced from the greater frequency of the tribes, and

---

[65] Robertson, b. iv. p. 155. Lettres Edif. tom. vi. p. 182, 360.

[66] Lettres Edif. tom. viii. p. 243. Les Chiriguanes multiplierent prodigieusement, et en assez peu d'années leur nombre monta à trente mille ames.

[67] Lafitau, tom. ii. p. 163.

[68] [In 1807 (Vol. I, p. 65) Malthus re-worded the beginning of this paragraph and added a footnote:

That the causes[(a)] which have been mentioned as affecting the population of the Americans, are principally regulated by the plenty or scarcity of subsistence ...

[(a)] These causes may perhaps appear more than sufficient to keep the population down to the level of the means of subsistence; and they certainly would be so, if the representations

the greater numbers in each, throughout all those parts of the country where, from the vicinity of lakes or rivers, the superior fertility of the soil, or further advances in improvement, food becomes more abundant. In the interior of the provinces bordering on the Oronoco, several hundred miles may be traversed in different directions, without finding a single hut, or observing the footsteps of a single creature. In some parts of North America, where the climate is more rigorous and the soil less fertile, the desolation is still greater. Vast tracts of some hundred leagues have been crossed through uninhabited plains and forests.[69] The missionaries speak of journeys of twelve days without meeting a single soul,[70] and of immense tracts of country in which scarcely three or four scattered villages were to be found.[71] Some of these deserts furnished no game,[72] and were therefore entirely desolate; others, which were to a certain degree stocked with it, were traversed in the hunting seasons by parties who encamped and remained in different spots according to the success they met with, and were therefore really inhabited in proportion to the quantity of subsistence which they yielded.[73]

Other districts of America are described as comparatively fully peopled; such as the borders of the great northern lakes, the shores of the Mississippi, Louisiana, and many provinces in South America. The villages here were large, and near each other, in proportion to the superior fruitfulness of the territory in game and fish, and the advances made by the inhabitants in agriculture.[74] The Indians of the great and populous empires of Mexico and Peru sprung undoubtedly from the same stock, and originally possessed the same customs as their ruder brethren; but from the moment when, by a fortunate train of circumstances, they were led to improve and extend their agriculture, a considerable population rapidly followed, in spite of the apathy of the men or the destructive habits of the women. These habits would indeed in a great measure yield to the change of circumstances; and the substitution of a more quiet and sedentary life for a life of perpetual wandering and hardship would immediately render the women more fruitful, and enable them at the same time to attend to the wants of a larger family.

In a general view of the American continent, as described by historians, the population seems to have been spread over the surface very nearly in proportion to the quantity of food which the inhabitants of the different

---

given of the unfruitfulness of the Indian women were universally, or even generally true. It is probable that some of the accounts are exaggerated, but it is difficult to say which; and it must be acknowledged that, even allowing for all such exaggerations, they are amply sufficient to establish the point proposed.

[69] Robertson, b. iv. p. 129, 130.   [70] Lettres Edif. tom. vi. p. 357.

[71] Lettres Edif. tom. vi. p. 321.

[72] Lettres Edif. tom. ix. p. 145.   [73] Lettres Edif. tom. vi. pp. 66, 81, 345. tom. ix. p. 145.

[74] Lettres Edif. tom. ix. p. 90, 142. Robertson, b. iv. p. 141.

parts, in the actual state of their industry and improvement, could obtain; and that, with few exceptions, it pressed hard against this limit, rather than fell short of it, appears from the frequent recurrence of distress for want of food in all parts of America.

Remarkable instances occur, according to Dr. Robertson, of the calamities which rude nations suffer by famine. As one of them, he mentions an account given by Alvar Nugnez Cabeca de Vaca, one of the Spanish adventurers, who resided almost nine years among the savages of Florida. He describes them as unacquainted with every species of agriculture, and living chiefly upon the roots of different plants, which they procure with great difficulty, wandering from place to place in search of them. Sometimes they kill game, sometimes they catch fish, but in such small quantities that their hunger is so extreme as to compel them to eat spiders, the eggs of ants, worms, lizards, serpents, and a kind of unctuous earth; and I am persuaded, he says, that if in this country there were any stones, they would swallow them. They preserve the bones of fishes and serpents, which they grind into powder and eat. The only season when they do not suffer much from famine is when a certain fruit like the opuntia, or prickly-pear, is ripe; but they are sometimes obliged to travel far from their usual place of residence in order to find it. In another place, he observes, that they are frequently reduced to pass two or three days without food.[75]

Ellis, in his voyage to Hudson's Bay, feelingly describes the sufferings of the Indians in that neighbourhood from extreme want. Having mentioned the severity of the climate, he says: 'Great as these hardships are which result from the rigour of the cold, yet it may justly be affirmed that they are much inferior to those which they feel from the scarcity of provisions, and the difficulty they are under of procuring them. A story which is related at the factories, and known to be true, will sufficiently prove this, and give the compassionate reader a just idea of the miseries to which these unhappy people are exposed.' He then gives an account of a poor Indian and his wife who, on the failure of game, having eaten up all the skins which they wore as clothing, were reduced to the dreadful extremity of supporting themselves on the flesh of two of their children.[76] In another place he says: 'It has sometimes happened that the Indians who come in summer to trade at the factories, missing the succours they expected, have been obliged to singe off the hair from thousands of beaver skins in order to feed upon the leather.'[77]

The Abbé Raynal, who is continually reasoning most inconsistently in his comparisons of savage and civilized life, though in one place he speaks of the savage as morally sure of a competent subsistence, yet in his account of the nations of Canada, he says that though they lived in a country abounding in

---

[75] Robertson, note 28. to p. 117. b. iv.   [76] p. 196.   [77] p. 194.

game and fish, yet in some seasons, and sometimes for whole years, this resource failed them; and famine then occasioned a great destruction among a people who were at too great a distance to assist each other.[78]

Charlevoix, speaking of the inconveniences and distresses to which the missionaries were subject, observes that not unfrequently the evils which he had been describing are effaced by a greater, in comparison of which all the others are nothing. This is famine. It is true, says he, that the savages can bear hunger with as much patience as they shew carelessness in providing against it; but they are sometimes reduced to extremities beyond their power to support.[79]

It is the general custom among most of the American nations, even those which have made some progress in agriculture, to disperse themselves in the woods at certain seasons of the year, and to subsist for some months on the produce of the chase, as a principal part of their annual supplies.[80] To remain in their villages exposes them to certain famine;[81] and in the woods they are not always sure to escape it. The most able hunters sometimes fail of success, even where there is no deficiency of game;[82] and in their forests, on the failure of this resource, the hunter or the traveller is exposed to the most cruel want.[83] The Indians, in their hunting excursions, are sometimes reduced to pass three or four days without food;[84] and a missionary relates an account of some Iroquois who, on one of these occasions, having supported themselves as long as they could, by eating the skins which they had with them, their shoes, and the bark of trees, at length, in despair, sacrificed some of the party to support the rest. Out of eleven, five only returned alive.[85]

The Indians, in many parts of South America, live in extreme want,[86] and are sometimes destroyed by absolute famines.[87] The islands, rich as they appeared to be, were peopled fully up to the level of their produce. If a few Spaniards settled in any district, such a small addition of supernumerary mouths soon occasioned a severe dearth of provisions.[88] The flourishing Mexican empire was in the same state in this respect; and Cortez often found the greatest difficulty in procuring subistence for his small body of soldiers.[89] Even the Missions of Paraguay, with all the care and foresight of the Jesuits, and notwithstanding that their population was kept down by frequent epidemics, were by no means totally exempt from the pressure of want. The

---

[78] Raynal, Hist. des Indes, tom. viii. l. xv. p. 22.   [79] Hist. N. Fr. tom. iii. p. 338.
[80] Lettres Edif. tom. vi. p. 66, 81, 345. ix. 145.
[81] Lettres Edif. tom. vi. 82, 196, 197, 215. ix. 151.
[82] Charlevoix, N. Fr. tom. iii. p. 201. Hennepin, Mœurs des Sauv. p. 78.
[83] Lettres Edif. tom. vi. pp. 167, 220.   [84] Id. tom. vi. p. 33.   [85] Id. tom. vi. p. 71.
[86] Id. tom. vii. p. 383. ix. 140.   [87] Id. tom. viii. p. 79.
[88] Robertson, b. iv. p. 121. Burke's America, vol. i. p. 30.
[89] Robertson, b. viii, p. 212.

Indians of the Mission of St. Michael are mentioned as having at one time increased so much that the lands capable of cultivation in their neighbourhood produced only half of the grain necessary for their support.[90] Long droughts often destroyed their cattle,[91] and occasioned a failure of their crops; and on these occasions some of the Missions were reduced to the most extreme indigence, and would have perished from famine but for the assistance of their neighbours.[92]

The late voyages to the north-west coast of America confirm these accounts of the frequent pressure of want in savage life, and shew the uncertainty of the resource of fishing, which seems to afford, in general, the most plentiful harvest of food that is furnished by unassisted nature. The sea on the coast near Nootka Sound is seldom or never so much frozen as to prevent the inhabitants from having access to it. Yet from the very great precautions they use in laying up stores for the winter, and their attention to prepare and preserve whatever food is capable of it, for the colder seasons, it is evident that the sea at these times yields no fish; and it appears, that they often undergo very great hardships from want of provisions in the cold months.[93] During a Mr. MacKay's stay at Nootka Sound, from 1786 to 1787, the length and severity of the winter occasioned a famine. The stock of dried fish was expended, and no fresh supplies of any kind were to be caught, so that the natives were obliged to submit to a fixed allowance, and the chiefs brought every day to our countrymen the stated meal of seven dried herrings' heads. Mr. Meares says that the perusal of this gentleman's journal would shock any mind tinctured with humanity.[94]

Captain Vancouver mentions some of the people to the north of Nootka Sound as living very miserably on a paste made of the inner bark of the pine tree, and cockles.[95] In one of the boat excursions, a party of Indians was met with who had some halibut, but, though very high prices were offered, they could not be induced to part with any. This, as Captain Vancouver observes, was singular, and indicated a very scanty supply.[96] At Nootka Sound, in the year 1794, fish had become very scarce and bore an exorbitant price; as, either from the badness of the season, or from neglect, the inhabitants had experienced the greatest distress for want of provisions during the winter.[97]

Pérouse describes the Indians in the neighbourhood of Port François as living during the summer in the greatest abundance by fishing, but exposed in the winter to perish from want.[98]

It is not, therefore, as Lord Kaimes imagines, that the American tribes

---

[90] Lettres Edif. tom. ix. p. 381.   [91] Id. tom. ix. p. 191.   [92] Id. tom. ix. p. 206, 380.
[93] Meares's Voy. ch. xxiv. p. 266.   [94] Id. ch. xi. p. 132.
[95] Vancouver's Voy. vol. ii. b. ii. c. ii. p. 273.
[96] Id. p. 282.   [97] Id. vol. iii. b. vi. c. i. p. 304.   [98] Voy. de Pérouse, ch. ix. p. 400.

have never increased sufficiently to render the pastoral or agricultural state necessary to them;[99] but, from some cause or other, they have not adopted in any great degree these more plentiful modes of procuring subsistence, and therefore have not increased so as to become populous. If hunger alone could have prompted the savage tribes of America to such a change in their habits, I do not conceive that there would have been a single nation of hunters and fishers remaining; but it is evident that some fortunate train of circumstances, in addition to this stimulus, is necessary for the purpose; and it is undoubtedly probable that these arts of obtaining food will be first invented and improved in those spots which are best suited to them, and where the natural fertility of the situation, by allowing a greater number of people to subsist together, would give the fairest chance to the inventive powers of the human mind.

Among most of the American tribes that we have been considering, so great a degree of equality prevailed that all the members of each community would be nearly equal sharers in the general hardships of savage life, and in the pressure of occasional famines. But in many of the more southern nations, as in Bagota,[100] and among the Natchez,[101] and particularly in Mexico and Peru, where a great distinction of ranks prevailed, and the lower classes were in a state of absolute servitude,[102] it is evident that,[103] on occasion of any failure of subsistence, these would be the principal sufferers, and the positive checks to population would act almost exclusively on this part of the community.

The very extraordinary depopulation that has taken place among the American Indians may appear to some to contradict the theory which is intended to be established; but it will be found that the causes of this rapid diminution may all be resolved into the three great checks to population which have been stated; and it is not asserted that these checks, operating from particular circumstances with unusual force, may not in some instances be more powerful even than the principle of increase.

The insatiable fondness of the Indians for spiritous liquors,[104] which, according to Charlevoix, is a rage that passes all expression,[105] by producing among them perpetual quarrels and contests which often terminate fatally, by exposing them to a new train of disorders which their mode of life unfits them to contend with, and by deadening and destroying the generative

---

[99] Sketches of the Hist. of Man. vol. i. p. 99, 105. 8vo. 2d edit.
[100] Robertson, b. iv. p. 141.
[101] Lettres Edif. tom. vii. p. 21. Robertson, b. iv. p. 139.
[102] Robertson, b. vii. pp. 190, 242.
[103] [In 1807 (Vol. i, p. 76) this was changed to:
       ..., it is probable that, on occasion ...
[104] Major Rogers's Account of North America, p. 210.   [105] Charlevoix, tom. iii. p. 302.

faculty in its very source, may alone be considered as a vice adequate to produce the present depopulation. In addition to this, it should be observed that almost everywhere the connexion of the Indians with Europeans has tended to break their spirit, to weaken or to give a wrong direction to their industry, and in consequence to diminish the sources of subsistence. In St. Domingo, the Indians neglected purposely to cultivate their lands in order to starve out their cruel oppressors.[106] In Peru and Chili, the forced industry of the natives was fatally directed to the digging into the bowels of the earth, instead of cultivating its surface; and among the northern tribes, the extreme desire to purchase European spirits directed the industry of the greatest part of them, almost exclusively, to the procuring of peltry for the purpose of this exchange,[107] which would prevent their attention to the more fruitful sources of subsistence, and at the same time tend rapidly to destroy the produce of the chase. The number of wild animals, in all the known parts of America, is probably even more diminished than the number of people.[108] The attention to agriculture has every where slackened, rather than increased, as might at first have been expected, from European connexion. In no part of America, either North or South, do we hear of any of the Indian nations living in great plenty in consequence of their diminished numbers. It may not, therefore, be very far from the truth to say that even now, in spite of all the powerful causes of destruction that have been mentioned, the average population of the American nations is, with few exceptions, on a level with the average quantity of food which in the present state of their industry they can obtain.

---

[106] Robertson, b. ii. p. 185. Burke's America, vol. i. p. 300.

[107] [In 1826 (Vol. 1, p. 65) a printer substituted the word *plenty* for *peltry* – skins and furs – and this mistake was repeated in all subsequent editions, until Pickering's of 1986, regardless of the fact that it made the passage quite meaningless.]

[108] The general introduction of fire-arms among the Indians has probably greatly contributed to the diminution of wild animals.

CHAPTER V

Of the Checks to Population in the Islands of the South Sea

The Abbé Raynal, speaking of the ancient state of the British isles, and of islanders in general, says of them: 'It is among these people that we trace the origin of that multitude of singular institutions that retard the progress of population. Anthropophagy, the castration of males, the infibulation of females, late marriages, the consecration of virginity, the approbation of celibacy, the punishments exercised against girls who become mothers at too early an age',[1] &c. These customs, caused by a superabundance of population in islands, have been carried, he says, to the continents, where philosophers of our days are still employed to investigate the reason of them. The Abbé does not seem to be aware that a savage tribe in America, surrounded by enemies, or a civilized and populous nation, hemmed in by others in the same state, is in many respects in a similar situation. Though the barriers to a further increase of population be not so well defined, and so open to common observation on continents, as on islands, yet they still present obstacles that are nearly as insurmountable: and the emigrant, impatient of the distresses which he feels in his own country, is by no means secure of finding relief in another. There is probably no island yet known, the produce of which could not be further increased. This is all that can be said of the whole earth. Both are peopled up to their actual produce. And the whole earth is in this respect like an island. But as the bounds to the number of people on islands, particularly when they are of small extent, are so narrow, and so distinctly marked, that every person must see and acknowledge them, an inquiry into the checks to population on those of which we have the most authentic accounts may perhaps tend considerably to illustrate the present subject. The question that is asked in Captain Cook's first Voyage, with respect to the thinly scattered savages of New Holland: 'By what means the inhabitants of this country are reduced to such a number as it can subsist?'[2] may be asked with equal propriety respecting the most populous islands in the South Sea or the best peopled countries in Europe and Asia. The

---

[1] Raynal, Hist. des Indes, vol. ii. liv. iii. p. 3. 10 vols. 8vo. 1795.

[*Anthropophagy* is cannibalism.]

[2] Cook's First Voyage, vol. iii. p. 240. 4to.

question, applied generally, appears to me to be highly curious, and to lead to the elucidation of some of the most obscure yet important points in the history of human society. I cannot so clearly and concisely describe the precise aim of the first part of the present work, as by saying that it is an endeavour to answer this question so applied.

Of the large islands of New Guinea, New Britain, New Caledonia, and the New Hebrides, little is known with certainty. The state of society in them is probably very similar to that which prevails among many of the savage nations of America. They appear to be inhabited by a number of different tribes who are engaged in frequent hostilities with each other. The chiefs have little authority; and private property being in consequence insecure, provisions have been rarely found on them in abundance.[3] With the large island of New Zealand we are better acquainted, but not in a manner to give us a favourable impression of the state of society among its inhabitants. The picture of it drawn by Captain Cook in his three different Voyages contains some of the darkest shades that are anywhere to be met with in the history of human nature. The state of perpetual hostility, in which the different tribes of these people live with each other, seems to be even more striking than among the savages of any part of America;[4] and their custom of eating human flesh, and even their relish for that kind of food, are established beyond a possibility of doubt.[5] Captain Cook, who is by no means inclined to exaggerate the vices of savage life, says of the natives in the neighbourhood of Queen Charlotte's Sound: 'If I had followed the advice of all our pretended friends, I might have extirpated the whole race; for the people of each hamlet or village, by turns, applied to me to destroy the other. One would have thought it almost impossible that so striking a proof of the divided state in which these miserable people live could have been assigned.'[6] And in the same chapter further on, he says: 'From my own observations, and the information of Taweiharooa, it appears to me that the New Zealanders must live under perpetual apprehensions of being destroyed by each other; there being few of their tribes that have not, as they think, sustained wrongs from some other tribes, which they are continually upon the watch to revenge. And perhaps the desire of a good meal may be no small incitement. . . . Their method of executing their horrible designs is by stealing upon the adverse party in the night; and if they find them unguarded (which, however, I believe is very seldom the case) they kill every one indiscriminately, not even

---

[3] See the different accounts of New Guinea and New Britain, in the Histoire des Navigations aux terres Australes; [DE BROSSES in the Alphabetical List] and of New Caledonia and the New Hebrides in Cook's Second Voyage, vol. ii, b. iii.

[4] Cook's First Voyage, vol. ii. p. 345. Second Voyage, vol. i. p. 101. Third Voyage, vol. i. p. 161, &c.

[5] Second Voyage, vol. i. p. 246.   [6] Third Voyage, vol. i. p. 124.

sparing the women and children. When the massacre is completed, they either feast and gorge themselves on the spot, or carry off as many of the dead bodies as they can, and devour them at home with acts of brutality too shocking to be described. . . . To give quarter, or to take prisoners, makes no part of the military law, so that the vanquished can only save their lives by flight. This perpetual state of war, and destructive method of conducting it, operates so strongly in producing habitual circumspection, that one hardly ever finds a New Zealander off his guard, either by night or by day.'[7]

As these observations occur in the last Voyage, in which the errors of former accounts would have been corrected, and as a constant state of warfare is here represented as prevailing to such a degree that it may be considered as the principal check to the population of New Zealand, little need be added on this subject. We are not informed whether any customs are practised by the women unfavourable to population. If such be known, they are probably never resorted to, except in times of great distress; as each tribe will naturally wish to increase the number of its members, in order to give itself greater power of attack and defence. But the vagabond life which the women of the southern island lead, and the constant state of alarm in which they live, being obliged to travel and work with arms in their hands,[8] must undoubtedly be very unfavourable to gestation, and tend greatly to prevent large families.

Yet, powerful as these checks to population are, it appears, from the recurrence of seasons of scarcity, that they seldom repress the number of people below the average means of subsistence. 'That such seasons there are (Captain Cook says) our observations leave us no room to doubt.'[9] Fish is a principal part of their food, which, being only to be procured on the sea coast, and at certain times,[10] must always be considered as a precarious resource. It must be extremely difficult to dry and preserve any considerable stores in a state of society subject to such constant alarms; particularly, as we may suppose, that the bays and creeks most abounding in fish would most frequently be the subject of obstinate contest to people who were wandering in search of food.[11] The vegetable productions are the fern root, yams, clams, and potatoes.[12] The three last are raised by cultivation, and are seldom found on the southern island, where agriculture is but little known.[13] On the occasional failure of these scanty resources from unfavourable seasons, it may be imagined that the distress must be dreadful. At such periods it does

---

[7] Cook's Third Voy. vol. i. p. 137.   [8] Id. Second Voy. vol. i. p. 127.
[9] Id. First Voy. vol. iii. p. 66.
[10] Id. p. 43.   [11] Id. Third Voy. vol. i. p. 157.
[12] Id. First Voy. vol. iii. p. 43.
    [For a note on clams, see COOK in the Alphabetical List, Vol. II, p. 272.]
[13] Id. First Voy. vol. ii. p. 405.

not seem improbable that the desire of a good meal should give additional force to the desire of revenge, and that they should be 'perpetually destroying each other by violence, as the only alternative of perishing by hunger'.[14]

If we turn our eyes from the thinly scattered inhabitants of New Zealand, to the crowded shores of Otaheite and the Society Islands, a different scene opens to our view. All apprehension of dearth seems at first sight to be banished from a country that is described to be fruitful as the garden of the Hesperides.[15] But this first impression would be immediately corrected by a moment's reflection. Happiness and plenty have always been considered as the most powerful causes of increase. In a delightful climate, where few diseases are known, and the women are condemned to no severe fatigues, why should not these causes operate with a force unparalleled in less favourable regions? Yet if they did, where could the population find room and food in such circumscribed limits? If the numbers in Otaheite, not 40 leagues in circuit, surprised Captain Cook, when he calculated them at two hundred and four thousand,[16] where could they be disposed of in a single century, when they would amount to above three millions, supposing them to double their numbers every twenty-five years.[17] Each island of the group would be in a similar situation. The removal from one to another would be a change of place, but not a change of the species of distress. Effectual emigration, or effectual importation, would be utterly excluded, from the situation of the islands and the state of navigation among their inhabitants.

The difficulty here is reduced to so narrow a compass, is so clear, precise, and forcible, that we cannot escape from it. It cannot be answered in the usual vague and inconsiderate manner, by talking of emigration and further cultivation. In the present instance we cannot but acknowledge that the one is impossible and the other glaringly inadequate. The fullest conviction must stare us in the face, that the people on this group of islands could not continue to double their numbers every twenty-five years; and before we proceed to inquire into the state of society on them, we must be perfectly certain that, unless a perpetual miracle render the women barren, we shall be able to trace some very powerful checks to population in the habits of the people.

The successive accounts that we have received of Otaheite and the

---

[14] Cook's First Voy. vol. iii. p. 45.

[15] Missionary Voy. Appendix, p. 347. [See WILSON in the Alphabetical List. Otaheite is now generally called Tahiti.]

[16] Cook's Second Voy. vol. i. p. 349.

[17] I feel very little doubt that this rate of increase is much slower than would really take place, supposing every check to be removed. If Otaheite, with its present produce, were peopled only with an hundred persons, the two sexes in equal numbers, and each man constant to one woman, I cannot but think, that for five or six successive periods, the increase would be

neighbouring islands leave us no room to doubt the existence of the Eareeoie societies[18] which have justly occasioned so much surprise among civilized nations. They have been so often described, that little more need be said of them here, than that promiscuous intercourse and infanticide appear to be their fundamental laws. They consist exclusively of the higher classes; 'and (according to Mr. Anderson)[19] so agreeable is this licentious plan of life to their disposition, that the most beautiful of both sexes thus commonly spend their youthful days, habituated to the practice of enormities that would disgrace the most savage tribes grass. . . . When an Eareeoie woman is delivered of a child, a piece of cloth dipped in water is applied to the mouth and nose which suffocates it.'[20] Captain Cook observes: 'It is certain that these societies greatly prevent the increase of the superior classes of people of which they are composed.'[21] Of the truth of this observation there can be no doubt.

Though no particular institutions of the same nature have been found among the lower classes; yet the vices which form their most prominent features are but too generally spread. Infanticide is not confined to the Eareeoies. It is permitted to all; and as its prevalence, among the higher classes of the people has removed from it all odium, or imputation of poverty, it is probably often adopted, rather as a fashion than a resort of necessity, and appears to be practised familiarly and without reserve.

It is a very just observation of Hume, that the permission of infanticide generally contributes to increase the population of a country.[22] By removing the fears of too numerous a family, it encourages marriage, and the powerful yearnings of nature prevent parents from resorting to so cruel an expedient except in extreme cases. The fashion of the Eareeoie societies in Otaheite and its neighbouring islands may have made them an exception to this observation, and the custom has probably here a contrary tendency.

The debauchery and promiscuous intercourse which prevail among the lower classes of people, though in some instances they may have been exaggerated, are established to a great extent on unquestionable authority. Captain Cook, in a professed endeavour to rescue the women of Otaheite from a too general imputation of licentiousness, acknowledges that there are

---

more rapid that in any instance hitherto known, and that they would probably double their numbers in less than fifteen years.

[18] Cook's First Voy. vol. ii. p. 207. & seq. Second Voy. vol. i. p. 352. Third Voy. vol. ii. p. 157. & seq. Missionary Voy. Appendix, p. 346. 4to.

[19] Mr. Anderson acted in the capacity of naturalist and surgeon in Cook's last voyage. Captain Cook and all the officers of the expedition seem to have had a very high opinion of his talents and accuracy of observation. His accounts therefore may be looked upon as of the first authority.

[20] Id. Third Voy. vol. ii. p. 158, 159.   [21] Id. Second Voy. vol. i. p. 352.

[22] Hume's Essays, vol. i. essay xi. p. 431. 8vo. 1764.

more of this character here than in any other countries, making at the same time a remark of a most decisive nature, by observing that the women who thus conduct themselves do not in any respect lower their rank in society, but mix indiscriminately with those of the most virtuous character.[23]

The common marriages in Otaheite are without any other ceremony than a present from the man to the parents of the girl. And this seems to be rather a bargain with them, for permission to try their daughter, than an absolute contract for a wife. If the father should think that he has not been sufficiently paid for his daughter, he makes no scruple of forcing her to leave her friend, and to cohabit with another person who may be more liberal. The man is always at liberty to make a new choice. Should his consort become pregnant, he may kill the child, and after that continue his connexion with the mother, or leave her, according to his pleasure. It is only when he has adopted a child, and suffered it to live, that the parties are considered as in the marriage state. A younger wife, however, may afterwards be joined to the first; but the changing of connexions is much more general than this plan, and is a thing so common that they speak of it with great indifference.[24] Libertinage before marriage seems to be no objection to a union of this kind ultimately.

The checks to population from such a state of society would alone appear sufficient to counteract the effects of the most delightful climate and the most exuberant plenty. Yet these are not all. The wars between the inhabitants of the different islands, and their civil contentions among themselves, are frequent, and sometimes carried on in a very destructive manner.[25] Besides the waste of human life in the field of battle, the conquerors generally ravage the enemy's territory, kill or carry off the hogs and poultry, and reduce as much as possible the means of future subsistence. The island of Otaheite which, in the years 1767 and 1768 swarmed with hogs and fowls, was in 1773 so ill supplied with these animals, that hardly any thing could induce the owners to part with them. This was attributed by Captain Cook principally to the wars which had taken place during that interval.[26] On Captain Vancouver's visit to Otaheite in 1791, he found that most of his friends that he had left in 1777 were dead; that there had been many wars since that time, in some of which the chiefs of the western districts of Otaheite had joined the enemy; and that the king had been for a considerable time completely worsted and his own districts entirely laid waste. Most of the animals, plants, and herbs, which Captain Cook had left, had been destroyed by the ravages of war.[27]

---

[23] Cook's Second Voy. vol. i. p. 187.   [24] Id. Third Voy. vol. ii. p. 157.

[25] Bouganville, Voy. autour du Monde, ch. iii. p. 217. Cook's First Voy. vol. ii. p. 244. Missionary Voy. p. 224.

[26] Id. Second Voy. vol. i. p. 182, 183. [In the Everyman Edition (1, 50) there is a misprint here, *1763* instead of '1773'.]

[27] Vancouver's Voy. vol. i. b. i. c. 6. p. 98. 4to.

The human sacrifices which are frequent in Otaheite, though alone sufficient strongly to fix the stain of barbarism on the character of the natives, do not probably occur in such considerable numbers as materially to affect the population of the country; and the diseases, though they have been dreadfully increased by European contact, were before peculiarly lenient; and even for some time afterwards, were not marked by any extraordinary fatality.[28]

The great checks to increase appear to be the vices of promiscuous intercourse, infanticide, and war, each of these operating with very considerable force. Yet powerful in the prevention and destruction of life as these causes must be, they have not always kept down the population to the level of the means of subsistence. According to Mr. Anderson: 'Notwithstanding the extreme fertility of the island, a famine frequently happens in which it is said many perish. Whether this be owing to the failure of some seasons, to over-population (which must sometimes almost necessarily happen) or wars, I have not been able to determine; though the truth of the fact may fairly be inferred from the great economy that they observe with respect to their food, even when there is plenty.'[29] After a dinner with a chief at Ulietea, Captain Cook observed that when the company rose many of the common people rushed in, to pick up the crumbs which had fallen, and for which they searched the leaves very narrowly. Several of them daily attended the ships, and assisted the butchers for the sake of the entrails of the hogs which were killed. In general, little seemed to fall to their share except offals. 'It must be owned', Captain Cook says, 'that they are exceedingly careful of every kind of provision, and waste nothing that can be eaten by man, flesh and fish especially.'[30]

From Mr. Anderson's account, it appears that a very small portion of animal food falls to the lot of the lower class of people, and then, it is either fish, sea-eggs, or other marine productions; for they seldom or never eat pork. The king or principal chief is alone able to furnish this luxury every day; and the inferior chiefs, according to their riches, once a week, fortnight, or month.[31] When the hogs and fowls have been diminished by wars, or too great consumption, a prohibition is laid upon these articles of food, which continues in force sometimes for several months, or even for a year or two, during which time, of course, they multiply very fast, and become again plentiful.[32] The common diet even of the Eareeoies, who are among the

---

[28] Cook's Third Voy. vol. ii. p. 148.   [29] Id. vol. ii. p. 153, 154.

[30] Id. Second Voy. vol. i. p. 176.

[31] Id. Third. Voy. vol. ii. p. 154. [A sea-egg is an *echinus* or sea-urchin; they were sometimes called sea-apples or sea-chestnuts.]

[32] Id. p. 155. [In the Everyman Edition (1. 51) there is a misprint here, *dogs and fowls* instead of 'hogs and fowls'.]

principal people of the islands, is, according to Mr. Anderson, made up of at least nine tenths of vegetable food.[33] And as a distinction of ranks is so strongly marked, and the lives and property of the lower classes of people appear to depend absolutely on the will of their chiefs, we may well imagine that these chiefs will often live in plenty while their vassals and servants are pinched with want.

From the late accounts of Otaheite, in the Missionary Voyage, it would appear that the depopulating causes above enumerated have operated with most extraordinary force since Captain Cook's last visit. A rapid succession of destructive wars, during a part of that interval, is taken notice of in the intermediate visit of Captain Vancouver;[34] and, from the small proportion of women remarked by the Missionaries,[35] we may infer that a greater number of female infants had been destroyed than formerly. This scarcity of women would naturally increase the vice of promiscuous intercourse and, aided by the ravages of European diseases, strike most effectually at the root of population.[36]

It is probable that Captain Cook, from the data on which he founded his calculation, may have overrated the population of Otaheite, and perhaps the Missionaries have rated it too low;[37] but I have no doubt that the population has very considerably decreased since Captain Cook's visit, from the different accounts that are given of the habits of the people, with regard to economy, at the different periods. Captain Cook and Mr. Anderson agree in describing their extreme carefulness of every kind of food; and Mr. Anderson, apparently after a very attentive investigation of the subject, mentions the frequent recurrence of famines. The Missionaries, on the contrary, though they strongly notice the distress from this cause in the Friendly Islands and the Marquesas, speak of the productions of Otaheite as being in the greatest profusion, and observe that, notwithstanding the horrible waste committed at feastings, and by the Eareeoie society, want is seldom known.[38]

It would appear from these accounts that the population of Otaheite is at present repressed considerably below the average means of subsistence, but it would be premature to conclude, that it will continue long so. The variations in the state of the island which were observed by Captain Cook, in his different visits, appear to prove that there are marked oscillations in its prosperity and population.[39] And this is exactly what we should suppose from theory. We cannot imagine that the population of any of these islands

---

[33] Id. p. 148.   [34] Vancouver's Voy. vol. i. b. i. c. 7. p. 137.

[35] Missionary Voyage, p. 192, & 385.

[36] Id. Appen. p. 347.   [37] Cook's Third Voy. vol vii ch. xiii. p. 212.

[38] Missionary Voy. p. 195. Appen. p. 385.

[39] Cook's Second Voy. vol. i. p. 182, & seq. & 346.

has, for ages past, remained stationary at a fixed number, or that it can have been regularly increasing, according to any rate, however slow. Great fluctuations must necessarily have taken place. Over-populousness would at all times increase the natural propensity of savages to war; and the enmities occasioned by aggressions of this kind would continue to spread devastation, long after the original inconvenience, which might have prompted them, had ceased to be felt.[40] The distresses experienced from one or two unfavourable seasons, operating on a crowded population, which was before living with the greatest economy, and pressing hard against the limits of its food, would, in such a state of society, occasion the more general prevalence of infanticide and promiscuous intercourse;[41] and these depopulating causes would, in the same manner, continue to act with increased force, for some time after the occasion which had aggravated them was at an end. A change of habits to a certain degree, gradually produced by a change of circumstances, would soon restore the population, which could not long be kept below its natural level without the most extreme violence. How far European contact may operate in Otaheite with this extreme violence, and prevent it from recovering its former population, is a point which experience only can determine. But should this be the case, I have no doubt that, on tracing the causes of it, we should find them to be aggravated vice and misery.

Of the other islands in the Pacific Ocean we have a less intimate knowledge than of Otaheite; but our information is sufficient to assure us that the state of society in all the principal groups of these islands is in most respects extremely similar. Among the Friendly and Sandwich islanders, the same feudal system and feudal turbulence, the same extraordinary power of the chiefs, and degraded state of the lower orders of society, and nearly the same promiscuous intercourse among a great part of the people, have been found to prevail, as at Otaheite.

In the Friendly Islands, though the power of the king was said to be unlimited, and the life and property of the subject at his disposal; yet it appeared, that some of the other chiefs acted like petty sovereigns, and frequently thwarted his measures, of which he often complained. 'But however independent' (Captain Cook says) 'of the despotic power of the king the great men may be, we saw instances enough to prove that the lower orders of people have no property nor safety for their persons, but at the will of the chiefs to whom they respectively belong.'[42] The chiefs often beat the

---

[40] Missionary Voy. p. 225.

[41] I hope I may never be misunderstood with regard to some of these preventive causes of overpopulation, and be supposed to imply the slightest approbation of them, merely because I relate their effects. A cause which may prevent any particular evil may be beyond all comparison worse than the evil itself.

[42] Cook's Third Voy. vol. i. p. 406.

inferior people most unmercifully;[43] and when any of them were caught in a theft on board the ships, their masters, far from interceding for them, would often advise the killing of them[44] which, as the chiefs themselves appeared to have no great horror of the crime of theft, could only arise from their considering the lives of these poor people as absolutely of no value.

Captain Cook, in his first visit to the Sandwich Islands, had reason to think that external wars and internal commotions were extremely frequent among the natives.[45] And Captain Vancouver, in his later account, strongly notices the dreadful devastations in many of the islands from these causes. Incessant contentions had occasioned alterations in the different governments since Captain Cook's visit. Only one chief of all that were known at that time was living; and, on inquiry, it appeared that few had died a natural death, most of them having been killed in these unhappy contests.[46] The power of the chiefs over the inferior classes of the people in the Sandwich Islands appears to be absolute. The people, on the other hand, pay them the most implicit obedience; and this state of servility has manifestly a great effect in debasing both their minds and bodies.[47] The gradations of rank seem to be even more strongly marked here than in the other islands, as the chiefs of higher rank behave to those who are lower in this scale in the most haughty and oppressive manner.[48]

It is not known that either in the Friendly or Sandwich Islands infanticide is practised, or that any institutions are established similar to the Eareeoie societies in Otaheite; but it seems to be stated on unquestionable authority that prostitution is extensively diffused, and prevails to a great degree among the lower classes of women;[49] which must always operate as a most powerful check to population. It seems highly probable, that the *toutous*, or servants, who spend the greatest part of their time in attendance upon the chiefs,[50] do not often marry; and it is evident that the polygamy allowed to the superior people must tend greatly to encourage and aggravate the vice of promiscuous intercourse among the inferior classes.

Were it an established fact that, in the more fertile islands of the Pacific Ocean, very little or nothing was suffered from poverty and want of food; as we could not expect to find among savages in such climates any great degree

---

[43] Cook's Third Voy. vol I, p. 232.
[44] p. 233. [In 1806 (Vol. I, p. 120) Malthus revised his judgement on this passage:
... considering the lives of these poor people as of little or no value.
[45] Cook's Third Voy. vol. ii. p. 247.   [46] Vancouver, vol. i. b. ii. c. ii. p. 187, 188.
[47] Cook's Third Voyage, vol. iii. p. 157.
[48] Ibid.
[49] Cook's Third Voy. vol. i. p. 401. Vol. ii. p. 543. Vol. iii. p. 130. Missionary Voy. p. 270.
[50] Cook's Third Voy. vol. i. p. 394.

of virtuous restraint,[51] the theory on the subject would naturally lead us to conclude that vice, including war, was the principal check to their population. The accounts which we have of these islands strongly confirm this conclusion. In the three great groups of islands which have been noticed, vice appears to be a most prominent feature. In Easter Island, from the great disproportion of the males to the females,[52] it can scarcely be doubted that infanticide prevails, though the fact may not have come to the knowledge of any of our navigators. Pérouse seemed to think that the women in each district were common property to the men of that district,[53] though the numbers of children which he saw[54] would rather tend to contradict this opinion. The fluctuations in the population of Easter Island appear to have been very considerable since its first discovery by Roggewein in 1722, though it cannot have been much affected by European intercourse. From the description of Pérouse, it appeared at the time of his visit to be recovering its population, which had been in a very low state, probably either from drought, civil dissensions, or the prevalence in an extreme degree of infanticide and promiscuous intercourse. When Captain Cook visited it in his second voyage, he calculated the population at six or seven hundred.[55] Pérouse at two thousand;[56] and, from the number of children which he observed, and the number of new houses that were building, he conceived that the population was on the increase.[57]

In the Marianne Islands, according to Pere Gobien, a very great number[58] of the young men remained unmarried, living like the members of the Eareeoie society in Otaheite, and distinguished by a similar name.[59] In the island of Formosa, it is said that the women were not allowed to bring children into the world before the age of thirty-five. If they were with child prior to that period, an abortion was effected by the priestess, and till the husband was forty years of age, the wife continued to live in her father's house, and was only seen by stealth.[60]

---

[51] [In 1817 (Vol. 1, p. 123) this was changed to:
    ... any great degree of moral restraint, ...
[52] Cook's Second Voy. vol. i. p. 289. Voyage de Pérouse, c. iv. p. 323. c. v. p. 336. 4to. 1794.
[53] Pérouse, c. iv. p. 326. c. v. p. 336.   [54] Pérouse, c. v. p. 336.
[55] Cook's Second Voy. vol. i. p. 289.
[56] Pérouse, c. v. p. 336.   [57] Ibid.
[58] Une infinité de jeunes gens. Hist. des Navigations aux terres Australes, vol. ii. p. 507. vol. ii. p. 158. note of the Editor. [See LEGOBIEN in the Alphabetical List.]
[59] Cook's Third Voyage, vol. ii. p. 158. note of the Editor.
[60] Harris's Collection of Voyages, 2 vols. folio. edit. 1744. vol. i. p. 794. This relation is given by John Albert de Mandesloe, a German traveller of some reputation for fidelity, though I believe in this instance he takes his account from the Dutch writers quoted by Montesquieu; (Esprit des Loix, liv. 23. ch. 17.) The authority is not perhaps sufficient to establish the existence of so strange a custom, though I confess that it does not appear to me wholly

The transient visits that have been made to some other islands, and the imperfect accounts that we have of them, do not enable us to enter into any particular detail of their customs; but from the general similarity of these customs, as far as has been observed, we have reason to think that, though they may not be marked by some of the more atrocious peculiarities which have been mentioned, vicious habits with respect to women, and wars, are the principal checks to their population.

These, however, are not all. On the subject of the happy state of plenty in which the natives of the South Sea islands have been said to live, I am inclined to think that our imaginations have been carried beyond the truth, by the exuberant descriptions which have sometimes been given of these delightful spots. The not unfrequent pressure of want, even in Otaheite, mentioned in Captain Cook's last voyage, has undeceived us with regard to the most fertile of all these islands; and from the Missionary Voyage it appears that at certain times of the year, when the bread fruit is out of season, all suffer a temporary scarcity. At Oheitahoo, one of the Marquesas, it amounted to hunger, and the very animals were pinched for want of food. At Tongataboo, the principal of the Friendly Islands, the chiefs, to secure plenty, changed their abodes to other islands,[61] and at times many of the natives suffered much from want.[62] In the Sandwich Islands, long droughts sometimes occur,[63] hogs and yams are often very scarce,[64] and visitors are received with an unwelcome austerity very different from the profuse benevolence of Otaheite. In New Caledonia, the inhabitants feed upon spiders,[65] and are sometimes reduced to eat great pieces of steatite to appease the cravings of their hunger.[66]

These facts strongly prove that, in whatever abundance the productions of these islands may be found at certain periods, or however they may be checked by ignorance, wars, and other causes, the average population, generally speaking, presses hard against the limits of the average food. In a

---

improbable. In the same account, it is mentioned that there is no difference of condition among these people, and that their wars are so bloodless that the death of a single person generally decides them. In a very healthy climate, where the habits of the people were favourable to population, and a community of goods was established, as no individual would have reason to fear *particular poverty* from a large family, the government would be in a manner compelled to take upon itself the suppression of the population by law; and as this would be the greatest violation of every natural feeling, there cannot be a more forcible argument against a community of goods.

[61] Missionary Voy. Appen. p. 385.   [62] Id. p. 270.
[63] Vancouver's Voy. vol. ii. b. iii. c. viii. p. 230.
[64] Id. c. vii. and viii.
[65] Voyage in search of Pérouse, ch. xiii. p. 420. Eng. transl. 4to. [See LABILLARDIÈRE in the Alphabetical List.]
[66] Id. ch. xiii. p. 400.

state of society where the lives of the inferior orders of the people seem to be considered by their superiors as absolutely of no value,[67] it is evident that we are very liable to be deceived with regard to the appearances of abundance; and we may easily conceive that hogs and vegetables might be exchanged in great profusion for European commodities by the principal proprietors, while their vassals and slaves were suffering severely from want.

I cannot conclude this general review of that department of human society, which has been classed under the name of savage life, without observing that the only advantage in it above civilized life, that I can discover, is the possession of a greater degree of leisure by the mass of the people. There is less work to be done, and consequently there is less labour. When we consider the incessant toil to which the lower classes of society in civilized life are condemned, this cannot but appear to us a striking advantage; but it is probably overbalanced by much greater disadvantages. In all those countries where provisions are procured with facility, a most tyrannical distinction of rank prevails. Blows, and violations of property, seem to be matters of course; and the lower classes of the people are in a state of comparative degradation much below what is known in civilized nations.

In that part of savage life where a great degree of equality obtains, the difficulty of procuring food, and the hardships of incessant war, create a degree of labour not inferior to that which is exerted by the lower classes of the people in civilized society, though much more unequally divided. But though we may compare the labour of these two classes of human society, their privations and sufferings will admit of no comparison. Nothing appears to me to place this in so striking a point of view as the whole tenor of education among the ruder tribes of savages in America. Everything that can contribute to teach the most unmoved patience under the severest pains and misfortunes, everything that tends to harden the heart, and narrow all the sources of sympathy, is most sedulously inculcated in the savage. The civilized man, on the contrary, though he may be advised to bear evil with patience when it comes, is not instructed to be always expecting it. Other virtues are to be called into action besides fortitude. He is taught to feel for his neighbour, or even his enemy, in distress; to encourage and expand his social affections; and in general, to enlarge the sphere of pleasurable emotions. The obvious inference, from these two different modes of education, is that the civilized man hopes to enjoy, the savage expects only to suffer.

The preposterous system of Spartan discipline, and that unnatural absorption of every private feeling in concern for the public, which has sometimes been so absurdly admired, could never have existed but among a

---

[67] [In 1807 (Vol. I, p. 106) this was altered to:
    ... considered by their superiors as of little or no value, ...

people exposed to perpetual hardships and privations from incessant war, and in a state under the constant fear of dreadful reverses of fortune. Instead of considering these phenomena as indicating any peculiar tendency to fortitude and patriotism in the disposition of the Spartans, I should merely consider them as a strong indication of the miserable and almost savage state of Sparta, and of Greece in general at that time. Like the commodities in a market, those virtues will be produced in the greatest quantity for which there is the greatest demand; and where patience, under pain and privations, and extravagant patriotic sacrifices, are the most called for, it is a melancholy indication of the misery of the people and the insecurity of the state.

CHAPER VI

Of the Checks to Population among the ancient Inhabitants of the North of Europe

A history of the early migrations and settlements of mankind, with the motives which prompted them, would illustrate in a striking manner the constant tendency in the human race to increase beyond the means of subsistence. Without some general law of this nature, it would seem as if the world could never have been peopled. A state of sloth, and not of restlessness and activity, seems evidently to be the natural state of man; and this latter disposition could not have been generated but by the strong goad of necessity, though it might afterwards be continued by habit, and the new associations that were formed from it, the spirit of enterprize, and the thirst of martial glory.

We are told that Abram and Lot had so great substance in cattle, that the land would not bear them both, that they might dwell together. There was strife between their herdsmen. And Abram proposed to Lot to separate, and said, 'Is not the whole land before thee? If thou wilt take the left hand, then I will go to the right; if thou depart to the right hand, then I will go to the left.'[1]

This simple observation and proposal is a striking illustration of that great spring of action which overspread the whole earth with people, and in the progress of time, drove some of the less fortunate inhabitants of the globe, yielding to irresistible pressure, to seek a scanty subsistence in the burning deserts of Asia and Africa, and the frozen regions of Siberia and North America. The first migrations would naturally find no other obstacles than the nature of the country; but when a considerable part of the earth had been peopled, though but thinly, the possessors of these districts would not yield them to others without a struggle; and the redundant inhabitants of any of the more central spots could not find room for themselves without expelling their nearest neighbours, or at least passing through their territories, which would necessarily give occasion to frequent contests.

The middle latitudes of Europe and Asia seem to have been occupied, at an early period of history, by nations of shepherds. Thucydides gave it as his opinion that the civilized states of Europe and Asia, in his time, could not

---

[1] Genesis, ch. xiii. [*Bible*, 1611.]

resist the Scythians united. [2]*Yet a country in pasture cannot possibly support so many inhabitants as a country in tillage; but what renders nations of shepherds so formidable is the power which they possess of moving altogether, and the necessity they frequently feel of exerting this power in search of fresh pasture for their herds. A tribe that is rich in cattle has an immediate plenty of food. Even the parent stock may be devoured in case of absolute necessity. The women live in greater ease than among nations of hunters, and are consequently more prolific. The men, bold in their united strength, and confiding in their power of procuring pasture for their cattle by change of place, feel probably but few fears about providing for a family. These combined causes soon produce their natural and invariable effect, an extended population. A more frequent and rapid change of place then becomes necessary. A wider and more extensive territory is successively occupied. A broader desolation extends all around them. Want pinches the less fortunate members of the society; and at length the impossibility of supporting such a number together becomes too evident to be resisted. Young scions are then pushed out from the parent stock, and instructed to explore fresh regions, and to gain happier seats for themselves by their swords.

> The world is all before them where to choose.

Restless from present distress, flushed with the hope of fairer prospects, and animated with the spirit of hardy enterprize, these daring adventurers are likely to become formidable adversaries to all who oppose them. The inhabitants of countries long settled, engaged in the peaceful occupations of trade and agriculture, would not often be able to resist the energy of men acting under such powerful motives of exertion. And the frequent contests with tribes in the same circumstances with themselves would be so many struggles for existence, and would be fought with a desperate courage, inspired by the reflection that death would be the punishment of defeat and life the prize of victory.*[2]

In these savage contests, many tribes must have been utterly exterminated. Many probably perished by hardships and famine. Others, whose leading star had given them a happier direction, became great and powerful tribes, and in their turn sent off fresh adventurers in search of other seats. These would at first owe allegiance to their parent tribe; but in a short time the ties that bound them would be little felt, and they would remain friends, or become enemies, according as their power, their ambition, or their convenience, might dictate.

---

[2] [Passages from 'Yet a country in pasture ...' to '... prize of victory' are taken almost verbatim from pp. 45–8 of the 1798 *Essay*. See MILTON in the Alphabetical List.]

The prodigious waste of human life occasioned by this perpetual struggle for room and food would be more than supplied by the mighty power of population, acting in some degree unshackled from the constant habit of migration. A prevailing hope of bettering their condition by change of place, a constant expectation of plunder, a power, even, if distressed, of selling their children as slaves, added to the natural carelessness of the Barbaric character, would all conspire to raise a population which would remain to be repressed afterwards by famine and war.

The tribes that possessed themselves of the more fruitful regions, though they might win them and maintain them by continual battles, rapidly increased in number and power, from the increased means of subsistence; till at length the whole territory, from the confines of China to the shores of the Baltic, was peopled by a various race of barbarians, brave, robust, and enterprising, inured to hardships and delighting in war.[3] While the different fixed governments of Europe and Asia, by superior population and superior skill, were able to oppose an impenetrable barrier to their destroying hordes, they wasted their superfluous numbers in contests with each other; but the moment that the weakness of the settled governments, or the casual union of many of these wandering tribes, gave them the ascendant in power, the storm discharged itself on the fairest provinces of the earth; and China, Persia, Egypt and Italy were overwhelmed at different periods in this flood of barbarism. These remarks are strongly exemplified in the fall of the Roman empire. The shepherds of the north of Europe were long held in check by the vigour of the Roman arms and the terror of the Roman name. The formidable irruption of the Cimbri in search of new settlements, though signalized by the destruction of five consular armies, was at length arrested in its victorious career by Marius; and the barbarians were taught to repent their rashness by the almost complete extermination of this powerful colony.[4] The names of Julius Cæsar, of Drusus, Tiberius, and Germanicus, impressed on their minds by the slaughter of their countrymen, continued to inspire them with a fear of encroaching on the Roman territory. But they were rather triumphed over than vanquished;[5] and though the armies or colonies which they sent forth were either cut off, or forced back into their original seats, the vigour of the great German nation remained unimpaired, and ready to pour

---

[3] The various branchings, divisions, and contests, of the great Tartar nation are curiously described in the genealogical history of the Tartars by the Khan Abul Ghazi; (translated into English from the French, with additions, in 2 vols. 8vo.) but the misfortune of all history is, that while the motives of a few princes and leaders, in their various projects of ambition, are sometimes detailed with accuracy, the motives which often crowd their standards with willing followers are totally overlooked.

[In 1806 (Vol. I, p. 138) *totally overlooked* was changed to 'almost entirely overlooked'.

[4] Tacitus de Moribus Germanorum, s. 37.   [5] Id., s. 37.

forth her hardy sons in constant succession, wherever they could force an opening for themselves by their swords. The feeble reigns of Decius, Gallus, Æmilianus, Valerian and Gallienus afforded such an opening, and were in consequence marked by a general irruption of barbarians. The Goths, who were supposed to have migrated in the course of some years from Scandinavia to the Euxine, were bribed to withdraw their victorious troops by an annual tribute. But no sooner was the dangerous secret of the wealth and weakness of the Roman empire thus revealed to the world, than new swarms of barbarians spread devastation through the frontier provinces, and terror as far as the gates of Rome.[6] The Franks, the Allemanni, the Goths, and adventurers of less considerable tribes, comprehended under these general appellations, poured like a torrent on different parts of the empire. Rapine and oppression destroyed the produce of the present, and the hope of future harvests. A long and general famine was followed by a wasting plague, which for fifteen years ravaged every city and province of the Roman empire; and, judging from the mortality in some spots, it was conjectured that in a few years war, pestilence and famine had consumed the moiety of the human species.[7] Yet the tide of emigration still continued at intervals to roll impetuously from the north, and the succession of martial princes, who repaired the misfortunes of their predecessors, and propped the falling fate of the empire, had to accomplish the labours of Hercules in freeing the Roman territory from these barbarous invaders. The Goths who, in the year 250 and the following years, ravaged the empire both by sea and land, with various success, but in the end, with the almost total loss of their adventurous bands,[8] in the year 269 sent out an emigration of immense numbers, with their wives and families, for the purposes of settlement.[9] This formidable body, which was said to consist at first of 320 000 barbarians,[10] was ultimately destroyed and dispersed by the vigour and wisdom of the emperor Claudius. His successor, Aurelian, encountered and vanquished new hosts of the same name that had quitted their settlements in the Ukraine; but one of the implied conditions of the peace was that he should withdraw the Roman forces from Dacia, and relinquish this great province to the Goths and Vandals.[11] A new and most formidable invasion of the Allemanni threatened soon after to sack the mistress of the world, and three great and bloody battles were fought by Aurelian before this destroying host could be exterminated and Italy be delivered from its ravages.[12]

The strength of Aurelian had crushed on every side the enemies of Rome. After his death, they seemed to revive with an increase of fury and numbers.

---

[6] Gibbon's Decline and Fall of the Roman Empire, vol. i. c. x. p. 407. et seq. 8vo. edit. 1783.
[7] Id. vol. i. c. x. p. 455, 456.   [8] Id. p. 431.   [9] Id. vol. ii. c. xi. p. 13.
[10] Id. p. 11.   [11] Id. p. 19. A. D. 270.   [12] Id. p. 26.

They were again vanquished on all sides by the active vigour of Probus. The deliverance of Gaul alone from German invaders is reported to have cost the lives of four hundred thousand barbarians.[13] The victorious emperor pursued his successes into Germany itself, and the princes of the country, astonished at his presence, and dismayed and exhausted by the ill success of their last emigration, submitted to any terms that the conquerors might impose.[14] Probus, and afterwards, Diocletian,[15] adopted the plan of recruiting the exhausted provinces of the empire, by granting lands to the fugitive or captive barbarians, and disposing of their superfluous numbers where they might be the least likely to be dangerous to the state: but such colonizations were an insufficient vent for the population of the north, and the ardent temper of the barbarians would not always bend to the slow labours of agriculture.[16] During the vigorous reign of Diocletian, unable to make an effectual impression on the Roman frontiers, the Goths, the Vandals, the Gepidæ, the Burgundians, and the Allemanni, wasted each other's strength by mutual hostilities, while the subjects of the empire enjoyed the bloody spectacle, conscious that, whoever vanquished, they vanquished the enemies of Rome.[17]

Under the reign of Constantine the Goths were again formidable. Their strength had been restored by a long peace, and a new generation had arisen which no longer remembered the misfortunes of ancient days.[18] In two successive wars great numbers of them were slain. Vanquished on every side, they were driven into the mountains; and, in the course of a severe campaign, above a hundred thousand were computed to have perished by cold and hunger.[19] Constantine adopted the plan of Probus and his successors, in granting land to those suppliant barbarians who were expelled from their own country. Towards the end of his reign, a competent portion in the provinces of Pannonia, Thrace, Macedonia, and Italy, was assigned for the habitation and subsistence of three hundred thousand Sarmatians.[20]

The warlike Julian had to encounter and vanquish new swarms of Franks and Allemanni who, emigrating from their German forests during the civil wars of Constantine, settled in different parts of Gaul, and made the scene of their devastations three times more extensive than that of their conquests.[21] Destroyed and repulsed on every side, they were pursued, in five expeditions, into their own country,[22] but Julian had conquered, as soon as he had penetrated into Germany; and in the midst of that mighty hive which had

---

[13] Gibbon, vol. ii. c. xii. p. 75.   [14] Id. p. 79. A.D. 277.   [15] Id. c. xiii. p. 132. A.D. 296.
[16] Id. c. xii. p. 84.   [17] Id. c. xiii. p. 130.   [18] Id. c. xiv. p. 254. A.D. 322.
[19] Id. vol. iii. c. xviii. p. 125. A.D. 332.   [20] Id. p. 127.
[21] Id. vol. iii. c. xix. p. 215. A.D. 356.
[22] Id. p. 228. and vol. iv. c. xxii. p. 17. from A.D. 357 to 359.

sent out such swarms of people, as to keep the Roman world in perpetual dread, the principal obstacles to his progress were almost impassable roads and vast unpeopled forests.[23]

Though thus subdued and prostrated by the victorious arms of Julian, this hydra-headed monster rose again after a few years; and the firmness, vigilance, and powerful genius of Valentinian were fully called into action, in protecting his dominions from the different irruptions of the Allemanni, the Burgundians, the Saxons, the Goths, the Quadi, and Sarmatians.[24]

The fate of Rome was at length determined by an irresistible emigration of the Huns from the east and north, which precipitated on the empire the whole body of the Goths;[25] and the continuance of this powerful pressure on the nations of Germany seemed to prompt them to the resolution of abandoning to the fugitives of Sarmatia their woods and morasses, or at least of discharging their superfluous numbers on the provinces of the Roman empire.[26] An emigration of four hundred thousand persons issued from the same coast of the Baltic, which had poured forth the myriads of Cimbri and Teutones during the vigour of the Republic.[27] When this host was destroyed by war and famine, other adventurers succeeded. The Suevi, the Vandals, the Alani, the Burgundians, passed the Rhine, never more to retreat.[28] The conquerors who first settled were expelled or exterminated by new invaders. [29]*Clouds of barbarians seemed to collect from all parts of the northern hemisphere. Gathering fresh darkness and terror as they rolled on, the congregated bodies at length obscured the sun of Italy, and sunk the western world in night.*[29]

In two centuries from the flight of the Goths across the Danube, barbarians of various names and lineage had plundered and taken possession of Thrace, Pannonia, Gaul, Britain, Spain, Africa, and Italy.[30] The most horrible devastations and an incredible destruction of the human species accompanied these rapid conquests; and famine and pestilence, which always march in the train of war when it ravages with such inconsiderate cruelty, raged in every part of Europe. The historians of the times, who beheld these scenes of desolation, labour and are at a loss for expressions to describe them; but beyond the power of language, the numbers and the destructive violence of these barbarous invaders were evinced by the total change which

---

[23] Gibbon, vol. iv. c. xxii. p. 17. and vol. iii. c. xix. p. 229.

[24] Id. vol. iv. c. xxv. from A.D. 364 to 375.

[25] Id. vol. iv. c. xxvi. p. 382. et seq. A. D. 376.   [26] Id. vol. v. c. xxx. p. 213.

[27] Id. p. 214. A. D. 406.

[28] Id. p. 224.

[29] [These two sentences are taken from p. 45 of the 1798 *Essay*, only then Malthus wrote:
     ... sunk the whole world in universal night.

[30] Robertson's Charles V. vol. i. sect. i. p. 7. 8vo. 1782.

took place in the state of Europe.[31] These tremendous effects, so long, and so deeply felt, throughout the fairest portions of the earth, may be traced to the simple cause of the superiority of the power of population to the means of subsistence.

Machiavel, in the beginning of his history of Florence, says: 'The people who inhabit the northern parts that lie between the Rhine and the Danube, living in a healthful and prolific climate, often increase to such a degree that vast numbers of them are forced to leave their native country, and go in search of new habitations. When any one of those provinces begins to grow too populous, and wants to disburthen itself, the following method is observed. In the first place, it is divided into three parts, in each of which there is an equal portion of the nobility and commonalty, the rich and the poor. After this they cast lots, and that division on which the lot falls quits the country and goes to seek its fortune, leaving the other two more room and liberty to enjoy their possessions at home. These emigrations proved the destruction of the Roman empire.'[32] Gibbon is of opinion that Machiavel has represented these emigrations too much as regular and concerted measures;[33] but I think it highly probable that he has not erred much in this respect, and that it was a foresight of the frequent necessity of thus discharging their redundant population which gave occasion to that law among the Germans, taken notice of by Cæsar and Tacitus, of not permitting their cultivated lands to remain longer than a year under the same possessors.[34] The reasons which Cæsar mentions as being assigned for this custom seem to be hardly adequate; but if we add to them the prospect of emigration, in the manner described by Machiavel, the custom will appear to be highly useful, and a double weight will be given to one of the reasons that Cæsar mentions;

---

[31] Robertson's Charles V, p. 10, 11, 12.   [32] Istorie Fiorentine Machiavelli, l. i. p. 1, 2.

[33] Gibbon, vol. i. c. ix. p. 360. note. Paul Diaconus, from whom it is supposed that Machiavel has taken this description, writes thus: Septentrionalis plaga quantò magis ab æstu solis remota est, et nivali frigore gelida, tantò salubrior corporibus hominum et propagandis gentibus magis coaptata. Sicut e contrario, omnis meridiana regio, quò solis est fervori vicinior eo morbis est abundantior, et educandis minus apta mortalibus ... Multæque quoque ex eâ, eo quod tantas mortalium turmas germinat, quantas alere vix sufficit, sæpe gentes egressæ sunt, quæ non solum partes Asiæ, sed etiam maxime sibi contiguam Europam afflixere. (De gestis Longobardorum, l. i. c. i.)

Intra hanc ergo constituti populi, dum in tantam multitudinem pullulassent, ut jam simul habitare non valerent, in tres (ut fertur) partes omnem catervam dividentes, quænam ex illis patriam effet relictura, ut novas sedes exquirerent, sorte disquirunt. Igitur ea pars, cui sors dederit genitale solum excedere, exteraque arva sectari, constitutis supra se duobus ducibus, Ibore scilicet, et Agione, qui et Germani erant, et juvenili ætate floridi, ceterisque prestantiores, ad exquirandas quas possint incolere terras, sedesque statuere, valedicentes suis simul et patriæ iter arripiunt. (c. ii.)

[For English translations, see PAULUS DIACONUS in the Alphabetical List.]

[34] De bello Gallico, vi. 22. De moribus German. s. xxvi.

namely, lest they should be led, by being accustomed to one spot, to exchange the toils of war for the business of agriculture.[35]

Gibbon very justly rejects, with Hume and Robertson, the improbable supposition, that the inhabitants of the north were far more numerous formerly than at present,[36] but he thinks himself obliged at the same time to deny the strong tendency to increase in the northern nations,[37] as if the two facts were necessarily connected. For a careful distinction should always be made between a redundant population and a population actually great. The Highlands of Scotland are probably more redundant in population than any other part of Great Britain; and though it would be admitting a palpable absurdity, to allow that the north of Europe, covered in early ages with immense forests, and inhabited by a race of people who supported themselves principally by their herds and flocks,[38] was more populous in those times than in its present state; yet the facts detailed in the Decline and Fall of the Roman empire, or even the very slight sketch of them that I have given, cannot rationally be accounted for, without the supposition of a most powerful tendency in these people to increase, and to repair their repeated losses by the prolific power of nature.

From the first irruption of the Cimbri, to the final extinction of the western empire, the efforts of the German nations to colonize or plunder were unceasing.[39] The numbers that were cut off during this period by war and famine were almost incalculable, and such as could not possibly have been supported with undiminished vigour by a country thinly peopled, unless the stream had been supplied by a spring of very extraordinary power.

Gibbon describes the labours of Valentinian in securing the Gallic frontier against the Germans; an enemy, he says, whose strength was renewed by a stream of daring volunteers which incessantly flowed from the most distant tribes of the north.[40] An easy adoption of strangers was probably a mode by which some of the German nations renewed their strength so suddenly,[41] after the most destructive defeats; but this explanation only removes the difficulty a little further off. It makes the earth rest upon the tortoise; but does not tell us on what the tortoise rests. We may still ask, what northern reservoir supplied this incessant stream of daring adventurers? Montesquieu's solution of the problem, will, I think, hardly be admitted. The swarms of barbarians which issued formerly from the north appear no more, he says, at present; and the reason which he gives is that the violence of the

---

[35] De bello Gallico vi. 22.　　　[36] Gibbon, vol. i. c. ix. p. 361.　　　[37] Id. p. 348.

[38] Tacitus de moribus German. s. v. Cæsar de bell. Gall. vi. 22.

[39] Cæsar found in Gaul a most formidable colony under Ariovistus, and a general dread prevailing that in a few years all the Germans would pass the Rhine. De bell. Gall. i. 31.

[40] Gibbon, vol. iv. c. xxv. p. 283.　　　[41] Ibid. note.

Romans had driven the people of the south into the north, who, as long as this force continued, remained there; but as soon as it was weakened, spread themselves again over every country.

The same phenomenon appeared after the conquests and tyrannies of Charlemagne, and the subsequent dissolution of his empire; and if a prince, he says, in the present days were to make similar ravages in Europe, the nations driven into the north, and resting on the limits of the universe,[42] would there make a stand, till the moment when they would inundate, or conquer, Europe a third time. In a note he observes: 'We see to what the famous question is reduced – why the north is no longer so fully peopled as in former times?'

If the famous question, or rather the answer to it, be reduced to this, it is reduced to a miracle; for without some supernatural mode of obtaining food, how these collected nations could support themselves in such barren regions, for so long a period, as during the vigour of the Roman empire, it is a little difficult to conceive; and one can hardly help smiling at the bold figure of these prodigious crowds making their last determined stand on the limits of the universe, and living, as we must suppose, with the most patient fortitude on air and ice for some hundreds of years, till they could return to their own homes, and resume their usual more substantial mode of subsistence.

The whole difficulty, however, is at once removed if we apply to the German nations at that time a fact, which is so generally known to have occurred in America, and suppose that, when not checked by wars and famine, they increased at a rate that would double their numbers in twenty-five or thirty years. The propriety, and even the necessity, of applying this rate of increase to the inhabitants of ancient Germany, will strikingly appear from that most valuable picture of their manners which has been left us by Tacitus. He describes them as not inhabiting cities, or even admitting of contiguous settlements. Every person surrounds his house with a vacant space;[43] a circumstance, which besides its beneficial effect as a security from fire, is strongly calculated to prevent the generation, and check the ravages, of epidemics. 'They content themselves almost universally with one wife. Their matrimonial bond is strict and severe, and their manners in this respect deserving of the highest praise.[44] They live in a state of well-guarded chastity, corrupted by no seducing spectacles or convivial incitements. Adultery is extremely rare, and no indulgence is shewn to a prostitute. Neither beauty, youth, nor riches can procure her a husband; for none there

---

[42] Les nations adossées au limites de l'univers y tiendroient fermue. Grandeur et Decad. des Rom. c. xvi. p. 187. [The nations with their backs against the limits of the universe would there hold fast.]

[43] Tacitus de moribus Germ. s. xvi.   [44] Id. s. xviii.

looks on vice with a smile, nor calls mutual seduction the way of the world. To limit the increase of children, or put to death any of the husband's blood, is accounted infamous; and virtuous manners have there more efficacy than good laws elsewhere.[45] Every mother suckles her own children, and does not deliver them into the hands of servants and nurses. The youths partake late of the sexual intercourse, and hence pass the age of puberty unexhausted. Nor are the virgins brought forward. The same maturity, the same full growth is required: the sexes unite equally matched and robust, and the children inherit the vigour of their parents. The more numerous are a man's kinsmen and relations, the more comfortable is his old age; nor is it any advantage to be childless.'[46]

With these manners, and a habit of enterprise and emigration, which would naturally remove all fears about providing for a family, it is difficult to conceive a society with a stronger principle of increase; and we see at once that prolific source of successive armies and colonies, against which the force of the Roman empire so long struggled with difficulty, and under which it ultimately sunk. It is not probable that for two periods together, or even for one, the population within the confines of Germany ever doubled itself in twenty-five years. Their perpetual wars, the rude state of agriculture, and particularly the very strange custom adopted by most of the tribes, of marking their barriers by extensive deserts,[47] would prevent any very great actual increase of numbers. At no one period could the country be called well-peopled, though it was often redundant in population. They abandoned their immense forests to the exercise of hunting, employed in pasturage the most considerable part of their lands, bestowed on the small remainder a rude and careless cultivation, and when the return of famine severely admonished them of the insufficiency of their scanty resources, they accused the sterility of a country which refused to supply the multitude of its inhabitants;[48] but instead of clearing their forests, draining their swamps, and rendering their soil fit to support an extended population, they found it more congenial to their martial habits and impatient dispositions, to go 'in quest of food, or plunder, or of glory'[49] into other countries. These adventurers either gained lands for themselves by their swords, or were cut off by the various accidents of war; were received into the Roman armies, or dispersed over the Roman territory; or perhaps, having relieved their country by their absence, returned home laden with spoils, and ready, after having recruited their diminished numbers, for fresh expeditions. The succession of human beings appears to have been most rapid, and as fast as

---

[45] Tacitus de moribus Germ, s. xix.   [46] Id. s. xx.   [47] Cæsar de bell. Gall. vi. 23.
[48] Gibbon, vol. i. c. ix. p. 360.
[49] Id. c. x. p. 417.

some were disposed of in colonies, or mowed down by the scythe of war and famine, others rose in increased numbers to supply their place.

According to this view of the subject, the North could never have been exhausted; and when Dr. Robertson, describing the calamities of these invasions, says, that they did not cease until the North, by pouring forth successive swarms, was drained of people, and could no longer furnish instruments of destruction,[50] he will appear to have fallen into the very error which he had before laboured to refute, and to speak as if the northern nations were actually very populous. For they must have been so, if the number of their inhabitants at any one period had been sufficient, notwithstanding the slaughter of war, to people in such a manner Thrace, Pannonia, Gaul, Spain, Africa, Italy, and England, as in some parts not to leave many traces of their former inhabitants. The period of the peopling of these countries, however, he himself mentions as two hundred years,[51] and in such a time new generations would arise that would more than supply every vacancy.

The true cause which put a stop to the continuance of northern emigration was the impossibility any longer of making an impression on the most desirable countries of Europe. They were then inhabited by the descendants of the bravest and most enterprising of the German tribes; and it was not probable, that they should so soon degenerate from the valour of their ancestors, as to suffer their lands to be wrested from them by inferior numbers and inferior skill, though perhaps superior hardihood.

Checked for a time by the bravery and poverty of their neighbours by land, the enterprising spirit and overflowing numbers of the Scandinavian nations soon found vent by sea. Feared before the reign of Charlemagne, they were repelled with difficulty by the care and vigour of that great prince, but during the distractions of the empire under his feeble successors, they spread like a devouring flame over Lower Saxony, Friezeland, Holland, Flanders, and the banks of the Rhine as far as Mentz.

After having long ravaged the coasts, they penetrated into the heart of France, pillaged and burnt her fairest towns, levied immense tributes on her monarchs, and at length obtained, by grant, one of the finest provinces of the kingdom. They made themselves even dreaded in Spain, Italy, and Greece, spreading every where desolation and terror. Sometimes they turned their arms against each other, as if bent on their own mutual destruction; at other times transported colonies to unknown or uninhabited countries, as if they were willing to repair, in one place, the horrid destruction of the human race occasioned by their furious ravages, in others.[52]

---

[50] Robertson's Charles V. vol. i. s. i. p. 11.   [51] Id. vol. i. s. i. p. 7.
[52] Mallet, Introd. a l'Histoire de Dannemarc, tom. i. c. x. p. 221, 223, 224. 12mo. 1766.

The mal-administration and civil wars of the Saxon kings of England produced the same effect as the weakness which followed the reign of Charlemagne in France,[53] and for two hundred years the British isles were incessantly ravaged, and often in part subdued, by these northern invaders. During the eighth, ninth and tenth centuries, the sea was covered with their vessels from one end of Europe to the other,[54] and the countries now the most powerful in arts and arms were the prey of their constant depredations. The growing and consolidating strength of these countries at length removed all further prospect of success from such invasions.[55] The nations of the north were slowly and reluctantly compelled to confine themselves within their natural limits, and to exchange their pastoral manners, and with them the peculiar facilities of plunder and emigration which they afforded, for the patient labours and slow returns of trade and agriculture. But the slowness of these returns necessarily effected an important change in the manners of the people.

In ancient Scandinavia, during the time of its constant wars and emigrations, few or none, probably, were ever deterred from marrying by the fear of not being able to provide for a family. In modern Scandinavia, on the contrary, the frequency of the marriage union is continually checked by the most imperious and justly founded apprehensions of this kind. This is most particularly the case in Norway, as I shall have occasion to remark in another place; but the same fears operate in a greater or less degree, though every where with considerable force, in all parts of Europe. Happily, the more tranquil state of the modern world does not demand such rapid supplies of human beings, and the prolific powers of nature cannot therefore be so generally called into action.

Mallet, in the excellent account of the northern nations which he has prefixed to his History of Denmark, observes that he had not been able to discover any proofs that their emigrations proceeded from want of room at home,[56] and one of the reasons which he gives is, that after a great emigration, the countries often remained quite deserted and unoccupied for a long time.[57] But instances of this kind I am inclined to think were rare, though they might occasionally happen. With the habits of enterprize and emigration which prevailed in those days, a whole people would sometimes move in search of a more fertile territory. The lands, which they before occupied, must of necessity be left desert for a time; and if there were any

---

[53] Mallet, Introd. a l'Histoire de Dannemarc, tom. i. c. x. p. 226.   [54] Id. p. 221.

[55] Perhaps the civilized world could not be considered as perfectly secure from another northern or eastern inundation, till the total change in the art of war, by the introduction of gunpowder, gave to improved skill and knowledge the decided advantage over physical force.

[56] Hist. Dan. tom. i. c. ix. p. 206.   [57] Id. p. 205, 206.

thing particularly ineligible in the soil or situation, which the total emigration of the people would seem to imply, it might be more congenial to the temper of the surrounding barbarians, to provide for themselves better by their swords, than to occupy immediately these rejected lands. Such total emigrations proved the unwillingness of the society to divide, but by no means that they were not straitened for room and food at home.

The other reason which Mallet gives is that in Saxony, as well as Scandinavia, vast tracts of land lay in their original uncultivated state, having never been grubbed up or cleared; and that, from the descriptions of Denmark in those times, it appeared that the coasts alone were peopled, but the interior parts formed one vast forest.[58] It is evident that he here falls into the common error of confounding a superfluity of inhabitants with great actual population. The pastoral manners of the people, and their habits of war and enterprize, prevented them from clearing and cultivating their lands,[59] and then these very forests, by restraining the sources of subsistence within very narrow bounds, contributed to a superfluity of numbers; that is, to a population beyond what the scanty supplies of the country could support.

There is another cause, not often attended to, why poor, cold, and thinly-peopled countries tend generally to a superfluity of inhabitants, and are strongly prompted to emigration. In warmer and more populous countries, particularly those abounding in great towns and manufactures, an insufficient supply of food can seldom continue long without producing epidemics, either in the shape of great and ravaging plagues, or of less violent, though more constant, sicknesses. In poor, cold, and thinly-peopled countries, on the contrary, from the antiseptic quality of the air, the misery arising from insufficient or bad food, may continue a considerable time without producing these effects, and consequently this powerful stimulus to emigration continues to operate for a much longer period.[60]

---

[58] Hist. Dan. tom. i. c. ix. p. 207.

[59] Nec arare terram aut expectare annum tam facile persuaseris, quam vocare hostes et vulnera mereri; pigrum quinimò et iners videtur sudore acquirere quod possis sanguine parare. Tacitus de mor. Germ.
[S. XIV. 'It would be much more difficult to persuade them to till the soil and wait for the year's harvest, than to challenge the enemy and be rewarded with wounds; indeed, it seems to them sluggish and unenterprising to get by your own sweat that which could be gained by shedding somebody else's blood.'] Nothing, indeed, in the study of human nature,[(a)] is more evident than the extreme difficulty with which habits are changed; and no argument therefore can be more fallacious than to infer, that those people are not pinched with want, who do not make a proper use of their lands.
[(a)] [In 1806 (Vol. 1, p. 166) *in the study of human nature* was replaced by 'in the history of mankind'.

[60] Epidemics have their seldomer or frequenter returns according to their sundry soils, situations, air, &c. Hence, some have them yearly, as Egypt and Constantinople; others, once in four or five years, as about Tripoli and Aleppo; others, scarce once in ten, twelve, or

I would by no means, however, be understood to say that the northern nations never undertook any expeditions unless prompted by straitened food or circumstances at home. Mallet relates, what was probably true, that it was their common custom to hold an assembly every spring, for the purpose of considering in what quarter they should make war;[61] and among a people who nourished so strong a passion for war, and who considered the right of the strongest as a right divine, occasions for it would never be wanting. Besides this pure and disinterested love of war and enterprize, civil dissensions, the pressure of a victorious enemy, a wish for a milder climate, or other causes, might sometimes prompt to emigration; but, in a general view of the subject, I cannot help considering this period of history as affording a very striking illustration of the principle of population; a principle which appears to me to have given the original impulse and spring of action, to have furnished the inexhaustible resources, and often prepared the immediate causes, of that rapid succession of adventurous irruptions and emigrations which occasioned the fall of the Roman empire; and afterwards, pouring from the thinly-peopled countries of Denmark and Norway, for above two hundred years ravaged and over-ran a great part of Europe. Without the supposition of a tendency to increase almost as great as among the Americans,[62] the facts appear to me not to be accounted for;[63] and with such a supposition, we cannot be at a loss to name the checks to the actual population, when we read the disgusting details of those unceasing wars, and of that prodigal waste of human life which marked these barbarous periods.

Inferior checks would undoubtedly concur; but we may safely pronounce that, among the shepherds of the north of Europe, war and famine were the principal checks that kept the population down to the level of their scanty means of subsistence.

---

thirteen years, as England; others, not in less than twenty years, as Norway and the Northern islands. Short, History of Air, Seasons, &c. vol. ii. p. 344.

[In 1806 (Vol. 1, p. 167) this footnote was amended thus:

Epidemics return more or less frequently, according to their various soils ... Hence some return yearly, as in Egypt and Constantinople; ...

[61] Hist. Dan. c. ix. p. 209.

[62] [In 1817 (Vol. 1, p. 169) this was altered to:

... as great as the United States of America.

[63] Gibbon, Robertson, and Mallet, seem all rather to speak of Jornandes's expression *vagina nationum* as incorrect and exaggerated; but to me it appears exactly applicable, though the other expression, *officina gentium*, at least their translation of it, *storehouse of nations*, may not be quite accurate.

Ex hac igitur Scanziâ insulâ, quasi officina gentium, aut certè velut vagina nationuma egressi, &c. Jornandes de rebus Geticis, p. 83.

[In 1826 (Vol. 1, p. 118) Malthus was more authoritative:

... their translation of it, *storehouse of nations*, is not accurate.

CHAPTER VII

Of the Checks to Population among modern Pastoral Nations

The pastoral tribes of Asia, by living in tents and moveable huts, instead of fixed habitations, are still less connected with their territory than the shepherds of the north of Europe. The camp, and not the soil, is the native country of the genuine Tartar. When the forage of a certain district is consumed, the tribe makes a regular march to fresh pastures. In the summer, it advances towards the north, in the winter returns again to the south; and thus, in a time of most profound peace, acquires the practical and familiar knowledge of one of the most difficult operations of war. Such habits would strongly tend to diffuse among these wandering tribes the spirit of emigration and conquest. The thirst of rapine, the fear of a too powerful neighbour, or the inconvenience of scanty pastures, have in all ages been sufficient causes to urge the hordes of Scythia boldly to advance into unknown countries, where they might hope to find a more plentiful subsistence or a less formidable enemy.[1]

In all their invasions, but more particularly when directed against the civilized empires of the south, the Scythian shepherds have been uniformly actuated by a most savage and destructive spirit. When the Moguls had subdued the northern provinces of China, it was proposed, in calm and deliberate council, to exterminate all the inhabitants of that populous country, that the vacant land might be converted to the pasture of cattle. The execution of this horrid design was prevented by the wisdom and firmness of a Chinese mandarin;[2] but the bare proposal of it exhibits a striking picture, not only of the inhuman manner in which the rights of conquest were abused, but of the powerful force of habit among nations of shepherds, and the consequent difficulty of the transition from the pastoral to the agricultural state.

To pursue, even in the most cursory manner, the tide of emigration and conquest in Asia, the rapid increase of some tribes, and the total extinction of others, would lead much too far. During the periods of the formidable irruptions of the Huns, the wide-extended invasions of the Moguls and Tartars, the sanguinary conquests of Attila, Zingis Khan and Tamerlane,

---

[1] Gibbon, vol. iv. c. xxvi. p. 348.   [2] Id. vol. vi. ch. xxxiv. p. 54.

and the dreadful convulsions which attended the dissolution, as well as the formation of their empires, the checks to population are but too obvious. In reading of the devastations of the human race in those times, when the slightest motive of caprice or convenience often involved a whole people in indiscriminate massacre,[3] instead of looking for the causes which prevented a further progress in population, we can only be astonished at the force of that principle of increase, which could furnish fresh harvests of human beings for the scythe of each successive conqueror. Our inquiries will be more usefully directed to the present state of the Tartar nations, and the ordinary checks to their increase, when not under the influence of these violent convulsions.

The immense country inhabited at present by those descendants of the Moguls and Tartars, who retain nearly the same manners as their ancestors, comprises in it almost all the middle regions of Asia, and possesses the advantage of a very fine and temperate climate. The soil is in general of great natural fertility. There are comparatively but few genuine deserts. The wide-extended plains without a shrub, which have sometimes received that appellation, and which the Russians call steppes, are covered with a luxuriant grass, admirably fitted for the pasture of numerous herds and flocks. The principal defect of this extensive country is a want of water; but it is said that the parts which are supplied with this necessary article would be sufficient for the support of four times the number of its present inhabitants, if it were properly cultivated.[4] Every Orda, or tribe, has a particular canton belonging to it, containing both its summer and winter pastures; and the population of this vast territory, whatever it may be, is probably distributed over its surface nearly in proportion to the degree of actual fertility in the different districts.

Volney justly describes this necessary distribution in speaking of the Bedoweens of Syria: 'In the barren cantons, that is, those which are ill furnished with plants, the tribes are feeble, and very distant from each other; as in the desert of Suez, that of the Red Sea, and the interior part of the Great Desert. When the soil is better covered, as between Damascus and the Euphrates, the tribes are stronger and less distant. And in the cultivable cantons, as the Pachalic of Aleppo, the Hauran, and the country of Gaza, the incampments are numerous and near each other.'[5] Such a distribution of inhabitants, according to the quantity of food which they can obtain in the actual state of their industry and habits, may be applied to Grand Tartary, as well as to Syria and Arabia, and is, in fact, equally applicable to the whole earth, though the commerce of civilized nations prevents it from being so obvious as in the more simple stages of society.

---

[3] Gibbon, vol. vi. ch. xxxiv. p. 55.   [4] Geneal. Hist. of Tartars, vol. ii. sec. i. 8vo. 1730.
[5] Voy. de Volney, tom. i. ch. xxiii. p. 351. 8vo. 1787.

The Mahometan Tartars, who inhabit the western parts of Grand Tartary, cultivate some of their lands, but in so slovenly and insufficient a manner as not to afford a principal source of subsistence.[6] The slothful and warlike genius of the Barbarian every where prevails, and he does not easily reconcile himself to the acquiring by labour what he can hope to acquire by rapine. When the annals of Tartary are not marked by any signal wars and revolutions, its domestic peace and industry are constantly interrupted by petty contests and mutual invasions for the sake of plunder. The Mahometan Tartars are said to live almost entirely by robbing and preying upon their neighbours, as well in peace as in war.[7]

The Usbecks, who possess as masters the kingdom of Chowarasm, leave to their tributary subjects, the Sarts and Turkmans, the finest pastures of their country, merely because their neighbours on that side are too poor, or too vigilant, to give them hopes of successful plunder. Rapine is their principal resource. They are perpetually making incursions into the territories of the Persians, and of the Usbecks of Great Bucharia; and neither peace nor truce can restrain them; as the slaves and other valuable effects which they carry off form the whole of their riches. The Usbecks, and their subjects the Turkmans, are perpetually at variance; and their jealousies, fomented often by the princes of the reigning house, keep the country in a constant state of intestine commotion.[8] The Turkmans are always at war with the Curds and the Arabs, who often come and break the horns of their herds, and carry away their wives and daughters.[9]

The Usbecks of Great Bucharia are reckoned the most civilized of all the Mahometan Tartars, yet are not much inferior to the rest in their spirit of rapine.[10] They are always at war with the Persians, and laying waste the fine plains of the province of Chorasan. Though the country which they possess is of the greatest natural fertility, and some of the remains of the ancient inhabitants practise the peaceful arts of trade and agriculture; yet neither the aptitude of the soil, nor the example which they have before them, can induce them to change their ancient habits; and they would rather pillage, rob, and kill their neighbours than apply themselves to improve the benefits which nature so liberally offers them.[11]

The Tartars of the Casatshia Orda in Turkestan, live in a state of continual warfare with their neighbours to the north and east. In the winter they make their incursions towards the Kalmucks, who, about that time, go to scour the frontiers of Great Bucharia and the parts to the south of their

---

[6] Geneal. Hist. Tart. vol. ii. p. 382.   [7] Id. p. 390.
[8] Id. p. 430, 431.
[9] Id. p. 426.   [10] Id. p. 459.   [11] Id. p. 455.

country. On the other side, they perpetually incommode the Cosacks of the Yaik and the Nogai Tartars. In the summer they cross the mountains of Eagles, and make inroads into Siberia. And though they are often very ill treated in these incursions, and the whole of their plunder is not equivalent to what they might obtain with very little labour from their lands, yet they choose rather to expose themselves to the thousand fatigues and dangers necessarily attendant on such a life, than apply themselves seriously to agriculture.[12]

The mode of life among the other tribes of Mahometan Tartars presents the same uniform picture, which it would be tiresome to repeat, and for which, therefore, I refer the reader to the Genealogical History of the Tartars and its valuable notes. The conduct of the author of this history, himself a Chan of Chowarasm, affords a curious example of the savage manner in which the wars, of policy, of revenge, or plunder, are carried on in these countries. His invasions of Great Bucharia were frequent, and each expedition was signalized by the ravage of provinces and the utter ruin and destruction of towns and villages. When at any time the number of his prisoners impeded his motions, he made no scruple to kill them on the spot. Wishing to reduce the power of the Turkmans who were tributary to him, he invited all the principal people to a solemn feast, and had them massacred to the number of two thousand. He burnt and destroyed their villages with the most unsparing cruelty, and committed such devastations that the effect of them returned on their authors, and the army of the victors suffered severely from dearth.[13]

The Mahometan Tartars in general hate trade, and make it their business to spoil all the merchants who fall into their hands.[14] The only commerce that is countenanced is the commerce in slaves. These form a principal part of the booty which they carry off in their predatory incursions, and are considered as a chief source of their riches. Those which they have occasion for themselves, either for the attendance on their herds, or as wives and concubines, they keep, and the rest they sell.[15] The Circassian and Daghestan Tartars, and the other tribes in the neighbourhood of Caucasus, living in a poor and mountainous country and, on that account, less subject to invasion, generally overflow with inhabitants; and when they cannot obtain slaves in the common way, steal from one another, and even sell their own wives and children.[16] This trade in slaves, so general among the Mahometan Tartars, may be one of the causes of their constant wars; as, when a prospect

---

[12] Geneal. Hist. Tart. vol. ii. p. 573, et. seq.   [13] Id. vol. i. c. xii.   [14] Id. vol. ii. p. 412.
[15] Id. p. 413.
[16] Id. vol. ii. p. 413, 414, and ch. xii.

of a plentiful supply for this kind of traffic offers itself, neither peace nor alliance can restrain them.[17]

The heathen Tartars, the Kalmucks, and Moguls, do not make much use of slaves, and are said in general to lead a much more peaceable and harmless life, contenting themselves with the produce of their herds and flocks, which form their sole riches. They rarely make war for the sake of plunder; and seldom invade the territory of their neighbours, unless to revenge a prior attack. They are not, however, without destructive wars. The inroads of the Mahometan Tartars oblige them to constant defence and retaliation; and feuds subsist between the kindred tribes of the Kalmucks and Moguls, which, fomented by the artful policy of the emperor of China, are carried on with such animosity as to threaten the entire destruction of one or other of these nations.[18]

The Bedoweens of Arabia and Syria do not live in greater tranquillity than the inhabitants of Grand Tartary. The very nature of the pastoral state seems to furnish perpetual occasions for war. The pastures which a tribe uses at one period form but a small part of its possessions. A large range of territory is successively occupied in the course of the year; and as the whole of this is absolutely necessary for the annual subsistence of the tribe, and is considered as appropriated, every violation of it, though the tribe may be at a great distance, is held to be a just cause of war.[19] Alliances and kindred make these wars more general. When blood is shed, more must expiate it; and as such accidents have multiplied in the lapse of years, the greatest part of the tribes have quarrels between them, and live in a state of perpetual hostility.[20] In the times which preceded Mahomet, seventeen hundred battles are recorded by tradition; and a partial truce of two months, which was religiously kept, might be considered, according to a just remark of Gibbon,

---

[17] 'They justify it as lawful to have many wives, because they say they bring us many children, which we can sell for ready money, or exchange for necessary conveniences; yet when they have not wherewithal to maintain them, they hold it a piece of charity to murder infants new born, as also they do such as are sick, and past recovery, because they say they free them from a great deal of misery.' Sir John Chardin's Travels. Harris's Col. b. iii. c. ii. p. 865.

[18] Geneal. Hist. Tart. vol. ii. p. 545.

[19] Ils se disputeront la terre inculte comme parmi nous les citoyens se disputent les heritages. Ainsi ils trouveront de frequentes occasions de guerre pour la nourriture de leur bestiaux, &c. … ils auront autant de choses à regler par le droit des gens qu'ils en auront peu à decider par le droit civil. Montes[quieu]. Esprit des Loix, l. xviii. c. xii. [They quarrelled over their uncultivated territory in the same way that our modern citizens quarrel over their inherited property. They had constant occasions for warfare over pasture for their animals, etc … They had as much to settle according to the law of nations as they had little to determine according to civil law.]

[20] Voy. de Volney, tom. i. c. xxii. p. 361, 362, 363.

as still more strongly expressive of their general habits of anarchy and warfare.[21]

The waste of life from such habits might alone appear sufficient to repress their population; but probably their effect is still greater in the fatal check which they give to every species of industry, and particularly to that, the object of which is to enlarge the means of subsistence. Even the construction of a well, or a reservoir of water, requires some funds and labour in advance; and war may destroy in one day the work of many months and the resources of a whole year.[22] The evils seem mutually to produce each other. A scarcity of subsistence might at first perhaps give occasion to the habits of war, and the habits of war in return powerfully contribute to narrow the means of subsistence.

Some tribes, from the nature of the deserts in which they live, seem to be necessarily condemned to a pastoral life;[23] but even those which inhabit soils proper for agriculture have but little temptation to practise this art while surrounded by marauding neighbours. The peasants of the frontier provinces of Syria, Persia, and Siberia, exposed as they are to the constant incursions of a devastating enemy, do not lead a life that is to be envied by the wandering Tartar or Arab. A certain degree of security is perhaps still more necessary than richness of soil, to encourage the change from the pastoral to the agricultural state; and where this cannot be attained, the sedentary labourer is more exposed to the vicissitudes of fortune than he who leads a wandering life and carries all his property with him.[24] Under the feeble yet oppressive government of the Turks, it is not uncommon for peasants to desert their villages and betake themselves to a pastoral state, in which they expect to be better able to escape from the plunder of their Turkish masters and Arab neighbours.[25]

It may be said, however, of the shepherd, as of the hunter, that if want alone could effect a change of habits, there would be few pastoral tribes remaining. Notwithstanding the constant wars of the Bedoween Arabs, and the other checks to their increase, from the hardships of their mode of life, their population presses so hard against the limits of their food, that they are compelled from necessity to a degree of abstinence which nothing but early and constant habit could enable the human constitution to support. According to Volney, the lower classes of the Arabs live in a state of habitual misery and famine.[26] The tribes of the desert deny that the religion of Mahomet was made for them. 'For how', they say, 'can we perform ablutions, when we have no water; how can we give alms, when we have no riches; or what occasion

---

[21] Gibbon, vol. ix. c. l. p. 238, 239.   [22] Voy. de Volney, tom. i. c. xxiii. p. 353.
[23] Id. p. 350.
[24] Id. p. 354.   [25] Id. p. 350.   [26] Id. p. 359.

can there be to fast during the month of Ramadan, when we fast all the year?'[27]

The power and riches of a Chaik consist in the number of his tribe. He considers it therefore as his interest to encourage population, without reflecting how it may supported. His own consequence greatly depends on a numerous progeny and kindred;[28] and in a state of society where power generally procures subsistence, each individual family derives strength and importance from its numbers. These ideas act strongly as a bounty upon population; and co-operating with a spirit of generosity which almost produces a community of goods,[29] contribute to push it to its utmost verge, and to depress the body of the people in the most rigid poverty.

The habits of polygamy, where there have been losses of men in war, tend perhaps also to produce the same effect. Niebuhr observes that polygamy multiplies families till many of their branches sink into the most wretched misery.[30] The descendants of Mahomet are found in great numbers all over the east, and many of them in extreme poverty. A Mahometan is in some degree obliged to polygamy from a principle of obedience to his prophet, who makes one of the great duties of man to consist in procreating children to glorify the Creator. Fortunately, individual interest corrects in some degree, as in many other instances, the absurdity of the legislator, and the poor Arab is obliged to proportion his religious obedience to the scantiness of his resources. Yet still the direct encouragements to population are extraordinarily great; and nothing can place in a more striking point of view the futility and absurdity of such encouragements than the present state of these countries. It is universally agreed that, if their population be not less than formerly, it is indubitably not greater; and it follows as a direct consequence that the great increase of some families has absolutely pushed the others out of existence. Gibbon, speaking of Arabia, observes that: 'The measure of population is regulated by the means of subsistence, and the inhabitants of this vast peninsula might be out-numbered by the subjects of a fertile and industrious province.'[31] Whatever may be the encouragements to marriage, this measure cannot be passed. While the Arabs retain their present manners, and the country remains in its present state of cultivation, the promise of Paradise to every man who had ten children would but little

---

[27] Voy. de Volney, tom. i. c. xxiii. p. 380.   [28] Id. p. 366.   [29] Id. p. 378.

[30] Niebuhr's Travels, vol. ii. c. v. p. 207.

[31] It is rather a curious circumstance that a truth so important, which has been stated and acknowledged by so many authors, should so rarely have been pursued to its consequences. People are not every day dying of famine. How then is the population regulated to the measure of the means of subsistence?

[This quotation may be found in chapter L, at the beginning of the paragraph marginally summarised 'Manners of the Bedoweens or pastoral Arabs'.]

increase their numbers, though it might greatly increase their misery. Direct encouragements to population have no tendency whatever to change these manners and promote cultivation. Perhaps, indeed, they have a contrary tendency, as the constant uneasiness from poverty and want which they occasion must encourage the marauding spirit[32] and multiply the occasions of war.

Among the Tartars, who from living in a more fertile soil are comparatively richer in cattle, the plunder to be obtained in predatory incursions is greater than among the Arabs. And as the contests are more bloody, from the superior strength of the tribes, and the custom of making slaves is general, the loss of numbers in war will be more considerable. These two circumstances united enable some hordes of fortunate robbers to live in a state of plenty, in comparison of their less enterprising neighbours. Professor Pallas gives a particular account of two wandering tribes subject to Russia, one of which supports itself almost entirely by plunder, and the other lives as peacefully as the restlessness of its neighbours will admit. It may be curious to trace the different checks to population that result from these different habits.

The Kirgisiens, according to Pallas,[33] live at their ease in comparison of the other wandering tribes that are subject to Russia. The spirit of liberty and independence which reigns amongst them, joined to the facility with which they can procure a flock sufficient for their maintenance, prevents any of them from entering into the service of others. They all expect to be treated as brothers, and the rich, therefore, are obliged to use slaves. It may be asked what are the causes which prevent the lower classes of people from increasing till they become poor?

Pallas has not informed us how far vicious customs with respect to women, or the restraints on marriage from the fear of a family, may have contributed to this effect; but perhaps the description which he gives of their civil constitution, and licentious spirit of rapine may be alone almost sufficient to account for it. The Chan cannot exercise his authority but through the medium of a council of principal persons, chosen by the people; and even the decrees thus confirmed are continually violated with impunity.[34] Though the

---

[32] Aussi arrive-t'il chaque jour des accidens, des enlèvements de bestiaux; et cette guerre de maraude est une de celles qui occupent d'avantage les Arabes. Voy. de Volney, tom. i. c. xxiii. p. 364. [Every day there are incidents, and animals stolen; and this form of marauding warfare is one in which the Arabs engage very successfully.]

[33] Not having been able to procure the work of Pallas on the history of the Mongol nations, I have here made use of a general abridgement of the works of the Russian travellers, in 4 vols. oct. published at Berne and Lausanne in 1781 and 1784, entitled, Decouvertes Russes, tom. iii. p. 399. [See PALLAS in the Alphabetical List.]

[34] Decouv. Russ. tom. iii. p. 389.

plunder and capture of persons, of cattle, and of merchandize, which the Kirgisiens exercise on their neighbours the Kazalpacs, the Bucharians, the Persians, the Truchemenes, the Kalmucks, and the Russians, are prohibited by their laws, yet no person is afraid to avow them. On the contrary, they boast of their successes in this way, as of the most honourable enterprizes. Sometimes they pass their frontiers alone, to seek their fortune, sometimes collect in troops under the command of an able chief, and pillage entire caravans. A great number of Kirgisiens, in exercising this rapine, are either killed, or taken into slavery; but about this the nation troubles itself very little. When these ravages are committed by private adventurers, each retains what he has taken, whether cattle or women. The male slaves and the merchandize are sold to the rich, or to foreign traders.[35]

With these habits, in addition to their national wars, which, from the fickle and turbulent disposition of the tribe, are extremely frequent,[36] we may easily conceive that the checks to population from violent causes may be so powerful as nearly to preclude all others. Occasional famines may sometimes attack them in their wars of devastation,[37] their fatiguing predatory incursions, or from long droughts and mortality of cattle; but in the common course of things the approach of poverty would be the signal for a new marauding expedition; and the poor Kirgisien would either return with sufficient to support him, or lose his life or liberty in the attempt. He who determines to be rich, or die, and does not scruple the means, cannot long live poor.

The Kalmucks, who before their migration in 1771 inhabited the fertile steppes of the Wolga, under the protection of Russia, lived in general in a different manner. They were not often engaged in any very bloody wars,[38] and the power of the Chan being absolute,[39] and the civil administration better regulated than among the Kirgisiens, the marauding expeditions of private adventurers were checked. The Kalmuck women are extremely prolific. Barren marriages are rare, and three or four children are generally seen playing round every hut. From which it may naturally be concluded, Pallas observes, that they ought to have multiplied greatly during the hundred and fifty years that they inhabited tranquilly the steppes of the

---

[35] Decouv. Russ. tom. iii. p. 396, 397, 398.   [36] Id. p. 378.

[37] Cette multitude devaste tout ce qui se trouve sur son passage, ils emmenent avec eux tout le betail qu'ils ne consomment pas, et reduisent a l'esclavage les femmes, les enfans, et les hommes, qu'ils n'ont pas massacrés. Id. p. 390.
   [This horde lays waste everything in its path, driving off the cattle they do not eat, taking for slaves the women and children, and the men they have not massacred.]

[38] Decouv. Russ. tom. iii. p. 221. The tribe is described here under the name of the Torgots, which was their appropriate appellation. The Russians called them by the more general name of Kalmucks.

[39] Id. p. 327.

Wolga. The reasons which he gives for their not having increased so much as might be expected are the many accidents occasioned by falls from horses, the frequent petty wars between their different princes and with their different neighbours; and, particularly, the numbers among the poorer classes who die of hunger, of misery, and every species of calamity, of which the children are most frequently the victims.[40]

It appears that when this tribe first put itself under the protection of Russia, it had separated from the Soongares, and was by no means numerous. The possession of the fertile steppes of the Wolga, and a more tranquil life, soon increased it, and in 1662 it amounted to fifty thousand families.[41] From this period to 1771, the time of its migration, it seems to have increased very slowly. The extent of pastures possessed would not probably admit of a much greater population as, at the time of its flight from these quarters, the irritation of the Chan at the conduct of Russia was seconded by the complaints of the people, of the want of pasture for their numerous herds. At this time the tribe amounted to between 55 and 60 000 families. Its fate in this curious migration was what has probably been the fate of many other wandering hordes who, from scanty pastures, or other causes of discontent, have attempted to seek for fresh seats. The march took place in the winter, and numbers perished on this painful journey from cold, famine, and misery. A great part were either killed or taken by the Kirghises; and those who reached their place of destination, though received at first kindly by the Chinese, were afterwards treated with extreme severity.[42]

Before this migration, the lower classes of the Kalmucks had lived in great poverty and wretchedness, and had been reduced habitually to make use of every animal, plant, or root from which it was possible to extract nourishment.[43] They very seldom killed any of their cattle that were in health, except indeed they were stolen, and then they were devoured immediately for fear of a discovery. Wounded or worn-out horses, and beasts that had died of any disease, except a contagious epidemic, were considered as most desirable food. Some of the poorest Kalmucks would eat the most putrid carrion, and even the dung of their cattle.[44] A great number of children perished of course from bad nourishment.[45] In the winter all the lower classes suffered severely

---

40 Decouv. Russ. tom. iii. p. 319, 320, 321.
41 Id. p. 221. Tooke's View of Russian Empire, vol. ii. b. ii. p. 30. Another instance of rapid increase presents itself in a colony of baptized Kalmucks, who received from Russia a fertile district to settle in. From 8695, which was its number in 1754, it had increased in 1771 to 14,000. Tooke's View of Rus. Em. vol. ii. b. ii. p. 32, 33. [See TOOKE, WILLIAM, in the Alphabetical List.]
42 Tooke's View of Rus. Emp. vol. ii. b. ii. p. 29, 30, 31. Decouv. Russ. tom. iii. p. 221.
43 Id. p. 275, 276.
44 Id. p. 272, 273, 274.   45 Id. p. 324.

from cold and hunger.[46] In general, one third of their sheep, and often much more, died in the winter, in spite of all their care; and if a frost came late in the season after rain and snow, so that the cattle could not get at the grass, the mortality among their herds became general, and the poorer classes were exposed to inevitable famine.[47]

Malignant fevers, generated principally by their putrid food and the putrid exhalations with which they were surrounded, and the small-pox, which is dreaded like the plague, sometimes thinned their numbers;[48] but in general, it appears, that their population pressed so hard against the limits of their means of subsistence, that want, with the diseases arising from it, might be considered as the principal check to their increase.

A person travelling in Tartary during the summer months, would probably see extensive steppes unoccupied, and grass in profusion, spoiling for want of cattle to consume it. He would infer, perhaps, that the country could support a much greater number of inhabitants, even supposing them to remain in their shepherd state. But this might be a hasty and unwarranted conclusion. A horse, or any other working animal, is said to be strong only in proportion to the strength of his weakest part. If his legs be slender and feeble, the strength of his body will be but of little consequence; or if he wants power in his back and haunches, the strength which he may possess in his limbs can never be called fully into action. The same reasoning must be applied to the power of the earth to support living creatures. The profusion of nourishment which is poured forth in the seasons of plenty cannot all be consumed by the scanty numbers that were able to subsist through the season of scarcity. When human industry and foresight are directed in the best manner, the population that the soil can support is regulated by the average produce throughout the year; but among animals, and in the uncivilized states of man, it will be much below this average. The Tartar would find it extremely difficult to collect and carry with him such a quantity of hay as would feed all his cattle well during the winter. It would impede his motions, expose him to the attacks of his enemies, and an unfortunate day might deprive him of the labours of a whole summer; as in the mutual invasions which occur, it seems to be the universal practice to burn and destroy all the forage and provisions which cannot be carried away.[49] The Tartar therefore provides only for the most valuable of his cattle during the

---

[46] Id. p. 310.   [47] Ibid. and p. 270.   [48] Id. p. 311, 312, 313.

[49] On mit le feu a toutes les meules de bled et de fourrage. ... Cent cinquante villages egalement encendiés. Memoires du Baron de Tott, tom. i. p. 272. He gives a curious description of the devastations of a Tartar army, and of its suffering in a winter campaign. Cette journée couta a l'armée plus de 3000 hommes, et 30 000 chevaux, qui perirent de froid, p. 267.

[For an English translation, see TOTT in the Alphabetical List.]

winter, and leaves the rest to support themselves by the scanty herbage which they can pick up. This poor living, combined with the severe cold, naturally destroys a considerable part of them.[50] The population of the tribe is measured by the population of its herds; and the average numbers of the Tartars, as of the horses that run wild in the desert, are kept down so low by the annual returns of the cold and scarcity of winter, that they cannot consume all the plentiful offerings of summer.

Droughts and unfavourable seasons have, in proportion to their frequency, the same effects as the winter. In Arabia,[51] and a great part of Tartary,[52] droughts are not uncommon; and if the periods of their return be not above six or eight years, the average population can never much exceed what the soil can support during these unfavourable times. This is true in every situation; but perhaps, in the shepherd state, man is peculiarly exposed to be affected by the seasons; and a great mortality of parent stock is an evil more fatal and longer felt than the failure of a crop of grain. Pallas and the other Russian travellers speak of epizooties as very common in these parts of the world.[53]

As among the Tartars a family is always honourable, and women are reckoned very serviceable in the management of the cattle and the household concerns, it is not probable that many are deterred from marriage from the fear of not being able to support a family.[54] At the same time, as all wives are bought of their parents, it must sometimes be out of the power of the poorer classes to make the purchase. The monk Rubruquis, speaking of this custom, says that as parents keep all their daughters till they can sell them, their maids are sometimes very stale before they are married.[55] Among the Mahometan Tartars female captives would supply the place of wives;[56] but among the pagan Tartars, who make but little use of slaves, the inability of buying a wife must frequently operate on the poorer classes as a check to marriage, particularly as their price would be kept up by the practice of polygamy among the rich.[57]

The Kalmucks are said not to be jealous,[58] and, from the general prevalence of the venereal disease among them,[59] we may infer that a certain degree of promiscuous intercourse prevails.

---

[50] Decouvertes Russes, vol. iii. p. 261.   [51] Voy. de Volney, vol. i. c. 23. p. 353.

[52] Decouv. Russ. tom. i. p. 467. ii. p. 10, 11, 12, &c. &c.

[53] Id. tom. i. p. 290, &c. ii. p. 11. iv. p. 304. [An *epizoon* is a parasitic animal which lives on the exterior of the body of another animal.]

[54] Geneal. Hist. Tartars, vol. ii. p. 407.

[55] Travels of Wm. Rubruquis in 1253. Harris's Collection of Voy. b. i. c. ii. p. 561.

[56] Decouv. Russ. tom. iii. p. 413.

[57] Pallas takes notice of the scarcity of women, or the superabundance of males among the Kalmucks, notwithstanding the more constant exposure of the male sex to every kind of accident. Decouv. Russ. tom. iii. p. 320.

[58] Decouv. Russ. tom. iii. p. 239.

[59] Id. p. 324. [In 1806 (Vol. 1, p. 169) *general prevalence* was changed to 'frequency'.

On the whole, therefore, it would appear that in that department of the shepherd life which has been considered in this chapter, the principal checks which keep the population down to the level of the means of subsistence are restraint, from inability to obtain a wife, vicious customs with respect to women, epidemics, wars, famine, and the diseases arising from extreme poverty. The three first checks and the last appear to have operated with much less force among the shepherds of the north of Europe.

CHAPTER VIII

Of the Checks to Population in different Parts of Africa

The parts of Africa visited by Park are described by him as neither well cultivated nor well peopled. He found many extensive and beautiful districts entirely destitute of inhabitants; and in general the borders of the different kingdoms were either very thinly peopled or perfectly deserted. The swampy banks of the Gambia, the Senegal, and other rivers towards the coast, appeared to be unfavourable to population, from being unhealthy;[1] but other parts were not of this description; and it was not possible, he says, to behold the wonderful fertility of the soil, the vast herds of cattle proper both for labour and food, and reflect on the means which presented themselves of vast inland navigation, without lamenting that a country so abundantly gifted by nature should remain in its present savage and neglected state.[2]

The causes of this neglected state clearly appear, however, in the description which Park gives of the general habits of the negroe nations. In a country divided into a thousand petty states, mostly independent and jealous of each other, it is natural to imagine, he says, that wars frequently originate from very frivolous provocations. The wars of Africa are of two kinds, one called Killi, that which is openly avowed; and the other, Tegria, plundering or stealing. These latter are very common, particularly about the beginning of the dry season, when the labours of harvest are over, and provisions are plentiful. These plundering excursions always produce speedy retaliation.[3]

The insecurity of property arising from this constant exposure to plunder, must necessarily have a most baneful effect on industry. The deserted state of all the frontier provinces sufficiently proves to what a degree it operates. The nature of the climate is unfavourable to the exertion of the negroe nations; and, as there are not many opportunities of turning to advantage the surplus produce of their labour, we cannot be surprised that they should in general content themselves with cultivating only as much ground as is necessary for their own support.[4] These causes appear adequately to account for the uncultivated state of the country.

---

[1] Park's Interior of Africa, c. xx. p. 261. 4to.   [2] Id. c. xxiii. p. 312.
[3] Id. c. xxii. p. 291. & seq.
[4] Id. c. xxi. p. 280.

The waste of life in these constant wars and predatory incursions must be considerable; and Park agrees with Buffon in stating that, independent of violent causes, longevity is rare among the negroes. At forty, he says, most of them became greyhaired and covered with wrinkles, and but few of them survive the age of fifty-five or sixty.[5] Buffon attributes this shortness of life to the premature intercourse of the sexes, and the very early and excessive debauchery.[6] On this subject perhaps he has been led into exaggerations; but, without attributing too much to this cause, it seems agreeable to the analogy of nature to suppose that, as the natives of hot climates arrive much earlier at maturity than the inhabitants of colder countries, they should also perish earlier.

According to Buffon, the negroe women are extremely prolific; but, it appears from Park, that they are in the habit of suckling their children two or three years, and as the husband, during this time, devotes the whole of his attention to his other wives, the family of each wife is seldom numerous.[7] Polygamy is universally allowed among the negro nations,[8] and consequently without a greater superabundance of women than we have reason to suppose, many will be obliged to live unmarried. This hardship will probably fall principally on the slaves, who, according to Park, are in the proportion of three to one to the free men.[9] A master is not permitted to sell his domestic slaves, or those born in his own house, except in case of famine, to support himself and family. We may imagine, therefore, that he will not suffer them to increase beyond the employment which he has for them. The slaves which are purchased, or the prisoners taken in war, are entirely at the disposal of their masters.[10] They are often treated with extreme severity, and in any scarcity of women arising from the polygamy of the free men, would of course be deprived of them without scruple. Few or no women, probably, remain in a state of strict celibacy; but, in proportion to the number married, the state of society does not seem to be favourable to increase.

Africa has been at all times the principal mart of slaves. The drains of its

---

[5] Park's Interior of Africa, c. xxii. p. 284.

[6] L'usage prématuré des femmes est peut-être la cause de la brieveté de leur vie; les enfans sont si debauchés, et si peu contraints par les pères et mères, que des leur plus tendre jeunesse ils se livrent à tout ce que la nature leur suggère, rien n'est si rare que de trouver dans ce peuple quelque fille qui puise se souvenir du tems auquel elle a cessé d'etre vierge. Histoire Naturelle de l'Homme, vol. vi. p. 235. 5th edit. 12mo. 31 vols. [For a contemporary English translation, see BUFFON in the Alphabetical List.]

[7] Park's *Africa*, c. xx. p. 265. As the accounts of Park, and those on which Buffon has founded his observations, are probably accounts of different nations, and certainly at different periods, we cannot infer that either is incorrect because they differ from each other: but as far as Park's observations extend, they are certainly entitled to more credit than any of the travellers which preceded him.

[8] Id. c. xx. p. 267.   [9] Id. c. xxii. p. 287.   [10] Id. 288.

population in this way have been great and constant, particularly since their introduction into the European colonies; but perhaps, as Dr. Franklin observes, it would be difficult to find the gap that has been made by a hundred years exportation of negroes which has blackened half America.[11] For, notwithstanding this constant emigration, the loss of numbers from incessant war, and the checks to increase from vice and other causes, it appears that the population is continually passing beyond the means of subsistence. According to Park, scarce years and famines are frequent. Among the four principal causes of slavery in Africa, he mentions famine next to war,[12] and the express permission given to masters to sell their domestic slaves for the support of their family, which they are not allowed to do on any less urgent occasion,[13] seems to imply the not infrequent recurrence of severe want. During a great scarcity, which lasted for three years in the countries of the Gambia, great numbers of people became slaves. Park was assured by Dr. Laidley that at that time many free-men came, and begged with great earnestness to be put upon his slave chain to save them from perishing with hunger.[14] While Park was in Manding, a scarcity of provisions was severely felt by the poor, as the following circumstance painfully convinced him. Every evening during his stay, he observed five or six women come to the Mansa's house, and receive each of them a certain quantity of corn. 'Observe that boy', said the Mansa to him, pointing to a fine child about five years of age – 'his mother has sold him to me for forty days provision for herself and the rest of her family. I have bought another boy in the same manner.'[15] In Sooseeta, a small Jallonka village, Mr. Park was informed by the master that he could furnish no provisions, as there had lately been a great scarcity in that part of the country. He assured him that, before they had gathered in their present crops, all the inhabitants of Kullo had been for twenty-nine days without tasting corn; during which time they had supported themselves entirely on the yellow powder which is found in the pods of the nitta (so called by the natives), a species of mimosa, and upon the seeds of the bamboo cane which, when properly pounded and dressed, taste very much like rice.[16]

It may be said perhaps that as, according to Park's account, much good land remains uncultivated in Africa, the dearths may be attributed to a want

---

[11] Franklin's Miscell. p. 9.   [12] Park's Africa, c. xxii. p. 295.   [13] Id. p. 288. note.

[14] Id. p. 295.

[15] Id. c. xix. p. 248. [The Mansa, a Muslim, was Park's landlord at Wonda, 'a small town with a mosque and surrounded by a high wall'. He 'acted in two capacities; as chief magistrate of the town, and schoolmaster to the children'. Op. cit. p. 247.]

[16] Id. c. xxv. p. 336.
[The nitta or nutta is a West African tree now known as *Parkia africana* or biglandula; it is also found in tropical Asia and has been introduced into the West Indies.]

of people; but if this were the case, we can hardly suppose that such numbers would yearly be sent out of the country. What the negroe nations really want is security of property, and its general concomitant, industry; and without these an increase of people would only greatly aggravate their distresses. If, in order to fill up those parts that appeared to be deficient in inhabitants, we were to suppose a high bounty given on children, the effects would probably be the increase of wars, the increase of the exportation of slaves, and a great increase of misery, but little or no real increase of population.[17]

The customs of some nations, and the prejudices of all, operate in some degree like a bounty of this kind. The Shangalla negroes, according to Bruce, hemmed in on every side by active and powerful enemies, and leading a life of severe labour and constant apprehension, feel but little desire for women. It is the wife, and not the man, that is the cause of their polygamy. Though they live in separate tribes or nations, yet these nations are again subdivided into families. In fighting, each family attacks and defends by itself, and theirs is the spoil and plunder who take it. The mothers therefore, sensible of the disadvantages of a small family, seek to multiply it by all the means in their power; and it is by their importunity that the husband suffers himself to be overcome.[18] The motives to polygamy among the Galla are described to be the same, and in both nations the first wife courts the alliance of a second for her husband; and the principal argument she makes use of is, that their

---

[17] [In 1807 (Vol. 1, p. 177) Malthus added a footnote here:

The two great requisites just mentioned for a real increase of population, namely, security of property, and its natural concomitant, industry, could not be expected to exist among the Negro nations while the traffic in slaves, on the coast, gave such constant encouragement to the plundering excursions which Park describes. Now that this traffic is happily soon to be at an end, we may rationally hope that before the lapse of any long period, future travellers will be able to give us a more favourable picture of the state of society among the African nations, than that which has been drawn by Park.

[Malthus's hope was based on the Grenville Ministry's Act of 1807: this did not abolish slavery, but forbade any further trading in slaves, throughout all the British dominions. It proved ineffective; the illicit commerce probably involved the human cargoes in more suffering than they had to endure when the trade was legal. It was not until almost the close of the nineteenth century, when slavery as an institution was given up in both North and South America, that the Atlantic slave trade came to an end. See also Malthus's footnote on slavery added to the Appendix of 1806.]

[In 1817 (Vol. 1, p. 211) there were small verbal changes, but in 1826 (Vol. 1, p. 150) the note had to be altered:

... security of property and its natural concomitant, industry, cannot be expected to exist among the negro nations while the traffic in slaves on the coast gives such constant encouragement to the plundering excursions ... Were this traffic at an end, we might rationally hope ... future travellers would be able to give us a more favourable picture ... than that drawn by Park.

[18] Bruce's Travels to discover the Source of the Nile, vol. ii. p. 556. 4to.

families may be joined together and be strong, and that her children, by being few in number, may not fall a prey to their enemies in the day of battle.[19] It is highly probable that this extreme desire of having large families defeats its own purpose; and that the poverty and misery which it occasions cause fewer children to grow up to maturity than if the parents had confined their attention to the rearing of a smaller number.

Bruce is a great friend to polygamy, and defends it in the only way in which it is capable of being defended, by asserting that, in the countries in which it principally prevails, the proportion of girls to boys born is two or three to one. A fact so extraordinary, however, cannot be admitted upon the authority of those vague inquiries on which he founds his opinion. That there are considerably more women living than men, in these climates, is in the highest degree probable. Even in Europe, where it is known with certainty that more boys are born than girls, the women in general exceed the men in number; and we may imagine that, in hot and unhealthy climates, and in a barbarous state of society, the accidents to which the men are exposed must be very greatly increased. The women, by leading a more sedentary life, would suffer less from the effects of a scorching sun and swampy exhalations. They would in general be more exempt from the disorders arising from debauchery; but above all, they would escape in great measure the ravages of war. In a state of society in which hostilities never cease, the drains of men, from this cause alone, must occasion a great disproportion of the sexes, particularly where it is the custom, as related of the Galla in Abyssinia,[20] to massacre indiscriminately all the males, and save only the marriageable women from the general destruction. The actual disproportion of the sexes arising from these causes, probably, first gave rise to the permission of polygamy, and has, perhaps, contributed to make us more easily believe that the proportion of male and female children in hot climates is very different from what we have experienced it to be in the temperate zone.

Bruce, with the usual prejudices on this subject, seems to think that the celibacy of a part of the women is fatal to the population of a country. He observes of Jidda that, on account of the great scarcity of provisions which is the result of an extraordinary concourse of people to a place almost destitute of the necessaries of life, few of the inhabitants can avail themselves of the privilege granted by Mahomet. They cannot, therefore, marry more than one wife; and from this cause, he says, the want of people and the large number of unmarried women.[21] But it is evident, that the want of people in this barren spot arises solely from the want of provisions, and that if each

---

[19] Bruce's Travels to discover the Source of the Nile, vol. ii. p. 223.   [20] Id. vol. iv. p. 411.
[21] Id. vol. i. c. xi. p. 280.

man had half a dozen wives, the number of people could not be much increased by it.[22]

In Arabia Felix, according to Bruce, where every sort of provision is exceedingly cheap, where the fruits of the ground, the general food of man, are produced spontaneously, the support of a number of wives costs no more than that of so many slaves or servants; their food is the same, and a blue cotton shirt, a habit common to them all, is not more chargeable for the one than the other. The consequence is, he says, that celibacy in women is prevented, and the number of people increased in a fourfold ratio by polygamy, to what it is in those countries that are monogamous.[23] And yet, notwithstanding this fourfold increase, it does not appear that any part of Arabia is really very populous.

The effect of polygamy in increasing the number of married women and preventing celibacy is beyond dispute; but how far this may tend to increase the actual population is a very different consideration. It may perhaps continue to press the population harder against the limits of the food; but the squalid and hopeless poverty which this occasions, is by no means favourable to industry; and in a climate in which there appears to be many predisposing causes of sickness, it is difficult to conceive that this state of wretchedness does not powerfully contribute to the extraordinary mortality which has been observed in some of these countries.

According to Bruce, the whole coast of the Red Sea, from Suez to Babelmandel, is extremely unwholesome, but more especially between the tropics. Violent fevers, called there Nedad, make the principal figure in this fatal list, and generally terminate the third day in death.[24] Fear frequently seizes strangers upon the first sight of the great mortality which they observe on their first arrival.

Jidda, and all the parts of Arabia adjacent to the eastern coast of the Red Sea, are in the same manner very unwholesome.[25]

In Gondar, fevers perpetually reign, and the inhabitants are all the colour of a corpse.[26]

In Sirè, one of the finest countries in the world, putrid fevers of the very worst kind are almost constant.[27] In the low grounds of Abyssinia, in general, malignant tertians occasion a great mortality.[28] And everywhere the small-

---

[22] [In 1806 (Vol. i, p. 180) this was corrected to:
  ... and that if each man had four wives, the number of people could not be permanently increased by it.

[23] Bruce, vol. i. c. xi. p. 281.   [24] Id. vol. iii. p. 33.   [25] Id. vol. i. 279.

[26] Id. vol. iii. p. 178.

[27] Id. p. 153.

[28] Id. vol. iv. p. 22. [A *tertian* is a fever or ague characterised by the occurrence of a paroxysm every third day.]

pox makes great ravages, particularly among the nations bordering on Abyssinia, where it sometimes extinguishes whole tribes.[29]

The effect of poverty, with bad diet, and its almost constant concomitant want of cleanliness, in aggravating malignant distempers, is well known; and this kind of wretchedness seems generally to prevail. Of Tchagassa, near Gondar, Bruce observes that the inhabitants, notwithstanding their three-fold harvests, are miserably poor.[30] At Adowa, the capital of Tigré, he makes the same remark, and applies it to all the Abyssinian farmers. The land is let yearly to the highest bidder and, in general, the landlord furnishes the seed and receives half of the produce; but it is said that he is a very indulgent master who does not take another quarter for the risk he has run; so that the quantity which comes to the share of the husbandman is not more than sufficient to afford a bare sustenance to his wretched family.[31] The Agows, one of the most considerable nations of Abyssinia in point of number, are described by Bruce as living in a state of misery and penury scarcely to be conceived. We saw a number of women, he says, wrinkled and sunburnt, so as scarcely to appear human, wandering about under a burning sun, with one and sometimes two children upon their backs, gathering the seeds of bent grass to make a kind of bread.[32] The Agow women begin to bear children at eleven years old. They marry generally about that age, and there is no such thing as barrenness known among them.[33] In Dixan, one of the frontier towns of Abyssinia, the only trade is that of selling children. Five hundred are exported annually to Arabia; and in times of scarcity, Bruce observes, four times that number.[34]

In Abyssinia polygamy does not regularly prevail. Bruce, indeed, makes rather a strange assertion on this subject, and says that though we read from the Jesuits a great deal about marriage and polygamy, yet that there is nothing which may be averred more truly than that there is no such thing as marriage in Abyssinia.[35] But however this may be, it appears clear that few or no women live a life of celibacy in Abyssinia, and that the prolific powers of nature are nearly all called into action, except as far as they are checked by promiscuous intercourse. This, however, from the state of manners described by Bruce, must operate very powerfully.[36]

The check to population from war appears to be excessive. For the last four hundred years, according to Bruce, it has never ceased to lay desolate this unhappy country,[37] and the savage manner in which it is carried on surrounds it with tenfold destruction. When Bruce first entered Abyssinia, he

---

[29] Bruce, vol. iii. c. iii. p. 68, c. vii. p. 178. vol. i. c. xiii. p. 353.   [30] Id. vol. iii. c. vii. p. 195.
[31] Id. vol. iii. c. v. p. 124.   [32] Id. c. xix. p. 738. ['Bent grass' is of the genus *Agrostis*.]
[33] Id. p. 739.   [34] Id. vol. iii. c. iii. p. 88.   [35] Id. c. xi. p. 306.   [36] Id. p. 292.
[37] Id. vol. iv. p. 110.

saw on every side ruined villages destroyed to the lowest foundations by Rass Michael in his march to Gondar.[38] In the course of the civil wars, while Bruce was in the country, he says: 'The rebels had begun to lay waste Dembea, and burnt all the villages in the plain, from south to west; making it like a desert between Michael and Fasil. ... The king often ascended to the top of the tower of his palace, and contemplated, with the greatest displeasure, the burning of his rich villages in Dembea.'[39] In another place, he says: 'The whole country of Degwessa was totally destroyed; men, women, and children, were entirely extirpated, without distinction of age or sex; the houses rased to the ground, and the country about it left as desolate as after the deluge. The villages belonging to the king were as severely treated; a universal cry was heard from all parts, but no one dared to suggest any means of help.'[40] In Maitsha, one of the provinces of Abyssinia, he was told that if ever he met an old man, he might be sure that he was a stranger, as all that were natives died by the lance young.[41]

If the picture of the state of Abyssinia drawn by Bruce be in any degree near the truth, it places, in a strong point of view, the force of that principle of increase which preserves a population fully up to the level of the means of subsistence, under the checks of war, pestilential diseases, and promiscuous intercourse, all operating in an excessive degree.

The nations which border on Abyssinia are universally short-lived. A Shangalla woman at twenty-two is, according to Bruce, more wrinkled and deformed by age than is an European woman at sixty.[42] It would appear, therefore, that in all these countries, as among the northern shepherds, in the times of their constant emigrations, there is a very rapid succession of human beings, and the difference in the two instances is that our northern ancestors died out of their own country, whereas these die at home. If accurate registers of mortality were kept among these nations, I have little doubt that it would appear that, including the mortality from wars, 1 in 17 or 18 at the least die annually, instead of 1 in 34 or 36, as in the generality of European states.[43]

The description which Bruce gives of some parts of the country which he passed through on his return home, presents a picture more dreadful even than the state of Abyssinia, and shews how little population depends on the birth of children, in comparison of the production of food, and of those circumstances of natural and political situation which influence this produce.

'At half past six', Bruce says, 'we arrived at Garigana, a village whose inhabitants had all perished with hunger the year before; their wretched

---

[38] Bruce, vol. iii. c. vii. p. 192.   [39] Id. vol. iv. c. v. p. 112.   [40] Id. vol. iv. p. 258.
[41] Id. c. i. p. 14.   [42] Id. vol. ii. p. 559.
[43] [In 1817 [Vol. I, p. 223) Malthus altered this to:
    ... instead of 1 in 34, 36, or 40, as in the generality of European states.

bones being all unburied, and scattered upon the surface of the ground where the village formerly stood. We encamped among the bones of the dead, no space could be found free from them.'[44]

Of another town or village in his route, he observes: 'The strength of Teawa was 25 horse. The rest of the inhabitants might be 1200, naked, miserable, and despicable Arabs, like the rest of those which live in villages. ... Such was the state of Teawa. Its consequence was only to remain till the Daveina Arabs should resolve to attack it, when its cornfields being burnt and destroyed in a night, by a multitude of horsemen, the bones of its inhabitants scattered upon the earth, would be all its remains, like those of the miserable village of Garigana.[45]

'There is no water between Teawa and Beyla. Once Ingedidema and a number of villages were supplied with water from wells, and had large crops of Indian corn sown about their possessions. The curse of that country the Daveina Arabs have destroyed Ingedidema, and all the villages about it; filled up their wells, burnt their crops, and exposed all the inhabitants to die by famine.'[46]

Soon after leaving Sennaar, he says: 'We began now to see the effects of the quantity of rain having failed. There was little corn sown, and that so late as to be scarcely above ground. It seems the rains begin later as they pass northward. Many people were here employed in gathering grass-seeds to make a very bad kind of bread. These people appear perfect skeletons, and no wonder, as they live upon such fare. Nothing increases the danger of travelling and prejudice against strangers, more than the scarcity of provisions in the country through which you are to pass.[47]

'Came to Eltic, a straggling village about half a mile from the Nile, in the north of a large bare plain; all pasture, except the banks of the river which are covered with wood. We now no longer saw any corn sown. The people here were at the same miserable employment as those we had seen before, that of gathering grass-seeds.'[48]

Under such circumstances of climate and political situation, though a greater degree of foresight, industry, and security might considerably better their condition, and increase their population, the birth of a greater number of children without these concomitants would only aggravate their misery, and leave their population where it was.

The same may be said of the once flourishing and populous country of Egypt. Its present depressed state has not been caused by the weakening of the principle of increase, but by the weakening of the principle of industry

---

[44] Bruce, vol. iv. p. 349.   [45] Id. p. 353.   [46] Id. vol. iv. p. 411.
[47] Id. p. 511.
[48] Id.

and foresight, from the insecurity of property consequent on a most tyrannical and oppressive government. The principle of increase in Egypt, at present, does all that is possible for it to do. It keeps the population fully up to the level of the means of subsistence; and, were its power ten times greater than it really is, it could do no more.

The remains of ancient works, the vast lakes, canals, and large conduits for water destined to keep the Nile under control, serving as reservoirs to supply a scanty year, and as drains and outlets to prevent the superabundance of water in wet years, sufficiently indicate to us that the ancients, by art and industry, contrived to fertilize a much greater quantity of land from the overflowings of their river than is done at present; and to prevent, in some measure, the distresses which are now so frequently experienced from a redundant or insufficient inundation.[49] It is said of the governor Petronius that, effecting by art what was denied by nature, he caused abundance to prevail in Egypt under the disadvantage of such a deficient inundation as had always before been accompanied by dearth.[50] A flood too great is as fatal to the husbandman as one that is deficient; and the ancients had, in consequence, drains and outlets to spread the superfluous waters over the thirsty sands of Lybia and render even the desert habitable. These works are now all out of repair, and by ill management often produce mischief instead of good. The causes of this neglect, and consequently of the diminished means of subsistence, are obviously to be traced to the extreme ignorance and brutality of the government and the wretched state of the people. The Mamelukes, in whom the principal power resides, think only of enriching themselves, and employ for this purpose what appears to them to be the simplest method, that of seizing wealth wherever it may be found, of wresting it by violence from the possessor, and of imposing continually new and arbitrary contributions.[51] Their ignorance and brutality, and the constant state of alarm in which they live, prevent them from having any views of enriching the country, the better to prepare it for their plunder. No public works therefore are to be expected from the government, and no individual proprietor dares to undertake any improvement which might imply the possession of capital, as it would probably be the immediate signal of his destruction. Under such circumstances, we cannot be surprised that the ancient works are neglected, that the soil is ill cultivated, and that the means of subsistence, and consequently the population, are greatly reduced. But

---

[49] Bruce, vol. iii. c. xvii. p. 710.

    [Not until 1826 (Vol. i, p. 161) did Malthus amend this oblique quotation:

      ... large conduits for water ... serving as reservoirs to supply a dry year ... sufficiently indicate to us that the former inhabitants of Egypt, by art and industry ...

[50] Voyage de Volney, tom. i. c. iii. p. 33. 8vo.   [51] Id. c. xii. p. 170.

such is the natural fertility of the Delta, from the inundations of the Nile, that even without any capital employed upon the land, without a right of succession, and consequently almost without a right of property, it still maintains a considerable population in proportion to its extent; sufficient, if property were secure, and industry well directed, gradually to improve and extend the cultivation of the country, and restore it to its former state of prosperity. It may be safely pronounced of Egypt, that it is not the want of population that has checked its industry, but the want of industry that has checked its population.

The causes which keep down the population to the level of the present contracted means of subsistence are but too obvious.[52] The peasants are allowed for their maintenance only sufficient to keep them alive.[53] A miserable sort of bread made of doura without leaven or flavour,[54] cold water, and raw onions, make up the whole of their diet. Meat and fat, of which they are passionately fond, never appear but on great occasions, and among those who are more at their ease. Their habitations are huts made of earth, where a stranger would be suffocated with the heat and smoke; and where the diseases that are generated by want of cleanliness, by moisture, and by bad nourishment, often visit them and commit great ravages. To these physical evils are added a constant state of alarm, the fear of the plunder of the Arabs, and the visits of the Mamelukes, the spirit of revenge that is transmitted in families, and all the evils of a continued civil war.[55]

In the year 1783 the plague was very fatal; and in 1784 and 1785 a dreadful famine reigned in Egypt, owing to a deficiency in the inundations of the Nile. Volney draws a frightful picture of the misery that was suffered on this occasion. The streets of Cairo, which at first were full of beggars, were soon cleared of all these objects, who either perished or fled. A vast number of unfortunate wretches, in order to escape death, spread themselves over all the neighbouring countries, and the towns of Syria were inundated with Egyptians. The streets and public places were crowded with extenuated and dying skeletons. All the most revolting modes of satisfying the cravings of hunger were resorted to; the most disgusting food was devoured with eagerness; and Volney mentions the having seen, under the walls of ancient Alexandria, two miserable wretches seated on the carcase of a camel, and

---

[52] [In 1806 (Vol. I, p. 192) this paragraph began:
The immediate causes ...
[53] Voyage de Volney, tom. i. c. xiii. p. 172.
[54] ['Doura' is a variant of *durra* or Indian millet, *Panicum miliaceum*.]
[55] Volney, tom. i. c. xii. p. 173. This sketch of the state of the peasantry in Egypt, given by Volney, seems to be nearly confirmed by all the other writers on the subject; and particularly in a valuable paper intitled, Considerations generales sur l'Agriculture de l'Egypte, par L. Reynier. (Memoirs sur l'Egypte, tom. iv. p. 1.)

disputing with the dogs its putrid flesh. The depopulation of the two years was estimated at one sixth of all the inhabitants.[56]

---

[56] Voy. de Volney, tom. i. c. xii. s. ii.

CHAPTER IX

Of the Checks to Population in Siberia, Northern and Southern

The inhabitants of the most northern parts of Asia subsist chiefly by hunting and fishing; and we may suppose, therefore, that the checks to their increase are of the same nature as those which prevail among the American Indians; except that the check from war is considerably less, and the check from famine perhaps greater, than in the temperate regions of America. M. de Lesseps, who travelled from Kamtschatka to Petersburgh with the papers of the unfortunate Perouse,[1] draws a melancholy picture of the misery that is sometimes suffered in this part of the world from a scarcity of food. He observes, while at Bolcheretsk, a village of Kamtschatka, 'very heavy rains are injurious in this country, because they occasion floods, which drive the fish from the rivers. A famine, the most distressing to the poor Kampscha-dales, is the result, as it happened last year in all the villages along the western coast of the peninsula. This dreadful calamity occurs so frequently in this quarter, that the inhabitants are obliged to abandon their dwellings, and repair with their families to the borders of the Kamtschatka river, where they hope to find better resources, fish being more plentiful in this river. M. Kasloff (the Russian officer who conducted M. de Lesseps) had intended to proceed along the western coast; but the news of this famine determined him, contrary to his wishes, to return, rather than be driven to the necessity of stopping half way, or perishing with hunger.'[2] Though a different route was pursued, yet in the course of the journey almost all the dogs which drew the sledges died for want of food; and every dog, as soon as he failed, was immediately devoured by the others.[3]

Even at Okotsk, a town of considerable trade, the inhabitants wait with hungry impatience for the breaking up of the river Okhota in the spring. When M. de Lesseps was there, the stock of dried fish was nearly exhausted. Meal was so dear that the common people were unable to purchase it. On drawing the seine prodigious numbers of small fish were caught, and the joy and clamour redoubled at the sight. The most famished were first served. M.

---

[1] [See DE LESSEPS and LA PÉROUSE in the Alphabetical List.]
[2] Travels in Kamtschatka, vol. i. p. 147. 8vo. Eng. trans. 1790.
[3] Id. p. 264.

de Lesseps feelingly says: 'I could not refrain from tears on perceiving the ravenousness of these poor creatures; ... whole families contended for the fish, which were devoured raw before my eyes.'[4]

Throughout all the northern parts of Siberia, the small-pox is very fatal. In Kampschatka, according to M. de Lesseps, it has carried off three fourths[5] of the native inhabitants.

Pallas confirms this account; and, in describing the Ostiacks on the Obi, who live nearly in the same manner, observes that this disorder makes dreadful ravages among them, and may be considered as the principal check to their increase.[6] The extraordinary mortality of the small-pox among these people is very naturally accounted for by the extreme heat, filth, and putrid air of their underground habitations. Three or four Ostiack families are crowded together in one yourt, and nothing can be so disgusting as their mode of living. They never wash their hands, and the putrid remains of the fish, and the excrements of the children, are never cleared away. From this description, says Pallas, one may easily form an idea of the stench, the fœtid vapours and humidity of their yourts.[7] They have seldom many children. It is a rare thing to see three or four in one family. The reason which Pallas gives is that so many die young on account of their bad nourishment.[8] To this, perhaps, should be added the state of miserable and laborious servitude to which the women are condemned,[9] which certainly prevents them from being prolific.

The Samoyedes, Pallas thinks, are not quite so dirty as the Ostiacks, because they are more in motion during the winter in hunting; but he describes the state of the women amongst them as a still more wretched and laborious servitude;[10] and consequently the check to population from this cause must be greater.

Most of the natives of these inhospitable regions live nearly in the same miserable manner which it would be, therefore, mere repetition to describe. From what has been said, we may form a sufficient idea of the principal checks that keep the actual population down to the level of the scanty means of subsistence which these dreary countries afford.

In some of the southern parts of Siberia, and in the districts adjoining the Wolga, the Russian travellers describe the soil to be of extraordinary fertility. It consists in general of a fine black mould of so rich a nature as not to require, or even to bear, dressing. Manure only makes the corn grow too

---

[4] Travels in Kamtshalka, vol. ii. p. 252, 253.   [5] Id. vol. i. p. 128.
[6] Voy. de Pallas, tom. iv. p. 68. 4to. 5 vols. 1788. Paris.
[7] Id. p. 60. [In 1817 (Vol. 1, p. 236) Malthus substituted 'one hut' for *one yourt*.]
[8] Id. tom. iv. p. 72.
[9] Id. p. 60.   [10] Id. p. 92.

luxuriantly, and subjects it to fall to the ground and be spoiled. The only mode of recruiting this kind of land which is practised is by leaving it one year out of three in fallow, and proceeding in this way, there are some grounds the vigour of which is said to be inexhaustible.[11] Yet notwithstanding the facility with which, as it would appear, the most plentiful subsistence might be procured, many of these districts are thinly peopled, and in none of them, perhaps, does population increase in the proportion that might be expected from the nature of the soil.

Such countries seem to be under that moral impossibility of increasing, which is well described by Sir James Steuart. [13]● Man, though he may often be produced without a sufficient demand for him, cannot really multiply and prosper unless his labour be wanted; and the reason that the population goes on so slowly in these countries is that there is very little demand for men.●[13] The mode of agriculture is described to be extremely simple, and to require very few labourers. In some places, the seed is merely thrown on the fallow.[14] The buck-wheat is a common culture; and though it is sown very thin, yet one sowing will last five or six years, and produce every year twelve or fifteen times the original quantity. The seed which falls during the time of the harvest is sufficient for the next year, and it is only necessary to pass a harrow once over it in the spring. And this is continued till the fertility of the soil begins to diminish. It is observed, very justly, that the cultivation of no kind of grain can so exactly suit the indolent inhabitants of the plains of Siberia.[15]

With such a system of agriculture and with few or no manufactures, the demand for men must be very easily satisfied. Corn will undoubtedly be very cheap; but labour will be in proportion still cheaper. Though the farmer may be able to provide an ample quantity of food for his own children, yet the wages of his labourer may not be sufficient to enable him to rear up a family with ease.

If, from observing the deficiency of population, compared with the fertility of the soil, we were to endeavour to remedy it by giving a bounty upon children, and thus enabling the labourer to rear up a greater number; what

---

[11] Voy. de Pallas, tom. iv. p. 5.   [12] Polit. Econ. b. i. c. v. p. 30. 4to.

[13] [In 1817 (Vol. 1, p. 239) this sentence was excised and Malthus's summary of Steuart's views was expanded thus:

If either from the nature of the government, or the habits of the people, obstacles exist to the settlement of fresh farms or the subdivision of the old ones, a part of the society may suffer want, even in the midst of apparent plenty. It is not enough that a country should have the power of producing food in abundance, but the state of society must be such as to afford the means of its proper distribution; and the reason why population goes on slowly in these countries is, that the small demand for labour prevents that distribution of the produce of the soil which, while the divisions of land remain the same, can alone make the lower classes of society partakers of the plenty which it affords. The mode of agriculture ...

[14] Voy. de Pallas, tom. i. p. 250.   [15] Decouv. Russ. vol. iv. p. 329. 8vo. 4 vols. Berne.

would be the consequence? Nobody would want the work of the supernumerary labourers that were thus brought into the market. Though the
ample subsistence of a man for a day might be purchased for a penny, yet
nobody will give these people a farthing for their labour. The farmer is
able to do all that he wishes, all that he thinks necessary in the cultivation of the soil, by means of his own family, and the one or two
labourers which he might have before. As these people, therefore, can
give him nothing that he wants, it is not to be expected that he should
overcome his natural indolence, and undertake a larger and more troublesome concern, merely to provide them gratuitously with food. In such a
state of things, when the very small demand for manufacturing labour is
satisfied, what are the rest to do? They are, in fact, as completely without
the means of subsistence as if they were living upon a barren sand. They
must either emigrate to some place where their work is wanted, or perish
miserably of poverty. Should they be prevented from suffering this last
extremity by a scanty subsistence given to them, in consequence of a
scanty and only occasional use of their labour, it is evident that though
they might exist themselves, they would not be in a capacity to marry
and continue to increase the population.

 ¹⁵●It might be supposed, perhaps, that if there were much good land
unused, the redundant population would naturally betake itself to the
cultivation of it, and raise its own food. But though there are many countries
where good land remains uncultivated, there are very few where it may be
obtained by the first person who chooses to occupy it. Even were this the
case, there would be still some obstacles remaining. The supernumerary
labourer whom I have described has no funds whatever that can enable him
to build a house, to purchase stock and utensils, and to subsist till he has
brought his new land into proper order and obtained an adequate return.
Even the children of the farmer, when they grow up, would find it very
difficult to obtain these necessary funds.●¹⁶

---

¹⁶ [In 1817 (Vol. I, p. 239) Malthus expanded and re-wrote this passage:
  If in the best cultivated and most populous countries of Europe the present divisions of land and
  farms had taken place, and had not been followed by the introduction of commerce and
  manufactures, population would long since have come to a stand from the total want of motive to
  further cultivation, and the consequent want of demand for labour; and it is obvious that the
  excessive fertility of the country now under consideration would rather aggravate than diminish
  the difficulty.
    It will probably be said that, if there were much good land unused, new settlements and
  divisions would of course take place, and that the redundant population would raise its own food,
  and generate the demand for it, as in America.
    This would, no doubt, be the case under favourable circumstances; if, for instance, in the first
  place, the land were of such a nature as to afford all the other materials of capital as well as corn;
  secondly, if such land were to be purchased in small lots, and the property well secured under a

In a state of society where the market for corn is extremely narrow, and the price very low, the cultivators are always poor; and though they may be able amply to provide for their family, in the simple article of food, yet they cannot realise a capital to divide among their children, and enable them to undertake the cultivation of fresh land. Though this necessary capital might be very small, yet even this small sum the farmer perhaps cannot acquire; for when he grows a greater quantity of corn than usual, he finds no purchaser for it,[17] and cannot convert it into any permanent article which will enable any of his children to command an equivalent portion of subsistence or labour in future.[18] In general, therefore, he contents himself with growing only what is sufficient for the immediate demands of his family and the narrow market to which he is accustomed. And if he has a large family, many of his children probably fall into the rank of labourers, and their further

---

free government; and, thirdly, if habits of industry and accumulation generally prevailed among the mass of the people. But the failure of any of these conditions would essentially check, or might altogether stop, the progress of population. Land that would bear the most abundant crops of corn might be totally unfit for extensive and general settlements from a want either of wood or of water. The accumulations of individuals would go most reluctantly and slowly to the land, if the tenures on which farms were held were either insecure or degrading; and no facility of production could effect a permanent increase and proper distribution of the necessaries of life under inveterate habits of indolence and want of foresight.

It is obvious that the favourable circumstances here alluded to have not been combined in Siberia; and even on the supposition of there being no physical defects in the nature of the soil to be overcome, the political and moral difficulties in the way of a rapid increase of population could yield but slowly to the best-directed efforts. In America the rapid increase of agricultural capital is occasioned in a great degree by the savings from the high wages of common labour. The command of thirty or forty pounds at the least is considered as necessary to enable an active young man to begin a plantation of his own in the back settlements. Such a sum may be saved in a few years without much difficulty in America, where labour is in great demand and paid at a high rate; but the redundant labourer of Siberia would find it extremely difficult to collect such funds as would enable him to build a house, to purchase stock and utensils, and to subsist till he could bring his new land into proper order and obtain an adequate return. Even the children of the farmer, when grown up, would not easily provide these necessary funds.

[17] Il y a fort peu de debit dans le pays, parce que le plupart des habitans sont cultivateurs et elevent eux memes des bestiaux. Voy. de Pallas, tom. iv. p. 4. [There is very little buying and selling in this country, because most of the inhabitants are cultivators, and raise their own animal products.]

[18] [In 1806 (Vol. I, p. 203) Malthus added a footnote here:

In addition to the causes here mentioned, I have lately been informed that one of the principal reasons why large tracts of rich land lie uncultivated in this part of the world is the swarm of locusts which at certain seasons covers these districts, and from the ravages of which it is impossible to protect the rising crop.

increase is checked, as in the case of the labourer before described, by a want of the means of subsistence.

It is not therefore a direct encouragement to the procreation and rearing of children that is wanted in these countries, in order to increase their population; but the creation of an effectual demand for the produce of the soil, by promoting the means of its distribution. [19]●This can only be effected either by the introduction of manufactures, and by inspiring the cultivator with a taste for them, which must necessarily be a work of time; or by assisting new colonists and the children of the old cultivators with capital, to enable them to occupy successively, and bring into cultivation, all the land that is fit for it.

The late Empress of Russia adopted both these means of increasing the population in her dominions. She encouraged both manufacturers and cultivators; and furnished to foreigners of either description, capital, and funds for subsistence,●[19] free of all interest for a certain term of years.[20] These well-directed efforts, added to what had been done by Peter I, had, as might be expected, a considerable effect; and the Russian territories, particularly the Asiatic part of them, which had slumbered for centuries, with a population nearly stationary, or at most increasing very languidly, seem to have made a sudden start of late years. Though the population of the more fertile provinces of Siberia be still very inadequate to the richness of the soil; yet in some of them, agriculture flourishes in no inconsiderable degree, and great quantities of corn are grown. In a general dearth which happened in 1769, the province of Isetsk was able, notwithstanding a scanty harvest, to supply in the usual manner the foundries and forges of Ural, besides preserving from the horrors of famine all the neighbouring provinces.[21] And in the territory of Krasnoyarsk, on the shores of the Yenissey, in spite of the

---

[19] [Malthus altered this passage twice. In 1807 (Vol. I, p. 304) he wrote:
 . . . bring into cultivation all the land that is fit for it, and thus enlarge the internal market.
[At the beginning of the next paragraph, *and funds for subsistence* was omitted.
[In 1826 (Vol. I, p. 174) the whole passage was abbreviated to two sentences:
 This can only be effected by the introduction of manufactures, and by inspiring the cultivator with a taste for them, and thus enlarging the internal market.
 The late empress of Russia encouraged both manufacturers and cultivators; and furnished to foreigners of either description capital free of all interest for a certain term of years.
[For the late Empress, see CATHERINE in the Alphabetical List.]

[20] Tooke's View of the Russian Empire, vol. ii. p. 242. [In 1807 (Vol I, pp. 204–5) this footnote was enlarged:
 The principal effect, perhaps, of these importations of foreigners was the introduction of free men instead of slaves, and of German industry instead of Russian indolence; but the introduction of that part of capital which consists in machinery would be a very great point, and the cheapness of manufactures would soon give the cultivators a taste for them.

[21] Voy. de Pallas, tom. iii. p. 10. [In the Everyman Edition (I, p. 106) this date is incorrectly given as 1796.]

indolence and drunkenness of the inhabitants, the abundance of corn is so great that no instance has ever been known of a general failure.[22] Pallas justly observes that, if we consider that Siberia not two hundred years ago was a wilderness utterly unknown, and in point of population even far behind the almost desert tracts of North America, we may reasonably be astonished at the present state of this part of the world, and at the multitude of its Russian inhabitants, who in numbers greatly exceed the natives.[23]

When Pallas was in Siberia, provisions in these fertile districts, particularly in the environs of Krasnoyarsk, were most extraordinarily cheap. A pood, or forty pounds, of wheaten flour, was sold for about twopence-half-penny, an ox for five or six shillings, and a cow for three or four.[24] This unnatural cheapness, owing to a want of vent for the products of the soil, was perhaps the principal check to the population.[25] In the period which has since elapsed, the prices have risen considerably;[26] and we may conclude, therefore, that the object principally wanted has been in a great measure attained, and that the population proceeds with rapid strides.

Pallas, however, complains that the intentions of the Empress respecting the peopling of Siberia were not always well fulfilled by her subordinate agents, and that the proprietors, to whose care this was left, often sent off colonists in every respect unfit for the purpose, in regard to age, disease, and want of industrious habits.[27] Even the German settlers in the districts near the Wolga are, according to Pallas, deficient in this last point,[28] and this is certainly a most essential one. It may, indeed, be safely asserted that the importation of industry is of infinitely more consequence to the population of a country than the importation of men and women, considered only with regard to numbers. Were it possible at once to change the habits of a whole people, and to direct its industry at pleasure, no government would ever be reduced to the necessity of encouraging foreign settlers. But to change long-existing habits is of all enterprizes the most difficult. Many years must elapse under the most favourable circumstances before the Siberian boor will possess the industry and activity of an English labourer. And though the Russian government has been incessant in its endeavours to convert the pastoral tribes of Siberia to agriculture, yet many obstinately persist in bidding defiance to any attempts that can be made to wean them from their injurious sloth.[29]

Many obstacles concur to prevent that rapid growth of the Russian colonies which the procreative power would permit.[30] Some of the low

---

22 Id. tom. iv. p. 3.   23 Voy. de Pallas, tom. iv. p. 6.   24 Id. p. 3.
25 [In 1806 (Vol. i, p. 206) *the principal check to the population* was altered to:
   ... the principal check to industry.
26 Tooke's View of Russian Empire, vol. iii. p. 239.   27 Voy. de Pallas, tom. v. p. 5.
28 Id. p. 253.   29 Tooke's Russian Empire, vol. iii. p. 313.
30 [In 1806 (Vol. i, p. 207) this paragraph began:
   Many other obstacles ...

countries of Siberia are unhealthy, from the number of marshes which they contain,[31] and great and wasting epizooties are frequent among the cattle.[32] In the districts near the Wolga, though the soil is naturally rich, yet droughts are so frequent that there is seldom more than one good harvest out of three.[33] The colonists of Saratof, after they had been settled for some years, were obliged to remove on this account to other districts, and the whole expense of building their houses, amounting to above a million of roubles, was remitted to them by the Empress.[34] For purposes either of safety or convenience, the houses of each colony are all built contiguous, or nearly so, and not scattered about upon the different farms. A want of room is, in consequence, soon felt in the immediate neighbourhood of the village, while the distant grounds remain in a state of very imperfect cultivation. On observing this in the colony of Kotschesnaia, Pallas proposed that a certain part should be removed by the Empress to other districts, that the remainder might be left more at their ease.[35] This proposal seems to prove that spontaneous divisions of this kind did not often take place, and that the children of the colonists might not always find an easy mode of settling themselves, and rearing up fresh families. In the flourishing colony of the Moravian brethren at Sarepta, it is said that the young people cannot marry without the consent of their priests; and that their consent is not in general granted till late.[36] It would appear, therefore, that among the obstacles to the increase of population, even in these new colonies, the preventive check has its share. Population can never increase with great rapidity but when the real price of common labour is very high, as in America; and from the state of society in this part of the Russian territories, and the consequent want of a

---

[31] Voy. de Pallas, tom. iii. p. 16. [In 1806 (Vol. 1, p. 208) a footnote was added here:

Though in countries where the procreative power is never fully called into action, unhealthy seasons and epidemics have but little effect on the average population, yet in new colonies, which are differently circumstanced in this respect, they materially impede its progress.

[In 1807 (Vol. 1, p. 208) this note was extended:

This point is not sufficiently understood. If in countries which were either stationary or increasing very slowly, all the immediate checks to population, which had been observed, were to continue in force, no abundance of food could materially increase the number of people. But the precise way in which such an abundance operates is by diminishing the immediate checks which before prevailed. Those, however, which may remain, either from the difficulty of changing habits, or from any unfavourable circumstances in the soil or climate, will still continue to operate in preventing the procreative power from producing its full effect.

[32] Id. p. 17, tom. v. p. 411.   [33] Id. tom. v. p. 252 et seq.

[34] Tooke's Russian Empire, vol. ii. p. 245.

[35] Voy. de Pallas, tom. v. p. 253.   [36] Id. p. 175.

proper vent for the produce of industry, this effect, which usually accompanies new colonies, and is essential to their rapid growth, does not take place in any considerable degree.[37]

---

[37] [In 1807 (Vol. i, p. 210) Malthus added a footnote to this chapter:

Other causes may concur in restraining the population of Siberia which have not been noticed by Pallas. In general, it should be observed, with regard to all the immediate checks to population, which I either have had or shall have occasion to mention, that, as it is evidently impossible to ascertain the extent to which each acts, and the proportion of the whole procreative power which it impedes, no accurate inferences respecting the actual state of population can be drawn from them *a priori*. The prevailing checks in two different nations may appear to be exactly the same as to kind, yet if they are different in degree, the rate of increase in each will, of course, be as different as possible. All that can be done, therefore, is to proceed as in physical inquiries; that is, first to observe the facts, and then account for them from the best lights that can be collected.

CHAPTER X

Of the Checks to Population in the Turkish Dominions and Persia

In the Asiatic parts of the Turkish dominions it will not be difficult, from the accounts of travellers, to trace the checks to population and the causes of its present decay; and as there is little difference in the manners of the Turks, whether they inhabit Europe or Asia, it will not be worth while to make them the subject of distinct consideration.

The fundamental cause of the low state of population in Turkey, compared with its extent of territory, is undoubtedly the nature of the government. Its tyranny, its feebleness, its bad laws, and worse administration of them, with the consequent insecurity of property, throw such obstacles in the way of agriculture that the means of subsistence are necessarily decreasing yearly, and with them, of course, the number of people. The miri, or general land-tax, paid to the sultan, is in itself moderate;[1] but, by abuses inherent in the Turkish government, the pachas and their agents have found out the means of rendering it ruinous. Though they cannot absolutely alter the impost which has been established by the sultan, they have introduced a multitude of changes which, without the name, produce all the effects of an augmentation.[2] In Syria, according to Volney, having the greatest part of the land at their disposal, they clog their concessions with burdensome conditions, and exact the half, and sometimes even two-thirds, of the crop. When the harvest is over, they cavil about losses and, as they have the power in their hands, they carry off what they think proper. If the season fail, they still exact the same sum, and expose every thing that the poor peasant possesses to sale. To these constant oppressions are added a thousand accidental extortions. Sometimes a whole village is laid under contribution for some real or imaginary offence. Arbitrary presents are exacted on the accession of each governor; grass, barley, and straw are demanded for his horses; and commissions are multiplied, that the soldiers who carry the orders may live upon the starving peasants, whom they treat with the most brutal insolence and injustice.[3]

---

[1] Voy. de Volney, tom. ii. c. xxxvii. p. 373. (8vo. 1787.)
[2] Ibid. [The word *changes* should be 'charges'; see VOLNEY in the Alphabetical List.]
[3] Id. c. xxxvii.

The consequence of these depredations is that the poorer class of inhabitants, ruined, and unable any longer to pay the miri, become a burden to the village, or fly into the cities; but the miri is unalterable, and the sum to be levied must be found somewhere. The portion of those who are thus driven from their homes falls on the remaining inhabitants, whose burden, though at first light, now becomes insupportable. If they should be visited by two years of drought and famine, the whole village is ruined and abandoned; and the tax which it should have paid is levied on the neighbouring lands.[4]

The same mode of proceeding takes place with regard to the tax on the Christians, which has been raised by these means from three, five, and eleven piastres, at which it was first fixed, to thirty-five and forty, which absolutely impoverishes those on whom it is levied, and obliges them to leave the country. It has been remarked that these exactions have made a rapid progress during the last forty years, from which time are dated the decline of agriculture, the depopulation of the country, and the diminution in the quantity of specie carried to Constantinople.[5]

The food of the peasants is almost everywhere reduced to a little flat cake of barley or doura, onions, lentils, and water. Not to lose any part of their corn, they leave in it all sorts of wild grain, which often produce bad consequences. In the mountains of Lebanon and Nablous, in time of dearth, they gather the acorns from the oaks, which they eat after boiling, or roasting them on the ashes.[6]

By a natural consequence of this misery, the art of cultivation is in the most deplorable state. The husbandman is almost without instruments, and those he has are very bad. His plough is frequently no more than the branch of a tree cut below a fork, and used without wheels. The ground is tilled by asses and cows, rarely by oxen, which would bespeak too much riches. In the districts exposed to the Arabs, as in Palestine, the countryman must sow with his musket in his hand; and scarcely does the corn turn yellow, before it is reaped and concealed in subterraneous caverns. As little as possible is employed for seed corn, because the peasants sow no more than is barely necessary for their subsistence. Their whole industry is limited to a supply of their immediate wants; and to procure a little bread, a few onions, a blue shirt, and a bit of woollen, much labour is not necessary. 'The peasant lives therefore in distress; but at least he does not enrich his tyrants, and the avarice of despotism is its own punishment.'[7]

This picture, which is drawn by Volney in describing the state of the

---

[4] Voy. de Volney, tom. ii. c. xxxvii. p. 375.   [5] Id. p. 376.
[6] Id. p. 377. [In 1826 (Vol. i, p. 182) *on the ashes* was changed to:
    ... roasting them in ashes.
[7] Id. p. 379.

peasants in Syria, seems to be confirmed by all the other travellers in these countries; and, according to Eton, it represents very nearly the condition of the peasants in the greatest part of the Turkish dominions.[8] Universally, the offices of every denomination are set up to public sale; and in the intrigues of the seraglio, by which the disposal of all places is regulated, everything is done by means of bribes. The pachas, in consequence, who are sent into the provinces, exert to the utmost their power of extortion; but are always outdone by the officers immediately below them who, in their turn, leave room for their subordinate agents.[9]

The pacha must raise money to pay the tribute, and also to indemnify himself for the purchase of his office; support his dignity, and make a provision in case of accidents; and as all power, both military and civil, centres in his person, from his representing the sultan, the means are at his discretion, and the quickest are invariably considered as the best.[10] Uncertain of to-morrow, he treats his province as a mere transient possession, and endeavours to reap, if possible, in one day, the fruit of many years, without the smallest regard to his successor, or the injury that he may do to the permanent revenue.[11]

The cultivator is necessarily more exposed to these extortions than the inhabitants of the towns. From the nature of his employment, he is fixed to one spot, and the productions of agriculture do not admit of being easily concealed. The tenure of the land and the right of succession are besides uncertain. When a father dies, the inheritance reverts to the sultan, and the children can only redeem the succession by a considerable sum of money. These considerations naturally occasion an indifference to landed estates. The country is deserted, and each person is desirous of flying to the towns, where he will not only in general meet with better treatment, but may hope to acquire a species of wealth which he can more easily conceal from the eyes of his rapacious masters.[12]

To complete the ruin of agriculture, a maximum is in many cases established, and the peasants are obliged to furnish the towns with corn at a fixed price. It is a maxim of Turkish policy, originating in the feebleness of the government and the fear of popular tumults, to keep the price of corn low in all the considerable towns. In the case of a failure in the harvest, every person who possesses any corn is obliged to sell it at the price fixed, under pain of death; and if there be none in the neighbourhood, other districts are ransacked for it.[13] When Constantinople is in want of provisions, ten

---

[8] Eton's Turkish Emp. c. viii. 2nd edit. 1799.   [9] Id. c. ii. p. 55.
[10] Voy. de Volney, tom. ii. c. xxxiii. p. 347.
[11] Id. p. 350.   [12] Id. c. xxxvi. p. 369.   [13] Id. c. xxxviii. p. 38.

provinces are perhaps famished for a supply.[14] At Damascus, during a scarcity in 1784, the people paid only one penny farthing a pound for their bread, while the peasants in the villages were absolutely dying with hunger.[15]

The effect of such a system of government on agriculture need not be insisted upon. The causes of the decreasing means of subsistence are but too obvious; and the checks which keep the population down to the level of these decreasing resources may be traced with nearly equal certainty, and will appear to include almost every species of vice and misery that is known.

It is observed, in general, that the Christian families consist of a greater number of children than the Mahometan families in which polygamy prevails.[16] This is an extraordinary fact; because though polygamy, from the unequal distribution of women which it occasions, be naturally unfavourable to the population of a whole country; yet the individuals who are able to support a plurality of wives ought certainly, in the natural course of things, to have a greater number of children than those who are confined to one. The way in which Volney principally accounts for this fact is that, from the practice of polygamy, and very early marriages, the Turks are enervated while young, and impotence at thirty is very common.[17] Eton notices an unnatural vice as prevailing in no inconsiderable degree among the common people, and considers it as one of the checks to the population,[18] but the five principal causes of depopulation which he enumerates, are,

1. The plague, from which the empire is never entirely free.

2. Those terrible disorders which almost always follow it, at least in Asia.

3. Epidemic and endemic maladies in Asia, which make as dreadful ravages as the plague itself, and which frequently visit that part of the empire.

4. Famine.

5. And lastly, the sicknesses which always follow a famine, and which occasion a much greater mortality.[19]

He afterwards gives a more particular account of the devastations of the plague in different parts of the empire, and concludes by observing that if the numbers of the Mahometans have decreased, this cause alone is adequate to the effect,[20] and that, things going on in their present train, the Turkish population will be extinct in another century.[21] But this inference, and the calculations which relate to it, are without doubt erroneous. The increase of population in the intervals of these periods of mortality is probably greater

[14] Voy. de Volney, tom. ii. c. xxxiii. p. 345. [15] Id. c. xxxviii. p. 381.
[16] Eton's Turkish Emp. c. vii. p. 275.
[17] Voy. de Volney, tom. ii. c. xl. p. 445. [18] Eton's Turkish Emp. c. vii. p. 275.
[19] Id. p. 264.
[20] Id. p. 291. [21] Id. p. 280.

than he is aware of. At the same time, it must be remarked that in a country where the industry of the husbandman is confined to the supply of his necessary wants, where he sows only to prevent himself from starving, and is unable to accumulate any surplus produce, a great loss of people is not easily recovered, as the natural effects from the diminished numbers cannot be felt in the same degree as in countries where industry prevails and property is secure.

According to the Persian legislator Zoroaster, to plant a tree, to cultivate a field, to beget children, are meritorious acts; but it appears, from the account of travellers, that many among the lower classes of people cannot easily attain the latter species of merit; and in this instance, as in numberless others, the private interest of the individual corrects the errors of the legislator. Sir John Chardin says that matrimony in Persia is very expensive, and that only men of estates will venture upon it, lest it prove their ruin.[22] The Russian travellers seem to confirm this account, and observe, that the lower classes of people are obliged to defer marriage till late; and that it is only among the rich that this union takes place early.[23]

The dreadful convulsions to which Persia has been continually subject for many hundred years must have been fatal to her agriculture. The periods of repose from external wars and internal commotions have been short and few, and even during the times of profound peace, the frontier provinces have been constantly subject to the ravages of the Tartars.

The effect of this state of things is such as might be expected. The proportion of uncultivated to cultivated land, in Persia, Sir John Chardin states to be ten to one;[24] and the mode in which the officers of the Shah and private owners let out their lands to husbandmen is not that which is best calculated to reanimate industry. The grain in Persia is also very subject to be destroyed by hail, drought, locusts, and other insects,[25] which probably tends rather to discourage the employment of capital in the cultivation of the soil.

The plague does not extend to Persia; but the small-pox is mentioned by the Russian travellers as making very fatal ravages.[26]

It will not be worth while to enter more minutely on the checks to population in Persia, as they seem to be nearly similar to those which have been just described in the Turkish dominions. The superior destruction of the plague in Turkey is perhaps nearly balanced by the greater frequency of internal commotions in Persia.

---

[22] Sir John Chardin's Travels. Harris's Collect. b. iii. c. ii. p. 870.
[23] Decouv. Russ. tom. ii. p. 293.
[24] Id. p. 902.   [25] Ibid.
[26] Decouv. Russ. tom. ii. p. 377.

CHAPTER XI

Of the Checks to Population in Indostan and Tibet

In the ordinances of Menu, the Indian legislator, which Sir Wm. Jones has translated and called the *Institutes of Hindu Law*, marriage is very greatly encouraged, and a male heir is considered as an object of the first importance.

'By a son, a man obtains victory over all people; by a son's son, he enjoys immortality; and afterwards, by the son of that grandson, he reaches the solar abode.'

'Since the son delivers his father from the hell, named Put, he was therefore called puttra by Brahma himself.'[1]

Among the different nuptial rites, Menu has ascribed particular qualities to each.

'A son of a *Bráhmì*, or wife by the first ceremony, redeems from sin, if he perform virtuous acts, ten ancestors, ten descendants, and himself, the twenty-first person.'

'A son born of a wife by the *Daiva* nuptials redeems seven and seven, in higher and lower degrees; of a wife by the *Arsha*, three and three; of a wife by the *Prájápatya*, six and six.'[2]

A housekeeper is considered as of the most eminent order.[3] 'The divine sages, the manes, the gods, the spirits, and guests, pray for benefits to masters of families.'[4] An elder brother not married before the younger is mentioned among the persons who are particularly to be shunned.[5]

Such ordinances would naturally cause marriage to be considered as a religious duty; yet it seems to be rather a succession of male heirs, than a very numerous progeny, that is the object so much desired.

---

[1] Sir Wm. Jones's Works, vol. iii. c. ix. p. 354. Speaking of the Indian laws, the Abbé Raynal says: 'La population est un devoir primitif, un ordre de la nature si sacré, que la loi permet de tromper, de mentir, de se parjurer pour favoriser un marriage.' Hist. des Indes, tom. i. l. i. p. 81. 8vo. 10 vols. Paris 1795.
['To propagate is a man's first duty, an ordinance of nature so sacred, that the law permits him to cheat, to lie, and to perjure himself to facilitate a marriage.']

[2] Sir Wm. Jones's Works, vol. iii. c. iii. p. 124.

[3] [A *housekeeper* here means a householder.]

[4] Id. p. 130. [*Manes* is a Latin word (familiar to children made to read Virgil) for the revered souls of dead ancestors.]

[5] Id. p. 141.

'The father, having begotten a son, discharges his debt to his own progenitors.'

'That son alone, by whose birth he discharges the debt, and through whom he attains immortality, was begotten from a sense of duty; all the rest are considered by the wife as begotten from love of pleasure.'[6]

A widow is, on some occasions, allowed to have one son by the brother, or some appointed kinsman of the deceased husband, but on no account a second. 'The first object of the appointment being obtained, according to law, both the brother and the sister must live together like a father and daughter by affinity.'[7]

In almost every part of the ordinances of Menu, sensuality of all kinds is strongly reprobated, and chastity inculcated as a religious duty.

'A man by the attachment of his organs to sensual pleasure incurs certain guilt; but having wholly subdued them, he thence attains heavenly bliss.'

'Whatever man may obtain all those gratifications, or whatever man may resign them completely, the resignation of all pleasures is far better than the attainment of them.'[8]

It is reasonable to suppose that such passages might, in some degree, tend to counteract those encouragements to increase, which have been before mentioned, and might prompt some religious persons to desist from further indulgencies when they had obtained one son, or to remain more contented than they otherwise would have been in an unmarried state. Strict and absolute chastity seems indeed to supersede the obligation of having descendants.

'Many thousands of Brahmens having avoided sensuality from their early youth, and having left no issue in their families, have ascended nevertheless to heaven.'

'And, like those abstemious men, a virtuous wife ascends to heaven, though she have no child, if after the decease of her lord she devote herself to pious austerity.'[9]

The permission to a brother, or other kinsman, to raise up an heir for the deceased husband, which has been noticed, extends only to women of the servile class.[10] Those of the higher classes are not even to pronounce the name of another man, but to

'Continue till death forgiving all injuries, performing harsh duties, avoiding every sensual pleasure, and cheerfully practising the incomparable rules of virtue.'[11]

Besides these strict precepts relating to the government of the passions,

---

[6] Sir Wm. Jones's Works, vol. iii. c. ix. p. 349.   [7] Id. p. 343.   [8] Id. c. ii. p. 96.
[9] Id. c. v. p. 221.   [10] Id. c. ix. p. 343.   [11] Id. c. v. p. 221.

other circumstances would perhaps concur to prevent the full effect of the ordinances which encourage marriage.

The division of the people into classes, and the continuance of the same profession in the same family, would be the means of pointing out to each individual, in a clear and distinct manner, his future prospects respecting a livelihood; and from the gains of his father, he would be easily enabled to judge whether he could support a family by the same employment. And though, when a man cannot gain a subsistence in the employments appropriate to his class, it is allowable for him, under certain restrictions, to seek it in another; yet some kind of disgrace seems to attach to this expedient, and it is not probable that many persons would marry with the certain prospect of being obliged thus to fall from their class, and to lower in so marked a manner their condition in life.

In addition to this, the choice of a wife seems to be a point of considerable difficulty. A man might remain unmarried for some time before he could find exactly such a companion as the legislator prescribes. Ten families of a certain description, be they ever so great, or ever so rich in kine, goats, sheep, gold, and grain, are studiously to be avoided. Girls with too little or too much hair, who are too talkative, who have bad eyes, a disagreeable name, or any kind of sickness, who have no brother, or whose father is not well known, are all, with many others, excluded; and the choice will appear to be in some degree confined when it must necessarily rest upon

'A girl, whose form has no defect; who has an agreeable name; who walks gracefully, like a phenicopteros or a young elephant; whose hair and teeth are moderate respectively in quantity and size; whose body has exquisite softness.'[12]

It is observed that a woman of the servile class is not mentioned, even in the recital of any ancient story, as the wife of a Brahmen or of a Cshatriya, though in the greatest difficulty to find a suitable match; which seems to imply such a difficulty might sometimes occur.[13]

Another obstacle to marriage, arising from the Hindoo customs, is that an elder brother who does not marry seems in a manner to confine all his other brothers to the same state; for a younger brother who marries before the elder incurs disgrace, and is mentioned among the persons who ought to be shunned.[14]

The character which the legislator draws of the manners and disposition of the women in India is extremely unfavourable. Among many other passages expressed with equal severity, he observes that,

---

[12] Sir William Jones's Works, vol. iii. c. iii. p. 120.
  [A phenicopteros is a flamingo.]
[13] Id. p. 121.   [14] Id. p. 141.

'Through their passion for men, their mutable temper, their want of settled affection, and their perverse nature, let them be guarded in this world ever so well, they soon become alienated from their husbands.'[15]

This character, if true, probably proceeded from their never being allowed the smallest degree of liberty,[16] and from the state of degradation to which they were reduced by the practice of polygamy; but however this may be, such passages tend strongly to show that illicit intercourse between the sexes was frequent, notwithstanding the laws against adultery. These laws are noticed as not relating to the wives of public dancers or singers, or of such base men as lived by the intrigues of their wives;[17] a proof that these characters were not uncommon, and were to a certain degree permitted. Add to this, that the practice of polygamy[18] among the rich would sometimes render it difficult for the lower classes of people to obtain wives; and this difficulty would probably fall particularly hard on those who were reduced to the condition of slaves.

From all these circumstances combined, it seems probable that among the checks to population in India the preventive check would have its share; but from the prevailing habits and opinions of the people, there is reason to believe that the tendency to early marriages was still always predominant and in general prompted every person to enter into this state who could look forward to the slightest chance of being able to maintain a family. The natural consequence of this was that the lower classes of people were reduced to extreme poverty, and were compelled to adopt the most frugal and scanty mode of subsistence. This frugality was still further increased, and extended in some degree to the higher classes of society, by its being considered as an eminent virtue.[19] The population would thus be pressed hard against the limits of the means of subsistence, and the food of the country would be meted out to the major part of the people in the smallest shares that could support life. In such a state of things, every failure in the crops from unfavourable seasons would be felt most severely; and India, as might be expected, has in all ages been subject to the most dreadful famines.

A part of the ordinances of Menu is expressly dedicated to the consideration of times of distress, and instructions are given to the different classes respecting their conduct during these periods. Brahmens pining with hunger and want are frequently mentioned,[20] and certain ancient and virtuous characters are described, who had done impure and unlawful acts, but who

---

[15] Sir William Jones's Works, vol. iii. c. ix. p. 337.   [16] Id. c. v. p. 219.
[17] Id. c. viii. p. 325.
[18] Id. c. ix. p. 346, 347.   [19] Id. c. iii. p. 133.
[20] Id. c. iv. p. 165. c. x. p. 397.

were considered by the legislator as justified, on account of the extremities to which they were reduced.

'Ajígarta, dying with hunger, was going to destroy his own son by selling him for some cattle; yet he was guilty of no crime, for he only sought a remedy against famishing.'

'Vámadéva, who well knew right and wrong, was by no means rendered impure, though desirous, when oppressed by hunger, of eating the flesh of dogs.'[21]

'Viswámitra too, than whom none knew better the distinctions between virtue and vice, resolved, when he was perishing with hunger, to eat the haunch of a dog, which he had received from a *Chandála*.'[22]

If these great and virtuous men of the highest class, whom all persons were under the obligation of assisting, could be reduced to such extremities, we may easily conjecture what must have been the sufferings of the lowest class.

Such passages clearly prove the existence of seasons of the most severe distress, at the early period when these ordinances were composed; and we have reason to think that they have occurred at irregular intervals ever since. One of the Jesuits says that it is impossible for him to describe the misery to which he was witness, during the two years famine in 1737 and 1738;[23] but the description which he gives of it, and of the mortality which it occasioned, is sufficiently dreadful without further detail. Another Jesuit, speaking more generally, says: 'Every year we baptize a thousand children, whom their parents can no longer feed, or who, being likely to die, are sold to us by their mothers in order to get rid of them.'[24]

The positive checks to population would of course fall principally upon the Sudrá class, and those still more miserable beings who are the outcasts of all the classes, and are not even suffered to live within the towns.[25]

On this part of the population the epidemics which are the consequences of indigence and bad nourishment, and the mortality among young children, would necessarily make great ravages; and thousands of these unhappy wretches would probably be swept off in a period of scarcity, before any considerable degree of want had reached the middle classes of the society. The Abbé Raynal says, on what authority I know not, that when the crops of rice fail, the huts of these poor outcasts are set on fire, and the flying inhabitants shot by the proprietors of the grounds, that they may not consume any part of the produce.[26]

---

[21] [Malthus cut this quotation, which reads:

    ... eating the flesh of dogs for the preservation of his life ...

[22] Id. c. x. p. 397, 398.   [23] Lettres Edif. tom. xiv. p. 178.   [24] Id. p. 284.

[25] Sir William Jones's Works, vol. iii. c. x. p. 390.

[26] Hist. des Indes, tom. i. liv. i. p. 97. 8vo. 10 vols. Paris, 1795.

The difficulty of rearing a family, even among the middle and higher classes of society, or the fear of sinking from their caste, has driven the people in some parts of India to adopt the most cruel expedients to prevent a numerous offspring. In a tribe on the frontiers of Junapore, a district of the province of Benares, the practice of destroying female infants has been fully substantiated. The mothers were compelled to starve them. The reason that the people gave for this cruel practice was the great expense of procuring suitable matches for their daughters. One village only furnished an exception to this rule, and in this village several old maids were living. It will naturally occur that the race could not be continued upon this principle; but it appeared that the particular exceptions to the general rule, and the intermarriages with other tribes, were sufficient for this purpose. Our East India Company obliged these people to enter into an engagement not to continue this inhuman practice.[27]

On the coast of Malabar the Nayrs do not enter into regular marriages, and the right of inheritance and succession rests in the mother of the brother, or otherwise goes to the sister's son, the father of the child being always considered as uncertain.

Among the Brahmens, when there are more brothers than one, only the elder or eldest of them marries. The brothers who thus maintain celibacy cohabit with Nayr women without marriage in the way of the Nayrs. If the eldest brother has not a son, then the next brother marries.

Among the Nayrs, it is the custom for one Nayr woman to have attached to her two males, or four, or perhaps more.

The lower casts, such as carpenters, ironsmiths, and others, have fallen into the imitation of their superiors, with this difference, that the joint concern in one woman is confined to brothers and male relations by blood, to the end that no alienation may take place in the course of the succession.[28]

Montesquieu takes notice of this custom of the Nayrs on the coast of Malabar, and accounts for it on the supposition that it was adopted in order to weaken the family ties of this cast that, as soldiers, they might be more at liberty to follow the calls of their profession; but I should think that it originated, more probably, in a fear of the poverty arising from a large family, particularly as the custom seems to have been adopted by the other classes.[29]

In Tibet, according to Turner's late account of it, a custom of this kind prevails generally. Without pretending absolutely to determine the question of its origin, Mr. Turner leans to the supposition that it arose from the fear of

---

[27] Asiatic Researches, vol. iv. p. 354. [In 1817 (Vol. I, p. 282) Malthus changed *Our* to 'The East India Company ...'

[28] Asiatic Researches, vol. v. p. 14. [For the correct references, see ASIATIC RESEARCHES in the Alphabetical List.]

[29] Esprit des Loix, liv. xvi. c. 5.

a population too great for an unfertile country. From travelling much in the east, he had probably been led to observe the effects necessarily resulting from an overflowing population, and is in consequence one among the very few writers who see these effects in their true light. He expresses himself very strongly on this subject, and, in reference to the custom above mentioned, says: 'It certainly appears that a superabundant population in an unfertile country must be the greatest of all calamities, and produce eternal warfare or eternal want. Either the most active and the most able part of the community must be compelled to emigrate, and to become soldiers of fortune or merchants of chance; or else, if they remain at home, be liable to fall a prey to famine, in consequence of some accidental failure in their scanty crops. By thus linking whole families together in the matrimonial yoke, the too rapid increase of population was perhaps checked, and an alarm prevented, capable of pervading the most fertile region upon the earth, and of giving birth to the most inhuman and unnatural practice, in the richest, the most productive, and the most populous country in the world. I allude to the empire of China, where a mother, not foreseeing the means of raising or providing for a numerous family, exposes her new-born infant to perish in the fields; a crime, however odious, by no means, I am assured, unfrequent.'[30]

In almost every country of the globe individuals are impelled, by considerations of private interest, to habits which tend to repress the natural increase of population; but Tibet is perhaps the only country where these habits are universally encouraged by the government, and where to repress, rather than to encourage population, seems to be a public object.

In the first career of life the Bootea is recommended to distinction by a continuance in a state of celibacy, as any matrimonial contract proves almost a certain hindrance to his rise in rank or his advancement to offices of political importance. Population is thus opposed by the two powerful bars of ambition and religion; and the higher orders of men, entirely engrossed by political or ecclesiastical duties, leave to the husbandman and labourer, to those who till the fields and live by their industry, the exclusive charge of propagating the species.[31]

Hence religious retirement is frequent,[32] and the number of monasteries and nunneries is considerable. The strictest laws exist to prevent a woman from accidentally passing a night within the limits of the one, or a man within those of the other; and a regulation is framed, completely to obviate abuse, and establish respect towards the sacred orders of both sexes.

---

[30] Turner's Embassy to Tibet, part ii. c. x. p. 351. [In 1817 (Vol I, p. 284) Malthus began this paragraph:
    In Tibet, according to Turner's account of that country, a custom of this kind ...
[31] Id. part ii. c. i. p. 172.   [32] Ibid.

The nation is divided into two distinct and separate classes, those who carry on the business of the world, and those who hold intercourse with heaven. No interference of the laity ever interrupts the regulated duties of the clergy. The latter, by mutual compact, take charge of all spiritual concerns; and the former, by their labours, enrich and populate the state.[33]

But, even among the laity, the business of population goes on very coldly. All the brothers of a family, without any restriction of age or of numbers, associate their fortunes with one female, who is chosen by the eldest, and considered as the mistress of the house; and whatever may be the profits of their several pursuits, the result flows into the common store.[34]

The number of husbands is not, apparently, defined, or restricted within any limits. It sometimes happens that in a small family there is but one male; and the number, Mr. Turner says, may seldom exceed that which a native of rank at Teshoo Loomboo pointed out to him in a family resident in the neighbourhood, in which five brothers were then living together very happily with one female under the same connubial compact. Nor is this sort of league confined to the lower ranks of people alone, it is found also frequently in the most opulent families.[35]

It is evident that this custom, combined with the celibacy of such a numerous body of ecclesiastics, must operate in the most powerful manner as a preventive check to population. Yet notwithstanding this excessive check it would appear, from Mr. Turner's account of the natural sterility of the soil, that the population is kept up to the level of the means of subsistence, and this seems to be confirmed by the number of beggars in Teshoo Loomboo. On these beggars, and the charity which feeds them, Mr. Turner's remark, though common, is yet so just and important that it cannot be too often repeated.

'Thus I unexpectedly discovered', he says, 'where I had constantly seen the round of life moving in a tranquil regular routine, a mass of indigence and idleness of which I had no idea. But yet it by no means surprised me, when I considered that wherever indiscriminate charity exists, it will never want objects on which to exercise its bounty, but will always attract expectants more numerous than it has the means to gratify. No human being can suffer want at Teshoo Loomboo. It is on this humane disposition that a multitude even of Musselmen, of a frame probably the largest and most robust in the world, place their reliance for the mere maintenance of a feeble life; and besides these, I am informed, that no less than three hundred Hindoos, Goseins, and Sunniasses, are daily fed at this place by the Lama's bounty.'[36]

---

[33] Turner's Embassy, part ii. c. viii. p. 312.   [34] Id. c. x. p. 348, 350.   [35] Id. p. 349.
[36] Id. c. ix. p. 330. ['Teshoo Loomboo', now spelt Tashi-Ihunpo, was the seat of a Lamaistic patriarch, the Hutukhtu: Lhasa was the seat of the Dalai Lama.]

CHAPTER XII

Of the Checks to Population in China and Japan

The account which has lately been given of the population of China is so extraordinary as to startle the faith of many readers, and tempt them to suppose, either that some accidental error must have crept into the calculations from an ignorance of the language, or that the mandarin who gave Sir George Staunton the information must have been prompted by a national pride (which is common everywhere, but is particularly remarkable in China) to exaggerate the power and resources of his country. It must be allowed that neither of these circumstances is very improbable; at the same time it will be found that the statement of Sir George Staunton does not very essentially differ from other accounts of good authority; and so far from involving any contradiction, is rendered probable by a reference to those descriptions of the fertility of China in which all the writers who have visited the country agree.

According to Duhalde, in the poll made at the beginning of the reign of Kang-hi, there were found 11 052 872 families, and 59 788 364 men able to bear arms; and yet, neither the princes, nor the officers of the court, nor the mandarins, nor the soldiers who had served and been discharged; nor the literati, the licentiates, the doctors, the bonzas, nor young persons under twenty years of age; nor the great multitudes living either on the sea, or on rivers in barks, are comprehended in this number.[1]

The proportion which the number of men of a military age bears to the whole population of any country is generally estimated as 1 to 4. If we multiply 59 788 364 by 4, the result will be 239 153 456; but in the general calculations on this subject, a youth is considered as capable of bearing arms before he is twenty. We ought therefore to have multiplied by a higher number. The exceptions to the poll seem to include almost all the superior classes of society, and a very greater number among the lower. When all these circumstances are taken into consideration, the whole population, according to Duhalde, will not appear to fall very short of the 333 000 000 mentioned by Sir George Staunton.[2]

---

[1] Duhalde's Hist. of China, 2 vols. folio, 1738. vol. i. p. 244.
[2] Embassy to China, vol. ii. Appen. p. 615. 4to.

The small number of families in proportion to the number of persons able to bear arms, which is a striking part of this statement of Duhalde, is accounted for by a custom noticed by Sir George Staunton as general in China. In the inclosure belonging to one dwelling, he observes that a whole family of three generations, with all their respective wives and children, will frequently be found. One small room is made to serve for the individuals of each family, sleeping in different beds, divided only by mats hanging from the ceiling. One common room is used for eating.[3] In China there is, besides, a prodigious number of slaves,[4] who will of course be reckoned as part of the families to which they belong. These two circumstances may perhaps be sufficient to account for what at first appears to be a contradiction in the statement.

To account for this population, it will not be necessary to recur to the supposition of Montesquieu, that the climate of China is in any peculiar manner favourable to the production of children, and that the women are more prolific than in any other part of the world.[5] The causes which have principally contributed to produce this effect appear to be the following:

First, the excellence of the natural soil, and its advantageous position in the warmest parts of the temperate zone, a situation the most favourable to the productions of the earth. Duhalde has a long chapter on the plenty which reigns in China, in which he observes that almost all that other kingdoms afford may be found in China, and that China produces an infinite number of things which are to be found nowhere else. This plenty, he says, may be attributed as well to the depth of the soil as to the painful industry of its inhabitants, and the great number of lakes, rivers, brooks and canals wherewith the country is watered.[6]

Secondly, the very great encouragement that from the beginning of the monarchy has been given to agriculture, which has directed the labours of the people to the production of the greatest possible quantity of human subsistence. Duhalde says that what makes these people undergo such incredible fatigues in cultivating the earth is not barely their private interest, but rather the veneration paid to agriculture, and the esteem which the emperors themselves have always had for it, from the commencement of the monarchy. One emperor of the highest reputation was taken from the plough to sit on the throne. Another found out the art of draining water from several low countries, which were till then covered with it, of conveying it in canals to the sea, and of using these canals to render the soil fruitful.[7] He besides wrote several books on the manner of cultivating land, by dunging, tilling, and watering it. Many other emperors expressed their zeal for this art and made

---

[3] Embassy to China, vol. ii. Appen. p. 155.
[4] Duhalde's China, vol. i. p. 278.   [5] Esprit des Loix, liv. viii. c. xxi.
[6] Duhalde's China, vol. i. p. 314.   [7] Id. p. 274.

laws to promote it; but none raised its esteem to a higher pitch than Ven-ti, who reigned 179 years before Christ. This prince, perceiving that his country was ruined by wars, resolved to engage his subjects to cultivate their lands, by the example of ploughing with his own hands the land belonging to his palace, which obliged all the ministers and great men of his court to do the same.[8]

A great festival, of which this is thought to be the origin, is solemnized every year in all the cities of China on the day that the sun enters the fifteenth degree of Aquarius, which the Chinese consider as the beginning of their spring. The emperor goes himself in a solemn manner to plough a few ridges of land, in order to animate the husbandman by his own example; and the mandarins of every city perform the same ceremony.[9] Princes of the blood, and other illustrious persons, hold the plough after the emperor, and the ceremony is preceded by the spring sacrifice which the emperor, as chief pontiff, offers to Shang-ti to procure plenty in favour of his people.

The reigning emperor, in the time of Duhalde, celebrated this festival with extraordinary solemnity, and in other respects shewed an uncommon regard for husbandmen. To encourage them in their labours, he ordered the governors of all the cities to send him notice every year of the person in this profession, in their respective districts, who was most remarkable for his application to agriculture, for unblemished reputation, for preserving union in his own family, and peace with his neighbours, and for his frugality and aversion to all extravagance.[10] The mandarins in their different provinces encourage with honours the vigilant cultivator, and stigmatize with disgrace the man whose lands are neglected.[11]

In a country in which the whole of the government is of the patriarchal kind, and the emperor is venerated as the father of his people and the fountain of instruction, it is natural to suppose that these high honours paid to agriculture would have a powerful effect. In the gradations of rank, they have raised the husbandman above the merchant or mechanic,[12] and the great object of ambition among the lower classes is to become possessed of a small portion of land. The number of manufacturers bears but a very inconsiderable proportion to that of husbandmen in China;[13] and the whole surface of the empire is, with trifling exceptions, dedicated to the production of food for man alone. There is no meadow, and very little pasture; neither are the fields cultivated in oats, beans or turnips for the support of cattle of any kind. Little land is taken up for roads, which are few and narrow, the chief communication being by water. There are no commons, or lands

---

[8] Duhalde's China, vol. i. p. 275.   [9] Id. p. 275.   [10] Id. p. 276.
[11] Lettres Edif. tom. xix. p. 132.
[12] Duhalde's China, vol. i. p. 272.   [13] Embassy to China, Staunton, vol. ii. p. 544.

suffered to lie waste by the neglect or the caprice, or for the sport, of great proprietors. No arable land lies fallow. The soil, under a hot and fertilizing sun, yields annually, in most instances, double crops, in consequence of adapting the culture to the soil, and of supplying its defects by mixture with other earths, by manure, by irrigation, and by careful and judicious industry of every kind. The labour of man is little diverted from that industry to minister to the luxuries of the opulent and powerful, or in employments of no real use. Even the soldiers of the Chinese army, except during the short intervals of the guards which they are called upon to mount, or the exercises or other occasional services which they perform, are mostly employed in agriculture. The quantity of subsistence is increased also by converting more species of animals and vegetables to that purpose than is usual in other countries.[14]

This account, which is given by Sir George Staunton, is confirmed by Duhalde, and the other Jesuits, who agree in describing the persevering industry of the Chinese, in manuring, cultivating, and watering their lands, and their success in producing a prodigious quantity of human subsistence.[15] The effect of such a system of agriculture on population must be obvious.

Lastly, the extraordinary encouragements that have been given to marriage, which have caused the immense produce of the country to be divided into very small shares, and have consequently rendered China more populous in proportion to its means of subsistence, than perhaps any other country in the world.

The Chinese acknowledge two ends in marriage,[16] the first is that of perpetuating the sacrifices in the temple of their fathers; and the second the multiplication of the species. Duhalde says that the veneration and submission of children to parents, which is the grand principle of their political government, continues even after death, and that the same duties are paid to them as if they were living. In consequence of these maxims, a father feels some sort of dishonour, and is not easy in his mind, if he do not marry off all his children; and an elder brother, though he inherit nothing from his father, must bring up the younger children, and marry them, lest the family should become extinct, and the ancestors be deprived of the honours and duties they are entitled to from their descendants.[17]

Sir George Staunton observes that whatever is strongly recommended, and generally practised, is at length considered as a kind of religious duty, and that the marriage union, as such, takes place in China wherever there is the least prospect of subsistence for a future family. This prospect, however,

---

[14] Embassy to China, Staunton, vol. ii. p. 545.
[15] Duhalde, chapter on agriculture, vol. i. p. 272. chapter on plenty, p. 314.
[16] Lettres Edif. et Curieuses, tom. xxiii. p. 448.   [17] Duhalde's China, vol. i. p. 303.

is not always realized, and the children are then abandoned by the wretched authors of their being;[18] but even this permission given to parents thus to expose their offspring tends undoubtedly to facilitate marriage and encourage population. Contemplating this extreme resource beforehand, less fear is entertained of entering into the married state, and the parental feelings will always step forwards to prevent a recurrence to it, except under the most dire necessity. Marriage with the poor is, besides, a measure of prudence, because the children, particularly the sons, are bound to maintain their parents.[19]

The effect of these encouragements to marriage among the rich is to subdivide property, which has in itself a strong tendency to promote population. In China there is less inequality in the fortunes than in the conditions of men. Property in land has been divided into very moderate parcels, by the successive distribution of the possessions of every father equally among his sons. It rarely happens that there is but one son to enjoy the whole property of his deceased parents; and, from the general prevalence of early marriages, this property would not often be increased by collateral succession.[20] These causes constantly tend to level wealth, and few succeed to such an accumulation of it as to render them independent of any efforts of their own for its increase. It is a common remark among the Chinese that fortunes seldom continue considerable in the same family beyond the third generation.[21]

The effect of the encouragements to marriage on the poor is to keep the reward of labour as low as possible, and consequently to press them down to the most abject state of poverty. Sir George Staunton observes, that the price of labour is generally found to bear as small a proportion everywhere to the rate demanded for provisions as the common people can suffer; and that notwithstanding the advantage of living together in large families, like soldiers in a mess, and the exercise of the greatest economy in the management of these messes, they are reduced to the use of vegetable food, with a very rare and scanty relish of any animal substance.[22]

Duhalde, after describing the painful industry of the Chinese, and the shifts and contrivances, unknown in other countries, to which they have recourse in order to gain a subsistence, says, 'yet it must be owned, that notwithstanding the great sobriety and industry of the inhabitants of China, the prodigious number of them occasions a great deal of misery. There are some so poor, that being unable to supply their children with common necessaries, they expose them in the streets. ... In the great cities, such as Pekin and Canton, this shocking sight is very common.'[23]

---

[18] Embassy to China, vol. ii. p. 157.   [19] Ibid.
[20] Id. p. 151.
[21] Id. p. 152.   [22] Id. p. 156.   [23] Duhalde's China, vol. i. p. 277.

The Jesuit Premare, writing to a friend of the same society, says: 'I will tell you a fact, which may appear to be a paradox,[24] but is nevertheless strictly true. It is, that the richest and most flourishing empire of the world is notwithstanding, in one sense, the poorest and the most miserable of all. The country, however extensive and fertile it may be, is not sufficient to support its inhabitants. Four times as much territory would be necessary to place them at their ease. In Canton there is, without exaggeration, more than a million of souls, and in a town three or four leagues distant, a still greater number. Who then can count the inhabitants of this province? But what is this to the whole empire, which contains fifteen great provinces all equally peopled? To how many millions would such a calculation amount? A third part of this infinite population would hardly find sufficient rice to support itself properly.

'It is well known that extreme misery impels people to the most dreadful excesses. A spectator in China, who examines things closely, will not be surprised that mothers destroy or expose many of their children; that parents sell their daughters for a trifle; that the people should be interested;[25] and that there should be such a number of robbers. The surprise is that nothing still more dreadful should happen, and that in the times of famine, which are here but too frequent, millions of people should perish with hunger, without having recourse to those dreadful extremities of which we read examples in the histories of Europe.

'It cannot be said in China, as in Europe, that the poor are idle, and might gain a subsistence if they would work. The labours and efforts of these poor people are beyond conception. A Chinese will pass whole days in digging the earth, sometimes up to his knees in water, and in the evening is happy to eat a little spoonful of rice, and to drink the insipid water in which it was boiled. This is all that they have in general.'[26]

A great part of this account is repeated in Duhalde, and, even allowing for some exaggeration, it shews, in a strong point of view, to what degree population has been forced in China, and the wretchedness which has been the consequence of it. The population which has arisen naturally from the fertility of the soil, and the encouragements to agriculture, may be considered as genuine and desirable; but all that has been added by the encouragements to marriage has not only been an addition of so much pure misery in itself, but has completely interrupted the happiness which the rest might have enjoyed.

---

[24] Lettres Edif. et Curieuses, tom. xvi. p. 394.

[25] [This is Malthus's direct translation of the French *intéressé*, which here means covetous, mercenary, or miserly.]

[26] Lettres Edif. et Curieuses, tom. xvi. p. 394. et seq.

The territory of China is estimated at about eight times the territory of France.[27] Taking the population of France only at 26 millions, eight times that number will give 208 000 000; and when the three powerful causes of population, which have been stated, are considered, it will not appear incredible that the population of China should be to the population of France, according to their respective superficies, as 333 to 208, or a little more than 3 to 2.

The natural tendency to increase is everywhere so great, that it will generally be easy to account for the height at which the population is found in any country. The more difficult, as well as the more interesting part of the inquiry, is to trace the immediate causes which stop its further progress. The procreative power would, with as much facility, double in twenty-five years the population of China, as that of any of the states of America; but we know that it cannot do this, from the palpable inability of the soil to support such an additional number. What then becomes of this mighty power in China? and what are the kinds of restraint, and the forms of premature death, which keep the population down to the level of the means of subsistence?

Notwithstanding the extraordinary encouragements to marriage in China, we should perhaps be led into an error if we were to suppose that the preventive check to population does not operate. Duhalde says that the number of bonzas is considerably above a million, of which there are two thousand unmarried at Pekin, besides three hundred and fifty thousand more in their temples established in different places by the emperor's patents, and that the literary bachelors alone are about ninety thousand.[28]

The poor, though they would probably always marry when the slightest prospect opened to them of being able to support a family and, from the permission of infanticide, would run great risks in this respect; yet they would undoubtedly be deterred from entering into this state under the certainty of being obliged to expose all their children, or to sell themselves and families as slaves; and from the extreme poverty of the lower classes of people, such a certainty would often present itself. But it is among the slaves themselves, of which, according to Duhalde, the misery in China produces a prodigious multitude, that the preventive check to population principally operates. A man sometimes sells his son, and even himself and wife, at a very moderate price. The common mode is to mortgage themselves with a condition of redemption, and a great number of men and maid servants are thus bound in a family.[29] Hume, in speaking of the practice of slavery among the ancients,

---

[27] Embassy to China, Staunton, vol. ii. p. 546. [28] Duhalde's China, vol. i. p. 244.

[29] Id. p. 278. La misere et le grand nombre d'habitans de l'empire y causent cette multitude prodigieuse d'esclaves: presque tous les valets, et generalement toutes les filles de service d'une maison sont esclaves. Lettres Edif. tom. xix. p. 145. [This tremendous number of

remarks very justly that it will generally be cheaper to buy a full grown slave than to rear up one from a child. This observation appears to be particularly applicable to the Chinese. All writers agree in mentioning the frequency of the dearths in China; and, during these periods, it is probable that slaves would be sold in great numbers for little more than a bare maintenance. It could very rarely therefore answer to the master of a family to encourage his slaves to breed; and we may suppose, in consequence, that a great part of the servants in China, as in Europe, remain unmarried.

The check to population arising from a vicious intercourse with the sex does not appear to be very considerable in China. The women are said to be modest and reserved, and adultery is rare. Concubinage is however generally practised, and in the large towns public women are registered; but their number is not great, being proportioned, according to Sir George Staunton, to the small number of unmarried persons, and of husbands absent from their families.[30]

The positive checks to population from disease, though considerable, do not appear to be so great as might be expected. The climate is in general extremely healthy. One of the missionaries goes so far as to say that plagues or epidemic disorders are not seen once in a century;[31] but this is undoubtedly an error, as they are mentioned by others as if they were by no means so infrequent. In some instructions to mandarins relating to the burying of the poor, who have in general no regular places of sepulture, it is observed that when epidemic diseases prevail the roads are found covered with bodies sufficient to infect the air to a great distance;[32] and the expression of years of contagion[33] occurs soon after it, in a manner which seems to imply that they are not uncommon. On the first and fifteenth day of every month the mandarins assemble, and give their people a long discourse, wherein every governor acts the part of a father who instructs his family.[34] In one of these discourses which Duhalde produces, the following passage occurs: 'Beware of those years which happen from time to time, when epidemic distempers, joined to a scarcity of corn, make all places desolate. Your duty is then to have compassion on your fellow citizens, and assist them with whatever you can spare.'[35]

It is probable that the epidemics, as is usually the case, fall severely on the children. One of the Jesuits, speaking of the number of infants whom the poverty of their parents condemns to death the moment that they are born,

---

slaves is due to the extremes of poverty and the very large population of the empire; almost all the men-servants in a household are slaves, as are usually all the maid-servants.]

[30] Embassy to China, vol. ii. p. 157.   [31] Lettres Edif. tom. xxii. p. 187.
[32] Id. tom. xix. p. 126.
[33] Id. p. 127.   [34] Duhalde's China, vol. i. p. 254.
[35] Id. p. 256.

writes thus: 'There is seldom a year in which the churches at Pekin do not reckon five or six thousand of these children purified by the waters of baptism. This harvest is more or less abundant according to the number of catechists which we can maintain. If we had a sufficient number, their cares need not be confined alone to the dying infants that are exposed. There would be other occasions for them to exercise their zeal, particularly at certain times of the year, when the small-pox or epidemic disorders carry off an incredible number of children.'[36] It is indeed almost impossible to suppose that the extreme indigence of the lower classes of people should not produce diseases, likely to be fatal to a considerable part of those children whom their parents might attempt to rear in spite of every difficulty.

Respecting the number of infants which are actually exposed, it is difficult to form the slightest guess; but, if we believe the Chinese writers themselves, the practice must be very common. Attempts have been made at different times by the government to put a stop to it, but always without success. In a book of instructions before alluded to, written by a mandarin celebrated for his humanity and wisdom, a proposal is made for the establishment of a foundling hospital in his district, and an account is given of some ancient establishments of the same kind,[37] which appear to have fallen into disuse. In this book, the frequency of the exposure of children, and the dreadful poverty which prompts it, are particularly described. We see, he says, people so poor that they cannot furnish the nourishment necessary for their own children. It is on this account that they expose so great a number. In the metropolis, in the capitals of the provinces, and in the places of the greatest commerce, their number is the most considerable; but many are found in parts that are less frequented, and even in the country. As the houses in towns are more crowded together, the practice is more obvious; but everywhere these poor unfortunate infants have need of assistance.[38]

In the same work, part of an edict to prevent the drowning of children runs thus: 'When the tender offspring just produced is thrown without pity into the waves, can it be said that the mother has given or that the child has received life, when it is lost as soon as it is begun to be enjoyed? The poverty of the parents is the cause of this crime. They have hardly enough to support themselves, much less are they able to pay a nurse and provide for the expenses necessary for the support of their children. This drives them to despair, and not being able to bring themselves to suffer two people to die that one may live, the mother, to preserve the life of her husband, consents to sacrifice her child. It costs much, however, to the parental feelings; but the resolution is ultimately taken, and they think that they are justified in disposing of the life of their child to prolong their own. If they exposed their

---

[36] Lettres Edif. tom. xix. p. 100.   [37] Id. p. 110.   [38] Id. p. 111.

children in a secret place, the babe might work upon their compassion with its cries. What do they do then? They throw it into the current of the river, that they may lose sight of it immediately, and take from it at once all chance of life.'[39]

Such writings appear to be most authentic documents respecting the general prevalence of infanticide.

Sir George Staunton has stated, from the best information which he could collect, that the number of children exposed annually at Pekin is about two thousand;[40] but it is highly probable that the number varies extremely from year to year, and depends very much upon seasons of plenty or seasons of scarcity. After any great epidemic or destructive famine, the number is probably very small; it is natural that it should increase gradually on the return to a crowded population; and it is without doubt the greatest when an unfavourable season takes place, at a period in which the average produce is already insufficient to support the overflowing multitude.

These unfavourable seasons do not appear to be infrequent, and the famines which follow them are perhaps the most powerful of all the positive checks to the Chinese population; though at some periods the checks from wars and internal commotions have not been inconsiderable.[41] In the annals of the Chinese monarchs, famines are often mentioned;[42] and it is not probable that they would find a place among the most important events and revolutions of the empire, if they were not desolating and destructive to a great degree.

One of the Jesuits remarks that the occasions when the mandarins pretend to show the greatest compassion for the people are when they are apprehensive of a failure in the crops, either from drought, from excessive rains, or from some other accident, such as a multitude of locusts, which sometimes overwhelms certain provinces.[43] The causes here enumerated are probably those which principally contribute to the failure of the harvests in China; and the manner in which they are mentioned seems to show that they are not uncommon.

Meares speaks of violent hurricanes, by which harvests are dissipated, and a famine follows. From a similar cause, he says, accompanied by excessive drought, a most dreadful dearth prevailed in 1787 throughout all the southern provinces of China, by which an incredible number of people perished. It was no uncommon thing at Canton to see the famished wretch breathing his last, while mothers thought it a duty to destroy their infant

---

[39] Lettres Edif. tom. xix. p. 124.   [40] Embassy to China, vol. ii. p. 159.
[41] Annals of the Chinese Monarchs. Duhalde's China, vol. i. p. 136.
[42] Ibid.   [43] Lettres Edif. tom. xix. p. 154.

children, and the young to give the stroke of fate to the aged, to save them from the agonies of such a dilatory death.[44]

The Jesuit Parennim, writing to a member of the Royal Academy of Sciences, says, 'another thing that you can scarcely believe is that dearths should be so frequent in China',[45] and in the conclusion of his letter he remarks that if famine did not, from time to time, thin the immense number of inhabitants which China contains, it would be impossible for her to live in peace.[46] The causes of these frequent famines he endeavours to investigate, and begins by observing, very justly, that in a time of dearth China can obtain no assistance from her neighbours, and must necessarily draw the whole of her resources from her own provinces.[47] He then describes the delays and artifices which often defeat the emperor's intentions to assist from the public granaries those parts of the country which are the most distressed. When a harvest fails in any province, either from excessive drought or a sudden inundation, the great mandarins have recourse to the public granaries; but often find them empty, owing to the dishonesty of the inferior mandarins who have the charge of them. Examinations and researches are then made, and an unwillingness prevails to inform the court of such disagreeable intelligence. Memorials are however at length presented. These memorials pass through many hands, and do not reach the emperor till after many days. The great officers of state are then ordered to assemble, and to deliberate on the means of relieving the misery of the people. Declarations full of expressions of compassion for the people are in the meantime published throughout the empire. The resolution of the tribunal is at length made known; but numberless other ceremonies delay its execution; while those who are suffering have time to die with hunger before the remedy arrives. Those who do not wait for this last extremity crawl as well as they can into other districts, where they hope to get support, but leave the greatest part of their number dead on the road.[48]

If, when a dearth occurs, the court do not make some attempt to relieve the people, small parties of plunderers soon collect, and their numbers increase by degrees, so as to interrupt the tranquillity of the province. On this account numerous orders are always given, and movements are continually taking place, to amuse the people till the famine is over; and as the motives to relieve the people are generally rather reasons of state than genuine compassion, it is not probable that they should be relieved at the time, and in the manner, that their wants require.[49]

The last cause of famine which is mentioned in this investigation, and on

---

[44] Meares's Voyage, ch. vii. p. 92.   [45] Lettres Edif. et Curieuses, tom. xxii. p. 174.
[46] Id. p. 186.
[47] Id. p. 175.   [48] Id. p. 180.   [49] Id. p. 187.

which the writer lays considerable stress, is the very great consumption of grain in making spirits;[50] but in stating this as a cause of famine, he has evidently fallen into a very gross error; yet, in the Abbé Grosier's general description of China, this error has been copied, and the cause above mentioned has been considered as one of the grand sources of the evil.[51] But,'. in reality, the whole tendency of this cause is in a contrary direction. The consumption of corn in any other way but that of necessary food checks the population before it arrives at the utmost limits of subsistence; and as the grain may be withdrawn from this particular use in the time of a scarcity, a public granary is thus opened, richer probably than could have been formed by any other means. When such a consumption has been once established, and has become permanent, its effect is exactly as if a piece of land with all the people upon it were removed from the country. The rest of the people would certainly be precisely in the same state as they were before, neither better nor worse in years of average plenty; but in a time of dearth the produce of this land would be returned to them, without the mouths to help them to eat it. China without her distilleries would certainly be more populous; but on a failure of the seasons, would have still less resource than she has at present, and as far as the magnitude of the cause would operate, would in consequence be more subject to famines, and those famines would be more severe.

The state of Japan resembles in so many respects that of China, that a particular consideration of it would lead into too many repetitions. Montesquieu attributes its populousness to the birth of a great number of females;[52] but the principal cause of this populousness is, without doubt, as in China, the persevering industry of the natives, directed, as it has always been, principally to agriculture.

In reading the preface to Thunberg's account of Japan, it would seem extremely difficult to trace the checks to the population of a country, the inhabitants of which are said to live in such happiness and plenty; but the continuation of his own work contradicts the impression of his preface; and in the valuable history of Japan by Kaempfer these checks are sufficiently obvious. In the extracts from two historical chronicles published in Japan, which he produces,[53] a very curious account is given of the different mortalities, plagues, famines, bloody wars, and other causes of destruction which have occurred since the commencement of these records. The Japanese are distinguished from the Chinese in being much more warlike,

---

[50] Lettres Edif. tom. xxii. p. 184.   [51] Vol. i. b. iv. c. iii. p. 396. 8vo. Eng. tran.

[52] Liv. xxiii. c. xii. It is surprising that Montesquieu, who appears sometimes to understand the subject of population, should at other times make such observations as this.

[53] Book ii.

seditious, dissolute, and ambitious; and it would appear, from Kaempfer's account, that the check to population from infanticide, in China, is balanced by the greater dissoluteness of manners with regard to the sex, and the greater frequency of wars and intestine commotions, which prevail in Japan. With regard to the positive checks to population from disease and famine, the two countries seem to be nearly on a level.

CHAPTER XIII

Of the Checks to Population among the Greeks

It has been generally allowed, and will not indeed admit of a doubt, that the more equal division of property among the Greeks and Romans, in the early period of their history, and the direction of their industry principally to agriculture, must have tended greatly to encourage population. Agriculture is not only, as Hume states,[1] that species of industry which is chiefly requisite to the subsistence of multitudes, but it is in fact the *sole* species by which multitudes can exist; and all the numerous arts and manufactures of the modern world, by which such numbers appear to be supported, have no tendency whatever to increase population, except so far as they tend to increase the quantity and to facilitate the distribution of the products of agriculture.

In countries where, from the operation of particular causes, property in land is divided into very large shares, these arts and manufactures are absolutely necessary to the existence of any considerable population. Without them, modern Europe would be unpeopled. But where property is divided into small shares, the same necessity for them does not exist. The division itself attains immediately one great object, that of distribution; and if the demand for men be constant, to fight the battles and support the power and dignity of the state, we may easily conceive that this motive, joined to the natural love of a family, might be sufficient to induce each proprietor to cultivate his land to the utmost, in order that it might support the greatest number of descendants.

The division of people into small states, during the early periods of Greek and Roman history, gave additional force to this motive. Where the number of free citizens did not perhaps exceed ten or twenty thousand, each individual would naturally feel the value of his own exertions; and knowing that the state to which he belonged, situated in the midst of envious and watchful rivals must depend chiefly on its population for its means of defence and safety, would be sensible, that in suffering the lands which were allotted to him to lie idle, he would be deficient in his duty as a citizen. These causes appear to have produced a considerable attention to agriculture, without the intervention of the artificial wants of mankind to encourage it. Population

---

[1] Essay xi. p. 467. 4to. edit.

followed the products of the earth with more than equal pace; and when the overflowing numbers were not taken off by the drains of war or disease, they found vent in frequent and repeated colonization. The necessity of these frequent colonizations, joined to the smallness of the states, which brought the subject immediately home to every thinking person, could not fail to point out to the legislators and philosophers of these times the strong tendency of population to increase beyond the means of subsistence; and they did not, like the statesmen and projectors of modern days, overlook the consideration of a question which so deeply affects the happiness and tranquillity of society. However we may justly execrate the barbarous expedients which they adopted to remove the difficulty, we cannot but give them some credit for their penetration in seeing it; and in being fully aware that, if not considered and obviated, it would be sufficient of itself to destroy their best planned schemes of republican equality and happiness.

The power of colonization is necessarily limited, and after the lapse of some time it might be extremely difficult, if not impossible, for a country, not particularly well situated for this purpose, to find a vacant spot proper for the settlement of its expatriated citizens. It was necessary, therefore, to consider of other resources besides colonization.

It is probable that the practice of infanticide had prevailed from the earliest ages in Greece. In the parts of America where it was found to exist, it appears to have originated from the extreme difficulty of rearing many children in a savage and wandering life, exposed to frequent famines and perpetual wars. We may easily conceive that it had a similar origin among the ancestors of the Greeks, or the native inhabitants of the country. And when Solon[2] permitted the exposing of children, it is probable that he only gave the sanction of law to a custom already prevalent.

In this permission he had, without doubt, two ends in view. First, that which is most obvious, the prevention of such an excessive population as would cause universal poverty and discontent; and, secondly, that of keeping the population up to the level of what the territory could support, by removing the terrors of too numerous a family and, consequently, the principal obstacle to marriage. From the effect of this practice in China, we have reason to think that it is better calculated to attain the latter than the former purpose. But if the legislator either did not see this, or if the barbarous habits of the times prompted parents invariably to prefer the murder of their children to poverty, the practice would appear to be very particularly calculated to answer both the ends in view, and to preserve, as completely and as constantly as the nature of the thing would permit, the requisite proportion between the food and the numbers which were to consume it.

---

[2] [See SOLON in the Alphabetical List.]

On the very great importance of attending to this proportion, and the evils that must necessarily result, of weakness on the one hand, or of poverty on the other, from the deficiency or the excess of population, the Greek political writers strongly insist; and propose in consequence various modes of maintaining the relative proportion desired.

Plato, in the republic which he considers in his books of *Laws*, limits the number of free citizens, and of habitations, to five thousand and forty; and this number he thinks may be preserved, if the father of every family choose one out of his sons for his successor to the lot of land which he has possessed, and disposing of his daughters in marriage according to law, distribute his other sons, if he have any, to be adopted by those citizens who are without children. But if the number of children upon the whole be either too great or too few, the magistrate is to take the subject particularly into his consideration, and to contrive so that the same number of five thousand and forty families should still be maintained. There are many modes, he thinks, of effecting this object. Procreation, when it goes on too fast, may be checked, or when it goes on too slow, may be encouraged, by the proper distribution of honours and marks of ignominy, and by the admonitions of the elders to prevent or promote it according to circumstances.[3]

In his philosophical *Republic*[4] he enters more particularly into this subject, and proposes that the most excellent among the men should be joined in marriage to the most excellent among the women, and the inferior citizens matched with the inferior females; and that the offspring of the first should be brought up, of the others, not. On certain festivals appointed by the laws, the young men and women who are betrothed are to be assembled, and joined together with solemn ceremonies. But the number of marriages is to be determined by the magistrates; that, taking into consideration the drains from wars, diseases, and other causes, they may preserve, as nearly as possible, such a proportion of citizens as will be neither too numerous nor too few, according to the resources and demands of the state. The children who are thus born from the most excellent of the citizens are to be carried to certain nurses destined to this office, inhabiting a separate part of the city; but those which are born from the inferior citizens, and any from the others which are imperfect in their limbs, are to be buried in some obscure and unknown place.

He next proceeds to consider the proper age for marriage, and determines it to be twenty for the women, and thirty for the men. Beginning at twenty, the woman is to bear children for the state till she is forty, and the man is to fulfil his duty in this respect from thirty to thirty-five. If a man produce a child into public either before or after this period, the action is to be

---

[3] Plato de Legibus, lib. v.   [4] Plato de Republicâ, lib. v.

considered in the same criminal and profane light as if he had produced one without the nuptial ceremonies, and instigated solely by incontinence. The same rule should hold, if a man who is of the proper age for procreation be connected with a woman who is also of the proper age, but without the ceremony of marriage by the magistrate; he is to be considered as having given to the state a spurious, profane, and incestuous offspring. When both sexes have passed the age assigned for presenting children to the state, Plato allows a great latitude of intercourse, but no child is to be brought to light. Should any infant by accident be born alive, it is to be exposed in the same manner as if the parents could not support it.[5]

From these passages it is evident that Plato fully saw the tendency of population to increase beyond the means of subsistence. His expedients for checking it are indeed execrable; but the expedients themselves, and the extent to which they were to be used, shew his conceptions of the magnitude of the difficulty. Contemplating, as he certainly must do in a small republic, a great proportional drain of people by wars; if he could still propose to destroy the children of all the inferior and less perfect citizens; to destroy also all that were born not within the prescribed ages and with the prescribed forms; to fix the age of marriage late, and after all to regulate the number of these marriages; his experience and his reasonings must have strongly pointed out to him the great power of the principle of increase, and the necessity of checking it.

Aristotle appears to have seen this necessity still more clearly. He fixes the proper age of marriage at thirty-seven for the men, and eighteen for the women; which must of course condemn a great number of women to celibacy, as there never can be so many men of thirty-seven as there are women of eighteen. Yet though he has fixed the age of marriage for the men at so late a period, he still thinks that there may be too many children, and proposes that the number allowed to each marriage should be regulated; and if any woman be pregnant after she has produced the prescribed number, that an abortion should be procured before the fœtus has life.

The period of procreating children for the state is to cease with the men at fifty-four or fifty-five, because the offspring of old men, as well as of men too young, is imperfect both in body and mind. When both sexes have passed the prescribed age, they are allowed to continue a connexion; but, as in Plato's republic, no child which may be the result is to be brought to light.[6]

In discussing the merits of the republic proposed by Plato in his books of laws, Aristotle is of opinion that he has by no means been sufficiently attentive to the subject of population, and accuses him of inconsistency in equalizing property without limiting the number of children. The laws on this subject,

---

[5] Plato de Repub. lib. v.   [6] Aristotelis Opera. De Repub. lib. vii. c. xvi.

Aristotle very justly observes, require to be much more definite and precise in a state where property is equalized than in others. Under ordinary governments an increase of population would only occasion a greater subdivision of landed property; whereas in such a republic the supernumeraries would be altogether destitute, because the lands, being reduced to equal and, as it were, elementary parts, would be incapable of further partition.[7]

He then remarks that it is necessary in all cases to regulate the proportion of children, that they may not exceed the proper number. In doing this, deaths and barrenness are of course to be taken into consideration. But, if, as in the generality of states, every person be left free to have as many children as he pleases, the necessary consequence must be poverty; and poverty is the mother of villainy and sedition. On this account Pheidon of Corinth, one of the most ancient writers on the subject of politics, introduced a regulation directly the reverse of Plato's, and limited population without equalizing possessions.[8]

Speaking afterwards of Phaleas of Chalcedon, who proposed, as a most salutary institution, to equalize wealth among the citizens, he adverts again to Plato's regulations respecting property, and observes that those who would thus regulate the extent of fortunes ought not to be ignorant that it is absolutely necessary at the same time to regulate the number of children. For if children multiply beyond the means of supporting them, the law will necessarily be broken, and families will be suddenly reduced from opulence to beggary – a revolution always dangerous to public tranquillity.[9]

It appears from these passages that Aristotle clearly saw that the strong tendency of the human race to increase, unless checked by strict and positive laws, was absolutely fatal to every system founded on equality of property; and there cannot surely be a stronger argument against any system of this kind than the necessity of such laws as Aristotle himself proposes.

From a remark which he afterwards makes respecting Sparta, it appears still more clearly that he fully understood the principle of population. From the improvidence of the laws relating to succession, the landed property in Sparta had been engrossed by a few, and the effect was greatly to diminish the populousness of the country. To remedy this evil, and to supply men for continual wars, the kings preceding Lycurgus had been in the habit of naturalizing strangers. It would have been much better however, according to Aristotle, to have increased the number of citizens by a nearer equalization

---

[7] De Repub. lib. ii. c. vi. Gillies's Aristotle, vol. ii. b. ii. p. 87. For the convenience of those who may not choose the trouble of consulting the original, I refer at the same time to Gillies's translation; but some passages he has wholly omitted, and of others he has not given the literal sense, his object being a free version.

[8] De Repub. lib. ii. c. vii. Gillies's Aristot. vol. ii. b. ii. p. 87.

[9] De Repub. lib. ii. c. vii. Gillies's Aristot. vol. ii. b. ii. p. 91.

of property. But the law relating to children was directly adverse to this improvement. The legislator wishing to have many citizens, had encouraged as much as possible the procreation of children. A man who had three sons was exempt from the night-watch, and he who had four enjoyed a complete immunity from all public burdens. But it is evident, as Aristotle most justly observes, that the birth of a great number of children, the division of the lands remaining the same, would necessarily cause only an accumulation of poverty.[10]

He here seems to see exactly the error, into which many other legislators besides Lycurgus have fallen, and to be fully aware that, to encourage the birth of children, without providing properly for their support, is to obtain a very small accession to the population of a country at the expense of a very great accession of misery.

The legislator of Crete[11] as well as Solon, Pheidon, Plato, and Aristotle, saw the necessity of checking population in order to prevent general poverty; and, as we must suppose that the opinions of such men, and the laws founded upon them, would have considerable influence, it is probable that the preventive check to increase, from later marriages and other causes, operated to a considerable degree among the free citizens of Greece.

For the positive checks to population, we need not look beyond the wars in which these small states were almost continually engaged, though we have an account of one wasting plague at least, in Athens; and Plato supposes the case of his republic being greatly reduced by disease.[12] Their wars were not only almost constant, but extremely bloody. In a small army, the whole of which would probably be engaged in close fight, a much greater number in proportion would be slain than in the large modern armies, a considerable part of which often remains untouched,[13] and as all the free citizens of these republics were generally employed as soldiers in every war, losses would be felt very severely, and would not appear to be very easily repaired.

---

[10] De Repub. lib. ii. c. ix. Gillies's Aristot. vol. ii. b. ii. p. 107.
[11] Aristot. de Repub. lib. ii. c. x. Gillies's Aristot. vol. ii. b. ii. p. 113.
[12] De legibus, lib. v.   [13] Hume, Essay xi. p. 451.

CHAPTER XIV

Of the Checks to Population among the Romans

The havoc made by war in the smaller states of Italy, particularly during the first struggles of the Romans for power, seems to have been still greater than in Greece. Wallace, in his dissertation on the numbers of mankind, after alluding to the multitudes which fell by the sword in these times, observes: 'On an accurate review of the history of the Italians during this period, we shall wonder how such vast multitudes could be raised as were engaged in those continual wars till Italy was entirely subdued.'[1] And Livy expresses his utter astonishment that the Volsci and Æqui, so often as they were conquered, should have been able to bring fresh armies into the field.[2] But these wonders will perhaps be sufficiently accounted for, if we suppose, what seems to be highly probable, that the constant drains from wars had introduced the habit of giving nearly full scope to the power of population; [3]●and that a much greater number of youths, in proportion to the whole people, were yearly rising into manhood, and becoming fit to bear arms, than is usual in other states not similarly circumstanced.●[3] It was without doubt the rapid influx of these supplies which enabled them, like the ancient Germans, to astonish future historians, by renovating in so extraordinary a manner their defeated and half-destroyed armies.

Yet there is reason to believe, that the practice of infanticide prevailed in Italy as well as in Greece from the earliest times. A law of Romulus forbad the exposing of children before they were three years old,[4] which implies that the custom of exposing them as soon as they were born had before prevailed. But this practice was of course never resorted to but when the drains from wars were insufficient to make room for the rising generation; and consequently, though it may be considered as one of the positive checks to the full power of increase, yet, in the actual state of things, it certainly contributed rather to promote than impede population.

---

[1] Dissertation, p. 62. 8vo. 1763, Edinburgh.   [2] Lib. vi. c. xii.
[3] [In 1826 (Vol. i, p. 243) this passage was altered:
    ... population; and that a much larger proportion of births, and of healthy children, were rising into manhood and becoming fit to bear arms ...
[4] Dionysius Halicarn. lib. ii. 15.

Among the Romans themselves, engaged as they were in incessant wars from the beginning of their republic to the end of it, many of which were dreadfully destructive, the positive check to population from this cause alone must have been enormously great. But this cause alone, great as it was, would never have occasioned that want of Roman citizens under the emperors, which prompted Augustus and Trajan to issue laws for the encouragement of marriage and of children, if other causes still more powerful in depopulation had not concurred.

When the equality of property, which had formerly prevailed in the Roman territory, had been destroyed by degrees, and the land had fallen into the hands of a few great proprietors, the citizens who were by this change successively deprived of the means of supporting themselves, would naturally have no resource to prevent them from starving but that of selling their labour to the rich, as in modern states; but from this resource they were completely cut off by the prodigious number of slaves which, increasing by constant influx with the increasing luxury of Rome, filled up every employment both in agriculture and manufactures. Under such circumstances, so far from being astonished that the number of free citizens should decrease, the wonder seems to be that any should exist besides the proprietors. And in fact many could not have existed but for a strange and preposterous custom, which, however, the strange and unnatural state of the city might perhaps require, that of distributing vast quantities of corn to the poorer citizens gratuitously. Two hundred thousand received this distribution in Augustus's time; and it is highly probable that a great part of them had little else to depend upon. It is supposed to have been given to every man of full years; but the quantity was not enough for a family and too much for an individual.[5] It could not therefore enable them to increase; and, from the manner in which Plutarch speaks of the custom of exposing children among the poor,[6] there is great reason to believe that many were destroyed in spite of the *jus trium liberorum*. The passage in Tacitus in which, speaking of the Germans, he alludes to this custom in Rome, seems to point to the same conclusion.[7] What effect, indeed, could such a law have among a set of people who appear to have been so completely excluded from all the means of acquiring a

---

[5] Hume, Essay xi. p. 488.   [6] De amore prolis.

[7] De moribus Germanorum, 19. How completely the laws relating to the encouragement of marriage and of children were despised, appears from a speech of Minucius Felix in Octavio, cap. 30. '*Vos enim video procreatos filios nunc feris et avibus exponere, nunc adstrangulatos misero mortis genere elidere; sunt quæ in ipsis visceribus medicaminibus epotis originem futuri hominis extinguant, et parricidium faciant antequam pariant.*'

This crime had grown so much into a custom in Rome that even Pliny attempts to excuse it; '*Quoniam aliquarum fecunditas plena liberis tali venia indiget.*' Lib. xxix. c. iv. [For English translations see FELIX and PLINY in the Alphabetical List.]

subsistence, except that of charity, that they would be scarcely able to support themselves, much less a wife and two or three children? If half of the slaves had been sent out of the country, and the people had been employed in agriculture and manufactures, the effect would have been to increase the number of Roman citizens with more certainty and rapidity than ten thousand laws for the encouragement of children.

It is possible that the *jus trium liberorum*, and the other laws of the same tendency, might have been of some little use among the higher classes of Roman citizens; and, indeed, from the nature of these laws, consisting as they did principally of privileges, it would appear that they were directed chiefly to this part of society. But vicious habits of every possible kind, preventive of population,[8] seem to have been so generally prevalent at this period, that no corrective laws could have any considerable influence. Montesquieu justly observes that 'the corruption of manners had destroyed the office of censor, which had been established itself to destroy the corruption of manners; but when the corruption of manners becomes general, censure has no longer any force'.[9] Thirty-four years after the passing of the law of Augustus respecting marriage, the Roman knights demanded its repeal. On separating the married and the unmarried, it appeared that the latter considerably exceeded in number the former; a strong proof of the inefficacy of the law.[10]

In most countries, vicious habits preventive of population appear to be a consequence rather than a cause of the infrequency of marriage; but in Rome the depravity of morals seems to have been the direct cause which checked the marriage union, at least among the higher classes. It is impossible to read the speech of Metellus Numidicus in his censorship without indignation and disgust. 'If it were possible', he says, 'entirely to go without wives, we would deliver ourselves at once from this evil; but as the laws of nature have so ordered it that we can neither live happy with them, nor continue the species without them, we ought to have more regard for our lasting security than for our transient pleasures.'[11]

Positive laws to encourage marriage and population, enacted on the urgency of the occasion, and not mixed with religion, as in China and some other countries, are seldom calculated to answer the end which they aim at, and therefore generally indicate ignorance in the legislator who proposes them; but the apparent necessity of such laws almost invariably indicates a

---

[8] Sed jacet aurato vix ulla puerpera lecto
Tantum artes hujus; tantum medicamina possunt.
Quæ steriles facit, atque homines in ventre necandos
Conducit. Juvenal, sat. vi. 593.
[For an English translation, see JUVENALIS in the Alphabetical List.]
[9] Esprit des Loix, liv. xxiii. c. 21.   [10] Ibid.
[11] Aulus Gellius, lib. i. c. 6. [See GELLIUS in the Alphabetical List.]

very great degree of moral and political depravity in the state; and in the countries in which they are most strongly insisted on, not only vicious manners will generally be found to prevail, but political institutions extremely unfavourable to industry, and consequently to population.

On this account, I cannot but agree with Wallace[12] in thinking that Hume was wrong in his supposition that the Roman world was probably the most populous during the long peace under Trajan and the Antonines.[13] We well know that wars do not depopulate much, while industry continues in vigour; and that peace will not increase the number of people when they cannot find the means of subsistence. The renewal of the laws relating to marriage under Trajan indicates the continued prevalence of vicious habits, and of a languishing industry, and seems to be inconsistent with the supposition of a great increase of population.

It might be said, perhaps, that the vast profusion of slaves would more than make up for the want of Roman citizens; but it appears that the labour of these slaves was not sufficiently directed to agriculture to support a very great population. Whatever might be the case with some of the provinces, the decay of agriculture in Italy seems to be generally acknowledged. The pernicious custom of importing great quantities of corn to distribute gratuitously among the people had given it a blow from which it never afterwards recovered. Hume observes that 'when the Roman authors complain that Italy, which formerly exported corn, became dependent on all the provinces for its daily bread, they never ascribe this alteration to the increase of its inhabitants, but to the neglect of tillage and agriculture.'[14] And in another place he says: 'All ancient authors tell us, that there was a perpetual influx of slaves to Italy from the remoter provinces, particularly Syria, Cilicia, Cappadocia, and the Lesser Asia, Thrace, and Egypt; yet the number of people did not increase in Italy; and writers complain of the continual decay of industry and agriculture.'[15] It seems but little probable that the peace under Trajan and the Antonines should have given so sudden a turn to the habits of the people as essentially to alter this state of things.

On the condition of slavery, it may be observed that there cannot be a stronger proof of its unfavourableness to the propagation of the species, in the countries where it prevails, than the necessity of this continual influx. This necessity forms at once a complete refutation of the observation of Wallace, that the ancient slaves were more serviceable in raising up people than the inferior ranks of men in modern times.[16] Though it is undoubtedly true, as he observes, that all our labourers do not marry, and that many of their

---

[12] Dissertation, Appendix, p. 247.   [13] Essay xi. p. 505.   [14] Id. p. 504.
[15] Id. p. 433.
[16] Dissert. on the numbers of mankind, p. 91.

children die, and become sickly and useless through the poverty and negligence of their parents;[17] yet notwithstanding these obstacles to increase, there is perhaps scarcely an instance to be produced where the lower classes of society in any country, if free, do not raise up people fully equal to the demand for their labour.

To account for the checks to population which are peculiar to a state of slavery, and which render a constant recruit of numbers necessary, we must adopt the comparison of slaves to cattle, which Wallace and Hume have made; Wallace to shew that it would be the interest of masters to take care of their slaves and rear up their offspring;[18] and Hume, to prove that it would more frequently be the interest of the master to prevent than to encourage their breeding.[19] If Wallace's observation had been just, it is not to be doubted that the slaves would have kept up their own numbers with ease by procreation; and as it is acknowledged that they did not do this, the truth of Hume's observation is clearly evinced. 'To rear a child in London, till he could be serviceable, would cost much dearer than to buy one of the same age from Scotland or Ireland, where he had been raised in a cottage, covered with rags, and fed on oatmeal and potatoes. Those who had slaves, therefore, in all the richer and more populous countries, would discourage the pregnancy of the females, and either prevent or destroy the birth.'[20] It is acknowledged by Wallace that the male slaves greatly exceeded in number the females,[21] which must necessarily be an additional obstacle to their increase. It would appear therefore that the preventive check to population must have operated with very great force among the Greek and Roman slaves; and as they were often ill-treated, fed perhaps scantily, and sometimes great numbers of them confined together in close and unwholesome ergastula or dungeons,[22] it is probable that the positive checks to population from disease were also severe, and that when epidemics prevailed they would be most destructive in this part of the society.

The unfavourableness of slavery to the propagation of the species in the country where it prevails is not, however, decisive of the question respecting the absolute population of such a country, or the greater question respecting the populousness of antient and modern nations. We know that some countries could afford a great and constant supply of slaves, without being in the smallest degree depopulated themselves; and if these supplies were

---

[17] Dissert. on the numbers of mankind, p. 88.   [18] Id. p. 89.   [19] Hume, Essay xi. p. 433.
[20] Id. p. 433.   [21] Appendix to Dissertation, p. 182.
[22] Hume, Essay, xi. p. 430. [*Ergastulum* (plural, *ergastula*) is a Latin word for 'a place of hard labour', used for a building or compound in which slaves were confined; in modern French *ergastule* (m.) means a special prison for slaves; the word is not in the Oxford English Dictionary.]

poured in, as they probably would be, exactly in proportion to the demand for labour in the nation which received them, the question respecting the populousness of this nation would rest precisely on the same grounds as in modern states, and depend upon the number of people which it could employ and support. Whether the practice of domestic slavery, therefore, prevail or not, it may be laid down as a position not to be controverted that, taking a sufficient extent of territory to include within it exportation and importation, and allowing some variation for the prevalence of luxury or of frugal habits, the population of these countries will always be in proportion to the food which the earth is made to produce. And no cause, physical or moral, unless it operate in an excessive and unusual manner,[23] can have any considerable and permanent effect on the population, except in as far as it influences the production and distribution of the means of subsistence.

In the controversy concerning the populousness of antient and modern nations, this point has not been sufficiently attended to; and physical and moral causes have been brought forward on both sides from which no just inference in favour of either party could be drawn. It seems to have escaped the attention of both writers that the more productive and populous a country is, in its actual state, the less probably will be its power of obtaining a further increase of produce, and consequently the more checks must necessarily be called into action to keep the population down to the level of this stationary or slowly-increasing produce. From finding such checks, therefore, in antient or modern nations, no inference can be drawn against the absolute populousness of either. On this account, the prevalence of the small-pox, and of other disorders unknown to the antients, can by no means be considered as an argument against the populousness of modern nations, though to these physical causes both Hume[24] and Wallace[25] allow considerable weight.

In the moral causes which they have brought forward, they have fallen into a similar error. Wallace introduces the positive encouragements to marriage among the antients as one of the principal causes of the superior populous-

---

[23] The extreme insalubrity of Batavia, and perhaps the plague in some countries, may be considered as physical causes operating in an excessive degree. The extreme and unusual attachment of the Romans to a vicious celibacy, and the promiscuous intercourse in Otaheite, may be considered as moral causes of the same nature. Such instances may perhaps form exceptions to the general observation.
[In 1807 (Vol. 1, p. 298) the last sentence in this note read:
    Such instances, and others which might perhaps be found, make it necessary to qualify the general proposition as in the text.
[In 1817 (Vol. 1, p. 356) it was changed again:
    Such instances, and others of the same kind, which might probably be found, make it necessary to qualify . . .
[24] Essay xi. p. 425.   [25] Dissertation, p. 80.

ness of the antient world;[26] but the necessity of positive laws to encourage marriage certainly rather indicates a want than an abundance of people; and in the instance of Sparta, to which he particularly refers, it appears from the passage in Aristotle, mentioned in the last chapter, that the laws to encourage marriage were instituted for the express purpose of remedying a marked deficiency of people. In a country with a crowded and overflowing population, a legislator would never think of making express laws to encourage marriage and the procreation of children. Other arguments of Wallace will be found upon examination to be almost equally ineffectual to his purpose.

Some of the causes which Hume produces are in the same manner unsatisfactory, and rather make against the inference which he has in view than for it. The number of footmen, housemaids, and other persons remaining unmarried in modern states, he allows to be an argument against their populousness.[27] But the contrary inference of the two appears to be the more probable. When the difficulties attending the rearing of a family are very great, and consequently many persons of both sexes remain single, we may naturally enough infer that population is stationary, but by no means that it is not absolutely great; because the difficulty of rearing a family may arise from the very circumstance of a great absolute population, and the consequent fullness of all the channels to a livelihood; though the same difficulty may undoubtedly exist in a thinly-peopled country, which is yet stationary in its population. The number of unmarried persons in proportion to the whole number may form some criterion by which we can judge whether population be increasing, stationary, or decreasing; but will not enable us to determine anything respecting absolute populousness. Yet even in this criterion we are liable to be deceived. In some of the southern countries early marriages are general, and very few women remain in a state of celibacy, yet the people not only do not increase, but the actual number is perhaps small. In this case the removal of the preventive check is made up by the excessive force of the positive check. The sum of all the positive and preventive checks, taken together, forms undoubtedly the immediate cause which represses population; but we never can expect to obtain and estimate accurately this sum in any country; and we can certainly draw no safe conclusion from the contemplation of two or three of these checks taken by themselves, because it so frequently happens that the excess of one check is balanced by the defect of some other. Causes which affect the number of births or deaths may or may not affect the average population, according to circumstances; but causes which affect the production and distribution of the

---

[26] Dissertation, p. 93.

[27] Essay xi. [Malthus deals with this more briefly and succinctly on pp. 58–9 of the 1798 *Essay*.]

means of subsistence must necessarily affect population; and it is therefore only on these causes, besides actual enumerations, on which we can with any certainty rely.[28]

All the checks to population which have been hitherto considered, in the course of this review of human society, are clearly resolvable into moral restraint, vice, and misery.

[29]●Of moral restraint, though it might be rash to affirm that it has not had some share in repressing the natural power of population, yet it must be allowed to have operated very feebly indeed, compared to the others. Of the preventive check, considered generally, and without reference to its producing vice, though its effect appears to have been very considerable in the later periods of Roman History, and in some few other countries,●[29] yet, upon the whole, its operation seems to have been inferior to the positive checks. A large portion of the procreative power appears to have been called into action, the redundancy from which was checked by violent causes. Among these, war is the most prominent and striking feature; and after this may be ranked famines and violent diseases. In most of the countries considered, the population seems to have been seldom measured accurately according to the average and permanent means of subsistence, but generally to have vibrated between the two extremes, and consequently the oscillations between want and plenty are strongly marked, as we should naturally expect among less civilized nations.

---

[28] [In 1817 (Vol. 1, p. 360) Malthus altered the final words of this paragraph:
   ... population; and it is therefore upon these latter causes alone (independently of actual enumerations) that we can with certainty rely.

[29] [In 1806 (Vol. 1, p. 302) Malthus altered the beginning of this paragraph:
   Of that branch of the preventive check, which I have denominated moral restraint, though it might be rash to affirm, that it has not had some share in repressing the natural power of population, yet it must be allowed to have operated very feebly indeed, compared with the others. Of the other branch of the preventive check, which comes under the head of vice, though its effect appears to have been very considerable in the later periods of Roman History, and in some other countries; yet, upon the whole ...
   [In 1817 (Vol. 1, p. 361) he changed it again:
   Of that branch of the preventive check which I have denominated moral restraint, though it has certainly had some share in repressing the natural power of population, yet, taken in its strict sense, it must be allowed to have operated feebly, compared with the others. Of the other branch ...

ESSAY, &c

BOOK II

OF THE CHECKS TO POPULATION IN THE DIFFERENT STATES OF MODERN EUROPE

CHAPTER I

Of the Checks to Population in Norway

In reviewing the states of modern Europe, we shall be assisted in our inquiries by registers of births, deaths, and marriages, which, when they are complete and correct, point out to us with some degree of precision whether the prevailing checks to population are of the positive or preventive kind. The habits of most European nations are of course much alike, owing to the similarity of the circumstances in which they are placed; and it is to be expected, therefore, that their tables of mortality should sometimes give the same results. Relying however too much upon this occasional coincidence, political calculators have been led into the error of supposing that there is, generally speaking, an invariable order of mortality in all countries; but it appears, on the contrary, that this order is extremely variable; that it is very different in different places of the same country and, within certain limits, depends upon circumstances which it is in the power of man to alter.

Norway, during nearly the whole of the last century, was in a peculiar degree exempt from the drains of people by war. The climate is remarkably free from epidemic sicknesses; and, in common years, the mortality is less than in any other country in Europe, the registers of which are known to be correct.[1] The proportion of the annual deaths to the whole population, on an average throughout the whole country, is only as 1 to 48.[2] Yet the population

---

[1] The registers for Russia give a smaller mortality: but it is supposed that they are defective.
   [In 1826 (Vol. i, p. 260) a sentence was added to this note:
      It appears, however, that in England and Wales during the ten years ending with 1820, the mortality was still less than in Norway.
[2] Thaarup's Statistik der Danischen Monarchie, vol. ii. p. 4.
   [Malthus took it for granted his readers would know that Norway and Sweden were united to

of Norway never seems to have increased with great rapidity. It has made a start within the last ten or fifteen years; but till that period its progress must have been very slow, as we know that the country was peopled in very early ages, and in 1769 its population was only 723 141.[3]

Before we enter upon an examination of its internal economy, we must feel assured that, as the positive checks to its population have been so small, the preventive checks must have been proportionably great; and we accordingly find from the registers that the proportion of yearly marriages to the whole population is as 1 to 130,[4] which is a smaller proportion of marriages than appears in the registers of any other country except Switzerland.

One cause of this small number of marriages is the mode in which the enrolments for the army have been conducted till within a very few years. Every man in Denmark and Norway born of a farmer or labourer is a soldier.[5] Formerly, the commanding officer of the district might take these peasants at any age he pleased, and he in general preferred those that were from twenty-five to thirty to such as were younger. After being taken into the service, a man could not marry without producing a certificate signed by the minister of the parish, that he had substance enough to support a wife and family; and even then it was further necessary for him to obtain the permission of the officer. The difficulty, and sometimes the expense, attendant on the obtaining of this certificate and permission,[6] generally deterred those who were not in very good circumstances, from thinking of marriage till

---

Denmark according to the Union of Kalmar in 1397; Sweden broke away in 1523, but Norway was part of the Danish dominions until the Treaty of Kiel in 1814, when the victorious powers transferred her crown from Denmark to Sweden.]

[3] Thaarup's Statistik der Danischen Monarchie, vol. ii. Table ii. p. 5.

[4] Id. vol. ii. p. 4. [In 1807 (Vol. 1, p. 307) Malthus added the following to this note:

The proportion of yearly marriages to the whole population is one of the most obvious criterions of the operation of the preventive check, though not quite a correct one. Generally speaking, the preventive check is greater than might be inferred from this criterion; because in the healthy countries of Europe, where a small proportion of marriages takes place, the greater number of old people living at the time of these marriages will be more than counterbalanced by the smaller proportion of persons under the age of puberty. In such a country as Norway, the persons from 20 to 50, that is, of the most likely age to marry, bear a greater proportion to the whole population than in most of the other countries of Europe; and consequently the actual proportion of marriages in Norway, compared with that of others, will not express the full extent in which the preventive check operates.

[5] The few particulars which I shall mention relating to Norway were collected during a summer excursion in that country in the year 1799. [Malthus's journal of his Norwegian tour is published in full in *The Travel Diaries of T. R. Malthus* (Cambridge University Press, 1966) pp. 83-221. In the first Appendix to this work (pp. 274-95) the reader may compare this chapter on Norway with actual passages in the journal; as with other authorities, Malthus on occasion quotes himself almost verbatim.]

[6] [In 1806 (Vol. 1, p. 308) this was altered to:

The difficulty, and sometimes the expense, of obtaining this certificate and permission, ...

their service of ten years was expired; and as they might be enrolled at any age under thirty-six, and the officers were apt to take the oldest first, it would often be late in life before they could feel themselves at liberty to settle.

Though the minister of the parish had no legal power to prevent a man from marrying who was not enrolled for service, yet it appears that custom had in some degree sanctioned a discretionary power of this kind, and the priest often refused to join a couple together when the parties had no probable means of supporting a family.

Every obstacle, however, of this nature, whether arising from law or custom, has now been entirely removed. A full liberty is given to marry at any age, without leave either of the officer or priest; and in the enrolments for the army, all those of the age of twenty are taken first, then all those of twenty-two, and so on till the necessary number is completed.

The officers in general disapprove of this change. They say that a young Norwegian has not arrived at his full strength, and does not make a good soldier, at twenty. And many are of opinion that the peasants will now marry too young, and that more children will be born than the country can support.

But, independently of any regulations respecting the military enrolments, the peculiar state of Norway throws very strong obstacles in the way of early marriages. There are no large manufacturing towns to take off the overflowing population of the country; and as each village naturally furnishes from itself a supply of hands more than equal to the demand, a change of place in search of work seldom promises any success. Unless, therefore, an opportunity of foreign emigration offer, the Norwegian peasant generally remains in the village in which he was born; and as the vacancies in houses and employments must occur very slowly, owing to the small mortality that takes place, he will often see himself compelled to wait a considerable time before he can attain a situation which will enable him to rear a family.

The Norway farms have in general a certain number of married labourers employed upon them, in proportion to their size, who are called house-men. They receive from the farmer a house and a quantity of land nearly sufficient to maintain a family; in return for which they are under the obligation of working for him at a low and fixed price whenever they are called upon. Except in the immediate neighbourhood of the towns, and on the seacoast, the vacancy of a place of this kind is the only prospect which presents itself of providing for a family. From the small number of people, and the little variety of employment, the subject is brought distinctly within the view of each individual; and he must feel the absolute necessity of repressing his inclinations to marriage till some such vacancy offer. If, from the plenty of materials, he should be led to build a house himself, it could not be expected that the farmer, if he had a sufficient number of labourers before, should give him an adequate portion of land with it; and though he would, in general, find employment for three or four months in the summer, yet there would be little chance of his earning enough to support a family during the whole year. It is probable that it was in cases of this kind, where the impatience of the parties prompted them to build, or propose to build, a house themselves, and trust to what they could earn, that the parish priests exercised the discretionary power of refusing to marry.

The young men and women therefore are obliged to remain with the farmers as unmarried servants, till a houseman's place becomes vacant: and of these unmarried servants there is in every farm and every gentleman's family a much greater proportion than the work would seem to require. There is but little division of labour in Norway. Almost all the wants of domestic economy are supplied in each separate household. Not only the common operations of brewing, baking, and washing, are carried on at home, but many families make, or import, their own cheese and butter, kill their own beef and mutton, import their own grocery stores; and the farmers and country people in general spin their own flax and wool, and weave their own linen and woollen clothes. In the largest towns, such as Christiania and Drontheim, there is nothing that can be called a market. It is extremely difficult to get a joint of fresh meat; and a pound of fresh butter is an article not to be purchased, even in the midst of summer. Fairs are held at certain seasons of the year, and stores of all kinds of provisions that will keep are laid in at these times; and if this care be neglected, great inconveniences are suffered, as scarcely anything is to be bought retail. Persons who make a temporary residence in the country, or small merchants not possessed of farms, complain heavily of this inconvenience; and the wives of merchants who have large estates say that the domestic economy of a Norway family is so extensive and complicated, that the necessary superintendence of it requires their whole attention, and that they can find no time for anything else.

It is evident that a system of this kind must require a great number of servants. It is said besides, that they are not remarkable for diligence, and that to do the same quantity of work, more are necessary than in other countries. [7]●The consequence is that in every establishment two or three times the number of servants will be found, as in a family living at the same rate in England; and it is not uncommon for a farmer in the country who, in his appearance, is not to be distinguished from any of his labourers, to have a household of twenty persons, including his own family.●[7]

---

[7] [In 1806 (Vol. I, pp. 312–13) Malthus altered this sentence:

The consequence is, that in every establishment, the proportion of servants will be found two or three times as great as in England; and a farmer in the country, who in his appearance

The means of maintenance to a single man are, therefore, much less confined than to a married man; and under such circumstances the lower classes of people cannot increase much, till the increase of mercantile stock, or the division and improvement of farms, furnishes a greater quantity of employment for married labourers. In countries more fully peopled this subject is always involved in great obscurity. Each man naturally thinks that he has as good a chance of finding employment as his neighbour, and that if he cannot get it in one place, he shall in some other.[8] He marries, therefore, and trusts to fortune; and the effect too frequently is that the redundant population occasioned in this manner is repressed by the positive checks of poverty and disease. In Norway the subject is not involved in the same obscurity. The number of additional families which the increasing demand for labour will support is more distinctly marked. The population is so small that, even in the towns, it is difficult to fall into any considerable error on this subject; and in the country the division and improvement of an estate, and the creation of a greater number of housemen's places, must be a matter of complete notoriety. If a man can obtain one of these places, he marries, and is able to support a family; if he cannot obtain one, he remains single. A redundant population is thus prevented from taking place, instead of being destroyed after it has taken place.

It is not to be doubted that the general prevalence of the preventive check to population, owing to the state of society which has been described, together with the obstacles thrown in the way of early marriages from the enrolments for the army, have powerfully contributed to place the lower classes of people in Norway in a better situation, than could be expected from the nature of the soil and climate. On the seacoast where, on account of the hopes of an adequate supply of food from fishing, the preventive check does not prevail in the same degree, the people are very poor and wretched and, beyond comparison, in a worse state than the peasants in the interior of the country.

The greatest part of the soil in Norway is absolutely incapable of bearing corn, and the climate is subject to the most sudden and fatal changes. There are three nights about the end of August which are particularly distinguished by the name of iron nights, on account of their sometimes blasting the promise of the fairest crops. On these occasions, the lower classes of people necessarily suffer; but as there are scarcely any independent labourers, except the housemen that have been mentioned, who all keep cattle, the

---

is not to be distinguished from any of his labourers, will sometimes have a household of twenty persons, ...

[8] [In 1806 (Vol. I, p. 313) this was changed to:
   ... and that, if he fail in one place, he shall succeed in some other.

hardship of being obliged to mix the inner bark of the pine with their bread is mitigated by the stores of cheese, of salt butter, of salt meat, salt fish, and bacon, which they were enabled to lay up[9] for winter provision. The period in which the want of corn presses the most severely is generally about two months before harvest; and at this time the cows, of which the poorest housemen have generally two or three, and many five or six, begin to give milk, which must be a great assistance to the family, particularly to the younger part of it. In the summer of the year 1799, the Norwegians appeared to wear a face of plenty and content, while their neighbours, the Swedes, were absolutely starving: and I particularly remarked, that the sons of housemen, and the farmers' boys, were fatter, larger, and had better calves to their legs, than boys of the same age and in similar situations in England.[10]

It is also, without doubt, owing to the prevalence of the preventive check to population, as much as to any peculiar healthiness of the air, that the mortality in Norway is so small. There is nothing in the climate, or the soil, that would lead to the supposition of its being in any extraordinary manner favourable to the general health of the inhabitants; but as in every country the principal mortality takes place among very young children, the smaller number of these in Norway, in proportion to the whole population, will naturally occasion a smaller mortality than in other countries, supposing the climate to be equally healthy.

It may be said, perhaps, and with truth, that one of the principal reasons of the small mortality in Norway is that the towns are inconsiderable and few, and that few people are employed in unwholesome manufactories. [11]●In some of the agricultural villages in England, where the preventive check to population does not prevail in the same degree, the mortality is as small as in Norway. But it should be recollected that the calculation, in this case, is for these particular villages alone; whereas in Norway the calculation of 1 in 48 is for the whole country. The redundant population of the villages in England●[11] is disposed of by constant emigrations to the towns, and the deaths of a great part of those that are born in the parish do not appear in the

---

9 [In 1806 (Vol. 1, p. 315) this was amended:
    ... which they are generally enabled to lay up ...

10 [In the 1798 *Essay* (p. 73) Malthus wrote of rural England:
    The sons and daughters of peasants will not be found such rosy cherubs in real life, as they are described to be in romances. ... And the lads who drive plough, which must certainly be a healthy exercise, are very rarely seen with any appearance of calves to their legs; a circumstance which can only be attributed to a want either of proper or of sufficient nourishment.]

11 [In 1806 (Vol. 1, pp. 316–17) Malthus altered this passage: *In some of the agricultural villages in England ...* was changed to 'In many of the agricultural villages of other countries ...' and *The redundant population of the villages in England ...* was changed to 'The redundant population of these villages ...'

registers. But in Norway all the deaths are within the calculation, and it is clear that if more were born than the country could support, a great mortality must take place in some form or other. If the people were not destroyed by disease, they would be destroyed by famine. It is indeed well known that bad and insufficient food will produce disease and death in the purest air and the finest climate. Supposing, therefore, no great foreign emigration, and no extraordinary increase in the resources of the country, nothing but the more extensive prevalence of the preventive check to population in Norway can secure to her a smaller mortality than in other countries, however pure her air may be, or however healthy the employments of her people.

Norway seems to have been anciently divided into large estates or farms, called Gores; and as, according to the law of succession, all the brothers divide the property equally, it is a matter of surprise, and a proof how slowly the population has hitherto increased, that these estates have not been more subdivided. Many of them are indeed now divided into half gores, and quarter gores, and some still lower, but it has in general been the custom, on the death of the father, for a commission to value the estate at a low rate, and if the eldest son can pay his brothers' and sisters'[12] shares, according to this valuation, by mortgaging his estate or otherwise, the whole is awarded to him; and the force of habit and natural indolence too frequently prompt him to conduct the farm after the manner of his forefathers, with few or no efforts at improvement.

Another great obstacle to the improvement of farms in Norway is a law which is called Odel's right, by which any lineal descendant can repurchase an estate which has been sold out of the family, by paying the original purchase-money. Formerly, collateral as well as lineal descendants had this power, and the time was absolutely unlimited, so that the purchaser could never consider himself as secure from claims. Afterwards the time was limited to twenty years, and in 1771 it was still further limited to ten years, and all the collateral branches were excluded. It must, however, be an uninterrupted possession of ten years; for if, before the expiration of this term, a person who has a right to claim under the law give notice to the possessor that he does not forego his claim, though he is not then in a condition to make the purchase, the possessor is obliged to wait six years more before he is perfectly secure. And as, in addition to this, the eldest in the lineal descent may reclaim an estate that had been purchased by a younger brother, the law, even in its present amended state, must be considered as a very great bar to improvement; and in its former state when the time was unlimited, and the sale of estates in this way was more frequent, it seems as if

---

[12] A daughter's portion is the half of the son's portion. [In 1806 (Vol. 1, p. 318) this was amended to 'a son's portion'.

it must have been a most complete obstacle to the amelioration of farms, and obviously accounts for the very slow increase of the population in Norway for many centuries.

A further difficulty in the way of clearing and cultivating the land arises from the fears of the great timber merchants respecting the woods. When a farm has been divided among children and grandchildren, as each proprietor has a certain right in the woods, each, in general, endeavours to cut as much as he can; and the timber is thus felled before it is fit, and the woods spoiled. To prevent this, the merchants buy large tracts of woods of the farmers, who enter into a contract that the farm shall not be any further subdivided or more housemen placed upon it; at least, that if the number of families be increased, they should have no right in the woods. It is said that the merchants who make these purchases are not very strict, provided the smaller farmers and housemen do not take timber for their houses. The farmers who sell these tracts of wood are obliged by law to reserve to themselves the right of pasturing their cattle, and of cutting timber sufficient for their houses, repairs, and firing.

A piece of ground round a houseman's dwelling cannot be enclosed for cultivation without an application, first, to the proprietor of the woods, declaring that the spot is not fit for timber, and afterwards to a magistrate of the district, whose leave on this occasion is also necessary, probably for the purpose of ascertaining whether the leave of the proprietor had been duly obtained.

In addition to these obstacles to improved cultivation, which may be considered as artificial, the nature of the country presents an insuperable obstacle to a cultivation and population in any respect proportioned to the surface of the soil. The Norwegians, though not in a nomadic state, are still in a considerable degree in the pastoral state, and depend very much upon their cattle. The high grounds that border on the mountains are absolutely unfit to bear corn, and the only use to which they can be put is to pasture cattle upon them for three or four months during the summer. The farmers accordingly send all their cattle to these grounds at this time of the year, under the care of a part of their families; and it is here that they make all their butter and cheese for sale, or for their own consumption. The great difficulty is to support their cattle during the long winter, and for this purpose it is necessary that a considerable proportion of the most fertile land in the valleys should be mowed for grass.[13] If too much of it were taken into tillage, the number of cattle must be proportionably diminished, and the greatest part of the higher grounds would become absolutely useless; and it might be a

---

[13] [In 1806 (Vol. I, p. 321) *grass* was changed to 'hay'.

question, in that case, whether the country upon the whole would support a greater population.

Notwithstanding, however, all these obstacles, there is a very considerable capacity of improvement in Norway, and of late years it has been called into action. I heard it remarked by a professor at Copenhagen, that the reason why the agriculture of Norway had advanced so slowly was that there were no gentlemen farmers to set examples of improved cultivation, and break the routine of ignorance and prejudice in the conduct of farms that had been handed down from father to son for successive ages. From what I saw of Norway I should say that this want is now, in some degree, supplied. Many intelligent merchants and well-informed general officers are at present engaged in farming. In the country round Christiania very great improvements have taken place in the system of agriculture; and even in the neighbourhood of Drontheim the culture of artificial grasses has been introduced, which, in a country where so much winter feed is necessary for cattle, is a point of the highest importance. Almost everywhere the cultivation of potatoes has succeeded, and they are growing more and more into general use, though in the distant parts of the country they are not yet relished by the common people.

It has been more the custom of late years than formerly to divide farms; and, as the vent for commodities in Norway is not perhaps sufficient to encourage the complete cultivation of large farms, this division of them has probably contributed to the improvement of the land. It seems indeed to be universally agreed, among those who are in a situation to be competent judges, that the agriculture of Norway in general has advanced considerably of late years; and the registers shew that the population has followed with more than equal pace. On an average of ten years, from 1775 to 1784, the proportion of births to deaths was 141 to 100.[14] But this seems to have been rather too rapid an increase; as the following year, 1785, was a year of scarcity and sickness, in which the deaths considerably exceeded the births; and for four years afterwards, particularly in 1789, the excess of births was not great. But in the five years from 1789 to 1794, the proportion of births to deaths was nearly 150 to 100.[15]

---

[14] Thaarup's Statistik der Danischen Monarchie, vol. ii. p. 4.
[15] Id. table i. p. 4. [In 1806 (Vol. 1, p. 323) Malthus added to this note:

In the Tableau Statistique des Etats Danois, since published, it appears that the whole number of births for the five years subsequent to 1794 was 138 799, of deaths 94 530, of marriages 34 313. These numbers give the proportion of births to deaths as 146 to 100, of births to marriages as 4 to 1, and of deaths to marriages as 275 to 100. The average proportion of yearly births is stated to be $\frac{1}{35}$, and of yearly deaths $\frac{1}{49}$ of the whole population. Vol. ii. ch. viii.

Many of the most thinking and best informed persons express their apprehensions on this subject, and on the probable result of the new regulations respecting the enrolments for the army, and the apparent intention of the court of Denmark to encourage, at all events, the population. No very unfavourable season has occurred in Norway since 1785; but it is feared that, in the event of such a season, the most severe distress might be felt from the increased population.[16]

Norway is, I believe, almost the only country in Europe where a traveller will hear any apprehensions expressed of a redundant population, and where the danger to the happiness of the lower classes of people from this cause is, in some degree, seen and understood. This obviously arises from the smallness of the population altogether, and the consequent narrowness of the subject. If our attention were confined to one parish, and there were no power of emigrating from it, the most careless observer could not fail to remark that if all married at twenty, it would be perfectly impossible for the farmers, however carefully they might improve their land, to find employment and food for those that would grow up; but, when a great number of these parishes are added together in a populous kingdom, the largeness of the subject, and the power of moving from place to place, obscure and confuse our view. We lose sight of a truth which before appeared completely obvious; and, in a most unaccountable manner, attribute to the aggregate quantity of land a power of supporting people beyond comparison greater than the sum of all its parts.

[The reference was not given until 1826 (Vol. I, p. 274). For a note on this work see CATTEAU-CALLEVILLE in the Alphabetical List.]

[16] [In 1806 (Vol. I, p. 324) this was changed to:

... the most severe distress might be felt from the rapid increase that has of late taken place.

CHAPTER II

Of the Checks to Population in Sweden

Sweden is, in many respects, in a state similar to that of Norway. A very large proportion of its population is, in the same manner, employed in agriculture; and in most parts of the country the married labourers who work for the farmers, like the housemen of Norway, have a certain portion of land for their principal maintenance, while the young men and women that are unmarried live as servants in the farmers' families. This state of things, however, is not so complete and general as in Norway; and from this cause, added to the greater extent and population of the country, the superior size of the towns, and the greater variety of employment, it has not occasioned, in the same degree, the prevalence of the preventive check to population; and consequently the positive check has operated with more force, or the mortality has been greater.

According to a paper published by M. Wargentin in the *Memoires abrégés de l'Academie Royale des Sciences de Stockholm*,[1] the yearly average mortality in all Sweden, for nine years, ending in 1763, was to the population as 1 to $34\frac{3}{4}$.[2] M. Wargentin furnished Dr. Price with a continuance of these tables, and an average of 21 years gives a result of 1 to $34\frac{3}{5}$, nearly the same.[3] This is undoubtedly a very great mortality, considering the large proportion of the population in Sweden which is employed in agriculture. It appears, from some calculations in Cantzlaer's account of Sweden, that the inhabitants of the towns are to the inhabitants of the country only as 1 to 13,[4] whereas in well-peopled countries, the proportion is often as 1 to 3 or above.[5] The superior mortality of towns, therefore, cannot much affect the general proportion in Sweden.

---

[1] 1 vol. 4to. printed at Paris, 1772.
[2] P. 27. [This date was wrongly printed as 1663 in all the editions preceding Pickering's of 1986.]
[3] Price's Observ. on Revers. Paym. vol. ii. p. 126. ['4th edit.' was added in 1826 (Vol. i, p. 278). See PRICE in the Alphabetical List.]
[4] Memoires pour servir a la connoissance des affaires politiques et économiques du Royaume de Suede, 4to. 1776, ch. vi. p. 187. This work is considered as very correct in its information, and is in great credit at Stockholm. [See CANZLER in the Alphabetical List.]
[5] Susmilch's Gottliche Ordnung, vol. i. ch. ii. sect. xxxiv. edit. 1798.

The average mortality of villages, according to Susmilch, is 1 in 40.[6] In Prussia and Pomerania, which include a number of great and unhealthy towns, and where the inhabitants of the towns are to the inhabitants of the country as 1 to 4, the mortality is less than 1 in 37.[7] The mortality in Norway, as has been mentioned before, is 1 in 48, which is in a very extraordinary degree less than in Sweden, though the inhabitants of the towns in Norway bear a greater proportion to the inhabitants of the country than in Sweden.[8] The towns in Sweden are indeed larger and more unhealthy than in Norway; but there is no reason to think that the country is naturally more unfavourable to the duration of human life. The mountains of Norway are in general not habitable. The only peopled parts of the country are the valleys. Many of these valleys are deep and narrow clefts in the mountains; and the cultivated spots in the bottom, surrounded as they are by almost perpendicular cliffs of a prodigious height,[9] which intercept the rays of the sun for many hours, do not seem as if they could be so healthy as the more exposed and drier soil of Sweden.

It is difficult, therefore, entirely to account for the mortality of Sweden, without supposing that the habits of the people, and the continual cry of the government for an increase of subjects, tend to press the population too hard against the limits of subsistence, and consequently to produce diseases which are the necessary effect of poverty and bad nourishment; and this, from observation, appears to be really the case.

Sweden does not produce food sufficient for its population. Its annual want in the article of grain, according to a calculation made from the years 1768 and 1772, is 440 000 tuns.[10] This quantity, or near it, has in general been imported from foreign countries, besides pork, butter, and cheese, to a considerable amount.[11]

The distillation of spirits in Sweden is supposed to consume above 400 000 tuns of grain; and when this distillation has been prohibited by government, a variation in defect appears in the tables of importations;[12] but no great

---

[6] Susmilch's Gottliche Ordnung, vol. i. ch. ii. sect. xxxv. p. 91.   [7] Id. vol. iii. p. 60.

[8] Thaarup's Statistik der Danischen Monarchie, vol. ii. tab. ii. p. 5. 1765. [This should be 1769.]

[9] Some of these valleys are strikingly picturesque. The principal road from Christiania to Drontheim leads, for nearly 180 English miles, through a continued valley of this kind, by the side of a very fine river, which in one part stretches out into the extensive lake Miosen. I am inclined to believe that there is not any river in all Europe, the course of which affords such a constant succession of beautiful and romantic scenery. It goes under different names in different parts. The verdure in the Norway valleys is peculiarly soft, the foliage of the trees luxuriant, and in summer no traces appear of a northern climate.

[10] Memoires du Royaume de Suede, table xvii. p. 174.   [11] Id. c. vi. p. 198.

[12] Id. table xlii. p. 418. c. vi. p. 201. I did not find out exactly the measure of the Swedish tun. It is rather less than our sack or half quarter.

variations in excess are observable, to supply the deficiencies in years of scanty harvests which, it is well known, occur frequently. In years the most abundant, when the distillation has been free, it is asserted, that 388 000 tuns have in general been imported.[13] It follows, therefore, that the Swedes consume all the produce of their best years, and nearly 400 000 more; and that, in their worst years, their consumption must be diminished by nearly the whole deficiency in their crops. The mass of the people appears to be too poor to purchase nearly the same quantity of corn at a very advanced price. There is no adequate encouragement, therefore, to corn merchants to import in great abundance; and the effect of a deficiency of one fourth or one third, in the crops, is to oblige the labourer to content himself with nearly three-fourths or two thirds of the corn which he used before, and to supply the rest by the use of any substitutes which necessity, the mother of invention, may suggest. I have said *nearly*, because it is difficult to suppose that the importations should not be something greater in years of scarcity than in common years, though no marked differences of this kind appear in the tables published by Cantzlaer. The greatest importation, according to these tables, was in the year 1768, when it amounted to 590 265 tuns of grain;[14] but even this greatest importation is only 150 000 tuns above the average wants of the country; and what is this, to supply a deficiency of one fourth or one third of a crop? The whole importation is indeed in this respect trifling.

The population of Sweden, at the time that Cantzlaer wrote, was about two millions and a half.[15] He allows four tuns of grain to a man.[16] Upon this supposition the annual wants of Sweden would be ten millions of tuns, and four or five hundred thousand would go but a little way in supplying a deficiency of two millions and a half or three millions; and, if we take only the difference from the average importation, it will appear that the assistance which the Swedes receive from importation in a year of scarcity is perfectly futile.

The consequence of this state of things is that the population of Sweden is in a peculiar manner affected by every variation of the seasons; and we cannot be surprised at a very curious and instructive remark of M. Wargentin, that the registers of Sweden show that the population and the mortality increase or decrease according as the harvests are abundant or deficient.[17] From the nine years of which he had given tables, he instances the following.

---

13 Memoires du Royaume de Suede, c. vi. p. 201.
14 Id. table xlii. p. 418.
15 Id. ch. vi. p. 184.   16 Id. p. 196.
17 [In 1806 (Vol. I, p. 332) Malthus altered this sentence:
    ... the registers of Sweden show that the births, marriages and deaths increase and decrease according to the state of the harvests.

		Marriages	Births	Deaths
Barren years	{ 1757	18 799	81 878	68 054
	{ 1758	19 584	83 299	74 370
Abundant years	{ 1759	23 210	85 579	62 662
	{ 1760	23 383	90 635	60 083[18]

Here it appears that in the year 1760 the births were to the deaths as 15 to 10; but in the year 1758 only as 11 to 10. By referring to the enumerations of the population in 1757 and 1760,[19] which M. Wargentin has given, it appears that the number of marriages in the year 1760, in proportion to the whole population, was as 1 to 101; in the year 1757, only as 1 to about 124. The deaths in 1760 were to the whole population as 1 to 39; in 1757 as 1 to 32, and in 1758 as 1 to 31.

In making some observations on the tables which had been produced,[20] M. Wargentin says that in the unhealthy years about 1 in 29 have died annually, and in the healthy years 1 in 39; and that, taking a middle term, the average mortality might be considered at 1 in 36.[21] But this inference does not appear to be just, as a mean between 29 and 39 would give 34; and indeed the tables, which he has himself brought forward, contradict an average mortality of 1 in 36, and prove that it is about 1 in $34\frac{3}{4}$.

The proportion of yearly marriages to the whole population appears to be, on an average, nearly as 1 to 112, and to vary between the extremes of 1 to 101, and 1 to 124, according to the temporary prospect of a support for a family. Probably, indeed, it varies between much greater extremes, as the period from which these calculations are made is merely for nine years.

In another paper which M. Wargentin published in the same collection, he again remarks that in Sweden the years which are the most fruitful in produce are the most fruitful in children.[22]

If accurate observations were made in other countries, it is highly probable that differences of the same kind would appear, though not to the same extent.[23] With regard to Sweden, they clearly prove that its population has a very strong tendency to increase; and that it is not only always ready to follow with the greatest alertness any average increase in the means of subsistence, but that it makes a start forwards at every temporary and occasional increase of food, by which means it is continually going beyond the average increase,

---

[18] Memoires Abrégés de l'Academie de Stockholm, p. 29.   [19] Id. p. 21, 22.

[20] [In 1806 (Vol. I, p. 333) this was changed to:
    In some observations on the Swedish registers, M. Wargentin says ...

[21] Memoires Abrégés de l'Academie de Stockholm, p. 29.

[22] Id. p. 31.

[23] This has been confirmed, with regard to England, by the abstracts of parish registers which have lately been published. The years 1795 and 1800 are marked by a diminution of marriages and births, and an increase of deaths.

and is repressed by the periodical returns of severe want and the diseases arising from it.

Yet notwithstanding this constant and striking tendency to overflowing numbers, strange to say! the government and the political economists of Sweden are continually calling out for population, population. Cantzlaer observes that the government, not having the power of inducing strangers to settle in the country, or of augmenting at pleasure the number of births, has occupied itself since 1748 in every measure which appeared proper to increase the population of the country.[24] But suppose that the government really possessed the power of inducing strangers to settle, or of increasing the number of births at pleasure, what would be the consequence? If the strangers were not such as to introduce a better system of agriculture, they would either be starved themselves or cause more of the Swedes to be starved; and if the yearly number of births were considerably increased, it appears to me perfectly clear, from the tables of M. Wargentin, that the principal effect would be merely an increase of mortality. The actual population might, perhaps, even be diminished by it, as when epidemics have once been generated by bad nourishment and crowded houses, they do not always stop when they have taken off the redundant population, but take off with it a part, and sometimes a very considerable part, of that which the country might be able properly to support.

In all very northern climates, in which the principal business of agriculture must necessarily be compressed into the small space of a few summer months, it will almost inevitably happen that during this period a want of hands is felt; but this temporary want should be carefully distinguished from a real and effectual demand for labour, which includes the power of giving employment and support through the whole year, and not merely for two or three months. The population of Sweden, in the natural course of its increase, will always be ready fully to answer this effectual demand; and a supply beyond it, whether from strangers or an additional number of births, could only be productive of misery.

It is asserted by Swedish authors that a given number of men and of days produces, in Sweden, only a third part of what is produced by the same number of each in some other countries;[25] and heavy accusations are in consequence brought against the national industry. Of the general grounds for such accusations a stranger cannot be a competent judge; but in the present instance, it appears to me that more ought to be attributed to the climate and soil than to an actual want of industry in the natives. For a large portion of the year their exertions are necessarily cramped by the severity of

---

[24] Memoires du Royaume de Suede, c. vi. p. 188.
[25] Id. (Cantzlaer) ch. vi. p. 191.

the climate; and during the time when they are able to engage in agricultural operations, the natural indifference of the soil, and the extent of surface
required for a given produce, inevitably employ a great proportional
quantity of labour. It is well known in England that a farm of large extent,
consisting of a poor soil, is worked at a much greater expense for the same
produce than a small one of rich land. The natural poverty of the soil in
Sweden, generally speaking, cannot be denied.[26]

In a journey up the western side of the country, and afterwards in crossing
it from Norway to Stockholm, and thence up the eastern coast to the passage
over to Finland, I confess that I saw fewer marks of a want of national
industry than I should have expected. As far as I could judge, I very seldom
saw any land uncultivated which would have been cultivated in England;
and I certainly saw many spots of land in tillage which never would have
been touched with a plough here. These were lands in which, every five or ten
yards, there were large stones or rocks, round which the plough must
necessarily be turned, or be lifted over them; and the one or the other is
generally done according to their size. The plough is very light, and drawn by
one horse, and in ploughing among the stumps of the trees when they are low,
the general practice is to lift it over them. The man who holds the plough
does this very nimbly, with little or no stop to the horse.

Of the value of those lands for tillage, which are at present covered with
immense forests, I could be no judge; but both the Swedes and the
Norwegians are accused of clearing these woods away too precipitately, and
without previously considering what is likely to be the real value of the land
when cleared. The consequence is that, for the sake of one good crop of rye,
which may always be obtained from the manure afforded by the ashes of the
burnt trees, much growing timber is sometimes spoiled, and the land perhaps
afterwards becomes almost entirely useless. After the crop of rye has been
obtained, the common practice is to turn cattle in upon the grass which may
accidentally grow up. If the land be naturally good, the feeding of the cattle
prevents fresh firs from rising; but if it be bad, the cattle of course cannot
remain long in it, and the seeds with which every wind is surcharged sow the
ground again thickly with firs.

On observing many spots of this kind both in Norway and Sweden, I could
not help being struck with the idea that, though for other reasons it was very
little probable, such appearances certainly made it seem possible that these
countries might have been better peopled formerly than at present; and that
lands which are now covered with forests might have produced corn a

---

[26] [In 1826 (Vol. i, p. 286) Malthus added the following note:
   Cantzlaer mentions the returns from land *effectivement ensemencé* [actually sown by the
   cultivator] as only three grains for one. ch. vi. p. 196.

thousand years ago. Wars, plagues, or that greater depopulator than either, a tyrannical government, might have suddenly destroyed or expelled the greatest part of the inhabitants, and a neglect of the land for twenty or thirty years in Norway or Sweden would produce a very strange difference in the face of the country. But this is merely an idea which I could not help mentioning, but which the reader already knows has not had weight enough with me to make me suppose the fact in any degree probable.

To return to the agriculture of Sweden. Independently of any deficiency in the national industry, there are certainly some circumstances in the political regulations of the country which tend to impede the natural progress of its cultivation. There are still some burdensome corvées remaining, which the possessors of certain lands are obliged to perform for the domains of the crown.[27] The posting of the country is undoubtedly very cheap and convenient to the traveller; but is conducted in a manner to occasion a great waste of labour to the farmer, both in men and horses. It is calculated by the Swedish economists that the labour which would be saved by the abolition of this system alone would produce annually 300 000 tuns of grain.[28] The very great distance of the markets in Sweden, and the very incomplete division of labour which is almost a necessary consequence of it, occasion also a great waste of time and exertion. And, if there be no marked want of diligence and activity among the Swedish peasants, there is certainly a want of knowledge as to the best modes of regulating the rotation of their crops, and of manuring and improving their lands.[29]

If the government were employed in removing these impediments, and in endeavours to encourage and direct the industry of the farmers, and circulate the best information on agricultural subjects, it would do much more for the population of the country than by the establishment of five hundred foundling hospitals.

According to Cantzlaer, the principal measures in which the government had been engaged for the encouragement of the population were the establishment of colleges of medicine, and of lying-in and foundling hospitals.[30] The establishment of colleges of medicine for the cure of the poor, gratis, may in many cases be extremely beneficial, and was so, probably, in the particular circumstances of Sweden; but the example of the hospitals of France, which have the same object, may create a doubt whether even such establishments are universally to be recommended. Lying-in hospitals, as far as they have an effect, are probably rather prejudicial than otherwise as, according to the principle on which they are generally conducted, their

---

[27] Memoires du Royaume de Suede, ch. vi. p. 202.   [28] Id. p. 204.
[29] Id. ch. vi.
[30] Id. p. 188.

tendency is certainly to encourage vice. Foundling hospitals, whether they attain their professed and immediate object or not, are in every view hurtful to the state; but the mode in which they operate, I shall have occasion to discuss more particularly in another chapter.

The Swedish government, however, has not been exclusively employed in measures of this nature. By an edict in 1776, the commerce of grain was rendered completely free throughout the whole interior of the country and, with regard to the province of Scania, which grows more than its consumption, exportation free of every duty was allowed.[31] Till this period, the agriculture of the southern provinces had been checked by the want of vent for their grain, on account of the difficulty of transport, and the absolute prohibition of selling it to foreigners at any price. The northern provinces are still under some little difficulties in this respect,[32] though, as they never grow a quantity sufficient for their consumption, these difficulties are not so much felt.[33] It may be observed, however, in general, that there is no check more fatal to improving cultivation, than any difficulty in the vent of its produce, which prevents the farmer from being able to obtain, in good years, a price for his corn, not much below the general average.

But what perhaps has contributed more than any other cause to the increasing population of Sweden is the abolition of a law in 1748 which limited the number of persons to each henman, or farm.[34] The object of this law appears to have been to force the children of the proprietors to undertake the clearing and cultivation of fresh lands, by which it was thought that the whole country would be sooner improved. But it appeared from experience that these children, being without sufficient funds for such undertakings, were obliged to seek their fortune in some other way; and great numbers, in consequence, are said to have emigrated. A father may now, however, not only divide his landed property into as many shares as he thinks proper; but these divisions are particularly recommended by the government; and, considering the immense size of the Swedish henmans, and the impossibility of their being cultivated completely by one family, such divisions must in every point of view be highly useful.

The population of Sweden in 1751, was 2 229 661.[35] In 1799, according to an account which I received in Stockholm from Professor Nicander, the successor to M. Wargentin, it was 3 043 731. This is a very considerable addition to the permanent population of the country, which has followed a proportional increase in the produce of the soil, as the imports of corn are not

[31] Memoires du Royaume de Suede, ch. vi. p. 204. [p. 202.]
[32] [In 1806 (Vol. I, p. 342) the word *little* was omitted.]
[33] Memoires du Royaume de Suede, ch. vi. p. 204.
[34] Id. p. 177.   [35] Id. p. 184.

greater than they were formerly, and there is no reason to think that the condition of the people is, on an average, worse.

This increase, however, has not gone forwards without periodical checks which, if they have not for a time entirely stopped its progress, have always retarded the rate of it. How often these checks have recurred during the last 50 years, I am not furnished with sufficient data to be able to say, but I can mention some of them. From the paper of M. Wargentin,[36] already quoted in this chapter, it appears that the years 1757 and 1758 were barren and comparatively mortal years. If we were to judge from the increased importation of 1768,[37] this would also appear to be an unproductive year. According to the additional tables with which M. Wargentin furnished Dr. Price, the years 1771, 1772, and 1773 were particularly mortal.[38] The year 1789 must have been very highly so, as in the accounts which I received from Professor Nicander, this year alone materially affected the average proportion of births to deaths for the twenty years ending in 1795. This proportion, including the year 1789, was 100 to 77; but abstracting it, was 100 to 75; which is a great difference for one year to make in an average of twenty. To conclude the catalogue, the year 1799, when I was in Sweden, must have been a very fatal one. In the provinces bordering on Norway, the peasants called it the worst that they had ever remembered. The cattle had all suffered extremely during the winter, from the drought of the preceding year; and, in July, about a month before the harvest, a considerable portion of the people was living upon bread made of the inner bark of the fir, and of dried sorrel, absolutely without any mixture of meal to make it more palatable and nourishing. The sallow looks and melancholy countenances of the people betrayed the unwholesomeness of their nourishment. Many had died, but the full effects of such a diet had not then been felt. They would probably appear afterwards in the form of some epidemic sickness.

The patience with which the lower classes of people in Sweden bear these severe pressures is perfectly astonishing, and can only arise from their being left entirely to their own resources, and from the belief that they are submitting to the great law of necessity, and not to the caprices of their rulers. Most of the married labourers, as has been before observed, cultivate a small portion of land; and when, from an unfavourable season, their crops fail or their cattle die, they see the cause of their want, and bear it as the visitation of providence. Every man will submit, with becoming patience, to evils which he believes to arise from the general laws of nature; but when the vanity and mistaken benevolence of the government and the higher classes of society

---

[36] Memoires de l'Academie de Stockholm, p. 29.
[37] Memoires du Royaume de Suede, table xlii.
[38] Price's Observ. on Revers. Pay. vol. ii. p. 125.

have, by a perpetual interference with the concerns of the lower classes, endeavoured to persuade them that all the good which they enjoy is conferred upon them by their rulers and rich benefactors, it is very natural that they should attribute all the evil which they suffer to the same sources, and patience, under such circumstances, cannot reasonably be expected. Though to avoid still greater evils, we may be allowed to repress this impatience by force, if it shew itself in overt acts, yet the impatience itself appears to be clearly justified in this case; and those are in a great degree answerable for its consequences whose conduct has tended evidently to encourage it.

Though the Swedes had supported the severe dearth of 1799 with extraordinary resignation; yet afterwards, on an edict of the government to prohibit the distillation of spirits, it is said that there were considerable commotions in the country. The measure itself was certainly calculated to benefit the people; and the manner in which it was received affords a curious proof of the different temper with which people bear an evil arising from the laws of nature, or a privation caused by the edicts of a government.

The sickly periods in Sweden which have retarded the rate of its increase in population, appear in general to have arisen from the unwholesome nourishment occasioned by severe want. And this want has been caused by unfavourable seasons falling upon a country which was without any reserved store, either in its general exports, or in the liberal division of food to the labourer in common years; and which was therefore peopled fully up to its produce before the occurrence of the scanty harvest. Such a state of things is a clear proof that if, as some of the Swedish economists assert, their country ought to have a population of nine or ten millions,[39] they have nothing further to do than to make it produce food sufficient for such a number, and they may rest perfectly assured that they will not want mouths to eat it, without the assistance of lying-in and foundling hospitals.

Notwithstanding the mortal year of 1789, it appeared from the accounts which I received from Professor Nicander that the general healthiness of the country had increased. The average mortality for the twenty years ending 1795, was 1 in 37, instead of 1 in less than 35, which had been the average of the preceding twenty years. As the rate of increase had not been accelerated in the twenty years ending in 1795, the diminished mortality must have been occasioned by the increased operation of the preventive check. Another calculation which I received from the professor seemed to confirm this supposition. According to M. Wargentin, as quoted by Susmilch,[40] 5 standing marriages produced yearly 1 child; but in the latter period, the proportion of standing marriages to annual births, was as $5\frac{1}{10}$ and subtrac-

---

39 Memoires du Royaume de Suede, ch. vi. p. 196.
40 Gottliche Ordnung, vol. i. c. vi. s. 120. p. 231.

ting illegitimate children, as $5\frac{3}{10}$ to 1; a proof that in the latter period the marriages had not been quite so early and so prolific.

[In 1826 (Vol. 1, pp. 296–8) Malthus added the following paragraphs:

1825

From subsequent accounts it appears that the healthiness of Sweden has continued to increase, from which we may fairly infer that the condition of the mass of the people has been improving.

In all Sweden and Finland during the five years ending with 1805, the mean number of the living at all ages was, males 1 564 611; females 1 683 457; both, 3 248 068. Annual average deaths of males 40 147; of females 39 266; that is, the annual mortality of males was 1 of 38.97; of females 1 of 42.87; mean, 1 of 40.92.[41]

The annual average births of males were 55 119; of females 52 762; both, 107 882; that is, the proportion of male births to the male population was 1 of 28.38; of female births to the female population of 1 of 31.92; mean, 1 of 30.15.

From a valuable table formed by Mr. Milne on these and other data, it appears that, according to the law of mortality which prevailed in Sweden during the five years ending with 1805, the expectation of life at birth would be for males 37.820, for females 41.019; both, 39.385: and that half of the males would live to very nearly 43 years of age, half of the females nearly to 48 years of age, and half of all the births taken together to 45 years.

A proportion of births as 1 to 30.15, and of deaths as 1 to 40.92, would give a yearly excess of births to the population as 1 to 114.5, which, if continued, would (according to Table II. at the end of Ch. xi. Bk. ii.) give a rate of increase such as to double the population in less than 80 years.

In the Revue Encyclopédique for March 1825, a short account is given of the result of a commission to inquire into the progress of population in Sweden since 1748, from which it appears that Sweden properly so called, exclusive of Finland, contained then 1 736 483 inhabitants; in 1773, 1 958 797; in 1798, 2 352 298; and in 1823, 2 687 457. In 1823, there had been 56 054 deaths, and 98 259 births. The excess of the births in that year alone was therefore 42 205, and it is stated that, supposing the same excess in the next year, 1824, the average annual excess of the last fifteen years would be 23 333. This would be in the proportion of 1 to 108 of the average population, an excess which, if continued, would double the population in about 75 years. According to the foregoing numbers, the proportion of the births to the population was in 1823 as 1 to 27.3, of the deaths as 1 to 47.9. The healthiness of the country, therefore, and the rate of its increase in population, has continued to advance since 1805. This increase is attributed to the progress of agriculture and industry, and the practice of vaccination.

The gradual diminution of mortality since the middle of the last century is very striking.

---

[41] Transactions of the Royal Academy of Sciences at Stockholm for the year 1809, and Supplement to the Encyclopædia Britannica, article Mortality, by Mr. Milne, Actuary to the Sun Life Assurance Society. The period of five years here noticed was free from any remarkable epidemics, and vaccination had commenced in 1804. [See NICANDER and MILNE in the Alphabetical List.]

CHAPTER III

Of the Checks to Population in Russia

The lists of births, deaths, and marriages in Russia present such extraordinary results that it is impossible not to receive them with a considerable degree of suspicion; at the same time, the regular manner in which they have been collected, and their agreement with each other in different years, entitle them to attention.

In a paper presented in 1786,[1] by B. F. Herman, to the academy of Petersburgh, and published in the *Nova Acta Academiæ, tom. iv.* a comparison is made of the births, deaths, and marriages in the different provinces and towns of the empire, and the following proportions are given:[2]

In Petersburgh the births are to the burials, as	13 to 10
In the government of Moscow,	21–10
District of Moscow, excepting the town,	21–10
Tver,	26–10
Novogorod,	20–10
Pskovsk,	22–10
Resan,	20–10
Veronesch,	29–10
Archbishopric of Vologda,	23–10
Kostroma,	20–10
Archangel,	13–10
Tobolsk,	21–10
Town of Tobolsk,	13–10
Reval,	11–10
Vologda,	12–10

Some of these proportions, it will be observed, are extraordinarily high. In Veronesch, for instance, the births are to the deaths nearly as 3 to 1, which is as great a proportion, I believe, as ever was known in America. The average result, however, of these proportions, has been confirmed by subsequent

---

[1] [In 1807 (Vol. 1, p. 350) this date was wrongly given as 1768, and the mistake has been repeated in all subsequent editions.]

[2] [This table is on p. 77 of Vol. iv.]

observations.[3] Mr. Tooke, in his View of the Russian Empire, makes the general proportion of births to burials throughout the whole country as 225 to 100,[4] which is $2\frac{1}{4}$ to 1; and this proportion is taken from the lists of 1793.[5]

From the number of yearly marriages, and yearly births, M. Herman draws the following conclusions:[6]

In Petersburgh one marriage yields	4 children,
In the government of Moscow, about	3
Tver,	3
Novogorod,	3
Pskovsk,	3
Resan,	3
Veronesch,	4
Vologda,	4
Kostroma,	3
Archangel,	4
Reval,	4
Government of Tobolsk,	4
Town of Tobolsk, from 1768 to 1778,	3
„ „ from 1779 to 1783,	5
„ „ in 1783,	6

M. Herman observes that the fruitfulness of marriages in Russia does not exceed that of other countries, though the mortality is much less; as appears from the following proportions, drawn from a rough calculation of the number of inhabitants in each government:

In Petersburgh,	1 in 28 dies annually
In the government of Moscow,	1–32
District of Moscow,	1 in 74
Tver,	1–75
Novogorod,	$1-68\frac{6}{7}$
Pskovsk,	$1-70\frac{4}{5}$
Resan,	1–50
Veronesch,	1–79
Archbishopric of Vologda,	1–65
Kostroma,	1–59
Archangel,	$1-28\frac{3}{5}$
Reval,	1–29
Government of Tobolsk,	1–44
Town of Tobolsk,	1–32
„ „ in 1783,	$1-22\frac{1}{4}$

[3] [In 1806 (Vol. I, p. 351) Malthus qualified this:
... has been, in some degree, confirmed by subsequent observations.
[4] Vol. ii. b. iii. p. 162.   [5] Id. p. 145.   [6] [This table is on pp. 81–2 of Vol. IV.]

It may be concluded, M. Herman says, that in the greatest number of the Russian provinces the yearly mortality is 1 in 60.[7]

This average number is so high, and some of the proportions in the particular provinces are so extraordinary, that it is almost impossible to believe them accurate. They have been nearly confirmed, however, by subsequent lists which, according to Mr. Tooke, make the general mortality in all Russia, 1 in 58.[8] But Mr. Tooke himself seems to doubt the accuracy of this particular department of the registers; and I have since heard, from good authority, that there is reason to believe that the omissions in the burials are in all the provinces much greater than the omissions in the births, and consequently, that the very great excess of births, and very small mortality, are more apparent than real. It is supposed that many children, particularly in the Ukraine, are privately interred by their fathers without information to the priest. The numerous and repeated levies of recruits take off great numbers whose deaths are not recorded. From the frequent emigrations of whole families to different parts of the empire, and the transportation of malefactors to Siberia, great numbers necessarily die on journeys, or in parts where no regular lists are kept; and some omissions are attributed to the neglect of the parish priests who have an interest in recording the births, but not the deaths.

To these reasons, I should add that the population of each province is probably estimated by the number of boors belonging to each estate in it; but it is well known that a great part of them has leave to reside in the towns. Their births, therefore, appear in the province, but their deaths do not. The apparent mortality of the towns is not proportionably increased by this emigration, because it is estimated according to actual enumeration. The bills of mortality in the towns express correctly the numbers dying out of a certain number known to be actually present in these towns; but the bills of mortality in the provinces, purporting to express the numbers dying out of the estimated population of the province, do really only express the numbers dying out of a much smaller population, because a considerable part of the estimated population is absent.

In Petersburgh, it appeared by an enumeration in 1784, that the number of males was 126 827, and of females only 65 619.[9] The proportion of males was therefore very nearly double, arising from the numbers who came to the town to earn their capitation tax, leaving their families in the country, and from the custom among the nobles of retaining a prodigious number of their boors as household servants in Petersburgh and Moscow.

---

[7] Nova Acta Academiæ, tom. iv. [For comment on this table see HERMANN in the Alphabetical List.]

[8] View of the Russian Empire, vol. ii. b. iii. p. 148.

[9] Memoire par W. L. Krafft, Nova Acta Academiæ, tom. iv.

The number of births in proportion to the whole population in Russia is not different from a common average in other countries, being about 1 in 26.[10]

According to the paper of M. Herman, already quoted, the proportion of boys dying within the first year is, at Petersburgh, $\frac{1}{5}$, in the government of Tobolsk $\frac{1}{10}$, in the town of Tobolsk $\frac{1}{8}$, in the Archbishopric of Vologda $\frac{1}{14}$, in Novogorod $\frac{1}{31}$, in Veronesch $\frac{1}{24}$, in Archangel $\frac{1}{5}$. The very small mortality of infants in some of these provinces, particularly as the calculation does not seem to be liable to much error, makes the smallness of the general mortality more credible. In Sweden, throughout the whole country, the proportion of infants which dies within the first year is $\frac{1}{5}$ or more.[11]

The proportion of yearly marriages in Russia to the whole population, is, according to M. Herman, in the towns about 1 in 100, and in the provinces about 1 in 70 or 80. According to Mr. Tooke, in the fifteen governments of which he had lists, the proportion was 1 in 92.[12] This is not very different from other countries. In Petersburgh, indeed, the proportion was 1 in 140;[13] but this is clearly accounted for, by what has already been said of the extraordinary number of the males in comparison of the females.

The registers for the city of Petersburgh are supposed to be such as can be entirely depended upon; and these tend to prove the general salubrity of the climate. But there is one fact recorded in them which is directly contrary to what has been observed in all other countries. This is a much greater mortality of female children than of male. In the period from 1781 to 1785, of 1000 boys born, 147 only died within the first year, but of the same number of girls 310.[14] The proportion is as 10 to 21, which is inconceivable, and must indeed have been in some measure accidental, as, in the preceding periods, the proportion was only as 10 to 14; but even this is very extraordinary, as it has been generally remarked that, in every stage of life, except during the period of childbearing, the mortality among females is less than among males. The climate of Sweden does not appear to be very different from that of Russia; and M. Wargentin observes, with respect to the Swedish tables, that it appears from them that the smaller mortality of females is not merely owing to a more regular and less laborious life, but is a natural law which operates constantly from infancy to old age.[15]

According to M. Krafft,[16] the half of all that are born in Petersburgh live to

---

[10] Tooke's View of Russian Empire, vol. ii. b. iii. p. 147.
[11] Memoires Abrégés de l'Academie de Stockholm, p. 28.
[12] View of Russ. Emp. vol. ii. b. iii. p. 146.
[13] Memoire par W. L. Krafft, Nova Acta Academiæ, tom. iv.
[14] Id. tom. iv.   [15] Memoires Abrégés de l'Academie de Stockholm, p. 28.
[16] Nova Acta Academiæ, tom. iv.

25; which shews a degree of healthiness in early life very unusual for so large a town; but after twenty, a mortality much greater than in any other town in Europe takes place, which is justly attributed to the immoderate use of brandy.[17] The mortality between 10 and 15 is so small, that only 1 in 47 males, and 1 in 29 females, die during this period. From 20 to 25, the mortality is so great that 1 in 9 males, and 1 in 13 females die. The tables show that this extraordinary mortality is occasioned principally by pleurisies, high fevers, and consumptions. Pleurisies destroy $\frac{1}{4}$, high fevers $\frac{1}{3}$, and consumptions $\frac{1}{6}$, of the whole population. The three together take off $\frac{5}{7}$ of all that die.

The general mortality during the period from 1781 to 1785, was, according to M. Krafft, 1 in 37. In a former period it has been 1 in 35, and in a subsequent period, when epidemic diseases prevailed, 1 in 29.[18] This average mortality is small for a large town; but there is reason to think, from a passage in M. Krafft's memoir,[19] that the deaths in the hospitals, the prisons, and in the *Maison des Enfans trouvés*, are either entirely omitted, or not given with correctness; and undoubtedly the insertion of these deaths might make a great difference in the apparent healthiness of the town.

In the *Maison des Enfans trouvés* alone, the mortality is prodigious. No regular lists are published, and verbal communications are always liable to some uncertainty. I cannot, therefore, rely upon the information which I collected on the subject; but, from the most careful inquiries which I could make of the attendants at the house in Petersburgh, I understood that 100 a month was the common average.[20] In the preceding winter, which was the winter of 1788,[21] it had not been uncommon to bury 18 a day. The average number received in the day is about 10; and though they are all sent into the country to be nursed three days after they have been in the house, yet, as many of them are brought in a dying state, the mortality must necessarily be great. The number said to be received appears, indeed, almost incredible; but, from what I saw myself, I should be inclined to believe that both this and the mortality before mentioned might not be far from the truth. I was at the house about noon, and four children had been just received, one of which was evidently dying, and another did not seem as if it would long survive.

A part of the house is destined to the purpose of a lying-in hospital, where

---

17 Tooke's View of the Russian Empire, vol. ii. b. iii. p. 155.   18 Id. p. 151.
19 See a Note in Tooke's View of Russ. Emp. vol. ii. b. iii. p. 150.
20 [Malthus and his friend William Otter visited St Petersburg in the course of their northern tour, in the autumn of 1799. This was during the brief reign of the mad Czar Paul, who had succeeded his mother, Catherine the Great, in 1796; he was assassinated in March 1801. Malthus's diary for this part of his tour – if he kept one – has not been found.]
21 [This was, in fact, the winter of 1798, and the mistake was repeated in all subsequent editions until Pickering's of 1986.]

every woman that comes is received, and no questions are asked. The children which are thus born are brought up by nurses in the house, and are not sent into the country like the others. A mother, if she choose it, may perform the office of nurse to her own child, in the house, but is not permitted to take it away with her. A child brought to the house may at any time be reclaimed by its parents, if they can prove themselves able to support it; and all the children are marked and numbered on being received, that they may be known and produced to the parents when required, who, if they cannot reclaim them, are permitted to visit them.

The country nurses receive only two roubles a month which, as the current paper rouble is seldom worth more than half a crown, is only about fifteen pence a week; yet the general expenses are said to be 100 000 roubles a month. The regular revenues belonging to the institution are not nearly equal to this sum; but the government takes on itself the management of the whole affair, and consequently bears all the additional expenses. As the children are received without any limit, it is absolutely necessary that the expenses should also be unlimited. It is evident that the most dreadful evils must result from an unlimited reception of children, and only a limited fund to support them. Such institutions, therefore, if managed properly, that is, if the extraordinary mortality do not prevent the rapid accumulation of expense, cannot exist long except under the protection of a very rich government; and even under such protection there must ultimately be a limit.[22]

At six or seven years old the children who have been sent into the country, return to the house, where they are taught all sorts of trades and manual operations. The common hours of working are from 6 to 12, and from 2 till 4. The girls leave the house at 18, and the boys at 20 or 21. When the house is too full, some of those which have been sent into the country are not brought back.

The principal mortality, of course, takes place among the infants who are just received, and the children which are brought up in the house; but there is a considerable mortality among those which are returned from the country, and are in the firmest stages of life. I was in some degree surprised at hearing this, after having been particularly struck with the extraordinary degree of neatness, cleanliness, and sweetness which appeared to prevail in every department. The house itself had been a palace, and all the rooms were large, airy, and even elegant. I was present while 180 boys were dining. They were all dressed very neatly; the table-cloth was clean, and each had a separate napkin to himself. The provisions appeared to be extremely good, and there

---

[22] [In 1806 (Vol. I, p. 361) this was changed to:
    ... and even under such protection of the period of failure cannot be very distant.

was not the smallest disagreeable smell in the room. In the dormitories there was a separate bed for each child; the bedsteads were of iron without tester[23] or curtains, and the coverlids and sheets particularly clean.

This degree of neatness, almost inconceivable in a large institution, was to be attributed principally to the present Empress Dowager,[24] who interested herself in all the details of the management and, when at Petersburgh, seldom passed a week without inspecting them in person. The mortality which takes place in spite of all these attentions is a clear proof that the constitution, in early youth, cannot support confinement and work for 8 hours in the day. The children had all rather a pale and sickly countenance, and if a judgment had been formed of the national beauty from the girls and boys in this establishment, it would have been most unfavourable.

It is evident that, if the deaths belonging to this institution be omitted, the bills of mortality for Petersburgh cannot give a representation, in any degree near the truth, of the real state of the city with respect to healthiness. At the same time, it should be recollected that some of the observations which attest its healthiness, such as the number dying in a thousand, &c. are not influenced by this circumstance; unless indeed we say, what is perhaps true, that nearly all those who would find any difficulty in rearing their children send them to the foundling hospital, and the mortality among the children of those who are in easy circumstances, and live in comfortable houses and airy situations, will of course be much less than a general average taken from all that are born.

The *Maison des Enfans trouvés*, at Moscow, is conducted exactly upon the same principle as that of Petersburgh; and Mr. Tooke gives an account of the surprising loss of children which it had sustained in twenty years, from the time of its first establishment to the year 1786. On this occasion, he observes that if we knew precisely the number of those who died immediately after reception, or who brought in with them the germ of dissolution, a small part only of the mortality would probably appear to be fairly attributable to the foundling-hospital; as none would be so unreasonable as to lay the loss of these certain victims to death to the account of a philanthropical institution, which enriches the country from year to year with an ever-increasing number of healthy, active, and industrious burghers.[25]

It appears to me, however, that the greatest part of this premature mortality is clearly to be attributed to these institutions, miscalled philanth-

---

[23] [A *tester* is the wooden canopy or 'roof' of a four-poster bed.]
[24] [The 'present Empress Dowager' was Maria Feodorovna (born Sophia Dorothea of Würtemberg) who in 1803 was the widow of the assassinated Czar Paul and the mother of Czar Alexander I (1777–1825). She herself did not die until 1828.]
[25] View of the Russian Empire, vol. ii. b. iii. p. 201.

ropic. If any reliance can be placed on the accounts which are given of the infant mortality in the Russian towns and provinces, it would appear to be unusually small. The greatness of it, therefore, at the foundling hospitals, may justly be laid to the account of institutions which encourage a mother to desert her child at the very time when, of all others, it stands most in need of her fostering care. The frail tenure by which an infant holds its life will not allow of a remitted attention, even for a few hours.

The surprising mortality which takes place at these two foundling hospitals of Petersburgh and Moscow, which are managed in the best possible manner (as all who have seen them, with one consent, assert) appears to me incontrovertibly to prove that the nature of these institutions is not calculated to answer the immediate end that they have in view, which I conceive to be the preservation of a certain number of citizens to the state, who might otherwise, perhaps, perish from poverty or false shame. It is not to be doubted that if the children received into these hospitals had been left to the management of their parents, taking the chance of all the difficulties in which they might be involved, a much greater proportion of them would have reached the age of manhood, and have become useful members of the state.

When we look a little deeper into this subject, it will appear that these institutions not only fail in their immediate object, but by encouraging, in the most marked manner, habits of licentiousness, discourage marriage, and thus weaken the main spring of population. All the well-informed men with whom I conversed on this subject, at Petersburgh, agreed invariably that the institution had produced this effect in a surprising degree. To have a child was considered as one of the most trifling faults which a girl could commit. An English merchant at Petersburgh told me that a Russian girl living in his family, under a mistress, who was considered as very strict, had sent six children to the foundling hospital without the loss of her place.

It should be observed, however, that generally speaking six children are not common in this kind of intercourse. Where habits of licentiousness prevail, the births are never in the same proportion to the number of people as in the married state; and therefore the discouragement to marriage, arising from this licentiousness, and the diminished number of births which is the consequence of it, will much more than counterbalance any encouragement to marriage from the prospect held out to parents of disposing of the children which they cannot support.

Considering the extraordinary mortality which occurs in the institutions, and the habits of licentiousness which they have an evident tendency to create, it may perhaps be truly said that, if a person wished to check population, and were not solicitous about the means, he could not propose a more effectual measure than the establishment of a sufficient number of foundling hospitals, unlimited in their reception of children. And with regard to the moral feelings of a nation, it is difficult to conceive that they must not be very sensibly impaired[26] by encouraging mothers to desert their offspring, and endeavouring to teach them, that their love for their new-born infants is a prejudice which it is the interest of their country to eradicate. An occasional child-murder, from false shame, is saved at a very high price, if it can only be done by the sacrifice of some of the best and most useful feelings of the human heart in a great part of the nation.

On the supposition that foundling hospitals attained their proposed end, the state of slavery in Russia would perhaps render them more justifiable in that country than in any other; because every child brought up at the foundling hospitals becomes a free citizen, and in this capacity is likely to be more useful to the state than if it had merely increased the number of slaves belonging to an individual proprietor. But in countries not similarly circumstanced, the most complete success in institutions of this kind would be a glaring injustice to other parts of the society. The true encouragement to marriage is the high price of labour, and an increase of employments which require to be supplied with proper hands; but if the principal part of these employments, apprenticeships, &c. be filled up by foundlings, the demand for labour among the legitimate part of the society must be proportionally diminished, the difficulty of supporting a family be increased, and the best encouragement to marriage removed.

Russia has great natural resources. Its produce is, in its present state, above its consumption; and it wants nothing but greater freedom of industrious exertion, and an adequate vent for its commodities in the interior parts of the country, to occasion an increase of population astonishingly rapid. The principal obstacle to this is the vassalage, or rather slavery, of the peasants, and the ignorance and indolence which almost necessarily accompany such a state. The fortune of a Russian nobleman is measured by the number of boors that he possesses, which in general are saleable, like cattle and not *adscripti glebæ*.[27] His revenue arises from a capitation tax on all the males. When the boors upon an estate are increasing, new divisions of land are made at certain intervals, and either more is taken into cultivation, or the old shares are subdivided. Each family is awarded such a portion of land as it can properly cultivate, and will enable it to pay the tax. It is evidently the interest of the boor not to improve his lands much, and appear to get considerably more than is necessary to support his family and pay the poll-tax; because the natural consequence will be that, in the next division which takes place, the farm which he before possessed will be considered as

---

26 [In 1826 (Vol. i, p. 313) Malthus excised the word *very*]. ['Sensibly' here does not mean according to common sense, but such as is obviously perceived by the senses, acutely felt.]

27 [Legally attached to a particular piece of land or estate.]

capable of supporting two families, and he will be deprived of the half of it. The indolent cultivation that such a state of things must produce is easily conceivable. When a boor is deprived of much of the land which he had before used, he makes complaints of inability to pay his tax, and demands permission for himself or his sons to go and earn it in the towns. This permission is in general eagerly sought after, and is granted without much difficulty by the seigneurs, in consideration of a small increase of the poll-tax. The consequence is that the lands in the country are left half cultivated, and the genuine spring of population impaired in its source.

A Russian nobleman at Petersburgh, of whom I asked some questions respecting the management of his estate, told me that he never troubled himself to inquire whether it was properly cultivated or not, which he seemed to consider as a matter in which he was not in the smallest degree concerned. *Cela m'est egal*, says he, *cela me fait ni bien ni mal*.[28] He gave his boors permission to earn their tax how and where they liked, and as long as he received it, he was satisfied. But it is evident that by this kind of conduct he sacrificed the future population of his estate, and the consequent future increase of his revenues, to considerations of indolence and present convenience.

It is certain, however, that of late years many noblemen have attended more to the improvement and population of their estates, instigated principally by the precepts and examples[29] of the empress Catherine, who made the greatest exertions to advance the cultivation of the country. Her immense importations of German settlers, not only contributed to people her state with free citizens, instead of slaves, but what was perhaps of still more importance, to set an example of industry, and of modes of directing that industry, totally unknown before to the Russian peasants.

These exertions have been crowned,[30] upon the whole, with great success; and it is not to be doubted, that, during the reign of the late empress, and since, a very considerable increase of cultivation and of population has been going forward, in almost every part of the Russian empire.

In the year 1763 an enumeration of the people, estimated by the poll-tax, gave a population of 14 726 696; and the same kind of enumeration in 1783 gave a population of 25 677 000, which, if correct, shews a very extraordinary increase; but it is supposed that the enumeration in 1783 was more correct and complete than the one in 1763. Including the provinces not subject to the poll-tax, the general calculation for 1763 was 20 000 000, and for 1796, 36 000 000.[31]

---

[28] ['It's all the same to me, I neither gain nor lose by it.']
[29] [In 1817 (Vol. I, p. 437) *examples* was replaced by 'example'.]
[30] [In 1817 (Vol. I, p. 438) *crowned* was replaced by 'attended'.]
[31] Tooke's View of the Russian Empire, vol. ii. book iii. sect. i. p. 126, et seq.

[In 1806 (Vol. 1, pp. 371–2) Malthus added the following paragraphs:

In a subsequent edition of Mr. Tooke's View of the Russian Empire, a table of the births, deaths, and marriages in the Greek Church is given for the year 1799, taken from a respectable German periodical publication, and faithfully extracted from the general returns received by the synod. It contains all the eparchies except Bruzlaw,[32] which, from the peculiar difficulties attending a correct list of mortality in that eparchy, could not be inserted. The general results are:

	Males	Females	Totals
Births	531 015	460 900	991 915
Deaths	275 582	264 807	540 389

Marriages 257 513

Overplus of births $\left\{ \begin{array}{ll} \text{Males} & 255\,433 \\ \text{Females} & 196\,093 \end{array} \right\}$ 451 525

To estimate the population Mr. Tooke multiplies the deaths by 58. But as this table has the appearance of being more correct than those which preceded it, and as the proportion of deaths compared with the births is greater in this table than in the others, it is probable that 58 is too great a multiplier. It may be observed that in this table the births are to the deaths nearly as 183 to 100, the births to marriages as 385 to 100, and the deaths to the marriages as 210 to 100.

These are all more probable proportions than the results of the former tables.

[In 1826 (Vol. 1, pp. 318–19) this chapter was extended with more up-to-date information:

1825

The population of Russia, including the wandering tribes and the acquired territories, was in 1822 estimated at 54 476 931. But the most interesting part of the population to examine is that where lists of the births, deaths, and marriages can be obtained.

The following table, which is given in the Encyclopædia Britannica, under the head of Russia, is formed from the reports published by the Synod, including only the members of the Orthodox Greek Church, the most numerous body of the people.

	1806	1810	1816	1820
Marriages	299 057	320 389	329 683	317 805
Births	1 361 286	1 374 926	1 457 606	1 570 399
Deaths	818 585	903 380	820 383	917 680

The population belonging to the Greek Church is estimated at 40 351 000.

If the average excess of the births above the deaths be applied to the 14 years

---

[32] [An *eparchy* is the equivalent of a diocese (a district administered by a bishop) in the Russian Church; Malthus's use of this word is quoted in the O.E.D., but the references are incorrect.]

ending with 1820, it will appear that, from this excess alone, the population had increased in that period, 8 064 616; and if the population in 1820 were 40 351 000, the population in 1806 was 32 286 384. Comparing the average excess of births with the average population during the 14 years, it will be found that the proportion is as 1 to 63, which (according to Table II. at the end of the 11th Chapter of this Book)· would double the population in less than 44 years; a most rapid rate of increase.

The proportion of births to marriages is a little above 4½ to 1; of births to deaths, as 5 to 3; of marriages to the population, as 1 to 114; of births to the population as 1 to 25.2; and of deaths to the population, or the mortality, as 1 to 41.9.

Most of these proportions are essentially different from those mentioned in the earlier part of this chapter; but there is good reason to believe that they are more accurate; and they certainly accord better with the very rapid increase of population which is known to be going on in Russia.

The apparent increase of mortality is to be attributed rather to the former inaccuracy of the registers than to increased unhealthiness. It is now allowed that the registers before 1796 were very imperfectly kept.

CHAPTER IV(a)

On the fruitfulness of Marriages[1]

Notwithstanding the extraordinary proportions of births to deaths in Russia, which have been noticed in the last chapter, and the confirmation of these proportions in a considerable degree by actual enumerations, which establish a very rapid increase, it appears that in most of the provinces each marriage yields only three children.

But if we reflect a moment, it will be clear that to prevent the population of a country from regularly decreasing, it is absolutely necessary that each marriage, on an average, should yield a marriage; that is, yield two children who live to be married. If the result fall short of this, the number of marriages must be gradually diminishing, and the number of children to each marriage remaining the same, the population, of course, will continue decreasing. If each marriage yield accurately two marrying children, the number of marriages and the number of children being the same in every generation, the population can be neither retrograde nor progessive, but must remain exactly stationary.

Supposing each marriage to produce three children, as appears to be the case, according to the lists in some of the provinces of Russia, it will be granted that one out of three is but a small proportion to allow for all who die in infancy and celibacy. But admitting this proportion, which may perhaps be true in the present instance, though it is very rarely so in other situations, it will follow that exactly two children, and no more, from every marriage, live to form a fresh union; in which case, from what has been before observed, no increase is possible. And yet in these same provinces the proportion of the births to the deaths is given as 26 to 10; 22 to 10; 21 to 10; 20 to 10, &c: which implies a very rapid increase. The lists therefore involve a most complete contradiction. Yet there is no reason to suspect the accuracy of the statements respecting the births and marriages; and, allowing for some

---

[1] [In 1806 (Vol. II, pp. 1–30) Malthus completely re-wrote this chapter; it then became chapter ix of Book II: see his 'Advertisement to the Third Edition'. When in 1817 he added two new chapters to Book II, on France and England, 'On the Fruitfulness of Marriages' became chapter xi. In this edition the re-written chapter is printed at the beginning of Vol. II.]

omissions in the burials, the excess of births will still be great; and indeed the increasing state of the population has been ascertained by the enumerations mentioned in the last chapter.

Contradictory as these lists appear, they do not involve a greater contradiction than the lists of other countries, which purport to express the number of births which each marriage yields. And it may perhaps contribute to the better understanding of the tables, which I shall have occasion to notice in the next chapter, if I endeavour to explain a very important error into which all the writers in political arithmetic that I have ever met with have fallen, relative to this subject.

These lists are, in reality, enumerations of the annual marriages and the annual births; and the proportion between them, of course, accurately expresses the proportion of births to marriages which takes place in the year; but this proportion has been assumed to express the number of births which each individual marriage in the course of its duration yields. On what grounds this assumption has been made will appear from the following considerations.

If, in a country where there were no exports or imports of people, we could obtain the number of births and of marriages that had taken place in the course of a very long period, it is evident that double the number of marriages or, which is the same thing, the number of married people, would express accurately the proportion of the born which had lived to be married; and the difference between this number and the number of births would also express accurately the proportion of the born which had died in infancy and celibacy. But the whole numbers of births and marriages, during this period, are evidently nothing more than the sum of the annual births and the sum of the annual marriages. If, therefore, in any country, an average proportion can be obtained between the annual births and annual marriages, this proportion will manifestly express the same thing as the whole numbers; that is, the number of persons annually married, compared with the number of annual births, will accurately express the proportion of the born which lives to be married; and the difference between them, the proportion of the born which dies in infancy and celibacy. For instance, if the average proportion of annual marriages to annual births in any country be as 1 to 4, this will imply that, out of four children born, two of them live to marry, and the other two die in infancy and celibacy. This is a most important and interesting piece of information, from which the most useful inferences are to be drawn; but it is totally different from the number of births which each individual marriage yields in the course of its duration; so much so, that on the supposition which has been just made, that half of the born live to be married, which is a very usual proportion, the annual marriages would be to the annual births as 1 to 4, whether each individual marriage yielded 4 births, 2 births, or 100 births.

If the latter number be taken, then, according to the present supposition, 50 would live to be married; and out of every 100 births there would be 25 marriages, and the marriages would still be to the births as 1 to 4. The same proportion would evidently hold good in the case of two births yielded by each marriage, as this proportion is not in the smallest degree affected by the number of children which a marriage in the course of its duration may yield, but merely relates to the number of these children who live to be married, or the number of births from which one marriage results.

The only case in which the proportion of annual births to annual marriages is the same as the proportion of births which each individual marriage yields, is when the births and deaths are exactly equal; and the reason of their being the same in this case is that, in order to make the births and deaths exactly equal, we must assume that each marriage yields exactly another marriage, and that whatever be the number of children born from each union, they all die in infancy and celibacy except one pair. Thus, if each marriage yield five children, two of which only live to form a fresh union, the proportion of annual marriages to annual births will be as 1 to 5, which is the same as the number of births yielded by each individual marriage, by hypothesis. But whenever each marriage yields either more or less than one marrying pair, that is, whenever the population is either increasing or decreasing, then the proportion of annual births to annual marriages can never be the same as the proportion of births yielded by each individual marriage in the course of its duration.

Hence it follows, that whenever we assume them to be the same, any increase of population is impossible. Thus, if the foregoing reasoning be admitted, and it be granted that the proportion of persons yearly married, to the number of children yearly born, truly expresses the proportion of the born which lives to be married; then, assuming at the same time, what is assumed by those who produce these lists, that they express the number of births yielded by each individual marriage, it is evident that all such lists prove that the population is stationary; whereas perhaps, from other accounts, it is known with certainty that a rapid increase is going forwards. Thus in Sweden, if we allow that the proportion of yearly marriages to yearly births, which is as 1 to 4 and $\frac{1}{10}$, expresses what it really does, that out of 4 and $\frac{1}{10}$ births, one pair lives to marry; and suppose, at the same time, according to Wargentin, Susmilch, Crome, Price, and others, that each marriage, in the course of its duration, yields only $4\frac{1}{10}$ births, it would follow that, out of $4\frac{1}{10}$ births, 2 and $\frac{1}{10}$ die in infancy and celibacy, and only two children from each marriage live to form a fresh union, in which case no increase would be possible though, from the excess of births above the deaths, and even from actual enumerations, it might be completely ascertained that the progress of the population was considerable.

Dr. Price had considered this subject sufficiently to see that, in countries where an increase or decrease of population was taking place, these lists did not accurately express the number of births yielded by each marriage; but that he was very far from coming at what I conceive to be the just conclusion on this point, appears from his observing that, on the supposition that half of the born live to marry, if the prolificness of marriages were to increase, the births would rise above quadruple the weddings;[2] whereas in fact, as long as exactly half of the born live to be married, the annual births will always be exactly quadruple the annual weddings, let the prolificness of marriages vary in any conceivable degree.[3]

As a further proof that Dr. Price did not understand this subject, though he has a long and elaborate note on it, he often mentions the lists of the yearly births and marriages, as expressing the number of children born to each marriage, and particularly notices the proportion in Sweden, as shewing the degree of prolificness in the marriages of that country.[4] He merely thought that the lists of annual births and marriages did not, in all cases, express accurately the prolificness of marriages; but he does not seem to have been in the smallest degree aware that they had absolutely nothing to do with it; and that, so far from being merely inaccurate, it would be impossible, from such lists, unaccompanied by other information, to tell with certainty whether the prolificness in the marriages of any country were such as to yield 2 births or 100 births in the course of their duration.

Such lists, therefore, considered as expressing the prolificness of marriages, must be rejected as perfectly useless; but considered as expressing the proportion of the born which lives to be married, should be preserved as highly valuable, and as giving a most interesting and desirable piece of information.

The late Empress Catherine, in her instructions for a new code of laws in Russia, says, 'our peasants have for the most part twelve, fifteen, and even as far as twenty children from one marriage'.[5] This is certainly an exaggeration; but the probability is that the assertion was founded on a knowledge that the Russian women were generally prolific; and yet, according to the lists which have been produced, it would appear that in most of the provinces, one

---

[2] Observations on Revers. Paym. vol. i. p. 270, note.

[3] That is, when a sufficient time has elapsed, to let the births affect the marriages. Before this period, indeed, Dr. Price's observation would be just; but, practically, it seldom happens that the women of a country become all at once more prolific than usual; and in the general tables of mortality from which the deductions are made, if they be not such, as for the births to affect the marriages, they cannot express a just average of any kind, and are in every point of view almost entirely useless.

[4] Observations on Revers. Paym. vol. i. p. 275.

[5] Chap. xii. p. 188. 4to. 1770. Petersburgh. [See CATHERINE II in the Alphabetical List.]

marriage yields only three children, which is perfectly irreconcilable with the assertions of the empress. But according to the foregoing reasonings, these lists merely express that, out of three children born, two live to be married, which agrees with the extraordinary healthiness in early life noticed in some of the provinces. The probability is that each marriage in these provinces yields about 6 births, 4 of which live to marry; and this supposition, which retains the proper proportion of the births to the marriages, according to the lists, will account for the excess of the births above the deaths and the rapid increase of the population.

In those provinces where the annual births are to the annual marriages as 4 to 1, there, according to the principles laid down, only 2 out of 4, instead of 2 out of 3, live to be married; and to produce the excess of births observed in some of these provinces, even after making great allowances for omissions in the burials,[6] it will be necessary to suppose that there were full as many as 8 births to each marriage in the course of its duration.

Taking the general proportion of annual births to marriages for the whole country, as given by Mr. Tooke, then it would appear that out of 362 births, 200 lived to marry;[7] and to produce a proportion of births to deaths, as 2 to 1, instead of $2\frac{1}{4}$ to 1, as given by Mr. Tooke; that is, allowing the $\frac{1}{4}$ for the omissions in the burials, it will be necessary to suppose 7 or $7\frac{1}{2}$ births to each marriage, which may in some degree justify the assertions of the empress.[8]

These are rough calculations, formed by constructing tables on the plan of one produced by Wallace, in his Dissertation on the Numbers of Mankind, and observing the proportions of births to deaths, which result from different suppositions respecting the number of children born and the number which live to be married. As this dissertation is not in every person's hands, I insert the table, in order that the reader may see the grounds on which I have gone in these calculations.

It sets out with a single pair, but of course it is the same thing, whether we begin with 2 people or 2 millions of people. There are 8 columns, the contents of which are explained at the top of each.

---

[6] I am inclined to believe that where only half of the born live to be married, the proportion of the births to the deaths can never rise quite so high as 2 to 1, whatever may be the number of children to a marriage. The lists, therefore, such as those of Veronesch, which imply that only half of the born live to be married, at the same time that the births are to the deaths in the proportion of above 2 to 1, can only be accounted for by great omissions in the deaths, and by emigrations.

[7] Tooke's View of Russian Empire, vol. ii. b. iii. p. 147.

[8] On the supposition that I have not assumed the proper proportions of births to deaths, which, from not knowing how to estimate the acknowledged omissions in the burials, is very probable, the results of course will be changed, and therefore too much stress should not be laid on them.

TABLE I

Periods of the scheme	Years of the scheme	Born since the last period	Of whom died since last period	And remain in life to propagate	Died since the last period at an advanced age	The sum of all who are alive at the respective periods	The sum of the last column collected
Col. 1	Col. 2	Col. 3	Col. 4	Col. 5	Col. 6	Col. 7	Col. 8
0	1	0	0	0	0	2	2
1	$33\frac{1}{3}$	6	2	4	0	2+4	6
2	$66\frac{2}{3}$	12	4	8	2	6+8−2	12
3	100	24	8	16	4	12+16−4	24
4	$133\frac{1}{3}$	48	16	32	8	24+32−8	48
5	$166\frac{2}{3}$	96	32	64	16	48+64−16	96
6	200	192	64	128	32	96+128−32	192

The object of Mr. Wallace, in this table, was merely to show the progress of population from a single pair, and the period of doubling; but if no essential fault be found with the construction of it, it may be applied more extensively and usefully.

The periods are taken at $33\frac{1}{3}$ years; but the real period of a generation will, of course, vary in different countries, according to the average age of marriage. Each marriage is supposed to yield 6 children, 2 of whom, or one third, die in infancy or celibacy; and 4, or two thirds, forming two marriages, are left alive to breed.

If we examine the numbers in the second period, we shall find 12 in the 3rd column, which expresses the births; 4 in the 4th column, which expresses the deaths in infancy and celibacy; and 2 in the 6th column, which expresses the deaths of the parents. Consequently the births are to the deaths, in the same period, as 12 to 4+2, as 12 to 6, or 2 to 1, and the proportions continue the same in all the other periods. From which, I think, we may safely infer that, if in any country the births be to the deaths as 2 to 1, and two thirds of the born live to marry, each marriage must yield exactly 6 children.

If we examine the births and marriages in any of the contemporaneous periods, we shall find, in the second period, 12 births and 8 marrying persons, or the proportion of 12 births to 4 marriages; in the third period, 24 births and 16 marrying persons, or the proportion of 24 births to 8 marriages; and so on, always in the proportion of 3 to 1. But the proportion of the sum of births to the sum of marriages, during these periods, must be the same as any correct annual average; and consequently the annual births are to the annual marriages as 3 to 1; from which, according to the usual mode of calculation, it would be inferred that each marriage yielded 3 children, though we set out with the supposition of 6 children to each marriage; a contradiction which strongly confirms the reasonings of the foregoing part of this chapter, and shows that the proportion of annual births to annual marriages does not express the number of children to each marriage, but a very different thing, namely, the number of the born which live to marry.

If, instead of two thirds, as in the present instance, we suppose that only half of the born live to marry, which is a more common proportion; then, for the second period, we shall have in the third column expressing the births, the number 9, and in the fifth column expressing the marrying persons $4\frac{1}{2}$: consequently, the marriages will be to the births as 1 to 4, which is the most usual average of Europe; though in the present instance we still suppose that each marriage yields six children in the course of its duration. On the same supposition, the births will be to the deaths, as 9 to $4\frac{1}{2}+2$, as 18 to 13, or about $13\frac{4}{5}$ to 10; and consequently it may be inferred that, when the births are to the deaths as $13\frac{4}{5}$ to 10, or 138 to 100, and half of the born live to marry, each marriage must yield six births.

If we suppose five births to a marriage, and that half of the born live to marry, then, according to the table, the births will be to the deaths as about $12\frac{1}{5}$ to 10; and consequently we may infer, in the same manner, that when the births are to the deaths as $12\frac{1}{5}$ to 10, and half of the born live to marry, each marriage must yield 5 children.

Upon these principles, if we can obtain in any country the proportion of births to deaths, and of births to marriages, we may calculate pretty nearly the number of children born to each marriage.[9] This number will indeed turn out to be very different from the results of the old mode of calculation; but this circumstance is rather in favour of its correctness; because the known facts respecting population cannot possibly be accounted for, according to the usual mode of estimating the number of births to a marriage, which gives less than four for the general average of Europe.

Buffon has inserted in his work some tables of mortality, which he means should be considered as applicable to the whole human race. By these, it appears that half of the born die under eight years and one month old.[10] If we apply the average of four children to a marriage to Buffon's estimate of mortality, it would appear that the population of Europe, instead of having a strong tendency to increase, is in danger of being extinct in the course of some years. Instead of increasing in a geometrical ratio, it would be decreasing in a geometrical ratio. If two out of the four children allowed to each marriage

---

[9] That is, upon the supposition, that there is no incorrectness in the construction of the table, or in the inferences which I think may be drawn from it. At present I do not see any.

[10] Histoire Naturelle de l'Homme, tom. iv. p. 420. 12mo. 1752.

were to die under 8 years and a month old, the utmost that we could possibly expect is that $1\frac{1}{2}$ should survive, to form a fresh union, or that four present marriages should yield three in the next generation; a ratio of decrease which would, in no very long period, unpeople Europe.

But the truth is that both the calculations are incorrect. Buffon's tables were taken from the registers of Paris and its neighbouring villages, and can by no means be considered as generally applicable. The source of the other error has been attempted to be pointed out in this chapter.

It is only in unhealthy towns, or villages very peculiarly circumstanced, that half of the born die under 8 or 9 years of age. Taking an average throughout Europe, I have little doubt that not only above half of the born live beyond the age of puberty, but that each marriage yields considerably above four births; I should think, more than five. The poverty which checks population tends much more powerfully to increase the number of deaths than to diminish the number of births.

In forming conclusions respecting the proportion of the born which lives to be married, from the lists of annual births and annual marriages which, according to the principles laid down, is the only point of view in which they are useful, there is one circumstance which, if not particularly attended to, may lead to considerable error.

In country parishes from which there are emigrations, the proportion which lives to be married will be given too small, and in towns which receive continually an accession of strangers, this proportion will be given much too great. The proportion of annual births to annual marriages is in general higher in the country than in towns; but if there were no changing of inhabitants, the proportion in the towns would be much the highest. If, in a country parish, the births be to the weddings as 4 or $4\frac{1}{2}$ to 1, this implies that, out of 4 or $4\frac{1}{2}$ births in that place, 2 lived to be married in that place; but many probably emigrated and married in other places, and therefore we cannot positively infer, from this proportion, that only 2 out of the 4, or $4\frac{1}{2}$, lived to be married.

In towns, the proportion of births to marriages is very often only 3 and $3\frac{1}{2}$ to 1, which would seem to imply that, out of 3 or $3\frac{1}{2}$ children, 2 lived to be married; but in these towns it is known, perhaps from the bills of mortality, that much above half of the born die under the age of puberty. The proportion which has been mentioned, therefore, cannot possibly express the real proportion of the children born in the town which lives to be married, but is caused by the accession of strangers, whose marriages appear in the registers, though not their births. In towns, where there is a great mortality in early life, if no marriages were registered but of those who were born in the place, the proportion of annual births to annual marriages would be greater than the proportion of children born to each marriage, in the course of its duration and would amount, perhaps, to 6 or 7 to 1, instead of 3 or $3\frac{1}{2}$ to 1.

In Leipsic, the proportion of births to weddings is only 2 and $\frac{8}{10}$ to 1;[11] and Susmilch, supposing this to imply that there were only 2 and $\frac{8}{10}$ children born to each marriage, puzzles himself to account for this extraordinary unfruitfulness; but this appearance in the registers, without doubt, arises either from a great accession of strangers, or from a custom among the inhabitants of the neighbouring country, of celebrating their marriages in the town.

At Geneva, where the registers are supposed to be kept with considerable care, the number of marriages, from the year 1701 to 1760, was 21 493, and the number of births in the same period, 42 076; from which it is inferred, that each marriage had yielded, on an average, less than two children. The author of a valuable paper in the Bibliotheque Britannique, who mentions these numbers,[12] naturally expresses some surprise at the result, but still adopts it as the measure of the fruitfulness of the Geneva women. The circumstance, however, arises undoubtedly from the constant influx of new settlers, whose marriages appear in the registers but not their births. If the number of children from each individual mother were traced with care in the bills of mortality at Geneva, I am confident that the result would be very different.

In Paris the proportion of annual births to annual marriages, is about $4\frac{1}{2}$ to 1,[13] and the women have, in consequence, been considered as more prolific than usual for a large town; but no such inference can properly be drawn from this proportion, which is probably caused merely by the infrequency of marriages among persons not born in the town, and the custom of celebrating marriages in the neighbouring villages. The small number of weddings which takes place in Paris, in proportion to the whole population,[14] and the more than usual number in the villages round Paris, seem to confirm this supposition.

The rapidity of the increase in population depends upon the number of children born to each marriage, and the proportion of that number which lives to form a fresh union. The measure of this rapidity is the proportion which the excess of the births above the deaths bears to the whole population.

---

[11] Susmilch's Gottliche Ordnung, vol. i. c. v. s. lxxxiii. p. 171.

[12] Tom. iv. p. 38. note. [See BARTON in the Alphabetical List.]

[13] Susmilch's Gottliche Ordnung, vol. i. c. v. s. lxxxv. p. 174.

[14] In Paris the proportion of annual marriages to the whole population is, according to Susmilch, 1 to 137; according to Crome, 1 to 160. In Geneva, it is as 1 to 64; and this extraordinary proportion of marriages is certainly owing principally to the great influx of foreign settlers. In places where the proportion of annual births to annual marriages is much influenced by new settlers or emigrations, few accurate inferences can be drawn from them in any way. They neither express the fruitfulness of marriages nor the proportion of the born which lives to be married.

That the reader may see at once the tendency to increase, and the period of doubling, which would result from any observed proportion of births to deaths, and of these to the whole population, I subjoin two tables from Susmilch, calculated by Euler, which I believe are very correct. The first is confined to the supposition of a mortality of 1 in 36, and therefore can only be applied to countries where such a mortality is known to take place. The other is general, depending solely upon the proportion which the excess of the births above the burials bears to the whole population, and therefore may be applied universally to all countries, whatever may be the degree of their mortality.

It will be observed that when the proportion between the births and burials is given, the period of doubling will be shorter, the greater the mortality; because the births, as well as deaths, are increased by this supposition, and they both bear a greater proportion to the whole population than if the mortality were smaller, and there were a greater number of people in advanced life.

The general mortality of Russia, according to Mr. Tooke, as has before been stated, is 1 in 58, and the proportion of births 1 in 26. Allowing something for the omissions in the burials, if we assume the mortality to be 1 in 52, then the births will be to the deaths as 2 to 1, and the proportion which the excess of births bears to the whole population will be $\frac{1}{52}$. According to Table III the period of doubling will, in this case, be about 36 years. But if we were to keep the proportion of births to deaths as 2 to 1, and suppose a mortality of 1 in 36, as in Table II, the excess of births above the burials would be $\frac{1}{36}$ of the whole population, and the period of doubling would be only 25 years.

It is evident that in countries which are very healthy, and where in consequence the number of grown up people is great, the births can never bear the same proportion to the whole population as where the number of grown people is smaller; and therefore the excess of births above the deaths cannot, in so short a time, produce a number equal to the former population.

TABLE II   *When in any country there are 100 000 persons living and the mortality is 1 in 36*

If the proportion of deaths to births be as	Then the excess of the births will be	The proportion of the excess of the births, to the whole population, will be	And therefore the period of doubling will be
11	277	$\frac{1}{360}$	250 years
12	555	$\frac{1}{180}$	125
13	833	$\frac{1}{120}$	$83\frac{1}{2}$
14	1110	$\frac{1}{90}$	$62\frac{3}{4}$
15	1388	$\frac{1}{72}$	$50\frac{1}{4}$
16	1666	$\frac{1}{60}$	42
10 { 17	1943	$\frac{1}{51}$	$35\frac{3}{4}$
18	2221	$\frac{1}{45}$	$31\frac{2}{3}$
19	2499	$\frac{1}{40}$	28
20	2777	$\frac{1}{36}$	$25\frac{3}{10}$
22	3332	$\frac{1}{30}$	$21\frac{1}{8}$
25	4165	$\frac{1}{24}$	17
30	5554	$\frac{1}{18}$	$12\frac{4}{5}$

TABLE III

The proportion of the excess of births above the deaths, to the whole of the living	Periods of doubling in years, and ten thousandth parts	The proportion of the excess of births above the deaths, to the whole of the living	Periods of doubling in years, and ten thousandth parts
10	7.2722	21	14.9000
11	7.9659	22	15.5932
12	8.6595	23	16.2864
13	9.3530	24	16.9797
14	10.0465	25	17.6729
1: { 15	10.7400	1: { 26	18.3662
16	11.4333	27	19.0594
17	12.1266	28	19.7527
18	12.8200	29	20.4458
19	13.5133	30	21.1391
20	14.2066		

TABLE III (*cont.*)

1:	32	22.5255	1:	210	145.9072
	34	23.9119		220	152.8387
	36	25.2983		230	159.7702
	38	26.6847		240	166.7017
	40	28.0711		250	173.6332
	42	29.4574		260	180.5647
	44	30.8438		270	187.4961
	46	32.2302		280	194.4275
	48	33.6165		290	201.3590
	50	35.0029		300	208.2905
1:	55	38.4687	1:	310	215.2220
	60	41.9345		320	222.1535
	65	45.4003		330	229.0850
	70	48.8661		340	236.0164
	75	52.3318		350	242.9479
	80	55.7977		360	249.8794
	85	59.2634		370	256.8109
	90	62.7292		380	263.7425
	95	66.1950		390	270.6740
	100	69.6607		400	277.6055
1:	110	76.5923	1:	410	284.5370
	120	83.5238		420	291.4685
	130	90.4554		430	298.4000
	140	97.3868		440	305.3314
	150	104.3183		450	312.2629
	160	111.2598		460	319.1943
	170	118.1813		470	326.1258
	180	125.1128		480	333.0573
	190	132.0443		490	339.9888
	200	138.9757		500	346.9202
			1:	1000	693.49

CHAPTER V

Of the Checks to Population in the middle parts of Europe[1]

I have dwelt longer on the northern states of Europe than their relative importance might, to some, appear to demand, because their internal economy is in many respects essentially different from our own, and a personal though slight acquaintance with these countries has enabled me to mention a few particulars which have not yet been before the public. In the middle parts of Europe the division of labour, the distribution of employments, and the proportion of the inhabitants of towns to the inhabitants of the country, differ so little from what is observable in England, that it would be in vain to seek for the checks to their population in any peculiarity of habits and manners sufficiently marked to admit of description. I shall, therefore, endeavour to direct the reader's attention principally to some inferences drawn from the lists of births, marriages, and deaths in different countries; and these data will, in many important points, give us more information respecting their internal economy than we could receive from the most observing traveller.

One of the most curious and instructive points of view in which we can consider lists of this kind appears to me to be in the dependence of the marriages on the deaths. It has been justly observed by Montesquieu, that wherever there is a place for two persons to live comfortably, a marriage will certainly ensue:[2] but in most of the countries in Europe, in the present state of their population, experience will not allow us to expect any sudden and great increase in the means of supporting a family. The place therefore for the new marriage must, in general, be made by the dissolution of an old one; and we find in consequence that, except after some great mortality, from whatever cause it may have proceeded, or some sudden change of policy peculiarly favourable to cultivation and trade, the number of annual marriages is regulated principally by the number of annual deaths. They reciprocally influence each other. There are few countries in which the common people have so much foresight as to defer marriage till they have a fair prospect of being able to support properly all their children. Some of the mortality

---

[1] [In 1806 and subsequent editions, this was chapter iv of Book ii.]
[2] Esprit des Loix, liv. xxiii. c. x.

therefore, in almost every country, is forced by the too great frequency of marriage; and in every country a great mortality, whether arising principally from this cause, or occasioned by the number of great towns and manufactories, and the natural unhealthiness of the situation, will necessarily produce a great frequency of marriage.

A most striking exemplification of this observation occurs in the case of some villages in Holland. Susmilch has calculated the mean proportion of annual marriages, compared with the number of inhabitants, as between 1 in 107, and 1 in 113, in countries which have not been thinned by plagues or wars, or in which there is no sudden increase in the means of subsistence.[3] And Crome, a later statistical writer, taking a mean between 1 in 92 and 1 in 122, estimates the average proportion of marriages to inhabitants as 1 to 108.[4] But in the registers of 22 Dutch villages, the accuracy of which, according to Susmilch, there is no reason to doubt, it appears that out of 64 persons there is 1 annual marriage.[5] This is a most extraordinary deviation from the mean proportion. When I first saw this number mentioned, not having then adverted to the mortality in these villages, I was much astonished; and very little satisfied with Susmilch's attempt to account for it, by talking of the great number of trades, and the various means of getting a livelihood, in Holland;[6] as it is evident that, the country having been long in the same state, there would be no reason to expect any great yearly accession of new trades and new means of subsistence, and the old ones would of course all be full. But the difficulty was immediately solved,[7] when it appeared that the mortality was between 1 in 22 and 1 in 23,[8] instead of being 1 in 36, as is usual when the marriages are in the proportion of 1 to 108. The births and deaths were nearly equal. The extraordinary number of marriages was not caused by the opening of any new sources of subsistence, and therefore produced no increase of population. It was merely occasioned by the rapid dissolution of the old marriages by death, and the consequent vacancy of some employment by which a family could be supported.

It might be a question, in this case, whether the too great frequency of

---

[3] Susmilch, Gottliche Ordnung, vol. i. c. iv. sect. lvi. p. 126.

[4] Crome, uber die Grösse und Bevölkerung der Europ. Staaten, p. 88. Leips. 1785.

[5] Susmilch, Gottliche Ordnung, vol. i. c. iv. sect. lviii. p. 127. [In 1807 (Vol. 1, p. 376) Malthus added a footnote here:

Such a proportion of marriages could not, however, be supplied in a country like Holland, from the births within the territory, but must be caused principally by the influx of foreigners; and it is known that such an influx, before the Revolution, was constantly taking place. Holland, indeed, has been called the grave of Germany.

[6] Susmilch, Gottliche Ordnung, vol. i. c. iv. sect. lviii. p. 128.

[7] [In 1817 (Vol. 1, p. 445) this was altered:

But the difficulty was in a great measure solved ...

[8] Susmilch, Gottliche Ordnung, vol. i. c. ii. sect. xxxvi. p. 92.

marriage, that is, the pressure of the population too hard against the limits of subsistence, contributed most to produce the mortality; or the mortality, occasioned naturally by the employments of the people and unhealthiness of the country, the frequency of marriage. In the present instance I should without doubt incline to the latter supposition; particularly as it seems to be generally agreed that the common people in Holland are, upon the whole, well off. The great mortality probably arises partly from the natural marshiness of the soil,[9] and the number of canals; and partly from the very great proportion of the people engaged in sedentary occupations, and the very small number in the healthy employments of agriculture.

A very curious and striking contrast to these Dutch villages, tending to illustrate the present subject, will be recollected in what was said respecting the state of Norway. In Norway, the mortality is 1 in 48, and the marriages are 1 in 130. In the Dutch villages, the mortality is 1 in 23 and the marriages 1 in 64. The difference both in the marriages and deaths is above double. They maintain their relative proportions in a very exact manner, and show how much the deaths and marriages mutually depend upon each other; and that, except where some sudden start in the agriculture of a country enlarges the means of subsistence, an increase of marriages will only produce an increase of mortality, and *vice versa*.[10]

In Russia this sudden start in agriculture has in great measure taken place; and consequently, though the mortality is very small, yet the proportion of marriages is not so. But in the progress of the population of Russia, if the proportion of marriages remain the same as at present, the mortality will inevitably increase, or if the mortality remain nearly the same, the proportion of marriages will diminish.

Susmilch has produced some striking instances of this gradual decrease in the proportional number of marriages, in the progress of a country to a fuller population,[11] and a more complete occupation of all the means of gaining a livelihood.

In the town of Halle, in the year 1700, the number of annual marriages was to the whole population as 1 to 77. During the course of the 55 following

---

9 [In 1806 (Vol. i, p. 377) Malthus re-wrote this passage:
   ... it seems to be generally agreed that the common people in Holland before the Revolution were, upon the whole, in a good state. The great mortality probably arose partly...
10 [In 1817 (Vol. i, p. 447) this was changed to:
   ... an increase of marriages must be accompanied by an increase of mortality and *vice versa*.
11 [In 1817 (Vol. i, p. 448) this sentence was expanded:
   ... in the progress of a country to a greater degree of cleanliness, healthiness, and population, and a more complete occupation ...

years, this proportion changed gradually, according to Susmilch's calculation, to 1 in 167.[12] This is a most extraordinary difference, and, if the calculation were quite accurate, would prove to what a degree the preventive check to population had operated,[13] and how completely it had measured itself to the means of subsistence. As, however, the number of people is estimated by calculation, and not taken from enumerations, this very great difference in the proportions may not be perfectly correct, or may be occasioned in part by other causes.

In the town of Leipsic, in the year 1620, the annual marriages were to the population as 1 to 82: from the year 1741 to 1756, they were as 1 to 120.[14]

In Augsburgh, in 1510, the proportion of marriages to the population was as 1 to 86; in 1750, as 1 to 123.[15]

In Dantzic, in the year 1705, the proportion was as 1 to 89; in 1745 as 1 to 118.[16]

In the dukedom of Magdeburgh in 1700, the proportion was as 1 to 87; from 1752 to 1755, as 1 to 125.

In the principality of Halberstadt, in 1690, the proportion was as 1 to 88; in 1756, as 1 to 112.

In the dukedom of Cleves, in 1705, the proportion was as 1 to 83; in 1755, 1 to 100.

In the Churmark of Brandenburgh, in 1700, the proportion was as 1 to 76; in 1755, 1 to 108.[17]

More instances of this kind might be produced; but these are sufficient to shew that, in countries where, from a sudden increase in the means of subsistence, arising either from a great previous mortality, or from improving cultivation and trade, room has been made for a number of marriages much beyond those dissolved by death; this additional number will annually decrease, in proportion as all the new employments are filled up,[18] and there is no further room for an increasing population.

But in countries which have long been fully peopled,[19] and in which no new sources of subsistence are opening, the marriages, being regulated principally by the deaths, will generally bear nearly the same proportion to

---

12 Susmilch, Gottliche Ordnung, vol. i. c. iv. sect. lxii. p. 132.
13 [In 1806 (Vol. I, p. 379) this was amended to:
　　... to what a degree the check to marriage had operated, ...
14 Susmilch, Gottliche Ordnung, vol. i. c. iv. sect. lxiii. p. 134.　　15 Id. sect. lxiv. p. 134.
16 Id. sect. lxv. p. 135.　　17 Id. sect. lxxi. p. 140.
18 [In 1817 (Vol. I, pp. 449–50) this passage was altered:
　　... improving cultivation and trade, room has been made for a great proportion of marriages, this proportion will annually decrease as the new employments are filled up ...
19 [In 1817 (Vol. I, p. 450) Malthus inserted a qualification here:
　　... fully peopled, in which the mortality continues the same, and ...

the whole population at one period as at another. And the same constancy will take place even in countries where there is an annual increase in the means of subsistence, provided this increase be uniform and permanent. Supposing it to be such, as for half a century, to allow every year of a fixed number of marriages beyond those dissolved by death, the population would then be increasing, and perhaps rapidly; but it is evident that the proportion of marriages to the whole population would remain the same during the whole period.[20]

This proportion Susmilch has endeavoured to ascertain in different countries and different situations. In the villages of the Churmark of Brandenburgh, 1 marriage out of 109 persons takes place annually;[21] and the general proportion for agricultural villages, he thinks, may be taken at between 1 in 108 and 1 in 115.[22] In the small towns of the Churmark where the mortality is greater, the proportion is 1 to 98:[23] in the Dutch villages mentioned before, 1 to 64: in Berlin 1 to 110:[24] in Paris 1 to 137:[25] according to Crome in the *unmarrying* cities of Paris and Rome the proportion is only 1 to 160.[26]

All general proportions however, of every kind, should be applied with considerable caution, as it seldom happens that the increase of food and of population is uniform; and when the circumstances of a country are varying, either from this cause, or from any change in the habits of the people with respect to prudence and cleanliness, it is evident that a proportion which is true at one period will not be so at another.

Nothing is more difficult than to lay down rules on these subjects that do not admit of exceptions. Generally speaking, it might be taken for granted that an increased facility in the means of gaining a livelihood, either from a great previous mortality, or from improving cultivation and trade, would produce a greater proportion of annual marriages; but this effect might not perhaps follow. Supposing the people to have been before in a very depressed state, and much of the mortality to have arisen from the want of foresight which usually accompanies such a state, it is possible that the sudden improvements of their condition might give them more of a decent and proper pride; and the consequence would be that the proportional number of marriages might remain nearly the same, but they would all rear more of their children, and the additional population that was wanted would be supplied by a diminished mortality, instead of an increased number of births.

---

[20] In 1806 (Vol. I, p. 381) this was changed to:
. . . the proportion of marriages might remain the same during the whole period.
[21] Susmilch, Gottliche Ordnung, vol. i. c. iv. sect. lvi. p. 125. [22] Id. sect. lxx. v. p. 147.
[23] Id. sect. lx. p. 129. [24] Ibid. [25] Id. sect. lxix. p. 137.
[26] Crome, uber die Grösse und Bevölkerung der Europaischen Staaten, p. 89.

In the same manner, if the population of any country had been long stationary, and would not easily admit of an increase, it is possible that a change in the habits of the people, from improved education or any other cause, might diminish the proportional number of marriages; but as fewer children would be lost in infancy from the diseases consequent on poverty, the diminution in the number of marriages would be balanced by the diminished mortality, and the population would be kept up to its proper level by a smaller number of births.

Such changes, therefore, in the habits of a people should evidently be taken into consideration.

The most general rule that can be laid down on this subject is, perhaps, that any *direct* encouragements to marriage must be accompanied by an increased mortality. The natural tendency to marriage is in every country so great that, without any encouragements whatever, a proper place for a marriage will always be filled up. Such encouragements, therefore, must either be perfectly futile, or produce a marriage where there is not a proper place for one, and the consequence must necessarily be increased poverty and mortality. Montesquieu, in his Lettres Persanes, says that, in the past wars of France, the fear of being inrolled in the militia tempted a great number of young men to marry, without the proper means of supporting a family, and the effect was the birth of a crowd of children, 'que l'on cherche encore en France, et que la misère, la famine et les maladies en ont fait disparoître'.[27]

After so striking an illustration of the necessary effects of direct encouragements to marriage, it is perfectly astonishing that, in his Esprit des Loix, he should say that Europe is still in a state to require laws which favour the propagation of the human species.[28]

Susmilch adopts the same ideas; and though he contemplates the case of the number of marriages coming necessarily to a stand, when the food is not capable of further increase, and examines some countries in which the number of contracted marriages is exactly measured by the number dissolved by death, yet he still thinks that it is one of the principal duties of government to attend to the number of marriages. He cites the examples of Augustus and Trajan, and thinks that a prince or a statesman would really merit the name of father of his people if, from the proportion of 1 to 120 or 125, he could increase the marriages to the proportion of 1 to 80 or 90.[29] But

---

[27] Lettre cxxii. [The children 'for whom one will search in vain in France today, who have disappeared as the result of poverty, starvation and disease.' There was a printer's error in 1806 (Vol. 1, p. 384) *Persannes* instead of the correct *Persanes*, which was repeated in all subsequent editions except those of 1872 and 1986.]

[28] Esprit des Loix, liv. xxiii. c. xxvi.

[29] Susmilch, Gottliche Ordnung, vol. i. c. iv. sect. lxxviii. p. 151.

as it clearly appears, from the instances which he himself produces, that in countries which have been long tolerably well peopled, death is the most powerful of all the encouragements to marriage, the prince or statesman who should succeed in thus greatly increasing the number of marriages might, perhaps, deserve much more justly the title of destroyer, than father, of his people.

The proportion of yearly births to the whole population must evidently depend principally upon the proportion of the people marrying annually; and therefore, in countries which will not admit of a great increase of population, must, like the marriages, depend principally on the deaths. Where an actual decrease of population is not taking place, the births will always supply the vacancies made by death, and exactly so much more as the increasing agriculture and trade of the country will admit.[30] In almost every part of Europe during the intervals of the great plagues, epidemics, or unusually[31] destructive wars, with which it is occasionally visited, the births exceed the deaths; but as the mortality varies very much in different countries and situations, the births will be found to vary in the same manner, though from the excess of births above deaths, which most countries can admit, not in the same degree.

In 39 villages of Holland, where the deaths are about 1 in 23, the births are also about 1 in 23.[32] In 15 villages round Paris, the births bear the same, or even a greater proportion to the whole population, on account of a still greater mortality. The births are 1 in $22\frac{7}{10}$, and the deaths the same.[33] In the small towns of Brandenburgh, which are in an increasing state, the mortality is 1 in 29, and the births 1 in $24\frac{7}{10}$.[34] In Sweden, where the mortality is about 1 in 35, the births are 1 in 28.[35] In 1056 villages of Brandenburgh, in which the mortality is about 1 in 39 or 40, the births are about 1 in 30.[36] In Norway, where the mortality is 1 in 48, the births are 1 in 34.[37] In all these instances, the births are evidently measured by the deaths, after making a proper allowance for the excess of births which the state of each country will admit. [38] ● In Russia this allowance must be great, as, although the mortality may perhaps be taken as only 1 in 48 or 50, the births are as high as 1 in 26, owing to the present rapid increase of the population.● [38]

Statistical writers have endeavoured to obtain a general measure of mortality for all countries taken together; but, if such a measure could be

---

[30] [In 1817 (Vol. I, p. 456) this was changed to:
        ... so much more as the increasing resources of the country will admit.
[31] [In 1806 (Vol. I, p. 385) the word *unusually* was omitted.]
[32] Susmilch, Gottliche Ordnung, vol. i. c. vi. s. cxvi. p. 225.
[33] Id. and c. ii. s. xxxvii. p. 93.   [34] Id. c. ii. s. xxviii. p. 80 and c. vi. s. cxvi. p. 225.
[35] Id. c. vi. s. cxvi. p. 225.   [36] Ibid.   [37] Thaarup's Statistik, vol. ii. p. 4.
[38] [This sentence was omitted in 1826 (Vol. I, p. 332).]

obtained, I do not see what good purpose it could answer. It would be but of little use in ascertaining the population of Europe, or of the world; and it is evident that in applying it to particular countries or particular places, we might be led into the grossest errors. When the mortality of the human race, in different countries, and different situations, varies so much as from 1 in 20 to 1 in 60, no general average could be used with safety in a particular case, without such a knowledge of the circumstances of the country, with respect to the number of towns, the habits of the people, and the healthiness of the situation, as would probably supersede the necessity of resorting to any general proportion, by the knowledge of the particular proportion suited to the country.

There is one leading circumstance, however, affecting the mortality of countries, which may be considered as very general, and which is, at the same time, completely open to observation. This is the number of towns in any state, which has been before alluded to, and the proportion of town to country inhabitants.[39] The unfavourable effects of close habitations and sedentary employments on the health are universal; and therefore on the number of people living in this manner, compared with the number employed in agriculture, will much depend the general mortality of the state. Upon this principle, it has been calculated that when the proportion of the people in the towns to those in the country is as 1 to 3, then the mortality is about 1 in 36, which rises to 1 in 35 or 1 in 33, when the proportion of townsmen to villagers is 2 to 5 or 3 to 7; and falls below 1 in 36 when this proportion is 2 to 7 or 1 to 4. On these grounds the mortality in Prussia is 1 in 38; in Pomerania, 1 in 37½; in the Neumark, 1 in 37; in the Churmark, 1 in 35; according to the lists for 1756.[40]

The nearest average measure of mortality for all countries, taking towns and villages together, is, according to Susmilch, 1 in 36.[41] But Crome thinks that this measure, though it might possibly have suited the time at which Susmilch wrote, is not correct at present, when in most of the states of Europe both the number and the size of towns have increased.[42] He seems to be of opinion, indeed, that this mortality was rather below the truth in Susmilch's time, and that now 1 in 30 would be found to be nearer the average measure. It is not improbable that Susmilch's proportion is too small, as he had a little tendency, with many other statistical writers, to throw out of his calculations epidemic years; but Crome has not advanced proofs sufficient to establish a general measure of mortality in opposition to that proposed by Susmilch. He

---

[39] In 1806 (Vol. 1, p. 388) this sentence was amended:

    This is the number of towns, and the proportion of town to country inhabitants.

[40] Susmilch, Gottliche Ordnung, vol. iii. p. 60.   [41] Vol. i. c. ii. s. xxxv. p. 91.

[42] Crome, uber die Grösse und Bevölkerung der Europaischen Staaten, p. 116.

quotes Busching, who states the mortality of the whole Prussian monarchy to be 1 in 30.[43] But it appears that this inference was drawn from lists for only three years, a period much too short to determine any general average. This proportion for the Prussian monarchy is, indeed, completely contradicted by subsequent observations mentioned by Crome. According to lists for five years, ending in 1784, the mortality was only 1 in 37.[44] During the same period the births were to the deaths as 131 to 100. In Silesia the mortality from 1781 to 1784 was 1 in 30; and the births to deaths as 128 to 100. In Gelderland the mortality from 1776 to 1781 was 1 in 27, and the births 1 in 26. These are the two provinces of the monarchy in which the mortality is the greatest. In some others it is very small. From 1781 to 1784 the average mortality in Neuffchatel and Ballengin was only 1 in 44, and the births 1 in 31. In the principality of Halberstadtz, from 1778 to 1784, the mortality was still less, being only 1 in 45 or 46, and the proportion of births to deaths 137 to 100.[45]

The general conclusion that Crome draws is that the states of Europe may be divided into three classes, to which a different measure of mortality ought to be applied. In the richest and most populous states, where the inhabitants of towns are to the inhabitants of the country in so high a proportion as 1 to 3, the mortality may be taken as 1 in 30. In those countries which are in a middle state with regard to population and cultivation, the mortality may be considered as 1 in 32. And in the thinly-peopled northern states, Susmilch's proportion of 1 in 36 may be applied.[46]

These proportions seem to make the general mortality rather too great, even after allowing epidemic years to have their full effect in the calculations.

[In 1806 (Vol. 1, p. 391) Malthus added a sentence to this chapter:

The improved habits of cleanliness, which appear to have prevailed in late years in most of the towns of Europe, have probably, in point of salubrity, more than counterbalanced their increased size.

[In 1826 (Vol. 1, pp. 335–6) he added the following two paragraphs:

1825

In a census which was made in 1817, of the population of Prussia in its present enlarged state, the number of inhabitants was found to be 10 536 571, of which 5 244 308 were males, and 5 320 535 were females. The births were 454 031, the deaths 306 484, and the marriages 112 034. Of the births 53 576, or 1/8.4, were illegitimate. The proportion of males to females born was as 20 to 19. Of the

---

[43] Crome, uber die Bevölkerung der Europaisch. Staat. p. 118.   [44] Id. p. 120.
[45] Id. p. 122.
[46] Id. p. 127.

illegitimate children 3 out of every 10 died in the first year after birth; of the legitimate 2 out of 10.[47]

The numbers here stated give a proportion of births to deaths as 149 to 100; of births to marriages as 4 to 1; of births to the population as 1 to 23.2; of deaths to the population, of males, as 1 to 33; of females, as 1 to 36; of both together, as 1 to 34½; and of marriages to the population as 1 to 94. The proportion of the excess of the births above the deaths to the population is as 1 to 62; an excess which, if continued, would double the population in about 43 years. As it is not however stated how long these proportions have continued, no very certain conclusions can be drawn from them; but there is little doubt that the population is proceeding with great rapidity.

---

[47] Supplement to the Encyclopædia Britannica, article Prussia. [See JACOB, WILLIAM, in the Alphabetical List.]

CHAPTER VI(a)

Effects of Epidemics on Tables of Mortality[1]

It appears clearly, from the very valuable tables of mortality which Susmilch has collected, and which include periods of 50 or 60 years, that all the countries of Europe are subject to periodical sickly seasons which check their increase; and very few are exempt from those great and wasting plagues which, once or twice, perhaps in a century, sweep off the third or fourth part of their inhabitants. The way in which these periods of mortality affect all the general proportions of births, deaths, and marriages is strikingly illustrated in the tables for Prussia and Lithuania, from the year 1692 to the year 1757.[2]

The table from which this is copied contains the marriages, births, and deaths for every particular year during the whole period; but to bring it into smaller compass, I have retained only the general average drawn from the shorter periods of five and four years, except where the numbers for the individual years presented any fact worthy of particular observation. The year 1711, immediately succeeding the great plague, is not included by Susmilch in any general average; but he has given the particular numbers, and if they be accurate, they show the very sudden and prodigious effect of a great mortality on the number of marriages.

Susmilch calculates that above one third of the people was destroyed by the plague; and yet, notwithstanding this great diminution of the population, it will appear, by a reference to the table, that the number of marriages in the year 1711 was very nearly double the average of the six years preceding the

---

[1] [In 1806 this became chapter x of Book II, entitled 'Effects of Epidemics on Registers of Births, Deaths, and Marriages'. The first part of the chapter is scarcely changed at all; that which was substantially re-written is given in Volume II, pp. 19–22, in order that readers who wish to do so may compare the two versions side by side.]

[2] Susmilch, Gottliche Ordnung, vol. i. table xxi. p. 83 of the tables.

TABLE IV

Annual average	Marriages	Births	Deaths	Proportion of births to marriages	Proportion of deaths to births
5 y^{rs} to 1697	5747	19 715	14 862	10:34	100:132
5 y^{rs}–1702	6070	24 112	14 474	10:39	100:165
6 y^{rs}–1708	6082	26 896	16 430	10:44	100:163
In 1709 and 1710	a plague	number destroyed in 2 years	247 733		
In 1711	12 028	32 522	10 131	10:27	100:320
In 1712	6267	22 970	10 445	10:36	100:220
5 y^{rs} to 1716	4968	21 603	11 984	10:43	100:180
5 y^{rs}–1721	4324	21 396	12 039	10:49	100:177
5 y^{rs}–1726	4719	21 452	12 863	10:45	100:166
5 y^{rs}–1731	4808	29 554	12 825	10:42	100:160
4 y^{rs}–1735	5424	22 692	15 475	10:41	100:146
In 1736	5280	21 859	26 371	Epidemic	
In 1737	5765	18 930	24 480	years	
5 y^{rs} to 1742	5582	22 099	15 255	10:39	100:144
4 y^{rs}–1746	5469	25 275	15 117	10:46	100:167
5 y^{rs}–1751	6423	28 235	17 272	10:43	100:163
5 y^{rs}–1756	5599	28 392	19 154	10:50	100:148
In the 16 y^{rs} before the plague	95 585	380 516	245 763	10:39	100:154
In 46 y^{rs} after the plague	248 777	108 387 2	690 324	10:43	100:157
In 62 good years	344 361	1 464 388 936 087	936 087	10:43	100:156
More born than died		528 301			
In the 2 plague y^{rs}	5477	23 977	247 733		
In all the 64 y^{rs} including the plague	340 838	1 488 365 1 183 820	1 183 820	10:42	100:125
More born than died		304 745			

plague.[3] To produce this effect, we must suppose[4] that almost all who were at the age of puberty were induced, from the demand for labour and the number of vacant employments, immediately to marry. This immense number of marriages in the year could not possibly be accompanied by a great proportional number of births, because we cannot suppose that the new marriages could each yield more than one birth in the year, and the rest must come from the marriages which had continued unbroken through the plague. We cannot therefore be surprised that the proportion of births to marriages in this year should be only 2 and $\frac{7}{10}$ to 1, or 27 to 10.[5] But though the proportion of births to marriages could not be great; yet, on account of the extraordinary number of marriages, the absolute number of births must be great; and as the number of deaths would naturally be small, the proportion of births to deaths is prodigious, being 320 to 100; an excess of births as great, perhaps, as has ever been known in America.

In the next year, 1712, the number of marriages must of course diminish exceedingly, because nearly all who were at the age of puberty having married the year before, the marriages of this year would be supplied principally by those who had arrived at this age subsequent to the plague. Still, however, as *all* who were marriageable had not probably married the year before, the number of marriages, in the year 1712, is great in proportion to the population; and, though not much more than half of the number which took place during the preceding year, is greater than the average number in the last period before the plague. The proportion of births to marriages in 1712, though greater than in the preceding year, on account of the smaller comparative number of marriages, is, with reference to other countries, not great, being as $3\frac{6}{10}$ to 1, or 36 to 10. But the proportion of births to deaths, though less than in the preceding year, when so very large a proportion of the people married is, with reference to other countries, still unusually great,

---

[3] The number of people before the plague, according to Susmilch's calculation, (vol. i. ch. ix. sect. 173) was 570 000; from which, if we subtract 247 733, the number dying in the plague, the remainder 322 267 will be the population after the plague; which, divided by the number of marriages and the number of births for the year 1711, makes the marriages about one twenty-sixth part of the population, and the births about one tenth part. Such extraordinary proportions could only occur, in any country, in an individual year. If they were to continue, they would double the population in less than ten years. [In 1807 (Vol. 1, p. 540) Malthus added to this note:

It is possible that there may be a mistake in the table, and that the births and marriages of the plague years are included in the year 1711; though as the deaths are carefully separated, it seems very strange that it should be so. It is however a matter of no great importance. The other years are sufficient to illustrate the general principle.

[4] [In 1807 (Vol. 1, p. 540) *must suppose* was changed to 'may suppose ...']
[5] [In 1806 (Vol. 11, pp. 35–48) fractions here expressed in tenths were written as decimals: 2.7 to 1, 3.6 to 1, and so on.]

being as 220 to 100; an excess of births which, calculated on a mortality of 1 in 36, would double the population of a country (according to Table II. page 192) in 21⅛ years.

From this period the number of annual marriages begins to be regulated by the diminished population, and of course to sink considerably below the average number of marriages before the plague, depending principally on the number of persons rising annually to a marriageable state. In the year 1720, about nine or ten years after the plague, the number of annual marriages, either from accident, or the beginning operation of the preventive check, is the smallest; and it is at this time, as might be expected,[6] that the proportion of births to marriages rises very high. In the period from 1717 to 1721 the proportion, as appears by the Table, is 49 to 10; and, in the particular years 1719 and 1720, it is 50 to 10, and 55 to 10.

Susmilch draws the attention of his readers to the fruitfulness of marriages in Prussia after the plague, and mentions the proportion of 50 annual births to 10 annual marriages as a proof of it. There are the best reasons for supposing that the marriages in Prussia at this time were very fruitful; but certainly this proportion by itself is no proof of it, being evidently caused by the smaller number of marriages taking place in the year, and not by the greater number of births.[7] In the two years immediately succeeding the plague, when the excess of births above the deaths was so astonishing, the births bore a small proportion to the marriages; and according to the usual mode of calculating, it would have followed that each marriage yielded only $2\frac{7}{10}$, or $3\frac{6}{10}$ children. In the last period of the table, from 1752 to 1756, the births are to the marriages as 5 to 1, and in the individual year 1756, as $6\frac{1}{10}$ to 1; and yet, during this period, the births are to the deaths only as 148 to 100; which could not have been the case if the high proportion of births to marriages had indicated a greater number of births than usual, instead of a smaller number of marriages.

The variations in the proportion of births to deaths, in the different periods of the 64 years included in the table, deserve particular attention. If we were to take an average of the four years immediately succeeding the plague, the births would be to the deaths in the proportion of above 22 to 10, which, supposing the mortality to be 1 in 36, would double the population in less

---

[6] [In 1806 (Vol. II, p. 36) the words *as might be expected* were omitted.]

[7] Susmilch, Gottliche Ordnung, vol. i. c. v. s. lxxxvi. p. 175. [In 1806 (Vol. II, pp. 36–7) [Malthus altered the end of this sentence:

   . . . very fruitful; but certainly the proportion of this individual year, or even period, is not a sufficient proof of it, being evidently caused by a smaller number of marriages taking place in the year, and not by a greater number of births.

than 21 years.[8] If we take the 20 years from 1711 to 1731, the average proportion of the births to deaths will appear to be about 17 to 10; a proportion which (according to Table II. page 192) would double the population in about 35 years. But if, instead of 20 years, we were to take the whole period of 64 years, the average proportion of births to deaths turns out to be but a little more than 12 to 10; a proportion which would not double the population in less than 125 years. If we were to include the mortality of the plague, or even of the epidemic years 1736 and 1737, in too short a period, the deaths might exceed the births, and the population would appear to be decreasing.

Susmilch thinks that, instead of 1 in 36, the mortality in Prussia after the plague might be 1 in 38; and it may appear perhaps to some of my readers that the plenty occasioned by such an event ought to make a still greater difference. Dr. Short has particularly remarked that an extraordinary healthiness generally succeeds any very great mortality,[9] and I have no doubt that the observation is just, comparing similar ages together. But under the most favourable circumstances, infants under three years are more subject to death than at other ages; and the extraordinary proportion of children which usually follows a very great mortality counterbalances the natural healthiness of the period, and prevents it from making much difference in the general mortality.

If we divide the population of Prussia after the plague, by the number of deaths in the year 1711, it will appear that the mortality was nearly 1 in 31, and was therefore increased rather than diminished, owing to the prodigious number of children born in that year.[10] And, in general, we shall observe, that, from this cause, a great previous mortality produces a much more sensible effect on the births than on the deaths. By referring to the table, it will appear that the number of annual deaths regularly increases with the increasing population, and nearly keeps up the same relative proportion all the way through. But the number of annual births is not very different during the whole period, though in this time the population had more than doubled

---

[8] [In 1817 (Vol. II, p. 176) this was changed to:
   ... would double the population in 21 years.
[9] History of air, seasons, &c. vol. ii. p. 344.
[10] [When he revised this chapter in 1806 (Vol. II, p. 39) Malthus inserted a sentence here:
   ... that year. But this greater mortality would certainly cease as soon as these children began to rise into the firmer stages of life, and then probably Susmilch's observations would be just. In general, however, we shall observe that a great previous mortality produces a more sensible effect on the births than on the deaths ... [*Sensible* here means noticeable, easily apparent.]

itself; and therefore the *proportion* of births to the whole population, at first, and at last, must have changed in an extraordinary degree.[11]

On an average of the 46 years after the plague, the proportion of annual births to annual marriages is as 43 to 10; that is, according to the principles laid down in the fourth chapter of this book, out of 43 children born, 20 of them live to be married. The average proportion of births to deaths during this period is 157 to 100. But to produce such an increase, on the supposition that only 20 children out of 43, or 2 out of $4\frac{3}{10}$ live to be married, each marriage, I am persuaded for the reasons given in that chapter, must have yielded 8 births.

Crome observes that when the marriages of a country yield less than 4 births, the population is in a very precarious state;[12] and, like the other writers on this subject, he estimates the number of children from each marriage by the proportion of yearly births to yearly marriages. But I should say, on the contrary, that the population was in a more precarious state when the yearly marriages in these lists appeared to give more than four children. If less than half of the born live to be married, which would then be the case, an extraordinary number of children to each marriage is necessary to produce any considerable increase. In Prussia, the marriages were so fruitful as to allow of a considerable mortality among the children without stopping the increase; but this mortality in itself cannot be considered as a favourable sign; and, in other countries in which a rapid increase is going on, the proportion of yearly births to yearly marriages is generally not so high as 4 to 1, or, according to the common mode of calculating, each marriage yields less than 4 children.

In the Churmark of Brandenburgh, for 15 years after 1694, the proportion of births to deaths was nearly 17 to 10, which, if it had continued, would have doubled the population in 35 years; yet the proportion of yearly births to yearly marriages was only 37 to 10. In the whole period from 1692 to 1756, in which the population had actually more than doubled itself, notwithstanding many epidemic years, this proportion was nearly the same, or about $37\frac{1}{2}$ to 10.[13]

In the dutchy of Pomerania from 1694 to 1756, the population had doubled itself, and the average proportion of yearly births to yearly marriages was 38 to 10.[14]

In the Newmark of Brandenburgh from 1694 to 1756, there were some

---

[11] [After this paragraph, Malthus virtually re-wrote the rest of this chapter in 1806 (Vol. II, pp. 31–48) and readers should turn to Volume II, pp. 19–22, of this edition, for the new version.]
[12] Uber die Bevölkerung der Europais. Staat. p. 91.
[13] Susmilch, Gottliche Ordnung, vol. i. table xxii. p. 88 of the tables.
[14] Id. table xxiii. p. 91.

periods of rapid increase, though it was checked more frequently and effectually by epidemics. In 30 years, to 1726, the average proportion of births to deaths was 148 to 100, and the proportion of annual births to annual marriages 38 to 10. In the whole period, the births were to the deaths as 136 to 100, and the proportion of births to marriages the same as in the period of thirty years.[15]

In Russia, we know that a very rapid increase is going forwards, though the proportion of annual births to annual marriages is only about 36 to 10. And, if we had lists for America, where the progress of population is still more rapid, I should expect to find that the proportion of annual births to annual marriages was less than 4 to 1.[16]

On the contrary, in Silesia, where the proportion of births to deaths is only 13 to 10, and where consequently the progress of the population is not rapid, the proportion of yearly births to yearly marriages is $4\frac{1}{10}$ to 1, or 41 to 10.[17] And in France this proportion before the revolution was $4\frac{1}{2}$ to 1, though the progress of population was slower than in Silesia. In Corsica the births are said to be to the marriages as 5 to 1, though the population of Corsica cannot possibly be in a continued state of rapid increase. The proportion of births to deaths in Norway is greater than in Sweden, though in

---

[15] Susmilch, Gottliche Ordnung, vol. i. table xxv. p. 99.

[16] From a paper in the Transactions of the Society at Philadelphia (vol. iii. N° vii. p. 25.) by Mr. Barton, entitled, Observations on the probability of life in the United States, which I have seen since this was written, I am not sure that I might not be disappointed in the expectation here expressed. If, indeed, Mr. Barton's calculations were to be considered as true for the United States in general, it would appear that half of the born die under 13 or 14; and therefore half of the born could not live to marry. But the fact is that Mr. Barton's calculations, which he applies generally, are merely taken from the town of Philadelphia, and one or two small towns or villages which are certainly not healthy. Our largest European towns are, of course, not so healthy as Philadelphia, where it appears that half of the born die under $12\frac{1}{2}$, but many of our moderate towns are much more healthy. Mr. Barton's calculations of a mortality of 1 in 45 at Philadelphia, and 1 in 47 at Salem, certainly contradict his other estimates, and can therefore only have been taken for short periods, and rejecting epidemic years; indeed, he acknowledges the having made this kind of rejection in one or two instances, and of course his calculations are not to be relied on. He mentions $6\frac{1}{2}$ births to a marriage, but his numbers give only $4\frac{1}{2}$: and, supposing this to be the true proportion of children to a marriage, if, at the same time, we were to suppose that half of the born die under 14, all increase in the population of America would be impossible. On the whole, though we cannot imagine that the calculations in this paper are applicable to the United States in general, and that half of the born die under 14, instead of living to 25 or 30 and above, as in Europe; yet if we suppose that they imply a considerable mortality under puberty, we must believe that each marriage yields full as many as 7 or 8 births, to account for the rapid progress of population which we know for a certainty is going forwards in America. Dr. Franklin supposes 8 births to a marriage in America, and that half of the born live to marry, which probably is not far from the truth. (Miscell. p. 3.)

[17] Susmilch, Gottliche Ordnung, vol. i. table xx. p. 81.

Norway the annual births are to the annual marriages as 38 to 10, and in Sweden as 41 to 10.

It cannot therefore be said that the population of a country is in a precarious state when the proportion of yearly births to yearly marriages is less than 4 to 1. Such a proportion is, on the contrary, favourable to population, and is found to exist in many countries where the increase of people is very rapid. A proportion greater than 4 to 1 is in itself unfavourable to the progress of population, and though it may occasionally exist in countries which are increasing rapidly, owing to an extraordinary fruitfulness of the marriages, yet it will be found more frequently in countries where the progress of population is slow.

I take every opportunity that occurs of illustrating this subject, because so many respectable writers have fallen into the error of estimating the number of children produced by each marriage, in the course of its duration, by the proportion of yearly births to yearly marriages, and I am willing to give ample reasons to the reader for differing from such united authority. All these writers themselves express their surprise at the results that the lists, which they thus make use of, give. Susmilch and Crome particularly remark that the average of 4 or 4½ children to a marriage contradicts the experience we have of the fruitfulness of particular women, many of whom bear above 12 children,[18] though a considerable part of them may die in the rearing. And Wargentin takes notice of the smallness of this number, in reference to the reputed fecundity of the Northern women.[19]

I feel strongly persuaded that it has been principally owing to this error, in the mode of estimating the fruitfulness of marriages, that Dr. Price and almost all the writers in political arithmetic have so totally misapprehended the principle of population. If indeed this mode of calculation were just, the fears of depopulation would really be well founded.

When it appears, from the lists of any country, that the annual births are to the annual marriages in a higher proportion than 4 to 1; that is, according to the principles laid down, when less than half of the born live to be married, it cannot be determined from such a proportion alone, whether this effect arises from a number of persons above the age of puberty dying unmarried, the operation of the preventive check; or from a considerable mortality among children, the operation of the positive check. But the proportion of deaths and births will generally ascertain to which class it ought to be referred. In Prussia, it is undoubtedly occasioned principally by the mortality among children; and it does not seem improbable that, where so many children are born to each marriage, many should perish for want of sufficient attention,

---

[18] Gottliche Ordnung, vol. i. c. v. s. lxxxiii. p. 169. Crome, p. 91.
[19] Susmilch, vol. i. c. v. s. lxxxv. p. 173.

though there might be no want of food. I think it is generally to be observed that when the women in the lower classes of life marry very young, they not only have more children, but lose a greater proportion of them than when they marry later and, from having a smaller number, are able to take better care of them. It appears, from a table given by Susmilch, that in Prussia, during this period, half of the born died under 24.[20] And as not much less than half of the born lived to be married, the marriages must have been early, and the preventive check could not have operated much.

In Sweden half of the born live to 33,[21] and as about half, or rather less, live to be married, the preventive check would operate much more than in Prussia, though still not to a great degree. In France, where a smaller proportion of the born lives to be married, the operation of the preventive check is probably not very different from what it is in Sweden, though I should think that it was certainly rather less. According to Necker,[22] the proportion of marriages to the population in France is as 1 to $113\frac{1}{3}$.

The operation of the preventive check is best measured by the proportion which the whole population bears to the yearly marriages;[23] but though this proportion be obtained by multiplying the number of annual births in proportion to each annual marriage, by the number of inhabitants in proportion to each annual birth; yet it does not follow that it will be small because less than half of the born live to be married, or be great because more than half of the born live to be married. In that part of the Prussian dominions included in the table that has been given, and during the period

---

[20] Gottliche Ordnung, vol. iii. tab. xxi. p. 29.

[21] Price's Observ. on Revers. Paym. tab. xliii. p. 132.

[22] De l'Administration des Finances, tom. i. c. ix. p. 255. 12mo. 1785.

[23] Even from this measure, the inferences are not entirely to be depended upon, as it is liable to be influenced by the fruitfulness of marriages, and the proportion of the population which is under the age of puberty. If all the marriages, which take place in a country, be they few or many, take place young, and be consequently prolific, it is evident that to produce the same proportion of births a smaller proportion of marriages will be necessary; or with the same proportion of marriages a greater proportion of births will be produced. This latter case seems to be applicable to France, where both the births and deaths are greater than in Sweden, though the proportion of marriages is nearly the same, or rather less. And when in two countries compared, one of them has a much greater proportion of its population under the age of puberty than the other, it is evident that any general proportion of annual marriages, to the whole population, will not imply the same operation of the preventive check among those of a marriageable age. It is, in part, the small proportion of the population in towns under the age of puberty, as well as the influx of strangers, which makes it appear in the registers that the preventive check operates less in towns than in the country; whereas there can be little doubt that the number of unmarried persons of a marriageable age is the greatest in towns. The converse of this will of course be true, and consequently, in such a country as America, where above half of the population is under sixteen, the proportion of yearly marriages to the whole population will not accurately express how little the preventive check really operates. The subject is intricate, and requires some attention.

there mentioned, less than half of the born lived to be married, yet the proportion of annual marriages to the whole population was as high as 1 to 92.[24] In Norway, where more than half of the born live to be married, the proportion of annual marriages to the whole population is as low as 1 to 130. The reason is that the proportion of the population to annual births, which is the multiplier, is, in the two cases, extremely different.

In Norway it is probable that half of the born live to forty-three, forty-four, or above; and therefore, though rather more than half of the born live to be married, there will necessarily be many persons between the ages of 20 and 44 living unmarried; that is, the preventive check will prevail to a considerable degree. In a part of the Pays de Vaud in Switzerland, half of the born live to 45; and therefore if none married before 40, and all married when they reached that age, more than half of the born would live to be married; yet all being unmarried under 40, the preventive check might be said to prevail to a very great degree.

It is evident, therefore, that we cannot infer the absence of the preventive check because a considerable proportion of the born lives to be married. And it is equally evident that we cannot infer the contrary.

In Holland, it would appear from the registers that more than half of the born live to be married;[25] yet, from the proportion of annual marriages, to the whole population in the Dutch villages mentioned before, it is clear that the preventive check cannot operate much. In the Churmark of Brandenburgh, from 1694 to 1756, more than half of the born lived to be married. But it appears from a table given by Susmilch that, in the Churmark, half of the born die under 22.[26] The marriages, therefore, must have been very early indeed. And, from the proportion of the marriages for the Churmark, which he has given in one place, it appears that it was greater in comparison of the whole population, than in any other country which he has mentioned, except Holland.[27] Still, however, if it be true that half of the born die under 22, it is rather difficult to conceive that more than half should live to be married.

There is one circumstance not yet noticed, which may contribute to

---

[24] Susmilch, Gottliche Ordnung, vol. i. c. iv. s. lxxi. p. 141.
[25] Id. vol. i. table xvii. p. 51.
[26] Id. vol. iii. table xxii. p. 35.
[27] Susmilch's proportions and calculations for the same countries appear now and then a little to contradict each other. This arises from their being formed at different periods. The proportion of marriages to the population for the Churmark of Brandenburgh, from 1700 to 1755, (vol. i. ch. iv. sec. lxxi. p. 141.) appears to be 1 in 90, and up to the year 1722, 1 in 87. But in another calculation, which includes only the period from 1738 to 1748, the proportion for the villages of the Churmark is 1 in 109, and for the small towns, 1 in 98, (sec. lx. p. 129).

The table, which makes half of the born in the Churmark die under 22, was not formed from the period when the increase was so rapid, and when the lists appeared to show that above half of the born lived to be married.

smooth this difficulty, and which should be attended to in all cases. This is the number of second and third marriages. In the dukedom of Pomerania, it was observed, during a period of seven years, from 1748 to 1754, that out of 23 324 marriages that were contracted, 6170 of them were between persons, one of which had been married before, and 1214 between persons, both of which had been married before.[28] The whole of the latter number, therefore, and half of the former, ought to be subtracted, in order to find the number of the born which lived to be married. And from this cause, all the lists will give the proportion of the born which lives to be married greater than the truth. In the present instance, probably, full as many as half of the born died unmarried; and this correction, I am persuaded, ought to be applied to the Dutch villages in particular, where the proportion of marriages is so great, as it is difficult to conceive that a mortality of 1 in 23 should not destroy more than half of the born before they reach the age of twenty. In addition to this, I have little doubt that many of the marriages in the Dutch villages are, as in towns, between persons not born in the place. There is a constant influx of strangers into all parts of Holland. It has been called the church-yard of Germany.

For the periodical, though irregular, returns of sickly seasons, I refer the reader to the valuable tables of mortality which Susmilch has collected. The common epidemical years that are interspersed throughout these tables, will not, of course, have the same effects on the marriages and births, as the great plague in the table for Prussia; but in proportion to their magnitude, their operation will in general be found to be similar. From the registers of many other countries, and particularly of towns, it appears that the visitations of the plague were frequent at the latter end of the 17th, and the beginning of the 18th centuries.

[29]*In contemplating the plagues and sickly seasons which occur in these tables, after a period of rapid increase, it is impossible not to be impressed with the idea that the number of inhabitants had, in these instances, exceeded the food and the accommodations necessary to preserve them in health. The mass of the people would, upon this supposition, be obliged to live more hardly, and a greater number of them would be crowded together in one house; and these natural causes would evidently contribute to produce sickness, even though the country, absolutely considered, might not be crowded and populous. In a country even thinly inhabited, if an increase of population take place, before more food is raised, and more houses are built, the inhabitants must be distressed for room and subsistence. If in the Highlands of Scotland, for the next ten or twelve years, the marriages were to

---

[28] Susmilch, Gottliche Ordnung, vol. i. c. v. s. xc. p. 185.

be either more frequent, or more prolific, and no emigration were to take place, instead of five to a cottage there might be seven, and this, added to the necessity of worse living, would evidently have a most unfavourable effect on the health of the common people.*[29]

---

[29] [This final paragraph of the chapter is the same in all the editions, and is almost exactly what Malthus wrote on pp. 116–17 of the 1798 *Essay*:

Is it not probable that ... the number of inhabitants had increased faster than the food and the accommodations necessary to preserve them in health? The mass of the people would, upon this supposition, be obliged to live harder, and a greater number would be crowded together in one house; and it is not surely improbable, that these were among the natural causes that produced the three sickly years. These causes may produce such an effect, though the country, absolutely considered, may not be extremely crowded and populous. In a country even thinly inhabited, if an increase of population take place, before more food is raised, and more houses are built, the inhabitants must be distressed in some degree for room and subsistence. Were the marriages in England, for the next eight or ten years, to be more prolific than usual, or even were a greater number of marriages than usual to take place, supposing the number of houses to remain the same; instead of five or six to a cottage, there must be seven or eight; and this, added to the necessity of harder living, would probably have a very unfavourable effect on the health of the common people.

CHAPTER VII

Of the Checks to Population in Switzerland[1]

The situation of Switzerland is in many respects so different from the other states of Europe, and some of the facts that have been collected respecting it are so curious, and tend so strongly to illustrate the general principles of this work, that it seems to merit a separate consideration.

About 35 or 40 years ago,[2] a great and sudden alarm appears to have prevailed in Switzerland respecting the depopulation of the country; and the transactions of the Economical Society of Berne, which had been established some years before, were crowded with papers deploring the decay of industry, arts, agriculture, and manufactures, and the imminent danger of a total want of people. The greater part of these writers considered the depopulation of the country as a fact so obvious as not to require proof. They employed themselves therefore chiefly in proposing remedies, and among others, the importation of midwives, the establishment of foundling hospitals, the portioning of young virgins, the prevention of emigration, and the encouragement of foreign settlers.[3]

A paper, containing very valuable material was, however, about this time published by Mons. Muret, minister of Vevey, who, before he proceeded to point out remedies, thought it necessary to substantiate the existence of the evil. He made a very laborious and careful research into the registers of different parishes up to the time of their first establishment, and compared the number of births which had taken place during three different periods of 70 years each, the first ending in 1620, the second in 1690, and the third in 1760.[4] Finding, upon this comparison, that the number of births was rather less in the second than in the first period, (and by the help of supposing some omissions in the second period, and some redundancies in the third,) that the number of births in the third was also less than in the second, he considered the evidence for a continued depopulation of the country from the year 1550 as incontrovertible.

---

[1] [This was chapter v of Book II in 1806 and subsequent editions.]

[2] [Malthus did not trouble to alter these figures, even in 1826.]

[3] See the different Memoirs for the year 1766. [These are Volumes VI and VII.]

[4] Memoires, &c. par la Societé Economique de Berne. Année 1766, premiere partie, p. 15. et seq. octavo. Berne.

Admitting all the premises, the conclusion is not perhaps so certain as he imagined it to be; and from other facts which appear in his memoir, I am strongly disposed to believe that Switzerland, during this period, came under the case supposed in the last chapter, and that the improving habits of the people, with respect to prudence, cleanliness, &c. had added gradually to the general healthiness of the country, and by enabling them to rear up to manhood a greater proportion of their children, had furnished the requisite increase of population with a smaller number of births. Of course the proportion of annual births to the whole population, in the latter period, would be less than in the former.

From accurate calculations of M. Muret, it appears that during the last period the mortality was extraordinarily small, and the proportion of children reared from infancy to puberty extraordinarily great.[5] In the former periods, this could not have been the case in the same degree. M. Muret himself observes that: 'The ancient depopulation of the country was to be attributed to the frequent plagues which in former times desolated it'; and adds, 'if it could support itself, notwithstanding the frequency of so dreadful an evil, it is a proof of the goodness of the climate, and of the certain resources which the country could furnish for a prompt recovery of its population.'[6] He neglects to apply this observation as he ought, and forgets that such a prompt repeopling could not take place without an unusual increase of births, and that, to enable a country to support itself against such a source of destruction, a greater proportion of births to the whole population would be necessary than at other times.

In one of his tables he gives a list of all the plagues that had prevailed in Switzerland,[7] from which it appears that this dreadful scourge desolated the country, at short intervals, during the whole of the first period, and extended its occasional ravages to within 22 years of the termination of the second.[8]

It would be contrary to every rule of probability to suppose that, during the frequent prevalence of this disorder, the country could be particularly healthy and the general mortality extremely small. Let us suppose it to have been such as at present takes place in many other countries which are exempt from this calamity, about 1 in 32, instead of 1 in 45, as in the last period. The births would, of course, keep their relative proportion, and instead of 1 in 36,[9] be about 1 in 26. In estimating the population of the country by the births, we should thus have two very different multipliers for the different periods; and

---

[5] Memoires, &c. par la Societé Economique de Berne. premiere partie, table xiii. p. 120. Année 1766.

[6] Id. Année 1766. premiere partie, p. 22.

[7] [In 1817 (Vol. I, p. 467) Malthus added here: 'since the year 1312'.

[8] Id. table iv. p. 22. [This table is in fact on pp. 44–50.]

[9] Id. table i. p. 21.

though the absolute number of births might be greater in the first period, yet the fact would by no means imply a greater population.

In the present instance, the sum of the births in 17 parishes, during the first 70 years, is given as 49 860, which annually would be about 712. This, multiplied by 26, would indicate a population of 18 512. In the last period, the sum of the births is given as 43 910,[10] which will be about 626 annually. This, multiplied by 36, will indicate a population of 22 536: and if the multipliers be just, it will thus appear that, instead of the decrease which was intended to be proved, there had been a considerable increase.

That I have not estimated the mortality too high during the first period, I have many reasons for supposing, particularly a calculation respecting the neighbouring town of Geneva, in which it appears that in the 16th century the probability of life, or the age to which half of the born live, was only 4.883, rather less than four years and $\frac{9}{10}$ths; and the mean life 18.511, about 18 years and a half. In the 17th century, the probability of life was 11.607, above 11 years and a half; the mean life 23.358. In the 18th century, the probability of life had increased to 27.183, 27 years and nearly a fifth, and the mean life to 32 years and a fifth.[11]

It is highly probable that a diminution of mortality of the same kind, though perhaps not in the same degree, should have taken place in Switzerland; and we know from the registers of other countries, which have been already noticed, and most particularly from that of Prussia, that the period of the greater mortality naturally produces a greater proportion of births.[12]

Of this dependence of the births on the deaths, M. Muret himself produces many instances; but not being aware of the true principle of population, they only serve to astonish him, and he does not apply them.

Speaking of the want of fruitfulness in the Swiss women, he says that Prussia, Brandenburgh, Sweden, France, and indeed every country, the registers of which he had seen, give a greater proportion of baptisms to the number of inhabitants than the Pays de Vaud, where this proportion is only as 1 to 36.[13] He adds, that from calculations lately made in the Lyonois, it appeared that in Lyons itself the proportion of baptisms was 1 in 28; in the small towns, 1 in 25; and in the parishes, 1 in 23 or 24. What a prodigious difference, he exclaims, between the Lyonois and the Pays de Vaud, where

---

[10] Memoires, &c. par la Societé Econ. de Berne. Année 1766. premiere partie, p. 16.
[11] See a paper in the Bibliotheque Britannique, published at Geneva. tom. iv. p. 328. [See BARTON, WILLIAM, in the Alphabetical List.]
[12] [In 1806 (Vol. I, p. 397) this sentence read:
   ... from the registers of other countries, which we have already noticed, that a greater mortality naturally produces a greater proportion of births.
[13] Memoires, &c. par la Societé Econ. de Berne. Année, 1766, premiere partie, pp. 47, 48.

the most favourable proportion, and that only in two small parishes of extraordinary fecundity, is not above 1 in 26, and in many parishes it is considerably less than 1 in 40.[14] *The same difference*, he remarks, takes place in the *mean life*. In the Lyonois, it is a little above 25 years, while in the Pays de Vaud the lowest mean life, and that only in a single marshy and unhealthy parish, is 29½ years, and in many places it is above 45 years.[15]

'But whence comes it', he says, 'that the country where children escape the best from the dangers of infancy, and where the mean life, in whatever way the calculation is made, is higher than in any other, should be precisely that in which the fecundity is the smallest? How comes it again that, of all our parishes, the one which gives the mean life the highest should also be the one where the tendency to increase is the smallest?

'To resolve this question, I will hazard a conjecture which, however, I give only as such. Is it not that, in order to maintain in all places the proper equilibrium of population, God has wisely ordered things in such a manner as that the force of life, in each country, should be in the inverse ratio of its fecundity.[16]

'In effect, experience verifies my conjecture. Leyzin (a village in the Alps) with a population of 400 persons, produces but a little above eight children a year. The Pays de Vaud in general, in proportion to the same number of inhabitants, produces 11, and the Lyonois 16. But if it happen that, at the age of 20 years, the 8, the 11, and the 16, are reduced to the same number, it will appear that the force of life gives in one place what fecundity does in another. And thus the most healthy countries, having less fecundity, will not overpeople themselves, and the unhealthy countries, by their extraordinary fecundity, will be able to sustain their population.'

We may judge of the surprise of M. Muret, at finding from the registers that the most healthy people were the least prolific, by his betaking himself to a miracle in order to account for it. But the *nodus* does not seem in the present instance to be worthy of such an interference.[17] The fact may be accounted for without resorting to so strange a supposition as that the fruitfulness of women should vary inversely as their health.

There is certainly a considerable difference in the healthiness of different countries, arising partly from the soil and situation, and partly from the habits and employments of the people. When, from these or any other causes

---

[14] Memoires, &c. par la Societé Econ. de Berne. Année 1766, premiere partie, p. 48.

[15] Ibid.

[16] Id. p. 48. et. seq.

[17] Nec deus intersit nisi dignus vindice nodus. [In 1817 (Vol. I, p. 472) the Latin word *nodus*, meaning a knot, and hence a knotty problem, was replaced by 'difficulty'. The Latin footnote was omitted in 1806 (Vol. I, p. 400); it might be loosely translated: God does not interfere (with the laws of nature) unless the situation truly requires such intervention.]

whatever, a great mortality takes place, a proportional number of births immediately ensues, owing both to the greater number of yearly marriages, from the increased demand for labour, and the greater fecundity of each marriage, from being contracted at an earlier, and naturally a more prolific, age.

On the contrary, when, from opposite causes, the healthiness of any country or parish is extraordinarily great; if, from the habits of the people, no vent for an overflowing population be found in emigration, the absolute necessity of the preventive check will be forced so strongly on their attention, that they must adopt it, or starve; and consequently, the marriages being very late, the number annually contracted will not only be small, in proportion to the population, but each individual marriage will naturally be less prolific.

In the parish of Leyzin, noticed by M. Muret, all these circumstances appear to have been combined in a very high degree.[18] Its situation in the Alps, but yet not too high, gave it probably the most pure and salubrious air; and the employments of the people being all pastoral, were consequently of the most healthy nature. From the calculations of M. Muret, the accuracy of which there is no reason to doubt, the probability of life in this parish, appeared to be so extraordinarily high as 61 years.[19] And the average number of the births being, for a period of 30 years, almost accurately equal to the number of deaths,[20] clearly proved that the habits of the people had not led them to emigrate, and that the resources of the parish for the support of population had remained nearly stationary. We are warranted, therefore, in concluding that the pastures were limited, and could not easily be increased, either in quantity or quality. The number of cattle which could be kept upon them would of course be limited; and, in the same manner, the number of persons required for the care of these cattle.

Under such circumstances, how would it be possible for the young men who had reached the age of puberty to leave their fathers' houses, and marry, till an employment of herdsman, dairy-man, or something of the kind, became vacant by death? And as, from the extreme healthiness of the people, this must happen very slowly, it is evident that the majority of them must wait during a great part of their youth in their bachelor state, or run the most obvious risk of starving themselves and their families. The case is still stronger than in Norway, and receives a particular precision from the circumstance of the births and deaths being so nearly equal.

---

[18] [In 1806 (Vol. I, p. 401) this was altered to:
    ... in an unusual degree.
[19] Memoires &c. par la Societé Econ. de Berne. Année 1766, table v. p. 64.
[20] Id. table i. p. 15.

If a father had, unfortunately, a larger family than usual, the tendency of it would be rather to decrease than increase the number of marriages. He might perhaps, with economy, be just able to support them all at home, though he could not probably find adequate employment for them on his small property; but it would evidently be long before they could quit him; and the first marriage among the sons would probably be after the death of the father; whereas, if he had had only two children, one of them might perhaps have married without leaving the parental roof, and the other on the death of the father. And, in a general view, it may be said that the absence or presence of four grown up unmarried people will make the difference of there being room, or not, for the establishment of another marriage and a fresh family.

As the marriages in this parish would, with few exceptions, be very late, and yet, from the extreme healthiness of the situation, be very slowly dissolved by the death of either of the parties, it is evident that a very large proportion of the subsisting marriages would be among persons so far advanced in life that most of the women would have ceased to bear children; and in consequence the whole number of subsisting marriages was found to be to the number of annual births in the very unusual proportion of 12 to 1. The births were only about a 49th part of the population; and the number of persons above sixteen was to the number below that age nearly as 3 to 1.[21]

As a contrast to this parish, and a proof how little the number of births can be depended upon for an estimate of population, M. Muret produces the parish of St. Cergue in the Jura, in which the subsisting marriages were to the annual births only in the proportion of 4 to 1, the births were a 26th part of the population, and the number of persons above and below sixteen just equal.[22]

Judging of the population of these parishes from the proportion of their annual births, it would appear, he says, that Leyzin did not exceed St. Cergue by above one fifth at most; whereas, from actual enumeration, the population of the former turned out to be 405, and of the latter only 171.[23]

I have chosen, he observes, the parishes where the contrast is the most striking; but though the difference be not so remarkable in the rest, yet it will always be found that, from one place to another, even at very small distances, and in situations apparently similar, the proportions will vary considerably.[24]

It is strange that, after making these observations, and others of the same tendency, which I have not produced, he should rest the whole proof of the depopulation of the Pays de Vaud on the proportion of births. There is no good reason for supposing that this proportion should not be different at

---

[21] Memoires, &c. par la Societé Econ. de Berne. Année 1766, p. 11 and 12.   [22] Ibid.
[23] Id. p. 11.   [24] Id. p. 13.

different periods, as well as in different situations. The extraordinary contrast in the fecundity of the two parishes of Leyzin and St. Cergue depends upon causes within the power of time and circumstances to alter. From the great proportion of infants which was found to grow up to maturity in St. Cergue, it appeared that its natural healthiness was not much inferior to that of Leyzin.[25] The proportion of its births to deaths, was 7 to 4,[26] but as the whole number of its inhabitants did not exceed 171, it is evident that this great excess of births could not have been regularly added to the population during the last two centuries. It must have arisen, therefore, either from a sudden increase of late years in the agriculture or trade of the parish, or from a habit of emigration. The latter supposition I conceive to be the true one, and it seems to be confirmed by the small proportion of adults which has already been noticed. The parish is situated in the Jura, by the side of the high road from Paris to Geneva, a situation which would evidently tend to facilitate emigration; and in fact it seems to have acted the part of a breeding parish for the towns and flat countries, and the annual drain of a certain portion of the adults made room for all the rest to marry and to rear a numerous offspring.

A habit of emigration in a particular parish will not only depend on situation, but probably often on accident. I have little doubt that three or four very successful emigrations have frequently given a spirit of enterprize to a whole village; and three or four unsuccessful ones a contrary spirit. If a habit of emigration were introduced into the village of Leyzin, it is not to be doubted that the proportion of births would be immediately changed; and at the end of twenty years an examination of its registers might give results as different from those at the time of M. Muret's calculations, as they were then, from the contrasted parish of St. Cergue. It will hence appear that other causes besides a greater mortality will concur to make an estimate of population, at different periods, from the proportion of births, liable to great uncertainty.

The facts which M. Muret has collected are all valuable, though his inferences cannot always be considered in the same light. He made some calculations at Vevey, of a nature really to ascertain the question, respecting the fecundity of marriages, and to show the incorrectness of the usual mode of estimating it, though without this particular object in view at the time. He found that 375 mothers had yielded 2093 children, all born alive, from which it followed, that each mother had produced $5\frac{10}{12}$, or nearly six children.[27] These, however, were all actually mothers, which every wife is not; but allowing for the usual proportion of barren wives at Vevey, which he had

---

[25] Memoires, &c. par la Societé Econ. de Berne. Année 1766, table xiii. p. 120.

[26] Id. table i. p. 11.

[27] Id. p. 29. et seq.

found to be 20 out of 478, it will still appear that the married women, one with another, produced above $5\frac{1}{3}$ children.[28] And yet this was in a town the inhabitants of which he seems to accuse of not entering into the marriage state at the period when nature called them, and when married, of not having all the children which they might have.[29] The general proportion of the annual marriages to the annual births in the Pays de Vaud is as 1 to 3.9,[30] and of course, according to the common mode of calculation, the marriages would appear to yield 3.9 children each.

In a division of the Pays de Vaud into eight different districts, M. Muret found that in seven towns the mean life was 36 years; and the probability of life, or the age to which half of the born live, 37. In 36 villages the mean life was 37, and the probability of life 42. In nine parishes of the Alps the mean life was 40, and the probability of life 47. In seven parishes of the Jura, these two proportions were 38 and 42: in 12 corn parishes, 37 and 40: in 18 parishes among the great vineyards, 34 and 37: in 6 parishes of mixed vines and hills, $33\frac{9}{10}$ and 36: and in one marshy parish, 29 and 24.[31]

From another table, it appears that the number of persons dying under the age of puberty[32] was less than $\frac{1}{5}$ in the extraordinary parish of Leyzin; and less than $\frac{1}{4}$ in many other parishes of the Alps and the Jura. For the whole of the Pays de Vaud it was about $\frac{1}{3}$.[33]

In some of the largest towns, such as Lausanne and Vevey, on account of the number of strangers above the age of puberty settling in them, the proportion of adults to those under 15 was nearly as great as in the parish of Leyzin, and not far from 3 to 1.[34] In the parishes from which there were not many emigrations, this proportion was about 2 to 1. And in those which furnished inhabitants for other countries, it approached more towards an equality.[35]

The whole population of the Pays de Vaud M. Muret estimated at 113

---

[28] [In 1806 (Vol. 1, p. 408) a footnote was added here:

On account of second and third marriages, the fecundity of marriages must always be less than the fecundity of married women. The mothers alone are here considered, without reference to the number of husbands.

[29] Memoires, &c. par la Societé Econ. de Berne. Année 1766, p. 32.   [30] Id. table i. p. 21.

[31] Id. table viii. p. 92 et seq.

[32] [In 1817 (Vol. 1, p. 482) this was altered to:

... dying under the age of fifteen.

[33] Memoires, &c. par la Societé Econ. de Berne. Année 1766, table xiii. p. 120. [In 1817 (Vol. 1, p. 482) Malthus changed this to:

... it was less than $\frac{1}{3}$.

[34] [In 1817 (Vol. 1, pp. 482-3) this sentence was altered:

In some of the largest towns ... on account of the number of strangers settling in them, the proportion of adults to those under 16 was nearly as great as in the parish of Leyzin ...

[35] Memoires, &c. par la Societé de Berne. Année 1766, table xiii.

thousand, of which 76 thousand were adults. The proportion of adults, therefore, to those under the age of puberty,[36] for the whole country, was 2 to 1. Among these 76 thousand adults, there were 19 thousand subsisting marriages, and consequently 38 thousand married persons; and the same number of persons unmarried, though of the latter number nine thousand, according to M. Muret, would probably be widows or widowers.[37] With such an average store of persons not in the actual state of marriage, amounting to the half of all the adults, there was little ground for apprehension that any probable emigrations, or military levies, would affect the number of annual marriages and check the progress of population.[38]

The proportion of annual marriages to inhabitants in the Pays de Vaud, according to M. Muret's tables, was only 1 to 140,[39] which is even less than in Norway.

All these calculations of M. Muret imply the operation of the preventive check to population in a considerable degree, throughout the whole of the district which he considered; and there is reason to believe that the same habits prevail in other parts of Switzerland, though varying considerably from place to place, according as the situation or the employments of the people render them more or less healthy, or the resources of the country make room, or not, for an increase.

In the town of Berne, from the year 1583 to 1654, the sovereign council had admitted into the Bourgeoisie 487 families, of which 379 became extinct in the space of two centuries, and in 1783 only 108 of them remained. During the hundred years from 1684 to 1784, 207 Bernoise families became extinct. From 1624 to 1712 the Bourgeoisie was given to 80 families. In 1623, the sovereign council united the members of 112 different families, of which 58 only remain.[40]

The proportion of unmarried persons in Berne, including widows and widowers, is considerably above the half of the adults, and the proportion of those below sixteen, to those above, is nearly as 1 to 3.[41] These are strong proofs of the powerful operation of the preventive check.

---

[36] [In 1817 (Vol. 1, p. 483) this was changed to:
... under the age of sixteen.
[37] Mem. Soc. de Berne, Année 1766, p. 27.
[38] [In 1807 (Vol. 1, p. 410) Malthus altered this sentence:
With such an average store of unmarried persons, notwithstanding the acknowledged emigrations, there was little ground for the supposition that these emigrations had essentially affected the number of annual marriages and checked the progress of population.
[39] Mem. Soc. de Berne, Année 1766, tab. i.
[40] Statistique de la Suisse, Durand, tom. iv. p. 405. 8vo. 4 vols. Lausanne, 1796.
[41] Beschreibung von Bern, vol. ii. tab. i. p. 35. 2 vols. 8vo. Bern, 1796. [See HEINZMANN in the Alphabetical List.]
[In 1817 (Vol. 1, p. 485) Malthus changed this:
... the proportion of those below sixteen to those above is not far from 1 to 3.

The peasants in the canton of Berne have always had the reputation of being rich, and without doubt it is greatly to be attributed to this cause. A law has for some time prevailed, which makes it necessary for every peasant to prove himself in possession of the arms and accoutrements necessary for the militia before he can obtain permission to marry. This at once excludes the very poorest from marriage; and a very favourable turn may be given to the habits of many others, from a knowledge that they cannot accomplish the object of their wishes without a certain portion of industry and economy. A young man who, with this end in view, had engaged in service either at home or in a foreign country, when he had gained the necessary sum, might feel his pride rather raised, and not be contented merely with what would obtain him permission to marry, but go on till he could obtain something like a provision for a family.

I was much disappointed, when in Switzerland, at not being able to procure any details respecting the smaller cantons, but the disturbed state of the country made it impossible.[42] It is to be presumed, however, that as they are almost entirely in pasture, they must resemble in a great measure the alpine parishes of the Pays de Vaud, in the extraordinary health of the people, and the absolute necessity of the preventive check; except where these circumstances may have been altered by a more than usual habit of emigration, or by the introduction of manufactures which has taken place in some parts.[43]

---

[42] [Malthus and a large family party, including his future wife Harriet Eckersall, toured France and Switzerland in the summer of 1802, during the short-lived Peace of Amiens. Napoleon, as First Consul, was at this time consolidating his position by organising 'republics' in Holland, northern Italy, and Switzerland, in which last there were a number of skirmishes. The Malthus party left Berne on 17th September, when the gates 'were allowed to remain open for an hour', and General d'Erlach's army of peasants captured the town on the following day.]

[43] [In 1806 (Vol. I, p. 413) Malthus omitted *which has taken place in some parts*. In 1826 (Vol. I, p. 354) he added a footnote here:

M. Prevost, of Geneva, in his translation of this work, gives some account of the small Canton of Glavis, in which the cotton-manufacture had been introduced. It appears that it had been very prosperous at first, and had occasioned a habit of early marriages, and a considerable increase of population; but consequently wages became extremely low, and a fourth part of the population was dependent upon charity for their support. The proportions of the births and deaths to the population, instead of being 1 to 36 and 1 to 45, as in the Pay' de Vaud, had become as 1 to 26 and 1 to 35. And, according to a later account in the last translation, the proportion of the births to the population, during the 14 years from 1805 to 1819, was as 1 to 24, and of the deaths as 1 to 30.

These proportions show the prevalence of early marriages, and its natural consequences in such a situation, and under such circumstances – great poverty and great mortality. M. Heer, who gave M. Prevost the information, seems to have foreseen these consequences early.

The limits to the population of a country strictly pastoral, are strikingly obvious. There are no grounds less susceptible of improvement than mountainous pastures. They must necessarily be left chiefly to nature; and when they have been adequately stocked with cattle, little more can be done. The great difficulty in these parts of Switzerland, as in Norway, is to procure a sufficient quantity of fodder for the winter support of the cattle which have been fed on the mountains in the summer. For this purpose, every bit of grass is collected with the greatest care.[44] In places inaccessible to cattle, the peasant sometimes makes hay with crampons on his feet; grass is cut not three inches high, in some places, three times a year;[45] and in the valleys, the fields are seen shaven as close as a bowling-green, and all the inequalities clipped as with a pair of scissors. In Switzerland, as in Norway, for the same reasons, the art of mowing seems to be carried to its highest pitch of perfection. As, however, the improvement of the lands in the valleys must depend principally upon the manure arising from the stock; it is evident that the quantity of hay and the number of cattle will be mutually limited by each other; and as the population will of course be limited by the produce of the stock, it does not seem possible to increase it beyond a certain point, and that at no great distance. Though the population, therefore, in the flat parts of Switzerland has increased during the last century, there is reason to believe that it has been stationary in the mountainous parts. According to M. Muret, it has decreased very considerably in the Alps of the Pays de Vaud; but his proofs of this fact have been noticed as extremely uncertain. It is not probable that the Alps are less stocked with cattle than they were formerly: and if the inhabitants be really rather fewer in number, it is probably owing to the smaller proportion of children, and to the improvement which has taken place in the mode of living.

In some of the smaller cantons, manufactures have been introduced which, by furnishing a greater quantity of employment, and at the same time a greater quantity of exports for the purchase of corn, have of course considerably increased their population. But the Swiss writers seem generally to agree that the districts where they have been established have, upon the whole, suffered in point of health, morals, and happiness.

It is the nature of pasturage to produce food for a much greater number of people than it can employ. In countries, strictly pastoral, therefore, many persons will be idle, or at most be very inadequately occupied. This state of things naturally disposes to emigration, and has been a chief cause that the

---

[44] [In 1807 (Vol. I, p. 413) Malthus omitted *every bit of* ...]
[45] [In 1817 (Vol. I, p. 487) this was altered to:
... his feet; in some place grass not three inches high is cut three times a year; ...

Swiss have been so much engaged in foreign service.[46] When a father had more than one son, it would rarely happen that some of the rest did not enrol themselves as soldiers or emigrate in some other way.[47]

It is possible, though not probable, that a more than usual spirit of emigration, operating upon a country in which, as it has appeared, the preventive check prevailed to a very considerable degree, might have produced a temporary check to increase at the period when there was such a universal cry about depopulation. If this were so, it without doubt contributed to improve the condition of the lower classes of people. All the foreign travellers in Switzerland, soon after this time, invariably take notice of the state of the Swiss peasantry as superior to that of other countries. In a late excursion to Switzerland, I was rather disappointed not to find it so superior as I had been taught to expect. The greatest part of the unfavourable change might justly be attributed to the losses and sufferings of the people during the late troubles; but a part, perhaps, to the ill-directed efforts of the different governments to increase the population, and to the ultimate consequences even of efforts well directed, and for a time, calculated to advance the comforts and happiness of the people.

I was very much struck with an effect of this last kind, in an expedition to the *Lac de Joux* in the Jura. The party had scarcely arrived at a little inn at the end of the lake when the mistress of the house began to complain of the poverty and misery of all the parishes in the neighbourhood. She said that the country produced little, and yet was full of inhabitants; that boys and girls were marrying who ought still to be at school; and that, while this habit of early marriages continued, they should always be wretched and distressed for subsistence.

The peasant, who afterwards conducted us to the source of the Orbe, entered more fully into the subject, and appeared to understand the principle of population almost as well as any man I ever met with. He said that the women were prolific, and the air of the mountains so pure and healthy that very few children died, except from the consequences of absolute want; that

---

[46] [In 1807 (Vol. I, p. 415) Malthus amended this:
    ... disposes to emigration, and is the principal reason why the Swiss have been so much engaged in foreign service.
[47] [Again in 1807 (Vol. I, p. 415) Malthus altered this sentence:
    When a father had more than one son, those who were not wanted on the farm would be powerfully tempted to enrol themselves as soldiers, or to emigrate in some other way, as the only chance of enabling them to marry.
    [In 1826 (Vol. I, p. 356) he changed to the present tense:
    When a father has more than one son, those who are not wanted on the farm are powerfully tempted ...

the soil, being barren, was inadequate to yield employment and food for the numbers that were yearly growing up to manhood; that the wages of labour were consequently very low, and totally insufficient for the decent support of a family; but that the misery and starving condition of the greatest part of the society did not operate properly as a warning to others, who still continued to marry and to produce a numerous offspring which they could not support. This habit of early marriages might really, he said, be called *le vice du pays*; and he was so strongly impressed with the necessary and unavoidable wretchedness that must result from it, that he thought a law ought to be made restricting men from entering into the marriage state before they were forty years of age, and then allowing it only with '*des vielles filles*', who might bear them two or three children instead of six or eight.

I could not help being diverted with the earnestness of his oratory on this subject, and particularly with his concluding proposition, [48]●which went far beyond even my ideas respecting the necessity of the preventive check.●[48] He must have seen and felt the misery arising from a redundant population most forcibly, to have proposed so violent a remedy. I found, upon inquiry, that he had himself married very young.

The only point in which he failed, as to his philosophical knowledge of the subject, was in confining his reasonings too much to barren and mountainous countries, and not extending them into the plains; in fertile situations, he thought, perhaps, that the plenty of corn and employment might remove the difficulty, and allow of early marriages. Not having lived much in the plains, it was natural for him to fall into this error; particularly as, in such situations, the difficulty is not only more concealed from the extensiveness of the subject, but is in reality less, from the greater mortality naturally occasioned by low grounds, towns, and manufactories.

On inquiring into the principal cause of what he had named the *predominant vice* of his country, he explained it with great philosophical precision. He said that a manufacture for the polishing of stones had been established some years ago, which for a time had been in a very thriving state, and had furnished high wages and employment to all the neighbourhood; that the facility of providing for a family, and of finding early employment for children, had encouraged, to a great degree, early marriages;[49] and that the same habit had continued when, from a change of fashion, accident, and

---

[48] [In 1806 (Vol. 1, p. 418) this sentence ended with the word 'proposition', Malthus having deleted the clause which followed it.

[49] [In 1807 (Vol. 1, p. 419) this read:
   had encouraged to a degree early marriages;
   [In 1817 (Vol. 1, p. 494) it was changed to:
   had greatly encouraged early marriages.

other causes, the manufacture was almost at an end. Very great emigrations, he said, had of late years taken place, but the breeding system went on so fast that they were not sufficient to relieve the country of its superabundant mouths, and the effect was such as he had described to me, and as I had in part seen.[50]

In other conversations which I had with the lower classes of people in different parts of Switzerland and Savoy, I found many who, though not sufficiently skilled in the principle of population to see its effects on society, like my friend of the *Lac de Joux*, yet saw them clearly enough as affecting their own individual interests, and were perfectly aware of the evils which they should probably bring upon themselves by marrying before they could have a tolerable prospect of being able to maintain a family. From the general ideas which I found to prevail on these subjects, I should by no means say that it would be a difficult task to make the common people comprehend the principle of population, and its effect in producing low wages and poverty.

Though there is no absolute provision for the poor in Switzerland, yet each parish generally possesses some seigneurial rights and property in land for the public use, and is expected to maintain its own poor. These funds, however, being limited, will of course often be totally insufficient, and occasionally voluntary collections are made for this purpose. But the whole of the supply being comparatively scanty and uncertain, it has not the same bad effects as the parish rates of England. Of late years much of the common lands belonging to parishes have been parcelled out to individuals, which has of course tended to improve the soil and increase the number of people; but, from the manner in which it has been conducted, it has operated perhaps too much as a systematic encouragement of marriage, and has contributed to increase the number of poor. In the neighbourhood of the richest *communes*, I often observed the greatest quantity of beggars.

There is reason to believe, however, that the efforts of the Economical Society of Berne to promote agriculture were crowned with some success, and that the increasing resources of the country have made room for an additional population, and furnished an adequate support for the greatest part, if not the whole, of that increase which has of late taken place.

In 1764, the population of the whole canton of Berne, including the Pays de Vaud, was estimated at 336 689. In 1791, it had increased to 414 420. From 1764 to 1777, its increase proceeded at the rate of 2000 each year; and, from 1778 to 1791, at the rate of 3109 each year.[51]

---

[50] [Harriet Eckersall's account of this episode is printed in *The Travel Diaries of T. R. Malthus*, p. 296; her unpublished manuscript journal of this tour is in the Cambridge University Library.]

[51] Beschreibung von Bern, vol. ii. p. 40.

CHAPTER VIII

Of the Checks to Population in France[1]

As the tables of mortality in France, before the revolution, were not kept with peculiar care,[2] nor for any great length of time, and as the few which have been produced, exhibit no very extraordinary results, I should not have made this country the subject of a distinct chapter, but for a circumstance attending the revolution which has excited considerable surprise. This is, the undiminished state of the population, in spite of the losses sustained during so long and destructive a contest.[3]

A great national work, founded on the reports of the Prefects in the different departments, is at present in some state of forwardness at Paris, and when completed it may reasonably be expected to form a very valuable accession to the materials of statistical science in general. The returns of all the Prefects are not, however, yet complete; but I was positively assured, by the person who has the principal superintendence of them, that enough is already known to be certain that the population of the old territory of France has rather increased than diminished during the revolution.[4]

Such an event, if true, very strongly confirms the general principles of this work; and assuming it for the present as a fact, it may tend to throw some light on the subject, to trace a little in detail the manner in which such an event might happen.

In every country there is always a considerable body of unmarried persons, formed by the gradual accumulation of the excess of the number rising annually to the age of puberty above the number of persons annually married. The stop to the further accumulation of this body is when its

---

[1] [This was chapter vi of Book ii in 1806 and subsequent editions.]
[2] [In 1806 (Vol. i, p. 422) this was changed to:
    As the parochial registers in France ...
    [In 1817 (Vol. ii, p. 1) *peculiar* was changed to 'particular'.
[3] [In 1826 (Vol. i, p. 362) Malthus added a footnote here:
    This chapter was written in 1802, and refers to the state of France before the peace of Amiens.
[4] [For the 'great national work' see Malthus's long footnote at the end of this chapter and ANALYSE DES PROCES-VERBAUX DES CONSEILS GENERAUX DE DEPARTMENT in the Alphabetical List.]

number is such that the yearly mortality equals the yearly accessions that are made to it. In the Pays de Vaud, as appeared in the last chapter, this body, including widows and widowers, persons who are not actually in the state of marriage, equals the whole number of married persons. But in a country like France, where both the mortality and the tendency to marriage are much greater than in Switzerland, this body does not bear so large a proportion to the population.

According to a calculation in an *Essai d'une Statistique Generale*, published at Paris in 1800, by M. Peuchet, the number of unmarried males in France between 18 and 50 is estimated at 1 451 063, and number of males, whether married or not, between the same ages, at 5 000 000.[5] It does not appear at what period exactly this calculation was made.[6] The number of unmarried persons seems to be too great for any period after some years of the revolution had elapsed; and rather too small for the period before the revolution. Let us suppose, however, that this number of 1 451 063 expresses the collective body of unmarried males of a military age at the commencement of the revolution.

The population of France, before the beginning of the war, was estimated by the National Assembly at 26 363 074;[7] and there is no reason to believe that this calculation was too high. Necker, though he mentions the number 24 800 000, expresses his firm belief that the yearly births, at that time, amounted to above a million, and consequently, according to his multiplier of $25\frac{3}{4}$, that the whole population was nearly 26 millions;[8] and this calculation was made ten years previous to the estimate of the National Assembly.

Taking then the annual births at rather above a million, and estimating that rather above $\frac{2}{5}$ would die under 18, which appears to be the case from some calculations of M. Peuchet,[9] it will follow that 600 000 persons will annually arrive at the age of 18.

The annual marriages, according to Necker, are 213 774;[10] but as this number is an average of ten years, taken while the population was increasing, it is probably too low. If we take 220 000, then 440 000 persons will be supposed to marry out of the 600 000 rising to a marriageable age; and

---

[5] P. 32. 8vo. 78 pages.
[6] [In 1807 (Vol. I, p. 424) Malthus altered the wording here:
... made; but as the author uses the expression *en tems ordinaire*, it is probable that he refers to the period before the revolution. Let us suppose, then, that this number of 1 451 063 expresses the collective body ...
[7] A. Young's Travels in France, vol. i. c. xvii. p. 466. 4to. 1792.
[In 1806 (Vol. I, p. 424) Malthus changed *National Assembly* to 'Constituent Assembly' throughout these pages.]
[8] De l'Administration des Finances, tom. i. c. ix. p. 256. 12mo. 1785.   [9] Essai, p. 31.
[10] De l'Administration des Finances, tom. i. c. ix. p. 255.

consequently the excess of those rising to the age of 18, above the number wanted to complete the usual proportion of annual marriages, will be 160 000, or 80 000 males. It is evident, therefore, that the accumulated body of 1 451 063, unmarried males, of a military age, and the annual supply of 80 000 youths of 18, might be taken for the service of the state, without affecting in any degree the number of annual marriages. But we cannot suppose that the 1 451 063 should be taken all at once, and many soldiers are married, and in a situation not to be entirely useless to the population. Let us suppose 600 000 of the corps of unmarried males to be embodied at once; and this number to be kept up by the annual supply of 150 000 persons, taken partly from the 80 000 rising annually to the age of 18, and not wanted to complete the number of annual marriages, and partly from the 851 063 remaining of the body of unmarried males which existed at the beginning of the war.

It is evident that, from these two sources, 150 000 might be supplied each year, for ten years, and yet allow of an increase in the usual number of annual marriages of above 10 000. It is true that, in the course of the 10 years, many of the original body of unmarried males will have passed the military age; but this will be balanced, and indeed much more than balanced, by their utility in the married life. From the beginning, it should be taken into consideration, that though a man of fifty be generally considered as past the military age, yet if he marry a fruitful subject, he may by no means be useless to the population; and in fact, the supply of 150 000 recruits each year would be taken principally from the 300 000 males rising annually to 18, and the annual marriages would be supplied, in great measure, from the remaining part of the original body of unmarried persons. Widowers and bachelors of forty and fifty who, in the common state of things, might have found it difficult to obtain an agreeable partner, would probably see these difficulties removed in such a scarcity of husbands; and the absence of 600 000 persons would of course make room for a very considerable addition to the number of annual marriages. This addition in all probability took place. Many, among the remaining part of the original body of bachelors, who might otherwise have continued single, would marry under this change of circumstances; and it is known that a very considerable portion of youths under 18, in order to avoid the military conscriptions, entered prematurely into the married state. This was so much the case, and contributed so much to diminish the number of unmarried persons that, in the beginning of the year 1798, it was found necessary to repeal the law which had exempted married persons from the conscriptions; and those who married subsequently to this new regulation were taken indiscriminately with the unmarried. And though after this the levies fell, in part, upon those who were actually engaged in the peopling of the country; yet the number of marriages untouched by these levies might still remain greater than the usual number of marriages before the revolution; and the marriages which were broken by the removal of the husband to the armies, would not probably have been entirely barren.

Sir Francis D'Ivernois, who had certainly a tendency to exaggerate, and probably has exaggerated considerably the losses of the French nation, estimates the total loss of the troops of France both by land and sea, up to the year 1799, at a million and a half.[11] The round numbers, which I have allowed for the sake of illustrating the subject, exceed Sir Francis D'Ivernois's estimate by six hundred thousand. He calculates, however, a loss of a million of persons more, from the other causes of destruction attendant on the revolution; but as this loss fell indiscriminately on all ages and both sexes, it would not affect the population in the same degree, and will be much more than covered by the 600 000 men in the full vigour of life, which remain above Sir Francis's calculation. It should be observed also that, in the latter part of the revolutionary war, the military conscriptions were probably enforced with still more severity in the newly acquired territories than in the old state; and as the population of these new acquisitions is estimated at 5 or 6 millions, it would bear a considerable proportion of the million and a half supposed to be destroyed in the armies. And although the law which facilitated divorces to so great a degree be radically bad,[12] both in a moral and political view; yet, under the circumstance of a great scarcity of men, it would operate a little like the custom of polygamy, and increase the number of children in proportion to the number of husbands. In addition to this, the women without husbands do not appear all to have been barren, as the proportion of illegitimate births is now raised to $\frac{1}{11}$ of the whole number of births, from $\frac{1}{47}$,[13] which it was before the revolution; and though this be a melancholy proof of the depravation of morals, yet it would certainly contribute to increase the number of births; and as the female peasants in France were enabled to earn more than usual during the revolution, on account of the scarcity of hands, it is probable that a considerable portion of these children would survive.

---

[11] Tableau des Pertes, &c. c. ii. p. 7. Mons. Garnier, in the notes to his edition of Adam Smith, calculates that only about a sixtieth part of the French population was destroyed in the armies. He supposes only 500 000 embodied at once, and that this number was supplied by 400 000 more in the course of the war; and allowing for the number which would die naturally, that the additional mortality occasioned by the war was only about 45 000 each year. Tom. v. note xxx. p. 284. If the actual loss were no more than these statements make it, a small increase of births would have easily repaired it; but I should think that these estimates are probably as much below the truth as Sir F. D'Ivernois's are above.

[12] [In 1817 (Vol. II, p. 9) this was altered to:
The law which facilitated divorces to so great a degree in the early part of the revolution was radically bad both in a moral and political view; ...

[13] Essai de Peuchet, p. 28.

Under all these circumstances, it cannot appear impossible, and scarcely even improbable, that the population of France should remain undiminished, in spite of all the causes of destruction which have operated upon it during the course of the revolution, provided that the agriculture of the country has been such as to continue the means of subsistence unimpaired. And it seems now to be generally acknowledged that, however severely the manufactures of France may have suffered, her agriculture has increased rather than diminished. At no period of the war can we suppose that the number of embodied troops exceeded the number of men employed before the revolution in manufactures. Those who were thrown out of work by the destruction of these manufactures, and who did not go to the armies, would of course betake themselves to the labours of agriculture; and it was always the custom in France for the women to work much in the fields, which custom was probably increased during the revolution. At the same time, the absence of a large portion of the best and most vigorous hands would raise the price of labour; and as, from the new land brought into cultivation, and the absence of a considerable part of the greatest consumers[14] in foreign countries, the price of provisions did not rise in proportion; this advance in the price of labour would not only operate as a powerful encouragement to marriage, but would enable the peasants to live better, and to rear a greater number of their children.

At all times, the number of small farmers and proprietors in France was great; and though such a state of things be by no means favourable to the clear surplus produce or disposable wealth of a nation; yet, sometimes, it is not unfavourable to the absolute produce, and it has always a most powerful tendency[15] to encourage population. From the sale and division of many of the large domains of the nobles and clergy, the number of landed proprietors has considerably increased during the revolution; and as a part of these domains consisted of parks and chases, new territory has been given to the plough. It is true that the land tax has been not only too heavy, but injudiciously imposed. It is probable, however, that this disadvantage has been nearly counter-balanced by the removal of the former oppressions under which the cultivator laboured, and that the sale and division of the great domains may be considered as a clear advantage on the side of agriculture, or, at any rate, of the gross produce, which is the principal point with regard to mere population.

---

[14] Supposing the increased number of children, at any period, to equal the number of men absent in the armies, yet these children being all very young, could not be supposed to consume a quantity equal to that which would be consumed by the same number of grown up persons.

[15] [In 1817 (Vol. I, p. 12) *most powerful* was changed to 'strong'.

These considerations make it appear probable that the means of subsistence have at least remained unimpaired, if they have not increased during the revolution; and a view of the cultivation of France in its present state certainly rather tends to confirm this supposition.

We shall not therefore be inclined to agree with Sir Francis D'Ivernois in his conjecture that the annual births in France have diminished by one seventh during the revolution.[16] On the contrary, it is much more probable that they have increased by this number. The average proportion of births to the population in all France, before the revolution, was, according to Necker, as 1 to $25\frac{3}{4}$.[17] It has appeared in the reports of some of the Prefects which have been returned, that the proportion in many country places was raised to 1 to 21, 22, $22\frac{1}{2}$, and 23;[18] and though these proportions might, in some degree, be caused by the absence of a part of the population in the armies, yet I have little doubt that they are principally to be attributed to the birth of a greater number of children than usual. If, when the reports of all the Prefects are put together, it should appear that the number of births has not increased in proportion to the population, and yet that the population is undiminished; it will follow, either that Necker's multiplier for the births was too small, which is extremely probable, as from this cause he appears to have calculated the population too low; or that the mortality among those not exposed to violent deaths has been less than usual; which, from the high price of labour, and the desertion of the towns for the country, is not unlikely.

According to Necker and Moheau, the mortality in France before the revolution was 1 in 30 or $30\frac{1}{8}$.[19] Considering that the proportion of the population which lives in the country is to that in the towns as $3\frac{1}{2}$ to 1;[20] this mortality is extraordinarily great, caused probably by the misery arising from an excess of population; and from the remarks of Arthur Young on the state of the peasantry in France,[21] which are completely sanctioned by Necker,[22] this appears to have been really the case. If we suppose that, from the removal of a part of this redundant population, the mortality should have decreased from 1 in 30 to 1 in 35,[23] this favourable change would go a considerable way in repairing the breaches made by war on the frontiers.

---

16 Tableau des Pertes, &c. c. ii. p. 14.
17 De l'Administration des Finances, tom. i. c. ix. p. 254.
18 Essai de Peuchet, p. 28.
19 De l'Administration des Finances, tom. i. c. ix. p. 255. Essai de Peuchet, p. 29.
20 Young's Travels in France, vol. i. c. xvii. p. 466.
21 See generally, vol. i. c. xvii. and the just observations on these subjects, interspersed in many other parts of his very valuable tour.
22 De l'Administration des Finances, tom. i. c. ix. p. 262. et seq.
23 If it should appear that the mortality among those remaining in the country has not diminished, it will be attributable to the greater proportion of infants, a circumstance

The probability is that both the causes mentioned have operated in part. The births have increased, and the deaths of those remaining in the country have diminished; so that, putting the two circumstances together, it will probably appear, when the results of all the reports of the Prefects are known, that, including those who have fallen in the armies and by violent means, the deaths have not exceeded the births in the course of the revolution.

The returns of the Prefects are to be given for the year 9 of the republic, and to be compared with the year 1789; but if the proportion of births to the population be given merely for the individual year 9, it will not shew with precision[24] the average proportion of births to the population during the course of the revolution. In the confusion occasioned by this event, it is not probable that any very exact registers should have been kept; but from theory I should be inclined to expect that, soon after the beginning of the war, and at other periods during the course of it, the proportion of births to the whole population would be greater, than in 1800 and 1801.[25] If it should appear by

---

noticed in reference to the Prussian table, in c. vi. of this book. [In 1806 (Vol. i, p. 434) this footnote was omitted, on account of the re-writing of the chapter 'On the Effects of Epidemics'.]

[24] [In 1817 (Vol. ii, p. 16) the words *with precision* were omitted.]

[25] [In 1806 (Vol. i, pp. 436–8) the following footnote was added; the passages in square brackets were inserted in 1817 (Vol. ii, p. 17):

In the *Statistique Générale et Particulière de la France, et de ses Colonies*, lately published, the returns of the prefects for the year ix are given and seem to justify this conjecture. The births are 955 430, the deaths 821 871, and the marriages 202 177. These numbers hardly equal Necker's estimates; and yet all the calculations in this work, both with respect to the whole population and its proportion to a square league, make the old territory of France more populous now than at the beginning of the revolution. The estimate of the population, at the period of the Constituent Assembly has already been mentioned; and at this time the number of persons to a square league was reckoned 996. In the year vi of the republic, the result of the Bureau de Cadastre gave a population of 26 048 254, and the number to a square league 1020. In the year vii Dépère calculated the whole population of France at 33 501 094, of which 28 810 694 belonged to ancient France; the number to a square league 1101; [but the calculations, it appears, were founded upon the first estimate made by the Constituent Assembly, which was afterwards rejected as too high.] In the year ix and x the addition of Piedmont and the isle of Elba raised the whole population to 34 376 313; the number to a square league 1086. [The number belonging to Old France is not stated. It seems to have been about 28 000 000.]

In the face of these calculations, the author takes a lower multiplier than Necker for the births, observing that though Necker's proportions remained true in the towns, yet in the country the proportion of births had increased to $\frac{1}{21}, \frac{1}{22}, \frac{1}{22}, \frac{1}{2}, \frac{1}{23}$, which he attributes to the premature marriages, to avoid the military levies; and on the whole, concludes with mentioning 25 as the proper multiplier. And yet, if we make use of this multiplier, we shall get a population under 25 millions, instead of 28 millions. It is true, indeed, that no just inferences can be drawn from the births of a single year; but, as these are the only births referred to, the contradiction is obvious. Perhaps the future returns may solve the difficulty, and the births in the following years be greater; but I am inclined to think, as I have mentioned in the text, that the greatest increase in the proportion of births was before

the returns, that the number of annual marriages has not increased during the revolution, the circumstance will be obviously accounted for by the extraordinary increase in the illegitimate births, mentioned before in this chapter, which amount at present to one eleventh of all the births, instead of one forty-seventh, according to the calculation of Necker before the revolution.[26]

Sir Francis D'Ivernois observes that 'those have yet to learn the first principles of political arithmetic, who imagine that it is in the field of battle, and the hospitals, that an account can be taken of the lives which a revolution or a war has cost. The number of men it has killed is of much less importance than the number of children which it has prevented, and will still prevent, from coming into the world. This is the deepest wound which the population of France has received.' – 'Supposing', he says, 'that of the whole number of men destroyed, only two millions had been united to as many females; according to the calculation of Buffon, these two millions of couples

---

the year IX and probably during the first six or seven years of the republic, while married persons were exempt from the military conscriptions. If the state of the agricultural part of the nation has been improved by the revolution, I am strongly inclined to believe that the proportions both of births and deaths will be found to diminish. In so fine a climate as France nothing but the very great misery of the lower classes could occasion a mortality of $\frac{1}{30}$, and a proportion of births as $\frac{1}{25}\frac{3}{4}$, according to Necker's calculations. And consequently, upon this supposition, the births for the year IX may not be incorrect, and in future, the births and deaths may not bear so large a proportion to the population. The contrast between France and England in this respect is quite wonderful.

The part of this work relating to population is not drawn up with much knowledge of the subject. One remark is very curious. It is observed that the proportion of marriages to the population is as 1 to 110, and of births as 1 to 25; from which it is inferred that one-fourth of the born live to marry. If this inference were just, France would soon be depopulated.

In calculating the value of lives, the author makes use of Buffon's tables, which are entirely incorrect, being founded principally on registers taken from the villages round Paris. They make the probability of life at birth only a little above eight years; which, taking the towns and the country together, is very short of the just average.

Scarcely anything worth noticing has been added in this work to the details given in the Essay of Peuchet, which I have already frequently referred to. On the whole I have not seen sufficient grounds to make me alter any of my conjectures in this chapter, though probably they are not well founded. Indeed, in adopting Sir F. d'Ivernois's calculations respecting the actual loss of men during the revolution, I never thought myself borne out by facts; but the reader will be aware that I adopted them rather for the sake of illustration than from supposing them strictly true.

[See STATISTIQUE GÉNÉRALE ET PARTICULIÈRE DE LA FRANCE in the Alphabetical List. The year IX of the Republic (these were given in Roman figures from 1806 onwards) was from 22 September 1800 to 21 September 1801.]

[26] Essai de Peuchet, p. 28. It is highly probable that this increase of illegitimate births occasioned a more than usual number of children to be exposed in those dreadful receptacles, *Les Hopiteaux des Enfans trouvés*, as noticed by Sir Francis D'Ivernois; but probably this cruel custom was confined to particular districts, and the number exposed, upon the whole, might bear no great proportion to the sum of all the births.

ought to bring into the world twelve millions of children, in order to supply, at the age of thirty-nine, a number equal to that of their parents. This is a point of view in which the consequences of such a destruction of men becomes almost incalculable; because they have much more effect with regard to the twelve millions of children, which they prevent from coming into existence, than with regard to the actual loss of the two millions and a half of men, for whom France mourns. It is not till a future period that they will be able to estimate this dreadful breach.'[27]

And yet, if the circumstances on which the foregoing reasonings are founded, should turn out to be true, it will appear that France has not lost a single birth by the revolution.[28] She has the most just reason to mourn the two millions and a half of individuals which she may have lost, but not their posterity: because, if these individuals had remained in the country, a proportionate number of children, born of other parents, which are now living in France, would not have come into existence. If, in the best governed country in Europe, we were to mourn the posterity which is prevented from coming into being, we should always wear the habit of grief.

It is evident that the constant tendency of the births in every country to supply the vacancies made by death, cannot, in a moral point of view, afford the slightest shadow of excuse for the wanton sacrifice of men. The positive evil that is committed in this case, the pain, misery, and wide-spreading desolation and sorrow that are occasioned to the existing inhabitants, can by no means be counterbalanced by the consideration that the numerical breach in the population will be rapidly repaired. We can have no other right, moral or political, except that of the most urgent necessity, to exchange the lives of beings in the full vigour of their enjoyments for an equal number of helpless infants.

It should also be remarked that, though the numerical population of France may not have suffered by the revolution, yet if her losses have been in any degree equal to the conjectures on the subject, her military strength cannot be unimpaired. Her population at present must consist of a much greater proportion than usual of women and children; and the body of unmarried persons of a military age must be diminished in a very striking manner. This indeed is known to be the case, from the returns of the Prefects which have already been received.

It has appeared that the point at which the drains of men will begin essentially to affect the population of a country is when the original body of

---

[27] Tableau des Pertes, &c. c. ii. p. 13, 14.

[28] [In 1817 (Vol. II, p. 21) this sentence was altered:

And yet, if the foregoing reasonings are well founded, France may not have lost a single birth by the revolution.

unmarried persons is exhausted, and the annual demands are greater than the excess of the number of males rising annually to the age of puberty, above the number wanted to complete the usual proportion of annual marriages. France was probably at some distance from this point at the conclusion of the war; but in the present state of her population, with an increased proportion of women and children, and a great diminution of males of a military age, she could not make the same gigantic exertions which were made at one period, without trenching on the sources of her population.

At all times the number of males of a military age in France was small in proportion to the population, on account of the tendency to marriage,[29] and the great number of children. Necker takes particular notice of this circumstance. He observes that the effect of the very great misery of the peasantry is to produce a dreadful mortality of infants under three or four years of age; and the consequence is that the number of young children will always be in too great a proportion to the number of grown up people. A million of individuals, he justly observes, will in this case neither present the same military force, nor the same capacity of labour, as an equal number of individuals in a country where the people are less miserable.[30]

Switzerland, before the revolution, could have brought into the field, or have employed in labour appropriate to grown up persons, one third more in proportion to her population than France at the same period.

[31]●It will be but of little consequence, if any of the facts or calculations which have been assumed in the course of this chapter, should turn out to be false. The reader will see that the reasonings are of a general nature, and may be true, though the facts taken to illustrate them may prove to be inapplicable.●[31] [32]

---

[29] The proportion of marriages to the population in France, according to Necker, is 1 to 113, tom. i. c. ix. p. 255.

[30] De l'Administration des Finances, tom. i. c. ix. p. 263.

[31] [In 1817 (Vol. II, p. 25) this paragraph was omitted, and Malthus's long footnote began after '... at the same period'.]

[32] Since I wrote this chapter I have had an opportunity of seeing the *Analyse des Procès Verbaux des Conseils Généraux de Departement*, which gives a very particular and highly curious account of the internal state of France for the year 8.[(a)] With respect to the population, out of 69 departments, the reports from which are given, in 16 the population is supposed to be increased; in 42 diminished; in 9 stationary; and in 2 the active population is said to be diminished, but the numerical to remain the same. It appears, however, that most of these

[(a)] [See ANALYSE DES PROCÈS-VERBAUX in the Alphabetical List. *L'aisance générale répandue sur le peuple* might be translated as 'the general prosperity diffused among the people', and *la division des grandes propriétés* refers to the splitting up of large estates into a number of small farms. *Prématurés*, when applied to marriages, can mean 'hasty' as well as 'early'; an increase in the number of marriages, to avoid military service, is discussed by Malthus in the main text on p. 231.]

reports are not founded on actual enumerations; and without such positive data, the prevailing opinions on the subject of population, together with the necessary and universally acknowledged fact of a very considerable diminution in the males of a military age, would naturally dispose people to think that the numbers upon the whole, must be diminished. Judging merely from appearances, the substitution of a hundred children for a hundred grown-up persons would certainly not produce the same impression with regard to population. I should not be surprised therefore if when the enumerations for the year 9 are completed, it should appear that the population upon the whole has not diminished. In some of the reports, *l'aisance generale répandue sur le peuple*, and *la division des grandes propriétés*, are mentioned as the causes of increase; and almost universally, *les mariages prématurés*, and *les mariages multipliées par la crainte des loix militaires*, are particularly noticed.

With respect to the state of agriculture, out of 78 reports, 6 are of opinion that it is improved; 10, that it is deteriorated; 70 demand that it should be encouraged in general; 32 complain *de la multiplicité des défrichements*; and 12 demand *des encouragements pour les défrichements*. One of the reports mentions, *la quantité prodigieuse de terres vagues mise en culture depuis quelque tems, et les travaux multipliées, au delà de ce peuvent exécuter les bras employés en agriculture*; and others speak of *les défrichements multipliées qui ont eu lieu depuis plusieurs années*, which appeared to be successful at first; but it was soon perceived that it would be more profitable to cultivate less and cultivate well. Many of the reports notice the cheapness of corn, and the want of sufficient vent for this commodity; and in the discussion of the question respecting the division of the *biens communaux*, it is observed that 'le partage en opérant le défrichement de ces biens, a sans doute produit une augmentation réelle de denrées, mais d'un autre côté, les vaines pâtures n'existent plus, et les bestiaux sont peutêtre diminués'. On the whole, therefore, I should be inclined to infer that though the agriculture of the country does not appear to have been conducted judiciously, so as to obtain a large *surplus*[b] produce, yet that the *absolute*[b] produce had by no means been diminished during the revolution, and that the attempt to bring so much new land under cultivation had contributed to make the scarcity of labourers still more sensible.[c] And if it be allowed that the food of the country did not decrease during the revolution, the high price of labour, which is very generally noticed, must have operated as a most powerful encouragement to population among the labouring part   of the society.[d]

The land tax, or *contribution foncière*, is universally complained of; indeed, it appears to be extremely heavy, and to fall very unequally. It was intended to be only a fifth of the net[e] produce; but, from the unimproved state of agriculture in general, the number of small proprietors, and particularly the attempt to cultivate too much surface in proportion to the

[b] [In 1817 (Vol. II, p. 26) Malthus altered these to 'neat' and 'gross' produce.

[c] [Malthus is here using *sensible* as though it were French: in eighteenth-century English it often had the French meaning – obvious to the senses, easily perceptible, strongly felt.]

[d] [*Défrichement* is the clearing of land for cultivation; the word is also used to designate a piece of land which has been cleared. The second sentence could be translated: 'One of the reports mentions the great extent of the waste land brought under cultivation some time ago, and the increased labour needed to work it, beyond the capacity of the number of hands employed in agriculture (Department of Aude, p. 128); and others speak of a great deal of land brought under cultivation several years before, which appeared to be successful ...' (Department of Seine Inférieure, p. 140). *Biens communaux* were similar to the common grazing land of an English village; the sharing out of these into small holdings – *le partage* – had produced a real increase in the amount of food available, but on the other hand the rough pasture-land had gone, and there were perhaps fewer cattle (Department of Vosges, pp. 703–4).]

[e] [In 1817 (Vol. II, p. 27) this was changed to 'neat produce'.

capital employed, it often amounts to a fourth, a third, or even a half. [f]●The state of agriculture in France has never been such as to yield a surplus produce in proportion to the gross produce, in any respect equal to what it yields in England; and therefore a land tax bearing the same relation to the gross produce would cause a very different degree of pressure in the two countries.●[f] And, when property is so much divided, that the rent and profit of a farm must be combined in order to support a family upon it, a land tax must necessarily greatly impede cultivation; though it has little or no effect of this kind when farms are large and let out to tenants, as is most frequently the case in England. Among the impediments to agriculture mentioned in the reports, the too great division of lands from the new laws of succession is noticed. The partition of some of the great domains would probably contribute to the improvement of agriculture; but subdivisions of the nature here alluded to would certainly have a contrary effect, and would tend most particularly to diminish surplus[g] produce and make a land tax both oppressive and unproductive. If all the land in England were divided into farms of 20l. a year, we should probably be more populous than we are at present; but, as a nation, we should be extremely poor. [h]●We should be almost without disposable revenue,●[h] and should be under a total inability of maintaining the same number of manufactures, or collecting the same taxes, as at present. All the departments demand a diminution of the *contribution foncière* as absolutely necessary to the prosperity of agriculture.

Of the state of the hospitals and charitable establishments, of the prevalence of beggary, and the mortality among the exposed children, a most deplorable picture is drawn in almost all the reports; from which, we should at first be disposed to infer a greater degree of poverty and misery among all the lower classes of people in general. It appears, however, that the hospitals and charitable establishments lost almost the whole of their revenues during the revolution; and this sudden subtraction of support from a great number of people who had no other reliance, together with the known failure of manufactures in the towns, and the very great increase of illegitimate children, might produce all the distressing appearances described in the reports, without impeaching the great fact of the ameliorated condition of agricultural labourers in general, necessarily arising from the acknowledged high price of labour and comparative cheapness of corn; and it is from this part of the society that the effective population of a country is principally supplied. If the poor's rates of England were suddenly abolished, there would undoubtedly be the most complicated distress among those who were before supported by them; but I should not expect that either the condition of the labouring part of the society in general, or the population of the country, would suffer from it. As the proportion of illegitimate children in France has risen so extraordinarily, as from $\frac{1}{47}$ of all the births to $\frac{1}{11}$, it is evident that more might be abandoned in hospitals, and more out of these die than usual, and yet a more than usual number be reared at home, and escape the mortality of these dreadful receptacles. It appears that from the low state of the funds in the hospitals the proper nurses could not be paid, and numbers of children died from absolute famine. Some of the hospitals, at last, very properly refused to receive any more.

The reports upon the whole do not present a favourable picture of the internal state of France; but something is undoubtedly to be attributed to the nature of these reports, which, consisting as they do of observations explaining the state of the different departments, and of particular demands with a view to obtain assistance or relief from government, it is to be

[f] [In 1807 (Vol. I, p. 445) this sentence was omitted, and the next began:
   When property is so much divided ...
[g] [In 1817 (Vol. II, p. 27) this was changed to 'neat produce'.
[h] [In 1826 (Vol. I, p. 381) this was omitted, and the previous sentence run on:
   ... we should be extremely poor, and should be under a total inability ...

expected that they should lean rather to the unfavourable side. When the question is respecting the imposition of new taxes, or the relief from old ones, people will generally complain of their poverty. On the subject of taxes, indeed, it would appear as if the French government must be a little puzzled. For though it very properly recommended to the *conseils généraux* not to indulge in vague complaints, but to mention specific grievances, and propose specific remedies, and particularly not to advise the abolition of one tax without suggesting another; yet all the taxes appear to me to be reprobated, and most frequently in general terms, without the proposal of any substitute. *La contribution foncière, la taxe mobilière, les barrières, les droits de douane*, all excite bitter complaints, and the only new substitute that struck me was a tax upon game which, being at present almost extinct in France, cannot be expected to yield a revenue sufficient to balance all the rest.[^i] The work, upon the whole, is extremely curious; and as shewing the wish of the government to know the state of each department, and to listen to every observation and proposal for its improvement, is highly creditable to the ruling power. It was published for a short time, but the circulation of it was soon stopped, and confined to the ministers, *les conseils généraux*, &c. Indeed the documents are evidently more of a private than of a public nature, and certainly have not the air of being intended for general circulation.

For the state of population in Spain, I refer the reader to the valuable and entertaining travels of Mr. Townsend in that country, in which he will often find the principle of population very happily illustrated. I should have made it the subject of a distinct chapter, but was fearful of extending this part of the work too much, and of falling, almost unavoidably, into too many repetitions, from the necessity of drawing the same kind of inference from so many different countries. I could expect, besides, to add very little to what has been so well done by Mr. Townsend.[^j]

[^i]: [The land tax was called *la contribution foncière* because land was basic or fundamental; *la taxe mobilière* was on movable personal property; the nearest English word to *barrières* in this context would be 'tolls', payments traditionally levied on merchandise entering a town or market; *les droits de douane* were the 'customs', or customary rights of the government to tax imports into the country.]

[^j]: [In 1817 (Vol. II, pp. 26–30) this final paragraph of the long footnote was printed in ordinary large type, as the concluding paragraph of the main text of the chapter.]

CHAPTER IX

Of the Checks to Population in France (continued)[1]

I have not thought it advisable to alter the conjectural calculations and suppositions of the preceding chapter, on account of the returns of the prefects for the year ix, as well as some returns published since by the government in 1813, having given a smaller proportion of births than I had thought probable; first, because these returns do not contain the early years of the revolution, when the encouragement to marriage and the proportion of births might be expected to be the greatest; and secondly, because they still seem fully to establish the main fact, which it was the object of the chapter to account for, namely, the undiminished population of France, notwithstanding the losses sustained during the revolution; although it may have been effected rather by a decreased proportion of deaths than an increased proportion of births.

According to the returns of the year ix, the proportions of the births, deaths, and marriages, to the whole population, are as follows:

Births	Deaths	Marriages
1 in 33	1 in $38\frac{1}{2}$	1 in 157.[2]

But these are in fact only the proportions of one year, from which no certain inference can be drawn. They are also applied to a population between three and four millions greater than was contained in ancient France, which population may have always had a smaller proportion of births, deaths, and marriages; and further, it appears highly probable from some of the statements in the *Analyse des Procès Verbaux*, that the registers had not been very carefully kept. Under these circumstances, they cannot be considered as proving what the numbers imply.

---

[1] [This chapter, added in 1817, was then and in 1826 chapter vii of Book II.]

[2] See a valuable note of M. Prevost of Geneva to his Translation of this Work, vol. ii. p. 88. M. Prevost thinks it probable that there are omissions in the returns of the births, deaths, and marriages, for the year ix. He further shews that the proportion of the population to the square league for Old France should be 1014, and not 1086. But if there is reason to believe that there are omissions in the registers, and that the population is made too great, the real proportions will be essentially different from those which are here given.

In the year IX, according to the Statistique Elémentaire by Peuchet, published subsequently to his *Essai*, an inquiry was instituted under the orders of M. Chaptal for the express purpose of ascertaining the average population of births to the population;[3] and such an inquiry, so soon after the returns of the year IX, affords a clear proof that these returns were not considered by the minister as correct. In order to accomplish the object in view, choice was made of those communes, in 30 departments distributed over the whole surface of France, which were likely to afford the most accurate returns. And these returns for the years VIII, IX, and X, gave a proportion of births as 1 in $28\frac{35}{100}$; of deaths, as 1 in $30\frac{9}{100}$; and of marriages, as 1 in $132\frac{78}{1000}$.[4]

It is observed by M. Peuchet that the proportion of population to the births is here much greater than had been formerly assumed, but he thinks that, as this calculation had been made from actual enumerations, it should be adopted in preference.

The returns published by the government in 1813 make the population of ancient France 28 786 911, which, compared with 28 000 000, the estimated population of the year IX, show an increase of about 800 000 in the 11 years from 1802 to 1813.

No returns of marriages are given, and the returns of births and deaths are given only for fifty departments.

In these fifty departments, during the ten years beginning with 1802 and ending with 1811, the whole number of births amounted to 5 478 669, and of deaths to 4 696 857, which, on a population of 16 710 719, indicates a proportion of births as 1 in $30\frac{1}{2}$, and of deaths as 1 in $35\frac{1}{2}$.

It is natural to suppose that these fifty departments were chosen on account of their showing the greatest increase. They contain indeed nearly the whole increase that had taken place in all the departments from the time of the enumeration in the year IX; and consequently the population of the other departments must have been almost stationary. It may further be reasonably conjectured that the returns of marriages were not published on account of their being considered as unsatisfactory, and showing a diminution of marriages and an increased proportion of illegitimate births.

From these returns, and the circumstances accompanying them, it may be concluded that, whatever might have been the real proportion of births before the revolution, and for the six or seven subsequent years, when the *mariages prématurés* are alluded to in the Procès Verbaux, and proportions of births as 1 in 21, 22, and 23 are mentioned in the Statistique Générale, the

---

[3] P. 331. Paris, 1805. [The year XI ran from 22 September 1802 to 21 September 1803.]
[4] [In 1826 (Vol. I, p. 386) these figures were expressed in decimals: 28.35, 30.09 and 132.078.]

proportions of births, deaths, and marriages are now all considerably less than they were formerly supposed to be.[5]

It has been asked, whether if this fact be allowed, it does not clearly follow that the population was incorrectly estimated before the revolution, and that it has been diminished rather than increased since 1792? To this question I should distinctly answer, that it does not follow. It has been seen, in many of the preceding chapters, that the proportions of births, deaths, and marriages are extremely different in different countries, and there is the strongest reason for believing that they are very different in the same country at different periods, and under different circumstances.

That changes of this kind have taken place in Switzerland has appeared to be almost certain. A similar effect from increased healthiness in our own country may be considered as an established fact. And if we give any credit to the best authorities that can be collected on the subject, it can scarcely be doubted that the rate of mortality has diminished during the last one or two hundred years in almost every country in Europe. There is nothing therefore that ought to surprise us in the mere fact of the same population being kept up, or even a decided increase taking place, under a smaller proportion of births, deaths, and marriages. And the only question is, whether the actual circumstances of France seem to render such a change probable.

Now it is generally agreed that the condition of the lower classes of people in France before the revolution was very wretched. The wages of labour were about 20 sous, or ten-pence a day, at a time when the wages of labour in England were nearly seventeen pence, and the price of wheat of the same quality in the two countries was not very different. Accordingly Arthur Young represents the labouring classes of France, just at the commencement of the revolution, as '76 per cent. worse fed, worse clothed, and worse supported, both in sickness and health, than the same classes in England'.[6] And though this statement is perhaps rather too strong, and sufficient allowance is not made for the real difference of prices, yet his work everywhere abounds with observations which show the depressed condition of the labouring classes in France at that time, and imply the pressure of the population very hard against the limits of subsistence.

On the other hand, it is universally allowed that the condition of the French peasantry has been decidedly improved by the revolution and the

---

[5] In the year 1792 a law was passed extremely favourable to early marriages. This was repealed in the year IX, and a law substituted which threw great obstacles in the way of marriage, according to Peuchet (p. 234). These two laws will assist in accounting for a small proportion of births and marriages in the ten years previous to 1813, consistently with the possibility of a large proportion in the first six or seven years after the commencement of the revolution.

[6] Young's Travels in France, vol. i. p. 437.

division of the national domains. All the writers who advert to the subject notice a considerable rise in the price of labour, partly occasioned by the demands of the army. In the Statistique Elémentaire of Peuchet, common labour is stated to have risen from 20 to 30 sous,[7] while the price of provisions appears to have remained nearly the same; and Mr. Birbeck, in his late Agricultural Tour in France,[8] says that the price of labour without board is twenty *pence* a day, and that provisions of all kinds are full as cheap again as in England. This would give the French labourer the same command of subsistence as an English labourer would have with three shillings and four-pence a day. But at no time were the wages of common day-labour in England so high as three shillings and four pence.

Allowing for some errors in these statements, they are evidently sufficient to establish a very marked improvement in the condition of the lower classes of people in France. But it is next to a physical impossibility that such a relief from the pressure of distress should take place without a diminution in the rate of mortality; and if this diminution in the rate of mortality has not been accompanied by a rapid increase of population, it must necessarily have been accompanied by a smaller proportion of births. In the interval between 1802 and 1813 the population seems to have increased, but to have increased slowly. Consequently a smaller proportion of births, deaths, and marriages, or the more general operation of prudential restraints, is exactly what the circumstances would have led us to expect. There is perhaps no proposition more incontrovertible than this, that, in two countries, in which the rate of increase, the natural healthiness of climate, and the state of towns and manufactures are supposed to be nearly the same, the one in which the pressure of poverty is the greatest will have the greatest proportion of births, deaths, and marriages.

It does not then by any means follow, as has been supposed, that because since 1802 the proportion of births in France has been as 1 in 30, Necker ought to have used 30 as his multiplier instead of $25\frac{3}{4}$. If the representations given of the state of the labouring classes in France before and since the revolution be in any degree near the truth, as the march of the population in both periods seems to have been nearly the same, the present proportion of births could not have been applicable at the period when Necker wrote. At the same time it is by no means improbable that he took too low a multiplier. It is hardly credible under all circumstances that the population of France should have increased in the interval between 1785 and 1802 so much as from $25\frac{1}{2}$ millions to 28. But if we allow that the multiplier might at that time have been 27 instead of $25\frac{3}{4}$, it will be allowing as much as is in any degree

---

[7] P. 391.   [8] P. 13.

probable, and yet this will imply an increase of nearly two millions from 1785 to 1813; an increase far short of the rate that has taken place in England, but still sufficient amply to shew the force of the principle of population in overcoming obstacles apparently the most powerful.

With regard to the question of the increase of births in the six or seven first years after the commencement of the revolution, there is no probability of its ever being determined. In the confusion of the times, it is scarcely possible to suppose that the registers should have been regularly kept; and as they were not collected in the year IX, there is no chance of their being brought forward in a correct state at a subsequent period.

[In 1826 (Vol. I, pp. 392–6) Malthus added the following:

1825

Subsequent to the last edition of this work, further details have appeared respecting the population of France.

Since 1817, regular returns have been made of the annual births, deaths, and marriages over the whole of the territory comprised in the limits of France, as settled in 1814 and 1815; and an enumeration was made of the population in 1820.

In the *Annuaire* of the *Bureau des Longitudes* for 1825,[9] the numbers of births, deaths, and marriages are given for six years ending with 1822. The sum of these are:

Births	Deaths	Marriages	Excess of births above deaths
5 747 249	4 589 089	1 313 502	1 158 160

The annual average:

Births	Deaths	Marriages	Average Excess of births
957 875	764 848	218 917	193 027

The population in 1820, according to an enumeration in each department, was 30 451 187.

From these numbers it appears that the proportion of annual births to the population is as 1 to 31.79, or nearly $\frac{1}{32}$; the annual mortality as 1 to 39.81, or nearly $\frac{1}{40}$; the proportion of annual marriages to the population is as 1 to 139; the proportion of births to deaths as 125.23 to 100, or very nearly as 5 to 4; and the proportion of marriages to births as 1 to 4.37. The proportion of illegitimate to legitimate births is as 1 to 14.6; the proportion of male to female births as 16 to 15; and the proportion of the annual excess of the births above the deaths to the whole population, which, if the returns are accurate, determines the rate of increase as 1 to 157.

To what degree the returns of the births, deaths, and marriages in the 6 years ending with 1822 are accurate, it is impossible to say. There is a regularity in them

---

[9] [See BUREAU DES LONGITUDES in the Alphabetical List.]

which has a favourable appearance. We well know, however, that with the same appearance of regularity there are great omissions in the births and deaths of our own registers. This is at once proved by the circumstance of the excess of the births above the deaths in the interval between two enumerations falling considerably short of the increase of population which appears by such enumerations to have taken place. The enumerations in France during the last twenty-five years have not been so regular, or so much to be depended upon, as those in England. The one in 1813, before noticed, may however be compared with that in 1820, and if they are both equally near the truth, it will appear that the population of France during the seven years from 1813 to 1820 must have increased considerably faster than during the six years ending with 1822, as determined by the excess of the births above the deaths. The whole of this excess during these six years, as above stated, was 1 158 160, the annual average of which is 193 027; which, compared with the mean population, or the population of 1820, reduced by the increase of a year, will give a proportion of annual increase to the population as 1 to about 156; and this proportion of the annual excess of the births above the deaths, to the population, will, according to Table II at the end of Ch. xi. Book ii,[10] give a rate of increase which would double the population in about 108 years.

On the other hand, as the population of Old France in 1813 was 28 786 911, and in 1820, 30 451 187, the difference or the increase of population during the seven years being 1 664 276, the annual average increase will be 237 753, instead of 193 026; and this greater annual increase, compared with the mean population of the seven years, will be as 1 to 124, instead of 1 to 156, and the rate of increase will be such as would double the population in about 86 years, instead of 108, showing the probability of considerable omissions in the returns of births and deaths in the 6 years ending with 1822. If, indeed, the two enumerations can be considered as equally near the truth, as there is no reason for supposing that any great difference in the proportion of births could have occurred in the three years preceding 1817, it follows that the French registers require the same kind of correction, though not to the same extent, as our own. In a subsequent chapter I have supposed that the returns of the births for England and Wales are deficient $\frac{1}{6}$, and of the burials $\frac{1}{12}$. This correction applied to the French returns would exceed what is necessary to account for the increase between 1813 and 1820. But if we suppose the births to be deficient $\frac{1}{10}$, and the deaths $\frac{1}{20}$, the proportion of the births to the population will then be $\frac{1}{29.1}$, and the proportion of the deaths $\frac{1}{38.1}$. These proportions will make the annual excess of the births above the deaths, compared with the population, as 1 to a little above 123; which, after a slight allowance for deaths abroad, will give the same period of doubling or the same rate of increase as that which took place in France between 1813 and 1820, supposing both enumerations to be equally near the truth.

It is worthy of remark that, after making the above allowances for omissions in the returns of births and deaths, the proportion of deaths appears to be smaller than in any of the registers before collected; and as the proportion of the births is also smaller than either before the revolution, or in the returns from the 30 departments in the

---

[10] [See chap. iv(b) of Book II in Vol. II of this edition.]

years VIII, IX, and X before noticed: and as there is every reason to believe that there were great omissions in the general returns of the year IX and that the omissions in the returns from the 50 departments in 1813 were not fewer than in the later registers, it may fairly be presumed that the proportion of births has diminished notwithstanding the increased rate at which the population has been proceeding of late years. This increased rate appears to be owing to a diminished mortality, occasioned by the improved situation of the labouring classes since the revolution, and aided probably by the introduction of vaccination. It shows that an acceleration in the rate of increase is quite consistent with a diminution in the proportion of births, and that such a diminution is likely to take place under a diminished mortality from whatever cause or causes arising.

As a curious and striking proof of the error into which we should fall, in estimating the population of countries at different periods by the increase of births, it may be remarkable that, according to Necker, the annual births in France on an average of six years, ending with 1780, were 958 586. The births for the same number of years ending with 1822 were, as above stated, 957 875. Estimating therefore the population by the births, it would appear that in 42 years it had rather diminished than increased, whereas, by enumeration, there is every reason to believe that it has increased in that time nearly four millions.

CHAPTER X

Of the Checks to Population in England[1]

*The most cursory view of society in this country must convince us that, throughout all ranks, the preventive check to population prevails in a considerable degree. Those among the higher classes, who live principally in towns, often want the inclination to marry, from the facility with which they can indulge themselves in an illicit intercourse with the sex. And others are deterred from marrying by the idea of the expenses that they must retrench, and the pleasures of which they must deprive themselves, on the supposition of having a family. When the fortune is large, these considerations are certainly trivial; but a preventive foresight of this kind has objects of much greater weight for its contemplation as we go lower.

A man of liberal education, with an income of just sufficient to enable him to associate in the rank of gentlemen, must feel absolutely certain that, if he marry and have a family, he shall be obliged if he mix in society to rank himself with farmers and tradesmen.[2] The woman, whom a man of education would naturally make the object of his choice, is one brought up in the same habits and sentiments with himself, and used to the familiar intercourse of a society totally different from that to which she must be reduced by marriage. Can a man easily content to place the object of his affection in a situation so discordant, probably, to her habits and inclinations? Two or three steps of descent in society, particularly at this round of the ladder, where education ends and ignorance begins, will not be considered by the generality of people as a chimerical, but a real evil. If society be desirable, it surely must be free, equal, and reciprocal society, where benefits are conferred as well as received, and not such as the dependent finds with his patron, or the poor with the rich.

These considerations certainly prevent a great number in this rank of life from following the bent of their inclinations in an early attachment. Others, influenced either by a stronger passion, or a weaker judgment, disregard these considerations; and it would be hard indeed, if the gratification of so

---

[1] [This was chapter ix of Book II in the quarto, chapter vii in 1806 and 1807, and chapter viii in 1817 and 1826.]

[2] [In 1807 (Vol. I, pp. 449–50) this was changed to:
... if he marry and have a family, he shall be obliged to give up all his former connections.

delightful a passion as virtuous love did not sometimes more than counter-balance all its attendant evils. But I fear that it must be acknowledged that the more general consequences of such marriages are rather calculated to justify than to disappoint the forebodings of the prudent.

The sons of tradesmen and farmers are exhorted not to marry, and generally find it necessary to comply with this advice, till they are settled in some business or farm, which may enable them to support a family. These events may not perhaps occur till they are far advanced in life. The scarcity of farms is a very general complaint; and the competition in every kind of business is so great, that it is not possible that all should be successful. Among the clerks in counting houses, and the competitors for all kinds of mercantile and professional employment, it is probable that the preventive check to population prevails more than in any other department of society.

The labourer who earns eighteen-pence or two shillings a day, and lives at his ease as a single man, will hesitate a little before he divides that pittance among four or five which seems to be not more than sufficient for one. Harder fare, and harder labour, he would perhaps be willing to submit to, for the sake of living with the woman he loves; but he must feel conscious that, should he have a large family and any ill fortune whatever, no degree of frugality, no possible exertion of his manual strength, would preserve him from the heart-rending sensation of seeing his children starve, or of being obliged to the parish for their support. The love of independence is a sentiment that surely none would wish to see eradicated; though the poor-laws of England, it must be confessed, are a system of all others the most calculated gradually to weaken this sentiment, and in the end will probably destroy it completely.

The servants who live in the families of the rich have restraints yet stronger to break through in venturing upon marriage. They possess the necessaries, and even the comforts of life, almost in as great plenty as their masters. Their work is easy and their food luxurious, compared with the work and food of the class of labourers; and their sense of dependence is weakened by the conscious power of changing their masters if they feel themselves offended. Thus comfortably situated at present, what are their prospects if they marry? Without knowledge or capital, either for business or farming, and unused and therefore unable to earn a subsistence by daily labour, their only refuge seems to be a miserable alehouse, which certainly offers no very enchanting prospect of a happy evening to their lives. The greater number of them, therefore, deterred by this uninviting view of their future situation, content themselves with remaining single where they are.*[3]

---

[3] [The first six paragraphs of this chapter are taken almost verbatim from pp. 63–9 of the 1798 *Essay*. In 1798, however, Malthus wrote of 'The servants who live in gentlemen's families ...' instead of 'the families of the rich'.]

If this sketch of the state of society in England be near the truth, it will be allowed that the preventive check to population operates with considerable force throughout all the classes of the community. And this observation is further confirmed by the abstracts from the registers returned in consequence of the late Population Act.[4] The results of these abstracts show that the annual marriages in England and Wales are to the whole population as 1 to $123\frac{1}{5}$,[5] a smaller proportion of marriages than obtains in any of the countries which have been examined, except Norway and Switzerland.

In the earlier part of the last century, Dr. Short estimated this proportion at about 1 to 115.[6] It is probable that this calculation was then correct, and the present diminution in the proportion of marriages, notwithstanding an increase of population more rapid than formerly, owing to the more rapid progress of commerce and agriculture, is partly a cause, and partly a consequence, of the diminished mortality that has been observed of late years.

The returns of the marriages, pursuant to the late act, are supposed to be less liable to the suspicion of inaccuracy than any other parts of the registers.

Dr. Short, in his *New Observations on Town and Country Bills of Mortality*, says he will 'conclude with the observation of an eminent Judge of this nation, that the growth and increase of mankind is more stinted from the cautious

---

[4] [In 1817 (Vol. II, p. 47) this was altered to:
   ... abstracts from the registers returned in 1800 in consequence of the Population Act.
[In 1826 (Vol. I, p. 400) this was changed again to:
   ... from the registers returned in consequence of the Population Act[a] passed in 1800.
[A footnote was added here: [a] This chapter was written in 1802, just after the first enumeration, the results of which were published in 1801.]
[For comment on these inaccurate statements, see RICKMAN in the Alphabetical List.]

[5] Observ. on the Results of the Population Act, p. 11. The answers to the Population Act have at length happily rescued the question of the population of this country from the obscurity in which it has been so long involved, and have afforded some very valuable data to the political calculator. At the same time, it must be confessed that they are not so complete as entirely to exclude reasonings and conjectures respecting the inferences which are to be drawn from them. It is earnestly to be hoped that the subject may not be suffered to drop after the present effort. Now that the first difficulty is removed, an enumeration every ten years might be rendered easy and familiar; and the registers of births, deaths, and marriages might be received every year, or at least every five years. I am persuaded that more inferences are to be drawn, respecting the internal state of a country, from such registers, than we have yet been in the habit of supposing.
[In 1817 (Vol. II, p. 47) Malthus added to this reference:
   ... Population Act, p. 11, printed in 1800.
[In 1826 (Vol. I, p. 400) he altered this to:
   ... printed in 1801.
[Both statements were incorrect; see RICKMAN in the Alphabetical List.]

[6] New Observ. on Bills of Mortality, p. 265. 8vo. 1750. [For a note on 'bills of mortality' see GRAUNT in the Alphabetical List.]

difficulty people make to enter on marriage, from the prospect of the trouble and expenses in providing for a family, than from anything in the nature of the species'. And, in conformity to this idea, Dr. Short proposes to lay heavy taxes and fines on those who live single, for the support of the married poor.[7]

The observation of the eminent Judge is, with regard to the numbers which are prevented from being born, perfectly just; but the inference that the unmarried ought to be punished does not appear to be equally so. [8]●It will not, I believe, be very far from the truth to say that, in this country, not more than half of the prolific power of nature is called into action, and yet that there are more children born than the country can properly support.

If we suppose that the yearly births were $\frac{1}{20}$ part of the population, a proportion which, for short periods, obtains frequently on the continent,[(a)] and constantly, perhaps, in many parts of America; and allowing one third for the mortality under 20, which is a moderate supposition, as, according to Dr. Short, this mortality in some places is only one fifth or one fourth,[(b)] then if all were to marry at 20, which is by no means so early an age as is possible, $\frac{1}{30}$th part of the population would, in that case, marry annually; that is, there would be one annual marriage out of 60 persons, instead of one marriage out of 123 persons, as is the case at present. It may fairly be said, therefore, that not more than one half of the prolific power of nature is called into action in this country.●[8] And yet, when we contemplate the insufficiency of the price of labour to maintain a large family, and the quantum[9] of mortality which arises directly and indirectly from poverty; and add to this, the crowds of children which are cut off prematurely in our great towns, our manufactories, and our workhouses, we shall be compelled to acknowledge that, if the number born annually were not greatly thinned by this premature mortality, the funds for the maintenance of labour must increase with much greater rapidity than they have ever done hitherto in this country, in order to find work and food for the additional numbers that would then grow up to manhood.

Those, therefore, who live single or marry late, do not by such conduct contribute in any degree to diminish the actual population; but merely to diminish the proportion of premature mortality which would otherwise be

---

[7] New Observ. on Bills of Mortality, p. 247.

[8] [In 1806 (Vol. i, p. 455) these passages were expunged, including footnotes 8(a) and 8(b), and replaced by a single sentence:

... equally so. The prolific power of nature is very far indeed from being called fully into action in this country. And yet, when we contemplate the insufficiency ...

[(a)] On an average of five years, after the plague in Prussia, rejecting the first extraordinary year, the proportion of births to the whole population was above 1 to 18, (table iv. page 253). In New Jersey, according to Dr. Price (Observ. on Revers. Paym. vol. i, p. 283.) it was 1 to 18, and in the back settlements probably 1 to 15.

[(b)] New Observ. on Bills of Mortality, p. 59.

[9] [In 1817 (Vol. ii, p. 49) *quantum* was changed to 'amount'.

excessive; and consequently in this point of view do not seem to deserve any very severe reprobation or punishment.

The returns of the births and deaths are supposed, on good grounds, to be deficient, and it will therefore be difficult to estimate, with any degree of accuracy, the proportion which they bear to the whole population.

If we divide the existing population of England and Wales by the average of burials for the five years ending in 1800, it would appear that the mortality was only 1 in 49;[10] but this is a proportion so extraordinarily small, considering the number of our great towns and manufactories, that it cannot be considered as approaching to the truth.

Whatever may be the exact proportion of the inhabitants of the towns to the inhabitants of the country, the southern part of this island certainly ranks in that class of states where this proportion is greater than 1 to 3; indeed, there is ample reason to believe that it is greater than 1 to 2. According to the rule laid down by Crome, the mortality ought consequently to be above 1 in 30;[11] according to Susmilch, above 1 in 33.[12] In the *Observations on the Results of the Population Act*,[13] many probable causes of deficiency in the registry of the burials are pointed out; but no calculation is offered respecting the sum of these deficiencies, and I have no data whatever to supply such a calculation. I will only observe, therefore, that if we suppose them altogether to amount to such a number as will make the present annual mortality about 1 in 40, this must appear to be the lowest proportion of deaths that can well be supposed, considering the circumstances of the country; and if true, would indicate a most astonishing superiority over the generality of other states, either in the habits of the people with respect to prudence and cleanliness, or in natural healthiness of situation.[14] Indeed, it seems to be nearly ascertained, that both these causes which tend to diminish mortality, operate in this country to a considerable degree. The small proportion of annual marriages before-mentioned indicates that habits of prudence, extremely

---

[10] The population is taken at 9 168 000, and the annual deaths at 186 000. (Obs. on the Results of Pop. Act. p. 6 & 9.)

[11] Uber die Bevölkerung der Europaischen Staaten, p. 127.

[12] Susmilch, Gottliche Ordnung, vol. iii. p. 60.

[13] P. 6.

[14] It is by no means surprising that our population should have been under-rated formerly, at least by any person who attempted to estimate it from the proportion of births or deaths. Till the late Population Act, no one would have imagined that the actual returns of annual deaths, which might naturally have been expected to be as accurate in this country as in others, would turn out to be less than a 49th part of the population. If the actual returns for France, even so long ago as the ten years ending with 1780, had been multiplied by 49, she would have appeared at that time to have a population of above 40 millions. The average of annual deaths was 818 491. Necker, de l'Administration des Finances, tom. i. c. ix. p. 255. 12mo. 1785.

favourable to happiness, prevail through a large part of the community, in spite of the poor-laws; and it appears from the clearest evidence that the generality of our country parishes are very healthy. Dr. Price quotes an account of Dr. Percival, collected from the ministers of different parishes and taken from positive enumerations, according to which, in some villages, only a 45th, a 50th, a 60th, a 66th, and even a 75th part, dies annually. In many of these parishes the births are to the deaths above 2 to 1, and in a single parish above 3 to 1.[15] These, however, are particular instances, and cannot be applied to the agricultural part of the country in general. In some of the flat situations, and particularly those near marshes, the proportions are found very different, and in a few the deaths exceed the births. In the 54 country parishes, the registers of which Dr. Short collected, choosing them purposely in a great variety of situations, the average mortality was as high as 1 in 37.[16] This is certainly much above the present mortality of our agricultural parishes in general. The period which Dr. Short took included some considerable epidemics, which may possibly have been above the usual proportion. But sickly seasons should always be included, or we shall fall into great errors. In 1056 villages of Brandenburgh which Susmilch examined, the mortality for 6 good years, was 1 in 43; for 10 mixed years, about 1 in 38½.[17] In the villages of England which Sir F. M. Eden mentions, the mortality seems to be about 1 in 47 or 48;[18] and in the late returns pursuant to the Population Act, a still greater degree of healthiness appears. Combining these observations together, if we take 1 in 46, or 1 in 48, as the average mortality of the agricultural part of the country including sickly seasons, this will be the lowest that can be supposed with any degree of probability. But this proportion will certainly be raised to 1 in 40, when we blend it with the mortality of the towns and the manufacturing part of the community in order to obtain the average for the whole kingdom.

The mortality in London, which includes so considerable a part of the inhabitants of this country, was, according to Dr. Price, at the time he made his calculations, 1 in 20¾; in Norwich 1 in 24½; in Northampton 1 in 26½; in Newbury 1 in 27½;[19] in Manchester 1 in 28; in Liverpool 1 in 27½, &c.[20] He observes that the number dying annually in towns is seldom so low as 1 in 28,

---

[15] Price's Observ. on Revers. Paym. vol. ii. note, p. 10. First additional Essay. In particular parishes, private communications are perhaps more to be depended upon than public returns; because in general those clergymen only are applied to, who are in some degree interested in the subject, and of course take more pains to be accurate.

[16] New Observations on bills of Mortality, table ix. p. 133.

[17] Gottliche Ordnung, vol. i. c. ii. s. xxi. p. 74.

[18] Estimate of the number of Inhabitants in G. Britain.

[19] Price's Observ. on Revers. Paym. vol. i. note p. 272.

[21] Id. vol. ii. First additional Essay, note, p. 4.

except in consequence of a rapid increase produced by an influx of people at those periods of life when the fewest die, which is the case with Manchester and Liverpool,[21] and other very flourishing manufacturing towns. In general he thinks, that the mortality in great towns may be stated at from 1 in 19[22] to 1 in 22 and 23; in moderate towns, from 1 in 24 to 1 in 28; and, in country villages, from 1 in 40, to 1 in 50.[23]

The tendency of Dr. Price to exaggerate the unhealthiness of towns may justly[24] be objected to these statements; but the objection seems to be only of weight with regard to London. The accounts from the other towns which are given are from documents which his particular opinions could not influence.[25] It should be remarked, however, that there is good reason to believe that not only London, but the other towns in England, and probably also country villages, were at the time of these calculations less healthy than at present. Dr. William Heberden remarks that the registers of the ten years from 1759 to 1768,[26] from which Dr. Price calculated the probabilities of life in London, indicate a much greater degree of unhealthiness than the registers of late years. And the returns pursuant to the Population Act, even after allowing for great omissions in the burials, exhibit in all our provincial towns, and in the country, a degree of healthiness much greater than had before been calculated. At the same time I cannot but think that 1 in 31, the proportion of mortality for London mentioned in the *Observations on the Results of the Population Act*,[27] is smaller than the truth. Five thousand may not, perhaps, be enough to allow for the omissions in the burials; or perhaps the absentees in the employments of war and commerce may not be included in these omissions.[28] In estimating the proportional mortality the resident population alone should be considered.

There certainly seems to be something in great towns, and even in moderate towns, peculiarly unfavourable to the very early stages of life; and the part of the community on which the mortality principally falls, seems to

---

[21] Price's Observ. on Revers. Paym. vol. First additional Essay, note, p. 4.

[22] The Mortality at Stockholm was, according to Wargentin, 1 in 19.

[23] Observ. on Revers. Paym. vol. ii. First additional Essay, p. 4.

[24] [In 1806 (Vol. I, p. 461) *justly* was changed to 'perhaps'.

[25] [In 1806 (Vol. I, p. 461) a footnote was added here:

An estimate of the population or mortality of London, before the late enumeration, always depended much on conjecture and opinion, on account of the great acknowledged deficiencies in the registers; but this was not the case in the same degree with other towns here named. Dr. Price, in allusion to a diminishing population, on which subject it appears that he has so widely erred, says very candidly that perhaps he may have been insensibly influenced to maintain an opinion once advanced.

[26] Increase and Decrease of Diseases, p. 32. 4to. 1801.   [27] P. 13.

[28] [In 1806 (Vol. I, p. 462) this sentence was altered:

Five thousand are not probably enough to allow for the omissions in the burials; and the absentees in the employment of war and commerce are not sufficiently adverted to.

indicate that it arises more from the closeness and foulness of the air, which may be supposed to be unfavourable to the tender lungs of children, and the greater confinement which they almost necessarily experience, than from the superior degree of luxury and debauchery usually and justly attributed to towns. A married pair with the best constitutions, who lead the most regular and quiet life, seldom find that their children enjoy the same health in towns as in the country.

In London, according to former calculations, one half of the born died under three years of age; in Vienna and Stockholm under two; in Manchester, under five; in Norwich, under five; in Northampton, under ten.[29] In country villages, on the contrary, half of the born live till thirty, thirty-five, forty, forty-six, and above. In the parish of Ackworth, in Yorkshire, it appears, from a very exact account kept by Dr. Lee of the ages at which all died there for 20 years, that half of the inhabitants live to the age of 46,[30] and there is little doubt, that if the same kind of account had been kept in some of those parishes before mentioned, in which the mortality is so small as 1 in 60, 1 in 66, and even 1 in 75, half of the born would be found to have lived till 50 or 55.

As the calculations respecting the ages to which half of the born live in towns depend more upon the births and deaths which appear in the registers than upon any estimates of the number of people, they are on this account less liable to uncertainty than the calculations respecting the proportion of the inhabitants of any place which dies annually.

To fill up the void occasioned by this mortality in towns, and to answer all further demands for population, it is evident that a constant supply of recruits from the country is necessary, and this supply appears, in fact, to be always flowing in from the redundant births of the country. Even in those towns where the births exceed the deaths, this effect is produced by the marriages of persons not born in the place. At a time when our provincial towns were increasing much less rapidly than at present, Dr. Short calculated that $\frac{9}{19}$ of the married were strangers.[31] Of 1618 married men, and 1618 married women, examined at the Westminster Infirmary, only 329 of the men and 495 of the women had been born in London.[32]

Dr. Price supposes that London, with its neighbouring parishes, where the deaths exceed the births, requires a supply of 10 000 persons annually. Graunt, in his time, estimated this supply for London alone at 6000;[33] and he

---

29 Price's Observ. on Revers. Paym. vol. i. p. 264–6.
30 Id. vol. i. p. 268. [According to Dr Percival (q.v. in the Alphabetical List) the Rev. Dr Lee was rector of the parish of Ackworth, near Ferrybridge.]
31 New Observations on Bills of Mortality, p. 76.
32 Price's Observ. on Revers. Paym. vol. ii. p. 17.
33 Short's New Observ. Abstract from Graunt, p. 277.

further observes that, let the mortality of the city be what it will, arising from plague or any other great cause of destruction, it always fully repairs its loss in two years.[34]

As all these demands, therefore, are supplied from the country, it is evident that we should fall into a very great error if we were to estimate the proportion of births to deaths for the whole kingdom by the proportion observed in country parishes from which there must be such numerous emigrations.

We need not, therefore, accompany Dr. Price in his apprehensions that the country will be depopulated by these emigrations, at least as long as the funds for the maintenance of agricultural labour remain unimpaired. The proportion of births, as well as the proportion of marriages, clearly proves that, in spite of our increasing towns and manufactories, the demand on the country for people is by no means very pressing.

If we divide the present population of England and Wales, by the average number of baptisms for the last five years,[35] it will appear that the baptisms are to the population, as 1 to very nearly 36;[36] but it is supposed, with reason, that there are great omissions in the baptisms; [37] ●and it is conjectured that these omissions are greater than in the burials. On this point, however, I should be inclined to think differently, at least with respect to the last twenty years, though probably it was the case formerly. It would appear, by the present proportion of marriages, that the more rapid increase of population, supposed to have taken place since the year 1780, has arisen more from the diminution of deaths than the increase of the births.●[37]

Dr. Short estimated the proportion of births to the population of England as 1 to 28.[38] In the agricultural report of Suffolk, the proportion of births to

---

[34] Short's New Observ. Abstract from Graunt, p. 276.

[35] [In 1817 (Vol. II, p. 62) a footnote was added here:
   This was written before the omitted returns were added in 1810. These additions make the births in 1800 amount to 263 000, instead of 255 426, and increase the proportion of registered births to 1 in 35. See the next chapter.

[36] Average medium of baptisms for the last five years 255 426. Pop. 9 168 000. (Observ. on Results, p. 9.)

[37] [In 1806 (Vol. I, p. 466–7) this passage was amended:
   ... the case formerly. The increase of population during this period, estimated from the births, is not greater than is warranted by the proportion of births to deaths, which would have been the case if the omissions in the births had been greater than in the deaths; and the absolutely stationary number of deaths during the last twenty years, notwithstanding a considerable increase of births, seems to be rather inconsistent with the idea of greater omissions in the births.
   [In 1817 (Vol. II, p. 62) all this was excised, the paragraph ending:
   ... baptisms; and that these omissions are greater than in the burials.
   [In 1826 (Vol. I, p. 411) there was a further cut, and the paragraph concluded:
   ... great omissions in the baptisms.

[38] New Observ. p. 267.

the population was calculated at 1 to 30. For the whole of Suffolk, according to the late returns, this proportion is not much less than 1 to 33.[39] According to a correct account of thirteen villages from actual enumerations, produced by Sir F. M. Eden, the proportion of births to the population was as 1 to 33; and from another account, on the same authority, taken from towns and manufacturing parishes, as 1 to $27\frac{3}{4}$.[40] If, combining all these circumstances, and adverting at the same time to the acknowledged deficiency in the registry of births, and the known increase of our population of late years, we suppose the true proportion of the births to the population to be as 1 to 30; then, assuming the present mortality to be 1 in 40, as before suggested, we shall nearly keep the proportion of baptisms to burials which appears in the late returns. The births will be to the deaths as 4 to 3 or $13\frac{1}{3}$ to 10, a proportion more than sufficient to account for the increase of population which has taken place since the American war, after allowing for those who may be supposed to have died abroad,[41] and for a greater general mortality in the earlier part of this period.

In the *Observations on the Results of the Population Act*, it is remarked that the average duration of life in England appears to have increased in the proportion of 117 to 100[42] since the year 1780. So great a change in so short a time, if true, would be a most striking phenomenon. But I am inclined to suspect that the whole of this proportional diminution of burials does not arise from increased healthiness, but is occasioned, in part, by the greater number of deaths which must necessarily have taken place abroad, owing to the very rapid increase of our foreign commerce since this period; and to the great number of persons absent in naval and military employments, during the late war,[43] and the constant supply of fresh recruits necessary to maintain undiminished so great a force. A perpetual drain of this kind would certainly have a tendency to produce the effect observed in the returns, and might keep the burials stationary, while the births and marriages were increasing with some rapidity. At the same time, as the increase of population since 1780 is incontrovertible, and the present mortality extraordinarily small, I should still be disposed to believe, that the greater part of the effect is to be attributed to increased healthiness.

---

[39] In private inquiries, dissenters, and those who do not christen their children, will not of course be reckoned in the population, and consequently such inquiries, as far as they extend, will more accurately express the true proportion of births; and we are fairly justified in making use of them, in order to estimate the acknowledged deficiency of births in the public returns.

[40] Estimate of the number of Inhabitants in G. Britain, &c. p. 27.

[41] [In 1806 (Vol. I, p. 468) this sentence ended here with
    ... died abroad.

[42] P. 6.

[43] [In 1806 (Vol. I, p. 469) the words *during the late war* were excised.]
    [Hostilities against France were officially resumed in May, 1803, after this chapter had been printed.]

[44]●If we suppose that the mortality about the year 1780 was 1 in 36, instead of 1 in 40 as at present, this will be making a great allowance for increased healthiness, though not so much as the proportion of 117 to 100; and assuming the proportion of births to have been nearly the same as at present, the births about the year 1780 will appear to have been to the deaths as 36 to 30, or 12 to 10; a proportion which, calculated on a mortality of 1 in 36, doubles the population of a country in 125 years, and is, therefore, as great a proportion as can be true for the average of the whole century. The highest estimates of our population do not make it double of what it was at the revolution.●[44]

We must not suppose, however, that this proportion of births to deaths, or of births and deaths to the whole population, continued uniform before 1780.[45] It appears from the registers of every country which have been kept for any length of time, that considerable variations occur at different periods. Dr. Short, about the middle of the century, estimated the proportion of births to deaths at 11 to 10;[46] and if the births were at the same time a twenty-eighth part of the population, the mortality was then as high as 1 in $30\frac{4}{5}$. We now suppose that the proportion of births to deaths is above 13 to 10; but if we were to assume this proportion as a criterion by which to estimate the increase of population for the next thirty or forty years,[47] we should probably fall into a very gross error. [48]●The effects of the late scarcities are strongly marked, in the returns of the *Population Act*, by a decrease of births and an increase of burials, and should such seasons frequently recur, they would soon destroy the great excess of births which has been observed during the last twenty years;●[48] and indeed we cannot reasonably suppose that the resources of this country should increase, for any long continuance, with such rapidity as to allow of a permanent proportion of births to deaths as 13 to 10, unless indeed this proportion were principally caused by great foreign drains.

---

[44] [By 'revolution' Malthus here means the deposition of King James II of England in 1688. In 1806 (Vol. 1, p. 469) this paragraph was re-written thus:

A mortality of 1 in 36 is perhaps too small a proportion of deaths for the average of the whole century; but a proportion of births to deaths as 12 to 10, calculated on a mortality of 1 in 36, would double the population of a country in 125 years, and is therefore as great a proportion of births to deaths as can be true for the average of the whole century. None of the late calculations imply a more rapid increase than this.

[45] [In 1806 (Vol. 1, p. 469) this was amended to:

... the whole population, has continued nearly uniform throughout the century.

[46] New Observ. tables ii. & iii. p. 22 & 44. Price's Observ. on Revers. Paym. vol. ii. p. 311.

[47] [In 1826 (Vol. 1, p. 414) this was altered to:

... for the next hundred years, we should probably fall into a very gross error.

[48] [In 1826 (Vol. 1, p. 414) this sentence was omitted; the next began:

We cannot reasonably suppose that the resources of this country ...

From all the data that could be collected, the proportion of births, to the whole population of England and Wales, has been assumed to be as 1 to 30; but this is a smaller proportion of births than has appeared, in the course of this review, to take place in any other country except Norway and Switzerland; and it has been hitherto usual with political calculators to consider a great proportion of births as the surest sign of a vigorous and flourishing state. It is to be hoped, however, that this prejudice will not last long. In countries circumstanced like America or Russia, or in other countries after any great mortality, a large proportion of births may be[49] a favourable symptom; but in the average state of a well-peopled territory there cannot well be a worse sign that a large proportion of births, nor can there well be a better sign than a small proportion.

Sir Francis D'Ivernois very justly observes that, 'if the various states of Europe kept and published annually an exact account of their population, noting carefully in a second column the exact age at which the children die, this second column would shew the relative merit of the governments, and the comparative happiness of their subjects. A simple arithmetical statement would then perhaps be more conclusive than all the arguments that could be adduced.'[50] In the importance of the inferences to be drawn from such tables, I fully agree with him: and to make these inferences, it is evident that we should attend less to the column expressing the number of children born, than to the column expressing the number which survived the age of infancy and reached manhood; and this number will, almost invariably, be the greatest where the proportion of the births to the whole population is the least. In this point we rank next after Norway and Switzerland, which, considering the number of our great towns and manufactories, is certainly a very extraordinary fact. As nothing can be more clear than that all our demands for population are fully supplied, if this be done with a small proportion of births, it is a decided proof of a very small mortality, a distinction on which we may justly pride ourselves. Should it appear from future investigations that I have made too great an allowance for omissions, both in the births and in the burials, I shall be extremely happy to find that this distinction which, other circumstances being the same, I consider as the surest test of happiness and good government, is even greater than I have supposed it to be. In despotic, miserable, or naturally unhealthy countries, the proportion of births to the whole population will generally be found very great.

---

[49] [In 1817 (Vol. II, p. 67) *may be* was changed to:
    ... is a favourable symptom; ...
[50] Tableau des Pertes, &c. c. ii. p. 16.

[51]●According to one of Sir F. M. Eden's calculations, taken from towns and manufacturing parishes, the annual births are to the annual marriages as 3 to 1.[(a)] In 111 agricultural parishes for 12 years, ending in 1799, the annual births are to the annual marriages in the proportion of above 4 to 1.[(b)] From which it might appear that, in our towns, more than half of the born live to be married, and in the country less. But for the reasons mentioned in page 188, the contrary is probably true. In our towns, from the mortality that takes place in the early stages of life, it is not to be doubted that less than half of the born live to be married, and the great proportion of marriages is occasioned merely by new settlers. In the country, on account of the emigrants that marry in other places, more than half of the born live to be married though, allowing for second and third marriages, probably not much more. But from what was said in page 211, the degree in which the preventive check operates cannot be determined by the proportion of the born which lives to be married; but depends upon the proportion of annual marriages, and the proportion of annual births, to the whole population; and till the first of these proportions rises from 1 in 123 to 1 in 80 or 1 in 70, and the second from 1 in 30 to 1 in 24, 22 or 20, it cannot be said that the towns draw hard upon the country for population.

If, taking the towns and country together, and rejecting at present second and third marriages and illegitimate children, we suppose that accurately half of the born live to be married, then, according to table 1, page 186, each marriage must yield five births, in order to produce a proportion of births to deaths as $12\frac{1}{5}$ to 10. And if the proportion of our births to deaths be above this, or $13\frac{1}{3}$ to 10, then, including all circumstances, it does not appear that we can allow less than $5\frac{1}{2}$ births to each marriage.

In judging of the proportion of the born which lives to be married, by the proportion of annual births to annual marriages, the number of second and third marriages, and the number of illegitimate children, tend to correct each other. The second and third marriages tend to give the proportion which lives to be married too great, and the illegitimate children too small. It must depend on the particular circumstances of the country, which of these two causes of irregularity preponderates.

According to the late returns, it would appear that, in this country, considerably more than half of the born live to be married; but when the deficiency in the births is assumed to be such as is suggested in this chapter, the result is rather on the contrary side.●[51]

On an average of the five years ending in 1780, the proportion of births to

---

[51] [In 1806 (Vol. I, p. 473) the following four paragraphs were omitted.]

[(a)] Estimate of the Number of Inhabitants in Great Britain, p. 10.

[(b)] Id. p. 79.

marriages is 350 to 100.[52] In 1760 it was 362 to 100, from which an inference is drawn that the registers of births, however deficient, were certainly not more deficient formerly than at present.[53] But a change of this nature, in the appearance of the registers, might arise from a cause totally unconnected with deficiencies. If from the acknowledged greater healthiness of the latter part of the century, compared with the middle of it, a greater number of children survived the age of infancy, a greater proportion of the born would of course live to marry; [54]●and this circumstance would produce exactly the effect observed in the registers. From what has already been said on this subject, the reader will be aware that this change may take place without diminishing the operation of the preventive check. If half of the born live to 40 instead of 30, it is evident that a greater proportion might live to marry and yet the marriages be later.●[54]

With regard to the general question, whether we have just grounds for supposing that the registry of births and deaths was in general more deficient in the former part of the century than in the latter part: I should say that the late returns tend to confirm the suspicion of former inaccuracy, and to show that the registers of the earlier part of the century, in every point of view, afford very uncertain data on which to ground any estimates of past population. In the years 1710, 1720, and 1730, it appears from the returns that the deaths exceeded the births; and taking the six periods ending in 1750,[55] including the first half of the century, if we compare the sum of the births with the sum of the deaths, the excess of the births is so small as to be perfectly inadequate to account for the increase of a million, which, upon a calculation from the births alone, is supposed to have taken place in that

---

[52] [In 1806 (Vol. 1, p. 473) this was altered to:
   On an average of the five years ending in 1800, the proportion of births to marriages is 347 to 100.

[53] Observations on the Results of the Population Act, p. 8.

[54] [In 1806 (Vol. 1, pp. 473-4) this paragraph was altered and continued thus:
   ... a greater proportion of the born would of course live to marry, and this circumstance would produce a greater present proportion of marriages compared with the births. On the other hand, if the marriages were rather more prolific formerly than at present, owing to their being contracted at an earlier age, the effect would be a greater proportion of births compared with the marriages. The operation of either or both of these causes would produce exactly the effect observed in the registers: and consequently from the existence of such an effect no inference can justly be drawn against the supposed increasing accuracy of the registers. The influence of the two causes just mentioned on the proportions of annual births to marriages will be explained in a subsequent chapter.
   [Malthus here means the re-written chapter on the fertility of marriages, chapter iv of Book II in the quarto, which became chapter ix in 1806.]

[56] Population Abstract Parish Registers. Final Summary, p. 455.

time.[56] Consequently, either the registers are very inaccurate, and the deficiencies in the births greater than in the deaths; or these periods, each at the distance of ten years, do not express the just average. These particular years may have been more unfavourable with respect to the proportion of births to deaths than the rest; indeed one of them, 1710, is known to have been a year of great scarcity and distress. But if this suspicion, which is very probable, be admitted, so as to affect the six first periods, we may justly suspect the contrary accident to have happened with regard to the three following periods ending with 1780; in which thirty years it would seem, by the same mode of calculation, that an increase of a million and an half had taken place.[57] At any rate it must be allowed that the three separate years, taken in this manner, can by no means be considered as sufficient to establish a just average; and what rather encourages the suspicion that these particular years might be more than usually favourable with regard to births, is, that the increase of births from 1780 to 1785 is unusually small,[58] which would naturally take place, without supposing a slower progress than before, if the births in 1780 had been accidentally above the average.

On the whole, therefore, considering the probable inaccuracy of the earlier registers, and the very great danger of fallacy, in drawing general inferences from a few detached years, I do not think that we can depend upon any estimates of past population, founded on a calculation from the births, till after the year 1780, when every following year is given, and a just average of the births may be obtained. As a further confirmation of this remark, I will just observe that, in the final summary of the abstracts from the registers of England and Wales, it appears that in the year 1790 the total number of births was 248 774, in the year 1795, 247 218, and 1800, 247 147.[59] Consequently, if we had been estimating the population from the births, taken at three separate periods of five years, it would have appeared that the population during the last ten years had been regularly decreasing, though we have very good reason to believe that it has increased considerably.

In the *Observations on the Results of the Population Act*,[60] a table is given of the population of England and Wales throughout the last century calculated from the births; but, for the reasons given above, little reliance can be placed on it, and for the population at the revolution, I should be inclined to place more dependence on the old calculations from the number of houses.

[In 1806 (Vol. I, pp. 477–9) two paragraphs were added here:

---

[56] Observations on the Results of the Population Act, p. 9.
[57] Ibid.   [58] Ibid.   [59] Population Abstract Parish Registers, p. 455.
[60] P. 9.

It is possible, indeed, though not probable, that these estimates of the population at the different periods of the century may not be very far from the truth, because opposite errors may have corrected each other; but the assumption of the uniform proportion of births on which they are founded is false on the face of the calculations themselves. According to these calculations the increase of population was more rapid in the period from 1760 to 1780 than from 1780 to 1800; yet it appears that the proportion of deaths about the year 1780 was greater than in 1800 in the ratio of 117 to 100. Consequently the proportion of births before 1780 must have been much greater than in 1800, or the population in that period could not possibly have increased faster. This overthrows at once the supposition of anything like uniformity in the proportion of births.

I should indeed have supposed from the analogy of other countries, and the calculations of Mr. King and Dr. Short, that the proportion of births at the beginning and in the middle of the century was greater than at the end. But this supposition would, in a calculation from the births, give a smaller population in the early part of the century than is given in the *Results of the Population Act*, though there are strong reasons for supposing that the population there given is too small. According to Davenant, the number of houses in 1690 was 1 319 215, and there is no reason to think that this calculation erred on the side of excess. Allowing only five to a house instead of $5\frac{2}{5}$, which is supposed to be the proportion at present, this would give a population of above six millions and a half, and it is perfectly incredible that from this time to the year 1710 the population should have diminished nearly a million and a half. It is far more probable that the omissions in the births should have been much greater than at present, and greater than in the deaths; and this is further confirmed by the observation before alluded to, that in the first half of the century the increase of population, as calculated from the births, is much greater than is warranted by the proportion of births to deaths. In every point of view, therefore, the calculations from the births are little to be depended on.

It must, indeed, have appeared to the reader, in the course of this work, that registers of births or deaths, excluding any suspicion of deficiencies, must at all times afford very uncertain data for an estimate of population. [61]●On account of the varying circumstances of every country, they are both very precarious guides in this respect; but of the two, perhaps the births still more so than the deaths; though from the greater apparent regularity of the former, political calculators have generally adopted them as the ground of their estimates, in preference to the latter.●[61] Necker, in estimating the population of France, observes that an epidemic disease, or an emigration, may occasion temporary differences in the deaths, and that therefore the number of births is the most certain criterion.[62] But the very circumstance of

---

[61] [In 1806 (Vol. I, p. 479) this sentence was amended:
   On account of the varying circumstances of every country, they are both precarious guides. From the greater apparent regularity of the births, political calculators have generally adopted them as the ground of their estimates in preference to the deaths.
[62] De l'Administration des Finances, tom. i. c. ix. p. 252. 12mo. 1785.

the apparent regularity of the births in the registers will now and then lead into the grossest errors.[63] If in any country we can obtain registers of burials for two or three years together, a plague or mortal epidemic will always show itself, from the very sudden increase of the deaths during its operation, and the still greater diminution of them afterwards. From these appearances we should of course be directed not to include the whole of a great mortality in any very short term of years. But there would be nothing of this kind to guide us in the registers of births; and after a country had lost an eighth part of its population by a plague, an average of the five or six subsequent years might show an increase in the number of births, and our calculations would give the population the highest at the very time that it was the lowest. This appears very strikingly in many of Susmilch's tables, and most particularly in the table for Prussia and Lithuania, which I have inserted in chap. vi. of this book,[64] where, in the year subsequent to the loss of one third of the population, the births were considerably increased, and in an average of five years but very little diminished; and this, at a time when, of course, the country could have made but a very small progress towards recovering its former population.

We do not know indeed of any extraordinary mortality which has occurred in England since 1700; and there are reasons for supposing that the proportions of the births and deaths to the population during the last century have not experienced such great variations as in many countries on the continent; at the same time it is certain that the sickly seasons which are known to have occurred would, in proportion to the degree of their fatality, produce similar effects; and the change which has been observed in the mortality of late years, should dispose us to believe that similar changes might formerly have taken place respecting the births, and should instruct us to be extremely cautious in applying any proportions which are observed to be true at present, to past or future periods.

---

[63] [In 1806 (Vol. i, p. 479) this was changed to:
... lead into great errors.

[64] [In 1806 (Vol. i, p. 480) after he had transferred his general statistical chapters towards the end of Book ii, Malthus altered this to:
... and Lithuania, which I shall insert in a following chapter; where, in the year subsequent to the loss of one third of the population ...
[In 1826 (Vol. i, pp. 422–3) he changed it again:
... a subsequent chapter; where, in the year following to the loss of one third ...

CHAPTER XI

Of the Checks to Population in England (continued) [1]

The returns of the Population Act in 1811 undoubtedly presented extraordinary results. They shewed a greatly accelerated rate of progress, and a greatly improved healthiness of the people, notwithstanding the increase of the towns and the increased proportion of the population engaged in manufacturing employments. They thus furnished another striking instance of the readiness with which population starts forwards, under almost any weight, when the resources of a country are rapidly increasing.

The amount of the population in 1800, together with the proportions of births, deaths and marriages given in the registers, made it appear that the population had been for some time increasing at a rate rather exceeding what would result from a proportion of births to deaths as 4 to 3, with a mortality of 1 in 40.

These proportions would add to the population of a country every year $\frac{1}{120}$th part; and if they were to continue, would (according to Table III, page 191) double the population in every successive period of $83\frac{1}{2}$ years.[2] This is a rate of progress which in a rich and well-peopled country might reasonably be expected to diminish rather than to increase. But instead of any such diminution, it appears that as far as 1810 it had been considerably accelerated.

In 1810, according to the returns from each parish, with the addition of $\frac{1}{30}$ for the soldiers, sailors, &c., the population of England and Wales was estimated at 10 488 000;[3] which, compared with 9 168 000, the population of 1800 estimated in a similar manner, shews an increase in the ten years of 1 320 000.

---

[1] [This chapter, added in 1817, was then and in 1826 chapter ix of Book II.]
[2] [In 1826 (Vol. I, p. 424) this was changed to:
... every year 120th part; and if they were to continue ...
[Table III, in the chapter on the fertility of marriages in 1803, became Table II when this chapter was re-written in 1806. Malthus's own reference here, in 1817, is to Table II in the revised chapter, which readers may find in Vol. II of this edition, p. 15. The tables themselves are identical.]
[3] See the Population Abstracts published in 1811 [in fact 1812] and the valuable Preliminary Observations by Mr Rickman.

The registered baptisms during ten years were 2 878 906, and the registered burials 1 950 189. The excess of the births is therefore 928 717, which falls very considerably short of the increase shewn by the two enumerations. This deficiency could only be occasioned either by the enumeration in 1800 being below the truth, or by the inaccuracy of the registers of births and burials, or by the operation of these two causes combined; as it is obvious that, if the population in 1800 were estimated correctly, and the registers contained all the births and burials, the difference must exceed rather than fall short of the real addition to the population; that is, it would exceed it exactly by the number of persons dying abroad in the army, navy, &c.

There is reason to believe that both causes had a share in producing the effect observed, though the latter, that is, the inaccuracy of the registers, in much the greatest degree.

In estimating the population throughout the century,[4] the births have been assumed to bear the same proportion at all times to the number of people. It has been seen that such an assumption might often lead to a very incorrect estimate of the population of a country at different and distant periods. As the population, however, is known to have increased with great rapidity from 1800 to 1810, it is probable that the proportion of births did not essentially diminish during that period. But if, taking the last enumeration as correct, we compare the births of 1810 with the births of 1800, the result will imply a larger population in 1800 than is given in the enumeration for that year.

Thus the average of the last five years' births to 1810 is 297 000, and the average of the five years' births to 1800 is 263 000. But 297 000 is to 263 000 as 10 488 000, the population of 1810, to 9 287 000, which must therefore have been the population in 1800 if the proportion of births be assumed to be the same, instead of 9 168 000, the result of the enumeration. It is further to be observed that the increase of population from 1795 to 1800 is according to the table unusually small, compared with most of the preceding periods of five years. And a slight inspection of the registers will shew that the proportion of births for five years from 1795, including the diminished numbers of 1796 and 1800, was more likely to be below than above the general average. For these reasons, together with the general impression on the subject, it is probable that the enumeration in 1800 was short of the truth, and perhaps the population at that time may be safely taken at as much as 9 287 000 at the least, or about 119 000 greater than the returns gave it.

But even upon this supposition, neither the excess of births above the

---

[4] See a table of the population throughout the century, in page xxv. of the Preliminary Observations to the Population Abstracts, printed in 1811.

deaths in the whole of the ten years, nor the proportion of births to deaths, as given in the registers, will account for an increase from 9 287 000 to 10 488 000. Yet it is not probable that the increase has been much less than is shown by the proportion of the births at the two periods. Some allowance must therefore necessarily be made for omissions in the registers of births and deaths, which are known to be very far from correct, particularly the registers of births.

There is reason to believe that there are few or no omissions in the register of marriages; and if we suppose the omissions in the births to be one-6th, this will preserve a proportion of the births to the marriages as 4 to 1, a proportion which appears to be satisfactorily established upon other grounds;[5] but if we are warranted in this supposition, it will be fair to take the omissions in the deaths at such a number as will make the excess of the births above the deaths in the ten years accord with the increase of population estimated by the increase of the births.

The registered births in the ten years, as was mentioned before, are 2 878 906, which increased by one-6th will be 3 358 723. The registered burials are 1 950 189, which increased by one-12th will be 2 112 704. The latter subtracted from the former will give 1 246 019 for the excess of births, and the increase of population in the ten years, which number added to 9 287 000, the corrected population of 1800, will give 10 533 019, forty-five thousand above the enumeration of 1810, leaving almost exactly the number which in the course of the ten years appears to have died abroad. This number has been calculated generally at about $4\frac{1}{4}$ per cent. of the male births; but in the present case there are the means of ascertaining more accurately the number of males dying abroad during the period in question. In the last population returns the male and female births and deaths are separated; and from the excess of the male births above the female births, compared with the male and female deaths, it appears that forty-five thousand males died abroad.[6]

The assumed omissions therefore in the births and burials seem to answer so far very well.

It remains to see whether the same supposition will give such a proportion of births to deaths, with such a rate of mortality, as will also account for an increase of numbers in ten years from 9 287 000 to 10 488 000.

If we divide the population of 1810 by the average births of the preceding

---

[5] See the Preliminary Observations on the Population Abstracts, p. xxvi.
[6] See Population Abstracts, 1811, page 196 of the Parish Register Abstract.

    It is certainly very extraordinary that a smaller proportion of males than usual should appear to have died abroad from 1800 to 1810; but as the registers for this period seem to prove it, I have made my calculations accordingly.

five years, with the addition of one-6th, it will appear that the proportion of births to the population is as 1 to 30. But it is obvious that if the population be increasing with some rapidity, the average of births for five years, compared with the population at the end of such period, must give the proportion of births too small. And further, there is always a probability that a proportion which is correct for five years may not be correct for ten years. In order to obtain the true proportion applicable to the progress of population during the period in question, we must compare the annual average of the births for the whole term with the average or mean population of the whole term.

The whole number of births, with the addition of $\frac{1}{6}$, is, as before stated, 3 358 723, and the annual average during the ten years 335 872. The mean population, or the mean between 10 488 000 (the population of 1810) and 9 287 000 (the corrected population of 1800) is 9 887 000: and the latter number divided by the average of the births will give a proportion of births to the population as 1 to rather less than 29½, instead of 30, which will make a considerable difference.

In the same manner, if we divide the population of 1810 by the average of the burials for the preceding five years, with the addition of one-12th, the mortality will appear to be as 1 in nearly 50; but upon the same grounds as with regard to the births, an average of the burials for five years, compared with the population at the end of such term, must give the proportion of burials too small; and further, it is known, in the present case, that the proportion of burials to the population by no means continued the same during the whole time. In fact the registers clearly shew an improvement in the healthiness of the country, and a diminution of mortality progressively through the ten years; and while the average number of annual births increased from 263 000 to 297 000, or more than one-8th, the burials increased only from 192 000 to 196 000, or one-48th. It is obviously necessary then for the purpose in view to compare the average mortality with the average or mean population.

The whole number of burials in the ten years, with the addition of one-12th, is, as was before stated, 2 112 704, and the mean population 9 887 000. The latter, divided by the former, gives the annual average of burials compared with the population as 1 to rather less than 47. But a proportion of births as 1 to 29½, with a proportion of deaths as 1 to 47, will add yearly to the numbers of a country one-79th of the whole, and in ten years will increase the population from 9 287 000 to 10 531 000, leaving 43 000 for the deaths abroad, and agreeing very nearly with the calculation founded on the excess of births.[7]

---

[7] A general formula for estimating the population of a country at any distance from a certain period, under given circumstances of births and mortality, may be found in Bridge's

We may presume therefore that the assumed omissions in the births and deaths from 1800 to 1810 are not far from the truth.

But if these omissions of one-6th for the births, and one-12th for the burials, may be considered as nearly right for the period between 1800 and 1810, it is probable that they may be applied without much danger of error to the period between 1780 and 1800, and may serve to correct some of the conclusions founded on the births alone. Next to an accurate enumeration, a calculation from the excess of births above the deaths is the most to be depended upon. Indeed, when the registers contain all the births and deaths, and these are the means of setting out from a known population, it is obviously the same as an actual enumeration; and where a nearly correct allowance can be made for the omissions in the registers, and for the deaths abroad, a much nearer approximation to it may be obtained in this way than from the proportion of births to the whole population, which is known to be liable to such frequent variations.

The whole number of births returned in the twenty years, from 1780 to 1800, is 5 014 899, and of the burials 3 840 455. If we add one-6th to the former, and one-12th to the latter, the two numbers will be 5 850 715 and 4 160 492; and subtracting the latter from the former, the excess of the births above the deaths will be 1 690 223. Adding this excess to the population of 1780, as calculated in Mr. Rickman's tables, from the births, which is 7 953 000, the result will be 9 643 000, a number which, after making a proper allowance for the deaths abroad, is very much above the population of

---

Elements of Algebra, p. 225.

$$\text{Log. A} = \text{log. P} + n \times \text{log } 1 + \frac{m - b}{m\,b}$$

A representing the required population at the end of any number of years; n the number of years; P the actual population at the given period; $\frac{1}{m}$ the proportion of yearly deaths to the population, or ratio of mortality; $\frac{1}{b}$ the proportion of yearly births to the population, or ratio of births.

In the present case, P = 9 287 000; n = 10; m = 47; b = $29\frac{1}{2}$.

$$\frac{m - b}{m\,b} = \tfrac{1}{79} \text{ and } 1 + \frac{m - b}{m\,b} = \tfrac{80}{79}$$

$$\text{The log. of } \tfrac{80}{79} = 00546; \therefore n \times \text{log. } 1 + \frac{m - b}{m\,b}$$

= 05460. Log. P. = 6.96787, which added to 05460 = 7.02247 the log. of A, the number answering to which is 10 531 000.

1800, as before corrected, and still more above the number which is given in the table as the result of the enumeration.

But if we proceed upon the safer ground just suggested, and, taking the corrected population of 1800 as established, subtract from it the excess of the births during the twenty years, diminished by the probable number of deaths abroad, which in this case will be about 124 000, we shall have the number 7 721 000 for the population of 1780, instead of 7 953 000; and there is good reason to believe that this is nearer the truth;[8] and that not only in 1780, but in many of the intermediate periods, the estimate from the births has represented the population as greater, and increasing more irregularly, than would be found to be true if recourse could be had to enumerations. This has arisen from the proportion of births to the population being variable, and, on the whole, greater in 1780, and at other periods during the course of the twenty years, than it was in 1800.

In 1795, for instance, the population is represented to be 9 055 000, and in 1800 9 168 000;[9] but if we suppose the first number to be correct, and add the excess of the births above the deaths in the five intervening years, even without making any allowance for omissions in the registers, we shall find that the population in 1800 ought to have been 9 398 000 instead of 9 168 000; or if we take the number returned for 1800 as correct, it will appear by subtracting from it the excess of births during the five preceding years, that the population in 1795 ought to have been 8 825 000, instead of 9 055 000. Hence it follows that the estimate from the births in 1795 cannot be correct.

To obtain the population at that period, the safest way is to apply the before-mentioned corrections to the registers, and, having made the allowance of 4¼ per cent. on the male births for the deaths abroad, subtract the remaining excess of the births from the corrected returns of 1800. The result in this case will be 8 831 086 for the population of 1795, implying an increase in the five years of 455 914, instead of only 113 000, as shewn by the table calculated from the births.

If we proceed in the same manner with the period from 1790 to 1795, we shall find that the excess of births above the deaths (after the foregoing corrections have been applied, and an allowance has been made of 4¼ per cent. upon the male births for the deaths abroad), will be 415 669, which, subtracted from 8 831 086, the population of 1795, as above estimated, leaves 8 415 417 for the population of 1790.

Upon the same principle, the excess of the births above the deaths in the

---

[8] The very small difference between the population of 1780 and 1785, as given in the table, seems strongly to imply that one of the two estimates is erroneous.

[9] Population Abstracts, 1811. Preliminary View, p. xxv.

interval between 1785 and 1790 will turn out to be 416 776. The population in 1785 will therefore be 7 998 641. And in like manner the excess of the births above the deaths in the interval between 1780 and 1785 will be 277 544, and the population in 1780 7 721 097.

The two tables therefore, of the population, from 1780 to 1810, will stand thus:

Table, calculated from the births alone, in the Preliminary Observations to the Population Abstracts printed in 1811		Table, calculated from the excess of the births above the deaths, after an allowance made for the omissions in the registers, and the deaths abroad	
Population in		Population in	
1780	7 953 000	1780	7 721 000
1785	8 016 000	1785	7 998 000
1790	8 675 000	1790	8 415 000
1795	9 055 000	1795	8 831 000
1800	9 168 000	1800	9 287 000
1805	9 828 000	1805	9 837 000
1810	10 488 000	1810	10 488 000

In the first table, or table calculated from the births alone, the additions made to the population in each period of five years are as follow:

From 1780 to 1785	63 000
From 1785 to 1790	659 000
From 1790 to 1795	380 000
From 1795 to 1800	113 000
From 1800 to 1805	660 000
From 1805 to 1810	660 000

In the second table, or table calculated from the excess of the births above the deaths, after the proposed corrections have been applied, the additions made to the population in each period of five years will stand thus:

From 1780 to 1785	277 000
From 1785 to 1790	417 000
From 1790 to 1795	416 000
From 1795 to 1800	456 000
From 1800 to 1805	550 000
From 1805 to 1810	651 000

The progress of the population, according to this latter table, appears much more natural and probable than according to the former.

It is no respect likely that, in the interval between 1780 and 1785, the increase of the population should only have been 63 000, and in the next

period 659 000; or that, in the interval between 1795 and 1800, it should have
been only 113 000, and in the next period 660 000. But it is not necessary to
dwell on probabilities; the most distinct proofs may be brought to shew that,
whether the new table be right or not, the old table must be wrong. Without
any allowances being made for omissions in the registers, the excess of the
births above the deaths, in the period from 1780 to 1785, shews an increase of
193 000, instead of 63 000. And, on the other hand, no allowances for
omissions in the registers, that could with the slightest degree of probability
be supposed, would make the excess of births above the deaths in the period
from 1785 to 1790 equal to 659 000. Making no allowance for omissions, this
excess only amounts to 317 406; and if we were to suppose the omissions in
the births one 4th, instead of one 6th, and that there were no omissions in the
registers of burials, and that no one died abroad, the excess would still fall
short of the number stated by many thousands.

The same results would follow if we were to estimate the progress of
population during these periods by the proportion of births to deaths, and the
rate of mortality. In the first period the increase would turn out to be very
much greater than the increase stated, and in the other very much less.

Similar observations may be made with regard to some of the other periods
in the old table, particularly that between 1795 and 1800, which has been
already noticed.

It will be found on the other hand that, if the proportion of births to deaths
during each period be estimated with tolerable accuracy, and compared with
the mean population, the rate of the progress of the population determined
by this criterion will, in every period, agree very nearly with the rate of
progress determined by the excess of the births above the deaths, after
applying the proposed corrections. And it is further worthy of remark that, if
the corrections proposed should be in some degree inaccurate, as is probable,
the errors arising from any such inaccuracies are likely to be very much less
considerable than those which must necessarily arise from the assumption on
which the old table is founded; namely, that the births bear at all times the
same proportion to the population.

Of course I do not mean to reject any estimates of population formed in
this way, when no better materials are to be found; but, in the present case,
the registers of the burials as well as baptisms are given every year, as far
back as 1780, and these registers, with the firm ground of the last enumeration to stand upon, afford the means of giving a more correct table of the
population from 1780 than was before furnished, and of shewing at the same
time the uncertainty of estimates from the births alone, particularly with a
view to the progress of population during particular periods. In estimating
the whole population of a large country, two or three hundred thousand are
not of much importance; but, in estimating the rate of increase during a

period of five or ten years, an error to this amount is quite fatal. It will be allowed, I conceive, to make an essential difference in our conclusions respecting the rate of increase for any five years which we may fix upon, whether the addition made to the population during the term in question is 63 000 or 277 000, 115 000 or 456 000, 659 000 or 417 000.

With regard to the period of the century previous to 1780, as the registers of the baptisms and burials are not returned for every year, it is not possible to apply the same corrections. And it will be obvious that, in the table calculated from the births previous to this period, when the registers are only given for insulated years at some distance from each other, very considerable errors may arise, not merely from the varying proportion of the births to the population, on averages of five years, but from the individual years produced not representing with tolerable correctness these averages.[10] A very slight glance at the valuable table of baptisms, burials and marriages, given in the Preliminary Observations to the Population Abstracts,[11] will show how very little dependence ought to be placed upon inferences respecting the population drawn from the number of births, deaths or marriages in individual years. If, for instance, we were estimating the population in the two years 1800 and 1801, compared with the two following years 1802 and 1803, from the proportion of marriages to the population, assuming this proportion to be always the same, it would appear that, if the population in the first two years were nine millions, in the second two years immediately succeeding it would be considerably above twelve millions, and thus it would seem to have increased above three millions, or more than one-third, in this short interval. Nor would the result of an estimate, formed from the births for the two years 1800 and 1801, compared with the two years 1803 and 1804, be materially different; at least such an estimate would indicate an increase of two millions six hundred thousand in three years.

The reader can hardly be surprised at these results, if he recollects that the births, deaths and marriages bear but a small proportion to the whole population; and that consequently variations in either of these, which may take place from temporary causes, cannot possibly be accompanied by similar variations in the whole mass of the population. An increase in the births of one-third, which might occur in a single year, instead of increasing the population one-third, would only perhaps increase it one-eightieth or ninetieth.

It follows therefore, as I stated in the last chapter, that the table of the

---

[10] From the one or the other of these causes, I have little doubt that the numbers in the table for 1760 and 1770, which imply so rapid an increase of population in that interval, do not bear the proper relation to each other. It is probable that the number given for 1770 is too great.

[11] P. 20.

population for the century previous to 1780, calculated from the returns of the births alone, at the distance of ten years each, can only be considered as a very rough approximation towards the truth, in the absence of better materials, and can scarcely in any degree be depended upon for the comparative rate of increase at particular periods.

The population in 1810, compared with that of 1800, corrected as proposed in this chapter, implies a less rapid increase than the difference between the two enumerations; and it has further appeared that the assumed proportion of births to deaths as 47 to 29½ is rather below than above the truth. Yet this proportion is quite extraordinary for a rich and well-peopled territory. It would add to the population of a country one 79th every year, and, were it to continue, would, according to table iii (p. 192 in this volume) double the number of inhabitants in less than fifty-five years.[12]

This is a rate of increase which, in the nature of things, cannot be permanent. It has been occasioned by the stimulus of a greatly-increased demand for labour, combined with a greatly-increased power of production, both in agriculture and manufactures. These are the two elements necessary to form an effective encouragement to a rapid increase of population. [13]●A failure of either of these must immediately weaken the stimulus; and there is but too much reason to fear the failure of one of them at present.●[13] But what has already taken place is a striking illustration of the principle of population, and a proof that in spite of great towns, manufacturing occupations, and the gradually-acquired habits of an opulent and luxuriant people, if the resources of a country will admit of a rapid increase, and if these resources are so advantageously distributed as to occasion a constantly-increasing demand for labour, the population will not fail to keep pace with them.

[In 1826 (Vol. 1, pp. 441–9) Malthus added the following:

1825

Since the publication of the last edition of this work in 1817, a third census of the population has taken place, and the results are highly worthy of our attention.

According to the enumeration in 1821, and the corrected returns of 1811 and 1801, as given in the preliminary observations to the published account by Mr. Rickman, the population of Great Britain was, in 1801, 10 942 646; in 1811, 12 596 803; and in 1821, 14 391 631.

These numbers taken as first stated, and including the very large numbers of males added in 1811 for the army and navy, give an increase of 15 per cent. in the ten years from 1800 to 1811, and only 14¼ per cent. from 1810 to 1821.[14] But it is calculated that

---

[12] [See note 2.]

[13] [In 1826 (Vol. 1, p. 441) this sentence was expunged; the next sentence began:
What has taken place is a striking illustration of the principle of population ...

[14] Preliminary Observations, p. viii.

out of the 640 500 males added for the army, navy, and merchant service above one-third must have been Irish and foreigners. Adding therefore only $\frac{1}{30}$ to the resident population in 1801 and 1811, and on account of the peace allowing only $\frac{1}{50}$ for the absent males in 1821, the population of England and Wales at the three different periods, without reference to any supposed deficiency in the first enumeration, will stand thus: in 1801, 9 168 000; in 1811, 10 502 500; and in 1821, 12 218 500, giving an increase in the interval between 1800 and 1811 of $14\frac{1}{2}$ per cent. and in the interval between 1810 and 1821 of $16\frac{1}{3}$ per cent. The first of these two rates of increase would double the population in 51 and the other in 46 years. As, however, there must always be some uncertainty respecting the proportion of the persons employed in the army, navy, and merchant service, properly belonging to the resident population, and as the male population is on other accounts more frequently on the move than the female, it has been judiciously proposed to estimate the rate of increase by the female population alone. The number of females in Great Britain was in 1801, 5 492 354; in 1811, 6 262 716; and in 1821, 7 253 728, giving an increase in the first period of 14.02 per cent. and in the second of 15.82.[15]

The increase of Scotland taken by itself was in the first period 13 per cent. and in the second $14\frac{1}{2}$. The increase of England and Wales exclusive of Scotland appears to be almost exactly the same; particularly in the second period, whether we estimate it from the females alone, or from the whole population, with the proposed allowances for the army and navy, etc., a proof that these allowances are not far from the truth. At the same time, it should perhaps be remarked that if, on account of the war, during the greater part of the period from 1800 to 1821, there must have been a greater portion of the male population destroyed than usual, the increase of the whole population ought not to be so great in proportion as the increase of the females; and that if such an increase appears, it is probably owing to too great a number of males having been added to the resident population for the army and navy, or to an influx from Scotland and Ireland.

The numbers above mentioned, and the rates of increase, have been stated as given by Mr. Rickman in the Preliminary Observations to the Population Abstracts. But in the former part of this chapter I assumed on what appeared to me to be sufficient ground that the first enumeration was not so correct as that of 1811, and it is probable that the enumeration of 1811 is not quite so correct as that of 1821. In this case the rates of increase in the two periods will not be so great as above stated, but still they will appear to be very extraordinary.

According to the assumed estimate, the population, as given in the enumeration of 1801, was about 119 000 short of the truth; and if on this ground we take the female population of the census in 1801 as deficient 60 000, and suppose that in 1811 it was deficient 30 000, the numbers of females in England and Wales at the different periods will stand thus: in 1801, 4 687 867; in 1811, 5 313 219; and in 1821, 6 144 709; giving an increase of 13.3 per cent. in the period from 1800 to 1811, and of 15.6 per cent. in the period from 1800 to 1821; making the rate of increase in the former period such as, if continued, would double the population in about 55 years,

---

[15] Preliminary Observations, p. viii.

and in the latter, such as would double it in 48 years. Taking the whole 20 years together, the rate of increase would be such as, if continued, would double the population in about 51 years.

This is no doubt a most extraordinary rate of increase, considering the actual population of the country compared with its territory, and the number of its great towns and manufactories. It is less, however, than that which is stated in the Preliminary Observations to the Population Abstracts. Yet even according to this slower rate of increase, it is necessary to suppose that the omissions in the parish registers, particularly in regard to the births, have latterly rather increased than diminished; and this is rendered probable by a statement of Mr. Rickman in the Preliminary Observations. He says, 'the question respecting unentered baptisms and burials showed a difference of nearly four to one in the degree of deficiency in the year 1811, the annual average number of unentered baptisms (as stated at the end of the several counties) having been 14 860; of burials (setting aside London) 3899; at present the proportion is five to one in the degree of deficiency, the annual average number of unentered baptisms (as stated at the end of the several counties) being 23 066; of burials (setting aside London) 4657'. And he goes on to say: 'Nor does this represent the full amount or proportion of unentered baptisms, the clergy of the most populous places, especially where many of the inhabitants are dissenters, usually declining to hazard an estimate.' A burial ground, on the contrary, is a visible object, and among the persons connected with it, the clergyman can usually procure an account (more or less accurate) of the number of interments.

On these grounds it would appear probable that, owing to the increasing number of dissenters or other causes, the omissions in the registers of births had been lately increasing rather than diminishing. Yet it has been thought that since the Act of 1812 the registers of births have been more carefully kept; and it is certain that, in the 10 years ending with 1820, the proportion of births to marriages is greater, though the proportions of births and marriages to the whole population are both less than they were either in 1800, or in the ten years ending with 1810. Under these circumstances, it may be advisable to wait for further documents before any fresh conclusion is drawn respecting the probable amount of omissions in the births and burials. What may be considered as certain is that, whereas the supposed admissions of one-sixth in the births and one-twelfth in the burials, with a proper allowance for the deaths abroad, are more than sufficient to account for the increase of population during the twenty years from 1781 to 1801, according to the numbers stated by Mr. Rickman, they are not sufficient to account for the increase of population in the 20 years from 1801 to 1821, according to the enumerations.

I have heard it surmised that the enumerations, particularly the two last, may by possibility exceed rather than fall short of the truth, owing to persons being reckoned more than once, from their having different places of residence. It must be allowed that this supposition would account for the fact of the diminished proportions of births and marriages to the whole population, notwithstanding the apparent increase of that population with extraordinary rapidity. But the same diminished proportions would take place owing to a diminished mortality; and as a diminished mortality has been satisfactorily established on other grounds, it will fairly account for much of what appears. And if anything can justly be attributed to over enumerations, it must be of trifling amount.

That there are great omissions both in the births and burials, and greater in the former than in the latter, it is quite impossible to doubt. The testimony of all the clergy concerned in making the returns was, according to Mr. Rickman, uniform in this respect. And if we suppose only the same proportion of omissions from 1801 to 1821 as we supposed from 1781 to 1801, and commence with the census of 1801, on the presumption that the number of double entries in that enumeration would be balanced probably by the number of deficiencies, it will appear that the excess of the births alone, excluding the deaths abroad, would bring the population to within 184 404 of the enumeration of 1821, and including the allowance for deaths abroad (which, in this case, from a comparison of the excess of male births with the male and female deaths, appears to be 128 651), to within 313 055.

On the supposition of such an amount of double entries unbalanced by deficiencies in the two last returns, the enumerations would still show a very extraordinary increase of population. The rate of increase in the period from 1801 to 1811 would be nearly 13 per cent. (12.88), which would double the population in about 57 years; and in the period from 1811 to 1821, it would be very nearly 15 per cent. (14.95), which would double the population in 50 years.

Under the uncertainty in which we must remain at present as to whether the enumerations partially err in defect or in excess, I have not thought it advisable to alter the amended table of the population from 1781 to 1811, given in the former part of this chapter. It is founded on a principle so very much safer than an estimate for the births alone that it must at any rate show the progress of the population more correctly than that given in the Preliminary Observations.

The more indeed the population returns are considered, the more uncertain will appear all estimates of the past population founded on the assumptions that the proportion of the births will always be nearly the same. If the population since the year 1801 were to be estimated in the same way as Mr. Rickman has estimated it before that year, it would appear that the population in 1821, instead of being, according to the enumeration, 12 218 500, would only be 11 625 334, that is, 593 166 or nearly 600 000 short of the enumeration of 1821. And the reason is, that the proportion of births to the population, which, estimated in the way suggested by Mr. Rickman, and without allowing for omissions, was in 1821 only as 1 to 36.58, was in 1801 as much as 1 to 34.8.

Supposing the enumerations to be correct, the varying proportions of the births (without allowance for omissions, and comparing the population at the end of each term with the average births for the five preceding years) would be for 1801 as 1 to 34.8, for 1811 as 1 to 35.3, and for 1821 as 1 to 36.58.

Similar and even greater variations will be found to take place in regard to the proportions of the marriages to the population.

In 1801, the proportion was 1 to 122.2, in 1811, 1 to 126.6, in 1821, 1 to 131.1; and if, assuming that, for the 20 years ending with 1820, the marriages, in which it is supposed that there are very few omissions, would remain in the same proportion to the population as in 1801, we had estimated the population by the marriages, the numbers in 1821, instead of being 12 218 500, would only have been 11 377 548, that is, 840 952 short of the enumeration of 1821.

It appears, then, that if we can put any trust in our enumerations,[16] no reliance can be placed on an estimate of past population founded on the proportions of the births, deaths, or marriages. The same causes which have operated to alter so essentially these proportions during the 20 years for which we have enumerations may have operated in an equal degree before; and it will be generally found true that the increasing healthiness of a country will not only diminish the proportions of deaths, but the proportions of births and marriages.

---

[16] The migrations into England from Ireland and Scotland may account for some portion of the excess of the enumerations above what is warranted by the excess of the births above the deaths.

CHAPTER XII

Of the Checks to Population in Scotland and Ireland[1]

An examination, in detail, of the statistical account of Scotland, would furnish numerous illustrations of the principle of population; but I have already extended this part of the work so much, that I am fearful of tiring the patience of my readers; and shall therefore confine my remarks in the present instance to a few circumstances which have happened to strike me.

On account of the acknowledged omissions in the registers of births, deaths, and marriages, in most of the parishes of Scotland, few just inferences can be drawn from them. Many give extraordinary results. In the parish of Crosmichael[2] in Kircudbright, the mortality appears to be only 1 in 98, and the yearly marriages 1 in 192. These proportions would imply the most unheard-of healthiness, and the most extraordinary operation of the preventive check; but there can be little doubt that they are principally occasioned by omissions in the registry of burials and the celebration of a part of the marriages in other parishes.

In general, however, it appears from registers that are supposed to be accurate, that in the country parishes the mortality is small; and that the proportions of 1 in 45, 1 in 50, and 1 in 55, are not uncommon. According to a table of the probabilities of life, calculated from the bills of mortality in the parish of Kettle, by Mr. Wilkie, the expectation of an infant's life is 46.6,[3] which is very high, and the proportion which dies in the first year is only $\frac{1}{10}$.[4] Mr. Wilkie further adds that, from 36 parish accounts, published in the first volume, the expectation of an infant's life appears to be 40.3. But in a table which he has produced in the last volume, calculated for the whole of Scotland from Dr. Webster's survey, the expectation at birth appears to be

---

[1] [This was originally chapter x of Book ii in 1803; it became chapter viii in 1806 and 1807, when the chapters on fertility and epidemics were placed after all those on the checks to population. In 1817 and 1826, when the additional chapters on France and England were included, it again became chapter x.]

[2] Statistical Account of Scotland, vol. i. p. 167. [See SINCLAIR in the Alphabetical List.]

[3] Id. vol. ii. p. 407.

[4] [In 1817 (Vol. ii, p. 106) this was changed to: ... only one-10th.]

only 31 years.[5] This, however, he thinks, must be too low, as it exceeds but little the calculations for the town of Edinburgh.

The Scotch registers appeared to be, in general, so incomplete, that the returns of 99 parishes only are published in the Population Abstracts of 1801; and, if any judgment can be formed from these, they show a very extraordinary degree of healthiness and a very small proportion of births. The sum of the population of these parishes in 1801 was 217 873;[6] the average of burials for 5 years ending in 1800 was about 3815; and of births, 4928:[7] from which it would appear that the mortality in these parishes was only 1 in 56, and the proportion of births 1 in 44. But these proportions are so extraordinary that it is difficult to conceive that they approach near the truth. Combining them with the calculations of Mr. Wilkie, it will not appear probable that the proportion of deaths and births in Scotland should be smaller than what has been allowed for England and Wales; namely, 1 in 40 for the deaths, and 1 in 30 for the births; and it seems to be generally agreed that the proportion of births to deaths is 4 to 3.[8]

With respect to the marriages, it will be still more difficult to form a conjecture. They are registered so irregularly, that no returns of them are given in the Population Abstracts. I should naturally have thought, from the Statistical Account, that the tendency to marriage in Scotland was upon the whole greater than in England; but if it be true that the births and deaths bear the same proportion to each other, and to the whole population, in both countries, the proportion of marriages cannot be very different. It should be remarked, however, that supposing the operation of the preventive check to be exactly the same in both countries, and the climates to be equally salubrious, a greater degree of want and poverty would take place in Scotland before the same mortality was produced as in England, owing to the smaller proportion of towns and manufactories in the former country than in the latter.

From a general view of the statistical accounts, the result seems clearly to be that the condition of the lower classes of people in Scotland has been considerably improved of late years. The price of provisions has risen; but almost invariably the price of labour has risen in a greater proportion; and it is remarked in most parishes that more butcher's meat is consumed among

---

[5] Statistical Account of Scotland, vol. xxi. p. 383.

[6] Population Abstract, Parish Registers, p. 459.

[7] Id. p. 458.

[8] Statistical Account of Scotland, vol. xxi. p. 383. [In 1826 (Vol. i, p. 452) Malthus added two sentences to this footnote:

The comparison with England here refers to the time of the first enumeration. There is little doubt that the mortality of Scotland has diminished, and the proportion of births to deaths increased since 1800.

the common people than formerly; that they are both better lodged and better clothed; and that their habits with respect to cleanliness are decidedly improved.

A part of this improvement is probably to be attributed to the increase of the preventive check. In some parishes a habit of later marriages is noticed, and in many places where it is not mentioned it may be fairly inferred, from the proportions of births and marriages and other circumstances. The writer of the account of the parish of Elgin[9] in enumerating the general causes of depopulation in Scotland, speaks of the discouragement to marriage from the union of farms, and the consequent emigration of the flower of their young men of every class and description, very few of whom ever return. Another cause that he mentions is the discouragement to marriage from luxury; at least, he observes, till people are advanced in years, and then a puny race of children are produced. 'Hence, how many men of every description remain single, and how many young women of every rank are never married, who, in the beginning of this century, or even so late as 1745, would have been the parents of a numerous and healthy progeny.'

In those parts of the country where the population has been rather diminished, by the introduction of grazing, or an improved system of husbandry which requires fewer hands, this effect has chiefly taken place; and I have little doubt that, in estimating the decrease of their population since the end of the last, or the beginning of the present century, by the proportion of births at the different periods, they have fallen into the error which has been particularly noticed with regard to Switzerland,[10] and have in consequence made the difference greater than it really is.[11]

The general inference on this subject which I should draw from the different accounts is, that the marriages are rather later than formerly. There are, however, some decided exceptions. In those parishes where manufactures have been introduced, which afford employment to children as soon as they have reached their 6th or 7th year, a habit of marrying early naturally follows; and while the manufacture continues to flourish and increase, the evil arising from it is not very perceptible; though humanity must confess with a sigh that one of the reasons why it is not so perceptible is that room is made for fresh families by the unnatural mortality which takes place among the children so employed.

There are other parts of Scotland, however, particularly the Western Isles and some parts of the Highlands, where population has considerably

---

[9] Vol. v. p. 1.   [10] [In 1817 (Vol. ii, p. 111) Malthus here inserted: and France, ...

[11] One writer takes notice of this circumstance, and observes that formerly the births seem to have born a greater proportion to the whole population than at present. Probably, he says, more were born, and there was a greater mortality. Parish of Montquitter, vol. vi. p. 121.

increased from the subdivision of possessions, and where perhaps the marriages may be earlier than they were formerly, though not caused by the introduction of manufactures. Here, the poverty which follows is but too conspicuous. In the account of Delting in Shetland,[12] it is remarked that the people marry very young, and are encouraged to this by their landlords, who wish to have as many men on their grounds as possible to prosecute the ling fishery;[13] but that they generally involve themselves in debt and large families. The writer further observes that formerly there were some old regulations called country acts, by one of which it was enacted that no pair should marry unless possessed of 40l. Scots, of free gear. This regulation is not now enforced. It is said that these regulations were approved and confirmed by the parliament of Scotland, in the reign of Queen Mary or James VI.[14]

In the account of Bressay Burra and Quarff in Shetland,[15] it is observed that the farms are very small, and few have a plough. The object of the proprietors is to have as many fishermen on their lands as possible – a great obstacle to improvements in agriculture. They fish for their masters, who either give them a fee totally inadequate, or take their fish at a low rate. The writer remarks that 'in most countries the increase of population is reckoned an advantage, and justly. It is, however, the reverse in the present state of Shetland. The farms are split. The young men are encouraged to marry without having any stock. The consequence is poverty and distress. It is believed that there is at present in these islands, double the number of people that they can properly maintain.'

The writer of the account of Auchterderran,[16] in the country of Fife, says that the meagre food of the labouring man is unequal to oppose the effects of incessant hard labour upon his constitution, and by this means his frame is worn down before the time of nature's appointment, and adds: 'That people continue voluntarily to enter upon such a hard situation by marrying shows how far the union of the sexes, and the love of independence, are principles of human nature.' In this observation, perhaps, the love of independence had better have been changed for the love of a progeny.

The island of Jura[17] appears to be absolutely overflowing with inhabitants in spite of constant and numerous emigrations. There are sometimes 50 or 60 on a farm. The writer observes that such a swarm of inhabitants, where

---

[12] Vol. i. p. 385.   [13] [The Latin name for ling is *molva*, a fish of the cod family, *gadidae*.]

[14] [*Free gear* in this context means movable property, which included clothes and tools as well as household furniture. Mary Queen of Scots reigned from 1542 to 1567, when she was forced to abdicate; her son (born in 1566) was James VI of Scotland from 1567 to 1625, and also James I of England after the death of Queen Elizabeth I in 1603.]

[15] Vol. x. p. 194.   [16] Vol. i. p. 449.   [17] Vol. xii. p. 317.

manufactures and many other branches of industry are unknown, are a very great load upon the proprietors, and useless to the state.

Another writer[18] is astonished at the rapid increase of population, in spite of a considerable emigration to America in 1770, and a large drain of young men during the late war. He thinks it difficult to assign adequate causes for it, and observes that, if the population continue to increase in this manner, unless some employment be found for the people, the country will soon be unable to support them. And in the account of the parish of Callander[19] the writer says that the villages of this place, and other villages in similar situations, are filled with naked and starving crowds of people, who are pouring down for shelter or for bread; and then observes that whenever the population of a town or village exceeds the industry of its inhabitants, from that moment the place must decline.

A very extraordinary instance of a tendency to rapid increase occurs in the register of the parish of Duthil,[20] in the county of Elgin; and as errors of excess are not so probable as errors of omission, it seems to be worthy of attention. The proportion of annual births to the whole population is as 1 to 12; of marriages, as 1 to 55; and of deaths the same. The births are to the deaths as 70 to 15, or $4\frac{2}{3}$ to 1. We may suppose some inaccuracy respecting the number of deaths, which seems to err on the side of defect; but the very extraordinary proportion of the annual births, amounting to $\frac{1}{10}$ of the whole population, does not seem to be easily liable to error; and the other circumstances respecting the parish tend to confirm the statement. Out of a population of 830, there were only 3 bachelors, and each marriage yielded 7 children. Yet with all this, the population is supposed to have decreased considerably since 1745; and it appears that this excessive tendency to increase had been occasioned by an excessive tendency to emigrate. The writer mentions very great emigrations; and observes that whole tribes, who enjoyed the comforts of life in a reasonable degree, had of late years emigrated from different parts of Scotland from mere humour, and a fantastical idea of becoming their own masters and freeholders.

Such an extraordinary proportion of births, caused evidently by habits of emigration, shows the extreme difficulty of depopulating a country merely by taking away its people. Take but away its industry, and the sources of its subsistence, and it is done at once.

It may be observed that in this parish the average number of children to a marriage is said to be 7, though from the proportion of annual births to annual marriages it would appear to be only $4\frac{2}{3}$. This difference occurs in many other parishes, from which we may conclude that the writers of these

---

18 Parish of Lochalsh, county of Ross, vol. xi. p. 422.   19 Vol. xi. p. 574.
20 Vol. iv. p. 308.

accounts very judiciously adopted some other mode of calculation than the proportion of annual births and marriages,[21] and probably founded the results they give either on personal inquiries, or researches into their registers, to find the number of children which had been born to each mother in the course of her marriage.

The women of Scotland appear to be prolific. The average of 6 children to a marriage is frequent; and of 7, and even $7\frac{1}{2}$, not very uncommon. One instance is very curious, as it appears as if this number was actually living to each marriage, which would of course imply that a much greater number had been and would be born. In the parish of Nigg,[22] in the county of Kincardine, the account says, that there are 57 land families and 405 children; which gives nearly $7\frac{1}{9}$ each; 42 fisher families, and 314 children; nearly $7\frac{1}{2}$ each. Of the land families which have had no children, there were 7; of the fishers, none. If this statement be just, I should conceive that each marriage must have yielded, or would yield, in the course of its duration, as many as 9 or 10 births.

When, from any actual survey, it appears that there are about 3 living children to each marriage, or 5 persons, or only $4\frac{1}{2}$ to a house, which are very common proportions, we must not infer that the average number of births to a marriage is not much above 3. We must recollect that all the marriages or establishments of the present year are of course without children; all of the year before have only one; all of the year before that can hardly be expected to have as many as two, and all of the fourth year preceding will certainly, in the natural course of things, have less than three. One out of five children is a very unusually small proportion to lose in the course of ten years; and after ten years, it may be supposed that the eldest begin to leave their parents; so that if each marriage be supposed accurately to yield 5 births in the course of its duration, the families which had increased to their full complement would only have 4 children, and a very large proportion of those which were in the earlier stages of increase would have less than three;[23] and consequently, taking into consideration the number of families where one of the parents may be supposed to be dead, I much doubt whether in this case a survey would give $4\frac{1}{2}$ to a family. In the parish of Duthil,[24] already noticed, the number of children to a marriage is mentioned as 7, and the number of persons to a house as only 5.

---

[21] [In 1806 (Vol. i, p. 492) this was altered to:

... some other mode of calculation than the mere uncorrected proportion of annual births to marriages; ...

[22] Vol. vii. p. 194.

[23] It has been calculated that, on an average, the difference of age in the children of the same family is about two years.

[24] Vol. iv. p. 308.

²⁵●I have taken notice of this circumstance to obviate an objection, which might perhaps appear to arise from the result of such surveys, to the proofs which have been adduced that marriages are in general more prolific than they have been usually supposed to be. The accounts of many of the parishes in Scotland, which mention 6, 7, and 7½, as the average number of children to a marriage, tend very strongly to confirm these proofs; and as, in these same parishes, the proportion of annual births to annual marriages is seldom above 3½, 4, or 4½, to 1, they prove at the same time the fallacy of this mode of estimating the fruitfulness of marriages. In those parishes where the authors have adopted this mode, they generally mention, as might be expected, 3, 3½, 4, and 4½ as the average number of children to a marriage.●²⁵

The poor of Scotland are in general supported by voluntary contributions, distributed under the inspection of the minister of the parish; and it appears, upon the whole, that they have been conducted with considerable judgment. Having no claim of right to relief,[26] and the supplies, from the mode of their collection, being necessarily uncertain, and never abundant, the poor have considered them merely as a last resource in cases of extreme distress, and not as a fund on which they might safely rely, and an adequate portion of which belonged to them, by the laws of their country, in all difficulties.

The consequence of this is that the common people make very considerable exertions to avoid the necessity of applying for such a scanty and precarious relief. It is observed, in many of the accounts, that they seldom fail of making a provision for sickness and for age; and, in general, the grown-up children and relations of persons who are in danger of falling upon the parish, step forward, if they be in any way able, to prevent such a degradation, which is universally considered as a disgrace to the family.

The writers of the accounts of the different parishes frequently reprobate, in very strong terms, the system of English assessments for the poor, and give a decided preference to the Scotch mode of relief. In the account of Paisley,[27] though a manufacturing town, and with a numerous poor, the author still reprobates the English system, and makes an observation on this subject, in

---

²⁵ [This paragraph was omitted in 1806 (Vol. 1, p. 495) after Malthus had re-written his chapter on the fruitfulness of marriages.]

²⁶ [In 1806 (Vol. 1, p. 495) a footnote was inserted here:

Mr Rose of the Treasury, in a late pamphlet on the subject of the Poor, has controverted this observation; but whatever may be the law on the subject, the practice is certainly as here represented; and it is the practice alone that concerns the present question.

[In 1807 (Vol. 1, p. 495) this footnote was altered to read as follows:

It has lately been stated in Parliament, that the poor-laws of Scotland are not materially different from those of England, though they have been very differently understood and executed; but, whatever may be the laws on the subject, the practice is generally as here represented; and it is ...

²⁷ Vol. vii. p. 74.

which perhaps he goes too far. He says that, though there are in no country such large contributions for the poor as in England, yet there is nowhere so great a number of them; and their condition, in comparison of *the poor of other countries, is truly most miserable.*

In the account of Caerlaverock,[28] in answer to the question, How ought the poor to be supplied? it is most judiciously remarked, 'that distress and poverty multiply in proportion to the funds created to relieve them; that the measures of charity ought to remain invisible, till the moment when it is necessary that they should be distributed; that in the country parishes of Scotland, in general, small occasional voluntary collections are sufficient; that the legislature has no occasion to interfere to augment the stream which is already copious enough; in fine, that the establishment of a poors rate would not only be unnecessary, but hurtful, as it would tend to oppress the landholder without bringing relief on the poor'.

These, upon the whole, appear to be the prevailing opinions of the clergy of Scotland. There are, however, some exceptions; and the system of assessments is sometimes approved, and the establishment of it proposed.[29] But this is not to be wondered at. In many of these parishes the experiment had never been made; and without being thoroughly aware of the principle of population, from theory, or having fully seen the evils of poor laws in practice, nothing seems, on a first view of the subject, more natural than the proposal of an assessment, to which the uncharitable as well as the charitable should be made to contribute, according to their abilities, and which might be increased or diminished according to the wants of the moment.

The endemic and epidemic diseases in Scotland fall chiefly, as is usual, on the poor. The scurvy is in some places extremely troublesome and inveterate; and in others it arises to a contagious leprosy, the effects of which are always dreadful, and not unfrequently mortal. One writer calls it the scourge and bane of human nature.[30] It is generally attributed to cold and wet situations, meagre and unwholesome food, impure air from damp and crowded houses, indolent habits, and the want of attention to cleanliness.

To the same causes, in great measure, are attributed the rheumatisms which are general, and the consumptions which are frequent among the common people. Whenever, in any place, from particular circumstances, the condition of the poor has been rendered worse, these disorders, particularly the latter, have been observed to prevail with greater force.

Low nervous fevers, and others of a more violent and fatal nature, are frequently epidemic, and sometimes take off considerable numbers; but the

---

[28] Vol. vi. p. 21.

[29] [In 1817 (Vol. II, p. 123) 'recommended' was substituted for *proposed.*

[30] Parishes of Forbes and Kearn, County of Aberdeen, vol. xi. p. 189.

most fatal epidemic, since the extinction of the plague which formerly visited Scotland, is the small-pox, the returns of which are in many places at regular intervals; in others irregular, but seldom at a greater distance than 7 or 8 years. Its ravages are dreadful, though in some parishes not so fatal as they were some time ago. The prejudices against inoculation are still great; and as the mode of treatment must almost necessarily be bad, in small and crowded houses, and the custom of visiting each other during the disorder still subsists in many places, it may be imagined that the mortality must be considerable, and the children of the poor the principal sufferers. In some parishes of the Western Isles and the Highlands, the number of persons to a house has increased from $4\frac{1}{2}$, and 5, to $6\frac{1}{2}$, and 7. It is evident that if such a considerable increase, without the proper accommodations for it, do not absolutely generate the disease,[31] it must give to its devastations tenfold force when it arrives.

Scotland has at all times been subject to years of scarcity, and occasionally even to dreadful famines. The years 1635, 1680, 1688, the concluding years of the last century,[32] the years 1740, 1756, 1766, 1778, 1782, and 1783, are all mentioned in different places, as years of very great sufferings from want. In the year 1680, so many families perished from this cause that for six miles, in a well-inhabited extent, there was not a smoke remaining.[33] The seven years at the end of the last century were called the ill years.[34] The writer of the account of the parish of Montquhitter[35] says that of 16 families on a farm in that neighbourhood, 13 were extinguished; and on another, out of 169 individuals, only 3 families, the proprietors included, survived. Extensive farms, now containing a hundred souls, being entirely desolated, were converted into a sheep walk. The inhabitants of the parish in general were diminished by death to one half or, as some affirm, to one fourth of the preceding number. Until 1709 many farms were waste. In 1740 another season of scarcity occurred, and the utmost misery was felt by the poor, though it fell short of death. Many offered in vain to serve for their bread. Stout men accepted thankfully twopence a day in full for their work. Great

---

[31] [In 1826 (Vol. 1, p. 464) ... *do not absolutely generate the disease,* was altered to: ... cannot generate the disease, ...

[32] [Here, as in n. 34, Malthus was distinctly muddled. In the *Errata* printed at the beginning of the quarto he wrote for page 332, lines 1 and 6, '*for* last *read* seventeenth'. In the edition of 1806, however, 'the last century' remained (Vol. 1, pp. 499 and 500). In 1807 (Vol. 1, same pagination) *the last century* was replaced by 'the 16th century'.

[33] Parish of Duthil, vol. iv. p. 308. [This example of the use of the word *smoke* is given in the O.E.D. It refers to the smoke rising from a domestic hearth or fire-place, relevant in the days when householders paid a tax on each hearth in their homes.]

[34] [In 1807 (Vol. 1, p. 500) Malthus altered this to:
    The seven years at the end of the 16th century ...

[35] Vol. vi. p. 121.

distress was also suffered in 1782 and 1783, but none died. 'If at this critical period', the author says, 'the American war had not ceased; if the copious magazines, particularly of pease, provided for the navy, had not been brought to sale, what a scene of desolation and horror would have been exhibited in this country!'

Many similar descriptions occur in different parts of the Statistical Account; but these will be sufficient to shew the nature and intensity of the distress which has been occasionally felt from want.

The year 1783 depopulated some parts of the Highlands, and is mentioned as the reason why in these places the number of people was found to have diminished since Dr. Webster's survey. Most of the small farmers in general, as might be expected, were absolutely ruined by the scarcity; and those of this description, in the Highlands, were obliged to emigrate to the Lowlands as common labourers,[36] in search of a precarious support. In some parishes at the time of the last survey, the effect of the ruin of the farmers during this bad year was still visible in their depressed condition, and the increased poverty and misery of the common people which is a necessary consequence of it.

In the account of the parish of Grange,[37] in the county of Banff, it is observed that the year 1783 put a stop to all improvements by green crops, and made the farmers think of nothing but raising grain. Tenants were most of them ruined. Before this period, consumptions were not near so frequent as they have been since. This may be justly attributed to the effects of the scarcity and bad victual in the year 1783, to the long inclement harvests in 1782 and 1787, in both which seasons the labourers were exposed to much cold and wet during the three months that the harvests continued; but principally to the change that has of late taken place in the manner of living among the lower ranks. Formerly every householder could command a draught of small beer, and killed a sheep now and then, out of his own little flock; but now the case is different. The frequent want of the necessaries of life among the poor, their damp and stinking houses, and dejection of mind among the middling classes, appear to be the principal causes of the prevailing distempers and mortality of this parish. Young people are cut off by consumptions, and the more advanced by dropsies and nervous fevers.

The state of this parish which, though there are others like it, may be considered as an exception to the average state of Scotland, was without doubt occasioned by the ruin of the tenants; and the effect is not to be wondered at, as no greater evil can easily happen to a country than the loss of agricultural stock and capital.

---

[36] Parish of Kincardine, County of Ross, vol. iii. p. 505.   [37] Vol. ix. p. 550.

We may observe that the diseases of this parish are said to have increased, in consequence of the scarcity and bad victual of 1783. The same circumstance is noticed in many other parishes, and it is remarked, that though few people died of absolute famine, yet that mortal diseases almost universally followed.

It is remarked, also, in some parishes, that the number of births and marriages are affected by years of scarcity and plenty.

Of the parish of Dingwall,[38] in the county of Ross, it is observed that, after the scarcity of 1783, the births were 16 below the average, and 14 below the lowest number of late years. The year 1787 was a year of plenty, and the following year the births increased in a similar proportion, and were 17 above the average, and 11 above the highest of the other years.

In the account of Dunrossness,[39] in Orkney, the writer says that the annual number of marriages depends much on the seasons. In good years they may amount to thirty or upwards; but when crops fail, will hardly come up to the half of that number.

The whole increase of Scotland, since the time of Dr. Webster's survey in 1755, is about 260 000,[40] for which a proportionate provision has been made in the improved state of agriculture and manufactures, and in the increased cultivation of potatoes, which in some places form two-thirds of the diet of the common people. It has been calculated that the half of the surplus of births in Scotland is drawn off in emigrations; and it cannot be doubted that this drain tends greatly to relieve the country, and to improve the condition of those which remain. Scotland is certainly still overpeopled, but not so much as it was a century or half a century ago, when it contained fewer inhabitants.

The details of the population of Ireland are but little known. I shall only observe, therefore, that the extended use of potatoes has allowed of a very rapid increase of it during the last century. But the cheapness of this nourishing root, and the small piece of ground which, under this kind of cultivation, will in average years produce the food for a family, joined to the ignorance and barbarism of the people,[41] which have prompted them to

---

[38] Vol. iii. p. 1.   [39] Vol. vii. p. 391.

[40] According to the returns in the late estimate, the whole population of Scotland is above 1 590 000, and therefore the increase up to the present time is above 320 000.

[In 1817 (Vol. ii, p. 130) this footnote was amended:

According to the returns in the estimate of 1800, the whole population of Scotland was above 1 590 000, and therefore the increase up to that time was above 320 000. In 1810 the population was 1 805 688.

[In 1826 (Vol. i, p. 468) Malthus added:

...; and in 1820, 2 093 456.

[41] [In 1826 (Vol. i, p. 469) after he had visited Ireland in 1817, Malthus changed this to:

... joined to the ignorance and depressed state of the people, ...

follow their inclinations with no other prospect than an immediate bare subsistence, have encouraged marriage to such a degree, that the population is pushed much beyond the industry and present resources of the country; and the consequence naturally is, that the lower classes of people are in the most depressed and miserable state.[42] The checks to the population are of course chiefly of the positive kind, and arise from the diseases occasioned by squalid poverty, by damp and wretched cabins, by bad and insufficient clothing, by the filth of their persons,[43] and occasional want. To these positive checks have, of late years, been added the vice and misery of intestine commotion, of civil war, and of martial law.

[44]●All the checks to population which have been observed to prevail in society, in the course of this review of it, are clearly resolvable into moral restraint, vice, and misery.●[44]

[In 1826 (Vol. I, p. 470) Malthus added the following:

1825

According to the late enumeration in 1821, the population of Ireland amounted to 6 801 827, and in 1695 it was estimated only at 1 034 000. If these numbers be correct it affords an example of continued increase for 125 years together, at such a rate as to double the population in about 45 years – a more rapid increase than has probably taken place in any other country of Europe during the same length of time.

In the peculiar circumstances of Ireland, it would be very interesting to know the average mortality, and the proportions of births and marriages to the population. But unfortunately no correct parochial registers have been kept, and the information, however much to be desired, is unattainable.

---

[42] [This was altered to:
    ... the most impoverished and miserable state.
[43] [Malthus expunged *by the filth of their persons*.]
[44] [In 1806 (Vol. I, p. 505) this short final paragraph was omitted.]

CHAPTER XIII

General deductions from the preceding view of Society[1]

That the checks which have been mentioned are the true[2] causes of the slow increase of population, and that these checks result principally from an insufficiency of subsistence, will be evident from the comparatively rapid increase which has invariably taken place whenever, by some sudden enlargement in the means of subsistence, these checks have been in any considerable degree removed.

It has been universally remarked that all new colonies, settled in healthy countries, where room and food were abundant, have constantly made a rapid progress in population. Many of the colonies from ancient Greece, in the course of one or two centuries, appear to have rivalled, and even surpassed, their mother cities. Syracuse and Agrigentum in Sicily; Tarentum and Locri in Italy; Ephesus and Miletus in Lesser Asia; were, by all accounts, at least equal to any of the cities of ancient Greece.[3] All these colonies had established themselves in countries inhabited by savage and barbarous nations which easily gave place to the new settlers who had of course plenty of good land. It is calculated that the Israelites, though they increased very slowly while they were wandering in the land of Canaan, on settling in a fertile district of Egypt doubled their numbers every fifteen years during the whole period of their stay.[4] But not to dwell on remote instances, the European settlements in America bear ample testimony to the truth of a remark that has never, I believe, been doubted. Plenty of rich land, to be had for little or nothing, is so powerful a cause of population as generally to overcome all obstacles.

No settlements could easily have been worse managed than those of Spain, in Mexico, Peru, and Quito. The tyranny, superstition, and vices of the mother country were introduced in ample quantities among her children. Exorbitant

---

[1] [This was chapter xi of Book II in the quarto, 1806 and 1807; it became chapter xiii in 1817 and 1826.]

[2] [In 1806 (Vol. II, p. 49) *true* was changed to 'immediate'.]

[3] Smith's Wealth of Nations, vol. ii. p. 360. [Also in 1806 (Vol. II, p. 49) this footnote was omitted.]

[4] Short's New Observ. on Bills of Mortality, p. 259, 8vo. 1750.

taxes were exacted by the crown; the most arbitrary restrictions were imposed on their trade; and the governors were not behindhand, in rapacity and extortion for themselves as well as their master. Yet under all these difficulties, the colonies made a quick progress in population. The city of Quito, which was but a hamlet of Indians, is represented by Ulloa as containing fifty or sixty thousand inhabitants above fifty years ago.[5] Lima, which was founded since the conquest, is mentioned by the same author as equally or more populous, before the fatal earthquake in 1746. Mexico is said to contain a hundred thousand inhabitants which, notwithstanding the exaggerations of the Spanish writers, is supposed to be five times greater than what it contained in the time of Montezuma.[6]

In the Portuguese colony of Brazil, governed with almost equal tyranny, there were supposed to be, above thirty years ago, six hundred thousand inhabitants of European extraction.[7]

The Dutch and French colonies, though under the government of exclusive companies of merchants, [8]●which, as Dr. Smith justly observes, is the worst of all possible governments,●[8] still persisted in thriving under every disadvantage.[9]

But the English North American colonies, now the powerful people of the United States of America, far outstripped all the others in the progress of their population. To the quantity of rich land, which they possessed in common with the Spanish and Portuguese colonies, they added a greater degree of liberty and equality. Though not without some restrictions on their foreign commerce, they were allowed the liberty of managing their own internal affairs. The political institutions which prevailed were favourable to the alienation and division of property. Lands which were not cultivated by the proprietor within a limited time were declared grantable to any other person. In Pennsylvania there was no right of primogeniture and, in the provinces of New England, the eldest son had only a double share. There were no tythes in any of the States, and scarcely any taxes. And on account of the extreme cheapness of good land,[10] a capital could not be more advantageously employed than in agriculture which, at the same time that it affords the greatest quantity of healthy work, supplies the most valuable produce to the society.

The consequence of these favourable circumstances united was a rapidity

[5] Voy. d'Ulloa, tom. i. liv. v. ch. v. p. 229. 4to. 1752.
[6] Smith's Wealth of Nations, vol. ii. b. iv. ch. vii. p. 363.
[7] Id. p. 365.   [8] [In 1807 (Vol. 1, p. 557) this clause was omitted.]
[9] Smith's Wealth of Nations, vol. ii. pp. 368, 369.
[10] [In 1826 (Vol. 1, p. 517) Malthus inserted here:
    ... and a situation favourable to the export of grain, ...

of increase almost without parallel in history. Throughout all the northern provinces the population was found to double itself in 25 years. The original number of persons which had settled in the four provinces of New England in 1643 was 21 200. Afterwards, it was calculated, that more left them than went to them. In the year 1760, they were increased to half a million. They had, therefore, all along, doubled their number in 25 years. In New Jersey the period of doubling appeared to be 22 years; and in Rhode Island still less. In the back settlements, where the inhabitants applied themselves solely to agriculture, and luxury was not known, they were supposed to double their number in fifteen years. Along the sea-coast, which would naturally be first inhabited, the period of doubling was about 35 years, and in some of the maritime towns the population was absolutely at a stand.[11] From the late census made in America it appears that, taking all the States together, they have still continued to double their numbers every 25 years,[12] and, as the

---

[11] Price's Observ. on Revers. Paym. vol. i. p. 282, 283, and vol. ii. p. 260. I have lately had an opportunity of seeing some extracts from the sermon of Dr. Styles, from which Dr. Price has taken these facts. Speaking of Rhode Island, Dr. Styles says that though the period of doubling for the whole colony is 25 years, yet that it is different in different parts, and within land is 20 and 15 years. The five towns of Gloucester, Situate, Coventry, Westgreenwich, and Exeter, were 5033, A.D. 1748, and 6986 A.D. 1755; which implies a period of doubling of 15 years only. He mentions afterwards that the county of Kent doubles in 20 years; and the county of Providence in 18 years.

●I have also lately seen a paper of *Facts and calculations respecting the population of the United States*, which makes the period of doubling for the whole of the States, since their first settlement, only 20 years. I know not of what authority this paper is; but far as it goes upon public facts and enumerations, I should think that it must be to be depended on. One period is very striking. From a return to Congress in 1782, the population appeared to be 2 389 300, and in the census of 1790, 4 000 000: increase in 9 years, 1 010 700: from which deduct ten thousand per annum for European settlers, which will be 90 000; and allow for their increase at 5 per cent. for 4½ years, which will be 20 250: the remaining increase during these 9 years, from procreation only, will be 1 500 450, which is very nearly 7 per cent.; and consequently the period of doubling at this rate would be less than 16 years.

If this calculation for the whole population of the States be in any degree near the truth, it cannot be doubted that, in particular districts, the period of doubling from procreation only has often been less than 15 years. The period immediately succeeding the war was likely to be a period of very rapid increase.●

[The last two paragraphs of this note were omitted in 1826 (Vol. 1, p. 518). The 'paper' was probably a 7-page octavo pamphlet entitled *Facts and Calculations respecting the Population and Territory of the United States of America*. According to Charles Evans's *American Bibliography* (vol. 13, 36051) it was published in Boston, 'printed by Russell for John Peck', on paper watermarked 1799.]

[12] [In 1826 (Vol. 1, p. 518) a footnote was added here:

See an article in the Supplement to the Encyclopædia Britannica on Population, p. 308; and a curious table, p. 310, calculated by Mr. Milne, Actuary to the Sun Life Assurance Office, which strikingly confirms and illustrates the computed rate of increase in the United States, and shows that it cannot be essentially affected by immigrations.

[The article on Population was written by Malthus himself.]

whole population is now so great as not to be materially affected by the emigrations from Europe; and as it is known that in some of the towns and districts near the sea-coast, the progress of population has been comparatively slow; it is evident that in the interior of the country in general the period of doubling, from procreation only, must have been considerably less than 25 years.

The population of the United States of America, according to the late census, is 5 172 312.[13] We have no reason to believe that Great Britain is less populous, at present, for the emigration of the small parent stock which produced these numbers. On the contrary a certain degree of emigration is known to be favourable to the population of the mother country. It has been particularly remarked that the two Spanish provinces from which the greatest number of people emigrated to America became in consequence more populous.

Whatever was the original number of British emigrants which increased so fast in North America, let us ask, Why does not an equal number produce an equal increase in the same time in Great Britain? The obvious reason to be assigned is the want of food; and that this want is the most efficient cause of the three great[14] checks to population which have been observed to prevail in all societies is evident from the rapidity with which even old states recover the desolations of war, pestilence, famine, and the convulsions of nature. They are then, for a short time, placed a little in the situation of new colonies, and the effect is always answerable to what might be expected. If the industry of the inhabitants be not destroyed, subsistence will soon increase beyond the wants of the reduced numbers; and the invariable consequence will be that population which before, perhaps, was nearly stationary, will begin immediately to increase, and will continue its progress till the former population is recovered.

The fertile province of Flanders, which has been so often the seat of the most destructive wars, after a respite of a few years, has always appeared as rich and as populous as ever. The undiminished population of France, which has before been noticed, is an instance very strongly in point. The tables of Susmilch afford continual proofs of a very rapid increase, after great mortalities; and the table for Prussia and Lithuania which I have inserted[15] is particularly striking in this respect. The effects of the dreadful plague in

---

[13] One small State is mentioned as being omitted in the census; and I understand that the population is generally considered at above this number. It is said to approach towards 6 000 000. But such vague opinions cannot of course be much relied on.

[This footnote was omitted in 1826 (Vol. I, p. 518) and the relevant sentence amended:

The population of the United States of America, according to the fourth census, in 1820, was 7 861 710.

[14] [In 1806 (Vol. II, p. 56) *great* was changed to 'immediate'].   [15] See p. 204.

London, in 1666, were not perceptible 15 or 20 years afterwards. It may even be doubted whether Turkey or Egypt are, upon an average, much less populous for the plagues which periodically lay them waste. If the number of people which they contain be considerably less now, than formerly, it is rather to be attributed to the tyranny and oppression of the governments under which they groan, and the consequent discouragements to agriculture, than to the losses which they sustain by the plague. The traces of the most destructive famines in China, Indostan, Egypt, and other countries, are by all accounts very soon obliterated; and the most tremendous convulsions of nature, such as volcanic eruptions and earthquakes, if they do not happen so frequently as to drive away the inhabitants, or destroy their spirit of industry, have been found to produce but a trifling effect on the average population of any state.[16]

It has appeared from the registers of different countries, which have already been produced, that the progress of their population is checked by the periodical though irregular returns of plagues and sickly seasons. Dr. Short, in his curious researches into bills of mortality, often uses the expression of 'terrible correctives of the redundance of mankind',[17] and in a table of all the plagues, pestilences, and famines, of which he could collect accounts, shews the constancy and universality of their operation.

The epidemical years in his table, or the years in which the plague or some great and wasting epidemic prevailed, for smaller sickly seasons seem not to be included, are 431,[18] of which 32 were before the Christian aera.[19] If we divide, therefore, the years of the present aera by 399, it will appear that the periodical returns of such epidemics, to some countries that we are acquainted with, have been on an average only at the interval of about $4\frac{1}{2}$ years.

Of the 254 great famines and dearths enumerated in the table, 15 were before the Christian aera,[20] beginning with that which occurred in Palestine in the time of Abraham. If, subtracting these 15, we divide the years of the present aera by the remainder, it will appear that the average interval between the visits of this dreadful scourge has been only about $7\frac{1}{2}$ years.

How far these 'terrible correctives to the redundance of mankind', have been occasioned by the too rapid increase of population, is a point which it would be very difficult to determine with any degree of precision. The causes of most of our diseases appear to us to be so mysterious, and probably are really so various, that it would rashness to lay too much stress on any single

---

[16] [Up to this point in this chapter, Malthus followed very closely pp. 100–12 of the 1798 *Essay*.]

[17] New Observ. on Bills of Mortality, p. 96.   [18] Hist. of Air, Seasons, &c. vol. ii. p. 366.

[19] Id. vol. ii. p. 202.   [20] Id. vol. ii. p. 206.

one: but it will not perhaps be too much to say that, *among* these causes, we ought certainly to rank crowded houses, and insufficient or unwholesome food, which are the natural consequences of an increase of population faster than the accommodations of a country with respect to habitations and food, will allow.

Almost all the histories of epidemics which we possess tend to confirm this supposition, by describing them in general as making their principal ravages among the lower classes of people. In Dr. Short's tables this circumstance is frequently mentioned;[21] and it further appears that a very considerable proportion of the epidemic years either followed or were accompanied by seasons of dearth and bad food.[22] In other places he also mentions great plagues as diminishing particularly the number of the lower or servile sort of people,[23] and, in speaking of different diseases, he observes that those which are occasioned by bad and unwholesome food generally last the longest.[24]

We know from constant experience that fevers are generated in our jails, our manufactories, our crowded workhouses, and in the narrow and close streets of our large towns; all which situations appear to be similar in their effects to squalid poverty: and we cannot doubt that causes of this kind, aggravated in degree, contributed to the production and prevalence of those great and wasting plagues formerly so common in Europe, but which now, from the mitigation of these causes, are everywhere considerably abated, and in many places appear to be completely extirpated.

Of the other great scourge of mankind, famine, it may be observed that it is not in the nature of things that the increase of population should absolutely produce one. This increase, though rapid, is necessarily gradual; and as the human frame cannot be supported, even for a very short time, without food, it is evident that no more human beings can grow up than there is provision to maintain. But though the principle of population cannot absolutely produce a famine, it prepares the way for one in the most complete manner; and, by obliging all the lower classes of people to subsist nearly on the smallest quantity of food that will support life,[25] turns even a slight deficiency from the failure of the seasons into a severe dearth; and may be fairly said, therefore, to be one of the principal causes of famine. Among the signs of an approaching dearth, Dr. Short mentions one or more years of luxuriant crops together,[26] and this observation is probably just, as we know that the general

---

[21] Hist. of Air, Seasons, &c. vol. ii. p. 206. et seq.   [22] Ibid. and p. 366.

[23] New Observ. p. 125.

[24] Id. p. 108.

[25] [In 1826 (Vol. i, p. 523) Malthus altered this:
    ... cannot absolutely produce a famine, it prepares a way for one; and by frequently obliging the lower classes of people to subsist on the smallest quantity of food ...

[26] Hist. of Air, Seasons, &c. vol. ii. p. 367.

effect of years of cheapness and abundance is to dispose a greater number of persons to marry, and under such circumstances the return to a year, merely of an average crop might produce a scarcity.

The small-pox, which at present may be considered as the most prevalent and fatal epidemic in Europe,[27] is of all others, perhaps, the most difficult to account for, though the periods of its return are in many places regular.[28] Dr. Short observes, that from the histories of this disorder, it seems to have very little dependence upon the past or present constitution of the weather or seasons, and that it appears epidemically at all times, and in all states of the air, though not so frequently in a hard frost. We know of no instances, I believe, of its being clearly generated under any circumstances of situation. I do not mean therefore to insinuate that poverty and crowded houses ever absolutely produced it; but I may be allowed to remark that in those places where its returns are regular, and its ravages among children, particularly among those of the lower class, are considerable, it necessarily follows that these circumstances, in a greater degree than usual, must always precede and accompany its appearance; that is, from the time of its last visit, the average number of children will be increasing, the people will in consequence be growing poorer, and the houses will be more crowded, till another visit removes this superabundant population.

In all these cases, how little soever force we may be disposed to attribute to the effects of the principle of population in the actual production of disorders, we cannot avoid allowing their force as predisposing causes to the reception of contagion, and as giving very great additional force to the extensiveness and fatality of its ravages.

It is observed by Dr. Short that a severe mortal epidemic is generally succeeded by an uncommon healthiness, from the late distemper having carried off most of the declining worn-out constitutions.[29] It is probable, also, that another cause of it may be the greater plenty of room and food, and the consequently ameliorated condition of the lower classes of the people. Sometimes, according to Dr. Short, a very fruitful year is followed by a very mortal and sickly one, and mortal ones often succeeded by very fruitful, as if Nature sought either to prevent or quickly repair the loss by death. In general the next year after sickly and mortal ones is prolific in proportion to the breeders left.[30]

This last effect we have seen most strikingly exemplified in the table for Prussia and Lithuania.[31] And from this and other tables of Susmilch, it also appears that when the increasing produce of a country and the increasing

---

[27] [In 1826 (Vol. 1, p. 524) the words *at present* were deleted.]
[28] Hist of Air, Seasons, &c. vol. ii. p. 411.
[29] Id. vol. ii. p. 344.   [30] New Observ. p. 191.   [31] p. 204.

demand for labour so far ameliorate the condition of the labourer as greatly to encourage marriage, the custom of early marriages is generally continued till the population has gone beyond the increased produce, and sickly seasons appear to be the natural and necessary consequence. The continental registers exhibit many instances of rapid increase interrupted in this manner by mortal diseases; and the inference seems to be that those countries where subsistence is increasing sufficiently to encourage population, but not to answer all its demands, will be more subject to periodical epidemics than those where the increase of population is more nearly accommodated to the average produce.

The converse of this will of course be true. In those countries which are subject to periodical sicknesses, the increase of population, or the excess of births above the deaths, will be greater, in the intervals of these periods than is usual in countries not so much subject to these diseases. If Turkey and Egypt have been nearly stationary in their average population for the last century in the intervals of their periodical plagues, the births must have exceeded the deaths in a much greater proportion than in such countries as France and England.

It is for these reasons that no estimates of future population or depopulation, formed from any existing rate of increase or decrease, can be depended upon. Sir William Petty calculated that in the year 1800 the city of London would contain 5 359 000 inhabitants,[32] instead of which it does not now contain a fifth part of that number. And Mr. Eton has lately prophesied the extinction of the population of the Turkish empire in another century,[33] an event which will certainly fail of taking place. If America were to continue increasing at the same rate as at present, for the next 150 years, her population would exceed the population of China; but though prophecies are dangerous, I will venture to say that such an increase will not take place in that time, though it may perhaps in five or six hundred years.

Europe was, without doubt, formerly more subject to plagues and wasting epidemics than at present, and this will account, in great measure, for the greater proportion of births to deaths in former times, mentioned by many authors, as it has always been a common practice to estimate these proportions from too short periods, and generally to reject the years of plague as accidental.

The highest average proportion of births to deaths in England may be considered as about 12 to 10, or 120 to 100.[34] The proportion in France for

---

[32] Political Arithmetick, p. 17.   [33] Survey of the Turkish Empire, c. vii. p. 281.
[34] [In 1817 (Vol. II, p. 208) this sentence read:
    The average proportion of births to deaths in England during the last century may be considered ...

ten years, ending in 1780, was about 115 to 100.[35] Though these proportions undoubtedly varied at different periods during the century, yet we have reason to think that they did not vary in any very considerable degree; and it will appear, therefore, that the population of France and England had accommodated itself more nearly to the average produce of each country than many other states. [36]*The operation of the preventive check, vicious manners,[37] wars, the silent, though certain, destruction of life in large towns and manufactories, and the close habitations and insufficient food of many of the poor, prevent population from outrunning the means of subsistence; and if I may use an expression, which certainly at first appears strange, supersede the necessity of great and ravaging epidemics to destroy what is redundant. If a wasting plague were to sweep off two millions in England, and six millions in France, it cannot be doubted that, after the inhabitants had recovered from the dreadful shock, the proportion of births to deaths would rise much above the usual average in either country during the last century.[38]

In New Jersey the proportion of births to deaths, on an average of 7 years, ending 1743, was 300 to 100. In France and England, the average proportion cannot be reckoned at more than 120 to 100. Great and astonishing as this difference is, we ought not to be so wonder-struck at it as to attribute it to the miraculous interposition of heaven. The causes of it are not remote, latent, and mysterious, but near us, round about us, and open to the investigation of every inquiring mind. It accords with the most liberal spirit of philosophy to believe that no stone can fall, or plant rise, without the immediate agency of divine power. But we know from experience that these operations of what we call nature have been conducted almost according to fixed laws. And since the world began, the causes of population and depopulation have been probably as constant as any of the laws of nature with which we are acquainted.

The passion between the sexes has appeared in every age to be so nearly the same that it may always be considered, in algebraic language, as a given quantity. The great law of necessity which prevents population from increasing in any country beyond the food which it can either produce or acquire, is a law so open to our view, so obvious and evident to our understandings, that we cannot for a moment doubt it. The different modes which nature takes to repress a redundant population do not indeed appear

---

[35] Necker, de l'Administration des Finances, tom. i. c. ix. p. 255.

[36] [From the beginning of this sentence until the word 'misery?' on p. 304 Malthus has closely followed pp. 125–41 of the 1798 *Essay*.]

[37] [In 1806 (Vol. II, p. 66) the words *vicious manners* were deleted.]

[38] This remark has been, to a certain degree, verified of late in France, by the increase of births which has taken place since the revolution. [In 1817 (Vol. II, p. 209) this footnote was omitted.]

to us so certain and regular; but though we cannot always predict the mode, we may with certainty predict the fact. If the proportion of the births to the deaths for a few years indicates an increase of numbers much beyond the proportional increased or acquired food of the country, we may be perfectly certain that, unless an emigration take place, the deaths will shortly exceed the births, and that the increase that had been observed for a few years, cannot be the real average increase of the population of the country. If there were no other depopulating causes, and if the preventive check did not operate very strongly, every country would without doubt be subject to periodical plagues or famines.

The only true criterion of a real and permanent increase in the population of any country is the increase of the means of subsistence. But even this criterion is subject to some slight variations, which however are completely open to our observation. In some countries population seems to have been forced; that is, the people have been habituated, by degrees, to live almost upon the smallest possible quantity of food. There must have been periods in such countries when population increased permanently without an increase in the means of subsistence. China, India, and the countries possessed by the Bedoween Arabs, as we have seen in the former part of this work, appear to answer to this description. The average produce of these countries seems to be but barely sufficient to support the lives of the inhabitants, and of course any deficiency from the badness of the seasons must be fatal. Nations in this state must necessarily be subject to famines.

In America, where the reward of labour is at present so liberal, the lower classes might retrench very considerably in a year of scarcity, without materially distressing themselves. A famine, therefore, seems to be almost impossible. It may be expected, that in the progress of the population of America, the labourers will in time be much less liberally rewarded. The numbers will in this case permanently increase without a proportional increase in the means of subsistence.

In the different countries of Europe, there must be some variations in the proportion of the number of inhabitants and the quantity of food consumed, arising from the different habits of living which prevail in each state. The labourers of the south of England are so accustomed to eat fine wheaten bread, that they will suffer themselves to be half-starved before they will submit to live like the Scotch peasants. They might perhaps, in time, by the constant operation of the hard law of necessity, be reduced to live even like the lower classes of the Chinese, and the country would then with the same quantity of food support a greater population. But to effect this must always be a difficult and, every friend to humanity will hope, an abortive attempt.

I have mentioned some cases where population may permanently increase without a proportional increase in the means of subsistence. But it is evident that the variation in different states, between the food and the numbers supported by it, is restricted to a limit beyond which it cannot pass. In every country, the population of which is not absolutely decreasing, the food must be necessarily sufficient to support and to continue the race of labourers.

Other circumstances being the same, it may be affirmed that countries are populous according to the quantity of human food which they produce or can acquire; and happy according to the liberality with which this food is divided, or the quantity which a day's labour will purchase. Corn countries are more populous than pasture countries, and rice countries more populous than corn countries. But their happiness does not depend either upon their being thinly or fully inhabited, upon their poverty or their riches, their youth or their age; but on the proportion which the population and the food bear to each other. This proportion is generally the most favourable in new colonies, where the knowledge and industry of an old state operate on the fertile unappropriated land of a new one. In other cases the youth or the age of a state is not, in this respect, of great importance. It is probable that the food of Great Britain is divided in more liberal shares to her inhabitants at the present period than it was two thousand, three thousand, or four thousand years ago. And it has appeared that the poor and thinly-inhabited tracts of the Scotch Highlands are more distressed by a redundant population than the most populous parts of Europe.

If a country were never to be over-run by a people more advanced in arts, but left to its own natural progress in civilization; from the time that its produce might be considered as an unit, to the time that it might be considered as a million, during the lapse of many thousand years, there would[39] not be a single period when the mass of the people could be said to be free from distress, either directly or indirectly, for want of food. In every state in Europe, since we have first had accounts of it, millions and millions of human existences have been repressed from this simple cause, though perhaps in some of these states an absolute famine may never have been known.

[40]●Famine seems to be the last, the most dreadful resource of nature. The power of population is so superior to the power in the earth to produce subsistence for man that, unless arrested by the preventive check, premature death must in some shape or other visit the human race. The vices of mankind are active and able ministers of depopulation. They are the precursors in the great army of destruction, and often finish the dreadful work themselves. But should they fail in this war of extermination, sickly seasons, epidemics, pestilence, and plague, advance in terrific array, and

---

[39] [In 1826 (Vol. I, p. 553) *would* was changed to 'might'.]

sweep off their thousands and ten thousands. Should success be still incomplete, gigantic inevitable famine stalks in the rear and, with one mighty blow, levels the population with the food of the world.●[40]

Must it not then be acknowledged, by an attentive examiner of the histories of mankind, that in every age, and in every state, in which man has existed, or does now exist,

The increase of population is necessarily limited by the means of subsistence:

Population invariably increases when the means of subsistence increase,[41] unless prevented by powerful and obvious checks:

These checks, and the checks which keep the population down to the level of the means of subsistence, are, moral restraint, vice, and misery?*

In comparing the state of society which has been considered in this second book with that which formed the subject of the first, I think it appears that in modern Europe the positive checks to population prevail less, and the preventive checks more, than in past times, and in the more uncivilized parts of the world.

War, the predominant check to the population of savage nations, has certainly abated, even including the late unhappy revolutionary contests: and since the prevalence of a greater degree of personal cleanliness, of better modes of clearing and building towns, and of a more equable distribution of the products of the soil from improving knowledge in political economy, plagues, violent diseases, and famines have been certainly mitigated, and have become less frequent.

With regard to the preventive checks to population, though it must be acknowledged, that moral restraint does not at present prevail much among the male part of society;[42] yet I am strongly disposed to believe that it prevails more than in those states which were first considered; and it can scarcely be doubted that, in modern Europe, a much larger proportion of

---

[40] [In 1807 (Vol. I, p. 578) this paragraph was omitted. It is taken verbatim from pp. 139–40 of the 1798 *Essay*.]

[41] [In 1817 (Vol. II, p. 216) a footnote was added here:

By an increase in the means of subsistence, as the expression is used here, is always meant such an increase as the mass of the population can command: otherwise it can be of no avail in encouraging an increase of people.

[42] [In 1817 (Vol. II, p. 217) Malthus altered this sentence:

With regard to the preventive check to population, though it must be acknowledged that that branch of it which comes under the head of moral restraint,[(a)] does not at present prevail much ...

[He added a footnote:

[(a)] The reader will recollect the confined sense in which I use this term.

[The reader must here refer to note 4 of chapter ii of Book I, added in 1806.]

women pass a considerable part of their lives in the exercise of this virtue than in past times and among uncivilized nations. But however this may be, taking the preventive check in its general acceptation, as implying an infrequency of the marriage union from the fear of a family, without reference to its producing vice, it may be considered in this light as the most powerful of the checks which in modern Europe keep down the population to the level of the means of subsistence.[43]

---

[43] This final sentence was amended twice. In 1806 (Vol. II, p. 75) it read:

But however this may be, if we consider only the general term which implies principally an infrequency of the marriage union from the fear of a family, without reference to consequences, it may be considered ...

[In 1817 (Vol. II, p. 218) this was changed to:

But however this may be, if we consider only the general term which implies principally a delay of the marriage union from prudential considerations, without reference to consequences, it may be considered ...

ESSAY, &c

BOOK III

OF THE DIFFERENT SYSTEMS OR EXPEDIENTS WHICH HAVE BEEN PROPOSED OR HAVE PREVAILED IN SOCIETY, AS THEY AFFECT THE EVILS ARISING FROM THE PRINCIPLE OF POPULATION

CHAPTER I

Of Systems of Equality. Wallace. Condorcet[1]

To a person who views the past and present states of mankind in the light in which they have appeared in the two preceding books, it cannot but be a matter of astonishment, that all the writers on the perfectibility of man and of society, who have noticed the argument of the principle of population, treat it always very slightly,[2] and invariably represent the difficulties arising from it, as at a great, and almost immeasurable distance. Even Mr. Wallace, who thought the argument itself of so much weight as to destroy his whole system of equality, did not seem to be aware that any difficulty would arise from this cause till the whole earth had been cultivated like a garden, and was incapable of any further increase of produce. Were this really the case, and were a beautiful system of equality in other respects practicable, I cannot think that our ardour in the pursuit of such a scheme ought to be damped by the contemplation of so remote a difficulty. An event at such a distance might fairly be left to providence. But the truth is, that if the view of the argument given in this essay be just, the difficulty, so far from being remote, would be[3] imminent and immediate. At every period during the progress of cultivation,

---

[1] [The whole of this chapter is based on pp. 142–72 of the 1798 *Essay*, chapters viii and ix.]
[2] [In 1817 (Vol. II, p. 219) this was altered to:
    ... very lightly.
[3] [In 1817 (Vol. II, p. 220) *would be* was changed to 'is'.

from the present moment to the time when the whole earth was become like a garden, the distress for want of food would be constantly pressing on all mankind, if they were equal. Though the produce of the earth would be increasing every year, population would be increasing much faster,[4] and the redundancy must necessarily be checked by the periodical or constant action of moral restraint, vice, or misery.

M. Condorcet's *Esquisse d'un tableau historique des progrès de l'esprit humain* was written, it is said, under the pressure of that cruel proscription which terminated in his death. If he had no hopes of its been seen during his life, and of its interesting France in his favour, it is a singular instance of the attachment of a man to principles which every day's experience was, so fatally for himself, contradicting. To see the human mind, in one of the most enlightened nations of the world, debased by such a fermentation of disgusting passions, of fear, cruelty, malice, revenge, ambition, madness, and folly, as would have disgraced the most savage nations in the most barbarous age, must have been such a tremendous shock to his ideas of the necessary and inevitable progress of the human mind, that nothing but the firmest conviction of the truth of his principles, in spite of all appearances, could have withstood.

This posthumous publication is only a sketch of a much larger work which he proposed should be executed. It necessarily wants, therefore, that detail and application which can alone prove the truth of any theory. A few observations will be sufficient to shew how completely this theory is contradicted, when it is applied to the real and not to an imaginary state of things.

In the last division of the work, which treats of the future progress of man towards perfection, M. Condorcet says, that, comparing in the different civilized nations of Europe the actual population with the extent of territory; and observing their cultivation, their industry, their divisions of labour, and their means of subsistence, we shall see that it would be impossible to preserve the same means of subsistence, and consequently the same population, without a number of individuals who have no other means of supplying their wants than their industry.

Having allowed the necessity of such a class of men, and adverting afterwards to the precarious revenue of those families that would depend so entirely on the life and health of their chief,[5] he says very justly: 'There exists

---

[4] [In 1817 (Vol. II, p. 221) this sentence was altered:
    Though the produce of the earth would be increasing every year, population would have the power of increasing much faster, and this superior power must necessarily be checked . . .
[5] To save time and long quotations, I shall here give the substance of some of M. Condorcet's sentiments, and I hope that I shall not misrepresent them; but I refer the reader to the work

then a necessary cause of inequality, of dependence, and even of misery, which menaces without ceasing the most numerous and active class of our societies.' The difficulty is just, and well stated; but his mode of removing it will, I fear, be found totally inefficacious.

By the application of calculations to the probabilities of life, and the interest of money, he proposes that a fund should be established, which should assure to the old an assistance produced in part by their own former savings, and in part by the savings of individuals who, in making the same sacrifice, die before they reap the benefit of it. The same, or a similar fund, should give assistance to women and children who lose their husbands or fathers; and afford a capital to those who were of an age to found a new family, sufficient for the development of their industry. These establishments, he observes, might be made in the name and under the protection of the society. Going still further, he says that, by the just application of calculations, means might be found of more completely preserving a state of equality, by preventing credit from being the exclusive privilege of great fortunes, and yet giving it a basis equally solid, and by rendering the progress of industry and the activity of commerce less dependent on great capitalists.

Such establishments and calculations may appear very promising upon paper; but when applied to real life they will be found to be absolutely nugatory. M. Condorcet allows that a class of people which maintains itself entirely by industry is necessary to every state. Why does he allow this? No other reason can well be assigned than because he conceives that the labour necessary to procure subsistence for an extended population will not be performed without the goad of necessity. If by establishments upon the plans that have been mentioned, this spur to industry be removed; if the idle and negligent be placed upon the same footing with regard to their credit, and the future support of their wives and families, as the active and industrious, can we expect to see men exert that animated activity in bettering their condition, which now forms the master-spring of public prosperity? If an inquisition were to be established to examine the claims of each individual, and to determine whether he had or had not exerted himself to the utmost, and to grant or refuse assistance accordingly, this would be little else than a repetition upon a larger scale of the English poor laws, and would be completely destructive of the true principles of liberty and equality.

But independently of this great objection to these establishments, and supposing for a moment that they would give no check to production, the greatest difficulty remains yet behind.

---

itself, which will amuse if it do not convince him. [In Dr Johnson's Dictionary (posthumous edition of 1792) 'to amuse' meant 'to entertain in tranquillity'; the verb had no risible connotation.]

Were every man sure of a comfortable provision for a family, almost every man would have one; and were the rising generation free from the 'killing frost'[6] of misery, population must increase with unusual rapidity.[7] Of this, M. Condorcet seems to be fully aware himself; and, after having described further improvements, he says,

'But in this progress of industry and happiness, each generation will be called to more extended enjoyments, and in consequence, by the physical constitution of the human frame, to an increase in the number of individuals. Must not there arrive a period then, when these laws, equally necessary, shall counteract each other; when the increase of the number of men surpassing their means of subsistence, the necessary result must be either a continual diminution of happiness and population – a movement truly retrograde; or, at least a kind of oscillation between good and evil? In societies arrived at this term, will not this oscillation be a constantly subsisting cause of periodical misery? Will it not mark the limit when all further amelioration will become impossible, and point out that term to the perfectibility of the human race, which it may reach in the course of ages, but can never pass?' He then adds,

'There is no person who does not see how very distant such a period is from us. But shall we ever arrive at it? It is equally impossible to pronounce for, or against, the future realization of an event which cannot take place but at an era when the human race will have attained improvements of which we can, at present, scarcely form a conception.'

M. Condorcet's picture of what may be expected to happen, when the number of men shall surpass their means of subsistence, is justly drawn. The oscillation which he describes will certainly take place, and will without doubt be a constantly subsisting cause of periodical misery. The only point in which I differ from M. Condorcet in this description is with regard to the period when it may be applied to the human race. M. Condorcet thinks that it cannot possibly be applicable but at an era extremely distant. If the proportion between the natural increase of population and food,[8] which was stated in the beginning of this essay, and which has received considerable confirmation from the poverty that has been found to prevail in every stage and department of human society, be in any degree near the truth; it will appear, on the contrary, that the period when the number of men surpass

---

6 [See SHAKESPEARE (1) in the Alphabetical List.]

7 [In 1817 (Vol. II, p. 226) this sentence was altered:

If every man were sure of a comfortable provision for a family, almost every man would have one; and if the rising generation were free from the fear of poverty, population must increase with unusual rapidity.

8 [In 1826 (Vol. II, p. 7) a qualification was introduced here:

If the proportion between the natural increase of population and of food in a limited territory, which was stated ...

their means of subsistence,[9] has long since arrived; and that this necessary oscillation, this constantly subsisting cause of periodical misery, has existed ever since we have had any histories of mankind, does exist at present, and will for ever continue to exist, unless some decided change take place in the physical constitution of our nature.[10]

M. Condorcet, however, goes on to say, that should the period which he conceives to be so distant ever arrive, the human race, and the advocates of the perfectibility of man, need not be alarmed at it. He then proceeds to remove the difficulty in a manner which I profess not to understand. Having observed that the ridiculous prejudices of superstition would by that time have ceased to throw over morals a corrupt and degrading austerity, he alludes either to a promiscuous concubinage, which would prevent breeding, or to something else as unnatural. To remove the difficulty in this way will surely, in the opinion of most men, be to destroy that virtue and purity of manners which the advocates of equality, and of the perfectibility of man, profess to be the end and object of their views.

The last question which M. Condorcet proposes for examination is the organic perfectibility of man. He observes, that if the proofs which have been already given, and which, in their development, will receive greater force in the work itself, are sufficient to establish the indefinite perfectibility of man, upon the supposition of the same natural faculties and the same organization which he has at present; what will be the certainty, what the extent of our hopes, if this organization, these natural faculties themselves, be susceptible of melioration?

From the improvement of medicine; from the use of more wholesome food and habitations; from a manner of living which will improve the strength of the body by exercise, without impairing it by excess; from the destruction of the two great causes of the degradation of man, misery, and too great riches; from the gradual removal of transmissible and contagious disorders by the improvement of physical knowledge, rendered more efficacious, by the progress of reason and of social order; he infers, that though man will not absolutely become immortal, yet that the duration between his birth and natural death will increase without ceasing, will have no assignable term, and may properly be expressed by the word indefinite. He then defines this word

---

[9] [In 1817 (Vol. II, p. 228) this was changed to:
   ... surpass their means of easy subsistence, ...

[10] [In 1806 (Vol. II, p. 85) Malthus amended this sentence, which he had taken verbatim from p. 153 of the 1798 *Essay*:
   ... cause of periodical misery, has existed ever since we have had any histories of mankind, and continues to exist at the present moment.
   [In 1817 (Vol. II, p. 228) he altered it again:
   ... misery, has existed in most countries ever since we have had any histories ...

to mean either a constant approach to an unlimited extent, without ever reaching it; or an increase in the immensity of ages to an extent greater than any assignable quantity.

But surely the application of this term in either of these senses to the duration of human life is in the highest degree unphilosophical, and totally unwarranted by any appearances in the laws of nature. Variations from different causes are essentially distinct from a regular and unretrograde increase. The average duration of human life will, to a certain degree, vary from healthy or unhealthy climates, from wholesome or unwholesome food, from virtuous or vicious manners, and other causes; but it may be fairly doubted, whether there has been really the smallest perceptible advance in the natural duration of human life since first we had any authentic history of man. The prejudices of all ages have indeed been directly contrary to this supposition; and though I would not lay much stress upon these prejudices, they will in some measure tend to prove[11] that there has been no marked advance in an opposite direction.

It may perhaps be said that the world is yet so young, so completely in its infancy, that it ought not to be expected that any difference should appear so soon.

If this be the case, there is at once an end of all human science. The whole train of reasonings from effects to causes will be destroyed. We may shut our eyes to the book of nature, as it will no longer be of any use to read it. The wildest and most improbable conjectures may be advanced with as much certainty as the most just and sublime theories founded on careful and reiterated experiments. We may return again to the old mode of philosophising, and make facts bend to systems, instead of establishing systems upon facts. The grand and consistent theory of Newton, will be placed upon the same footing as the wild and eccentric hypotheses of Descartes. In short, if the laws of nature be thus fickle and inconstant; if it can be affirmed, and be believed, that they will change, when for ages and ages they have appeared immutable; the human mind will no longer have any incitements to inquiry, but must remain fixed[12] in inactive torpor, or amuse itself only in bewildering dreams and extravagant fancies.

The constancy of the laws of nature, and of effects and causes, is the foundation of all human knowledge; and if, without any previous observable symptoms or indications of a change, we can infer that a change will take place, we may as well make any assertion whatever, and think it as unreasonable to be contradicted, in affirming that the moon will come in

---

[11] [In 1817 (Vol. II, p. 231) this was changed to:
    ... they must have some tendency to prove ...
[12] [In 1817 (Vol. II, p. 232) *fixed* was changed to 'sunk'.

contact with the earth to-morrow, as in saying that the sun will rise at its appointed time.[13]

With regard to the duration of human life, there does not appear to have existed, from the earliest ages of the world to the present moment, the smallest permanent symptom or indication of increasing prolongation. The observable effects of climate, habit, diet, and other causes, on length of life, have furnished the pretext for asserting its indefinite extension; and the sandy foundation on which the argument rests is, that because the limit of human life is undefined; because you cannot mark its precise term, and say so far exactly shall it go, and no further; that therefore its extent may increase for ever, and be properly termed indefinite or unlimited. But the fallacy and absurdity of this argument will sufficiently appear from a slight examination of what M. Condorcet calls the organic perfectibility or degeneration of the race of plants and animals, which, he says, may be regarded as one of the general laws of nature.

I am told that it is a maxim among the improvers of cattle,[14] that you may breed to any degree of nicety you please; and they found this maxim upon another, which is, that some of the offspring will possess the desirable qualities of the parents in a greater degree. In the famous Leicestershire breed of sheep, the object is to procure them with small heads and small legs. Proceeding upon these breeding maxims, it is evident that we might go on till the heads and legs were evanescent quantities; but this is so palpable an absurdity that we may be quite sure that the premises are not just, and that there really is a limit, though we cannot see it, or say exactly where it is. In this case, the point of the greatest degree of improvement, or the smallest size of the head and legs, may be said to be undefined; but this is very different from unlimited, or from indefinite, in M. Condorcet's acceptation of the term. Though I may not be able, in the present instance, to mark the limit at which further improvement will stop, I can very easily mention a point at which it will not arrive. I should not scruple to assert, that were the breeding

---

[13] [After following the 1798 *Essay* very closely, Malthus omitted here a passage from pp. 159–60:

... the foundation of all human knowledge; though far be it from me to say, that the same power which framed and executes the laws of nature, may not change them all in a moment, in the twinkling of an eye.[(a)] Such a change may undoubtedly happen. All that I mean to say is that it is impossible to infer it from reasoning. If without any previous observable symptoms ...

[(a)] St. Paul's First Epistle to the Corinthians, xv, 52, Bible of 1611.]

[In 1817 (Vol. II, p. 233) Malthus wrote:

... the sun will rise at its expected time.

[14] [In 1806 (Vol. II, p. 90) this was changed to:

I have been told that it is a maxim among some of the improvers of cattle ...

to continue for ever, the heads and legs of these sheep would never be so small as the head and legs of a rat.

It cannot be true, therefore, that among animals, some of the offspring will possess the desirable qualities of the parents in a greater degree; or that animals are indefinitely perfectible.

The progress of a wild plant to a beautiful garden flower is perhaps more marked and striking than any thing that takes place among animals; yet even here, it would be the height of absurdity to assert that the progress was unlimited or indefinite. One of the most obvious features of the improvement is the increase of size. The flower has grown gradually larger by cultivation. If the progress were really unlimited, it might be increased ad infinitum; but this is so gross an absurdity that we may be quite sure that among plants, as well as among animals, there is a limit to improvement, though we do not exactly know where it is. It is probable that the gardeners who contend for flower-prizes have often applied stronger dressing without success. At the same time, it would be highly presumptuous in any man to say that he had seen the finest carnation or anemone that could ever be made to grow. He might however assert without the smallest chance of being contradicted by a future fact, that no carnation or anemone could ever by cultivation be increased to the size of a large cabbage; and yet there are assignable quantities greater than a cabbage. No man can say that he has seen the largest ear of wheat, or the largest oak that could ever grow; but he might easily, and with perfect certainty, name a point of magnitude at which they would not arrive. In all these cases, therefore, a careful distinction should be made between an unlimited progress, and a progress where the limit is merely undefined.

It will be said, perhaps, that the reason why plants and animals cannot increase indefinitely in size is that they would fall by their own weight. I answer, how do we know this but from experience? from experience of the degree of strength with which these bodies are formed. I know that a car-nation, long before it reached the size of a cabbage, would not be supported by its stalk; but I only know this from my experience of the weakness, and want of tenacity in the materials of a carnation stalk. There are many substances in nature, of the same size, that would support as large a head as a cabbage.[15]

The reasons of the mortality of plants are at present perfectly unknown to us. No man can say why such a plant is annual, another biennial, and another endures for ages. The whole affair in all these cases, in plants, animals, and in the human race, is an affair of experience; and I only

---

[15] [In 1806 (Vol. II, p. 93) Malthus was more cautious:
    There might be substances of the same size that would support as large a head as a cabbage.

conclude that man is mortal, because the invariable experience of all ages has proved the mortality of those materials of which his visible body is made.[16]

What can we reason but from what we know?[17]

Sound philosophy will not authorize me to alter this opinion of the mortality of man on earth till it can be clearly proved that the human race has made, and is making, a decided progress towards an illimitable extent of life. And the chief reason why I adduced the two particular instances from animals and plants was to expose and illustrate, if I could, the fallacy of that argument which infers an unlimited progress merely because some partial improvement has taken place, and that the limit of this improvement cannot be precisely ascertained.

The capacity of improvement in plants and animals, to a certain degree, no person can possibly doubt. A clear and decided progress has already been made; and yet I think it appears that it would be highly absurd to say that this progress has no limits. In human life, though there are great variations from different causes, it may be doubted whether, since the world began, any organic improvement whatever of the human frame can be clearly ascertained. The foundations, therefore, on which the arguments for the organic perfectibility of man rest, are unusually weak, and can only be considered as mere conjectures. It does not, however, by any means seem impossible that, by an attention to breed, a certain degree of improvement, similar to that among animals, might take place among men. Whether intellect could be communicated may be a matter of doubt: but size, strength, beauty, complexion, and perhaps even longevity, are in a degree transmissible. The error does not seem to lie in supposing a small degree of improvement possible,[18] but in not discriminating between a small improvement, the limit of which is undefined, and an improvement really unlimited. As the human race, however, could not be improved in this way without condemning all the bad specimens to celibacy, it is not probable that an attention to breed should ever become general; indeed I know of no well-directed attempts of the kind, except in the ancient family of the Bickerstaffs, who are said to have been very successful in whitening the skins, and increasing the height of their race by prudent marriages, particularly by that very judicious cross with Maud the milk-maid, by which some capital defects in the constitutions of the family were corrected.[19]

---

[16] [In 1817 (Vol. II, p. 237) this was altered to:
   ... the mortality of that organised substance of which his visible body is made.
[17] [See POPE in the Alphabetical List.]
[18] [In 1817 (Vol. II, p. 239) this became:
  The error does not lie in supposing ...
[19] [See THE TATLERS in the Alphabetical List.]

It will not be necessary, I think, in order more completely to shew the improbability of any approach in man towards immortality on earth, to urge the very great additional weight that an increase in the duration of life would give to the argument of population.

M. Condorcet's book may be considered not only as a sketch of the opinions of a celebrated individual, but of many of the literary men in France at the beginning of the revolution. As such, though merely a sketch, it seems worthy of attention.

Many, I doubt not, will think that the attempting gravely to controvert so absurd a paradox as the immortality of man on earth, or indeed, even the perfectibility of man and society, is a waste of time and words; and that such unfounded conjectures are best answered by neglect. I profess, however, to be of a different opinion. When paradoxes of this kind are advanced by ingenious and able men, neglect has no tendency to convince them of their mistakes. Priding themselves on what they conceive to be a mark of the reach and size of their own understandings, of the extent and comprehensiveness of their views; they will look upon this neglect merely as an indication of poverty and narrowness in the mental exertions of their contemporaries; and only think that the world is not yet prepared to receive their sublime truths.

On the contrary, a candid investigation of these subjects accompanied with a perfect readiness to adopt any theory warranted by sound philosophy, may have a tendency to convince them that, in forming improbable and unfounded hypotheses, so far from enlarging the bounds of human science, they are contracting it; so far from promoting the improvement of the human mind, they are obstructing it: they are throwing us back again almost into the infancy of knowledge; and weakening the foundations of that mode of philosophising, under the auspices of which science has of late made such rapid advances. The late rage for wide and unrestrained speculation[20] seems to have been a kind of mental intoxication, arising, perhaps, from the great and unexpected discoveries which had been made in various branches of science. To men elate and giddy with such successes, everything appeared to be within the grasp of human powers; and under this illusion they confounded subjects where no real progress could be proved with those where the progress had been marked, certain, and acknowledged. Could they be persuaded to sober themselves with a little severe and chastized thinking, they would see that the cause of truth and of sound philosophy cannot but suffer, by substituting wild flights and unsupported assertions, for patient investigation and well authenticated proofs.[21]

---

[20] [In 1798 (footnote, p. 162) Malthus had written:
  The present rage ...
[21] [In 1817 (Vol. II, p. 242) *well authenticated proofs* was changed to:
  ... well-supported proofs.

CHAPTER II

Of Systems of Equality. Godwin[1]

In reading Mr. Godwin's ingenious work on political justice, it is impossible not to be struck with the spirit and energy of his style, the force and precision of some of his reasonings, the ardent tone of his thoughts, and particularly with that impressive earnestness of manner which gives an air of truth to the whole. At the same time it must be confessed that he has not proceeded in his inquiries with the caution that sound philosophy requires. His conclusions are often unwarranted by his premises. He fails sometimes in removing objections which he himself brings forward. He relies too much on general and abstract propositions which will not admit of application. And his conjectures certainly far outstrip the modesty of nature.

The system of equality which Mr. Godwin proposes is, on a first view, the most beautiful and engaging of any that has yet appeared. An amelioration of society to be produced merely by reason and conviction gives more promise of permanence than any change effected and maintained by force. The unlimited exercise of private judgement is a doctrine grand and captivating, and has a vast superiority over those systems where every individual is in a manner the slave of the public. The substitution of benevolence, as the masterspring and moving principle of society, instead of self-love, appears at first sight to be a consummation devoutly to be wished. In short, it is impossible to contemplate the whole of this fair picture without emotions of delight and admiration, accompanied with an ardent longing for the period of its accomplishment. But alas! that moment can never arrive. The whole is little better than a dream – a phantom of the imagination. These 'gorgeous palaces' of happiness and immortality, these 'solemn temples' of truth and virtue, will dissolve, 'like the baseless fabric of a vision', when we awaken to real life and contemplate the genuine situation of man on earth.[2]

Mr. Godwin, at the conclusion of the third chapter of his eighth book, speaking of population, says: 'There is a principle in human society, by which population is perpetually kept down to the level of the means of subsistence. Thus, among the wandering tribes of America and Asia, we

---

[1] [This chapter follows closely chapter x (pp. 173–209) of the 1798 *Essay*.]
[2] [See SHAKESPEARE (2) in the Alphabetical List.]

316

never find, through the lapse of ages, that population has so increased as to render necessary the cultivation of the earth.'[3] This principle, which Mr. Godwin thus mentions as some mysterious and occult cause, and which he does not attempt to investigate, has appeared to be the grinding law[4] of necessity – misery, and the fear of misery.

The great error under which Mr. Godwin labours throughout his whole work is the attributing of almost all the vices and misery that prevail in civil society to human institutions. Political regulations and the established administration of property are, with him, the fruitful sources of all evil, the hotbeds of all the crimes that degrade mankind. Were this really a true state of the case, it would not seem an absolutely hopeless task, to remove evil completely from the world; and reason seems to be the proper and adequate instrument for effecting so great a purpose. But the truth is, that though human institutions appear to be the obvious and obtrusive causes of much mischief to mankind, they are, in reality, light and superficial in comparison with those deeper-seated causes of evil which result from the laws of nature.[5]

In a chapter on the benefits attendant upon a system of equality, Mr. Godwin says: 'The spirit of oppression, the spirit of servility, and the spirit of fraud, these are the immediate growth of the established administration of property. They are alike hostile to intellectual improvement.[6] The other vices of envy, malice, and revenge, are their inseparable companions. In a state of society where men lived in the midst of plenty, and where all shared alike the bounties of nature, these sentiments would inevitably expire. The narrow principle of selfishness would vanish. No man being obliged to guard his little store, or provide with anxiety and pain for his restless wants, each would lose his individual existence in the thought of the general good. No man would be an enemy to his neighbours, for they would have no subject of contention: and of consequence philanthropy would resume the empire which reason assigns her. Mind would be delivered from her perpetual anxiety about corporal support, and free to expatiate in the field of thought which is congenial to her. Each would assist the inquiries of all.'[7]

This would indeed be a happy state. But that it is merely an imaginary

---

[3] P. 460. 8vo. 2nd edit.   [4] [In 1817 (Vol. II, p. 245) the word *grinding* was omitted.]

[5] In 1807 (Vol. II, pp. 24–5) this sentence was altered:

But the truth is, that though human institutions appear to be, and indeed often are, the obvious and obtrusive causes of much mischief to society, they are, in reality, light and superficial in comparison with those deeper-seated causes of evil which result from the laws of nature and the passions of mankind.

[6] [Professor Antony Flew points out in the Pelican edition of the 1798 *Essay* (p. 280) that what Godwin actually wrote was 'hostile to intellectual and moral improvement'.]

[7] Political Justice, b. viii. c. iii. p. 458.

picture, with scarcely a feature near the truth, the reader, I am afraid, is already too well convinced.

Man cannot live in the midst of plenty. All cannot share alike the bounties of nature. Were there no established administration of property, every man would be obliged to guard with force his little store. Selfishness would be triumphant. The subjects of contention would be perpetual. Every individual would be under a constant anxiety about corporal support, and not a single intellect would be left free to expatiate in the field of thought.

How little Mr. Godwin has turned his attention to the real state of human society will sufficiently appear from the manner in which he endeavours to remove the difficulty of an overcharged population.[8] He says: 'The obvious answer to this objection is, that to reason thus is to foresee difficulties at a great distance. Three-fourths of the habitable globe is now uncultivated. The parts already cultivated are capable of immeasurable improvement. Myriads of centuries of still increasing population may pass away, and the earth be still found sufficient for the subsistence of its inhabitants.'[9]

I have already pointed out the error of supposing that no distress or difficulty would arise from a redundant population before the earth absolutely refused to produce any more. But let us imagine, for a moment, Mr. Godwin's system of equality realized in its utmost extent,[10] and see how soon this difficulty might be expected to press, under so perfect a form of society. A theory that will not admit of application cannot possibly be just.

Let us suppose all the causes of vice and misery in this island removed. War and contention cease. Unwholesome trades and manufactories do not exist. Crowds no longer collect together in great and pestilent cities for purposes of court intrigue, of commerce, and vicious gratification. Simple, healthy, and rational amusements take place of drinking, gaming, and debauchery. There are no towns sufficiently large to have any prejudicial effects on the human constitution. The greater part of the happy inhabitants of this terrestrial paradise live in hamlets and farm-houses scattered over the face of the country. All men are equal. The labours of luxury are at an end; and the necessary labours of agriculture are shared amicably among all. The number of persons and the produce of the island we suppose to be the same as at present. The spirit of benevolence guided by impartial justice will divide this produce among all the members of society according to their wants. Though it would be impossible that they should all have animal food every day, yet vegetable food, with meat occasionally, would satisfy the desires of a

---

8 [In 1817 (Vol. II, p. 248) this was changed to:
      . . . a superabundant population.
9 Polit. Justice, b. viii. c. ix. p. 510.
10 [In 1826 (Vol. II, p. 22) the words *in its utmost extent* were excised.]

frugal people, and would be sufficient to preserve them in health, strength, and spirits.

Mr. Godwin considers marriage as a fraud and a monopoly.[11] Let us suppose the commerce of the sexes established upon principles of the most perfect freedom. Mr. Godwin does not think himself that this freedom would lead to a promiscuous intercourse; and in this I perfectly agree with him. The love of variety is a vicious, corrupt, and unnatural taste, and could not prevail in any great degree in a simple and virtuous state of society. Each man would probably select for himself a partner, to whom he would adhere, as long as that adherence continued to be the choice of both parties. It would be of little consequence, according to Mr. Godwin, how many children a woman had, or to whom they belonged. Provisions and assistance would spontaneously flow from the quarter in which they abounded, to the quarter in which they were deficient.[12] And every man, according to his capacity, would be ready to furnish instruction to the rising generation.

I cannot conceive a form of society so favourable, upon the whole, to population. The irremediableness of marriage, as it is at present constituted, undoubtedly deters many from entering into this state. An unshackled intercourse, on the contrary, would be a most powerful incitement to early attachments: and as we are supposing no anxiety about the future support of children to exist, I do not conceive that there would be one woman in a hundred, of twenty-three years of age, without a family.

With these extraordinary encouragements to population, and every cause of depopulation, as we have supposed, removed, the numbers would necessarily increase faster than in any society that has ever yet been known. I have before mentioned that the inhabitants of the back settlements of America appear to double their numbers in fifteen years. England is certainly a more healthy country than the back settlements of America; and as we have supposed every house in the island to be airy and wholesome, and the encouragements to have a family greater even than in America, no probable reason can be assigned why the population should not double itself in less, if possible, than fifteen years. But to be quite sure that we do not go beyond the truth, we will only suppose the period of doubling to be twenty-five years; a ratio of increase which is well known to have taken place throughout all the northern states of America.[13]

There can be little doubt, that the equalization of property which we have supposed, added to the circumstance of the labour of the whole community being directed chiefly to agriculture, would tend greatly to augment the

---

[11] Polit. Justice, b. viii. c. viii. p. 498. et seq.   [12] Id. b. viii. c. viii. p. 504.
[13] [In 1817 (Vol. II, p. 252) this was changed to:
    ... all the United States of America.

produce of the country. But to answer the demands of a population increasing so rapidly, Mr. Godwin's calculation of half an hour a day would certainly not be sufficient. It is probable that the half of every man's time must be employed for this purpose. Yet with such or much greater exertions, a person who is acquainted with the nature of the soil in this country, and who reflects on the fertility of the lands already in cultivation, and the barrenness of those that are not cultivated, will be very much disposed to doubt whether the whole average produce could possibly be doubled in twenty-five years from the present period. The only chance of success would be from the ploughing up most of the grazing countries, and putting an end almost entirely to animal food. Yet this scheme would probably defeat itself. The soil of England will not produce much without dressing; and cattle seem to be necessary to make that species of manure which best suits the land.

Difficult however as it might be to double the average produce of the island in twenty-five years, let us suppose it effected. At the expiration of the first period therefore, the food, though almost entirely vegetable, would be sufficient to support in health the doubled population of 22 millions.[14]

During the next period, where will the food be found to satisfy the importunate demands of the increasing numbers? Where is the fresh land to turn up? Where is the dressing necessary to improve that which is already in cultivation? There is no person with the smallest knowledge of land, but would say that it was impossible that the average produce of the country could be increased during the second twenty-five years by a quantity equal to what it at present yields. Yet we will suppose this increase, however improbable, to take place. The exuberant strength of the argument allows of almost any concession. Even with this concession, however, there would be eleven millions at the expiration of the second term unprovided for. A quantity equal to the frugal support of 33 millions would be to be divided among 44 millions.

Alas! what becomes of the picture where men lived in the midst of plenty, where no man was obliged to provide with anxiety and pain for his restless wants; where the narrow principle of selfishness did not exist; where the mind was delivered from her perpetual anxiety about corporeal support, and free to expatiate in the field of thought which is congenial to her? This beautiful fabric of the imagination vanishes at the severe touch of truth. The spirit of benevolence, cherished and invigorated by plenty, is repressed by the chilling breath of want. The hateful passions that had vanished reappear.

---

[14] [In 1826 (Vol. II, p. 26) this was altered to:
    ... to support in health the population increased from 11 to 22 millions.
    [A footnote was added:
    The numbers here mentioned refer to the enumeration of 1800.

The mighty law of self-preservation expels all the softer and more exalted emotions of the soul. The temptations to evil are too strong for human nature to resist. The corn is plucked before it is ripe, or secreted in unfair proportions; and the whole black train of vices that belong to falsehood are immediately generated. Provisions no longer flow in for the support of a mother with a large family. The children are sickly from insufficient food. The rosy flush of health gives place to the pallid cheek and hollow eye of misery. Benevolence, yet lingering in a few bosoms, makes some faint expiring struggles, till at length self-love resumes his wonted empire and lords it triumphant over the world.

No human institutions here existed, to the perverseness of which Mr. Godwin ascribes the original sin of the worst men.[15] No opposition had been produced by them between public and private good. No monopoly had been created of those advantages which reason directs to be left in common. No man had been goaded to the breach of order by unjust laws. Benevolence had established her reign in all hearts. And yet in so short a period as fifty years, violence, oppression, falsehood, misery, every hateful vice and every form of distress, which degrade and sadden the present state of society, seem to have been generated by the most imperious circumstances, by laws inherent in the nature of man, and absolutely independent of all human regulations.

If we be not yet too well convinced of the reality of this melancholy picture, let us look for a moment into the next period of twenty-five years, and we shall see 44 millions of human beings without the means of support: and at the conclusion of the first century, the population would be 176 millions, and the food only sufficient for 55 millions, leaving 121 millions unprovided for. In these ages, want, indeed, would be triumphant, and rapine and murder must reign at large:[16] and yet all this time we are supposing the produce of the earth absolutely unlimited, and the yearly increase greater than the boldest speculator can imagine.

This is undoubtedly a very different view of the difficulty arising from the principle of population from that which Mr. Godwin gives, when he says: 'Myriads of centuries of still increasing population may pass away, and the earth be still found sufficient for the subsistence of its inhabitants.'

I am sufficiently aware that the redundant millions which I have men-

---

[15] Polit. Justice, b. viii. c. iii. p. 340.

[16] [In 1817 (Vol. II, p. 257) this paragraph was substantially altered:

... let us but look for a moment into the next period of twenty-five years, and we shall see that, according to the natural increase of population, 44 millions of human beings would be without the means of support; and at the conclusion of the first century the population would have had the power of increasing to 176 millions, while the food was only sufficient for 55 millions, leaving 121 millions unprovided for; and yet all this time we are supposing the produce of the earth absolutely unlimited ...

tioned could never have existed. It is a perfectly just observation of Mr. Godwin, that 'there is a principle in human society by which population is perpetually kept down to the level of the means of subsistence.' The sole question is, what is this principle? Is it some obscure and occult cause? Is it some mysterious interference of heaven, which at a certain period strikes the men with impotence and the women with barrenness? Or is it a cause open to our researches, within our view; a cause which has constantly been observed to operate, though with varied force, in every state in which man has been placed? Is it not misery, and the fear of misery, the necessary and inevitable results of the laws of nature,[17] which human institutions, so far from aggravating, have tended considerably to mitigate, though they can never remove?

It may be curious to observe, in the case that we have been supposing, how some of the principal laws which at present govern civilized society would be successively dictated by the most imperious necessity. As man, according to Mr. Godwin, is the creature of the impressions to which he is subject, the goadings of want could not continue long before some violations of public or private stock would necessarily take place. As these violations increased in number and extent, the more active and comprehensive intellects of the society would soon perceive that, while population was fast increasing, the yearly produce of the country would shortly begin to diminish. The urgency of the case would suggest the necessity of some immediate measures being taken for the general safety. Some kind of convention would then be called, and the dangerous situation of the country stated in the strongest terms. It would be observed that while they lived in the midst of plenty, it was of little consequence who laboured the least, or who possessed the least, as every man was perfectly willing and ready to supply the wants of his neighbour. But that the question was no longer whether one man should give to another that which he did not use himself; but whether he should give to his neighbour the food which was absolutely necessary to his own existence. It would be represented that the number of those who were in want very greatly exceeded the number and means of those who should supply them; that these pressing wants, which from the state of the produce of the country could not all be gratified, had occasioned some flagrant violations of justice; that these violations had already checked the increase of food, and would, if they were not by some means or other prevented, throw the whole community into confusion; that imperious necessity seemed to dictate that a yearly increase of produce should, if possible, be obtained at all events; that, in order to effect

---

[17] [In 1817 (Vol. II, p. 258) there was a qualifying insertion here:
    ... inevitable results of the laws of nature, in the present state of man's existence, which human institutions ...

this first great and indispensable purpose, it would be advisable to make a more complete division of land, and to secure every man's property against violation, by the most powerful sanctions.

It might be urged perhaps by some objectors, that, as the fertility of the land increased, and various accidents occurred, the shares of some men might be much more than sufficient for their support; and that, when the reign of self-love was once established, they would not distribute their surplus produce without some compensation in return. It would be observed in answer that this was an inconvenience greatly to be lamented; but that it was an evil which would bear no comparison to the black train of distresses which would inevitably be occasioned by the insecurity of property; that the quantity of food which one man could consume was necessarily limited by the narrow capacity of the human stomach; that it was certainly not probable that he should throw away the rest; and if he exchanged his surplus produce for the labour of others, this would be better than that these others should absolutely starve.

It seems highly probable, therefore, that an administration of property, not very different from that which prevails in civilized states at present, would be established, as the best (though inadequate) remedy, for the evils which were pressing on the society.

The next subject which would come under discussion, intimately connected with the preceding, is the commerce of the sexes. It would be urged by those who had turned their attention to the true cause of the difficulties under which the community laboured, that while every man felt secure that all his children would be well provided for by general benevolence, the powers of the earth would be absolutely inadequate to produce food for the population which would inevitably ensue;[18] that even if the whole attention and labour of the society were directed to this sole point, and if by the most perfect security of property, and every other encouragement that could be thought of, the greatest possible increase of produce were yearly obtained; yet still the increase of food would by no means keep pace with the much more rapid increase of population; that some check to population, therefore, was imperiously called for; that the most natural and obvious check seemed to be to make every man provide for his own children; that this would operate in some respect as a measure and a guide in the increase of population, as it might be expected that no man would bring beings into the world for whom he could not find the means of support; that, where this notwithstanding was the case, it seemed necessary, for the example of others, that the disgrace and inconvenience attending such a conduct should fall upon that individual who

---

[18] [In 1807 (Vol. II, p. 38) the word *inevitably* was omitted.]

had thus inconsiderately plunged himself and his innocent children into want and misery.

The institution of marriage, or at least of some express or implied obligation on every man to support his own children, seems to be the natural result of these reasonings in a community under the difficulties that we have supposed.

The view of these difficulties presents us with a very natural reason why the disgrace which attends a breach of chastity should be greater in a woman than in a man. It could not be expected that women should have resources sufficient to support their own children. When, therefore, a woman had lived with a man, who had entered into no compact to maintain her children; and aware of the inconveniences that he might bring upon himself, had deserted her, these children must necessarily fall upon the society for support, or starve. And to prevent the frequent recurrence of such an inconvenience, as it would be highly unjust to punish so natural a fault by personal restraint or infliction, the men might agree to punish it with disgrace. The offence is, besides, more obvious and conspicuous in the woman, and less liable to any mistake. The father of a child may not always be known; but the same uncertainty cannot easily exist with regard to the mother. Where the evidence of the offence was most complete, and the inconvenience to the society, at the same time, the greatest, there it was agreed that the largest share of blame should fall. The obligation on every man to support his children, the society would enforce by positive laws; and the greater degree of inconvenience or labour to which a family would necessarily subject him, added to some portion of disgrace which every human being must incur, who leads another into unhappiness, might be considered as a sufficient punishment for the man.

That a woman should, at present, be almost driven from society for an offence which men commit nearly with impunity, seems undoubtedly to be a breach of natural justice. But the origin of the custom, as the most obvious and effectual method of preventing the frequent recurrence of a serious inconvenience to a community, appears to be natural, though not perhaps perfectly justifiable. This origin is now lost in the new train of ideas that the custom has since generated. What at first might be dictated by state necessity is now supported by female delicacy; and operates with the greatest force on that part of the society where, if the original intention of the custom were preserved, there is the least real occasion for it.

When these two fundamental laws of society, the security of property and the institution of marriage, were once established, inequality of conditions must necessarily follow. Those who were born after the division of property would come into a world already possessed. If their parents, from having too large a family, were unable to give them sufficient for their support, what could they do in a world where everything was appropriated? We have seen the fatal effects that would result to society if every man had a valid claim to an equal share of the produce of the earth. The members of a family which was grown too large for the original division of land appropriated to it could not then demand a part of the surplus produce of others as a debt of justice. It has appeared that, from the inevitable laws of human nature, some human beings will be exposed to want. These are the unhappy persons who in the great lottery of life have drawn a blank. The number of these persons would soon exceed the ability of the surplus produce to supply. Moral merit is a very difficult criterion, except in extreme cases. The owners of surplus produce would in general seek some more obvious mark of distinction; and it seems to be both natural and just that, except upon particular occasions, their choice should fall upon those, who were able, and professed themselves willing, to exert their strength in procuring a further surplus produce, which would at once benefit the community and enable the proprietors to afford assistance to greater numbers. All who were in want of food would be urged by imperious necessity[19] to offer their labour in exchange for this article, so absolutely necessary to existence. The fund appropriated to the maintenance of labour would be the aggregate quantity of food possessed by the owners of land beyond their own consumption. When the demands upon this fund were great and numerous, it would naturally be divided into very small shares. Labour would be ill paid. Men would offer to work for a bare subsistence; and the rearing of families would be checked by sickness and misery. On the contrary, when this fund was increasing fast; when it was great in proportion to the number of claimants, it would be divided in much larger shares. No man would exchange his labour without receiving an ample quantity of food in return. Labourers would live in ease and comfort, and would consequently be able to rear a numerous and vigorous offspring.

On the state of this fund, the happiness, or the degree of misery, prevailing among the lower classes of people, in every known state, at present chiefly depends; and on this happiness, or degree of misery, depends principally the increase, stationariness, or decrease, of population.

And thus it appears that a society constituted according to the most beautiful form that imagination can conceive, with benevolence for its moving principle, instead of self-love, and with every evil disposition in all its members corrected by reason, not force, would, from the inevitable laws of nature, and not from any original depravity of man or of human institu-

---

[19] [In 1817 (Vol. ii, p. 267) the word *imperious* was excised.]

tions,[20] degenerate in a very short period into a society constructed upon a plan not essentially different from that which prevails in every known state at present; a society divided into a class of proprietors and a class of labourers, and with self-love for the mainspring of the great machine.

In the supposition which I have made, I have undoubtedly taken the increase of population smaller, and the increase of produce greater, than they really would be. No reason can be assigned why, under the circumstances supposed, population should not increase faster than in any known instance. If, then, we were to take the period of doubling at fifteen years instead of twenty-five years, and reflect upon the labour necessary to double the produce in so short a time, even if we allow it possible; we may venture to pronounce with certainty that, if Mr. Godwin's system of society were established in its utmost perfection,[21] instead of myriads of centuries, not thirty years could elapse before its utter destruction from the simple principle of population.

I have taken no notice of emigration in this place, for obvious reasons. If such societies were instituted in other parts of Europe, these countries would be under the same difficulties with regard to population, and could admit no fresh members into their bosoms. If this beautiful society were confined to our island, it must have degenerated strangely from its original purity, and administer but a very small portion of the happiness it proposed, before any of its members would voluntarily consent to leave it, and live under such governments as at present exist in Europe, or submit to the extreme hardships of first settlers in new regions.

---

[20] [This wording is that of the 1798 *Essay* (p. 207). In 1817 (Vol. II, p. 268) it was altered:
... from the inevitable laws of nature, and not from any fault in human institutions, degenerate ...

[21] [In 1826 (Vol. II, p. 36) the words *in its utmost perfection* were excised.]

CHAPTER III(a)

Observations on the Reply of Mr. Godwin

Mr. Godwin, in a late publication, has replied to those parts of the Essay on the Principle of Population which he thinks bear the hardest on his system. A few remarks on this reply will be sufficient.

In a note to an early part of his pamphlet, he observes that the main attack of the essay is not directed against the principles of his work, but its conclusion.[1] It may be true indeed that, as Mr. Godwin had dedicated one particular chapter towards the conclusion of his work, to the consideration of the objections to his system from the principle of population, this particular chapter is most frequently alluded to: but certainly if the great principle of the essay be admitted, it affects his whole work, and essentially alters the foundations of political justice. A great part of Mr. Godwin's book consists of an abuse of human institutions, as productive of all, or most of, the evils which afflict society. The acknowledgment of a new and totally unconsidered cause of misery would evidently alter the state of these arguments, and make it absolutely necessary that they should be either newly modified or entirely rejected.

In the first book of Political Justice, chap. iii. entitled: 'The Spirit of Political Institutions', Mr. Godwin observes, that: 'Two of the greatest abuses relative to the interior policy of nations which at this time prevail in the world, consist in the irregular transfer of property, either first by violence, or secondly by fraud.' And he goes on to say that if there existed no desire in individuals to possess themselves of the substance of others, and if every man could, with perfect facility, obtain the necessaries of life, civil society might become what poetry has feigned of the golden age. Let us inquire, he says, into the principles to which these evils are indebted for existence. After acknowledging the truth of the principal argument in the essay on population, I do not think he could stop in this inquiry at mere human institutions. Many other parts of his work would be affected by this consideration in a similar manner.

As Mr. Godwin seems disposed to understand, and candidly to admit the

---

[1] Reply to the attacks of Dr. Parr, Mr. Mackintosh, the author of an Essay on Population, and others, p. 10.

truth of the principal argument in the essay, I feel the more mortified that he should think it a fair inference from my positions, that the political superintendents of a community are bound to exercise a paternal vigilance and care over the two great means of advantage and safety to mankind, misery and vice; and that no evil is more to be dreaded than that we should have too little of them in the world, to confine the principle of population within its proper sphere.[2] I am at a loss to conceive what class of evils Mr. Godwin imagines is yet behind, which these salutary checks are to prevent. For my own part, I know of no stronger or more general terms than vice and misery; and the sole question is respecting a greater or less degree of them.[3] The only reason why I object to Mr. Godwin's system is my full conviction that an attempt to execute it would very greatly increase the quantity of vice and misery in society. If Mr. Godwin will undo this conviction and prove to me, though it be only in theory, provided that theory be consistent, and founded on a knowledge of human nature, that his system will really tend to drive vice and misery from the earth, he may depend upon having me one of its steadiest and warmest advocates.

Mr. Godwin observes that he should naturally be disposed to pronounce that man strangely indifferent to schemes of extraordinary improvement in society, who made it a conclusive argument against them that, when they were realized, they might peradventure be of no permanence and duration. And yet what is morality, individual or political, according to Mr. Godwin's own definition of it, but a calculation of consequences? Is the physician the patron of pain, who advises his patient to bear a present evil, rather than betake himself to a remedy which, though it might give momentary relief, would afterwards greatly aggravate all the symptoms? Is the moralist to be called an enemy to pleasure, because he recommends to a young man just entering into life, not to ruin his health and patrimony in a few years, by an excess of present gratifications, but to economize his enjoyments, that he may spread them over a longer period? Of Mr. Godwin's system, according to the present arguments by which it is supported, it is not enough to say, *peradventure* it will be of no permanence; but we can pronounce with *certainty* that it will be of no permanence: and under such circumstances an attempt to execute it would unquestionably be a great political immorality.

Mr. Godwin observes, that after recovering from the first impression made by the Essay on Population, the first thing that is apt to strike every reflecting

---

[2] Reply, &c. p. 60.
[3] [In 1806 (Vol. II, p. 124) this sentence was amended:
   For my own part, I know of no greater evils than vice and misery; and the sole question is respecting the most effectual mode of diminishing them.

mind, is that the excess of power in the principle of population over the principle of subsistence has never, in any past instance, in any quarter or age of the world, produced those great and astonishing effects, that total breaking-up of all the structures and maxims of society, which the essay lead us to expect from it in certain cases in future.[4] This is undoubtedly true; and the reason is that in no past instance, nor in any quarter or age of the world, has an attempt been made to establish such a system as Mr. Godwin's, and without an attempt of this nature, none of these great effects will follow. The convulsions of the social system, described in the last chapter, appeared by a kind of irresistible necessity to terminate in the establishment of the laws of property and marriage; but in countries where these laws are already established, as they are in all the common constitutions of society with which we are acquainted, the operation of the principle of population will always be silent and gradual, and not different to what we daily see in our own country. Other persons besides Mr. Godwin have imagined that I looked to certain periods in the future, when population would exceed the means of subsistence in a much greater degree that at present, and that the evils arising from the principle of population were rather in contemplation than in existence; but this is a total misconception of the argument.[5] Poverty, and not absolute famine, is the specific effect of the principle of population, as I have before endeavoured to show. Many countries are now suffering all the evils that can ever be expected to flow from this principle, and even if we were arrived at the absolute limit to all further increase of produce, a point which we shall certainly never reach, I should by no means expect that these evils would be in any marked manner aggravated. The increase of produce in most European countries is so very slow, compared with what would be required to support an unrestricted increase of people, that the checks which are constantly in action to repress the population to the level of a produce increasing so slowly would have very little more to do in wearing it down to a produce absolutely stationary.

But Mr. Godwin says, that if he looks into the past history of the world, he does not see that increasing population has been controlled and confined by vice and misery alone. In this observation I cannot agree with him. I will thank Mr. Godwin to name to me any check which in past ages has contributed to keep down the population to the level of the means of subsistence, that does not fairly come under some form of vice or misery; except indeed the check of moral restraint, which I have mentioned in the course of this work; and which, to say the truth, whatever hopes we may

---

[4] Reply, p. 70.   [5] In other parts of his Reply, Mr. Godwin does not fall into this error.

entertain of its prevalence in future, has undoubtedly in past ages operated with very inconsiderable force.[6]

I do not think that I should find it difficult to justify myself in the eyes of my readers from the imputation of being the patron of vice and misery; but I am not clear that Mr. Godwin would find such a justification so easy. For though he has positively declared that he does not 'regard them with complacency', and 'hopes that it may not be considered as a taste absolutely singular in him that he should entertain no vehement partialities for vice and misery';[7] yet he has certainly exposed himself to the suspicion of having this singular taste, by suggesting the organization of a very large portion of them for the benefit of society in general. On this subject I need only observe that I have always ranked the two checks[8] which he first mentions among the worst forms of vice and misery.

In one part of his Reply, Mr. Godwin makes a supposition respecting the number of children that might be allowed to each prolific marriage; but as he has not entered into the detail of the mode by which a greater number might be prevented, I shall not notice it further than merely to observe that, although he professes to acknowledge the geometrical and arithmetical ratios of population and food, yet in this place he appears to think that, practically applied, these different ratios of increase are not of a nature to make the evil resulting from them urgent, or alarmingly to confine the natural progress of population.[9] This observation seems to contradict his former acknowledgment.

The last check which Mr. Godwin mentions, and which, I am persuaded,

---

[6] [In 1806 (Vol. II, p. 128) Malthus added a footnote here:

It should be recollected always, that by moral restraint I mean a restraint from marriage from prudential motives, which is not followed by irregular gratifications. In this sense, I am inclined to believe that the expression I have here used is not too strong.

[7] Reply, p. 76.

[8] Mr. Godwin does not acknowledge the justice of Hume's observation respecting infanticide; and yet the extreme population and poverty in China, where this custom prevails, tends strongly to confirm the observation. It is still, however, true, as Mr. Godwin observes, that the expedient is, in its own nature, adequate to the end for which it was cited (p. 66.); but, to make it so in fact, it must be done by the magistrate, and not left to the parents. The almost invariable tendency of this custom to increase population, when it depends entirely on the parents, shews the extreme pain which they must feel, in making such a sacrifice, even when the distress arising from excessive poverty may be supposed to have deadened in great measure their sensibility. What must this pain be then, upon the supposition of the interference of a magistrate or of a positive law, to make parents destroy a child, which they feel the desire, and think they possess the power, of supporting? The permission of infanticide is bad enough, and cannot but have a bad effect on the moral sensibility of a nation; but, I cannot conceive anything much more detestable, or shocking to the feelings, than any direct regulation of this kind, although sanctioned by the names of Plato and Aristotle.

[9] Reply, p. 70.

is the only one which he would seriously recommend, is, 'that sentiment, whether virtue, prudence, or pride, which continually restrains the universality and frequent repetition of the marriage contract'.[10] On this sentiment, which I have already noticed under the name of moral restraint, and of the more comprehensive title, the preventive check, it will appear that in the sequel of this work I shall lay considerable stress.[11] Of this check therefore itself, I entirely approve; but I do not think that Mr. Godwin's system of political justice is by any means favourable to its prevalence. The tendency to early marriages is so strong that we want every possible help that we can get to counteract it; and a system which in any way whatever tends to weaken the foundation of private property, and to lessen in any degree the full advantage and superiority which each individual may derive from his prudence, must remove the only counteracting weight to the passion of love that can be depended upon for any essential effect. Mr. Godwin acknowledges that in his system 'the ill consequences of a numerous family will not come so coarsely home to each man's individual interest as they do at present'.[12] But I am sorry to say that, from what we know hitherto of the human character, we can have no rational hopes of success, without this coarse application to individual interest which Mr. Godwin rejects. If the whole effect were to depend merely on a sense of duty, considering the powerful antagonist that is to be contended with in the present case, I confess that I should absolutely despair. At the same time, I am strongly of opinion that a sense of duty, superadded to a sense of interest, would by no means be without its effect. There are many noble and disinterested spirits who, though aware of the inconveniences which they may bring upon themselves by the indulgence of an early and virtuous passion, feel a kind of repugnance to listen to the dictates of mere worldly prudence, and a pride in rejecting these low considerations. There is a kind of romantic gallantry in sacrificing all for love, naturally fascinating to a young mind; and to say the truth, if all is to be sacrificed, I do not know in what better cause it can be done. But if a strong sense of duty could, in these instances, be added to prudential suggestions, the whole question might wear a different colour. In delaying the gratification of passion from a sense of duty, the most disinterested spirit, the most delicate honour, might be satisfied. The romantic pride might take a different direction, and the dictates of worldly prudence might be followed with the cheerful consciousness of making a virtuous sacrifice.

---

[10] Reply, p. 72.
[11] [In 1806 (Vol. II, p. 131) this sentence was altered:
    On this sentiment, which I have already noticed, it will appear that in the sequel of this work I shall lay considerable stress.
[12] Reply, p. 74.

If we were to remove or weaken the motive of interest, which would be the case in Mr. Godwin's system, I fear we should have but a weak substitute in a sense of duty. But if to the present beneficial effects, known to result from a sense of interest, we could superadd a sense of duty, which is the object of the latter part of this work, it does not seem absolutely hopeless that some partial improvement in society should result from it.

CHAPTER III(b)

Of Systems of Equality (continued)[1]

It was suggested to me some years since by persons for whose judgment I have a high respect, that it might be advisable, in a new edition, to throw out the matter relative to systems of equality, to Wallace, Condorcet and Godwin, as having in a considerable degree lost its interest, and as not being strictly connected with the main subject of the Essay, which is an explanation and illustration of the theory of population. But independently of its being natural for me to have some little partiality for that part of the work which led to those inquiries on which the main subject rests; I really think that there should be somewhere on record an answer to systems of equality founded on the principle of population; and perhaps such an answer is as appropriately placed, and is likely to have as much effect, among the illustrations and applications of the principle of population, as in any other situation to which it could be assigned.

The appearances in all human societies, particularly in all those which are the furthest advanced in civilization and improvement, will ever be such as to inspire superficial observers with a belief that a prodigious change for the better might be effected by the introduction of a system of equality and of common property. They see abundance in some quarters, and want in others; and the natural and obvious remedy seems to be an equal division of the produce. They see a prodigious quantity of human exertion wasted upon trivial, useless, and sometimes pernicious objects, which might either be wholly saved or more effectively employed. They see invention after invention in machinery brought forward, which is seemingly calculated, in the most marked manner, to abate the sum of human toil. Yet with these apparent means of giving plenty, leisure and happiness to all, they still see the labours of the great mass of society undiminished, and their condition, if not deteriorated, in no very striking and palpable manner improved.

Under these circumstances, it cannot be a matter of wonder that proposals for systems of equality should be continually reviving. After periods when the subject has undergone a thorough discussion, or when some great experi-

---

[1] [This chapter, in 1817, replaced chapter iii (a) of Book III, which had appeared in 1803, 1806 and 1807.]

ment in improvement has failed, it is likely that the question should lie dormant for a time, and that the opinions of the advocates of equality should be ranked among those errors which had passed away, to be heard of no more. But it is probable that if the world were to last for any number of thousand years, systems of equality would be among those errors, which like the tunes of a barrel organ, to use the illustration of Dugald Stewart,[2] will never cease to return at certain intervals.

I am induced to make these remarks, and to add a little to what I have already said on systems of equality, instead of leaving out the whole discussion, by a tendency to a revival of this kind at the present moment.[3]

A gentleman for whom I have a very sincere respect, Mr. Owen of Lanark, has lately published a work entitled *A New View of Society*, which is intended to prepare the public mind for the introduction of a system involving a community of labour and of goods. It is also generally known that an idea has lately prevailed among some of the lower classes of society, that the land is the people's farm, the rent of which ought to be equally divided among them; and that they have been deprived of the benefits which belong to them from this their natural inheritance, by the injustice and oppression of their stewards, the landlords.

Mr. Owen is, I believe, a man of real benevolence, who has done much good; and every friend to humanity[4] must heartily wish him success in his endeavours to procure an Act of Parliament for limiting the hours of working among the children in the cotton manufactories, and preventing them from being employed at too early an age. He is further entitled to great attention on all subjects relating to education, from the experience and knowledge which he must have gained in an intercourse of many years with two thousand manufacturers, and from the success which is said to have resulted from his modes of management. A theory professed to be founded on such experience is no doubt worthy of much more consideration than one formed in a closet.

The claims to attention possessed by the author of the new doctrines relating to land are certainly very slender; and the doctrines themselves indicate a very great degree of ignorance; but the errors of the labouring classes of society are always entitled to great indulgence and consideration. They are the natural and pardonable results of their liability to be deceived by first appearances, and by the arts of designing men, owing to the nature of

---

[2] Preliminary Dissertation to Supplement to the Encyclopædia Britannica, p. 121.

[3] [In 1826 (Vol. II, p. 40) a footnote was added:
    Written in 1817.

[4] [In 1826 (Vol. II, p. 40) this was changed to:
    ... every friend of humanity.

their situation, and the scanty knowledge which in general falls to their share. And, except in extreme cases, it must always be the wish of those who are better informed, that they should be brought to a sense of the truth, rather by patience and the gradual diffusion of education and knowledge, than by any harsher methods.

After what I have already said on systems of equality in the preceding chapters, I shall not think it necessary to enter into a long and elaborate refutation of these doctrines. I merely mean to give an additional reason for leaving on record an answer to systems of equality, founded on the principle of population, together with a concise restatement of this answer for practical application.

Of the two decisive arguments against such systems, one is the unsuitableness of a state of equality, both according to experience and theory, to the production of those stimulants to exertion which can alone overcome the natural indolence of man, and prompt him to the proper cultivation of the earth and the fabrication of those conveniences and comforts which are necessary to his happiness.

And the other, the inevitable and necessary poverty and misery in which every system of equality must shortly terminate from the acknowledged tendency of the human race to increase faster than the means of subsistence, unless such increase be prevented by means infinitely more cruel than those which result from the laws of private property, and the moral obligations imposed on every man by the commands of God and nature to support his own children.

The first of these arguments has, I confess, always appeared to my own mind sufficiently conclusive. A state, in which an inequality of conditions offers the natural rewards of good conduct, and inspires widely and generally the hopes of rising and the fears of falling in society, is unquestionably the best calculated to develop the energies and faculties of man, and the best suited to the exercise and improvement of human virtue.[5] And history, in every case of equality that has yet occurred, has uniformly borne witness to the depressing and deadening effects which arise from the want of this stimulus. But still perhaps it may be true that neither experience nor theory on this subject is quite so decisive as to preclude all plausible arguments on the other side. It may be said that the instances which history records of systems of equality really carried into execution are so few, and those in societies so little advanced from a state of barbarism, as to afford no fair conclusions relative to periods of great civilization and improvement; that in

---

[5] See this subject very ably treated in a work on the Records of the Creation, and the Moral Attributes of the Creator, by the Rev. John Bird Sumner, not long since published; a work of very great merit, which I hope soon to see in as extensive circulation as it deserves.

other instances in ancient times, where approaches were made toward a tolerable equality of conditions, examples of considerable energy of character in some lines of exertion are not unfrequent; and that in modern times some societies, particularly of Moravians,[6] are known to have had much of their property in common without occasioning the destruction of their industry. It may be said that, allowing the stimulus of inequality of conditions to have been necessary, in order to raise man from the indolence and apathy of the savage to the activity and intelligence of civilized life, it does not follow that the continuance of the same stimulus should be necessary when this activity and energy of mind has been once gained. It may *then* be allowable quietly to enjoy the benefit of a regimen which, like many other stimulants, having produced its proper effect at a certain point must be left off, or exhaustion, disease and death will follow.

These observations are certainly not of a nature to produce conviction in those who have studied the human character; but they are to a certain degree plausible, and do not admit of so definite and decisive an answer as to make the proposal for an experiment in modern times utterly absurd and unreasonable.

The peculiar advantage of the other argument against systems of equality, that which is founded on the principle of population, is, that it is not only still more generally and uniformly confirmed by experience, in every age and in every part of the world, but it is so pre-eminently clear in theory, that no tolerably plausible answer can be given to it; and consequently no decent pretence can be brought forward for an experiment. The affair is a matter of the most simple calculation applied to the known properties of land, and the proportion of births to deaths which takes place in almost every country village. There are many parishes in England, where, notwithstanding the actual difficulties attending the support of a family which must *necessarily* occur in every well-peopled country, and making no allowances for omissions in the registers, the births are to the deaths in the proportion of 2 to 1. This proportion, with the usual rate of mortality in country places, of about 1 in 50, would continue doubling the population in 41 years, if there were no emigrations from the parish. But in any system of equality, either such as that proposed by Mr. Owen, or in parochial partnerships in land, not only would there be no means of emigration to other parishes with any prospect of relief, but the rate of increase at first would of course be much greater than in the present state of society. What then, I would ask, is to prevent the division

---

[6] [Moravia is the English name for part of Bohemia (in the Austro-Hungarian Empire in Malthus's time) whence a Protestant episcopal sect spread to Germany, England and North America, as the result of renewed persecution in the early eighteenth century. Malthus would have known of them as outstandingly successful settlers in the United States.]

of the produce of the soil to each individual from becoming every year less and less, till the whole society and every individual member of it are pressed down by want and misery?[7]

This is a very simple and intelligible question. And surely no man ought to propose or support a system of equality, who is not able to give a rational answer to it, at least in theory. But even in theory, I have never yet heard any thing approaching to a rational answer to it.

It is a very superficial observation which has sometimes been made, that it is a contradiction to lay great stress upon the efficacy of moral restraint in an improved and improving state of society, according to the present structure of it, and yet to suppose that it would not act with sufficient force in a system of equality, which almost always presupposes a great diffusion of information and a great improvement of the human mind. Those who have made this observation do not see that the encouragement and motive to moral restraint are at once destroyed in a system of equality and community of goods.

Let us suppose that in a system of equality, in spite of the best exertions to procure more food, the population is pressing hard against the limits of subsistence, and all are becoming very poor. It is evidently necessary under these circumstances, in order to prevent the society from starving, that the rate at which the population increases should be retarded. But who are the persons that are to exercise the restraint thus called for, and either to marry late or not at all? It does not seem to be a necessary consequence of a system of equality that all the human passions should be at once extinguished by it; but if not, those who might wish to marry would feel it hard that they should be among the number forced to restrain their inclinations. As all would be equal, and in similar circumstances, there would be no reason whatever why one individual should think himself obliged to practise the duty of restraint more than another. The thing however must be done, with any hope of avoiding universal misery; and in a state of equality, the necessary restraint could only be effected by some general law. But how is this law to be

---

[7] In the Spencean system, as published by the secretary of the Society of Spencean Philanthropists, it unfortunately happens that after the *proposed allowances* have been made for the expenses of the government, and of the other bodies in the state which are intended to be supported, there would be absolutely no remainder; and the people would not derive a single sixpence from their estate, even at first, and on the supposition of the national debt being entirely abolished, without the slightest compensation to the national creditors.

The annual rent of the land, houses, mines and fisheries, is estimated at 150 millions, about three times its real amount; yet, even upon this extravagant estimate, it is calculated that the division would only come to about four pounds a head, not more than is sometimes given to individuals from the poor's rates; a miserable provision! and yet constantly diminishing. [See SPENCE, THOMAS, in the Alphabetical List.]

supported, and how are the violations of it to be punished? Is the man who marries early to be pointed at with the finger of scorn? is he to be whipped at the cart's tail? is he to be confined for years in a prison? is he to have his children exposed? Are not all direct punishments for an offence of this kind shocking and unnatural to the last degree? And yet, if it be absolutely necessary, in order to prevent the most overwhelming wretchedness, that there should be some restraint on the tendency to early marriages, when the resources of the country are only sufficient to support a slow rate of increase, can the most fertile imagination conceive one at once so natural, so just, so consonant to the laws of God and to the best laws framed by the most enlightened men, as that each individual should be responsible for the maintenance of his own children; that is, that he should be subjected to the natural inconveniences and difficulties arising from the indulgence of his inclinations, and to no other whatever?

That this natural check to early marriages arising from a view of the difficulty attending the support of a large family operates very widely throughout all classes of society in every civilized state, and may be expected to be still more effective, as the lower classes of people continue to improve in knowledge and prudence, cannot admit of the slightest doubt. But the operation of this natural check depends exclusively upon the existence of the laws of property, and succession; and in a state of equality and community of property could only be replaced by some artificial regulation of a very different stamp, and a much more unnatural character. Of this Mr. Owen is fully sensible, and has in consequence taxed his ingenuity to the utmost to invent some mode by which the difficulties arising from the progress of population could be got rid of, in the state of society to which he looks forward. His absolute inability to suggest any mode of accomplishing this object that is not unnatural, immoral,[8] or cruel in a high degree, together with the same want of success in every other person, ancient[9] or modern, who has made a similar attempt, seem to shew that the argument against systems of equality founded on the principle of population does not admit of a plausible answer, even in theory. The fact of the tendency of population to increase beyond the means of subsistence may be seen in almost every register of a country parish in the kingdom. The unavoidable effect of this tendency to depress the whole body of the people in want and misery, unless

---

[8] [In the Everyman edition of the Essay on Population (Vol. II, p. 29) the word *immoral* has been omitted here.]

[9] The reader has already seen in ch. xiii bk. i. the detestable means of checking population proposed by some ancient lawgivers in order to support their systems of equality. [This is the chapter about Greece.]

the progress of the population be somehow or other retarded, is equally obvious; and the impossibility of checking the rate of increase in a state of equality, without resorting to regulations that are unnatural, immoral or cruel, forms an argument at once conclusive against every such system.

CHAPTER IV

Of Emigration

Although the resource of emigration seems to be excluded from such a society as Mr. Godwin has imagined;[1] yet in that partial degree of improvement which alone can rationally be expected, it may fairly enter into our consideration. And as it is not probable that human industry should begin to receive its best direction throughout all the nations of the earth at the same time, it may be said that, in the case of a redundant population in the more cultivated parts of the world, the natural and obvious remedy that presents itself is emigration to those parts that are uncultivated. As these parts are of great extent and very thinly peopled, this resource might appear, on a first view of the subject, an adequate remedy, or at least of a nature to remove the evil to a distant period: but, when we advert to experience, and to the actual state of the uncivilized parts of the globe, instead of any thing like an adequate remedy, it will appear but a very weak palliative.[2]

In the accounts which we have received of the peopling of new countries, the dangers, difficulties, and hardships that the first settlers have had to struggle with,[3] appear to be even greater than we can well imagine that they could be exposed to in their parent state. The endeavour to avoid that degree of unhappiness arising from the difficulty of supporting a family might long have left the new world of America unpeopled by Europeans, if those more powerful passions, the thirst of gain, the spirit of adventure, and religious enthusiasm, had not directed and animated the enterprize. These passions enabled the first adventurers to triumph over every obstacle; but in many instances in a way to make humanity shudder, and to defeat the true end of emigration. Whatever may be the character of the Spanish inhabitants of

---

[1] [In 1817 (Vol. ii, p. 287) following the substitution of chapter iii(b) for chapter iii(a) on Godwin's *Reply*, this opening was altered:

Although the resource of emigration seems to be excluded from such perfect societies as the advocates of equality generally contemplate, yet in that imperfect state of improvement, which alone can rationally be expected, ...

[2] [In 1806 (Vol. ii, p. 135) this was changed to:

... but a slight palliative.

[3] [In 1806 (Vol. ii, p. 135) this was amended to:

... hardships with which the first settlers have had to struggle, ...

Mexico and Peru at the present moment, we cannot read the accounts of the first conquests of these countries without feeling strongly that the race destroyed was, in moral worth as well as numbers, highly superior[4] to the race of their destroyers.

The parts of America settled by the English, from being thinly peopled, were better adapted to the establishment of new colonies; yet even here the most formidable difficulties presented themselves. In the settlement of Virginia, begun by Sir Walter Raleigh, and established by Lord Delaware, three attempts completely failed. Nearly half of the first colony was destroyed by the savages, and the rest, consumed and worn down by fatigue and famine, deserted the country and returned home in despair. The second colony was cut off to a man, in a manner unknown; but they were supposed to be destroyed by the Indians. The third experienced the same dismal fate; and the remains of the fourth, after it had been reduced by famine and disease, in the course of six months, from 500 to 60 persons, were returning in a famishing and desperate condition to England, when they were met in the mouth of the Chesapeak bay by Lord Delaware, with a squadron loaded with provisions, and every thing for their relief and defence.[5]

The first puritan settlers in New England were few in number. They landed in a bad season, and they were only supported by their private funds. The winter was premature, and terribly cold; the country was covered with wood, and afforded very little for the refreshment of persons sickly with such a voyage, or for the sustenance of an infant people. Nearly half of them perished by the scurvy, by want, and the severity of the climate; yet those who survived were not dispirited by their hardships; but, supported by their energy of character, and the satisfaction of finding themselves out of the reach of the spiritual arm, reduced this savage country by degrees to yield them a comfortable subsistence.[6]

Even the plantation of Barbadoes, which increased afterwards with such extraordinary rapidity, had at first to contend with a country utterly desolate, an extreme want of provisions, a difficulty in clearing the ground unusually great from the uncommon size and hardness of the trees, a most disheartening scantiness and poverty in their first crops, and a slow and precarious supply of provisions from England.[7]

The attempt of the French, in 1663, to form at once a powerful colony in Guiana, was attended with the most disastrous consequences. Twelve thousand men were landed in the rainy season, and placed under tents and miserable sheds. In this situation, inactive, weary of existence, and in want of

---

[4] [In 1806 (Vol. II, p. 135) the word *highly* was omitted.]
[5] Burke's America, vol. ii. p. 219. Robertson, b. ix. p. 83, 86.
[6] Id. vol. ii. p. 144.   [7] Id. p. 85.

all necessaries, exposed to contagious distempers, which are always occasioned by bad provisions, and to all the irregularities which idleness produces among the lower classes of society, almost the whole of them ended their lives in all the horrors of despair. The attempt was completely abortive. Two thousand men, whose robust constitutions had enabled them to resist the inclemency of the climate, and the miseries to which they had been exposed, were brought back to France; and the 25 000 000 of livres which had been expended in the expedition were totally lost.[8]

In the last settlement at Port Jackson, in New Holland, a melancholy and affecting picture is drawn by Collins of the extreme hardships with which, for some years, the infant colony had to struggle before the produce was equal to its support. These distresses were undoubtedly aggravated by the character of the settlers; but those which were caused by the unhealthiness of a newly-cleared country, the failure of first crops, and the uncertainty of supplies from so distant a mother country, were of themselves sufficiently disheartening to place in a strong point of view the necessity of great resources, as well as unconquerable perseverance, in the colonization of savage countries.

The establishment of colonies in the more thinly peopled regions of Europe and Asia would evidently require still greater resources. From the power and warlike character of the inhabitants of these countries, a considerable military force would be necessary to prevent their utter and immediate destruction. Even the frontier provinces of the most powerful states are defended with considerable difficulty from such restless neighbours; and the peaceful labours of the cultivator are continually interrupted by their predatory incursions. The late Empress Catharine of Russia found it necessary to protect, by regular fortresses, the colonies which she had established in the districts near the Wolga; and the calamities which her subjects suffered by the incursions of the Crim Tartars furnished a pretext, and perhaps a just one, for taking possession of the whole of the Crimea, and expelling the greatest part of these turbulent neighbours, and reducing the rest to a more tranquil mode of life.

The difficulties attending a first establishment, from soil, climate, and the want of proper conveniences, are of course nearly the same in these regions as in America. Mr. Eton, in his account of the Turkish Empire, says that 75 000 Christians were obliged by Russia to emigrate from the Crimea, and sent to inhabit the country abandoned by the Nogai Tartars; but the winter coming on before the houses built for them were ready, a great part of them had no other shelter from the cold, than what was afforded them by holes dug in the

---

[8] Raynal, Hist. des Indes, tom. vii. liv. xiii. p. 43. 10 vols 8vo. 1795. [In 1807 (Vol. II, p. 62) this figure was corrected to 26 000 000.]

ground, covered with what they could procure, and the greatest part of them perished. Only seven thousand remained a few years afterwards. Another colony from Italy to the banks of the Borysthenes had, he says, no better fate, owing to the bad management of those who were commissioned to provide for them.[9]

It is needless to add to these instances, as the accounts given of the difficulties experienced in new settlements are all nearly similar. It has been justly observed, by a correspondent of Dr. Franklin,[10] that one of the reasons why we have seen so many fruitless attempts to settle colonies at an immense public and private expense, by several of the powers of Europe is, that the moral and mechanical habits adapted to the mother country are frequently not so to the new-settled one, and to external events, many of which are unforeseen; and that it is to be remarked that none of the English colonies became any way considerable, till the necessary manners were born and grew up in the country. Pallas particularly notices the want of proper habits in the colonies established by Russia as one of the causes why they did not increase so fast as might have been expected.

In addition to this, it may be observed that the first establishment of a new colony generally presents an instance of a country peopled considerably beyond its actual produce; and the natural consequence seems to be that this population, if not amply supplied by the mother country, should at the commencement be diminished to the level of the first scanty productions, and not begin permanently to increase till the remaining numbers had so far cultivated the soil as to make it yield a quantity of food more than sufficient for their own support; and which consequently they could divide with a family. The frequent failures in the establishment of new colonies tend strongly to show the order of precedence between food and population.

It must be acknowledged, then, that the class of people on whom the distress arising from a too rapidly increasing population would principally fall could not possibly begin a new colony in a distant country. From the nature of their situation, they must necessarily be deficient in those resources which alone could ensure success: and unless they could find leaders among the higher classes, urged by the spirit of avarice or enterprize; or of religious or political discontent; or were furnished with means and support by government; whatever degree of misery they might suffer in their own country from the scarcity of subsistence, they would be absolutely unable to take possession of any of those uncultivated regions, of which there is yet such an extent on the earth.[11]

---

[9] [The reference to Eton's work is given under his name in the Alphabetical List.]
[10] [See FRANKLIN in the Alphabetical List.]
[11] [In 1806 (Vol. II, p. 142) the word *yet* was omitted.]

When new colonies have been once securely established, the difficulty of emigration is indeed very considerably diminished; yet, even then, some resources are necessary to provide vessels for the voyage, and support and assistance till the emigrants can settle themselves, and find employment in their adopted country. How far it is incumbent upon a government to furnish these resources may be a question; but whatever be its duty in this particular, perhaps it is too much to expect that, except where any particular colonial advantages are proposed, emigration should be actively assisted.

The necessary resources for transport and maintenance are, however, frequently furnished by individuals or private companies. For many years before the American war, and for some few since, the facilities of emigration to this new world, and the probable advantages in view, were unusually great; and it must be considered undoubtedly as a very happy circumstance for any country to have so comfortable an asylum for its redundant population. But I would ask whether, even during these periods, the distress among the common people in this country was little or nothing, and whether every man felt secure before he ventured on marriage that, however large his family might be, he should find no difficulty in supporting it without parish assistance? The answer, I fear, could not be in the affirmative.

It will be said that, when an opportunity of advantageous emigration is offered, it is the fault of the people themselves if, instead of accepting it, they prefer a life of celibacy or extreme poverty in their own country. Is it then a fault for a man to feel an attachment to his native soil, to love the parents that nurtured him, his kindred, his friends, and the companions of his early years? Or is it no evil that he suffers, because he consents to bear it, rather than snap these cords which nature has wound in close and intricate folds round the human heart? The great plan of providence seems to require, indeed, that that these ties should sometimes be broken; but the separation does not, on that account, give less pain; and though the general good may be promoted by it, it does not cease to be an individual evil. Besides, doubts and uncertainty must ever attend all distant emigrations, particularly in the apprehensions of the lower classes of people. They cannot feel quite secure that the representations made to them of the high price of labour, or the cheapness of land, are accurately true. They are placing themselves in the power of the persons who are to furnish them with the means of transport and maintenance, who may perhaps have an interest in deceiving them; and the sea which they are to pass appears to them like the separation of death from all their former connexions, and in a manner to preclude the possibility of return in case of failure, as they cannot expect the offer of the same means to bring them back. We cannot be surprised

344

then, that, except where a spirit of enterprise is added to the uneasiness of poverty, the consideration of these circumstances should frequently

> Make them rather bear the ills they suffer,
> Than fly to others which they know not of.[12]

If a tract of rich land as large as this island were suddenly annexed to it, and sold in small lots, or let out in small farms, the case would be very different, and the amelioration of the state of the common people would be sudden and striking; though the rich would be continually complaining of the high price of labour, the pride of the lower classes, and the difficulty of getting work done. These, I understand, are not unfrequent complaints among the men of property in America.

Every resource, however, from emigration, if used effectually, as this would be, must be of short duration. There is scarcely a state in Europe, except perhaps Russia, the inhabitants of which do not often endeavour to better their condition by removing to other countries. As these states therefore have nearly all rather a redundant than deficient population, in proportion to their produce, they cannot be supposed to afford any effectual resources of emigration to each other. Let us suppose for a moment that, in this more enlightened part of the globe, the internal economy of each state were so admirably regulated that no checks existed to population, and the different governments provided every facility for emigration. Taking the population of Europe, excluding Russia, at a hundred millions, and allowing a greater increase of produce than is probable, or even possible, in the mother countries, the redundancy of parent stock in a single century would be eleven hundred millions, which, added to the natural increase of the colonies during the same time, would be more than double what has been supposed to be the present population of the whole earth.

Can we imagine that in the uncultivated parts of Asia, Africa, or America, the greatest exertions and the best directed endeavours could, in so short a period, prepare a quantity of land sufficient for the support of such a population? If any sanguine person should feel a doubt upon the subject, let him only add 25 or 50 years more, and every doubt must be crushed in overwhelming conviction.

It is evident, therefore, that the reason why the resource of emigration has so long continued to be held out as a remedy to redundant population is because, from the natural unwillingness of people to desert their native country, and the difficulty of clearing and cultivating fresh soil, it never is or can be adequately adopted. If this remedy were indeed really effectual, and had power so far to relieve the disorders of vice and misery in old states, as to

---

[12] [See SHAKESPEARE (3) in the Alphabetical List.]

place them in the condition of the most prosperous new colonies, we should soon see the phial exhausted, and when the disorders returned with increased virulence, every hope from this quarter would be for ever closed.

It is clear, therefore, that with any view of making room for an unrestricted increase of population, emigration is perfectly inadequate; but as a partial and temporary expedient, and with a view to the more general cultivation of the earth, and the wider spread of civilization, it seems to be both useful and proper; and if it cannot be proved that governments are bound actively to encourage it, it is not only strikingly unjust, but in the highest degree impolitic in them to prevent it. There are no fears so totally ill-grounded as the fears of depopulation from emigration. The *vis inertiæ* of people in general,[13] and their attachment to their homes, are qualities so strong and general, that we may rest assured that they will not emigrate unless, from political discontents or extreme poverty, they are in such a state as will make it as much for the advantage of their country as of themselves that they should go out of it. The complaints of high wages in consequence of emigrations are of all others the most unreasonable, and ought the least to be attended to. If the wages of labour in any country be such as to enable the lower classes of people to live with tolerable comfort, we may be quite certain that they will not emigrate; and if they be not such, it is cruelty and injustice to detain them.

[In 1817 (Vol. ii, pp. 303–5) the following long paragraph was added:

In all countries the progress of wealth must depend mainly upon the industry, skill and success of individuals, and upon the state and demands of other countries. Consequently, in all countries, great variations may take place at different times in the rate at which wealth increases, and in the demand for labour. But though the progress of population is mainly regulated by the effective demand for labour, it is obvious that the number of people cannot conform itself immediately to the state of this demand. Some time is required to bring more labour into the market when it is wanted; and some time to check the supply when it is flowing in with too great rapidity. If these variations amount to no more than that natural sort of oscillation noticed in an early part of this work, which seems almost always to accompany the progress of population and food, they should be submitted to as a part of the usual course of things. But circumstances may occasionally give them great force, and then, during the period that the supply of labour is increasing faster than the demand, the labouring classes are subject to the most severe distress. If, for instance, from a combination of external and internal causes, a very great stimulus should be given to the population of a country for ten or twelve years together, and it should then comparatively cease, it is clear that labour will continue flowing into the market, with

---

[13] [In 1817 (Vol. ii, p. 303) *people in general* was changed to:
     ... the great body of the people, ...

almost undiminished rapidity, while the means of employing and paying it have been essentially contracted. It is precisely under these circumstances that emigration is most useful as a temporary relief; and it is in these circumstances that Great Britain finds herself placed at present.[14] Though no emigration should take place, the population will by degrees conform itself to the state of the demand for labour; but the interval must be marked by the most severe distress, the amount of which can scarcely be reduced by any human efforts; because, though it may be mitigated at particular periods, and as it affects particular classes, it will be proportionably extended over a larger space of time and a greater number of people. The only real relief in such a case is emigration; and the subject at the present moment is well worthy the attention of the government, both as a matter of humanity and policy.

---

[14] 1816 and 1817.

CHAPTER V

Of the English Poor Laws[1]

To remedy the frequent distresses of the poor, laws to enforce their relief have been instituted; and in the establishment of a general system of this kind, England has particularly distinguished herself. But it is to be feared that, though it may have alleviated a little the intensity of individual misfortune, it has spread the evil over a much larger surface.

It is a subject often started in conversation, and mentioned always as a matter of great surprise, that, notwithstanding the immense sum which is annually collected for the poor in this country, there is still so much distress among them. Some think that the money must be embezzled for private use; others, that the churchwardens and overseers consume the greatest part of it in feasting. All agree that somehow or other it must be very ill managed. In short the fact that, even before the late scarcities, three millions were collected annually for the poor, and yet that their distresses were not removed, is the subject of continual astonishment. But a man who looks a little below the surface of things would be much more astonished if the fact were otherwise than it is observed to be; or even if a collection universally of eighteen shillings in the pound, instead of four, were materially to alter it.

Suppose, that by a subscription of the rich, the eighteen-pence or two shillings, which men earn now, were made up to five shillings; it might be imagined, perhaps, that they would then be able to live comfortably, and have a piece of meat every day for their dinner. But this would be a very false conclusion. The transfer of three additional shillings a day to each labourer would not increase the quantity of meat in the country. There is not at present enough for all to have a moderate share. What would then be the consequence? The competition among the buyers in the market of meat

---

[1] [In 1806 this chapter became simply 'Of Poor Laws'. The first eight paragraphs are based on pp. 74–82 of the 1798 *Essay*. The English Poor Laws dated from the 43rd year of the reign of Elizabeth I (1601) and did not apply to Scotland, which was then a separate kingdom; in that year parliament made permanent and compulsory certain practices which had developed gradually in different parts of the country during the previous three decades. The unit of civil administration was the ecclesiastical parish, of which there were some 15 000. Each parish was obliged to appoint Overseers of the Poor, who were to levy a rate to support the helpless and to provide work for the unemployed.]

would rapidly raise the price from eight-pence or nine-pence to two or three shillings in the pound, and the commodity would not be divided among many more than it is at present. When an article is scarce, and cannot be distributed to all, he that can show the most valid patent, that is, he that offers the most money, becomes the possessor. If we can suppose the competition among the buyers of meat to continue long enough for a greater number of cattle to be reared annually, this could only be done at the expense of the corn, which would be a very disadvantageous exchange; for it is well known that the country could not then support the same population; and when subsistence is scarce in proportion to the number of people, it is of little consequence whether the lowest members of the society possess two shillings or five. They must, at all events, be reduced to live upon the hardest fare and in the smallest quantity.

It might be said, perhaps, that the increased number of purchasers in every article would give a spur to productive industry, and that the whole produce of the island would be increased. But the spur that these fancied riches would give to population would more than counterbalance it; and the increased produce would be to be divided among a more than proportionably increased number of people.

A collection from the rich, of eighteen shillings in the pound, even if distributed in the most judicious manner, would have an effect similar to that resulting from the supposition which I have just made; and no possible sacrifices of the rich, particularly in money, could for any time prevent the recurrence of distress among the lower members of society, whoever they were. Great changes might indeed be made. The rich might become poor, and some of the poor rich; but while the present proportion between population and food continues, a part of society must necessarily find it difficult to support a family, and this difficulty will naturally fall on the least fortunate members.

It may at first appear strange, but I believe it is true, that I cannot by means of money raise the condition of a poor man, and enable him to live much better than he did before, without proportionably depressing others in the same class. If I retrench the quantity of food consumed in my house, and give him what I have cut off, I then benefit him without depressing any but myself and family, who perhaps may be well able to bear it. If I turn up a piece of uncultivated land, and give him the produce, I then benefit both him and all the members of society, because what he before consumed is thrown into the common stock, and probably some of the new produce with it. But if I only give him money, supposing the produce of the country to remain the same, I give him a title to a larger share of that produce than formerly, which share he cannot receive without diminishing the shares of others. It is evident that this effect in individual instances must be so small as to be totally imperceptible; but still it must exist, as many other effects do, which, like some of the insects that people the air, elude our grosser perceptions.

Supposing the quantity of food in any country to remain the same for many years together, it is evident that this food must be divided according to the value of each man's patent, or the sum of money which he can afford to spend in this commodity so universally in request. It is a demonstrative truth, therefore, that the patents of one set of men could not be increased in value without diminishing the value of the patents of some other set of men. If the rich were to subscribe, and give five shillings a day to five hundred thousand men, without retrenching their own tables, no doubt can exist that as these men would live more at their ease, and consume a greater quantity of provisions, there would be less food remaining to divide among the rest; and consequently, each man's patent would be diminished in value, or the same number of pieces of silver would purchase a smaller quantity of subsistence, and the price of provisions would universally rise.

These general reasonings have been strikingly confirmed during the late scarcities.[2] The supposition which I have made, of a collection from the rich of eighteen shillings in the pound, has been nearly realized; and the effect has been such as might have been expected. If the same distribution had been made when no scarcity existed, a considerable advance in the price of provisions would have been a necessary consequence; but following as it did a scarcity, its effect must have been doubly powerful. No person, I believe, will venture to doubt that, if we were to give three additional shillings a day to every labouring man in the kingdom, as I before supposed, in order that he might have meat for his dinner, the price of meat would rise in the most rapid and unexampled manner. But surely, in a deficiency of corn, which renders it impossible for every man to have his usual share, if we still continue to furnish each person with the means of purchasing the same quantity as before, the effect must be in every respect similar.

It seems, in great measure, to have escaped observation that the price of corn, in a scarcity, will depend much more upon the obstinacy with which the same degree of consumption is persevered in, than on the degree of the actual deficiency. A deficiency of one half of a crop, if the people could immediately consent to consume only one half of what they did before, would produce little or no effect on the price of corn. A deficiency of one twelfth, if exactly the same consumption were to continue for ten or eleven months, might raise the price of corn to almost any height. The more is given in parish assistance, the more power is furnished of persevering in the same

---

[2] [Here Malthus departs from the 1798 *Essay*. In 1817 (Vol. II, p. 311) a footnote was added:
    The scarcities referred to in this chapter were those of 1800 and 1801.

consumption; and, of course, the higher will the price rise before the necessary diminution of consumption is effected.

It has been asserted by some people that high prices do not diminish consumption. If this were really true, we should see the price of a bushel of corn at a hundred pounds or more, in every deficiency which could not be fully and completely remedied by importation. But the fact is that high prices do ultimately diminish consumption; but, on account of the riches of the country, the unwillingness of the people to resort to substitutes, and the immense sums which are distributed by parishes, this object cannot be attained till the prices become excessive, and force even the middle classes of society, or at least those immediately above the poor, to save in the article of bread from the actual inability of purchasing it in the usual quantity. The poor who were assisted by their parishes had no reason whatever to complain of the high price of grain; because it was the excessiveness of this price, and this alone, which, by enforcing such a saving, left a greater quantity of corn for the consumption of the lowest classes, which corn the parish allowances enabled them to command. The greatest sufferers in the scarcity were undoubtedly the classes immediately above the poor; and these were in the most marked manner depressed by the excessive bounties given to those below them. Almost all poverty is relative; and I much doubt whether these people would have been rendered so poor, if a sum equal to half of these bounties had been taken directly out of their pockets, as they were by that new distribution of the money of the society which actually took place.[3] This distribution, by giving to the poorer classes a command of food so much greater than their degree of skill and industry entitled them to,[4] in the actual circumstances of the country, diminished, exactly in the same proportion, that command over the necessaries of life which the classes above them, by their superior skill and industry, would naturally possess; and it may be a question whether the degree of assistance which the poor received, and which

---

[3] Supposing the lower classes to earn on an average ten shillings a week, and the classes just above them, twenty, it is not to be doubted that, in a scarcity, these latter would be more straightened in their power of commanding the necessaries of life, by a donation of ten shillings a week to those below them, than by the subtraction of five shillings a week from their own earnings. In the one case, they would be all reduced to a level; the price of provisions would rise in an extraordinary manner from the greatness of the competition; and all would be straightened for subsistence. In the other case, the classes above the poor would still maintain a considerable part of their relative superiority; the price of provisions would by no means rise in the same degree; and their remaining fifteen shillings would purchase much more than their twenty shillings in the former case.

[4] [In 1806 (Vol. II, p. 157) this was amended to:
  ... so much greater than that to which their degree of skill and industry entitled them ...
[In 1826 (Vol. II, p. 70) this was changed to:
  ... degree of skill and industry entitle them ...

prevented them from resorting to the use of those substitutes which, in every other country on such occasions, the great law of necessity teaches, was not more than overbalanced by the severity of the pressure on so large a body of people from the extreme high prices, and the permanent evil which must result from forcing so many persons on the parish, who before thought themselves almost out of the reach of want.

If we were to double the fortunes of all those who possess above a hundred a year, the effect on the price of grain would be slow and inconsiderable; but if we were to double the price of labour throughout the kingdom, the effect in raising the price of grain would be rapid and great. The general principles on this subject will not admit of dispute; and that in the particular case which we have been considering, the bounties to the poor were of a magnitude to operate very powerfully in this manner will sufficiently appear, if we recollect that before the late scarcities the sum collected for the poor was estimated at three millions, and that during the year 1801 it was said to be ten millions. An additional seven millions acting at the bottom of the scale,[5] and employed exclusively in the purchase of provisions, joined to a considerable advance in the price of wages in many parts of the kingdom, and increased by a prodigious sum expended in voluntary charity, must have had a most powerful effect in raising the price of the necessaries of life, if any reliance can be placed on the clearest general principles, confirmed as much as possible by appearances. A man with a family has received, to my knowledge, fourteen shillings a week from the parish. His common earnings were ten shillings a week, and his weekly revenue, therefore, twenty-four. Before the scarcity, he had been in the habit of purchasing a bushel of flour a week with eight shillings, perhaps, and consequently had two shillings out of his ten to spare for other necessaries. During the scarcity, he was enabled to purchase the same quantity at nearly three times the price. He paid twenty-two shillings for his bushel of flour and had, as before, two shillings remaining for other wants. Such instances could not possibly have been universal without raising the price of wheat very much higher than it really was during any part of the dearth. But similar instances were by no means infrequent, and the system itself, of measuring the relief given by the price of grain, was general.

---

[5] See a small pamphlet published in November 1800, entitled, *An investigation of the cause of the present high price of provisions.* This pamphlet was mistaken by some for an inquiry into the cause of the scarcity, and as such it would naturally appear to be incomplete, adverting, as it does, principally to a single cause. But the sole object of the pamphlet was to give the principal reason for the extreme high price of provisions, in proportion to the degree of the scarcity, admitting the deficiency of one fourth, as stated in the Duke of Portland's letter which, I am much inclined to think, was very near the truth.
[The pamphlet, published anonymously, was by Malthus himself. See PORTLAND in the Alphabetical List.]

If the circulation of the country had consisted entirely of specie, which could not have been immediately increased, it would have been impossible to have given such an additional sum as seven millions to the poor without embarrassing, to a great degree, the operations of commerce.[6] On the commencement, therefore, of this extensive relief, which would necessarily occasion a proportionate expenditure in provisions throughout all the ranks of society, a great demand would be felt for an increased circulating medium. The nature of the medium then principally in use was such that it could be created immediately on demand. From the accounts of the bank of England,[7] as laid before Parliament, it appeared that no very great additional issues of paper took place from this quarter. The three millions and a half added to its former average issues were not probably much above what was sufficient to supply the quantity of specie that had been withdrawn from the circulation. If this supposition be true (and the small quantity of gold which made its appearance at that time, furnishes the strongest reason for believing that as much as this must have been withdrawn) it would follow that the part of the circulation originating in the bank of England, though changed in its nature, had not been increased in its quantity;[8] and with regard to the effect of the circulating medium on the price of all commodities, it cannot be doubted that it would be precisely the same, whether it were made up principally of guineas, or of pound notes and shillings, which would pass current for guineas.

The demand, therefore, for an increased circulating medium was left to be supplied by the country banks,[9] and it could not be expected that they should hesitate in taking advantage of so profitable an opportunity. The paper issues of a country bank are, as I conceive, measured by the quantity of its notes which will remain in circulation; and this quantity is again measured, supposing a confidence to be established, by the sum of what is wanted to carry on all the money transactions of the neighbourhood. From the high price of provisions, all these transactions became more expensive. In the single article of the weekly payment of labourers' wages, including the parish

---

[6] [This and the four subsequent paragraphs follow very closely pp. 23–5 of Malthus's anonymous pamphlet *An Investigation of the Cause of the present High Price of Provisions* (London, 1800). In February 1797, following rumours of a French invasion and a run on gold, the Bank Act was suspended: this meant that the Bank of England was no longer obliged to pay out gold coins, on demand, in exchange for its own notes of the equivalent face value.]

[7] [Not until 1826 (Vol. II, p. 72) did the Bank of England merit a capital B.]

[8] [In 1806 (Vol. II, p. 161) this was modified:
... furnishes the strongest reason for believing that nearly as much as this must have been withdrawn) ... the part of the circulation originating in the bank of England ... had not been much increased in its quantity ...

[9] [In 1806 (Vol. II, p. 161) this was changed to:
... left to be supplied principally by the country banks ...

allowances, it is evident that a very great addition to the circulating medium of the neighbourhood would be wanted.[10] Had the country banks attempted to issue the same quantity of paper without such a particular demand for it, they would quickly have been admonished of their error by its rapid and pressing return upon them; but at this time it was wanted for immediate and daily use, and was therefore eagerly absorbed into the circulation.

It may even admit of a question, whether, under similar circumstances, the country banks would not have issued nearly the same quantity of paper if the bank of England had not been restricted from payment in specie. Before this event, the issues of the country banks in paper were regulated by the quantity which the circulation would take up; and after, as well as before, they were obliged to pay the notes which returned upon them in bank of England circulation. The difference in the two cases would arise principally from the pernicious custom, adopted since the restriction of the bank, of issuing one and two pound notes, and from the little preference that many people might feel, if they could not get gold, between country bank paper and bank of England paper.

The very great issue of country bank paper during the years 1800 and 1801 was evidently, therefore, in its origin, rather a consequence than a cause of the high price of provisions; but being once absorbed into the circulation, it must necessarily affect the price of all commodities, and throw very great obstacles in the way of returning cheapness.[11] This is the great mischief of the system. During the scarcity itself, it is not to be doubted that the increased circulation, by preventing the embarrassments which commerce and specu- lation must otherwise have felt, enabled the country to continue all the branches of its trade with less interruption, and to import a much greater quantity of grain, than it could have done otherwise; but to overbalance these temporary advantages, a lasting evil might be entailed upon the community, and the prices of a time of scarcity might become permanent, from the difficulty of re-absorbing this increased circulation.

In this respect, however, it is much better that the great issue of paper should have come from the country banks, than from the bank of England.

---

[10] A rise of wages or of parish allowances, amounting to any particular sum, would occasion a much greater demand for the current circulating medium than an increase of commercial transactions to the same amount; because, in the first case, it is the common currency alone which can be used; in the latter, much is done by the bills of exchange, &c.; in the first also, much money is actually wanted, in proportion to the amount of the increased payments; in the latter, a little will go a great way. [In 1806 (Vol. II, p. 162) this footnote was omitted.]

[11] It does not appear to me that Mr. Thornton, in his valuable publication on paper credit, has taken sufficient notice of the effects of the great paper issues of the country banks, in raising the price of commodities, and producing an unfavourable state of exchange with foreigners. [In 1806 (Vol. II, p. 163) this footnote was omitted.]

During the restriction of payment in specie, there is no possibility of forcing the bank to retake its notes when too abundant; but with regard to the country banks, as soon as their notes are not wanted in the circulation, they will be returned; and if the bank of England notes be not increased, which they probably will not be,[12] the whole circulating medium will thus be diminished.

We may consider ourselves as peculiarly fortunate that the two years of scarcity were succeeded by two events the best calculated to restore plenty and cheapness – an abundant harvest, and a peace;[13] which, together, produced a general conviction of plenty in the minds both of buyers and sellers; and by rendering the first slow to purchase, and the others eager to sell, occasioned a glut in the market and a consequent rapid fall of price, which has enabled parishes to take off their allowances to the poor, and thus to prevent a return of high prices when the alarm among the sellers was over.

If the two years of scarcity had been succeeded merely by years of average crops, I am strongly disposed to believe that, as no glut would have taken place in the market, the price of grain would have fallen only in an inconsiderable degree, the parish allowances could not have been resumed,[14] the increased quantity of paper would still have been wanted, and the prices of all commodities might by degrees have been regulated permanently according to the increased circulating medium.

If instead of giving the temporary assistance of parish allowances, which might be withdrawn on the first fall of price, we had raised universally the wages of labour, it is evident that the obstacles to a diminution of the circulation, and to returning cheapness, would have been still further increased; and the high price of labour would have become permanent, without any advantage whatever to the labourer.

There is no one that more ardently desires to see a real advance in the price of labour than myself; but the attempt to effect this object by forcibly raising the nominal price, which was practised to a certain degree, and recommended almost universally during the late scarcities, every thinking man must reprobate as puerile and ineffectual.

The price of labour, when left to find its natural level, is a most important political barometer, expressing the relation between the supply of provisions, and the demand for them; between the quantity to be consumed, and the number of consumers; and taken on the average, independently of accidental circumstances, it further expresses clearly the wants of society respecting population; that is, whatever may be the number of children to a marriage

---

12 [In 1806 (Vol. ii, p. 164) this clause, *which they probably will not be*, was excised.]

13 [This was the Peace of Amiens, which lasted from March 1802 until May 1803.]

14 [*Resumed* here means to take back (or take off) something previously given or granted.]

necessary to maintain exactly the present population, the price of labour will be just sufficient to support this number, or be above it, or below it, according to the state of the real funds for the maintenance of labour, whether stationary, progressive, or retrograde. Instead, however, of considering it in this light, we consider it as something which we may raise or depress at pleasure, something which depends principally upon His Majesty's justices of the peace. When an advance in the price of provisions already expresses that the demand is too great for the supply, in order to put the labourer in the same condition as before, we raise the price of labour, that is, we increase the demand, and are then much surprised that the price of provisions continues rising. In this, we act much in the same manner, as if, when the quicksilver in the common weather-glass stood at *stormy*, we were to raise it by some forcible pressure to *settled fair*,[15] and then be greatly astonished that it continued raining.

Dr. Smith has clearly shown that the natural tendency of a year of scarcity is either to throw a number of labourers out of employment, or to oblige them to work for less than they did before, from the inability of masters to employ the same number at the same price. The raising of the price of wages tends necessarily to throw more out of employment, and completely to prevent the good effects which, he says, sometimes arise from a year of moderate scarcity, that of making the lower classes of people do more work, and become more careful and industrious. The number of servants out of place, and of manufacturers wanting employment during the late scarcities, were melancholy proofs of the truth of these reasonings. If a general rise in the wages of labour had taken place proportioned to the price of provisions, none but farmers and a few gentlemen could have afforded to employ the same number of workmen as before. Additional crowds of servants and manufacturers would have been turned off; and those who were thus thrown out of employment would of course have no other refuge than the parish. In the natural order of things, a scarcity must tend to lower, instead of to raise, the price of labour.

After the publication and general circulation of such a work as Dr. Smith's, I confess that it appears to me strange that so many men, who would yet aspire to be thought political economists, should still think that it is in the power of the justices of the peace, or even of the omnipotence of parliament, to alter by a *fiat* the whole circumstances of the country; and when the demand for provisions is greater than the supply, by publishing a particular edict, to make the supply at once equal to or greater than the demand. Many men who would shrink at the proposal of a maximum, would propose

---

[15] [In 1806 (Vol. II, p. 166) this was changed to:
... raise it by some mechanical pressure ...

themselves that the price of labour should be proportioned to the price of provisions, and do not seem to be aware that the two proposals are very nearly of the same nature, and that both tend directly to famine. It matters not whether we enable the labourer to purchase the same quantity of provisions which he did before, by fixing their price, or by raising in proportion the price of labour. The only advantage on the side of raising the price of labour is that the rise in the price of provisions, which necessarily follows it, encourages importation: but putting importation out of the question, which might possibly be prevented by war, or other circumstances, a universal rise of wages in proportion to the price of provisions, aided by adequate parish allowances to those who were thrown out of work, would, by preventing any kind of saving, in the same manner as a maximum, cause the whole crop to be consumed in nine months, which ought to have lasted twelve, and thus produce a famine.

[In 1806 (Vol. II, p. 169) – as he stated in the 'Advertisement to the Third Edition' – Malthus added a passage here:

At the same time we must not forget that both humanity and true policy imperiously require that we should give every assistance to the poor on these occasions that the nature of the case will admit. If provisions were to continue at the price of scarcity, the wages of labour must necessarily rise, or sickness and famine would quickly diminish the number of labourers; and the supply of labour being unequal to the demand, its price would soon rise in a still greater proportion than the price of provisions. But even one or two years of scarcity, if the poor were left entirely to shift for themselves, might produce some effect of this kind, and consequently it is our interest, as well as our duty, to give them temporary aid in such seasons of distress. It is on such occasions that every cheap substitute for bread and every mode of economising food should be resorted to. Nor should we be too ready to complain of that high price of corn, which by encouraging importation increases the supply.

As the inefficacy of poor laws, and of attempts forcibly to raise the price of labour, is most conspicuous in a scarcity, I have thought myself justified in considering them under this view; and as these causes of increased price received great additional force during the late scarcity from the increase of the circulating medium, I trust that the few observations which I have made on this subject, will be considered as an allowable digression.

CHAPTER VI

Subject of Poor Laws continued[1]

Independently of any considerations respecting a year of deficient crops, it is evident that an increase of population, without a proportional increase of food, must lower the value of each man's earnings. The food must necessarily be distributed in smaller quantities, and consequently, a day's labour will purchase a smaller quantity of provisions. An increase in the price of provisions will arise, either from an increase of population faster than the means of subsistence, or from a different distribution of the money of the society. The food of a country which has been long peopled, if it be increasing, increases slowly and regularly, and cannot be made to answer any sudden demands; but variations in the distribution of the money of the society are not unfrequently occurring, and are undoubtedly among the causes which occasion the continual variations in the prices of provisions.

The poor laws of England tend to depress the general condition of the poor in these two ways. Their first obvious tendency is to increase population without increasing the food for its support. A poor man may marry with little or no prospect of being able to support a family without parish assistance. They may be said, therefore, to create the poor which they maintain; and as the provisions of the country must, in consequence of the increased population, be distributed to every man in smaller proportions, it is evident that the labour of those who are not supported by parish assistance will purchase a smaller quantity of provisions than before, and consequently more of them must be driven to apply for assistance.

Secondly, the quantity of provisions consumed in workhouses, upon a part of the society that cannot in general be considered as the most valuable part, diminishes the shares that would otherwise belong to more industrious and more worthy members, and thus, in the same manner, forces more to become dependent. If the poor in the workhouses were to live better than they do now, this new distribution of the money of the society would tend more

---

[1] [In 1817 this chapter became simply 'Of Poor-Laws (continued)'. Here Malthus returns again to the 1798 *Essay* (pp. 82–94) and follows it closely for the first 13 paragraphs of this chapter.]

conspicuously to depress the condition of those out of the workhouses by occasioning an advance in the price of provisions.

Fortunately for England, a spirit of independence still remains among the peasantry. The poor laws are strongly calculated to eradicate this spirit. They have succeeded in part; but had they succeeded as completely as might have been expected, their pernicious tendency would not have been so long concealed.

Hard as it may appear in individual instances, dependent poverty ought to be held disgraceful. Such a stimulus seems to be absolutely necessary to promote the happiness of the great mass of mankind; and every general attempt to weaken this stimulus, however benevolent its apparent intention, will always defeat its own purpose. If men be induced to marry from the mere prospect of parish provision, they are not only unjustly tempted to bring unhappiness and dependence upon themselves and children, but they are tempted, without knowing it, to injure all in the same class with themselves.

The parish laws of England[2] appear to have contributed to raise the price of provisions, and to lower the real price of labour. They have therefore contributed to impoverish that class of people whose only possession is their labour. It is also difficult to suppose that they have not powerfully contributed to generate that carelessness and want of frugality observable among the poor, so contrary to the disposition generally to be remarked among petty tradesmen and small farmers. The labouring poor, to use a vulgar expression, seem always to live from hand to mouth. Their present wants employ their whole attention; and they seldom think of the future. Even when they have an opportunity of saving, they seldom exercise it; but all that they earn beyond their present necessities goes, generally speaking, to the alehouse. The poor laws may, therefore, be said to diminish both the power and the will to save among the common people, and thus to weaken one of the strongest incentives to sobriety and industry, and consequently to happiness.

It is a general complaint among master manufacturers that high wages ruin all their workmen; but it is difficult to conceive that these men would not save a part of their high wages for the future support of their families, instead of spending it in drunkenness and dissipation, if they did not rely on parish assistance for support in case of accidents. And that the poor employed in manufactures consider this assistance as a reason why they may spend all the wages which they earn, and enjoy themselves while they can, appears to be evident from the number of families that, upon the failure of any great manufactory, immediately fall upon the parish; when, perhaps, the wages earned in this manufactory while it flourished were sufficiently above the

---

[2] [In 1807 (Vol. II, p. 97) this was changed to:
The poor laws of England ...

price of common country labour to have allowed them to save enough for their support, till they could find some other channel for their industry.

A man who might not be deterred from going to the alehouse, from the consideration that, on his death or sickness, he should leave his wife and family upon the parish, might yet hesitate in thus dissipating his earnings, if he were assured that in either of these cases his family must starve, or be left to the support of casual bounty.

The mass of happiness among the common people cannot but be diminished, when one of the strongest checks to idleness and dissipation is thus removed; and positive institutions, which render dependent poverty so general, weaken that disgrace which for the best and most humane reasons ought to be attached to it.

The poor laws of England were undoubtedly instituted for the most benevolent purpose; but it is evident that they have failed in attaining it. They certainly mitigate some cases of severe distress which might otherwise occur, though the state of the poor who are supported by parishes, considered in all its circumstances, is very miserable. But one of the principal objections to the system, is, that for the assistance which some of the poor receive, in itself almost a doubtful blessing, the whole class of the common people of England is subjected to a set of grating, inconvenient, and tyrannical laws, totally inconsistent with the genuine spirit of the constitution. The whole business of settlements, even in its present amended state, is contradictory to all ideas of freedom. The parish persecution of men whose families are likely to become chargeable, and of poor women who are near lying-in, is a most disgraceful and disgusting tyranny. And the obstructions continually occasioned in the market of labour, by these laws, have a constant tendency to add to the difficulties of those who are struggling to support themselves without assistance.

These evils attendant on the poor laws seem to be irremediable. If assistance be to be distributed to a certain class of people, a power must be lodged somewhere of discriminating the proper objects, and of managing the concerns of the institutions that are necessary; but any great interference with the affairs of other people is a species of tyranny; and, in the common course of things, the exercise of this power may be expected to become grating to those who are driven to ask for support. The tyranny of justices, churchwardens, and overseers, is a common complaint among the poor;[3] but the fault does not lie so much in these persons who, probably, before they were in power, were not worse than other people, but in the nature of all such institutions.

---

[3] [In 1807 (Vol. II, p. 101) the *justices* were omitted; the sentence began:
The tyranny of churchwardens and overseers is a common complaint ...

It will scarcely admit of a doubt,[4] that if the poor laws had never existed in this country, though there might have been a few more instances of very severe distress, the aggregate mass of happiness among the common people would have been much greater than it is at present.

The radical defect of all systems of the kind is that of tending to increase population, without increasing the means for its support, and by thus depressing the condition of those that are not relieved by parishes, to create more poor.[5] If, indeed, we examine some of our statutes, strictly with reference to the principle of population, we shall find that they attempt an absolute impossibility; and we cannot be surprised, therefore, that they should constantly fail in the attainment of their object.

The famous 43rd of Elizabeth, which has been so often referred to and admired, enacts that the overseers of the poor, 'shall take order from time to time, by and with the consent of two or more justices, for setting to work the children of all such whose parents shall not, by the said persons, be thought able to keep and maintain their children; and also such persons married or unmarried, as, having no means to maintain them, use no ordinary and daily trade of life to get their living by. And also to raise, weekly or otherwise, by taxation of every inhabitant, and every occupier of lands in the said parish, (in such competent sums as they shall think fit,) a convenient stock of flax, hemp, wool, thread, iron, and other necessary ware and stuff, to set the poor to work.'

What is this but saying that the funds for the maintenance of labour in this country may be increased at will, and without limit, by a *fiat* of government or an assessment of the overseers? Strictly speaking, this clause is as arrogant and as absurd as if it had enacted that two ears of wheat should in future grow where one only had grown before. Canute, when he commanded the waves not to wet his princely foot, did not in reality assume a greater power over the laws of nature. No directions are given to the overseers how to increase the funds for the maintenance of labour; the necessity of industry, economy, and enlightened exertion in the management of agricultural and commercial capital is not insisted on for this purpose; but it is expected that a miraculous increase of these funds should immediately follow an edict of the government, used at the discretion of some ignorant parish officers.

If this clause were really and *bona fide* put in execution, and the shame attending the receiving of parish assistance worn off, every labouring man

---

[4] [In 1806 (Vol. ii, p. 177) this was altered to:
  I feel persuaded that ...

[5] [In 1807 (Vol. ii, p. 101) this sentence was re-written:
  The radical defect of all systems of the kind is that of tending to depress the condition of those that are not relieved by parishes, and to create more poor.

might marry as early as he pleased, under the certain prospect of having all his children properly provided for; and as, according to the supposition, there would be no check to population from the consequences of poverty after marriage, the increase of people would be rapid beyond example in old states. After what has been said in the former parts of this work, it is submitted to the reader, whether the utmost exertions of the most enlightened government could, in this case, make the food keep pace with the population, much less a mere arbitrary edict, the tendency of which is certainly rather to diminish than to increase the funds for the maintenance of productive labour.

In the actual circumstances of every country, the principle of population[6] seems to be always ready to exert nearly its full force; but, within the limit of possibility, there is nothing perhaps more improbable, or more out of the power of any government to effect,[7] than the direction of the industry of its subjects in such a manner as to produce the greatest quantity of human sustenance that the earth could bear. It evidently could not be done without the most complete violation of the law of property, from which everything that is valuable to man has hitherto arisen. Such is the disposition to marry, particularly in very young people, that if the difficulties of providing for a family were entirely removed, very few would remain single at twenty-two. But what statesman or rational government could propose that all animal food should be prohibited, that no horses should be used for business or pleasure, that all the people should live upon potatoes, and that the whole industry of the nation should be exerted in the production of them, except what was required for the mere necessaries of clothing and houses. Could such a revolution be effected, would it be desirable? Particularly as in a few years, notwithstanding all these exertions, want, with less resource than ever, would inevitably recur.

After a country has once ceased to be in the peculiar situation of a new colony, we shall always find that, in the actual state of its cultivation, or in that state which may rationally be expected from the most enlightened government, the increase of its food can never allow, for any length of time, an unrestricted increase of population; and therefore the due execution of the clause in the 43rd of Elizabeth, as a permanent law, is a physical impossibility.

It will be said, perhaps, that the fact contradicts the theory, and that the clause in question has remained in force, and has been executed, during the

---

[6] [In 1806 (Vol. II, p. 180) *the principle of population* was altered to:
    ... the prolific power of nature ...

[7] [On the same page, Malthus also changed *out of the power of any government* to:
    ... out of the reach of any government ...

last two hundred years. In answer to this I should say without hesitation that it has not really been executed; and that it is merely owing to its incomplete execution that it remains on our statute book at present.

The scanty relief granted to persons in distress, the capricious and insulting manner in which it is sometimes distributed by the overseers, and the natural and becoming pride not yet quite extinct among the peasantry of England, have deterred the more thinking and virtuous part of them from venturing on marriage, without some better prospect of maintaining their families than mere parish assistance. The desire of bettering our condition and the fear of making it worse, like the *vis medicatrix naturæ* in physic, is the *vis medicatrix reipublicæ* in politics, and is continually counteracting the disorders arising from narrow human institutions. In spite of the prejudices in favour of population, and the direct encouragements to marriage from the poor laws, it operates as a preventive check to increase; and happy for this country is it that it does so.

[In 1806 (Vol. II, pp. 182–3) Malthus added a passage here:

But besides that spirit of independence and prudence which checks the frequency of marriage, notwithstanding the encouragements of the poor-laws, these laws themselves occasion a check of no inconsiderable magnitude, and thus counteract with one hand what they encourage with the other. As each parish is obliged to maintain its own poor, it is naturally fearful of increasing their number; and every landholder is in consequence more inclined to pull down than to build cottages, (except when the demand for labourers is really urgent.) This deficiency of cottages operates necessarily as a strong check to marriage; and this check is probably the principal reason why we have been able to continue the system of the poor-laws so long.

[The clause given in brackets here was inserted in 1807 (Vol. II, p. 106) without brackets.]

Those who are not deterred for a time from marriage, by considerations of this nature,[8] are either relieved very scantily at their own homes, where they suffer all the consequences arising from squalid poverty; or they are crowded together in close and unwholesome workhouses, where a great mortality almost universally takes place, particularly among the young children. The dreadful account given by Jonas Hanway of the treatment of parish children in London, is too well known to need a comment; and it appears from Mr. Howlett, and other writers, that in some parts of the country they are not

---

[8] [In 1806 (Vol. II, p. 183) this was changed to:
    Those who are not prevented for a time from marrying by these causes, are either . . .

very much better off.[9] A great part of the redundant population occasioned by the poor laws is thus taken off by the operation of the laws themselves, or at least by their ill execution. The remaining part which survives, by causing the funds for the maintenance of labour to be divided among a greater number than can be properly maintained by them, and by turning a considerable share from the support of the diligent and careful workman to the support of the idle and the negligent, depresses the condition of all those who are out of the workhouses, forces more every year into them, and has ultimately produced the enormous evil which we all so justly deplore, that of the great and unnatural proportion of the people which is now become dependent upon charity.

If this be a just representation of the manner in which the clause in question has been executed, and of the effects which it has produced, it must be allowed that we have practised an unpardonable deceit upon the poor, and have promised what we have been very far from performing. [10]●It may be asserted, without danger of exaggeration, that the poor laws have destroyed many more lives than they have preserved.●[10]

The attempts to employ the poor on any great scale in manufactures have almost invariably failed, and the stock and materials have been wasted. In those few parishes which, by better management or larger funds, have been enabled to persevere in this system, the effect of these new manufactures in the market must have been to throw out of employment many independent workmen who were before engaged in fabrications of a similar nature. This effect has been placed in a strong point of view by Daniel de Foe, in an address to parliament, entitled *Giving alms no charity*. Speaking of the employment of parish children in manufactures, he says: 'For every skein of worsted these poor children spin, there must be a skein the less spun by some poor family that spun it before; and for every piece of baize so made in London, there must be a piece the less made at Colchester, or somewhere else.'[11] Sir F. M. Eden, on the same subject, observes that 'whether mops and brooms are made by parish children, or by private workmen, no more can be sold than the public is in want of'.[12]

---

9 [In 1806 (Vol. II, p. 183) this was altered to:
   The dreadful account given by Jonas Hanway of the treatment of parish children in London is well known; and it appears from Mr Howlett and other writers, that in some parts of the country their situation is not very much better.

10 [In 1807 (Vol. II, p. 108) this sentence was excised.]

11 See extracts from Daniel de Foe, in Sir F. M. Eden's valuable work on the poor, vol. i. p. 261.

12 Sir F. Eden, speaking of the supposed right of the poor to be supplied with employment while able to work, and with a maintenance when incapacitated from labour, very justly remarks, 'It may, however, be doubted whether any right, the gratification of which seems to

It will be said, perhaps, that the same reasoning might be applied to any new capital brought into competition in a particular trade or manufacture, which can rarely be done without injuring, in some degree, those that were engaged in it before. But there is a material difference in the two cases. In this the competition is perfectly fair, and what every man on entering into business must lay his account to. He may rest secure that he will not be supplanted unless his competitor possess superior skill and industry. In the other case, the competition is supported by a great bounty; by which means, notwithstanding very inferior skill and industry on the part of his competitors, the independent workman may be undersold, and unjustly excluded from the market. He himself, perhaps, is made to contribute to this competition against his own earnings; and the funds for the maintenance of labour are thus turned, from the support of a trade which yields a proper profit, to one which cannot maintain itself without a bounty. It should be observed, in general, that when a fund for the maintenance of labour is raised by assessment, the greatest part of it is not a new capital brought into trade, but an old one, which before was much more profitably employed, turned into a new channel. The farmer pays to the poor's rates, for the encouragement of a bad and unprofitable manufacture, what he would have employed on his land with infinitely more advantage to his country. In the one case, the funds for the maintenance of labour are daily diminished; in the other, daily increased. And this obvious tendency of assessments for the employment of the poor to decrease the real funds for the maintenance of labour in any country, aggravates the absurdity of supposing that it is in the power of a government to find employment for all its subjects, however fast they may increase.

It is not intended that these reasonings should be applied against every mode of employing the poor on a limited scale, and with such restrictions, as may not encourage, at the same time, their increase. I would never wish to push general principles too far, though I think that they ought to be kept in view. In particular cases, the individual good to be obtained may be so great, and the general evil so slight, that the former may clearly overbalance the latter.

The intention is merely to show[13] that the poor laws, as a general system,

---

be impracticable, can be said to exist', vol. i. p. 447. No man has collected so many materials for forming a judgment on the effects of the poor laws as Sir F. Eden, and the result he thus expresses: 'Upon the whole, therefore, there seems to be just grounds for concluding that the sum of good to be expected from a compulsory maintenance of the poor will be far outbalanced by the sum of evil which it will inevitably create', vol. i. p. 467. I am happy to have the sanction of so practical an inquirer to my opinion of the poor laws.

[13] [In 1817 (Vol. II, p. 350) this paragraph began:
My intention is merely to show ...

are founded on a gross error; and that the common declamation on the subject of the poor, which we see so often in print, and hear continually in conversation, namely that the market price of labour ought always to be sufficient decently to support a family, and that employment ought to be found for all those who are willing to work, is in effect to say that the funds for the maintenance of labour, in this country, are not only infinite, [14]●but might be made to increase with such rapidity that, supposing us to have at present six millions of labourers, including their families, we might have 96 millions in another century; or if these funds had been properly managed since the beginning of the reign of Edward I, supposing that there were then only two millions of labourers, we might now have possessed above four million millions of labourers, or about four thousand times as many labourers as it has been calculated that there are people now on the face of the earth.●[14]

---

[14] [In 1817 (Vol. II, p. 350) this concluding paragraph finished thus:

. . . are not only infinite, but not subject to variation; and that, whether the resources of a country be rapidly progressive, slowly progressive, stationary, or declining, the power of giving full employment and good wages to the labouring classes must always remain exactly the same – a conclusion which contradicts the plainest and most obvious principles of supply and demand, and involves the absurd position that a definite quantity of territory can maintain an infinite population.

CHAPTER VII

Of Poor-Laws, continued

The remarks made in the last chapter on the nature and effects of the poor-laws have been in the most striking manner confirmed by the experience of the years 1815, 1816 and 1817.[1] During these years, two points of the very highest importance have been established, so as no longer to admit of a doubt in the mind of any rational man.

The first is that the country does not in point of fact fulfil the promise which it makes to the poor in the poor-laws, to maintain and find in employment, by means of parish assessments, those who are unable to support themselves or their families, either from want of work or any other cause.

And secondly, that with a very great increase of legal parish assessments, aided by the most liberal and praiseworthy contributions of voluntary charity, the country has been wholly unable to find adequate employment for the numerous labourers and artificers who were able as well as willing to work.

It can no longer surely be contended that the poor-laws really perform what they promise, when it is known that many almost starving families have been found in London and other great towns, who are deterred from going on the parish by the crowded, unhealthy and horrible state of the workhouses into which they would be received, if indeed they could be received at all; when it is known that many parishes have been absolutely unable to raise the necessary assessments, the increase of which, according to the existing laws, have tended only to bring more and more persons upon the parish, and to make what was collected less and less effectual; and when it is known that there has been an almost universal cry from one end of the kingdom to the other for voluntary charity to come in aid of the parochial assessments.

These strong indications of the inefficiency of the poor-laws may merely[2] be considered not only as incontrovertible proofs of the fact that they do not perform what they promise, but as affording the strongest presumption that

---

[1] [In 1826 (Vol. II, p. 96) a footnote was added here:
   This chapter was written in 1817.
[2] [In 1826 (Vol. II, p. 97) the word *merely* was omitted.

they cannot do it. The best of all reasons for the breach of a promise is the absolute impossibility of executing it; indeed it is the only plea that can ever be considered as valid. But though it may be fairly pardonable not to execute an impossibility, it is unpardonable knowingly to promise one. And if it be still thought advisable to act upon these statutes as far as is practicable, it would surely be wise so to alter the terms in which they are expressed, and the general interpretation given to them, as not to convey to the poor a false notion of what really is within the range of practicability.

It has appeared further as a matter of fact, that very large voluntary contributions, combined with greatly increased parochial assessments, and aided by the most able and incessant exertions of individuals, have failed to give the necessary employment to those who have been thrown out of work by the sudden falling off of demand which has occurred during the last two or three years.

It might perhaps have been foreseen that, as the great movements of society, the great causes which render a nation progressive, stationary or declining, for longer or shorter periods, cannot be supposed to depend much upon parochial assessments or the contributions of charity, it could not be expected that any efforts of this kind should have power to create in a stationary or declining state of things that effective demand for labour which only belongs to a progressive state. But to those who did not see this truth before, the melancholy experience of the last two years[3] must have brought it home with an overpowering conviction.

It does not however by any means follow that the exertions which have been made to relieve the present distresses have been ill directed. On the contrary, they have not only been prompted by the most praiseworthy motives; they have not only fulfilled the great moral duty of assisting our fellow-creatures in distress; but they have in point of fact done great good, or at least prevented great evil. Their partial failure does not necessarily indicate either a want of energy or a want of skill in those who have taken the lead in these efforts, but merely that a part only of what has been attempted is practicable.

It is practicable to mitigate the violence and relieve the severe pressure of the present distress, so as to carry the sufferers through to better times, though even this can only be done at the expense of some sacrifices, not

---

[3] [In 1826 (Vol. II, p. 98) a footnote was added here:
   The years 1816 and 1817.
   [The very wet summer of 1816 resulted in a bad harvest and an epidemic of typhus; the cessation of the Napoleonic wars led to a steep fall in demand, for labour, and for such commodities as had already been manufactured in anticipation of high profits. There were outbreaks of destructive violence all over the country, as well as more rational agitation for parliamentary reform.]

merely of the rich, but of other classes of the poor. But it is impracticable by any exertions, either individual or national, to restore at once that brisk demand for commodities and labour which has been lost by events that, however, they may have originated, are now beyond the power of control.

The whole subject is surrounded on all sides by the most formidable difficulties, and in no state of things is it so necessary to recollect the saying of Daniel de Foe quoted in the last chapter. The manufacturers all over the country, and the Spitalfields weavers in particular, are in a state of the deepest distress, occasioned immediately and directly by the want of demand for the produce of their industry, and the consequent necessity felt by the masters of turning off many of their workmen, in order to proportion the supply to the contracted demand. It is proposed however, by some well-meaning people, to raise by subscription a fund for the express purpose of setting to work again those who have been turned off by their masters, the effect of which can only be to continue glutting a market already much too fully supplied. This is most naturally and justly objected to by the masters, as it prevents them from withdrawing the supply, and taking the only course which can prevent the total destruction of their capitals, and the necessity of turning off all their men instead of a part.

On the other hand, some classes of merchants and manufacturers clamour very loudly for the prohibition of all foreign commodities which may enter into competition with domestic products, and interfere, as they intimate, with the employment of British industry. But this is most naturally and most justly deprecated by other classes of British subjects, who are employed to a very great extent in preparing and manufacturing those commodities which are to purchase our imports from foreign countries. And it must be allowed to be perfectly true that a court-ball, at which only British stuffs are admitted, may be the means of throwing out of employment in one quarter of the country just as many persons as it furnishes with employment in another.

Still, it would be desirable if possible to employ those that are out of work, if it were merely to avoid the bad moral effects of idleness, and of the evil habits which might be generated by depending for a considerable time on mere alms. But the difficulties just stated will show that we ought to proceed in this part of the attempt with great caution, and that the kinds of employment which ought to be chosen are those, the results of which will not interfere with existing capitals. Such are public works of all descriptions, the making and repairing of roads, bridges, railways,[4] canals, &c.; and now

---

[4] [In 1817 there were about 160 miles of rail-road in the United Kingdom, used mainly for the transport of coal, timber, limestone and iron-ore, in wagons pulled by horses. Malthus would certainly have heard of the early experiments with steam locomotives, made by Trevithick

perhaps, since the great loss of agricultural capital, almost every sort of labour upon the land, which could be carried on by public subscription.

Yet even in this way of employing labour, the benefit to some must bring with it disadvantages to others. That portion of each person's revenue, which might go in subscriptions of this kind, must of course be lost to the various sorts of labour which its expenditure in the usual channels would have supported; and the want of demand thus occasioned in these channels must cause the pressure of distress to be felt in quarters which might otherwise have escaped it. But this is an effect which, in such cases, it is impossible to avoid; and, as a temporary measure, it is not only charitable but just to spread the evil over a larger surface, in order that its violence on particular parts may be so mitigated as to be made bearable by all.

The great object to be kept in view, is to support the people through their present distresses, in the hope (and I trust a just one) of better times. The difficulty is without doubt considerably aggravated by the prodigious stimulus which has been given to the population of the country of late years, the effects of which cannot suddenly subside. But it will be seen probably, when the next returns of the population are made, that the marriages and births have diminished, and the deaths increased in a still greater degree than in 1800 and 1801; and the continuance of this effect to a certain degree for a few years will retard the progress of the population, and combined with the increasing wants of Europe and America from their increasing riches, and the adaptation of the supply of commodities at home to the new distribution of wealth occasioned by the alteration of the circulating medium, will again give life and energy to all our mercantile and agricultural transactions, and restore the labouring classes to full employment and good wages.[5]

On the subject of the distresses of the poor, and particularly the increase of pauperism of late years, the most erroneous opinions have been circulated. During the progress of the war, the increase in the proportion of persons requiring parish assistance was attributed chiefly to the high price of the

---

and Hedley in 1804 and 1813; their inventions were to some extent stimulated by the war-time shortage of horses and fodder.]

[5] [In 1826 (Vol. II, p. 102) a footnote was added here:

1825. This has, in a considerable degree, taken place; but it has been owing rather to the latter causes noticed than to the former. It appeared, by the returns of 1821, that the scarce years of 1817 and 1818 had but a slight effect in diminishing the number of marriages and births, compared with the effect of the great proportion of plentiful years in increasing them; so that the population proceeded with great rapidity during the ten years ending with 1820. But this great increase of the population has prevented the labouring classes from being so fully employed as might have been expected from the prosperity of commerce and agriculture during the last two or three years.

necessaries of life. We have seen these necessaries of life experience a great and sudden fall, and yet at the same time a still larger proportion of the population requiring parish assistance.

It is now said that taxation is the sole cause of their distresses, and of the extraordinary stagnation in the demand for labour; yet I feel the firmest conviction that if the whole of the taxes were removed to-morrow, this stagnation, instead of being at an end, would be considerably aggravated. Such an event would cause another great and general rise in the value of the circulating medium, and bring with it that discouragement to industry with which such a convulsion in society must ever be attended. If, as has been represented, the labouring classes now pay more than half of what they receive in taxes, he must know very little indeed of the principles on which the wages of labour are regulated, who can for a moment suppose that, when the commodities on which they are expended have fallen one half by the removal of taxes, these wages themselves would still continue of the same nominal value. Were they to remain but for a short time the same, while all commodities had fallen, and the circulating medium had been reduced in proportion, it would be quickly seen that multitudes of them would be at once thrown out of employment.

The effects of taxation are no doubt in many cases pernicious in a very high degree; but it may be laid down as a rule which has few exceptions, that the relief obtained by taking off a tax is in no respect equal to the injury inflicted in laying it on; and generally it may be said that the specific evil of taxation consists in the check which it gives to production, rather than the diminution which it occasions in demand. With regard to all commodities indeed of home production and home demand, it is quite certain that the conversion of capital into revenue, which is the effect of loans, must necessarily increase the proportion of demand to the supply; and the conversion of the revenue of individuals into the revenue of the government, which is the effect of taxes properly imposed, however hard upon the individuals so taxed, can have no tendency to diminish the general amount of demand. It will of course diminish the demands of the persons taxed by diminishing their powers of purchasing; but to the exact amount that the powers of these persons are diminished, will the powers of the government and of those employed by it be increased. If an estate of five thousand a year has a mortgage upon it of two thousand, two families, both in very good circumstances, may be living upon the rents of it, and both have considerable demands for houses, furniture, carriages, broad-cloth, silks, cottons, &c. The man who owns the estate is certainly much worse off than if the mortgage-deed was burnt, but the manufacturers and labourers who supply the silks, broad-cloth, cottons, &c., are so far from being likely to be benefited by such burning, that it would be a considerable time before the new wants and tastes of the enriched owner had restored the former demand; and if he were to take a fancy to spend his additional income in horses, hounds and menial servants, which is probable, not only would the manufacturers and labourers who had before supplied their silks, cloths and cottons be thrown out of employment, but the substituted demand would be very much less favourable to the increase of the capital and general resources of the country.

The foregoing illustration represents more nearly than may generally be imagined the effects of a national debt on the labouring classes of society, and the very great mistake of supposing that, because the demands of a considerable portion of the community would be increased by the extinction of the debt, these increased demands would not be balanced, and often more than balanced, by the loss of the demand from the fundholders[6] and government.

It is by no means intended by these observations to intimate that a national debt may not be so heavy as to be extremely prejudicial to a state. The division and distribution of property, which is so beneficial when carried only to a certain extent, is fatal to production when pushed to extremity. The division of an estate of five thousand a year will generally tend to increase demand, stimulate production and improve the structure of society; but the division of an estate of eighty pounds a year will generally be attended with effects directly the reverse.

But, besides the probability that the division of property occasioned by a national debt may in many cases be pushed too far, the process of the division is effected by means which sometimes greatly embarrass production. This embarrassment must necessarily take place to a certain extent in almost every species of taxation; but under favourable circumstances it is overcome by the stimulus given to demand.[7] During the late war, from the prodigious increase of produce and population, it may fairly be presumed that the power of production was not essentially impeded, notwithstanding the enormous amount of taxation; but in the state of things which has occurred since the peace, and under a most extraordinary fall of the exchangeable value of the raw produce of the land, and a great consequent diminution of the circulating medium, the very sudden increase of the weight and pressure of taxation must greatly aggravate the other causes which discourage production. This effect has been felt to a considerable extent on the land; but the distress in this

---

[6] [The fund-holders were those who had money invested in government stock. In 1751 a number of public securities had been consolidated into a single fund, bearing interest at 3 per cent; those who derived their income from this source were regarded as parasites on the rest of the community by William Cobbett and other radical writers.]

[7] [In 1826 (Vol. II, p. 105) Malthus inserted three words here:
     ... stimulus given to demand compared with supply.

quarter is already much mitigated;[8] and among the mercantile and manufacturing classes, where the greatest numbers are without employment, the evil obviously arises not so much from the want of capital and the means of production, as the want of a market for the commodity when produced – a want for which the removal of taxes, however proper, and indeed absolutely necessary as a permanent measure, is certainly not the immediate and specific remedy.

The principal causes of the increase of pauperism, independently of the present crisis, are, first, the general increase of the manufacturing system and the unavoidable variations of manufacturing labour; and secondly, and more particularly, the practice which has been adopted in some counties, and is now spreading pretty generally all over the kingdom, of paying a considerable portion of what ought to be the wages of labour out of the parish rates. During the war, when the demand for labour was great and increasing, it is quite certain that nothing but a practice of this kind could for any time have prevented the wages of labour from rising fully in proportion to the necessaries of life, in whatever degree these necessaries might have been raised by taxation. It was seen, consequently, that in those parts of Great Britain where this practice prevailed the least, the wages of labour rose the most. This was the case in Scotland, and some parts of the North of England, where the improvement in the condition of the labouring classes, and their increased command over the necessaries and conveniences of life, were particularly remarkable. And if, in some other parts of the country, where the practice did not greatly prevail, and especially in the towns, wages did not rise in the same degree, it was owing to the influx and competition of the cheaply raised population of the surrounding counties.

It is a just remark of Adam Smith, that the attempts of the legislature to raise the pay of curates had always been ineffectual, on account of the cheap and abundant supply of them, occasioned by the bounties given to young persons educated for the church at the universities. And it is equally true that no human efforts can keep up the price of day-labour so as to enable a man to support on his earnings a family of a moderate size, so long as those who have more than two children are considered as having a valid claim to parish assistance.

If this system were to become universal, and I own it appears to me that the poor-laws naturally lead to it, there is no reason whatever why parish assistance should not by degrees begin earlier and earlier; and I do not hesitate to assert that, if the government and constitution of the country were in all

---

[8] [In 1826 (Vol. II, p. 106) a footnote was added here:
    Written in 1817. It increased again afterwards from another great fall in the price of corn,
    subsequent to 1818.

other respects as perfect as the wildest visionary thinks he could make them; if parliaments were annual, suffrage universal, wars, taxes and pensions unknown, and the civil list fifteen hundred a year,[9] the great body of the community might still be a collection of paupers.

I have been accused of proposing a law to prohibit the poor from marrying.[10] This is not true. So far from proposing such a law, I have distinctly said that, if any person chooses to marry without having a prospect of being able to maintain a family, he ought to have the most perfect liberty so to do; and whenever any prohibitory propositions have been suggested to me as advisable by persons who have drawn wrong inferences from what I have said, I have steadily and uniformly reprobated them. I am indeed most decidedly of opinion that any positive law to limit the age of marriage would be both unjust and immoral; and my greatest objection to a system of equality and the system of the poor-laws (two systems which, however different in their outset, are of a nature calculated to produce the same results) is, that the society in which they are effectively carried into execution, will ultimately be reduced to the miserable alternative of choosing between universal want and the enactment of *direct* laws against marriage.

What I have really proposed is a very different measure. It is the *gradual* and *very gradual* abolition of the poor-laws.[11] And the reason why I have ventured to suggest a proposition of this kind for consideration is my firm conviction that they have lowered very decidedly the wages of the labouring classes, and made their general condition essentially worse than it would have been if these laws had never existed. Their operation is every where depressing; but it falls peculiarly hard upon the labouring classes in great towns. In country parishes the poor do really receive some compensation for their low wages; their children, beyond a certain number, are really supported by the parish; and though it must be a most grating reflection to a labouring man, that it is scarcely possible for him to marry without becoming the father of paupers; yet if he can reconcile himself to this prospect, the compensation, such as it is, is no doubt made to him. But in London and all

---

[9] [The word *pension* here does not refer to the modern retirement pension, but to 'regular payments to persons of rank, royal favourites, etc., to enable them to maintain their state'. (O.E.D.). The civil list was formerly a list of the charges to be defrayed by the government; in Malthus's time it meant the sum voted by parliament for what were traditionally the personal expenses of the monarch, including the payment of pensions, as above. Like the fund-holders (see n.6) the pensioners were not popular.]

[10] [In this and the following paragraph Malthus virtually assumes that readers of this chapter are familiar with earlier editions of the *Essay*, and know already about the plan for the gradual abolition of the poor laws which he had put forward in the quarto, chapter viii of Book IV in this edition.]

[11] So gradual as not to affect any individuals at present alive, or who will be born within the next two years.

the great towns of the kingdom, the evil is suffered without the compensation. The population raised by bounties in the country naturally and necessarily flows into the towns, and as naturally and necessarily tends to lower wages in them; while, in point of fact, those who marry in towns, and have large families, receive no assistance from their parishes unless they are actually starving; and altogether the assistance which the manufacturing classes obtain for the support of their families, in aid of their lowered wages, is perfectly inconsiderable.

To remedy the effects of this competition from the country, the artificers and manufacturers in towns have been apt to combine, with a view to keep up the price of labour and to prevent persons from working below a certain rate. But such combinations are not only illegal,[12] but irrational and ineffectual; and if the supply of workmen in any particular branch of trade be such as would naturally lower wages, the keeping them up forcibly must have the effect of throwing so many out of employment, as to make the expense of their support fully equal to the gain acquired by the higher wages, and thus render these higher wages in reference to the whole body perfectly futile.

It may be distinctly stated to be an *absolute impossibility* that all the different classes of society should be both well paid and fully employed, if the supply of labour on the whole exceed the demand; and as the poor-laws tend in the most marked manner to make the supply of labour exceed the demand for it, their effect must be, either to lower universally all wages, or, if some are kept up artificially, to throw great numbers of workmen out of employment, and thus constantly to increase the poverty and distress of the labouring classes of society.

If these things be so (and I am firmly convinced that they are) it cannot but be a subject of the deepest regret to those who are anxious for the happiness of the great mass of the community, that the writers which are now most extensively read among the common people should have selected for the subject of reprobation exactly that line of conduct which can alone generally improve their condition, and for the subject of approbation that system which must inevitably depress them in poverty and wretchedness.

---

[12] [In 1826 (Vol. II, p. 110) a footnote was added here:

This has since been altered; but the subsequent part of the passage is particularly applicable to the present time – the end of the year 1825. The workmen are beginning to find that, if they could raise their wages above what the state of the demand and the prices of goods will warrant, it is absolutely impossible that all, or nearly all, should be employed. The masters could not employ the same number as before without inevitable ruin.

[The Combination Acts of 1799 and 1800 had amounted to a general law against all trade unions; there had previously been many statutes forbidding combinations of workmen in particular trades. All such Acts were repealed in 1825. Malthus himself had given evidence,

They are taught that there is no occasion whatever for them to put any sort of restraint upon their inclinations, or exercise any degree of prudence in the affair of marriage; because the parish is bound to provide for all that are born. They are taught that there is as little occasion to cultivate habits of economy, and make use of the means afforded them by saving-banks, to lay by their earnings while they are single, in order to furnish a cottage when they marry, and enable them to set out in life with decency and comfort; because, I suppose, the parish is bound to cover their nakedness, and to find them a bed and a chair in a work-house.

They are taught that any endeavour on the part of the higher classes of society to inculcate the duties of prudence and economy can only arise from a desire to save the money which they pay in poor-rates; although it is absolutely certain that the *only* mode, consistent with the laws of morality and religion, of giving to the poor the largest share of the property of the rich, without sinking the whole community in misery, is the exercise on the part of the poor of prudence in marriage, and of economy both before and after it.

They are taught that the command of the Creator to increase and multiply is meant to contradict those laws which he has himself appointed for the increase and multiplication of the human race; and that it is equally the duty of a person to marry early, when, from the impossibility of adding to the food of the country in which he lives, the greater part of his offspring must die prematurely, and consequently no multiplication follow from it, as when the children of such marriages can all be well maintained, and there is room and food for a great and rapid increase of population.

They are taught that, in relation to the condition of the labouring classes, there is no other difference between such a country as England, which has been long well peopled, and where the land which is not yet taken into cultivation is comparatively barren, and such a country as America, where millions and millions of acres of fine land are yet to be had for a trifle, except what arises from taxation.

And they are taught, O monstrous absurdity! that the only reason why the American labourer earns a dollar a day, and the English labourer earns two shillings, is that the English labourer pays a great part of these two shillings in taxes.

Some of these doctrines are so grossly absurd that I have no doubt they are rejected at once by the common sense of many of the labouring classes. It cannot but strike them that, if their main dependence for the support of their children is to be on the parish, they can only expect parish fare, parish clothing, parish furniture, a parish house and parish government, and they

in May 1824, to the Select Committee on Artisans and Machinery that recommended the abolition of these restrictive laws, laws which were in any case almost impossible to enforce.]

must know that persons living in this way cannot possibly be in a happy and prosperous state.

It can scarcely escape the notice of the common mechanic, that the scarcer workmen are upon any occasion, the greater share do they retain of the value of what they produce for their masters; and it is a most natural inference, that prudence in marriage, which is the only moral means of preventing an excess of workmen above the demand, can be the only mode of giving to the poor permanently a large share of all that is produced in the country.

A common man, who has read his Bible, must be convinced that a command given to a rational being by a merciful God cannot be intended so as to be interpreted as to produce only disease and death instead of multiplication; and a plain sound understanding would make him to see that if, in a country in which little or no increase of food is to be obtained, every man were to marry at eighteen or twenty, when he generally feels most inclined to it, the consequence must be increased poverty, increased disease and increased mortality, and not increased numbers, as long at least as it continues to be true (which he will hardly be disposed to doubt) that additional numbers cannot live without additional food.

A moderately shrewd judgment would prompt any labourer acquainted with the nature of land to suspect that there must be some great difference, quite independent of taxation, between a country such as America, which might easily be made to support fifty times as many inhabitants as it contains at present, and a country such as England, which could not without extraordinary exertions be made to support two or three times as many. He would at least see that there would be a prodigious difference in the power of maintaining an additional number of cattle, between a small farm already well stocked, and a very large one which had not the fiftieth part of what it might be made to maintain; and as he would know that both rich and poor must live upon the produce of the earth as well as all other animals, he would be disposed to conclude that what was so obviously true in one case could not be false in the other. These considerations might make him think it natural and probable that in those countries where there was a great want of people, the wages of labour would be such as to encourage early marriages and large families, for the best of all possible reasons, because all that are born may be very easily and comfortably supported; but that in those countries which were already nearly full, the wages of labour cannot be such as to give the same encouragement to early marriages, for a reason surely not much worse, because the persons so brought into the world cannot be properly supported.

There are few of our mechanics and labourers who have not heard of the high prices of bread, meat and labour in this country compared with the nations of the continent, and they have generally heard at the same time that these high prices were chiefly occasioned by taxation, which, though it had raised among other things the money wages of labour, had done harm rather than good to the labourer, because it had before raised the price of the bread and beer and other articles on which he spent his earnings. With this amount of information, the meanest understanding would revolt at the idea that the very same cause which had kept the money price of labour in all the nations of Europe much lower than in England, namely, the absence of taxation, had been the means of raising it to more than double in America. He would feel quite convinced that, whatever might be the cause of the high money wages of labour in America, which he might not perhaps readily understand, it must be something very different indeed from the mere absence of taxation, which could only have an effect exactly opposite.

With regard to the improved condition of the lower classes of people in France since the revolution, which has also been much insisted upon; if the circumstances accompanying it were told at the same time, it would afford the strongest presumption against the doctrines which have been lately promulgated. The improved condition of the labouring classes in France since the revolution has been accompanied by a greatly diminished proportion of births, which has had its natural and necessary effect in giving to these classes a greater share of the produce of the country, and has kept up the advantage arising from the sale of the church lands and other national domains, which would otherwise have been lost in a short time. The effect of the revolution in France has been to make every person depend more upon himself and less upon others. The labouring classes are therefore become r...re industrious, more saving and more prudent in marriage than formerly; and it is quite certain that without these effects the revolution would have done nothing for them. An improved government has, no doubt, a natural tendency to produce these effects, and thus to improve the condition of the poor. But if an extensive system of parochial relief, and such doctrines as have lately been inculcated, counteract them, and prevent the labouring classes from depending upon their own prudence and industry, then any change for the better in other respects becomes comparatively a matter of very little importance; and, under the best form of government imaginable, there may be thousands on thousands out of employment and half starved.

If it be taught that all who are born have a *right* to support on the land, whatever be their number, and that there is no occasion to exercise any prudence in the affair of marriage so as to check this number, the temptations, according to all the known principles of human nature, will inevitably be yielded to, and more and more will gradually become dependent on parish assistance. There cannot therefore be a greater inconsistency and contradiction than that those who maintain these doctrines respecting the poor should still complain of the number of paupers. Such doctrines and a crowd of paupers are unavoidably united; and it is utterly beyond the power of any revolution or change of government to separate them.

CHAPTER VIII

Of increasing Wealth as it affects the Condition of the Poor[1]

The professed object of Dr. Smith's inquiry is the nature and causes of the wealth of nations. There is another, however, perhaps still more interesting,[2] which he occasionally mixes with it, the causes which affect the happiness and comfort of the lower orders of society, which is the most numerous class in every nation. I am sufficiently aware of the near connexion of these two subjects, and that, generally speaking, the causes which contribute to increase the wealth of a state tend also to increase the happiness of the lower classes of the people. But perhaps Dr. Smith has considered these two inquiries as still more nearly connected than they really are; at least, he has not stopped to take notice of those instances where the wealth of a society may increase, according to his definition of wealth, without having any tendency to increase the comforts of the labouring part of it.[3]

I do not mean to enter into any philosophical discussion of what constitutes the proper happiness of man, but shall merely consider two universally acknowledged ingredients, the command of the necessaries and comforts of life, and the possession of health.

The comforts of the labouring poor must necessarily depend upon the funds destined for the maintenance of labour; and will generally be in proportion to the rapidity of their increase. The demand for labour which such increase occasions will of course raise the value of labour; and till the additional number of hands required are reared, the increased funds will be distributed to the same number of persons as before, and therefore every labourer will live comparatively at his ease. The error of Dr. Smith lies in representing every increase of the revenue or stock of a society as an increase of these funds. Such surplus stock or revenue will indeed always be

---

[1] [The beginning of this chapter follows closely chapter xvi of the 1798 *Essay* (pp. 303–10). Some of this was retained in the re-written version of 1817; see in this edition Vol. ii, Book iii, chapter F.]

[2] [In 1817 (Vol. iii, p. 1) the word *perhaps* was excised.]

[3] [In 1806 (Vol. ii, p. 189) this was altered to:
  ... without having a proportional tendency to increase the comforts ...

considered, by the individual possessing it, as an additional fund from which he may maintain more labour: but it will not be a real and effectual fund for the maintenance of an additional number of labourers, unless the whole, or at least a great part of it, be convertible into a proportional quantity of provisions;[4] and it will not be so convertible where the increase has arisen merely from the produce of labour, and not from the produce of land. A distinction will in this case occur[5] between the number of hands which the stock of the society could employ, and the number which its territory can maintain.

Dr. Smith defines the wealth of a state to be the annual produce of its land and labour. This definition evidently includes manufactured produce, as well as the produce of the land. Now, supposing a nation, for a course of years, to add what is saved from its yearly revenue to its manufacturing capital solely, and not to its capital employed upon land; it is evident that it might grow richer according to the above definition, without a power of supporting a greater number of labourers, and therefore without any increase in the real funds for the maintenance of labour. There would notwithstanding be a demand for labour, from the power that each manufacturer would possess, or at least think he possessed, of extending his old stock in trade or of setting up fresh works.[6] This demand would of course raise the price of labour; but if the yearly stock of provisions in the country were not increasing, this rise would soon turn out to be merely nominal, as the price of provisions must necessarily rise with it. The demand for manufacturing labourers might, indeed, entice many from agriculture, and thus tend to diminish the annual produce of the land;[7] but we will suppose any effects of this kind to be compensated by improvements in the instruments or mode of agriculture, and the quantity of provisions therefore to remain the same. Improvements in manufacturing machinery would of course take place; and this circumstance, added to the greater number of hands employed in manufactures,

---

[4] [In 1806 (Vol. II, p. 190) this sentence was amended:
... maintain more labour; but with regard to the whole country, it will not be an effectual fund for the maintenance of an additional number of labourers, unless part of it be convertible into an additional quantity of provisions; and it will not be so convertible ...
[In 1807 (Vol. II, p. 114) this was modified:
...; and it may not be so convertible ...

[5] [In 1806 (Vol. II, p. 191) this was changed to:
A distinction may in this case occur ...

[6] [In 1806 (Vol. II, p. 191) this sentence was abbreviated:
There would notwithstanding be a demand for labour, from the extension of manufacturing capital.

[7] [In 1806 (Vol. II, p. 191) this sentence was altered:
The demand for manufacturing labourers would probably entice some from private service, and some even from agriculture; but we will suppose ...

would augment considerably the annual produce of the labour of the country. The wealth, therefore, of the country would be increasing annually, according to the definition, and might not be increasing very slowly.[8]

The question is how far wealth, increasing in this way, has a tendency to better the condition of the labouring poor. It is a self-evident proposition that any general advance in the price of labour, the stock of provisions remaining the same, can only be a nominal advance, as it must shortly be followed by a proportional rise in provisions. The increase in the price of labour which we have supposed, would have no permanent effect therefore in giving to the labouring poor a greater command over the necessaries of life. In this respect they would be nearly in the same state as before. In some other respects they would be in a worse state. A greater proportion of them would be employed in manufactures, and fewer consequently in agriculture.[9] And this exchange of professions will be allowed, I think by all, to be very unfavourable in respect of health, one essential ingredient of happiness, and also with regard to the greater uncertainty of manufacturing labour,[10] arising from the capricious taste of man, the accidents of war, and other causes, which occasionally produce very severe distress among the lower classes of society. On the state of the poor employed in manufactories, with respect to health and other circumstances which affect their happiness, I will beg to quote a passage from Dr. Aikin's description of the country round Manchester.

'The invention and improvements of machines to shorten labour have had a surprising influence to extend our trade, and also to call in hands from all parts, especially children for the cotton mills. It is the wise plan of Providence that in this life there shall be no good without its attendant inconvenience. There are many which are too obvious in these cotton mills and similar factories, which counteract that increase of population usually consequent on

---

[8] [In 1806 (Vol. II, p. 192) a footnote was added here:

I have supposed here a case which, in a landed nation, I allow to be very improbable in fact; but approximations to it are perhaps not unfrequently taking place. My intention is merely to show that the funds for the maintenance of labour do not increase exactly in proportion to the increase in the produce of the land and labour of a country, but with the same increase of produce, may be more or less favourable to the labourer, according as the increase has arisen principally from agriculture or from manufactures. On the supposition of a physical impossibility of increasing the food of a country, it is evident that by improvements in machinery it might grow yearly richer in the exchangeable value of its manufactured produce; but the labourer, though he might be better clothed and lodged, could not be better fed.

[9] [In 1806 (Vol. II, p. 193) this was changed to:
... employed in manufactures, and a smaller proportion in agriculture.

[10] [In 1806 (Vol. II, p. 193) this was altered:
... to be very unfavourable to health, one essential ingredient of happiness, and to be further disadvantageous on account of the greater uncertainty ...

the improved facility of labour. In these, children of very tender age are employed, many of them collected from the workhouses in London and Westminster, and transported in crowds as apprentices to masters resident many hundred miles distant, where they serve unknown, unprotected, and forgotten by those to whose care nature, or the laws, had consigned them. These children are usually too long confined to work in close rooms, often during the whole night. The air they breath from the oil, &c. employed in the machinery, and other circumstances, is injurious; little attention is paid to their cleanliness; and frequent changes from a warm and dense to a cold and thin atmosphere are predisposing causes to sickness and disability, and particularly to the epidemic fever which is so generally to be met with in these factories. It is also much to be questioned if society does not receive detriment, from the manner in which children are thus employed during their early years. They are not generally strong to labour, or capable of pursuing any other branch of business when the term of their apprenticeship expires. The females are wholly uninstructed in sewing, knitting, and other domestic affairs, requisite to make them notable and frugal wives and mothers. This is a very great misfortune to them and the public, as is sadly proved by a comparison of the families of labourers in husbandry and those of manufacturers in general. In the former we meet with neatness, cleanliness and comfort; in the latter, with filth, rags, and poverty, although their wages may be nearly double to those of the husbandman. It must be added that the want of early religious instruction and example, and the numerous and indiscriminate association in these buildings, are very unfavourable to their future conduct in life.'[11]

In addition to the evils mentioned in this passage, we all know how subject particular manufactures are to fail, from the caprice of taste or the accident of war. The weavers of Spitalfields were plunged into the most severe distress by the fashion of muslins instead of silks; and numbers of the workmen in Sheffield and Birmingham were for a time thrown out of employment, from the adoption of shoe-strings and covered buttons, instead of buckles and metal buttons. Our manufactures, taken in the mass, have increased with great rapidity, but in particular places they have failed, and the parishes

---

[11] P. 219. Endeavours have been made, Dr Aikin says, to remedy these evils, and in some factories they have been attended with success. An act of parliament has of late also passed on this subject, from which it is hoped that much good will result. [This was the Health and Morals of Apprentices Act of 1802, which limited their daily hours of work to twelve and (amongst other improvements) made the annual white-washing of their living quarters a statutory requirement; enforcement was entrusted to visiting magistrates and clergymen, and the Act was quite ineffective. A Bill to protect the 'free children', and not merely the paupers, was rejected by Parliament in 1815. The first effective Factory Act was that of 1833, when provision was made for the appointment of four full-time salaried inspectors.]

where this has happened are invariably loaded with a crowd of poor, in the most distressed and miserable condition. In the work of Dr. Aikin just alluded to, it appears that the register for the collegiate church at Manchester, from Christmas 1793 to Christmas 1794, stated a decrease of 168 marriages, 538 christenings, and 250 burials. And in the parish of Rochdale, in the neighbourhood, a still more melancholy reduction, in proportion to the number of people, took place. In 1792, the births were 746, the burials 646, and the marriages 339. In 1794, the births were 373, the burials 671, and the marriages 199. The cause of this sudden check to population was the commencement of the war, and the failure of commercial credit, which occurred about this time; and such a check could not have taken place, in so sudden a manner, without being occasioned by the most severe distress.

Under such circumstances of situation, unless the increase of the riches of a country from manufactures give the lower classes of the society, on an average, a decidedly greater command over the necessaries and conveniences of life, it will not appear that their condition is improved.

It will be said, perhaps, that the advance in the price of provisions will immediately turn some additional capital into the channel of agriculture, and thus occasion a much greater produce. But from experience it appears that this is an effect which takes place very slowly, particularly when, as in the present instance, an advance in the price of labour had preceded the advance in the price of provisions, and would therefore tend to impede the good effects upon agriculture which the increased value of the produce of land might otherwise have occasioned.[12]

It may also be said, that the additional capital of the nation would enable it to import provisions, sufficient for the maintenance of those whom its stock could employ. A small country, with a large navy, and great accommodations for inland carriage, may indeed import and distribute an effectual quantity of provisions: but in large landed nations, if they may be so called, an importation adequate at all times to the demand is scarcely possible. It seems in great measure to have escaped attention that a nation which, from its extent of territory and population, must necessarily support the greater part of its people on the produce of its own soil; but which yet, on average years, draws a small portion of its corn from abroad, is in a much more precarious situation with regard to the constancy of its supplies than such states as draw almost the whole of their provisions from other countries. The demands of Holland and Hamburgh may be known with considerable

---

[12] [In 1806 (Vol. ii, pp. 197–8) this sentence was altered:
   But from experience it appears that this is an effect which sometimes follows very slowly, particularly if heavy taxes that affect agricultural industry, and an advance in the price of labour, had preceded the advance in the price of provisions.

accuracy by those who supply them. If they increase, they increase gradually, and are not subject, from year to year, to any great and sudden variations. But it is otherwise with such a country as England. Supposing it, in average years, to want about four hundred thousand quarters of wheat. Such a demand will of course be very easily supplied. But a year of deficient crops occurs, and the demand is suddenly two millions of quarters. If the demand had been, on an average, two millions, it might perhaps have been adequately supplied, from the extended agriculture of those countries which are in the habit of exporting corn: but we cannot expect that it can easily be answered thus suddenly; and indeed we know from experience that an unusual demand of this nature, in a nation capable of paying for it, cannot exist without raising the price of wheat very considerably in the ports of Europe. Hamburgh, Holland, and the ports of the Baltic, felt very sensibly the high prices of England during the late scarcity; and I have been informed from very good authority that the price of bread in New York was little inferior to the highest price in London.

A nation possessed of a large territory is unavoidably subject to this uncertainty in its means of subsistence, when the commercial part of its population is either equal to, or has increased beyond, the surplus produce of its cultivators. No reserve being, in these cases, left in exportation,[13] the full effect of every deficiency from unfavourable seasons must necessarily be felt; and though the riches of such a country may enable it, for a certain period, to continue raising the nominal price of wages, so as to give the lower classes of the society a power of purchasing imported corn at a high price; yet, as a sudden demand can very seldom be fully answered, the competition in the market will invariably raise the price of provisions, in full proportion to the advance in the price of labour; the lower classes will be but little relieved; and the dearth will operate severely throughout all the ranks of society.

According to the natural order of things, years of scarcity must occasionally recur, in all landed nations. They ought always therefore to enter into our consideration; and the prosperity of any country may justly be considered as precarious, in which the funds for the maintenance of labour are liable to great and sudden fluctuations, from every unfavourable variation in the seasons.

But putting, for the present, years of scarcity out of the question; when the commercial population of any country increases so much beyond the surplus produce of the cultivators, that the demand for imported corn is not easily supplied, and the price rises in proportion to the price of wages, no further

---

[13] [In 1807 (Vol. II, p. 124) this was altered to:

No reserve being in these cases left in the store destined for exportation, the full effect of every deficiency ...

increase of riches will have any tendency to give the labourers a greater command over the necessaries of life. In the progress of wealth, this will naturally take place; either from the largeness of the supply wanted; the increased distance from which it is brought, and consequently the increased expense of importation; the greater consumption of it in the countries in which it is usually purchased; or what must unavoidably happen, the necessity of a greater distance of inland carriage, in these countries. Such a nation, by increasing industry, and increasing ingenuity in the improvement of machinery, may still go on increasing the yearly quantity of its manufactured produce; but its funds for the maintenance of labour, and consequently its population, will be perfectly stationary. This point is the natural limit to the population of all commercial states.[14]

[In 1806 (Vol. II, pp. 201–2) this passage was inserted here:

In countries at a great distance from this limit, an effect approaching to what has been here described will take place whenever the march of commerce and manufactures is more rapid than that of agriculture. During the last ten or twelve years it cannot be doubted, that the annual produce of the land and labour of England has very rapidly increased, and in consequence the nominal wages of labour have greatly increased; but the real recompense of the labourer, though increased, has not increased in proportion.

That every increase of the stock or revenue of a nation cannot be considered as an increase of the real funds for the maintenance of labour, and therefore cannot have the same good effect upon the condition of the poor, will appear in a strong light if the argument be applied to China.[15]

Dr. Smith observes that China has probably long been as rich as the nature of her laws and institutions will admit; but that, with other laws and institutions, and if foreign commerce were held in honour, she might still be much richer. The question is, would such an increase of wealth be an increase of the real funds for the maintenance of labour, and consequently tend to place the lower classes of people in China in a state of greater plenty?

If trade and foreign commerce were held in great honour in China, it is

---

[14] Sir James Steuart's Political Oeconomy, vol. i. b. i. c. xviii. p. 119. [In 1806 (Vol. II, pp. 201–2) Malthus added to this note:

It is probable that Holland before the revolution had nearly reached this point, not so much however from the difficulty of obtaining more foreign corn, but from the very heavy taxes which were imposed on this first necessary of life. All the great landed nations of Europe are certainly at a considerable distance from this point at present.

[The revolution referred to here is the French Revolution of 1789; the Batavian Republic, under French domination, was established in 1795.]

[15] [From this paragraph about China until the end of the chapter Malthus followed very closely pp. 321–6 of the 1798 *Essay*.]

evident that, from the great number of labourers and the cheapness of labour, she might work up manufactures for foreign sale to an immense amount. It is equally evident that, from the great bulk of provisions, and the amazing extent of her inland territory, she could not in return import such a quantity as would be any sensible addition to the annual stock of subsistence in the country. Her immense amount of manufactures, therefore, she would[16] exchange chiefly for luxuries collected from all parts of the world. At present it appears that no labour whatever is spared in the production of food. The country is rather overpeopled in proportion to what its stock can employ, and labour is therefore so abundant that no pains are taken to abridge it. The consequence of this is probably the greatest production of food that the soil can possibly afford; for it will be generally[17] observed, that processes for abridging labour,[18] though they may enable a farmer to bring a certain quantity of grain cheaper to market, tend[19] rather to diminish than increase the whole produce. An immense capital could not be employed in China, in preparing manufactures for foreign trade, without taking off so many labourers from agriculture as to alter this state of things, and in some degree to diminish the produce of the country. The demand for manufacturing labourers would naturally raise the price of labour; but as the quantity of subsistence would not be increased, the price of provisions would keep pace with it, or even more than keep pace with it, if the quantity of provisions were really decreasing. The country would, however, be evidently advancing in wealth; the exchangeable value of the annual produce of its land and labour would be annually augmented; yet the real funds for the maintenance of labour would be stationary, or even declining; and consequently the increasing wealth of the nation would tend rather to depress than to raise the condition of the poor.[20] With regard to the command over the necessaries of life, they would be in the same, or rather worse state, than before; and a great part of them would have exchanged the healthy labours of agriculture for the unhealthy occupations of manufacturing industry.

---

16 [In 1807 (Vol. II, p. 127) this was changed to:
    ... she could exchange chiefly for luxuries ...
17 [In 1807 (Vol. II, p. 127) the word *generally* was omitted.]
18 [In 1806 (Vol. II, p. 204) this was altered to:
    ... processes for abridging agricultural labour, ...
19 [In 1807 (Vol. II, p. 128) this was modified to:
    ... sometimes tend rather to diminish ...
20 The condition of the poor in China is, indeed, very miserable at present; but this is not owing to their want of foreign commerce, but to their extreme tendency to marriage and increase; and if this tendency were to continue the same, the only way in which the introduction of a greater number of manufacturers could possibly make the lower classes of people richer would be by increasing the mortality amongst them, which is certainly not a very desirable mode of growing rich.

The argument, perhaps, appears clearer when applied to China, because it is generally allowed that its wealth has been long stationary, and its soil cultivated nearly to the utmost. With regard to any other country, it might always be a matter of dispute, at which of the two periods compared, wealth was increasing the fastest, as it is upon the rapidity of the increase of wealth at any particular period that, Dr. Smith says, the condition of the poor depends. It is evident, however, that two nations might increase exactly with the same rapidity in the exchangeable value of the annual produce of their land and labour; yet, if one had applied itself chiefly to agriculture, and the other chiefly to commerce, the funds for the maintenance of labour, and consequently the effect of the increase of wealth in each nation, would be extremely different. In that which had applied itself chiefly to agriculture, the poor would live in greater plenty, and population would rapidly increase. In that which had applied itself chiefly to commerce, the poor would be comparatively but little benefited, and consequently, population would either be stationary, or increase very slowly.[21]

---

[21] [In 1806 (Vol. II, p. 206) a footnote was added here:

The condition of the labouring poor, supposing their habits to remain the same, cannot be very essentially improved but by giving them a greater command over the means of subsistence. But any advantage of this kind must from its nature be temporary, and is therefore really of less value to them than any permanent change in their habits. But manufactures by inspiring a taste for comforts, tend to promote a favourable change in these habits, and in this way perhaps counterbalance all their disadvantages. The labouring classes of society in nations merely agricultural are generally on the whole poorer than in manufacturing nations, though less subject to those occasional variations which among manufacturers often produce the most severe distress. But the considerations which relate to a change of habits in the poor belong more properly to a subsequent part of this work.

CHAPTER IX

Of the Definitions of Wealth. Agricultural and Commercial Systems

[1]*A question seems naturally to arise here, whether the exchangeable value of the annual produce of the land and labour is the proper definition of the wealth of a country, or whether merely the produce of land, according to the French Economists,[2] may not be a more correct definition. Certain it is that every increase of wealth, according to this definition, will be an increase of the funds for the maintenance of labour, and consequently will always tend to ameliorate the condition of the labouring poor, and increase population; though an increase of wealth, according to Dr. Smith's definition, will by no means invariably have the same tendency. And yet it may not follow, from this consideration, that Dr. Smith's definition is false.

The Economists consider all labour employed in manufactures as unproductive; and in endeavouring to disprove this position, Dr. Smith has been accused of arguing obscurely and inconclusively. He appears to me, however, only incorrect in applying his own definition to try the reasoning by which the Economists support theirs; when, in fact, the question was respecting the truth or falsehood of the definitions themselves; and, of course, one could not be applied as a test to the other. Nothing can be more clear than that manufactures increase the wealth of a state according to Dr. Smith's definition; and it is equally clear, that they do not increase it according to the definition of the Economists. The question of the productiveness or unproductiveness of manufactures is allowed by the Economists to be a question respecting net produce; and the determination of this question either way would not affect Dr. Smith's definition, which includes produce of every kind, whether net or otherwise. And in the same manner, the proof of a net produce arising to individuals from manufactures would

---

[1] [The opening of this chapter corresponds with pp. 327–35 of the 1798 *Essay*. Then, in 1806, Malthus excised the first eleven paragraphs, and started the chapter with the paragraph beginning: 'There are none of the definitions of the wealth of a state that are not liable to some objections.' (Vol. II, p. 207 in 1806; Vol. I, p. 392 in this edition).]

[2] [These were the *Économistes* or *Physiocrates*, whose principal exponent was François Quesnay (1694–1774). The excision of these passages suggests that Malthus's opinion of their doctrines had changed fundamentally in the three years between the writing of the quarto and the edition of 1806.]

not really invalidate the definition of the Economists, though they have laid themselves open to objections from this quarter, by the manner in which they have defended their position.

They say that labour employed upon land is productive, because the produce, over and above completely paying the labourer and the farmer, affords a clear rent to the landlord; and that the labour employed upon a piece of lace is unproductive, because it merely replaces the provisions that the workman had consumed while making it, and the stock of his employer, without affording any clear rent whatever. But supposing the value of the wrought lace to be such, as that besides paying in the most complete manner the workman and his employer, it could afford a clear rent to a third person, the state of the case would not really be altered. Though, according to this mode of reasoning, the man employed in the manufacture of lace would, upon the present supposition, appear to be a productive labourer; yet according to their definition of the wealth of a state, he ought not to be considered in that light. He will have added nothing to the produce of the land. He has consumed a portion of this produce, and has left a piece of lace in return; and though he may sell this piece of lace for three times the quantity of provisions which he consumed while he was making it, and thus be a very productive labourer with regard to himself; yet he has added nothing by his labour to the essential wealth of the state.

Suppose that two hundred thousand men, who are now employed in producing manufactures that only tend to gratify the vanity of a few rich people, were to be employed on some barren uncultivated land, and to produce only half of the quantity of food that they themselves consumed; they might still be considered, in some respects, as more productive labourers than they were before. In their former employment, they consumed a certain portion of the food of the country, and left in return some silks and laces. In their latter employment, they consumed the same quantity of food, and left in return provision for a hundred thousand men. There can be little doubt which of the two legacies would be the most really beneficial to the country, and which, according to the definition of the Economists, would add the most to the wealth of the state.

A capital employed upon land may be unproductive to the individual that employs it, and yet be productive to the society. A capital employed in trade, on the contrary, may be highly productive to the individual, and yet be almost totally unproductive to the society. It is indeed impossible to see the great fortunes that are made in commerce and, at the same time, the liberality with which so many merchants live, and yet agree in the statement of the Economists, that manufacturers can only grow rich by depriving themselves of the funds destined for their support. In many branches of trade the profits are so great as would allow of a clear rent to a third person; but as there is no third person in the case, and all the profits centre in the merchant or master manufacturer, he seems to have a fair chance of growing rich without much privation, and we consequently see large fortunes acquired in trade by persons who have not been remarked for their parsimony.

These fortunes, however, by which individuals are greatly enriched, do not enrich proportionally the whole society and, in some respects, have even a contrary tendency. The home trade of consumption is by far the most important trade of every nation. Putting then, for a moment, foreign trade out of the question, the man who, by an ingenious manufacture, obtains a double portion out of the old stock of provisions, will certainly not be so useful to the state as the man who, by his labour, adds a single share to the former stock. And this view of the subject shows that manufactures are essentially different from the produce of the land, and that the question respecting their productiveness or unproductiveness by no means depends entirely upon the largeness of the profits upon them, or upon their yielding or not yielding a clear rent. If the Economists would allow, which, from the manner in which they express themselves, they might be sometimes supposed to do, that the value yielded by manufacturers was of the same nature as the produce of the land, though it were allowed to be only accurately equal to the value of their consumption, they certainly could not maintain the position that land is the only source of wealth. A marriage which produces two children, though it contain in itself no principle of increase, yet it adds to the sum of the actual population, which would have been less by two persons if the marriage had been really barren. But the fact is, that though the language of the Economists has fairly warranted this illustration which Dr. Smith gives; yet the illustration itself is incorrect. In the case of the marriage, the two children are really a new production, a completely new creation. But manufactures, strictly speaking, are no new production, no new creation, but merely a modification of an old one, and when sold must be paid for out of a revenue already in existence, and consequently the gain of the seller is the loss of the buyer. A revenue is transferred, but not created.

If, in asserting the productiveness of the labour employed upon land, we look only to the clear monied rent yielded to a certain number of proprietors, we undoubtedly consider the subject in a very contracted point of view. The quantity of the surplus produce of the cultivators is, indeed, measured by this clear rent; but its real value consists in its capability of supporting a certain number of people, or millions of people, according to its extent, all exempted from the labour of procuring their own food, and who may, therefore, either live without manual exertions, or employ themselves in modifying the raw produce of nature into the forms best suited to the gratification of man.

A net monied revenue, arising from manufactures, of the same extent, and to the same number of individuals, would by no means be accompanied by the same circumstances. It would throw the country in which it existed into an absolute dependence upon the surplus produce of others; and if this foreign revenue could not be obtained, the clear monied rent, which we have supposed, would be absolutely of no value to the nation.

As manufactures are not a new production, but the modification of an old one, the most natural and obvious way of estimating them is by the labour which this modification costs. At the same time, it may be doubted whether we can say positively that the price of this labour, added to the price of the raw material, is exactly their real value. The ultimate value of everything, according to the general reasoning of the Economists, consists in being *propre à la jouissance*.[3] In this view, some manufactures are of very high value; and in general they may be said to be worth to the purchaser what that purchaser will consent to give. In the actual state of things, from monopolies, from superior machinery, or other causes, they are generally sold at a price above what the Economists consider as their real worth; and with regard to a mere monied revenue to an individual, there is no apparent difference between a manufacture which yields very large profits and a piece of land which is farmed by the proprietor.[4]

Land, in an enlarged view of the subject, is incontrovertibly the sole source of all riches; but when we take individuals or particular nations into our view, the state of the question is altered, as both nations and individuals may be enriched by a transfer of revenue without the creation of a new one.*[1]

There are none of the definitions of the wealth of a state that are not liable to some objections.[5] If we take the gross produce of the land, it is evident that the funds for the maintenance of labour, the population, and the wealth, may increase very rapidly, while the nation is apparently poor, and has very little disposable revenue. If we take Dr. Smith's definition, wealth may increase as has before been shewn, without tending to increase the funds for the maintenance of labour and the population. If we take the clear surplus produce of the land, according to most of the Economists; in this case, the funds for the maintenance of labour and the population may increase,

---

[3] [A literal translation is 'suitable for enjoyment'. The phrase roughly corresponds to the statement that the ultimate value of anything consists in its utility.]

[4] I do not mean to say that the Economists do not fully comprehend the true distinction between the labour employed upon land, and the labour employed in manufactures, and really understand the value of the surplus produce of the cultivators, as totally distinct from the net monied revenue which it yields; but it appears to me that they have exposed themselves to be misunderstood, in their reasonings respecting the productiveness of land, and the unproductiveness of manufactures, by dwelling too much on the circumstance of a net rent to individuals. In an enlarged sense, it is certainly true, that land is the only source of net rent.

[5] [This is the opening sentence of this chapter in the editions of 1806 (Vol. ii, p. 207) and 1807 (Vol. ii, p. 131).]

without an increase of wealth, as in the instance of the cultivation of new lands which will pay a profit but not a rent; and, *vice versa*, wealth may increase, without increasing the funds for the maintenance of labour, and the population, as in the instance of improvements in agricultural instruments, and in the mode of agriculture, which may make the land yield the same produce with fewer persons employed upon it; and consequently the disposable wealth, or revenue, would be increased, without a power of supporting a greater number of people.

The objections, however, to the two last definitions do not prove that they are incorrect; but merely that an increase of wealth, though generally, is not necessarily and invariably accompanied by an increase of the funds for the maintenance of labour; and consequently by the power of supporting a greater number of people, or of enabling the former number to live in greater plenty and happiness.

⁶●Whichever of these two definitions is adopted as the best criterion of the wealth, power, and prosperity of a state, the great position of the Economists will always remain true, that the surplus produce of the cultivators is the great fund which ultimately pays all those who are not employed upon the land.●⁶ Throughout the whole world, the number of manufacturers, of proprietors, and of persons engaged in the various civil and military professions, must be exactly proportioned to this surplus produce, and cannot in the nature of things increase beyond it. If the earth had been so niggardly of her produce as to oblige all her inhabitants to labour for it, no manufacturers or idle persons could ever have existed. But her first intercourse with man was a voluntary present; not very large indeed, but sufficient as a fund for his subsistence, till by the proper exercise of his faculties he could procure a greater. In proportion as the labour and ingenuity of man, exercised upon the land, have increased this surplus produce, leisure has been given to a greater number of persons to employ themselves in all the inventions which embellish civilized life. And though, in its turn, the desire to profit by these inventions has greatly contributed to stimulate the cultivators to increase their surplus produce; yet the order of precedence is clearly the surplus produce; because the funds for the subsistence of the manufacturer must be advanced to him, before he can complete his work: and if we were to imagine that we could command this surplus produce, whenever we willed it, by forcing manufactures, we should

---

⁶ [In 1807 (Vol. II, p. 132) this sentence was altered:

Whichever of these two definitions is adopted as the best criterion of the wealth, power, and prosperity of a state, it must always be true that the surplus produce of the cultivators measures and limits the growth of that portion of the society which is not employed upon the land.

be quickly admonished of our gross error by the inadequate support which the workman would receive, in spite of any rise that might take place in his nominal wages.

[In 1806 (Vol. II, p. 210) the following passages were inserted here:

... in his nominal wages. If in asserting the peculiar productiveness of labour employed upon land, we look only to the clear monied rent yielded to a certain number of proprietors, we undoubtedly consider the subject in a very contracted point of view. The quantity of the surplus produce of the cultivators is indeed in part measured by this clear rent, but its real value consists in its affording the means of subsistence, and the materials of clothing and lodging to a certain number of people, according to its extent, some of whom may live without manual exertions, and others employ themselves in modifying the raw materials of nature into the forms best suited to the gratification of man.

A clear monied revenue, arising from manufactures, of the same extent and to the same number of individuals, would by no means be accompanied by the same circumstances. It would throw the country in which it existed into an absolute dependence for food and materials on the surplus produce of other nations, and if this foreign supply were by any accident to fail, the revenue would immediately cease.

The skill to modify the raw materials produced from the land would be absolutely of no value, and the individuals possessing it would immediately perish, if these raw materials, and the food necessary to support those who are working them up, could not be obtained; but if the materials and the food were secure, it would be easy to find the skill sufficient to render them of considerable value.

According to the system of the Economists, manufactures are an object on which revenue is spent, and not any part of the revenue itself.[7] But though

---

[7] Even upon this system, there is one point of view in which manufactures appear greatly to add to the riches of a state. The use of a revenue, according to the Economists, is to be spent; and a great part of it will of course be spent in manufactures. But if, by the judicious employment of manufacturing capital, these commodities grow considerably cheaper, the surplus produce becomes proportionably of so much greater value, and the real revenue of the nation is virtually increased.[(a)(b)] There is no light, perhaps, in which we can view manufactures, where they appear to be so productive as in this; and if it do not completely justify Dr. Smith in calling manufacturing labour *productive* in the strict sense of that term; it fully warrants all the pains he has taken in explaining the nature and effects of commercial capital, and of the division of manufacturing labour.

[(a)] [In 1806 (Vol. II, p. 211) the final sentence of this note was altered:
... virtually increased. If this view of the subject do not, in the eyes of the Economists, completely justify Dr. Smith in calling manufacturing labour *productive*, in the strict sense of that term, it must fully warrant all the pains he has taken in explaining the nature and effects of commercial capital, and of the division of manufacturing labour.

[(b)] [In 1807 (Vol. II, p. 135) the note was re-written:
This account of manufactures and revenue is not in my opinion correct; because, if we measure the revenue of the whole state by its whole consumption, or even by the consumption of those who live upon surplus produce, manufactures evidently form a considerable part of

from this description of manufactures, and the epithet sterile sometimes applied to them, they seem rather to be degraded by the terms of the Economists, it is a very great error to suppose that their system is really unfavourable to them. On the contrary, I am disposed to believe that it is the only system by which commerce and manufactures can prevail to a very great extent, without bringing with them, at the same time, the seeds of their own ruin. Before the late revolution in Holland, the high price of the necessaries of life had destroyed many of its manufactures.[8] Monopolies are always subject to be broken; and even the advantage of capital and machinery, which may yield extraordinary profits for a time, is liable to be greatly lessened by the competition of other nations. In the history of the world, the nations whose wealth has been derived principally from manufactures and commerce have been perfectly ephemeral beings, compared with those the basis of whose wealth has been agriculture. It is in the nature of things, that a state which subsists upon a revenue furnished by other countries must be infinitely more exposed to all the accidents of time and chance than one which produces its own.

No error is more frequent than that of mistaking effects for causes. We are so blinded by the showiness of commerce and manufactures as to believe that they are almost the sole cause of the wealth, power, and prosperity of England. But perhaps they may be more justly considered as the consequences than the cause of this wealth. According to the definition of the Economists, which considers only the produce of land, England is the richest country in Europe in proportion to her size. Her system of agriculture is beyond comparison better, and consequently her surplus produce is more considerable. France is very greatly superior to England in extent of territory and population; but when the surplus produce or disposable revenue of the two nations are compared, the superiority of France almost vanishes. And it is this great surplus produce in England, arising from her agriculture, which enables her to support such a vast body of manufactures, such formidable

---

it; and the raw produce alone would not be an adequate representation either of its quantity or of its value. But even upon this system, there is one point of view in which manufactures appear greatly to add to the riches of a state. The use of a revenue, according to the Economists, is to be spent; and a great part of it will of course be spent in manufactures. But if, by the judicious employment of manufacturing capital, these commodities grow considerably cheaper, the surplus produce becomes proportionably of so much greater value, and the real revenue of the nation is virtually increased. If this view of the subject do not, in the eyes of the Economists, completely justify Dr Smith in calling manufacturing labour *productive*, in the strict sense of that term, it ought, even according to their own definition, fully to warrant all the pains he has taken in explaining the nature and effects of commercial capital, and the division of manufacturing labour.

[8] Smith's Wealth of Nations, vol. iii. b. v. c. ii. p. 392.

fleets and armies, such a crowd of persons engaged in the liberal professions, and a proportion of the society living on money rents, very far beyond what has ever been known in any other country of the world. According to the returns lately made of the population of England and Wales, it appears that the number of persons employed in agriculture is considerably less than a fifth part of the whole. There is reason to believe that the classifications in these returns are incorrect; but making very great allowances for errors of this nature, it can scarcely admit of a doubt that the number of persons employed in agriculture is very unusually small in proportion to the actual produce. Of late years, indeed, the part of the society not connected with agriculture has unfortunately increased beyond this produce; but the average importation of corn, as yet, bears but a small proportion to that which is grown in the country, and consequently the power which England possesses of supporting so vast a body of idle consumers must be attributed principally to the greatness of her surplus produce.

It will be said that it was her commerce and manufactures which encouraged her cultivators to obtain this great surplus produce, and therefore indirectly, if not directly, created it. That commerce and manufactures produce this effect in a certain degree is true; but that they sometimes produce a contrary effect, and generally so when carried to excess, is equally true.[9] Undoubtedly agriculture cannot flourish without a vent for its commodities, either at home or abroad; but when this want has been adequately supplied, the interests of agriculture demand nothing more. When too great a part of a nation is engaged in commerce and manufactures, it is a clear proof that, either from undue encouragement or from other particular causes, a capital is employed in this way to much greater advantage than on land;[10] and under such circumstances, it is impossible that the land should not be robbed of much of the capital which would naturally have fallen to its share. Dr. Smith justly observes that the navigation act, and the monopoly of the colony trade, necessarily forced into a particular and not very advantageous channel a greater proportion of the capital of Great Britain than would otherwise have gone to it; and by thus taking capital from other employments, and at the same time universally

---

[9] [In 1806 (Vol. II, p. 214) this sentence was altered:
    That commerce and manufactures produce this effect in a great degree is true; but that they sometimes produce a contrary effect when carried to excess is equally true.
[In 1807 (Vol. II, pp. 138–9) there was a further change:
    . . . is true; but that they sometimes fail to produce it, when carried to excess, is equally true.
[10] [In 1806 (Vol. II, p. 215) this was changed to:
    . . . much greater advantage than in domestic agriculture; . . .

raising the rate of British mercantile profit, discouraged the improvement of the land.[11] If the improvement of land, he goes on to say, affords a greater profit than what can be drawn from an equal capital in any mercantile employment, the land will draw capital from mercantile employments. If the profit be less, mercantile employments will draw capital from the improvement of land. The monopoly, therefore, by raising the rate of British mercantile profit, and thus discouraging agricultural improvement, has necessarily retarded the natural increase of a great original source of revenue, the rent of land.[12]

The East and West Indies are indeed so great an object, and afford employment with high profits to so great a capital, that it is impossible that they should not draw capital from other employments, and particularly from the cultivation of the soil, the profits upon which, in general, are unfortunately very small.[13]

All corporations, patents, and exclusive privileges of every kind, which abound so much in the mercantile system, have in proportion to their extent the same effect. And the experience of the last twenty years seems to warrant us in concluding that the high price of provisions arising from the abundance of commercial wealth, accompanied, as it has been, by very great variations, and by a great rise in the price of labour, does not operate as an encouragement to agriculture sufficient to make it keep pace with the rapid strides of commerce.

It will be said, perhaps, that land is always improved by the redundancy of commercial capital. But this effect is late and slow, and in the nature of things cannot take place till this capital is really redundant, which it never is, while the interest of money and the profits of mercantile stock are high. We cannot look forwards to any considerable effect of this kind till the interest of money sinks to 3 per cent. When men can get 5 or 6 per cent. for their money, without any trouble, they will hardly venture a capital upon land, where, including risks, and the profits upon their own labour and attendance, they may not get much more. Wars and loans, as far as internal circumstances are concerned, impede but little the progress of those branches of commerce where the profits of stock are high; but affect very considerably the increase of that more essential and permanent source of wealth, the improvement of the land. It is in this point, I am inclined to believe, that the national debt of England has been most injurious to bear. By absorbing the redundancy of commercial capital, and keeping up the rate of interest, it has prevented this

---

[11] Wealth of Nations, vol. ii. b. iv. c. vii. p. 435.
[12] Id. p. 436.
[13] [In 1806 (Vol. II, p. 216) the word *unfortunately* was omitted.]

capital from overflowing upon the soil. And a large mortgage[14] has thus been established on the lands of England, the interest of which is drawn from the payment of productive labour, and dedicated to the support of idle consumers.

---

[14] One of the principal errors of the French Economists appears to be on the subject of taxation. Admitting, as I shall be disposed to do, that the surplus produce of the land is the fund which pays everything besides the food of the cultivators; yet it seems to be a mistake to suppose that the owners of land are the sole proprietors of this surplus produce. It appears to me that every man who has realized a capital in money, on which he can live without labour, has virtually a mortgage on the land for a certain portion of the surplus produce. This mortgage may not indeed be so well secured as those which usually bear this title, or as the money rent of the land-owner; but while the power of obtaining this monied interest remains, its effect, or command over the surplus produce, is exactly the same. The landholders, therefore, are not the sole proprietors of surplus produce; and their joint proprietors, those who live upon the interest of money, certainly pay a general tax in the same manner as the landholders, and cannot throw it off from their shoulders, like those who live upon the profits of stock or the wages of labour. Practically, indeed, it cannot be doubted that even the profits of stock and the wages of labour, particularly of professional labour, pay some taxes on necessaries, and many on luxuries, for a very considerable time. †The real surplus produce of this country, or all the produce not actually consumed by the cultivators, is a very different thing, and should carefully be distinguished from the sum of the net rents of the landlords. This sum, it is supposed, does not much exceed a fifth part of the gross produce. The remaining four fifths is certainly not consumed by the labourers and horses employed in agriculture; but a very considerable portion of it is paid by the farmer in taxes, in the instruments of agriculture, and in the manufactures used in his own family, and in the families of his labourers. It is in this manner that a kind of mortgage is ultimately established on the land, by taxes, and the progress of commercial wealth,† and in this sense, all taxes certainly fall upon the land. Before the existence of national debts, and the accumulation of monied capitals, the simple territorial impost would be the fairest and most eligible of all taxes; but when these mortgages alluded to have been actually established, and the interest of them cannot be changed with every new tax, which in many instances is the case, particularly with regard to government annuitants, the mortgagee will really and *bonâ fide* pay a part of the taxes on consumption; and though these taxes may still fall wholly on the land, they will not fall wholly on the landholders. It seems a little hard, therefore, in taxing surplus produce, to make the landlords pay for what they do not receive. At the same time it must be confessed that, independently of these considerations, which make a land tax partial, it is the best of all taxes, as it is the only one which does not tend to raise the price of commodities. Taxes on consumption, by which alone monied revenues can be reached without an income tax, necessarily raise all prices to a degree greatly injurious to the country. A land tax, or tax upon net rent, has little or no effect in discouraging the improvement of land, as many have supposed. It is only a tithe or a tax in proportion to the gross produce, which does this. No man in his senses will be deterred from getting a clear profit of 20l. instead of 10l. because he is always to pay a fourth or fifth of his clear gains; but when he is to pay a tax in proportion to his gross produce, which, in the case of capital laid out in improvements, is scarcely ever accompanied with a proportional increase of his clear gains, it is a very different thing, and must necessarily impede in a great degree the progress of cultivation. I am astonished that so obvious and easy a commutation for tithes, as a land tax on improved rents, has not been adopted. Such a tax would be paid by the same person as before, only in a better form; and the change would not be felt, except in the advantage that would accrue to all the parties concerned, the landlord, the tenant, and the clergyman. Tithes undoubtedly operate as a high bounty on pasture, and a great discouragement to

It must be allowed, therefore, upon the whole, that our commerce has not done much for our agriculture; but that our agriculture has done a great deal for our commerce;[15] and that the improved system of cultivation which has taken place, in spite of considerable discouragements, creates yearly a surplus produce, which enables the country, with but little assistance, to support so vast a body of people engaged in pursuits unconnected with the land.

---

tillage, which in the present peculiar circumstances of the country is a very great disadvantage.

[This footnote was altered twice. In 1806 (Vol. II, pp. 217–20) it was divided into three paragraphs. The first ran thus:

The principal error of the French Economists appears to be on the subject of taxation. Admitting that the surplus produce of the land is the fund which pays everything besides the food of the cultivators; yet it seems to be a mistake to suppose that the owners of land are the sole proprietors of this surplus produce. It appears to me that every man who has realized a capital in money has virtually a mortgage on the land for a certain portion of the surplus produce; and as long as the conditions of this mortgage remain unaltered (and the taxes which affect him only in the character of a consumer, do not alter these conditions) the mortgagee pays a tax in the same manner as the landholder, finally. As consumers indeed it cannot be doubted, that even those who live upon the profits of stock and the wages of labour, particularly of professional labour, pay some taxes on necessaries for a very considerable time, and many on luxuries permanently; because the consumption of individuals, who possess large shares of the wealth which is paid in profits and wages, may be curtailed and turned into another channel, without impeding, in any degree, the continuance of the same quantity of stock or the production of the same quantity of labour.

[The second paragraph in 1806 began at the first† with 'The real surplus ...' and the text was unchanged until the second† when it continued:

... and in this sense, all taxes may be said to fall wholly upon the land, though not wholly upon the landholders.

[All the next sentence, *Before the existence of national debts* ... was omitted, and the passage continued with 'It seems a little hard ...'. The second paragraph concluded with '... greatly injurious to the country'. The remainder of this note, unaltered, became the third paragraph.]

[In 1807 (Vol. II, p. 142) the opening sentences of this footnote were changed again:

The great practical error of the Economists appears to be on the subject of taxation; and this error does not necessarily flow from their confined and inadequate definition of wealth, but is a false inference from their own premises. Admitting that the surplus produce of the land is the fund which pays everything besides the food of the cultivators; yet it seems to be a mistake to suppose that the owners of land are the sole proprietors of this surplus produce. Every man who has realised a capital in money has virtually a mortgage ...

[Malthus also made a further alteration at (b):

... in this sense, all taxes may be said to fall upon the land, though not on the landholders.

15 [Malthus altered this twice. In 1806 (Vol. II, p. 220) he wrote:

It must be allowed, therefore, upon the whole, that our commerce has not done so much for our agriculture as our agriculture has for our commerce; and that the improved system ...

[In 1807 (Vol. II, p. 144) this was changed to:

It must be allowed, therefore, upon the whole, that our commerce has not done more for our agriculture, than our agriculture has for our commerce; ...

CHAPTER X

Different Effects of the Agricultural and Commercial Systems

About the middle of the last century, we were genuinely, and in the strict sense of the Economists, an agricultural nation.[1] Our commerce and manufactures were, however, then in a very respectable and thriving state; and if they had continued to bear the same relative proportion to our agriculture, they would evidently have gone on increasing considerably,[2] with the improving cultivation of the country. There is no apparent limit to the quantity of manufactures which might in time be supported in this way. The increasing wealth of a country in such a state seems to be out of the reach of all common accidents. There is no discoverable germ of decay in the system; and in theory, there is no reason to say that it might not go on increasing in wealth and prosperity for thousands of years.

We have now, however, stepped out of the agricultural system into a state in which the commercial system clearly predominates; and there is but too much reason to fear that even our commerce and manufactures will ultimately feel the disadvantage of the change. It has been already observed, that we are exactly in that situation in which a country feels most fully the effect of those common years of deficient crops which, in the natural course of things, are to be expected. The competition of increasing commercial wealth, operating upon a supply of corn not increasing in the same proportion, must at all times greatly[3] tend to raise the price of labour; but when scarce years are taken into the consideration, its effect in this way must ultimately be prodigious.[4] We know how extremely difficult it is in England to lower the wages of labour after they have once been raised.[5] [6]●During the late scarcities, the price of labour has been continually rising – not to fall again; the rents of land have been every where advancing – not to fall again; and of

---

[1] [In 1807 (Vol. II, p. 145) this was altered to:
... we were genuinely an agricultural nation.

[2] [In 1807 (Vol. II, p. 145) this read:
... increasing constantly with the improving cultivation of the country.

[3] [In 1806 (Vol. II, p. 222) the word *greatly* was omitted.]

[4] [In 1806 (Vol. II, p. 222) *prodigious* was changed to 'very great'.]

[5] [In 1806 (Vol. II, p. 222) this sentence was omitted.]

course the price of produce must rise – not to fall again; as, independently of a particular competition from scarcity, or the want of competition from plenty, its price is necessarily regulated by the wages of labour and the rent of land. We have no reason whatever for supposing that we shall be exempt in future from such scarcities as we have of late experienced. On the contrary, upon our present system, they seem to be unavoidable. And if we go on, as we have done lately, the price of labour and of provisions must soon increase in a manner out of all proportion to their price in the rest of Europe; and it is impossible that this should not ultimately check all our dealings with foreign powers, and give a fatal blow to our commerce and manufactures. The effect of capital, skill, machinery, and establishments in their full vigour is great; so great, indeed, that it is difficult to guess at its limit; but still it is not infinite, and without doubt has this limit. The principal states of Europe, except this fortunate island, have of late suffered so much by the actual presence of war that their commerce and manufactures have been nearly destroyed, and we may be said in a manner to have the monopoly of the trade of Europe. All monopolies yield high profits, and at present, therefore, the trade can be carried on to advantage in spite of the high price of labour. But when the other nations of Europe shall have had time to recover themselves, and gradually to become our competitors, it would be rash to affirm that, with the prices of provisions and of labour still going on increasing from what they are at present, we shall be able to stand the competition. Dr. Smith says that, in his time, merchants frequently complained of the high price of British labour as the cause of their manufactures being undersold in foreign markets.[6(a)] If such complaints were in any degree founded at that time, how will they be aggravated twenty years hence! And have we not some reason to fear that our present great commercial prosperity is temporary, and belongs a little to that worst feature of the commercial system, the rising by the depression of others.

When a country, in average years, grows more corn than it consumes, and is in the habit of exporting a part of it, its price, and the price of labour as depending on it, can never rise in any very extraordinary degree above the common price in other commercial countries;●[6] and under such circum-

---

[6(a)] Wealth of Nations, vol. ii. b. iv. c. vii. p. 413.

[6] [In 1806 (Vol. II, pp. 222–5) the preceding passage was re-written, from 'During the late ...' on p. 400:

    ... During the late scarcities the price of labour has been continually rising, and it will not readily fall again. In every country there will be many causes, which, in practice, operating like friction in mechanics, prevent the price of labour from rising and falling exactly in proportion to the price of its component parts. But besides these causes, there is one very powerful cause in theory, which operates to prevent the price of labour from falling when once it has been raised. Supposing it to be raised by a temporary cause, such as a scarcity of

stances, England would have nothing to fear from the fullest and most open competition. The increasing prosperity of other countries would only open to her a more extensive market for her commodities, and give additional spirit to all her commercial transactions.

The high price of corn and of rude produce in general, as far as it is occasioned by the freest competition among the nations of Europe, is a very great advantage, and is the best possible encouragement to agriculture; but when occasioned merely by the competition of monied wealth at home, its effect is totally[7] different. In the one case, a great encouragement is given to production in general; and the more is produced, the better. In the other case, the produce is necessarily confined to the home consumption. The cultivators are justly afraid of growing too much corn, as a considerable loss will be sustained upon that part of it which is sold abroad; and a glut in the home market will universally make the price fall below the fair and proper recompence to the grower. It is impossible that a country, under such circumstances, should not be subject to great and frequent variations in the price of corn,[8] and occasionally to severe scarcities.

---

provisions, it is evident that it will not fall again, unless some kind of stagnation take place in the competition among the purchasers of labour; but the power which the increase of the real price of labour, on the return of plenty, gives to the labour of purchasing a greater quantity both of rude and manufactured produce, tends to prevent this stagnation, and strongly to counteract that fall in the price which would otherwise take place.

Labour is a commodity the price of which will not be so readily affected by the price of its component parts as any other. The reason why the consumer pays a tax on any commodity, or an advance in the price of any of its component parts, is because if he cannot or will not pay this advance of price, the commodity will not be produced in the same quantity, and the next year there will be only such a proportion in the market as is accommodated to the number of persons that will consent to pay the advance. But in the case of labour, the operation of withdrawing the commodity is much slower and more painful. Although the purchasers refuse to pay the advanced price, the same supply will necessarily remain in the market, not only the next year, but for some years to come. Consequently, if no increase take place in the demand, and the tax or advance in the price of provisions be not so great as to make it immediately obvious that the labourer cannot support his family, it is probable that he will continue to pay this advance, till a relaxation in the rate of the increase of population causes the market to be under supplied with labour, and then of course the competition among the purchasers will raise the price above the proportion of the advance, in order to restore the necessary supply. In the same manner, if an advance in the price of labour take place during two or three years of scarcity, it is probable that on the return of plenty the real recompence of labour will continue higher than the usual average, till a too rapid increase of population causes a competition among the labourers, and a consequent diminution of the price of labour below the usual rate.

When a country in average years grows more corn than it consumes, and is in the habit of exporting a part of it, those great variations of price which, from the competition of commercial wealth, often produce lasting effects, cannot occur to the same extent. The wages of labour can never rise very much above the common price in other commercial countries; ...

[7] [In 1806 (Vol. II, p. 225) the word *totally* was excised.]

[8] [In 1806 (Vol. II, p. 226) this sentence ended here.]

If we were to endeavour to lower the price of labour by encouraging the importation of foreign corn, we should probably aggravate the evil tenfold. Experience warrants us in saying that, from political fears or other causes, the fall in the price of labour would be uncertain; but the ruin of our agriculture would be certain.[9] The British grower of corn could not, in his own markets, stand the competition of the foreign grower, in average years. We should be daily thrown more and more into a dependence upon other countries for our support.[10] Arable lands of a moderate quality would not pay the expense of cultivation.[11] Rich soils alone would yield a rent. Round all our towns, the appearances would be the same as usual; but in the interior of the country, half of the lands[12] would be neglected, and almost universally, where it was practicable, pasture would take place of tillage. [13]●How dreadfully precarious would our commerce and manufactures, and even our very existence be, under such circumstances! It could hardly be expected that a century should elapse without seeing our population repressed within the limits of our scanty cultivation; and suffering the same melancholy reverse as the once flourishing population of Spain.

Nothing perhaps will shew more clearly the absurdity of that artificial system, which prompts a country with a large territory of its own, to depend upon others for its food, than the supposition of the same system being pursued by many other states. If France, Germany and Prussia were to become manufacturing nations, and to consider agriculture as a secondary concern, how would their wants, in the indispensable article of food, be supplied? The increasing demand for corn would tend certainly to encourage the growth of it in Russia and America; but we know that in these countries at present, particularly in America, the natural progress of population is not very greatly checked; and that, as their towns and manufactories increase, the demand for their own corn will of course increase with them. The Russian nobleman, whose revenue depends upon the number of his boors, will hardly be persuaded to check their increase in order to accommodate other nations; and the independent cultivator of America will surely feed his own family and servants, and probably supply the home market, before he begins to export. But allowing that at first, and for some time, the increasing demands

---

[9] [In 1806 (Vol. II, p. 226) this sentence read:
    Experience warrants us in saying that the fall in the price of labour would be slow and uncertain; but the decline of our agriculture would be certain.

[10] [In 1806 (Vol. II, p. 226) this sentence was omitted.]

[11] [In 1806 (Vol. II, p. 226) this was altered to:
    ... would hardly pay the expence of cultivation.

[12] [In 1806 (Vol. II, p. 226) this read:
    ... much of the land would be neglected, ...

could not in the nature of things last long. The manufacturers, from the decay of agriculture in their own countries, would annually want more; and Russia and America, from their rapidly increasing population, and the gradual establishment of manufactures at home, would annually be able to spare less. From these causes and the necessity of drawing a part of such vast supplies of corn from a much greater distance inland, and loaded perhaps with the expense of land carriage, the price would ultimately rise so extravagantly high, that the poor manufacturers would be totally unable to pay it, and want and famine would convince them too late of the precarious and subordinate nature of their wealth. They would learn, by painful experience, that though agriculture may flourish considerably, and give plenty and happiness to great numbers, without many manufactures; yet that manufactures cannot stir a single step without their agricultural pay-masters, either at home or abroad; and that therefore it is the height of folly and imprudence to have these pay-masters at a great distance, with different interests, and their payments precarious, instead of at home, with the same interests, and their payments always ready and certain. Nothing can be so hateful to a liberal mind, as the idea of being placed in a situation in which the growing prosperity of your neighbours will be the signal of your own approaching ruin. Yet this would be the situation of the principal countries of Europe, if they depended chiefly upon Russia and America or any other nations for their corn. A system which, like the present commercial system of England, throws a country into this state, without any physical necessity for it, cannot be founded on the genuine principles of the wealth of nations.

It seems almost impossible that a country possessed of a considerable territory should have its means of subsistence well assured without growing at home more corn than it consumes. Nor can it be exempt from those great and sudden variations of price, which produce such severe distress throughout so large a part of the community, and are often attended with great and lasting disadvantages; unless this superfluity of produce bear some considerable proportion to the common deficiencies of unfavourable years.●[13]

---

[13] [In 1806 (Vol. II, pp. 226–9) the preceding passage was re-written from 'How dreadfully precarious ...' on p. 403:

... pasture would take place of tillage. This state of things would continue, till the equilibrium was restored, either by the fall of British rent and wages, or an advance in the price of foreign corn, or, what is more probable, by the union of both causes. But a period would have elapsed of considerable relative encouragement to manufactures, and relative discouragement to

It has been almost universally acknowledged that there is no branch of trade, more profitable to a country, even in a commercial point of view, than the sale of rude produce. In general, its value bears a much greater proportion to the expense incurred in procuring it, than that of any other commodity whatever, and the national profit on its sale is in consequence greater. This is often noticed by Dr. Smith; but in combating the arguments of the Economists, he seems for a moment to forget it, and to speak of the superior advantage of exporting manufactures.

---

agriculture. A certain portion of capital would be taken from the land, and when the equilibrium was at length restored, the nation would probably be found dependant upon foreign supplies for a great portion of her subsistence; and unless some particular cause were to occasion a foreign demand greater than the home demand, her independence, in this respect, could not be recovered. During this period even her commerce and manufactures would be in a most precarious state; and circumstances by no means improbable in the present state of Europe might reduce her population within the limits of her reduced cultivation.[a]

In the natural course of things, a country which depends for a considerable part of its supply of corn upon its poorer neighbours may expect to see this supply gradually diminish, as these countries increase in riches and population, and have less surplus of their rude produce to spare.

The political relations of such a country may expose it, during a war, to have that part of its supplies of provisions which it derives from foreign states suddenly stopped or greatly diminished; an event which could not take place without producing the most calamitous effects.

A nation in which commercial wealth predominates has an abundance of all those articles which form the principal consumption of the rich, but is exposed to be straightened in its supplies of that article which is absolutely necessary to all, and in which by far the greatest portion of the revenue of the industrious classes is expended.

A nation in which agricultural wealth predominates, though it may not produce at home such a surplus of luxuries and conveniences as the commercial nation, and may therefore be exposed possibly to some want of these commodities, has, on the other hand, a surplus of that article which is essential to the well being of the whole state, and is therefore secure from want in what is of the greatest importance.

And if we cannot be so sure of the supply of what we derive from others, as of what we produce at home, it seems to be an advantageous policy in a nation, whose territory will allow of it, to secure a surplus of that commodity, a deficiency of which would strike most deeply at its happiness and prosperity.

[a] Though it be true that the high price of labour or taxes on agricultural capital ultimately fall on the rent, yet we must by no means throw out of our consideration the current leases. In the course of twenty years, I am inclined to believe that the state of agriculture in any country might be very flourishing, or very much the reverse, according as the current leases had tended to encourage or discourage improvement. A general fall in the rent of land would be preceded by a period most unfavourable to the investment of agricultural capital; and consequently every tax which affects agricultural capital is peculiarly pernicious. Taxes which affect capitals in trade are almost immediately shifted off on the consumer; but taxes which affect agricultural capital fall, during the current leases, wholly on the farmer.

He observes that a trading and manufacturing country exports what can subsist and accommodate but very few, and imports the subsistence and accommodation of a great number. The other, exports the subsistence and accommodation of a great number, and imports that of a very few only. The inhabitants of the one must always enjoy a much greater quantity of subsistence than what their own lands in the actual state of their cultivation could afford. The inhabitants of the other must always enjoy a much smaller quantity.[14]

In this passage he does not seem to argue with his usual accuracy. Though the manufacturing nation may export a commodity which, in its actual shape, can only subsist and accommodate a very few; yet it must be recollected that, in order to prepare this commodity for exportation, a considerable part of the revenue of the country had been employed in subsisting and accommodating a great number of workmen. And with regard to the subsistence and accommodation which the other nation exports, whether it be of a great or a small number, it is certainly no more than sufficient to replace the subsistence that had been consumed in the manufacturing nation, together with the profits of the master manufacturer and merchant, which probably are not so great as the profits of the farmer and the merchant in the agricultural nation. And though it may be true, that the inhabitants of the manufacturing nation enjoy a greater quantity of subsistence than what their own lands, in the actual state of their cultivation, could afford; yet an inference in favour of the manufacturing system by no means follows, because the adoption of the one or the other system will make the greatest difference in their actual state of cultivation. If, during the course of a century, two landed nations were to pursue these two different systems, that is, if one of them were regularly to export manufactures and import subsistence; and the other to export subsistence, and import manufactures, there would be no comparison at the end of the period between the state of cultivation in the two countries; and no doubt could rationally be entertained that the country which exported its raw produce would be able to subsist and accommodate a much greater population than the other.

[15]●In the ordinary course of things, the exportation of raw produce is sufficiently profitable to the individuals concerned in it. But with regard to national profit, it possesses two peculiar and eminent advantages above any other kind of export. In the first place, raw produce, and more particularly corn, pays from its own funds the expenses of procuring it, and the whole of what is sold is a clear national profit. If I set up a new manufacture, the

---

[14] Wealth of Nations, vol. iii. b. iv. c. ix. p. 27.

persons employed in it must be supported out of the funds of subsistence already existing in the country, the value of which must be deducted from the price for which the commodity is sold, before we can estimate the clear national profit; and of course this profit can only be the profit of the master manufacturer and the exporting merchant. But if I cultivate fresh land, or employ more men in the improvement of what was before cultivated, I increase the general funds of subsistence in the country. With a part of this increase I support all the additional persons employed, and the whole of the remainder which is exported and sold is a clear national gain; besides the advantage to the country of supporting an additional population equal to the additional number of persons so employed, without the slightest tendency to diminish the plenty of the rest.

Secondly, it is impossible always to be secure of having enough if we have not, in general, too much; and the habitual exportation of corn seems to be the only practicable mode of laying by a store of sufficient magnitude to answer the emergencies that are to be expected. The evil of scarcity is so dreadful, that any branch of commerce, the tendency of which is to prevent it, cannot but be considered, in a national point of view, as pre-eminently beneficial.

These two advantages, added to that which must necessarily accrue to manufactures from the steady and comparatively low price of provisions and of labour, are so striking, that it must be a point of the first consequence to the permanent prosperity of any country to be able to carry on the export trade of corn, as one considerable branch of its commercial transactions.●[15]

But how to give this ability, how to turn a nation from the habit of importing corn to the habit of exporting it, is the great difficulty. It has been generally acknowledged, and is frequently noticed by Dr. Smith, that the policy of modern Europe has led it to encourage the industry of the towns more than the industry of the country, or, in other words, trade more than agriculture. In this policy, England has certainly not been behind the rest of

---

[15] [In 1806 (Vol. II, pp. 231–4) the preceding passage was re-written from 'In the ordinary course of things ...' on p. 406:

In the ordinary course of things, the exportation of corn is sufficiently profitable to the individuals concerned in it. But with regard to national advantage, there are four very strong reasons why it is to be preferred to any other kind of export. In the first place, corn pays from its own funds the expences of procuring it, and the whole of what is sold is a clear national profit. If I set up a new manufacture, the persons employed in it must be supported out of the funds of subsistence already existing in the country, the value of which must be deducted from the price for which the commodity is sold, before we can estimate the clear national profit. But if I cultivate fresh land, or employ more men in the improvement of what was before cultivated, I

Europe; perhaps, indeed, except in one instance,[16] it may be said that she has been the foremost. If things had been left to take their natural course, there is no reason to think that the commercial part of the society would have increased beyond the surplus produce of the cultivators; but the high profits of commerce, from monopolies and other peculiar encouragements, have altered this natural course of things; and the body politic is in an artificial, and in some degree, diseased state, with one of its principal members out of proportion to the rest. Almost all medicine is in itself bad; and one of the great evils of illness is the necessity of taking it. No person can well be more averse to medicine in the animal economy, or a system of expedients in political economy, than myself; but in the present state of the country

increase the general funds of subsistence in the country. With a part of this increase I support all the additional persons employed, and the whole of the remainder which is exported and sold is a clear national gain; besides the advantage to the country of supporting an additional population equal to the additional number of persons so employed, without the slightest tendency to diminish the plenty of the rest.

Secondly, in all wrought commodities, the same quantity of capital, skill, and labour employed will produce the same (or very nearly the same) quantity of complete manufacture. But owing to the variations of the seasons, the same quantity of capital, skill, and labour in husbandry may produce in different years very different quantities of corn. Consequently, if the two commodities were equally valuable to man, from the greater probability of the occasional failure of corn than of manufactures, it would be of more consequence to have an average surplus of the former than of the latter.

Thirdly, corn being an article of the most absolute necessity, in comparison with which all others will be sacrificed, a deficiency of it must necessarily produce a much greater advance of price than a deficiency of any other kind of produce; and as the price of corn influences the price of so many other commodities, the evil effects of a deficiency will not only be more severe and more general, but more lasting, than the effects of a deficiency in any other commodity.

Fourthly, there appear to be but three ways of rendering the supplies of corn in a particular country more equable, and of preventing the evil effects of those deficiencies from unfavourable seasons, which in the natural course of things must be expected occasionally to recur. These are, 1. An immediate supply from foreign nations, as soon as the scarcity occurs. 2. Large public granaries. 3. The habitual growth of a quantity of corn for a more extended market than the average home consumption affords.[(a)] Of the first, experience has convinced us that the suddenness of the demand prevents it from being effectual. To the second, it is acknowledged by all that these are very great and weighty objections. There remains then only the third.

These considerations seem to make it a point of the first consequence to the happiness and permanent prosperity of any country, to be able to carry on the export trade of corn as one considerable branch of its commercial transactions.

---

[16] The bounty on the exportation of corn.

[(a)] [In 1807 (Vol. ii, p. 158) Malthus added a footnote here:
A plan has lately been suggested in Mr Oddy's European Commerce (page 511), of making this country an entrepôt of foreign grain, to be opened only for internal sale when corn is above the importation price, whatever that may be. To this plan, if it can be executed, I see no objection; and it certainly deserves attention. It would not interfere with the home growth of corn, and would be a good provision against years of scarcity.

something of the kind may be necessary to prevent greater evils. It is a matter of very little comparative importance whether we are fully supplied with broadcloth, linens and muslins, or even with tea, sugar and coffee; and no rational politician, therefore, would think of proposing a bounty upon such commodities. But it is certainly a matter of the very highest importance, whether we are fully supplied with food; and if a bounty would produce such a supply, the most liberal political economist might be justified in proposing it; considering food as a commodity distinct from all others, and pre-eminently valuable.

CHAPTER XI

Of Bounties on the Exportation of Corn

[1]●It is acknowledged by Dr. Smith, that the encouragement given to the industry of the towns has turned more capital into that channel than would otherwise have gone to it; and if this be true, it follows that the land must have had less than its natural share; and under such a discouragement, we cannot reasonably expect that agriculture should be able to keep pace with manufactures. The corn laws, as they were established in 1688 and 1700, did not do more than place them upon an equality.

The regulations respecting importation and exportation adopted in these corn laws seemed to have the effect of giving that encouragement to agriculture which it so much wanted, and the apparent result was gradually to produce a growth of corn in the country considerably above the wants of the actual population, and consequently to lower greatly the prices of it, and give a steadiness to these prices that had never been experienced before.●[1]

[In 1806 (Vol. II, pp. 237–9) Malthus replaced these two opening paragraphs by the following six:

In discussing the policy of a bounty on the exportation of corn, it should be premised that the private interests of the farmers and proprietors should never enter in the question. The sole object of our consideration ought to be the permanent interest of the consumer, in the character of which is comprehended the whole nation.

According to the general principles of political economy, it cannot be doubted that it is for the interest of the civilized world that each nation should purchase its commodities wherever they can be had the cheapest.

According to these principles, it is rather desirable that some obstacles should exist to the excessive accumulation of wealth in any particular country, and that rich nations should be tempted to purchase their corn of poorer nations, as by these means the wealth of the civilized world will not only be more rapidly increased but more equably diffused.

It is evident, however, that local interests and political relations may modify the application of these general principles; and in a country with a territory fit for the production of corn, an independent, and at the same time a more equable supply of this necessary of life, may be an object of such importance as to warrant a deviation from them.

It is undoubtedly true, that every thing will ultimately find its level, but this level is sometimes effected in a very harsh manner. England may export corn a hundred years hence without the assistance of a bounty; but this is much more likely to happen from the destruction of her manufactures than from the increase of her agriculture; and a policy which, in so important a point, may tend to soften the harsh corrections of general laws, seems to be justifiable.

The regulations respecting importation and exportation adopted in the corn laws that were established in 1688 and 1700 seemed to have the effect of giving that encouragement to agriculture which it so much wanted, and the apparent result was gradually to produce a growth of corn in the country considerably above the wants of the actual population, to lower the average price of it, and give a steadiness to prices that had never been experienced before.

[In 1807 (Vol. II, pp. 162–3) the final part of this last paragraph was altered:

... encouragement to agriculture, which it so much wanted; at least they were followed by a growth of corn in the country considerably above the wants of the actual population, by a lower average price, and by a steadiness of prices that had never been experienced before.

During the seventeenth century, and indeed the whole period of our history previous to it, the prices of wheat were subject to great fluctuations, and the average price was very high. For fifty years before the year 1700, the average price of wheat per quarter was 3l. 11d. and before 1650 it was 6l. 8s. 10d.[2] From the time of the completion of the corn laws in 1700 and 1706, the prices became extraordinarily steady; and the average price for forty years previous to the year 1750 sunk so low as 1l. 16s. per quarter. This was the period of our greatest exportations. In the year 1757 the laws were suspended, and in the year 1773 they were totally altered. The exports of corn have since been regularly decreasing, and the imports increasing. The average price of wheat for the forty years ending in 1800, was 2l. 9s. 5d; and for the last five years of this period, 3l. 6s. 6d. During this last term, the balance of the imports of all sorts of grain is estimated at 2 938 357,[3] and the dreadful fluctuations of price which have occurred of late years we are but too well acquainted with.

It is at all times dangerous to be hasty in drawing general inferences from partial experience; but, in the present instance, the period that has been considered is of so considerable an extent, and the changes from fluctuating and high prices, to steady and low prices, with a return to fluctuating and high prices again, correspond so accurately with the establishment and full vigour of the corn laws, and with their subsequent alterations and inefficacy,

---

[2] Dirom's Inquiry into the Corn Laws, Appendix, No. 1. [In 1807 (Vol. II, p. 163) Malthus changed *fifty* to 'sixty-three' and the reference to Dirom was omitted.]

[3] Anderson's Investigation of the Circumstances which led to Scarcity, table, p. 40.

that it was certainly rather a bold assertion in Dr. Smith to say that the fall in the price of corn must have happened in spite of the bounty, and could not possibly have happened in consequence of it.[4] We have a right to expect that he should defend a position, so contrary to all apparent experience, by the most powerful arguments.[5] As in the present state of this country the subject seems to be of the highest importance, it will be worth while to examine the validity of these arguments.

He observes that, both in years of plenty and in years of scarcity, the bounty necessarily tends to raise the money price of corn somewhat higher that it otherwise would be in the home market.[6]

That it does so in years of plenty is undoubtedly true; but that it does so in years of scarcity appears to me as undoubtedly false. The only argument, by which Dr. Smith supports this latter position, is by saying that the exportation prevents the plenty of one year from relieving the scarcity of another. But this is certainly a very insufficient reason. The scarce year may not immediately follow the most plentiful year; and it is totally contrary to the habits and practice of farmers to save the superfluity of six or seven years for a contingency of this kind. Great practical inconveniences generally attend the keeping of so large a reserved store. Difficulties often occur from a want of proper accommodations for it. It is at all times liable to damage from vermin and other causes. When very large, it is apt to be viewed with a jealous and grudging eye by the common people. And in general the farmer may either not be able to remain so long without his returns; or may not be willing to employ so considerable a capital in a way in which the returns must necessarily be distant and precarious. On the whole, therefore, we cannot reasonably expect that, upon this plan, the reserved store should in any degree be equal to that which in a scarce year would be kept at home, in a country which was in the habit of constant exportation to a considerable amount; and we know that even a very little difference in the degree of deficiency will often make a very great difference in the price.

Dr. Smith then proceeds to state, very justly, that the defenders of the corn laws do not insist so much upon the price of corn in the actual state of tillage, as upon their tendency to improve this actual state, by opening a more extensive foreign market to the corn of the farmer, and securing to him a better price than he could otherwise expect for his commodity: which double encouragement they imagine must, in a long period of years, occasion such

---

[4] Wealth of Nations, vol. ii. b. iv. c. v. p. 264.

[5] [In 1807 (Vol. II, p. 164) this was expanded:

... consequence of it. From a view of the facts, it does not at any rate seem probable, that the causes, whatever they may be, which have produced this effect, should have been continually impeded by the laws in question; and we have a right to expect ...

[6] Wealth of Nations, vol. ii. b. iv. c. v. p. 265.

an increase in the production of corn as may lower its price in the home market much more than the bounty can raise it, in the state of tillage then actually existing.[7]

In answer to this, he observes that whatever extension of the foreign market can be occasioned by the bounty, must, in every particular year, be altogether at the expense of the home market; as every bushel of corn, which is exported by means of the bounty, and which would not have been exported without the bounty, would have remained in the home market to increase the consumption and to lower the price of that commodity.

In this observation he appears to me a little to misuse the term market. Because, by selling a commodity below its natural price, it is possible to get rid of a greater quantity of it, in any particular market, than would have gone off otherwise, it cannot justly be said that by this process such a market is proportionally extended. Though the removal of the two taxes mentioned by Dr. Smith, as paid on account of the bounty, would certainly rather increase the power of the lower classes to purchase; yet in each particular year the consumption must be ultimately limited by the population; and the increase of consumption from the removal of these taxes might by no means be sufficient to take off the whole superfluity of the farmers, without lowering the general price of corn, so as to deprive them of their fair recompense.[8]

[9]•Suppose that the cultivators in England had a million quarters of wheat beyond what would supply the country, at a price for which they must sell their whole crop or lose their fair profits. And suppose, at the same time, that from the high price of land, the great taxes on consumption, and the consequent high price of labour, the British farmer cannot grow corn at the average price in Europe, which is always true when a bounty upon exportation is rendered necessary. Under these circumstances, if the cultivators endeavoured to force the additional million of quarters on the home market, it is perfectly clear that not only the price of this additional million, but the price of their whole crop, would fall very considerably; and without a bounty it could not answer to the farmer to export, till the prices in the home market had fallen below the average price in Europe, which we supposed to be lower than what would properly pay to the British farmer the expenses of cultivation. The purchasers in the home market would undoubtedly live for this year in great plenty. They might eat as much bread as they pleased themselves, and perhaps even feed their hogs and their horses on wheat corn;

---

[7] Wealth of Nations, vol. ii. b. iv. c. v. p. 265.

[8] [In 1806 (Vol. II, p. 244) a sentence was added here:
    ... their fair recompense. If the price of British corn in the home market rise in consequence of the bounty, it is an unanswerable proof that the effectual market for British corn is extended by it; and that the diminution of demand at home, whatever it may be, is more than counterbalanced by the extension of the demand abroad.

but the farmers in the mean time would be ruined, and would dread, as the greatest of all evils, the growing of too much corn. Finding, therefore, that tillage would not answer to them, they would of course neglect the plough, and gradually lay more of their land into pasture, till the return of scarcity, or at least the total removal of the superfluity, had again raised the prices to such a height as would make it answer to them to grow corn, provided that they never overstocked the home market. An individual farmer cannot know the quantity of corn that is sown by his brother farmers in other counties. The state of the future supply, in proportion to the future demand, remains in a great measure concealed till the harvest; and the cheapness or dearness of the current year can alone regulate the conduct of the farmer in the management of his land for the following year. Under such circumstances, great variations in the supply of corn, and consequently in its price, must necessarily occur. ●[9]

There cannot be a greater discouragement to the production of any commodity in a large quantity, than the fear of overstocking the market with it.[10] Nor can there be a greater encouragement to such a production, than the certainty of finding an effectual market for any quantity, however great, that can be obtained. [11]●It is obvious, that in the case of which we have supposed, nothing but a bounty upon corn can extend the effectual market for it to the British farmer.●[11]

Dr. Smith goes on to say that if the two taxes paid by the people on account of the bounty namely, the one to the government to pay this bounty, and the other paid in the advanced price of the commodity, in the actual state of the crop, do not raise the price of labour, and thus return upon the farmer; they must reduce the ability of the labouring poor to bring up their children and, by thus restraining the population and industry of the country, must tend to stunt and restrain the gradual extension of the home market, and thereby, in the long run, rather to diminish than to augment the whole market and consumption of corn.[12]

I think it has been shewn, and indeed it will scarcely admit of a doubt, that the system of exportation arising from the bounty has an evident tendency in

---

[9] [In 1806 (Vol. ii, p. 244) this whole paragraph was omitted.]

[10] I am sufficiently aware that, in common years, the farmer is apt to proceed in a regular routine of crops, without much attention to prices; but we cannot doubt for a moment that this routine will yield to extreme cases. No man in his senses will long go on with any species of cultivation by which he loses. [In 1806 (Vol. ii, p. 244) this footnote was omitted.]

[11] [In 1806 (Vol. ii, p. 244) this sentence was re-written:
    ... can be obtained. It should be observed further, that one of the principal objects of the bounty is to obtain a surplus above the home consumption which may supply the deficiency of unfavourable years; but it is evident that no possible extension of the home market can attain this object.

[12] Wealth of Nations, vol. ii. b. iv. c. v. p. 267.

years of scarcity to increase the supplies of corn, or to prevent their being so much diminished as they otherwise would be, which comes to the same thing. Consequently the labouring poor will be able to live better, and the population will be less checked in these particular years, than they would have been without the system of exportation arising from the bounty. But if the effect of the bounty, in this view of the subject, be only to repress a little the population in years of plenty, while it encourages it comparatively in years of scarcity, its effect is evidently to regulate the population more equally according to that quantity of subsistence which can permanently, and without occasional defalcations, be supplied. And this effect, I have no hesitation in saying, is one of the greatest advantages which can possibly occur to a society, and contributes more to the happiness of the labouring poor than can easily be conceived by those who have not deeply considered the subject. In the whole compass of human events, I doubt if there be a more fruitful source of misery, or one more invariably productive of disastrous consequences, than a sudden start of population from two or three years of plenty, which must necessarily be repressed on the first return of scarcity, or even of average crops. [13]●With the present high price of labour, and the existing habits of the poor in this country, I should consider it as a great misfortune if, from the late alarms respecting scarcity, and the unusual quantity of corn sown in consequence of them, the price of wheat for the next two years were to fall to ten or twelve pounds the load. It is not to be doubted that in this case a more than usual number of marriages would take place among the common people. The mouths would be rapidly increasing; but as this price of corn, with the present advanced rents of land, accumulated taxes on consumption, and high price of labour, would certainly not repay the farmer, the supplies would be rapidly decreasing, and the consequences are but too obvious.●[13]

---

[13] [In 1806 (Vol. II, pp. 246–7) this passage was altered:

... average crops. It has been suggested, that if we were in the habit of exporting corn in consequence of a bounty, the price would fall still lower in years of extraordinary abundance, than without such a bounty and such exportation; because the exuberance belonging to that part of the crop usually exported would fall upon the home market. But there seems to be no reason for supposing that this would be the case. The quantity annually exported would by no means be fixed, but would depend upon the state of the crop and the demands of the home market. One great advantage of a foreign market, both with regard to buying and selling, is the improbability that years of scarcity, or years of abundance, should in many different countries occur at the same time. In a year of abundance the fixed sum of the bounty would always bear a greater proportion to the cost of production. A greater encouragement would therefore be given to export, and a very moderate lowering of price would probably enable the farmer to dispose of the whole of his excess in foreign markets.

The most plausible argument that Dr. Smith adduces against the corn laws is, that as the money price of corn regulates that of all other home-made commodities, the advantage to the proprietor from the increased money price is merely apparent, and not real; since what he gains in his sales he must lose in his purchases.[14]

This position, however, is not true, without many limitations.[15] [16]●The money price of corn, in a particular country, is undoubtedly by far the most powerful ingredient in regulating the price of labour, and of all other commodities; but it is not the sole ingredient. Many parts of the raw produce of land, though affected by the price of corn, do not by any means rise and fall exactly in proportion to this price. When great improvements in manufacturing machinery have taken place in any country, the part of the expense arising from the wages of labour will bear a comparatively small proportion to the whole value of the wrought commodity, and consequently the price of it, though affected by the price of corn, will not be affected proportionally. When great and numerous taxes on consumption exist in any country, those who live by the wages of labour must always receive wherewithal to pay them, at least all those upon necessaries, such as soap, candles, leather, salt, &c. A fall in the price of corn, therefore, though it would decrease that part of the wages of labour which resolves itself into food, evidently would not decrease the whole in the same proportion. And besides these, and other limitations that might be named, the experienced difficulty of lowering wages when once they have been raised should be taken into consideration, before the position can be practically applied.

During the first half of the eighteenth century, the price of corn gradually fell, and that in a very considerable degree; but it does not appear that the price of labour fell in consequence of it. If this effect therefore did not take place in the course of fifty years, we could hardly expect that it would in seven or eight. And if, with the view of lowering the price of labour, the farmers were to push their superfluity on the home market, the disappointment of this view would clearly disable them from growing the same quantity of corn in future: and under such circumstances, it is obvious that a bounty alone could encourage them to continue the same growth of corn, and that this bounty is a great positive advantage to them, and far from being merely apparent, as Dr. Smith endeavours to prove.

Even supposing that, either by glutting the home market with British corn,

---

[14] Wealth of Nations, vol. ii. b. iv. c. v. p. 269.

[15] In the Physiocratie, by Dupont de Nemours, it is proposed as a problem in political economy to determine whether an advance in the money price of corn is a real or only nominal advantage: and the question is resolved, I think justly, on the side of the reality of the advantage. Tom. ii. [This footnote was omitted in 1806 (Vol. ii, p. 247).]

Even supposing that, either by glutting the home market with British corn, or by the importation of foreign corn duty free, we could succeed in lowering the wages of labour, the expenses of the British farmer in raising corn, and bringing it to market, would not be lowered in proportion. One of the principal ingredients in the price of British corn is the high rent of land; another, the numerous taxes on consumption which the farmer pays in his instruments of agriculture, his horses, his windows, and the necessary expenses of his establishment. While these ingredients of price remained the same, a fall in the wages of labour could not proportionally affect the price at which British corn could be brought to market:[(a)] and the British farmer would labour under a very considerable disadvantage in a competition with the farmers of America and the shores of the Baltic, where these two ingredients of price are comparatively trifling.●[16]

When Dr. Smith says that the nature of things has stamped upon corn a real value, which cannot be altered by merely altering the money price; and

---

[(a)] The immense tax paid in this country for the support of the poor forms undoubtedly another powerful ingredient in the price of British corn; but I have not mentioned it in the text, because it would always diminish immediately with the price of corn, which the other two ingredients would not.

[16] [In 1806 (Vol. II, pp. 247–50) these three paragraphs were almost entirely excised, and the following two long paragraphs substituted for them:

This position however, is not true, without many limitations. The money price of corn in a particular country is undoubtedly by far the most powerful ingredient in regulating the price of labour and of all other commodities; but it is not enough for Dr. Smith's position, that it should be the most powerful ingredient; it must be shown that other causes remaining the same, the price of every article will rise and fall exactly in proportion to the price of corn, and this does not appear to be the case. Dr. Smith himself excepts all foreign commodities; but when we reflect upon the sum of our imports, and the quantity of foreign articles used in our manufactures, this exception alone is of very great importance. Wool and raw hides, two most important materials of home growth, do not, according to Dr. Smith's own reasonings, (Book i. c. xi. p. 363 et seq.) depend much upon the price of corn and the rent of land; and the price of flax is of course greatly influenced by the quantity we import. But woollen cloths, leather, linen, cottons, tea, sugar, &c. which are comprehended in the above named articles, form almost the whole of the clothing and luxuries of the industrious classes of society. Consequently, although that part of the wages of labour which is expended in food will rise in proportion to the price of corn, the whole of the wages will not rise in the same proportion. When great improvements in manufacturing machinery have taken place in any country, that part of the price of the wrought commodity which pays the interest of the fixed capital employed in producing it, as this capital had been accumulated before the advance in the price of labour, will not rise in consequence of this advance, except as it requires gradual renovation. And in the case of great and numerous taxes on consumption, as those who live by the wages of labour must always receive wherewithal to pay them, at least all those upon necessaries, a rise or fall in the price of corn, though it would increase or decrease that

that no bounty upon exportation, no monopoly of the home market, can raise that value; nor the freest competition lower it,[17] it is evident, that he changes the question from the profits of the growers of corn [18]●in any particular country, to the physical and absolute value of corn in itself. Nothing can be more obvious than that the competition of farmers who pay few or no taxes, and little comparative rent for their land, must lower the profits of those who labour under these disadvantages, and other things being equal, must ultimately jostle them out of the market. And it is also obvious that the bounty to those who labour under these disadvantages must tend to raise their profits, and given them a fairer chance of standing the competition with the others. But all this while, undoubtedly, the physical value of corn remains just the same, untouched either by competition, or bounty. I certainly do not mean to say that the bounty alters the physical value of corn, and makes a bushel of it support a greater number of labourers for a day than it did before: but I certainly do mean to say that the bounty to the British cultivator does, in the actual state of things, really increase his profits on this commodity; and by thus making the growth of corn answer to him, encourages him to sow more than he otherwise would do, and enables him in consequence to employ more bushels of corn in the maintenance of a greater number of labourers. For, even supposing that the part of the price of labour which depends directly upon corn were to rise and fall exactly with the variations in the price of this commodity, it is demonstrably evident that, the other two principal ingredients in the price remaining the same, every rise in the money price of corn would be a positive gain to the grower or proprietor, and every fall a positive loss. And were we to go still further, and suppose that the rent of land would vary in the same way, which might be the case in the long run; yet still the money taxes on consumption remaining unaltered, the effect of a rise or

---

part of the wages of labour which resolves itself into food, evidently would not increase or decrease that part which was destined for the payment of taxes.

It cannot then be admitted as a general position, that the money price of corn in any country is an accurate measure of the real value of silver in that country. But all these considerations, though of great weight to the owners of land, will not influence the growth of corn beyond the current leases. At the expiration of a lease, any particular advantage which the farmer had received from a favourable proportion between the price of corn and of labour would be taken from him, and any disadvantage from an unfavourable proportion made up to him. The sole cause which would determine the quantity of effective capital employed in agriculture would be the extent of the effectual demand for corn, and if the bounty had really enlarged this demand, which it certainly would have done, it is impossible to suppose that more capital would not be employed upon the land.

[17] Wealth of Nations, vol. ii. b. iv. c. v. p. 278.

fall in the money price of corn would be to benefit or injure the grower or proprietor, though in a less degree than before. But in applying a theory to practice, all circumstances should certainly be taken into consideration; and in judging of the practical effects of the corn laws, or the opposite system of importation duty free; not only, as was before observed, the difficulty of lowering the price of labour should be attended to; but also the length of time which it would require to lower the rents of land, and the probable ruin of agriculture before these two objects could be effected.

If Dr. Smith's theory be just, and if it be impossible in the nature of things to encourage the growth of corn by bounties or any other human institutions, then it follows clearly that every rich country must cease to grow corn as soon as the price of labour, the rents of land, and the taxes on consumption rise so high as to exceed the advantages of superior skill and a home market. As we cannot force people to raise a commodity which will not pay them, this point evidently forms an impassable limit to the agriculture of all modern countries which have a free intercourse with others; and, from this period, they must daily grow more and more dependent upon their less rich neighbours for their subsistence.

But if the reasons that have been adduced against this theory be judged valid, then it will appear that, though agriculture be not altogether so manageable as manufactures, yet that it is still capable of being encouraged and protected by human institutions. And that consequently a system of laws respecting bounties upon exportation and duties upon importation, framed according to the circumstances of a particular country, with reference to the expense of bringing corn to market at home, and the average price of foreign corn, may make the production of this commodity answer to the farmers of such a country, however high may be the taxes on consumption, the rent of land, and the price of labour.

And if it be admitted that the cultivation of corn is susceptible of being encouraged by a bounty like other commodities, it will scarcely fail to follow that the greater plenty, occasioned by this encouragement, will in the long run lower the price.

After all the circumstances which have been before mentioned as affecting price have had their due weight, another cause must enter into our consideration, capable of producing the greatest variations, and in its immediate effects more powerful than all the rest combined. This is the proportion of the supply to the demand. A degree of plenty, indeed, which forces farmers to sell their corn below prime cost, evidently cannot last long; but the effects of scarcity are often permanent. The practical difficulty of lowering wages has before been noticed, but the same difficulty by no means exists with regard to raising them. Two or three years of high price from accidental causes are generally sufficient to do this; and when they are followed, as they generally are, by a rise in the rents of land, the extreme difficulty of a return to the former state of cheapness is obvious. Though it be allowed, therefore, that the growing of more corn, in average years, than is wanted for home consumption, in consequence of a bounty upon exportation, cannot permanently sink the price below what will fairly pay the British farmer; yet if it prevent that continual and often permanent rise, occasioned by every slight deficiency of supply or increase of demand,[a] its effect will clearly be, to keep the average price of corn lower than it otherwise would be. When a habit of considerable exportation prevails in consequence of a bounty, a slight increase of demand or deficiency of supply will produce scarcely any perceptible effect in the price of corn in the home market. This price can never exceed the average price in the ports of the commercial world, with the addition of the bounty, whatever that may be; and this addition will be absolutely nothing compared with the increase of price which arises from the slightest deficiency of supply; a deficiency which the system of importation in a large, rich, and populous country, such as Great Britain, will always render probable, not only in the home market, but in all the ports of the commercial world, as we have lately experienced to our cost.

And if the ultimate tendency of the bounty be clearly to lower the average price of corn in the home market, all Dr. Smith's just reasonings respecting the disadvantage of the cheapness of silver in any particular country, or the dearness of all other commodities, return upon himself, and are applicable in favour of the corn laws, not against them.

We are now indeed feeling the disadvantage of the cheapness of silver in this country, and in a few years, when our commercial competitors have recovered from their late depression, shall probably feel it much more than we do at present; but it certainly is not owing to a system of exporting corn in consequence of the corn laws; but, apparently, to our having altered these corn laws in such a manner as to make them fail in producing the effect of exportation.●[18]

---

[a] An occasional increase of demand for the supply of government stores produces, in the present state of things, a great effect upon the price of corn, but under a system of exportation it would not be felt.

[18] [In 1806 (Vol. II pp. 250–68) Malthus re-wrote the preceding seven paragraphs as follows:

When Dr. Smith says that the nature of things has stamped upon corn a real value, which cannot be altered by merely altering the money price; and that no bounty upon exportation, no monopoly of the home market, can raise that value, nor the freest competition lower it, it is evident that he changes the question from the profits of the growers of corn, or the proprietors of land, to the physical and absolute value of corn in itself. I certainly do not mean to say that the bounty

in itself. I certainly do not mean to say that the bounty alters the physical value of corn, and makes a bushel of it support a greater number of labourers for a day than it did before; but I certainly do mean to say that the bounty to the British cultivator does, in the actual state of things, really increase the demand for British corn; and thus encourages him to sow more than he otherwise would do, and enables him in consequence to employ more bushels of corn in the maintenance of a greater number of labourers.

If Dr. Smith's theory were strictly true, and the real price of corn, or its price in the sum of all other commodities, never suffered any variation, it would be difficult to give a reason why we grow more corn now that we did 200 years ago. If no rise in the nominal price of corn were a real rise, or could enable the farmer to cultivate better or determine more of the national capital of the land, it would appear that agriculture was indeed in a most unfortunate situation, and that no adequate motive could exist to the further investment of capital in this branch of industry. But surely we cannot doubt that the real price of corn varies, though it may not vary so much as the real price of other commodities, and that there are periods when all wrought commodities are cheaper, and periods when they are dearer, in proportion to the price of corn; and in the one case capital flows from manufactures to agriculture, and in the other from agriculture to manufactures. To overlook these periods, or consider them of slight importance, is unpardonable, because in every branch of trade these periods form the grand encouragement to an increase of supply. Undoubtedly the profits of trade in any particular branch of industry can never long remain higher than in others, but how are they lowered except by influx of capital occasioned by these high profits? It never can be a national object permanently to increase the profits of any particular set of dealers. The national object is the increase of supply; but this object cannot be attained but by previously increasing the profits of these dealers, and thus determining a greater quantity of capital to this particular employment. The ship-owners and sailors do not make greater profits now than they did before the navigation act; but the object of the nation was not to increase the profits of ship-owners and sailors, but the quantity of shipping and seamen, and this could not be done but by a law which, by increasing the demand for them, raised the profits of the capital before employed in this way, and determined a greater quantity to flow into the same channel.[(b)] The object of the nation in the corn laws is not the increase of the profits of the farmers or the rents of the landlords, but the determination of a greater quantity of the national capital to the land, and the consequent increase of supply; and though in the case of an advance in the price of corn from an increased demand, the rise of wages, the rise of rents, and the fall of silver, tend to obscure in some degree our view of the subject; yet we cannot refuse to acknowledge, that the real price of corn varies during periods sufficiently long to affect the determination of capital, or we shall be reduced to the dilemma of owning that no motive can exist to the further investment of capital in the production of corn.

The mode in which a bounty upon the exportation of corn operates seems to be this. Let us suppose that the price at which the British grower can afford to sell his corn in average years is 55 shillings, and the price at which the foreign grower can sell it, 53 shillings. Thus circumstanced, it is evident that the British grower cannot export corn, even in years

[(b)] [A series of Navigation Acts was passed from 1381 onwards, to protect English ship-owners from foreign competition. Malthus probably had in mind Cromwell's Navigation Act of 1651, aimed against the Dutch carrying trade, which was elaborated into a code of some five hundred petty regulations, not repealed until 1849; the important coasting trade remained an English monopoly until 1853. In Malthus's time, only English and colonial ship-owners were allowed to bring non-European commodities into the country. European commodities could only be imported in English vessels or in ships of the country where the goods originated. Adam Smith thought that these restrictive measures were justified in the interests of national defence, although it is now doubtful whether the navy did in fact benefit from them. Nelson's death and victory at Trafalgar on 21 October 1805, and his public funeral in St Paul's on 9 January 1806, were possibly fresh in Malthus's memory when he was writing these paragraphs.]

considerably above an average crop. In this state of things let a bounty of five shillings per quarter be granted on exported corn. Immediately as this bounty was established the exportation would begin, and go on till the price in the home market had risen to the price at which British corn could be sold abroad with the addition of the bounty. The abstraction of a part of the home supply, or even the apprehension of it, would soon raise the price in the home market, and it is probable that the quantity exported before this rise had taken place would not, at the most, bear such a proportion to the whole quantity in the ports of Europe, as to lower the general price more than a shilling in the quarter. Consequently the British grower would sell his corn abroad for 52 shillings, which with the addition of the bounty would be 57 shillings, and what was sold at home would bear exactly the same price, throwing out of our consideration at present the expenses of freight, &c. The British grower therefore, instead of 55 shillings at which he could afford to sell, would get 57 shillings for his whole crop. Dr. Smith has supposed that a bounty of five shillings would raise the price of corn in the home market four shillings, but this is evidently upon the supposition that the growing price of corn was not lower abroad than at home, and in this case his supposition would probably be correct. In the case before supposed, however, the extra profits of the farmer would be only two shillings. As far as this advance would go, it would raise the profits of farming and encourage him to grow more corn. The next year therefore the supply would be increased in proportion to the number of purchasers of the year before, and to make this additional quantity go off the price must fall; and it would of course fall both in the foreign and the home market; as while any exportation continues, the price in the home market will be regulated by the price in foreign markets with the addition of the bounty. This fall may be inconsiderable, but still the effect will be in this direction; and after the first year, the price of corn will for some time continue to fall towards its former level. In the meantime, however, the cheapness of corn abroad might gradually tend to increase the number of purchasers and extend the effectual demand for corn, not only at the late reduced prices, but at the original or even higher prices. But every extension of this kind would tend to raise the price of corn abroad to a nearer level with the growing price at home, and consequently would give the British farmer a greater advantage from the bounty. If the demand abroad extended only in proportion to the cheapness, the effect would be that part of the agriculture of foreign countries would be checked to make room for the increased agriculture of Britain, and some of the foreign growers, who traded upon the smallest profits, would be justled out of the markets.

At what time the advanced price at home would begin to affect the price of labour and of all other commodities, it would be very difficult to say; but it is probable that the interval might be considerable, because the first and greatest rise, upon the supposition that has been made, would not be above threepence in the bushel, and this advance would for some time diminish every year. But after the full effect from this advance, whatever it might be, had taken place, the influence of the bounty would by no means be lost. For some years it would give the British grower an absolute advantage over the foreign grower. This advantage would of course gradually diminish, because it is the nature of all effectual demand to be ultimately supplied, and to oblige the producers to sell at the lowest price that they can afford. But after having experienced a period of very decided encouragement, the British grower will find himself at last on a level with the foreign grower, which he was not before the bounty, and in the habit of supplying a larger market than his own upon equal terms with his competitors. And after this, if the foreign and British markets continued to extend themselves equally, the British grower would continue to proportion his supplies to both, because unless a particular increase of demand were to take place at home, he could never withdraw his foreign supply without lowering the price of his whole crop; and the nation would thus be in possession of a constant store for years of scarcity.

To the present state of things, indeed, the supposition here made will not apply. In average years we do not grow enough for our own consumption. Our first object must therefore be to supply our own wants before we aim at obtaining an excess, and the restrictive laws on importation are strongly calculated to produce this effect. It is difficult to conceive a more decided encouragement to the investment of capital in agriculture, than the certainty that, for many years to come, the price will never fall so low as the growing price.[c] If such a certainty has no tendency to give encouragement to British agriculture, on account of the advance it may occasion in the price of labour, it may safely be pronounced that no possible increase of wealth and population can ever encourage the production of corn.[d] In a nation which never imported corn except in a scarcity, commerce could never get the start of agriculture; and restrictive laws on importation, as far as they go, tend to give a relative discouragement to manufactures and a relative encouragement to agriculture. If without diminishing manufactures, they were merely to determine a greater part of the future annual accumulation to fall on the land, the effect would undoubtedly be in the highest degree desirable; but even allowing that the present very rapid march of wealth in general were to suffer a slight relaxation in its progress, if there be any foundation whatever for the alarms that have of late been expressed respecting the advantageous employment of so rapidly increasing a capital, we might surely be willing to sacrifice a small portion of present riches, in order to attain a greater degree of security, independence and permanent prosperity.

Having considered the effect of the bounty on the farmer, it remains to consider its effect on the consumer. It must be allowed that all the direct effects of the bounty are to raise, and not to lower, the price of corn to the consumer; but its indirect effects are both to lower the average price, and to prevent the variations above and below that price. If we take any period of some length prior to the establishment of the bounty, we shall find that the average price of corn is most powerfully affected by years of scarcity. From 1637 to 1700, both inclusive, the average price of corn, according to Dr. Smith, was 2l. 11s. 0½; yet in 1688 the growing price, according to an estimate of Gregory King, which Dr. Smith supposes to be correct, was only 1l. 8s. It appears, therefore, that during this period it was the monopoly price from deficiency of supply,[e] rather than the growing price which influenced the general average. But this high average price would not proportionally encourage the cultivation of corn. Though the farmer might feel very sanguine during one or two years of high price, and project many improvements, yet the glut in the market which would follow would depress him in the same degree, and destroy all his projects. Sometimes, indeed, a year of high price really tends to impoverish the land, and prepare the way for future scarcity. The period is too short to determine more capital to the land, and a temporary plenty is often restored by sowing ground that is not ready for it, and thus injuring the permanent interests of agriculture. It may easily happen therefore that a very fluctuating price, although the general average be high, will not tend to encourage the determination of capital to the land in the same degree as a steadier price with a lower general average, provided that this average is above the growing price. And if the bounty has any tendency to encourage a

[c] [In 1807 (Vol. II, p. 181) this was changed to:
     ... so low as the growing price according to the existing leases.
[d] If the operation of the corn laws, as they were established in 1700, had continued uninterrupted, I cannot bring myself to believe that we should be now in the habit of importing so much corn as we do at present. Putting the bounty on exportation out of the question, the restrictive laws on importation alone would have made it impossible. The demand for British corn would, for the last 30 years, have been both greater and more uniform than it has been; and it is contrary to every principle of supply and demand to suppose that this would not have occasioned a greater growth. Dr. Smith's argument clearly proves too much, which is as bad as proving too little.
[e] [In 1807 (Vol. II, p. 183) this was altered to:
     ... during this period it was the price of scarcity, rather than the growing price, which influenced the general average.

greater supply, and to cause the general average to be more affected by the growing price than the price of scarcity, it may produce a benefit of very high magnitude to the consumer, while at the same time it furnishes a better encouragement to the farmer, two objects which have been considered as incompatible, though not with sufficient reason. For let us suppose that the growing price in this country is 55 shillings per quarter, and that for three years out of the last ten the price from scarcity had been five guineas, for four years 55 shillings, and for the remaining three years 52 shillings. In this case the average of the ten years will be a little above 3l. 9s. This is a most encouraging price, but the three years which were below the growing price would destroy, in a great measure, its effect, and it cannot be doubted that agriculture would have received a much more beneficial impulse, if the price had continued steadily at 3 guineas during the whole time. With regard to the consumer, the advantage of the latter average need not be insisted on.

When Dr. Smith asserted that a fall in the price of corn could not possibly happen in consequence of a bounty, he overlooked a distinction which it is necessary to make in this case between the growing price of corn in years of common plenty, and the average price of a period including years of scarcity, which are in fact two very different things. Supposing the wages of labour to be regulated more frequently by the former than the latter price, which perhaps is the case, it will readily be allowed that the bounty could not lower the growing price, though it might very easily lower the average price of a long period, and I have no doubt whatever had this effect in a considerable degree during the first half of the last century.

The operation of the bounty on the value of silver is, in the same manner, in its direct effects to depreciate it, but its indirect effects may perhaps tend more powerfully to prevent it from falling. In the progress of wealth, when commerce outstrips agriculture, there is a constant tendency to a depreciation of silver, and a tendency to an opposite effect when the balance leans to the side of agriculture. During the first half of the last century agriculture seemed to flourish more than commerce and silver, according to Dr. Smith, seemed to rise in value in most of the countries in Europe. During the latter half of the century commerce seemed to have got the start of agriculture and, the effect not being counteracted by a deficiency of circulating medium, silver has been very generally depreciated. As far as this depreciation is common to the commercial world, it is comparatively[f] of little importance; but undoubtedly those nations will feel it most where this cause has prevailed in the greatest degree, and where the nominal price of labour has risen the highest, and has been most affected by the competition of commercial wealth, operating on a comparative deficiency of corn. It will certainly be allowed that those landed nations which supply the ports of Europe with corn will be the least liable to this disadvantage, and even those small states whose wants are known will probably suffer less than those whose wants, at the same time that they are quite uncertain, may be very considerable. That England is in the latter situation, and that the rapid progress of commercial wealth, combined with years of scarcity, has raised the nominal price of wages more than in any other country of Europe, will not be denied;

[f] Even the depreciation which is common to the commercial world produces much evil to individuals who have fixed incomes, and one important national evil, that of indisposing landlords to let long leases of farms. With regard to leases, the operation of the bounty would certainly be favourable. It has appeared that, after the advance occasioned on its first establishment, the price of corn would for many years tend to fall towards its former level and, if no other causes intervened, a very considerable time might elapse before it had regained the height from which it began to sink. Consequently, after the first depreciation, future depreciation would be checked, and of course long leases more encouraged. The absolute depreciation occasioned by the establishment of the bounty would be perfectly inconsiderable, compared with the other causes of depreciation which are constantly operating in this country. Independently of the funding system, the extended use of paper, the influx of commercial wealth, and the comparative deficiency of corn, every tax on the necessaries of life tends to lower the value of silver.

and the natural consequence is, that silver is more depreciated here than in the rest of Europe.

If the bounty has any effect in weakening this cause of depreciation, by preventing the average price of corn from being so much affected by the price of scarcity, the ultimate advantage which its indirect operation occasions, with regard to the value of silver, may more than counterbalance the present disadvantage of its direct operation.

On the whole therefore it appears, that the corn laws by opening a larger, but more particularly, by opening a steadier demand for British corn, must give a decided encouragement to British agriculture.[g]

This, it will be allowed, is an advantage of considerable magnitude; but this advantage cannot be attained without the attendant evil of establishing a fixed difference between the price of corn in Britain and in the ports of Europe, and as far as the nominal price of corn regulates the price of all other commodities, a proportional difference in the value of silver. With regard to the *permanent* interests of commerce, there is a great reason to believe that this disadvantage would be more than counterbalanced by the tendency of a fuller and steadier supply of corn to prevent the future depreciation of silver in this country, but still it is a present evil; and the good and evil of the system must be compared with the good and evil of a perfect freedom in the commerce of grain, the name of which is undoubtedly most fascinating.

The advantages of an unlimited freedom of importation and exportation are obvious. The specific evil to be apprehended from it in a rich and commercial country is that the rents of land and the wages of labour would not fall in proportion to the fall in the price of corn. If land yielded no other produce than corn, the proprietors would be absolutely obliged to lower their rents exactly in proportion to the diminished demand and diminished price; because, universally, it is price that determines rent, not rent that determines price; but in a country where the demands for the products of pasture are very great, and daily increasing, the rents of land would not be entirely determined by the price of corn; and though they would fall with a fall in the price of corn, they would not fall in proportion.

In the same manner the wages of labour, being influenced not only by the price of corn but by the competition of commercial wealth, and the other causes before enumerated, though they would probably fall with a fall in the price of corn, would not fall in proportion. During the first half of the last century the average price of corn fell considerably but, owing to the demand for labour arising from an increasing commerce, the price of labour did not fall with it. High rents and high wages occasioned by an increased demand and an increased price of corn cannot possibly stop cultivation, for the obvious reason that the power of paying the advance is given previous to the advance taking place; but high rents and high wages supported by other causes than the price of corn tend most powerfully to stop it. Under these circumstances, land on which little labour has been bestowed will generally yield a higher rent than that on which much has been bestowed, and

[g] On account of the tendency of population to increase in proportion to the means of subsistence, it has been supposed by some that there would always be a sufficient demand at home for any quantity of corn which could be grown. But this is an error. It is undoubtedly true that if the farmers could gradually increase their growth of corn to any extent, and could sell it *sufficiently cheap*, that a population would arise at home to demand the whole of it. But in this case the great increase of demand arises solely from the cheapness, and must therefore be totally of a different nature from such a demand as, in the actual circumstances of the country, would encourage an increased supply. If the makers of superfine broad cloths would sell their commodity for a shilling a yard instead of a guinea, it cannot be doubted that the demand would increase more than ten fold; but the certainty of such an increase of demand, in such a case, would have no tendency whatever, in the actual circumstances of any known country, to encourage the manufacture of broad cloths.

That we can readily, and with perfect facility,[19] turn ourselves from an importing to an exporting nation, in the article of corn, I would by no means pretend to say; but both theory, and the experience of the first half of the last century, warrant us in concluding it practicable; and we cannot but allow that it is worth the experiment, as the continuance of our national greatness and commercial prosperity seem absolutely to depend upon it.[20] If we proceed in our present course, let us but for a moment reflect on the probable consequences. There cannot be a doubt that, in the course of a few years,[21] we shall draw from America, and the nations bordering on the Baltic, as much as two million quarters of wheat, besides other corn, the support of above two millions of people. If, under these circumstances, any commercial discussion or other dispute were to arise with these nations, with what a weight of power they would negotiate! Not the whole British navy could offer a more convincing argument than the simple threat of shutting all

---

the bringing of fresh land under cultivation is most powerfully checked. A rich and commercial nation is thus by the natural course of things led more to pasture than tillage, and is tempted to become daily more dependent upon others for its supplies of corn.

If all the nations of Europe could be considered as one great country, and if any one state could be as secure of its supplies from others, as the pasture districts of a particular state are from the corn districts in their neighbourhood, there would be no harm in this dependence, and no person would think of proposing corn laws. But can we safely consider Europe in this light? The fortunate situation of this country, and the excellence of its laws and government, exempt it above any other nation from foreign invasion and domestic tumult, and it is a pardonable love of one's country, which under such circumstances produces an unwillingness to expose it, in so important a point as the supply of its principal food, to share in the changes and chances which may happen to the continent. How would the miseries of France have been aggravated during the revolution if she had been dependent on foreign countries for the support of two or three millions of her people.[h]

[h] [In 1807 (Vol. II, p. 192) Malthus added an exclamation mark to the conclusion of this paragraph. Much of this revised material was used again when the chapter on export bounties was re-written in 1817: see Vol. II, pp. 48–60.]

[19] [In 1806 (Vol. II, p. 268) this phrase was omitted, and the sentence read:
That we can readily turn ourselves from an importing to an exporting nation, in the article of corn ...

[20] [In 1806 (Vol. II, p. 268) this was altered to:
... worth the experiment, as the permanence of our national prosperity may depend upon it.
[A footnote was added:
Since this was first written, a new system of corn laws has been established by the legislature, but it is not so powerful in its operation as that of 1688 and 1700. The new laws tend strongly to encourage the growth of an independent supply of corn, but not so strongly the production of an excess. An independent supply however is certainly the first and most important object.
[By the 'new system of corn laws' Malthus meant the introduction of a sliding scale of duties on imported corn, the amount paid becoming progressively less as the home price of corn increased. The scheme was intended to stabilise prices as well as to ensure supplies, and the discussion of it in 1804, with the usual spate of pamphlets, must have influenced Malthus when he revised these chapters in 1806.]

[21] [In 1806 (Vol. II, p. 268) this was changed to:
We can hardly doubt that in the course of some years ...

their ports. I am not unaware that, in general, you[22] may securely depend upon people's not acting directly contrary to their interest. But this consideration, all-powerful as it is, will sometimes yield voluntarily to national indignation, and is sometimes forced to yield to the resentment of a sovereign. It is of sufficient weight in practice, when applied to manufactures; because a delay in their sale is not of such immediate consequence, and from their smaller bulk, they are easily smuggled. But in the case of corn, a delay of three or four months may produce the most complicated misery; and from the great bulk of corn, it will generally be in the power of a sovereign to execute almost completely his resentful purpose. Small commercial states which depend nearly for the whole of their supplies on foreign powers will always have many friends. They are not of sufficient consequence to excite any general indignation against them, and if they cannot be supplied from one quarter, they will from another. But this is by no means the case with such a country as Great Britain, whose commercial ambition is peculiarly calculated to excite a general jealousy, and in fact has excited it to a very great degree. If our commerce continue increasing for a few years, and our commercial population with it, we shall be laid so bare to the shafts of fortune that nothing but a miracle can save us from being struck. The periodical return of such seasons of dearth, as those which we have of late experienced, I consider as absolutely certain, upon our present importing system: but, excluding from the question, at present, the dreadful distress that they occasion, which however no man of humanity can long banish from his mind, I would ask, is it politic, merely with a view to our national greatness, to render ourselves thus dependent upon others for our support, and put it in the power of a combination against us to diminish our population two millions?

To restore our independence, and build our national greatness and commercial prosperity on the sure foundation of agriculture; it is evidently not sufficient, to propose premiums for tillage, to cultivate this or that waste, or even to pass a general inclosure bill, though these may be all good as far as they go.[23] If the increase of the commercial population keep pace with these efforts, we shall only be where we were before with regard to the necessity of importation. The object required is to alter the relative proportion between the commercial and the agricultural population of the country, which can only be done by some system which will permanently raise the profits of agriculture, encourage cultivators to employ more labour in the growing of corn, and completely secure them from all apprehensions of

---

[22] [In 1806 (Vol. II, p. 269) Malthus substituted 'we' for *you*.
[23] [In 1806 (Vol. II, p. 271) this was changed to:
    ... though these are all excellent as far as they go.

overstocking the market.[24] I see no other way, at present, of effecting this object, but by a system of corn laws adapted to the peculiar circumstances of the country and the state of foreign markets.[25] All systems of peculiar restraints and encouragements are undoubtedly disagreeable, and the necessity of resorting to them may justly be lamented. But the objection which Dr. Smith brings against bounties in general, that of forcing some part of the industry of the country into a channel less advantageous than that in which it would run of its own accord,[26] does not apply in the present instance, on account of the pre-eminent qualities of the products of agriculture, and the dreadful consequences that attend the slightest failure of them. The nature of things has, indeed, stamped upon corn a peculiar value;[27] and this remark, made by Dr. Smith for another purpose, may fairly be applied to justify the exception of this commodity from the objections against bounties in general.

If, throughout the commercial world, every kind of trade were perfectly free, one should undoubtedly feel the greatest reluctance in proposing any interruption to such a system of general liberty; and indeed, under such circumstances, agriculture would not need peculiar encouragements. But under the present universal prevalence of the commercial system, with all its different expedients of encouragement and restraint, it is folly to except from our attention the great manufacture of corn which supports all the rest. The high duties paid on the importation of foreign manufactures are so direct an encouragement to the manufacturing part of the society, that nothing but some encouragements of the same kind, operating with the same force,[28] can place the manufacturers and cultivators of this country on a fair footing. Any system of encouragement, therefore, which might be found necessary for the commerce of grain, would evidently be owing to the prior encouragements which had been given to manufactures. [29]●We consider the woollen manufacture of England as of the first importance, and protect and encourage it

---

[24] [In 1806 (Vol. II, p. 271) this was altered to:
  ... some system, which will determine a greater proportion of the national capital to the land.

[25] [In 1806 (Vol. II, p. 271) this was changed to:
  ... but by corn laws adapted to the peculiar circumstances ...
  [In 1807 (Vol. II, p. 195) a footnote was added:
  I do not mean to assert that any laws of this kind would have sufficient power, in the present state of things, to restore the balance between our agricultural and commercial population; but I am decidedly of opinion that they have this tendency. They should of course be supported by a general enclosure bill if possible, and by every relief that can safely be granted from taxes, tithes, and poor rates, in the cultivation of fresh lands.

[26] Wealth of Nations, vol. ii. b. iv. c. v. p. 278.
[27] Id.
[28] [In 1806 (Vol. II, p. 272) this qualification, *operating with the same force*, was omitted.]
[29] [In 1806 (Vol. II, p. 273) this sentence was excised.]

with peculiar care; but can any thinking man compare its influence on the strength of the state with the manufacture of corn, the scarcity or failure of which will involve in it the failure of the favourite manufacture itself. ●[29] If all be free, I have nothing to say; but if we protect and encourage, it seems to be folly not to encourage that production, which of all others is the most important and valuable.[30]

Let it not, however, be imagined that the most enlightened system of agriculture, though it will undoubtedly be able to produce food beyond the demands of the actual population, can ever be made to keep pace with an unchecked population. The errors that have arisen from the constant appearance of a full supply, produced by the agricultural system, and the source of some other prejudices on the subject of population, will be noticed in the following chapter.

---

[30] Though I have dwelt much on the importance of raising a quantity of corn in the country beyond the demands of the home consumption, yet I do not mean to recommend that general system of ploughing which takes place in most parts of France, and defeats its own purpose. A large stock of cattle is not only necessary as a very valuable part of the food of the country, and as contributing very greatly to the comforts of a considerable portion of its population; but it is also necessary in the production of corn itself. A large surplus produce, in proportion to the number of persons employed, can never be obtained without a great stock of cattle.[(a)] At the same time, it does not follow, that we should throw all the land that is fit for it into pasture. It is an observation of Arthur Young, and I should think a just one, that the first and most obvious improvement in agriculture is to make the fallows of a country support the additional cattle and sheep wanted in it. (Travels in France, vol. i. p. 361.) I am by no means sanguine, however, as to the practicability of converting England again into an exporting country, while the demands for the products of pasture are daily increasing, from the increasing riches of the commercial part of the nation. But should this be really considered as impracticable, it seems to point out to us one of the great causes of the decay of nations. We have always heard that states and empires have their periods of declension; and we learn from history that the different nations of the earth have flourished in a kind of succession; and that poor countries have been continually rising on the ruins of their richer neighbours. Upon the commercial system, this kind of succession seems to be in the natural and necessary course of things, independently of the effects of war. If from the increasing riches of the commercial part of any nation and the consequently increasing demands for the products of pasture, more land were daily laid down to grass, and more corn imported from other countries, the unavoidable consequence seems to be that the increasing prosperity of these countries, which their exportation of corn would contribute to accelerate, must ultimately destroy[(b)] the population and power of the countries which had fostered them. The ancients always attributed this natural weakness and old age of states to luxury. But the moderns, who have generally considered luxury as a principal encouragement to commerce and manufactures, and consequently a powerful instrument of prosperity, have with great appearance of reason, been unwilling to consider it as a cause of decline. But allowing with the moderns, all the advantages of luxury; and when it falls short of actual

[(a)] [This passage is a reminder of the importance of animal manure before the introduction of chemical fertilizers, which were almost unknown in Britain (apart from lime) until the second half of the nineteenth century.]

[(b)] [In 1806 (Vol. ii, p. 274) *destroy* was changed to 'diminish'.]

vice, they are certainly great; there seems to be a point, beyond which it must necessarily become prejudicial to a state, and bring with it the seeds of weakness and decay. This point is when it is pushed so far as to trench on the funds necessary for its support, and to become an impediment instead of an encouragement to agriculture. I should be much misunderstood if, from anything that I have said in the four last chapters, I should be considered as not sufficiently aware of the advantages derived from commerce and manufactures. I look upon them as the most distinguishing characteristics of civilization, the most obvious and striking marks of the improvement of society, and calculated to enlarge our enjoyment and add to the sum of human happiness. No great surplus produce of agriculture could exist without them, and if it did exist, it would be comparatively of very little value. But still they are rather the ornaments and embellishments of the political structure than its foundations. While these foundations are perfectly secure, we cannot be too solicitous to make all the apartments convenient and elegant; but if there be the slightest reason to fear that the foundations themselves may give way, it seems to be folly to continue directing our principal attention to the less essential parts. ^(c)●The most determined friend of commerce and manufactures must allow that the persons employed in them cannot exist without the food to support them; and I cannot persuade myself to believe that they can be sufficiently secure of this food, if they depend for it principally on other countries.●^(c) There has never yet been an instance in history of a large nation continuing, with undiminished vigour, to support four or five milions of its people on imported corn; nor do I believe that there ever will be such an instance in future. England is, undoubtedly, from her insular situation and commanding navy, the most likely to form an exception to this rule; ^(d)●but considering the subject as a general question in political economy, these advantages must evidently be looked upon as peculiar and incidental; and what might be applicable to England would not be so to other countries.●^(d) In spite, however, of the peculiar advantages of England, it appears to me clear that if she continue yearly to increase her importations of corn, she cannot ultimately escape that decline which seems to be the natural and necessary consequence of excessive commercial wealth; ^(c)●and the growing prosperity of those countries which supply her with corn must, in the end, diminish her population, her riches, and her power.●^(c) I am not now speaking of the next twenty or thirty years, but of the next two or three hundred. And though we are little in the habit of looking so far forwards, yet it may be questioned, whether we have a right knowingly to adopt a system^(f) which must necessarily terminate in the weakness and decline of our posterity. But whether we make any practical application of such a discussion or not, it is curious to contemplate the causes of those reverses in the fates of empires, which so frequently changed the face of the world in past times, and may be expected to produce similar, though perhaps not such violent, changes in future. War was undoubtedly, in ancient times, the principal cause of these changes; but it frequently only finished a work which excess of luxury and the neglect of agriculture had begun.^(g) With regard to ourselves, we should recollect that it is only within the last twenty or thirty years that we have become an importing nation. In so short a period it could hardly be expected that the evils of the system should be perceptible. We have, however, already felt some of its inconveniences; and if we persevere in it, its evil consequences may by no means be a matter of remote speculation. ^(h)●It has been before observed that, if from the beginning every kind of trade had been left to find its own level, agriculture would probably never have wanted any particular support; but when once this general and desirable liberty has been infringed, it seems to be clearly our interest to attend principally to those parts of the political structure which, in the actual circumstances of the country, appear to be comparatively the weakest; and, upon this principle, we should be justified in giving particular encouragement to manufactures in such countries as Poland and the southern parts of Siberia, and the same kind of encouragement to agriculture in England.●^(h)

^(c) [In 1806 (Vol. II, p. 275) this sentence was omitted.]

(d) [In 1806 (Vol. II, p. 275) this was excised, and the sentence read:
   ... exception to this rule; but in spite even of the peculiar advantages of England, it appears to me ...
(e) [In 1806 (Vol. II, p. 275) this was omitted, and the sentence ended with '... excessive commercial wealth'.]
(f) [In 1806 (Vol. II, p. 276) this was altered to:
   ... it may be questioned whether we are not bound in duty to make some exertions to avoid a system ...
(g) [In 1806 (Vol. II, p. 276) Malthus added a passage here:
   ... had begun. Foreign invasions, or internal convulsions, produce but a temporary and comparatively slight effect on such countries as Lombardy, Tuscany and Flanders, but are fatal to such states as Holland and Hamburgh; and though the commerce and manufactures of England will probably always be supported in a great degree by her agriculture, yet that part which is not so supported will still remain subject to the reverses of dependent states.
(h) [In 1806 (Vol. II, p. 277) this passage was omitted.]

CHAPTER XII

Of the principal Sources of the prevailing Errors on the Subject of Population[1]

It has been observed, that many countries at the period of their greatest degree of populousness, have lived in the greatest plenty, and have been able to export corn; but at other periods, when their population was very low, have lived in continual poverty and want, and have been obliged to import corn. Egypt, Palestine, Rome, Sicily, and Spain are cited as particular exemplifications of this fact: and it has been inferred that an increase of population in any state, not cultivated to the utmost, will tend rather to augment than diminish the relative plenty of the whole society; and that, as Lord Kaimes observes, a country cannot easily become too populous for agriculture; because agriculture has the signal property of producing food in proportion to the number of consumers.[2]

The general facts, from which these inferences are drawn, there is no reason to doubt; but the inferences by no means follow from the premises. It is the nature of agriculture,[3] particularly when well conducted, to produce support for a considerable number above that which it employs; and consequently if these members of the society, or as Sir James Steuart calls them, the free hands, do not increase so as to reach the limit of the number which can be supported by the surplus produce, the whole population of the country may continue for ages increasing with the improving state of agriculture, and yet always be able to export corn. But this increase, after a certain period, will be very different from the natural and unrestricted increase of population; it will merely follow the slow augmentation of produce from the gradual improvement of agriculture; and population will still be checked by the difficulty of procuring subsistence. [4]●It is very justly observed by Sir James Steuart that the population of England in the middle

---

[1] [In 1806 this chapter was entitled 'Of the prevailing Errors respecting Population and Plenty'. In 1817 (when this had become chapter xiv) the heading was changed to 'General Observations'.]

[2] Sketches of the History of Man, b. i. sketch i. p. 106, 107. 8vo. 1788.

[3] [In 1817 (Vol. III, p. 28) Malthus added a parenthesis here:
   ... the nature of agriculture (as it has before been observed) particularly when well conducted ...

of the last century, when the exports of corn were considerable, was still checked for want of food.●[4] The precise measure of the population in a country thus circumstanced will not, indeed, be the quantity of food, because part of it is exported, but the quantity of employment. The state of this employment, however, will necessarily regulate the wages of labour, on which depends the power of the lower classes of people to procure food; and according as the employment in the country is increasing, whether slowly or rapidly, these wages will be such as either to check or to encourage early marriages; such as to enable a labourer to support only two or three, or as many as five or six children.

[In 1817 (Vol. III, pp. 29–34) nine paragraphs were inserted here:

In stating that in this, and all the other cases and systems which have been considered, the progress of population will be mainly regulated and limited by the real wages of labour, it is necessary to remark that, practically, the current wages of labour estimated in the necessaries of life do not always correctly represent the quantity of these necessaries which it is in the power of the lower classes to consume; and that sometimes the error is in excess and sometimes in defect.

In a state of things when the prices of corn and of all sorts of commodities are rising, the money wages of labour do not always rise in proportion; but this apparent disadvantage to the labouring classes is sometimes more than counterbalanced by the plenty of employment, the quantity of task-work[5] that can be obtained, and the opportunity given to women and children to add considerably to the earnings of the family. In this case, the power of the labouring classes to command the necessaries of life is much greater than is implied by the current rate of their wages, and will of course have a proportionably greater effect on the population.

On the other hand, when prices are generally falling, it often happens that the current rate of wages does not fall in proportion; but this apparent advantage is in the same manner often more than counterbalanced by the scarcity of work, and the impossibility of finding employment for all the members of a labourer's family who are able and willing to be industrious. In this case, the powers of the labouring classes to command the necessaries of life will evidently be less than is implied by the current rate of their wages.

In the same manner parish allowances distributed to families, the habitual practice of task-work, and the frequent employment of women and children, will affect population like a rise in the real wages of labour. And, on the other hand, the paying of every sort of labour by the day, the absence of employment for women and children, and the practice among labourers of not working more than three or four days in the week, either from inveterate indolence, or any other cause, will affect population like a low price of labour.

In all these cases the real earnings of the labouring classes throughout the year,

---

[4] Polit. Econ. vol. i. b. i. c. xv. p. 100. [This sentence was omitted in 1817 (Vol. III, p. 29).]
[5] [This is now called piece-work.]

estimated in food, are different from the apparent wages; but it will evidently be the average earnings of the families of the labouring classes throughout the year on which the encouragement to marriage, and the power of supporting children, will depend, and not merely the wages of day-labour estimated in food.

An attention to this very essential point will explain the reason why, in many instances, the progress of population does not appear to be regulated by what are usually called the real wages of labour; and why this progress may occasionally be greater, when the price of a day's labour will purchase rather less than the medium quantity of corn, than when it will purchase rather more.

In our own country, for instance, about the middle of the last century, the price of corn was very low; and for twenty years together, from 1735 to 1755, a day's labour would, on an average, purchase a peck of wheat. During this period, population increased at a moderate rate; but not by any means with the same rapidity as from 1790 to 1811, when the average wages of day-labour would not in general purchase quite[6] so much as a peck of wheat. In the latter case, however, there was a more rapid accumulation of capital, and a greater demand for labour; and though the continued rise of provisions still kept them rather ahead of wages, yet the fuller employment for every body that would work, the greater quantity of task-work done, the higher relative value of corn compared with manufactures, the increased use of potatoes, and the greater sums distributed in parish allowances, unquestionably gave to the lower classes of society the power of commanding a greater quantity of food, and will account for the more rapid increase of population in the latter period, in perfect consistency with the general principle.

On similar grounds if, in some warm climates and rich soils, where corn is cheap, the quantity of food earned by a day's labour be such as to promise a more rapid progress in population than is really known to take place, the fact will be fully accounted for, if it be found that inveterate habits of indolence, fostered by a vicious government, and a slack demand for labour, prevent anything like constant employment.[7] It would of course require high corn wages of day-labour even to keep up the supply of a stationary population, where the days of working would only amount to half of the year.

In the case also of the prevalence of prudential habits, and a decided taste for the conveniences and comforts of life, as, according to the supposition, these habits and tastes do not operate as an encouragement to early marriages, and are not in fact spent almost entirely in the purchase of corn, it is quite consistent with the general principles laid down, that the population should not proceed at the same rate as is usual, *cæteris paribus*, in other countries, where the corn wages of labour are equally high.

The quantity of employment in any country will not of course vary from year to year, in the same manner as the quantity of produce must necessarily

---

[6] [In 1826 (Vol. II, p. 233) the word *quite* was deleted.]

[7] This observation is exemplified in the slow progress of population in some parts of the Spanish dominions in America, compared with its progress in the United States.

do, from the variation of the seasons; and consequently the check from want of employment will be much more steady in its operation, and be much more favourable to the lower classes of people, than the check from the immediate want of food. The first will be the preventive check; the second the positive check. When the demand for labour is either stationary, or increasing very slowly, people, not seeing any employment open by which they can support a family, or the wages of common labour being inadequate to this purpose, will of course be deterred from marrying. But if a demand for labour continue increasing with some rapidity, although the supply of food be uncertain, on account of variable seasons and a dependence on other countries, the population will evidently go on, till it is positively checked by famine or the diseases arising from severe want.

Scarcity and extreme poverty, therefore, may or may not accompany an increasing population, according to circumstances. But they must necessarily accompany a permanently declining population; because there never has been, nor probably ever will be, any other cause than want of food which makes the population of a country permanently decline. In the numerous instances of depopulation which occur in history, the causes of it may always be traced to the want of industry, or the ill direction of that industry arising from violence, bad government, ignorance, &c., which first occasion a want of food, and of course depopulation follows. When Rome adopted the custom of importing all her corn, and laying all Italy into pasture, she soon declined in population. The causes of the depopulation of Egypt and Turkey have already been alluded to;[8] and, in the case of Spain, it was certainly not the numerical loss of people, occasioned by the expulsion of the Moors, but the industry and capital thus expelled, which permanently injured her population. When a country has been depopulated by violent causes, if a bad government, with its usual concomitant, insecurity of property, ensue, which has generally been the case in all those countries which are now less peopled than formerly; neither the food nor the population can recover themselves,[9] and the inhabitants will probably live in severe want. But when an accidental depopulation takes place, in a country which was before populous and industrious, and in the habit of exporting corn, if the remaining inhabitants be left at liberty to exert, and do exert, their industry in the same direction as before, it is a strange idea to entertain, that they would then be unable to supply themselves with corn in the same plenty; particularly as the diminished numbers would, of course, cultivate principally the more fertile parts of their territory, and not be obliged, as in their more populous state, to apply to ungrateful soils. Countries in this situation would evidently have the same

---

[8] [In 1817 (Vol. III, p. 36) *alluded to* was replaced by 'adverted to'.]
[9] [In 1807 (Vol. II, p. 206) *themselves* was changed to 'itself'.]

chance of recovering their former number, as they had originally of reaching this number; and indeed if absolute populousness were necessary to relative plenty, as some agriculturists have supposed,[10] it would be impossible for new colonies to increase with the same rapidity as old states.

The prejudices on the subject of population bear a very striking resemblance to the old prejudices about specie, and we know how slowly, and with what difficulty, these last have yielded to juster conceptions. Politicians, observing that states which were powerful and prosperous were almost invariably populous, have mistaken an effect for a cause, and concluded that their population was the cause of their prosperity, instead of their prosperity being the cause of their population; as the old political economists concluded that the abundance of specie was the cause of national wealth, instead of being the effect of it. The annual produce of the land and labour, in both these instances, became in consequence a secondary consideration; and its increase, it was conceived, would naturally follow the increase of specie in the one case, or of population in the other. The folly of endeavouring by forcible means to increase the quantity of specie in any country, and the absolute impossibility of accumulating it beyond a certain level by any human laws that can be devised, are now fully established, and have been completely

---

[10] Among others, I allude more particularly to Mr. Anderson, who, in a *Calm Investigation of the Circumstances which have led to the present Scarcity of Grain in Britain*, (published in 1801,) has laboured, with extraordinary earnestness, and I believe with the best intentions possible,[a] to impress this curious truth on the minds of his countrymen. The particular position which he attempts to prove is, *that an increase of population in any state whose fields have not been made to attain their highest possible degree of productiveness, (a thing that probably has never yet been seen on this globe,) will necessarily have its means of subsistence rather augmented, than diminished, by that augmentation of its population; and the reverse.* The proposition is, to be sure, expressed rather obscurely; but, from the context, his meaning evidently is, that every increase of population tends to increase relative plenty, and vice versa. He concludes his proofs by observing, that, if the facts which he has thus brought forward and connected, do not serve to remove the fears of those who doubt the possibility of this country producing abundance to sustain its increasing population, were it to augment in a ratio greatly more progressive than it has yet done, he should doubt, whether they could be convinced of it, were one even to rise from the dead to tell them so. [b]●Mr. A. is, perhaps, justified in this doubt, from the known incredulity of the age, which might cause people to remain unconvinced in both cases.●[b] I agree with Mr. A. however, entirely, respecting the importance of directing a greater part of the national industry to agriculture; but from the circumstance of its being possible for a country with a certain direction of its industry, always to export corn,[c] although it may be very populous, he has been led into the strange error of supposing, that an agricultural country could support an unchecked population.

[a] [In 1817 (Vol. III, p. 37) the word *possible* was deleted.]
[b] [In 1817 (Vol. III, p. 38) this sentence was omitted.]
[c] [In 1817 (Vol. III, p. 38) this was altered to:
    ... direction of its industry, always to grow corn sufficient for its own supplies, although it may be very populous ...

exemplified in the instances of Spain and Portugal; but the illusion still remains respecting population; and under this impression, almost every political treatise has abounded in proposals to encourage population, with little or no comparative reference to the means of its support. Yet surely the folly of endeavouring to increase the quantity of specie in any country, without an increase of the commodities which it is to circulate, is not greater than that of endeavouring to increase the number of people, without an increase of the food which is to maintain them; and it will be found that the level above which no human laws can raise the population of a country, is a limit more fixed and impassable than the limit to the accumulation of specie. However improbable in fact, it is possible to conceive that means might be invented of retaining a quantity of specie in a state, greatly beyond what was demanded by the produce of its land and labour;[11] but when, by great encouragements, population has been raised to such a height that this produce is meted out to each individual in the smallest portions that can support life, no stretch of ingenuity can even conceive the possibility of going further.

It has appeared, I think, clearly, in the review of different societies given in the former part of this work, that those countries, the inhabitants of which were sunk in the most barbarous ignorance, or oppressed by the most cruel tyranny, however low they might be in actual population, were very populous in proportion to their means of subsistence; and upon the slightest failure of the seasons generally suffered the severities of want. Ignorance and despotism seem to have no tendency to destroy the passion which prompts to increase; but they effectually destroy the checks to it from reason and foresight. The improvident barbarian who thinks only of his present wants, or the miserable peasant who, from his political situation, feels little security of reaping what he has sown, will seldom be deterred from gratifying his passions by the prospect of inconveniences which cannot be expected to press on him under three or four years. But though this want of foresight, which is fostered by ignorance and despotism, tend thus rather to encourage the procreation of children, it is absolutely fatal to the industry which is to support them. Industry cannot exist without foresight and security. The indolence of the savage is well known; and the poor Egyptian or Abyssinian farmer without capital, who rents land which is let out yearly to the highest bidder, and who is constantly subject to the demands of his tyrannical masters, to the casual plunder of an enemy, and not unfrequently to the violation of his miserable contract, can have no heart to be industrious, and if

---

[11] [In 1817 (Vol. III, p. 40) there was an insertion here:
      ... the produce of its land and labour, and the relative state of other countries. But when ...

he had, could not exercise that industry with success. Even poverty itself, which appears to be the great spur to industry, when it has once passed certain limits, almost ceases to operate. The indigence which is hopeless destroys all vigorous exertion, and confines the efforts to what is sufficient for bare existence. It is the hope of bettering our condition, and the fear of want, rather than want itself, that is the best stimulus to industry, and its most constant and best directed efforts will almost invariably be found among a class of people above the class of the wretchedly poor.

The effect of ignorance and oppression will therefore always be to destroy the springs of industry, and consequently to diminish the annual produce of the land and labour in any country; and this diminution will inevitably be followed by a decrease of the population, in spite of the birth of any number of children whatever annually. The desire of immediate gratification, and the removal of the restraints to it from prudence, may perhaps, in such countries, prompt universally to early marriages; but when these habits have once reduced the people to the lowest possible state of poverty, they can evidently have no further effect upon the population. Their only effect must be on the degree of mortality; and there is no doubt that, if we could obtain accurate bills of mortality in those southern countries, where very few women remain unmarried, and all marry young, the proportion of the annual deaths would be 1 in 17, 18, or 20, instead of 1 in 34, 36, or 40, as in European states, where the preventive check operates.

That an increase of population, when it follows in its natural order, is both a positive good in itself,[12] and absolutely necessary to a further increase in the annual produce of the land and labour of any country, I should be the last to deny. The only question is, what is the natural[13] order of its progress? In this point Sir James Steuart, who has in general explained this subject so well, appears to me to have fallen into an error. He determines that multiplication is the efficient cause of agriculture, and not agriculture of multiplication.[14] But though it may be allowed that the increase of people, beyond what could easily subsist on the natural fruits of the earth, first prompted man to till the ground; and that the view of maintaining a family, or of obtaining some valuable consideration in exchange for the products of agriculture, still operates as the principal stimulus to cultivation; yet it is clear that these products, in their actual state, must be beyond the lowest wants of the existing population, before any permanent increase can possibly be supported. And we know that multiplication has in numberless instances taken

---

[12] [In 1806 (Vol. II, p. 288) this was changed to:
 ... a great positive good in itself, ...
[13] [In 1817 (Vol. III, p. 44) the word *natural* was deleted.]
[14] Polit. Econ. vol. i. b. i. c. xviii. p. 114.

place,[15] which has produced no effect upon agriculture, and has merely been followed by an increase of diseases; but perhaps there is no instance where a permanent increase of agriculture has not effected a permanent increase of population somewhere or other. Consequently, agriculture may with more propriety be termed the efficient cause of population, than population of agriculture,[16] though they certainly re-act upon each other, and are mutually necessary to each other's support. This indeed seems to be the hinge on which the subject turns, and all the prejudices respecting population have, perhaps, arisen from a mistake about the order of precedence.

The author of *L'Ami des Hommes*, in a chapter on the effects of a decay of agriculture upon population, acknowledges that he had fallen into a fundamental error in considering population as the source of revenue; and that he was afterwards fully convinced that revenue was the source of population.[17] From a want of attention to this most important distinction, statesmen, in pursuit of the desireable object of population, have been led to encourage early marriages, to reward the fathers of families, and to disgrace celibacy; but this, as the same author justly observes, is to dress and water a piece of land without sowing it,[18] and yet to expect a crop.

[In 1817 (Vol. III, pp. 46–50) Malthus inserted five paragraphs here:

What is here said of the order of precedence with respect to agriculture and population, does not invalidate what was said in an earlier part of this work on the tendency to an oscillation or alternation in the increase of population and food in the natural course of their progress. In this progress nothing is more usual than for the population to increase at certain periods faster than food; indeed it is a part of the general principle that it should do so; and when the money wages of labour are prevented from falling by the employment of the increasing population in manufactures, the rise in the price of corn which the increased competition for it occasions is practically the most natural and frequent stimulus to agriculture. But then it must be recollected that the greater relative increase of population absolutely implies a previous increase of food at some time or other greater than the lowest wants of the people. Without this, the population could not possibly have gone forward.[19]

---

15 [In 1806 (Vol. II, p. 289) this was corrected to:
   ... a multiplication of births has in numberless instances ...
16 Sir James Steuart explains himself afterwards, by saying that he means principally the multiplication of those persons who have some valuable consideration to give for the products of agriculture; but this is evidently not mere increase of population, and such an explanation seems to admit the incorrectness of the general proposition.
17 Tom. viii. p. 84. 12mo. 9 vols. 1762. [See MIRABEAU in the Alphabetical List.]
18 [To 'dress' a piece of land meant to spread manure over it.]
19 According to the principle of population, the human race has a tendency to increase faster than food. It has therefore a constant tendency to people a country fully up to the limits of subsistence; but by the laws of nature it can never go beyond them; meaning, of course, by

Universally, when the population of a country is for a longer or shorter time stationary, owing to the low corn wages of labour, a case which is not unfrequent, it is obvious that nothing but a previous increase of food, or at least an increase of the portion awarded to the labourer, can enable the population again to proceed forwards.

And, in the same manner, with a view to any essential improvement in the condition of the labourer, which is to give him a greater effective command over the means of comfortable subsistence, it is absolutely necessary that, setting out from the lowest point, the increase of food must precede and be greater than the increase of population.

Strictly speaking then, as man cannot live without food, there can be no doubt that in the order of precedence food must take the lead; although when, from the state of cultivation and other causes, the average quantity of food awarded to the labourer is considerably more than sufficient to maintain a stationary population, it is quite natural that the diminution of this quantity, from the tendency of population to increase, should be one of the most powerful and constant stimulants to agriculture.

It is worthy also of remark that on this account a stimulus to the increase of agriculture is much more easy when, from the prevalence of prudential restraint, or any other cause, the labourer is well paid; as in this case a rise in the price of corn, occasioned either by the increase of population or a foreign demand, will increase for a time the profits of the farmer, and often enable him to make permanent improvements; whereas, when the labourer is paid so scantily that his wages will not allow even of any temporary diminution without a diminution of population, the increase of cultivation and population must from the first be accompanied with a fall of profits. The prevalence of the preventive check to population and the good average wages of the labourer will rather promote than prevent that occasional increase and decrease of them, which as a stimulus seems to be favourable to the increase both of food and population.

Among the other prejudices which have prevailed on the subject of population, it has been generally thought that, while there is either waste among the rich, or land remaining uncultivated in any country, the complaints for want of food cannot be justly founded or, at least, that the pressure of distress upon the poor is to be attributed to the ill-conduct of the higher classes of society and the bad management of the land. The real effect, however, of these two circumstances, is merely to narrow the limit of the actual population; but they have little or no influence on what may be called the average pressure of distress on the poorer members of society. If our ancestors had been so frugal and industrious, and had transmitted such habits to their posterity, that nothing superfluous was now consumed by the higher classes, no horses were used for pleasure, and no land was left

---

these limits, the lowest quantity of food which will maintain a stationary population. Population, therefore, can never, strictly speaking, precede food.

uncultivated, a striking difference would appear in the state of the actual population; but probably none whatever in the state of the lower classes of people, with respect to the price of labour, and the facility of supporting a family. The waste among the rich, and the horses kept for pleasure, have indeed a little the effect of the consumption of grain in distilleries, noticed before with regard to China.[20] On the supposition that the food consumed in this manner may be withdrawn on the occasion of a scarcity, and be applied to the relief of the poor, they operate, certainly, as far as they go, like granaries, which are only opened at the time that they are most wanted, and must therefore tend rather to benefit than to injure the lower classes of society.

With regard to uncultivated land, it is evident that its effect upon the poor is neither to injure nor to benefit them. The sudden cultivation of it will indeed tend to improve their condition for a time, and the neglect of lands before cultivated will certainly make their situation worse for a certain period; but when no changes of this kind are going forward, the effect of uncultivated land on the lower classes operates merely like the possession of a smaller territory. It is, indeed, a point of very great importance to the poor,[21] whether a country be in the habit of exporting or importing corn; but this point is not necessarily connected with the complete or incomplete cultivation of the whole territory, but depends upon the proportion of the surplus produce to those who are supported by it; and in fact this proportion is generally the greatest in countries which have not yet completed the cultivation of all their territory. If every inch of land in this country were well cultivated, there would be no reason to expect, merely from this circumstance, that we should be able to export corn. Our power in this respect would depend entirely on the proportion of the surplus produce to the commercial population; and this, of course, would in its turn depend on the direction of capital to agriculture or commerce.

It is not probable that any country with a large territory should ever be completely cultivated; and I am inclined to think that we often draw very inconsiderate conclusions against the industry and government of states from the appearance of uncultivated lands in them. It seems to be the clear and express duty of every government to remove all obstacles and give every facility to the inclosure and cultivation of land; but when this has been done, the rest must be left to the operation of individual interest; and, upon this principle, it cannot be expected that any new land should be brought into

---

[20] [See p. 131 and GROSIER in the Alphabetical List.]
[21] [In 1817 (Vol. III, p. 52) this sentence began:
  It may indeed be a point of some importance to the poor, whether a country be in the habit of importing or exporting corn ...

cultivation, the manure and the labour necessary for which might be employed to greater advantage on the improvement of land already in cultivation; and this is a case which will very frequently occur. In countries possessed of a large territory, there will always be a great quantity of land of a middling quality, which requires constant dressing to prevent it from growing worse; but which would admit of very great improvement if a greater quantity of manure and labour could be employed upon it. The great obstacle to the amelioration of land is the difficulty, the expense, and sometimes the impossibility, of procuring a sufficient quantity of dressing. As this instrument of improvement, therefore, is in practice limited, whatever it may be in theory, the question will always be, how it may be most profitably employed; and in any instance where a certain quantity of dressing and labour employed to bring new land into cultivation, would have yielded a permanently greater produce if employed upon old land, both the individual and the nation are losers. Upon this principle, it is not uncommon for farmers in some situations never to dress their poorest land, but to get from it merely a scanty crop every three or four years, and to employ the whole of their manure, which they practically feel is limited, on those parts of their farms where it will produce a greater proportional effect.

The case will be different, of course, in a small territory with a great population, supported on funds not derived from their own soil. In this case there will be little or no choice of land, and a comparative superabundance of manure; and under such circumstances the poorest soils may be brought under cultivation. But for this purpose, it is not mere population that is wanted, but a population which can obtain the produce of other countries, while it is gradually improving its own; otherwise it would be immediately reduced in proportion to the limited produce of this small and barren territory; and the amelioration of the land might perhaps never take place; or if it did, it would take place very slowly indeed, and the population would always be exactly measured by this tardy rate, and could not possibly increase beyond it.

This subject is illustrated in the cultivation of the Campine in Brabant, which, according to the Abbé Mann,[22] consisted originally of the most barren and arid sand. Many attempts were made by private individuals to bring it under cultivation, but without success; which prove that, as a farming project, and considered as a sole dependence, the cultivation of it would not answer. Some religious houses, however, at last settled there, and being supported by other funds, and improving the land merely as a secondary object, they by degrees, in the course of some centuries, brought

---

[22] Memoir on the Agriculture of the Netherlands, published in vol. i. of Communications to the Board of Agriculture, p. 225.

nearly the whole under cultivation, letting it out to farmers as soon as it was sufficiently improved.

There is no spot, however barren, which might not be made rich this way, or by the concentrated population of a manufacturing town; but this is no proof whatever that with respect to population and food, population has the precedence; because this concentrated population could not possibly exist without the preceding existence of an adequate quantity of food in the surplus produce of some other district.

In a country like Brabant or Holland, where territory is the principal want, and not manure, such a district as the Campine is described to be, may perhaps be cultivated with advantage. But in countries, possessed of a large territory, and with a considerable quantity of land of a middling quality, the attempt to cultivate such a spot would be a palpable misdirection and waste, both of individual and national resources.

The French have already found their error in bringing under cultivation too great a quantity of poor land. They are now sensible that they have employed in this way a portion of labour and dressing, which would have produced a permanently better effect, if it had been applied to the further improvement of better land. Even in China, which is so fully cultivated and so fully peopled, barren heaths have been noticed in some districts; which proves that, distressed as the people appear to be for subsistence, it does not answer to them to employ any of their manure on such spots. These remarks will be still further confirmed, if we recollect that, in the cultivation of a large surface of bad land, there must necessarily be a very great waste of seed corn.[23]

We should not, therefore, be too ready to make inferences against the internal economy of a country, from the appearance of uncultivated heaths, without other evidence. But the fact is, that as no country has ever reached, or probably ever will reach, its highest possible acme of produce, it appears always as if the want of industry, or the ill-direction of that industry, was the actual limit to a further increase of produce and population, and not the absolute refusal of nature to yield any more; but a man who is locked up in a room may be fairly said to be confined by the walls of it, though he may never touch them; and with regard to the principle of population, it is never the question whether a country will produce *any more*, but whether it may be made to produce a sufficiency to keep pace with an unchecked increase of people.[24] In China, the question is not whether a certain additional quantity of rice might be raised by improved culture, but whether such an addition

---

23 [In 1817 (Vol. III, p. 57) the word *very* was deleted.]
24 [In 1817 (Vol. III, p. 58) this was changed to:
   ... to keep pace with a nearly unchecked increase of people.

could be expected during the next twenty-five years, as would be sufficient to support an additional three hundred millions of people. And in this country, it is not the question, whether by cultivating all our commons, we could raise considerably more corn that at present; but whether we could raise sufficient for a population of twenty millions in the next twenty-five years, and forty millions, in the next fifty years.

The allowing of the produce of the earth to be absolutely unlimited, scarcely removes the weight of a hair from the argument, which depends entirely upon the differently increasing ratios of population and food: and all that the most enlightened governments, and the most persevering and best guided efforts of industry can do, is to make the necessary checks to population operate more equably, and in a direction to produce the least evil; but to remove them, is a task absolutely hopeless.

[In 1817 (Vol. III, p. 59) Malthus added a footnote here, which was printed in the volume of *Additions* (pp. 249–51) as a continuation of the main text:

It may be thought that the effects here referred to as resulting from greatly increased resources could not take place in a country where there were towns and manufactories; and that they are not quite consistent with what was said in a former part of this work, namely, that the ultimate check to population (the want of food) is never the immediate check, except in cases of actual famine.

If the expressions are unguardedly strong, they will certainly allow of considerable mitigation, without any sensible diminution in the practical force and application of the argument. But I am inclined to think that, although they are unquestionably strong, they are not very far from the truth. The great cause which fills towns and manufactories is an insufficiency of employment, and consequently of the means of support in the country; and if each labourer, in the parish where he was born, could command food, clothing, and lodging for ten children, the population of the towns would soon bear but a small proportion to the population in the country. And if to this consideration we add that, in the case supposed, the proportion of births and marriages in towns would be greatly increased, and all the mortality arising from poverty almost entirely removed, I should by no means be surprised (after a short interval for the change of habits) at an increase of population, even in China, equal to that which is referred to in the text.

With regard to this country, as it is positively known that the rate of increase has changed from that which would double the population in 120 years, or more, to that which would double it in 55 years, under a great increase of towns and manufactures, I feel very little doubt that, if the resources of the country were so augmented and distributed, as that every man could marry at 18 or 20, with a certainty of being able to support the largest family, the population of the British Isles would go on increasing at a rate which would double the population in 25 years. It appears, from our registers, that England is a healthier country than America. At the time that America was increasing with extraordinary rapidity, in some of her towns the deaths exceeded the births. In the English towns, with their present improvements, I do not think this would ever be the case, if all the lower classes could marry as soon as they pleased, and there was little or no premature mortality from the consequences of poverty.

But whether the habits and customs of an old state could be so changed by an abundance of food, as to make it increase nearly like a new colony, is a question of mere curiosity. The argument only requires that a change from scanty to abundant means of supporting a family should occasion, in old states, a marked increase of population; and this, it is conceived, cannot possibly be denied.